W9-BME-893

LIST OF KEY POINTS AND LANGUAGE AND CULTURE BOXES

KEY POINTS BOXES

LANGUAGE AND CULTURE BOXES

THE OPEN HANDBOOK

Keys for Writers

ANN RAIMES

Hunter College, City University of New York

with

Maria Jerskey

Baruch College, City University of New York

Houghton Mifflin Company
Boston   New York

For Asa Raimes Bry and Gene Jerskey-Long,
who teach us what learning is all about.

Publisher: Patricia Coryell
Sponsoring Editor: Suzanne Phelps-Weir
Development Editor: Meg Botteon
Assistant Editor: Jane Acheson
Editorial Assistant: John McHugh
Senior Project Editor: Rosemary Winfield
Editorial Assistant: Katherine Leahey
Art and Design Coordinator: Jill Haber
Photo Editor: Jennifer Meyer Dare
Composition Buyer: Chuck Dutton
Manufacturing Coordinator: Karen Fawcett
Marketing Manager: Cindy Graff Cohen
Marketing Associate: Kelly Kunert

Printed in the U.S.A.
Library of Congress Catalog Card Number 2003109853
Instructor's exam copy ISBN: 0-618-73060-5, 978-0-618-73060-5
For orders, use student text ISBNs: 0-618-60715-3, 978-0-618-60715-0

2 3 4 5 6 7 8 9 -DOC- 09 08 07 06

Preface

What will make you want to keep a writing handbook **open**?

If you are a *student,* a handbook can provide help as you write; it can also provide practical exercises to help you improve specific features of your writing. But no reference tool is of any use to anyone if it is buried in a book bag or a car trunk. Here are some of the many reasons for you to keep this book **open** next to you:

- You'll find clear and extensive help with college writing such as essays, research papers, arguments, literature papers, oral reports, e-portfolios, and assignments across the curriculum.

- You'll learn about the "Seven Sins of Plagiarism" and how to avoid them.

- You'll see from edited examples how to fix incorrect grammar or punctuation—and you can try out what you learn with exercises built around interesting topics.

- The mysteries of documentation (MLA and APA) are fully explained, with many up-to-date examples and extensive coverage of how to cite online databases and Web sites.

- Eight annotated images of print and online source materials, called Source Shots, show (not just tell) you how to evaluate and cite your sources in a research paper.

- The pages are visually appealing, with boxes and images summarizing main points and illustrating the text; a four-color section shows graphics to their best advantage.

Once the book is literally open, you'll notice that its approach is **open** too, inclusive of all students whatever their cultural, linguistic, and educational background, whatever version of English they bring to the classroom, wherever they are on the journey from novice writer to expert.

If you are an *instructor,* you look to a handbook to provide readily accessible information and practice for your students as well as support for your own teaching; you want students to use a handbook so that you don't have to reinvent the wheel with every issue that arises in class. After all, you surely have enough to do with preparing your classes and commenting on your students' papers.

As the *authors* of this book and as dedicated writing teachers, we are committed to helping writers communicate more effectively. The success of the *Keys for Writers* handbook series has inspired us to develop *The Open Handbook* as a new alternative for a new generation of students needing a concise reference with exercises—a no-nonsense handbook designed for today's writing challenges. With our many years of teaching devoted to undergraduate writing, we have aimed to be constantly **open** to ideas of educational change and linguistic flux, **open** to the benefits that current technology brings to the writing process, **open** to the fact that writing happens in many forms outside the academic world, **open** to the diversity of the students in today's classrooms, and **open** to the expansion of literacy to include not just text but images.

We hope you will appreciate this openness as you use this handbook.

FEATURES

Sound advice and a friendly voice   A hallmark of the *Keys for Writers* handbook series is a style at once authoritative and approachable. Each edition of a *Keys* handbook features a richly illustrated discussion of style, including the unique "5 C's of Style" (you'll find it here in chapter 8). We believe that a writing handbook should itself model those principles—especially connection, commitment, and even delight. *The Open Handbook* strives to be both useful and pleasurable to read.

Clear and candid discussion of plagiarism   You will find extensive coverage of plagiarism, including a distinctive chapter that explains the many ways in which plagiarism happens; succinct guidance on using sources responsibly; an engaging and enlightening list of "The Seven Sins of Plagiarism"; and exercises on summary, paraphrase, and defining the boundaries of a citation.

Rich and varied exercise program   *The Open Handbook* contains 103 exercises, all clearly numbered and titled, with many designed for collaborative or group work. To add interest and context, the topics of continuous discourse exercises are drawn from a range of disciplines and multicultural perspectives. Each sentence set looks at a contemporary issue, debate, development, or discovery in the humanities, social sciences, or sciences. A partial Answer Key at the end of the book provides suggested answers to selected exercise items (indicated by an **A**), thus supporting individual student practice. A full Answer Key is included on the instructor-only portion of the Web site. The partial as well as the full Answer Keys indicate from which discipline each exercise topic is drawn. Additional exercises are available at *The Open Handbook* Web site at <http://college.hmco.com/keys.html>.

 Distinctive and thorough help for today's multicultural writers   We bring to *The Open Handbook* our experience and expertise in teaching culturally and linguistically diverse undergraduate populations. In the Language and Culture boxes, in the content of exercises, and in Part 5, Editing for Writers with Other Languages (ESL), Other Englishes, we acknowledge and support the diversity of students and diversity of languages and Englishes they bring to their writing. Our approach focuses on difference, not deficit. Specific support includes guides to editing vernacular Englishes and multilingual transfer errors as well as the ESL Notes throughout the text.

An emphasis on visuals, with four-color examples   *The Open Handbook* is the only handbook in its category to include four-color examples in its discussion of document design. Visuals are used as the authors recommend students should use them. Just as all student essays in *The Open Handbook* are written by real students, the tables and charts are also authentic. Some were prepared by students for use in a paper or presentation, and all have source and retrieval information. Visuals are attractive and informative—not just decorative.

 A substantive Web site   This distinctive icon indicates additional content on *The Open Handbook's* content-rich Web site at <http://college .hmco.com/keys.html>, which is available to all students who use the text. The Web site features additional exercises, tutorials, a module on collaboration, templates and checklists for peer review and research, a hyperlinked list of sources in twenty-seven research areas, and much more. The instructor's Web site also includes a complete Answer Key for all exercises in the print text of *The Open Handbook* as well as all online exercises.

Style, with substance   A complete chapter on Style includes the distinctive and popular 5 C's of Style section, which advises students in a straightforward and memorable way to Cut, Check for Action, Connect, Commit, and Choose the Right Words.

 Key Points boxes   This useful feature provides seventy easy-to-review summaries, tips, and checklists.

Intuitive and easy flowchart guide to MLA and APA citation   A simple and distinctive flowchart opens each section devoted to the list of sources used in MLA and APA styles. This visual approach eliminates confusion for students about whether a print article found in an online database is to be cited as a print work or an online work. Clear and complete discussions of finding sources in online databases and on citing articles from online library subscription databases are accompanied by annotated screen shots.

Writing in new contexts   *The Open Handbook* includes coverage of blogs, on-line discussions, preparation of online papers (with a full, linked student paper on the book's Web site), a student's PowerPoint presentation, e-portfolios, and oral reports.

Annotated screen shots   Eight Source Shots help students with understanding the anatomy of a Web site, finding information to help in evaluating a source, and knowing what to cite from print and online sources.

TechToolkit   This feature pays attention to the bells and whistles of the computer and online tools that writers use. TechToolkit notes give help with word processing tools useful in academic writing and provide relevant Web links.

A COMPLETE SUPPORT PACKAGE

Technology Tools for Student Writers

Along with the free Web site at <http://college.hmco.com/keys.html> that supports *The Open Handbook,* you and your students have many technology options to enhance the teaching and learning of writing.

HelpDesk for Writers   This powerful ensemble of technology products provides four convenient electronic aids for self-paced and personalized writing instruction on the computer.

- **Digital Keys 4.0 student CD-ROM**   This CD-ROM has a host of interactive tools and resources to help students work on all aspects of their writing, including grammar, punctuation, mechanics, and style. The core of this writing aid is an easily navigated handbook of writing instruction, practice exercises, examples, diagnostic tests, KeyTabs® for bookmarking, and hotlinks.

- **Digital Keys Online passkey**   Students receive a twelve-month subscription for a Web version of the CD-ROM (without diagnostic tests).

- **WriteSpace online writing environment registration code**   An easy-to-use Web-based writing program, WriteSpace delivers writing tutorials, interactive exercises, diagnostic tests, assignments, models, and more. Built within our Eduspace® platform and powered by Blackboard, the program can be used in online, distance learning courses, in wired classrooms, and as an easily integrated enhancement to traditional courses.

- **SMARTHINKING™ online writing tutoring program** Embedded in the WriteSpace program, Smarthinking links students to a Web-based writing center, staffed by experienced composition instructors. Tutors interact with students in real-time during afternoon and evening homework hours, five days a week, and answer questions and offer helpful feedback on drafts.

For more information about adopting the HelpDesk for Writers supplement with *The Open Handbook* or to sign up for online instructor demonstrations of these writing tools, instructors can contact their Houghton Mifflin sales representative or call 1-800-733-1717, extension 4020.

Other Technology Tools

In addition to the above HelpDesk for Writers (electronic writing tools that can be packaged together with the print handbook), students can also access other resources at the Web site for *The Open Handbook* at <http://college.hmco.com/keys.html>.

Internet Research Guide This online guide by Jason Snart of College of DuPage presents six extended learning modules with practice exercises (tutorials) for using the Internet as a research tool. Topics include evaluating Web information, building an argument with Web research, and plagiarism and documentation.

e-Exercises This rich e-library of enjoyable self-quizzes lets students hone their grammar skills, go at their own pace, and work wherever is convenient for them—home, computer lab, or classroom. Exercises cover thirty areas within the broad categories of punctuation, mechanics, parts of speech, spelling, and sentence problems.

Print Supplements for Students

Raimes and Flanagan, *Exercise Booklet,* Fourth Edition This well-regarded print booklet contains eighty-two well-crafted editing exercises.

THEA (formerly TASP) and CLAST preparation manuals These exercises and review booklets include practice tests to help students pass the Texas Higher Education Assessment Test and Florida's College Level Academic Skills Test.

The American Heritage College Dictionary, **Fourth Edition**   This best-selling reference is an indispensable tool and desk reference.

The American Heritage English as a Second Language Dictionary This reference is specially designed with additional sample sentences to suit the needs of intermediate to advanced ESL students.

Technology Tools for Instructors

WriteSpace online writing environment   WriteSpace (preview at <http://www.writespace.com>) includes a complete classroom management system with diagnostic skills tests; flexible tools for building customized grade books, syllabi, bulletin boards, and assignments; virtual-classroom features including online chat functions, interactive whiteboards synchronous and asynchronous class discussions, the ability to receive and post student papers, and online office hours.

Print Supplements for Instructors

Teaching Writing with Computers: An Introduction   Edited with an introduction by Pamela Takayoshi and Brian Huot, both of the University of Louisville, this book is an up-to-date resource on integrating technology into writing instruction.

Finding Our Way: A Writing Teacher's Sourcebook   Edited with an introduction by the late Wendy Bishop and Deborah Coxwell Teague of Florida State University in Tallahassee, this collection of essays is a unique and powerful guide for new or relatively new composition teachers.

The Essentials of Tutoring: Helping College Students Develop Their Writing Skills   Paul Gary Phillips and Joyce B. Phillips of Grossmont College have written this supportive and comprehensive guide for writing tutors.

A Student Guide to Authoring Your Own Work: Understanding Plagiarism   This handy supplement by Rosemarie Menager-Beeley and Lyn Paulos is a comprehensive yet concise guide to avoiding plagiarism in your writing. With helpful tips, a wealth of examples, and a special emphasis on MLA and APA documentation, students will learn to properly paraphrase, summarize, and integrate quotations. The book concludes with a practice quiz.

Houghton Mifflin Readers can also be packaged at a discount with *The Open Handbook*. Popular rhetorically organized readers include *The Essay Connection*, Eighth Edition, by Lynn Z. Bloom, and *The Riverside Reader*, Eighth Edition, by Joseph Trimmer. Thematic readers include *Many Americas: Reading and Writing across the Cultural Divide* and *The New World Reader*, both by Gilbert H. Muller; *Challenging Perspectives: Reading Critically about Ethics and Values* by Deborah Holdstein; and *The Well-Crafted Argument*, Second Edition, by Fred White and Simone Billings. Cross-disciplinary readers include *The New Humanities Reader*, Second Edition, by Richard Miller and Kurt Spellmeyer, and *Making Sense: Essays on Art, Science, and Culture* by Bob Coleman, Rebecca Brittenham, Scott Campbell, and Stephanie Girard. For information about packaging any readers or other supplements with *The Open Handbook* or for information on the new Riverside Select custom reader option, instructors can contact their Houghton Mifflin sales representative or call 1-800-733-1717, extension 4020.

ACKNOWLEDGMENTS

We are grateful to the teachers and students at Hunter College and Baruch College, City University of New York, whose suggestions, comments, and reactions to our teaching materials have taught us a great deal about writers and writing—and about what is needed in a handbook. Faculty members and students from around the country have also helped shape this book with their comments on other handbooks in the *Keys* series. We offer special thanks to the following reviewers for sharing with us their wisdom, experience, and critical analysis:

Greg Barnhisel, Duquesne University
Carl Singleton, Fort Hays State University
Barbara A. Rasnick, Arizona State University
K. F. Lisovsky, UCLA Writing Programs
Eve Dunbar, Vassar College
Joan Cashion, Marymount College, Palos Verdes
Patricia Lonchar, University of the Incarnate Word
Sharleen Pisciotta, University of Colorado at Colorado Springs
Deanne Gute, University of Northern Iowa
Jane Tainow Feder, NYC College of Technology
Nancy Drescher, Minnesota State University Mankato
Shari Horner, Shippensburg University
Jeffrey Andelora, Mesa Community College
Loren P. Q. Baybrook, University of Wisconsin Oshkosh
Robert Johnson, Midwestern State University
Jason Horn, Gordon College

Lesli St. Martin, College of the Canyons
Anne L. Legge, Lord Fairfax Community College
Peter Kratzke, University of Colorado/Boulder
Robbin Zeff, The George Washington University
Cathy J. Hunter, Ball State University
Professor Claire Berger, Camden County College
Sandra Dihlmann Lunday, Coconino Community College
Mary M. Hubbard, North West Arkansas Community College

For his expert advice on technological matters and his prompt, thoughtful replies to our many e-mails, we are deeply grateful to Manfred Kuechler at Hunter College. From Baruch College, we thank Cheryl Smith and Suresh Canagarajah and the tutors in the Writing Center for the many conversations about teaching students who are learning to write in English as a second language. For their contribution of inventive exercises, we are grateful to Carolyn Lengel and Anna Tomasino. Thanks go, too, to the librarians whose work and advice is so crucial for all students and teachers, especially to Jean Jacques Strayer and Tony Doyle at Hunter College, and Alan Bailin formerly at Baruch College, all of whom kept us abreast of sources and trends, and to Trudi Jacobson at the University of Albany, State University of New York, who so expertly revised and updated our *Keys* list of resources in twenty-seven subject areas.

We are proud of what we see as a special feature of *Keys* handbooks: authentic student writing, produced in a classroom setting and frequently in an introductory course. We give special thanks to Tiffany Brattina, Lindsay Camp, Zhe Chen, Diana Fatakhova, Jennifer Hopper, Christel Hyden, Todd Kray, Patricia Lee, Emily Luo, Juana Mere, Brad Thompson, Angela Tolano, and Tatyana Shchensek for so graciously giving us permission to use their work in this book and on the book's Web site.

Our colleagues at Houghton Mifflin have been a pleasure to work with. They are unfailingly warm, supportive, responsive, and incredibly knowledgeable about textbook publishing. Special thanks go to Patricia Coryell, Vice President, and Suzanne Phelps Weir, Editor in Chief, for their leadership, energy, and enthusiasm for the project; to Sarah Helyar Chester, Development Manager, for her keen eye for design and content; to Meg Botteon, Senior Development Editor, for keeping us focused and helping us resolve problems; to Rosemary Winfield, Senior Project Editor, for calmly making sure that our manuscript met a deadline to become a book; and to Cindy Graff Cohen, Senior Marketing Manager, for keeping us attuned to market needs and handbook trends. We also are grateful for the help and professionalism of all on the large *Keys* team: Jane Acheson, Janet Edmonds, John McHugh, Katherine Leahey, Jill Haber, Tony Saizon, Karen Fawcett, Vici Casana, Linda McLatchie, Deborah Prato, Patricia Herbst, Nancy Fulton, and Bruce Crabtree. Thanks, too, to Sam Davison and her team at New England Typographic Service for so ably converting our complex manuscript into handsome pages.

On a personal level, we want to thank our friends (Jane Ashdown and Brian Jermusyk were of particular help to Maria), colleagues, and family, who put up with our stress level and distraction and made sure we were able to find diversions. Two people were especially important to us: Gene Jerskey-Long and James Raimes had to put up with irregular schedules, wildly irregular mealtimes, and every surface covered with piles of paper. They knew when to let us be obsessive and when to say "Enough!" Without them, you would not now be holding this book in your hands.

AR
MJ

PART 1 The Writing Process

Through writing, you do not just *display* what you know; you can also *discover* what you know and think. The process of writing helps you have ideas, make connections, and raise questions, whether you are working on an e-mail message or a research report. Use the time that the writing process affords to discover as well as to present, to learn as well as to fulfill an assignment.

Writing involves the following:

Planning
- critical thinking and reading
- determining your purpose and audience
- generating ideas
- establishing a topic and thesis
- gathering information and support

Drafting
- organizing and developing ideas
- writing drafts (preliminary versions)

Revising
- revising and checking for clarity, coherence, and unity
- editing and proofreading

These planning, drafting, and revising activities are often characterized as steps in a linear process in order to make them easier to talk about. In reality, however, virtually no one embarking on a writing project marches neatly through a series of distinct steps. In fact, the most important features to bear in mind are these:

The writing process is not linear.

Writing is a messy adventure; nothing is done according to a formula.

Few writers achieve perfection on the first draft.

The very act of writing helps you generate ideas.

This process of discovery can be exciting.

For some, writing an essay brings along with it a set of fears: of laying out our ideas, of exposing those ideas to criticism, of being judged and found wanting.

In its favor, however, writing is less intimidating than public speaking and has distinct advantages. When expressing ourselves in writing, we will not lose our audience because we happen to have bronchitis or a bad case of nerves. Instead we write, for the most part, for an imagined audience, for readers who do not see us or know us. We can thus present to our readers an image of a person we would like to be, a person we admire and hope others will admire, too. Writing brings this freedom to invent ourselves anew. As journalist Adam Gopnik says fondly of writing, "It's you there, but not quite you."

1 Define the Writing Task.

"I'm not sure what I'm supposed to be doing." "I wish I had a clearer sense of what my instructor wants." Have you often found yourself thinking or saying things like this? If so, you are not alone. In fact, a big part of getting a writing task done is understanding and fulfilling the terms of the assignment: its purpose, readers, requirements, tone, and language.

1a Purpose

Before you begin writing, consider this question: "What is the main purpose of this piece of writing?"

Among the categories in the Key Points box, the overlap can be considerable. Some assignments may require you to explore and test concepts and opinions against what you already know. Other assignments may ask you to blend explanation with persuasion. Whatever you determine to be the main purpose or purposes of a given assignment should guide you as you write, along with any detailed instructions you receive.

KEY POINTS

Asking about Purpose

1. Is your main purpose to explain an idea, analyze, or provide information? Writing with this purpose is called *expository writing*.

2. Is your main purpose to persuade readers to see things your way or to move readers to action? This aim leads to *persuasive writing* or *argumentation*.

3. Is your main purpose to describe an experiment or a detailed process or to report on laboratory results? Writing with this purpose is frequently referred to as *scientific* or *technical writing*.

4. Is your main purpose to record and express your own experience, observations, ideas, and feelings? In the humanities, such accounts are known as *expressive, autobiographical,* or *personal writing*.

5. Is your main purpose to create an original work, such as a poem, story, play, or novel? Writing with this purpose is known as *creative writing*.

1b Audience

Sometimes thoughts about a reader, especially an instructor who will give you a grade based on the quality of your work, can be intimidating. Obviously readers and their expectations must be taken into account. The question is when. Writing is not just the final product or words on a page or screen. It is the process that gets you there. And because you can learn from writing, generate ideas from writing, and discover what you want to say and what you need to find out, readers do not have to play a major role from the very beginning. Consider beginning your writing for yourself alone.

Writing for yourself Write to create a record of your thinking for your eyes only. That way, you will not worry excessively about style, accuracy, spelling, and other details. You will concentrate instead on using your writing to generate and organize your ideas. After you review your draft, think of revising that draft so that it will interest you if you pick it up in a few years' time.

Writing for others   Before too long in the process, of course, it is helpful to formulate a picture of readers and their expectations. A good writer connects with his or her audience and keeps readers in mind as if in a face-to-face communication. Achieving this connection, however, often proves challenging because not all readers have the same characteristics. Readers come from different regions, communities, ethnic groups, organizations, and academic disciplines. They have different social and economic backgrounds and varied interests. Also, readers' approaches to what they are reading depend on the context or conventions of the material before them. Conventions vary, for instance, in informal letters, scholarly or scientific writing, Internet writing, newspapers and magazines, business interactions, and college papers in various disciplines.

LANGUAGE AND CULTURE
Assessing Readers' Expectations

- What kinds of texts do your readers usually read and write, and what are the conventions of those texts? For example, if you are writing a business letter to a company in another country, consult a business communications book to find out what readers there expect in a business letter.

- Will readers expect formal or informal language?

- What characteristics do you and your readers have in common: nationality, language, culture, race, class, ethnicity, or gender? Consider what limitations writing for these readers places on your use of dialect (for example, Australian English is different from Caribbean English, and African American Vernacular—AAV—is different from Standard English), punctuation (British English and American English treat quotations differently—see 26d), vocabulary, and political and cultural expectations. Cultivate common ground, and try not to alienate readers.

- What kinds of information and evidence will readers expect to find? Some cultures value the unattributed presentation of traditional wisdom from classic texts, while others (the North American academic culture, for example) expect discussion of controversies and evidence for one position. Different approaches to writing are not necessarily better or worse—but you should be aware of the differences when you write.

Writing for your instructor   Regard your instructor not as an expert but as a stand-in for a larger audience of general readers who are familiar with some of the basic information and the terminology of a particular discipline but not with detailed facts or the precise focus of your assigned or chosen topic. For the writing that you do in college, a unique set of conventions prevails. Even if you are certain that the reader (your instructor) knows what article, concept, or story you are writing about, the conventions of academic writing require you to identify the author and title and not simply begin by referring to "This story" or "This article."

KEY POINTS

Writing for Your Instructor

1. Ask your instructor about special guidelines for the paper: What background information should be included and what can be safely omitted? For example, for a paper analyzing an article or story, find out if your instructor envisions an audience that has read the work and so does not expect a detailed summary or an audience that has not read the work and would benefit from a summary. For a science paper, find out if you need to include tables or charts.

2. Find out if your instructor is willing to look at an early outline or draft of your paper.

3. Follow carefully any instructions about length, format, organization, and date of delivery.

4. Ask your instructor if you can see model papers for the course, ideally a paper that would earn an A and a model of an unsatisfactory paper.

5. Before you begin, find out what level of formality your instructor expects. For example, how acceptable will informal language and abbreviations be?

For more on writing about literature or writing in academic disciplines, see 52b–52d.

Writing and preparing presentations for individuals with disabilities When you prepare your texts for presentation in class, at work, or on the Web, consider that some of your audience may need special accommodations.

> ## KEY POINTS
>
> ### Taking Disabilities into Account
>
> 1. With shared hard-copy texts, if you have a reader with impaired vision, prepare a special copy in a larger type size.
>
> 2. With online texts, consider whether you need to limit visuals for vision-impaired audience members who have to use a screen-reader program such as Microsoft's Job Action with Speech (JAWS), which reads aloud what is on a computer screen. An alternative is to provide text descriptions of any visuals.
>
> 3. Pay attention to your use of color in visuals; contrasting shades will work better for some readers than entirely different colors.
>
> 4. In a multimedia presentation, provide alternatives to sound for those who do not hear well.
>
> 5. When you present your work via e-mail or on the Web, consult *WebAim* at <http://www.webaim.org> to ensure that you make your documents accessible to those with physical or cognitive disabilities. (Such strategies include providing a zoom function, allowing the possibility for enlarging text, and adding text to all visual material so that it can be read by screen-reader programs.) The *WebAim* site also contains strategies not only for considering readers but also for helping writers with physical and cognitive disabilities. A useful site that will test your own Web documents for accessibility is the *Bobby* site at <http://bobby.watchfire.com>.

1c Requirements, assignments, and schedules

Requirements The expectations of readers depend not only on the purpose of the piece of writing but also on the requirements of the context and the specific task. Use these questions to help you establish what you need to do in any writing task in a college, community, or business setting.

- What is the assigned task?
- Who will read what you write?
- What directions have been supplied, if any?
- What do you already know about the type of writing required?

- Have you been given detailed instructions about content and format, or are you free to find your own topic and your own way of approaching it?
- What sources of information are appropriate for the task (for example, interviews with experts, statistics, or critical essays), and what style are you expected to use to cite those sources (MLA, APA)?
- Will you present your writing on paper or online?
- How long do you have to complete the task?
- How will the written product be evaluated?

Assignments Always read the assignment carefully, and make sure you understand what you are being asked to do. Essay assignments often use the following verbs:

analyze: divide into parts and discuss each part

argue: make a claim and point out your reasons

classify: organize people, objects, or concepts into groups

compare: point out similarities

contrast: point out differences

define: give the meaning of

discuss: state important characteristics and main points

evaluate: define criteria for judgment and examine good and bad points, strengths and weaknesses

explain: give reasons or make clear by analyzing, defining, contrasting, illustrating, and so on

illustrate: give examples from experience and reading

relate: point out and discuss connections

Schedules Knowing the requirements helps you plan how to meet them. Radio host Ira Glass considers himself someone who thrives on deadlines, commenting, "There are people who are fundamentally lazy, who only get anything done because they put themselves under dreadful deadline pressure. Those people are all my brothers." You may agree with Glass that delaying and working in a last-minute frenzy is the only way to get anything done, but you will be pleasantly surprised at how much better you can do if you take the rush and panic out of the process. Section 38b provides detailed guidelines for setting a schedule for a research paper, but even a much simpler writing project deserves planning.

As soon as you know what the assignment is and when the final draft is due, work backward from that date to establish a schedule that allows you to do what needs to be done. Here is a sample four-day schedule for a short essay assignment in an English course.

Monday through Tuesday: Find and narrow a topic, brainstorm ideas, and make a scratch outline.

Wednesday: Write a first draft. Get feedback from a classmate, tutor, or study group. Read and analyze the draft, and plan revisions.

Thursday: Find any necessary additional information. Revise, edit, format, proofread, and print or post online.

Adapt this plan to fit the requirements of the writing project, your study and work schedule, and the length of time available. You can also build in rewards for yourself as you complete a part of the task.

"I wrote another five hundred words. Can I have another cookie?"

1d Tone

Choosing the right tone means fitting the structure and language you use to the type of writing you are doing, your purpose in doing the writing, and the expectations of readers. Tone can also be explained as the attitude of the writer toward the subject and the audience.

Using the appropriate tone in academic writing can increase your credibility; readers will be suspicious of a writer whose tone takes attention away from the content. Similarly, a casual e-mail message to a friend calls for a tone different from that of an informative business report for your boss. The content and language will be different; in addition, word choice can determine a humorous, sarcastic, ironic, serious, tongue-in-cheek, technical, formal, or conversational tone. For more on tone, see 8d, item 2.

EXERCISE 1.1   Match the tone of passages to the intended readers.

Read the following passages, and identify the tone of each passage. Then describe the audience or audiences that you think the writer had in mind. (**A** = See Answer Key.)

A 1. It's a bit oversimplified, but substantially true: A 30-minute walk a day helps keep the doctor away. That's the gist of the 278-page *Physical Activity and Health: A Report of the Surgeon General*, issued in 1996, which urged Americans to get 30 minutes of moderate activity on most days of the week. It's also the central finding of a Harvard University study, published last August in the *New England Journal of Medicine*, which concluded that walking can reduce the risk of heart attacks in women to the same degree as vigorous exercise.

—Carol Krucoff, "A Walk a Day"

Tone:_____   Audience:_____

2. The health benefits of physical activity have achieved international recognition following the publication of the 1996 US Surgeon General's report on physical activity and health. Given the high prevalence of inactivity, the promotion of physical activity appears to be at least as important in coronary heart disease prevention as efforts to reduce high cholesterol or high blood pressure, and more important than these factors in contributing to the overall burden of disease. . . . Physical activity is also associated with aspects of injury prevention [and with] positive mental health and reduces the risk of developing colon and probably breast and prostate cancer and possibly lung cancer. . . .

—Adrian Bauman, Neville Owen, and Eva Leslie, "Physical Activity and Health Outcomes: Epidemiological Evidence, National Guidelines and Public Health Initiatives"

Tone:_____   Audience:_____

3. There's a reason we're born with limbs. They're supposed to move. They *need* to move. And they need to move more than just three times a week when we put on special neon-colored clothes and stand on a machine that looks like the command cabin of the Space Shuttle *Atlantis*.

The active use of our physical bodies has to be more a part of our everyday lives. We need to get into the habit of using our bodies every minute by engaging our bodies in work, in play, in our errands, in all our daily rituals.

—Loretta LaRoche, *Life Is Not a Stress Rehearsal*

Tone:_____   Audience:_____

1e   Standard English and other Englishes

In an academic or business environment, the norm for written and spoken English is called Standard English. *Standard English* is defined by the *American Heritage Dictionary* (*AHD*) as the "variety of English that is generally acknowledged as the model for the speech and writing of educated speakers." A Usage Note in the *AHD,* however, continues, "A form that is considered standard in one region may be nonstandard in another," and points out that *standard* and *nonstandard* are relative terms, depending largely on context. The Note concludes, "Thus while the term can serve a useful descriptive purpose providing the context makes its meaning clear, it shouldn't be construed as conferring any absolute positive evaluation."

In short, the concept of Standard English is complex. It is inextricably entwined with the region, race, class, education, and gender of both the speaker (or writer) and the listener (or reader).

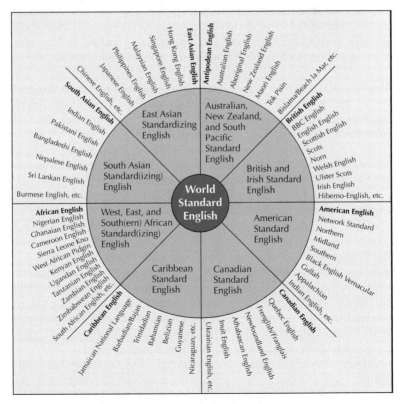

The Circle of World English
—Tom McArthur, "The English Languages," *English Today* 11 (July 1987): 11. Reprinted with the permission of Cambridge University Press.

The Circle of World English shows just some of the ways in which Standard English is being supplemented and challenged by other ways of speaking and writing. Note, though, that the influences are not only geographical; language variation is also influenced by technology, popular culture, race, gender, and sexual politics. (To learn more about Englishes around the world, see 32a.) But despite the complexity and fluidity of Standard English with all its quirks, irregularities, rules, and exceptions, in the academic and business world its conventions remain relatively rigid, with only subtle variation from country to country, region to region. Its prescribed forms are still politically and sociologically branded as the language of those in power in society; its practices are what most readers expect. Therefore, even if your ideas are original and insightful, readers may soon become impatient if you do not express those ideas in sentences that follow the conventions determined by the history of the language and the prescriptive power of the majority of its educated readers.

In your daily interactions with language, you will, however, come across examples of variation in usage, language change, and the coinage of new words. Scholars now see Englishes—varieties of English—instead of a monolithic English with an immutable set of rules.

The Englishes of North America   The Englishes of North America are living repositories of rich cultural heritages. Dialects as diverse as African American Vernacular (also known as Black English Vernacular), Gullah, Chicano English, and Newfoundland English have developed over generations while contemporary cultural movements and technological advances have spawned new uses of language such as hip-hop and cyber speech.

The polyphony of dialects, vernaculars, colloquialisms, slang expressions, and jargons that make up North American Englishes allows us to participate in multiple conversations. Think about the different Englishes you draw on in your day-to-day life. Compare the English you use when speaking with your family with the English you use with college professors, your employer, or your friends. Compare the English you read in a novel written 150 years ago with the English in your favorite magazine that came out last week, or compare the English you hear on the news with that of a late night comedy program on television. How does the English you write for a term paper compare with the English you write in an e-mail or blog?

Even if English is your only language, you might well consider yourself multilingual when you think about all the Englishes you move back and forth among and how and when you use academic English. As author Amy Tan writes in her essay "Mother Tongue," "I am fascinated by language in daily life. I spend a great deal of my time thinking about the power of language—the way it can evoke an emotion, a visual image, a complex idea, or a simple truth. Language is the tool of my trade. And I use them all—all the Englishes I grew up with."

1f In your own words: Resisting the lure of copy and paste

One of the downsides of the information explosion is the availability of so much information. Yes, that can be a downside, especially when you are short of time to finish an assignment and you know how easy it is to cut the perfect passage from an online site ✄ and paste it 📋 into your own document as if it were your own. When you are rushing to meet a deadline, it's also easy to not take the time to paraphrase or to select short, appropriate quotations.

The bottom line of this short section on the ease of cutting and pasting is this:

Don't do it.

It is better to be late with an assignment than to fall into the copying trap, especially since the penalties for plagiarizing are far worse than those for lateness. Turn to chapters 37 and 40 for useful strategies to help you plan your time and manage your source information.

2 Think Critically about Reading and Writing.

"I wonder where she gets that from? I don't understand that point. She hasn't convinced me at all." Just as we think critically about what we read, readers think critically when they read what we write, sometimes making comments like these. Thinking is inextricably tied to reading and writing, so much so that thinking critically is essential to being a good reader and a good writer.

Critical thinking leads us to ask questions about what we see, hear, or read. When we think critically, we do not accept everything at face value just because it is written on a page or screen. Thinking critically does not mean thinking negatively in order to criticize someone—unless, of course, we intend to criticize. Instead, it means questioning, discussing, and looking at an issue from a number of sides.

If you think of discussions you have had with friends about movies, music, TV programs, video games, Web sites, and books, you will realize that you already have the basic tools for thinking critically as you watch, listen, read, and write. You can then develop and refine those basic tools as you do reading and writing for college courses.

For more on thinking critically about visuals, see 11a and 11b.

2a How to read critically

How are you going to read what someone else has written? Imagine sitting down with a newspaper, comic book, poem, novel, letter from a relative, and a detailed instruction booklet on assembling a complex new grill, computer, or drum set. You will read each piece in a different way, depending on its purpose, your plans, and the response required. For instance, you may decide to skim the newspaper, admire the visual style used in the comic book's illustrations, memorize the poem, read the novel as an entertaining escape, answer immediately the letter from the relative, and study the instruction manual with an intent expression.

Now imagine that you are reading a passage that you are then going to analyze and write about, which is often the case in college. You may be looking for pieces of information, a general overview, the claim the author is making, the author's use of language, or specific details. Use the tactics in the Key Points box.

KEY POINTS

Tactics for Effective Reading

1. With an informational work (not a work of literature), skim when you want to know "Is this worth a detailed reading?" Look at the table of contents, any blurb or summary, preface, chapter introductions and conclusions, and index, in order to get a sense of whether the work meets your needs and how long it will take you to read and digest it.

2. Establish what background knowledge you need: What knowledge and information does the writer expect you to have? You may need to do some preliminary reading.

3. Give yourself large blocks of time for a long work, allowing yourself to become immersed. Reading quickly in short sessions will lead to a sketchy or superficial understanding of a work. As Woody Allen puts it, "I took a course in speed reading and I've just finished *War and Peace*. It pertains to Russia."

4. Predict as you read. Literacy theorist Kenneth Goodman has called reading a "psycholinguistic guessing game." See how

accurately you can predict what a writer will say next and how he or she will say it.

5. When doing focused research, read with the goal of finding a specific piece of information.

6. As you read, make inferences about what the writer intends and what assumptions the writer makes. Making an inference means "deriving conclusions that are not explicit in what is said" (*American Heritage Dictionary*).

7. Write as you read—comments, notes, questions, highlighting of main points. See the Key Points box on page 16.

8. Read more than once, especially for a challenging text, so that you are sure you have grasped all the text's complexities and so that you can review its main points.

9. Read aloud a poem, drama, short creative work, or any section of a work that you find difficult to follow. Doing this will help you hear the writer's voice more vividly.

10. Use a dictionary to find the meanings of words you do not know.

2b Annotating a reading

When you read, annotate. Read with a pencil in hand or a keyboard along with you so you can capture and record your ideas, questions, and associations. These annotations can be helpful starting points if you need to write a response to a particular reading.

While reading the following passage about the Ultimatum Game, for example, a student annotated the passage as she read it, increasing her interaction with the article.

Imagine that somebody offers you $100. All you have to do is agree with some other anonymous person on how to share the sum. The rules are strict. The two of you are in separate rooms and cannot exchange information. A coin toss decides which of you will propose how to share the money. Suppose that you are the proposer. You can make a single offer of how to split the sum, and the other person—the responder—can say yes or no. The responder also knows the rules and the total amount of money at stake. If her answer is yes, the deal goes ahead. If her answer is no, neither of you gets anything. In both cases, the game is over and will not be repeated. What will you do?

I like the direct approach!

Critical point

Authors use feminine pronoun here

—Excerpt from "Economics of Fair Play," by Karl Sigmund. Copyright © 2002 by Scientific American, Inc. All rights reserved.

Have the authors researched this assumption?

Instinctively, many people feel they should offer 50 percent, because such a division is "fair" and therefore likely to be accepted. More daring people, however, think they might get away with offering somewhat less than half the sum.

Or more greedy?

But the organizers will know what I offer, so it's not entirely between two anonymous people.

Before making a decision, you should ask yourself what you would do if you were the responder. The only thing you can do as the responder is say yes or no to a given amount of money. If the offer were 10 percent, would you take $10 and let someone walk away with $90, or would you rather have nothing at all? What if the offer were only 1 percent? Isn't $1 better than no dollars? And remember, haggling is strictly forbidden. Just one offer by the proposer; the responder can take it or leave it.

So what will you offer?

—Karl Sigmund, Ernst Fehr, and Martin A. Nowak,
"The Economics of Fair Play"

It is a good idea to get into the habit of writing your responses to what you read. In this way, your critical reading becomes more systematic and helpful to you. Try the techniques listed in the Key Points box.

KEY POINTS

Using Writing to Respond to a Reading

1. If you own the book or a copy of an article, read with a pencil and highlighter in hand. Highlight sparingly—only the most important passages or useful quotations. Write comments and questions in the margins and on self-stick notes.

2. Read, pause, and make notes. Read a paragraph or a page at a time, pause, and write a brief summary and your own comments.

3. Write a summary or paraphrase of a significant work or passage on index cards or in computer files (40e).

4. Write questions about the writer's claims and assumptions (6f).

5. Write challenges to the writer's views: "But what about . . .?"

6. Record in a journal or research notebook your reactions to what you have read.

7. Use a double-entry notebook to summarize the writer's ideas and how they relate to your own ideas and experiences (3b).

EXERCISE 2.1   Respond to reading by annotating.
Annotate the following excerpt from Stephen L. Carter's "The Insufficiency of Honesty." Go to *The Open Handbook* at <http://college.hmco.com/keys.html>, and click on Writing Process to download this excerpt if you would like to change the line spacing or use Track Changes to make your annotations.

A couple of years ago I began a university commencement address by telling the audience that I was going to talk about integrity. The crowd broke into applause. Applause! Just because they had heard the word "integrity"; that's how starved for it they were. . . .

When I refer to integrity, I have something very specific in mind. Integrity, as I will use the term, requires three steps: (1) *discerning* what is right and what is wrong; (2) *acting* on what you have discerned, even at personal cost; and (3) *saying openly* that you are acting on your understanding of right and wrong. The first criterion captures the idea that integrity requires a degree of moral reflectiveness. The second brings in the ideal of a person of integrity as steadfast, a quality that includes keeping one's commitments. The third reminds us that a person of integrity is unashamed of doing the right thing.

2c Critical reading of your own writing

When you read critically, imagine other readers doing the same thing when they read what you write. In order to pass readers' tests, you need to examine your drafts with great care and subject them to rigorous questioning. While doing your initial drafting, do not worry too much about readers' reactions, but after you have put something down on paper, examine it from a critical reader's perspective. Try putting your draft away for a while so that you can look at it with fresh eyes and see it as a new reader might see it—warts and all.

While it is important not to stop and try to perfect every word as you write, you may find that your difficulty in choosing the right words comes from not really knowing what you are trying to say. Experiment with speaking your ideas aloud before you write them, as if explaining them to a friend.

As you write, if you feel uncertain about the information you include, the stance you take, the effectiveness of your style, or just the choice of a word, do not stop to try to get it perfect. Keep going with your train of thought, but mark the questionable passage with a symbol (such as * or #). That will remind you to return to it later and ponder it anew. You can also ask a classmate or friend to read a draft and put a question mark by anything that seems unclear or wrong.

When you read your own draft, do some role-playing. Imagine you are your professor. What comments would he or she make?

3 Generate Ideas.

Whether you have to generate your own idea for a topic or you already have a topic to explore in detail, you need strategies other than staring at the ceiling or waiting for inspiration to fly in through the window. Professional writers use a variety of techniques to generate ideas at various stages of the process. Diane Ackerman, in her article "Oh Muse! You Do Make Things Difficult!" reports that the poet Dame Edith Sitwell used to lie in an open coffin; French novelist Colette picked fleas from her cat; statesman Benjamin Franklin soaked in the bathtub; and German dramatist Friedrich Schiller sniffed rotten apples stored in his desk.

Perhaps you have developed your own original approach to generating ideas. Perhaps you were taught a more formal way to begin a writing project, such as constructing an outline. If what you do now doesn't seem to produce good results, or if you are ready for a change, try some of the methods described in 3a–3e and see how they work. Not every method works equally well for every project or for every writer. Experimenting is a good idea.

TechToolkit   Web Sites for Generating Ideas

Some Web sites for writers include useful information on generating ideas and planning. Try, for example, the following:

- Planning/Starting to Write section at the Purdue University Online Writing Lab site at <http://owl.english.purdue.edu/handouts/general/index.html#planning>
- Getting Started page of the CUNY (City University of New York) WriteSite at <http://writesite.cuny.edu/projects/stages/start/index.html>
- Discovering What to Write page of the Paradigm Online Writing Assistant at <http://www.powa.org/discover/index.html> ■

Exercise 3.1   Write about your own writing process.
Think about the most recent essay you have written. Write an account of what the assignment was, how you generated ideas, how you wrote the essay, where you did your writing, and whether you wrote it with a word processing program or not. How much time was given between the assignment and the due date, and how did you use that time? How did you feel as you wrote the essay? Be complete and frank in describing your writing process. The point is to examine the way you write. Read your account aloud to a group of classmates. Then discuss any differences between their accounts and yours. A sample answer is in the Answer Key.

3a Finding a topic

Finding a topic "What on earth am I going to write about?" is a question frequently voiced or at least thought in college classrooms, especially in those classrooms in which students are free to write about any topic that interests them.

Using the strategies in 3b–3e will help you find topics. In addition, think about what matters to you. Reflect on issues raised in your college courses; read newspapers and magazines for current issues; consider campus, community, city, state, and nationwide issues; and look at the Library of Congress Subject Headings to get ideas (see chapter 39). Sometimes, browsing an online library catalog, a Web directory, or a site devoted to research such as the Brookings Institution at <http://www.brookings.org/index/research.htm> can produce good ideas for choosing a topic, but it is usually better to begin with something that has caught your interest elsewhere and has some connection to your life.

 TECHTOOLKIT   Using Web Directories to Find a Topic

Academic Web directories assembled by librarians and academic institutions provide reliable sources for finding good academic subjects. Try, for example, Librarians' Index to the Internet at <http://lii.org>, Academic Info at <http://www.academicinfo.net>, and Voice of the Shuttle, a University of California at Santa Barbara directory for humanities research at <http://vos.ucsb.edu>. For more on using search engines and directories, see 39a; for evaluating online materials, see 39f. ■

General Internet search engines and directories such as Yahoo! at <http://www.yahoo.com> and Google at <http://www.google.com> offer subject categories that you can explore and successively narrow down to find a topic suitable for an essay. For example, one Yahoo! search beginning with "Education" produced forty different categories, as shown in the screenshot on page 20. Clicking on *reform* produced links to twenty-one site listings (such as *computers as tutors*, *National Clearinghouse for Comprehensive School Reform*, *EducationReform.net*, and *No Child Left Behind*). Many of the sites linked to Web pages on topics such as "voucher programs" and "charter schools," as well as to many other sites, some with bibliographies with further online links. Such directories can suggest a wide range of interesting topics for you to explore.

Once you have a topic in mind, discussing it with others, conducting an interview, administering a questionnaire or survey, and doing a preliminary library and Web search will help you determine whether enough material is available and whether what is available is relevant and interesting.

Refining a topic   The strategies described in 3b–3e can help you find a topic and then generate ideas to include in an essay. While finding a topic is a necessary step, it is only a beginning. The topic has then to be tailored and adapted to make it appropriate for the length and type of essay you intend to write; then, for an opinion essay or an argument, you need to formulate what point of view you will express on the topic, in the form of a thesis. You also need to generate specific and concrete details to use as evidence and support for the thesis (4a).

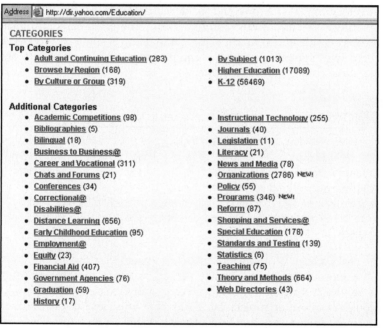

| Address | http://dir.yahoo.com/Education/ |

CATEGORIES

Top Categories
- Adult and Continuing Education (283)
- Browse by Region (168)
- By Culture or Group (319)
- By Subject (1013)
- Higher Education (17089)
- K-12 (56469)

Additional Categories
- Academic Competitions (98)
- Bibliographies (5)
- Bilingual (18)
- Business to Business@
- Career and Vocational (311)
- Chats and Forums (21)
- Conferences (34)
- Correctional@
- Disabilities@
- Distance Learning (656)
- Early Childhood Education (95)
- Employment@
- Equity (23)
- Financial Aid (407)
- Government Agencies (76)
- Graduation (59)
- History (17)
- Instructional Technology (255)
- Journals (40)
- Legislation (11)
- Literacy (21)
- News and Media (78)
- Organizations (2786) NEW!
- Policy (55)
- Programs (346) NEW!
- Reform (87)
- Shopping and Services@
- Special Education (178)
- Standards and Testing (139)
- Statistics (6)
- Teaching (75)
- Theory and Methods (664)
- Web Directories (43)

—Reproduced with permission of Yahoo! Inc. *Yahoo!* and the Yahoo! logo are trademarks of Yahoo! Inc.

What if you are assigned a topic that you are not interested in? That can happen, but do not despair. Read as much as you can on the topic until something strikes you and captures your interest. You can try taking the opposite point of view from that of one of your sources, challenging the point of view. Or you can set yourself the task of showing readers exactly why the topic has not grabbed people's interest—maybe the literature and the research have been just too technical or inaccessible? If you can, find a human angle.

Go to *The Open Handbook* at <http://college/hmco.com/keys.html>, and click on Research and Documentation for a tutorial on how to focus a topic by using search engines.

3b ▶ Journals, blogs, and online conversations

A *journal* can be far more than a personal diary. Many writers carry a notebook and write in it every day; others maintain a Web log or *blog*. Journal entries can be observations, references, quotations, questions for research, notes on events, and ideas about assigned texts or topics, as well as specific pieces of writing in progress. A journal can also serve as a review for final examinations or essay tests, reminding you of areas of special interest or subjects you did not understand.

The *double-entry* or *dialectical journal* provides a formalized way for you to think critically about readings and lectures. Two pages or two columns or open windows in your word processor provide the space for interaction. On the left-hand side, write summaries, quotations, and accounts of readings, lectures, and class discussions—that is, record as exactly and concisely as you can what you read or heard. The left-hand side, in short, is reserved for information about the material. On the right-hand side, record your own comments, reactions, and questions about the material (see 2b on annotating a reading). The right-hand side is the place to make your own connections between the reading or lecture and your own experience and knowledge. Go to *The Open Handbook* at <http://college.hmco
.com/keys.html>, and click on Writing Process for an example of a student's double-entry journal.

A *blog* also gives you the opportunity to think aloud—in public. Not only can others read your posting; they can respond to it as well. It is easy to set up a blog using an automated publishing system like <http://www.blogger.com> or <http://www.typepad.com>. Blogs are posted in reverse chronological order but otherwise function similarly to a writer's journal. The unedited blog, entitled "The *Life* of a Salesman" (p. 22), demonstrates how Tiffany Brattina, a student at Seton Hill University, works out a personal, original, and critical point of view as she considers an alternative interpretation of the character Willie Loman in Arthur Miller's play *Death of a Salesman*. Brattina largely avoids the colloquial nature of instant messaging and informal e-mail and begins to move to the conventions of public discourse suitable for her academic audience (see 9e). Knowing that other students in her English course will be reading her blog, Brattina openly asks what others think. For examples of *online conversations* on Blackboard, go to *The Open Handbook* at <http://college.hmco.com/keys.html>, and click on Writing Process.

March 16, 2004

The *Life* of a Salesman

Ok. So. I'm sure during class today everyone talked about how crazy Willie was, and I am the first to agree. Willie was insane, in the end. However, what about his life?

In *Death of a Salesman* we see the end of Willie's life as a salesman. He went through his entire life just working on the road selling things to buyers, he didn't know how to do anything else. Don't you think that would make you go crazy? If a company you worked for your entire life took you off of salary and put you on commission like you were just starting out wouldn't you feel like you were unworthy? Then there is the fact that Willie and his family didn't really have any money to their names at all. Willie kept borrowing money from Charley so that Linda wouldn't know that he wasn't getting paid anymore. Then the company he worked for fired him! I feel bad for Willie, I really do. His kids thought that he was insane and wanted nothing to do with him. The people he worked for his entire life turned him away. Willie was old, tired, and worn out and people including his family turned their backs on him.

Let me make this personal for a minute. My dad recently went through something very similar at his place of work. The company he worked for came into new management and they tried to put my dad on commission. My dad has major tenure where he works considering he is now 56 and has been working there for 40 years making him the longest member still working at the company. He took the new management to court and won his case. I know that while my dad was going through that time he was a total mess, so seeing my dad I can understand what Willie was going through.

What do you guys think? Do you feel bad for Willie or do you think he was just a jerk? Why or why not?

3c   Freewriting

If you do not know what to write about or how to approach a broad subject, try doing from five to ten minutes of *freewriting* either on paper or on the computer. When you freewrite, you let one idea lead to another in free association, thinking only about ideas and what you can say on the topic. The important thing is to keep writing.

Zhe Chen selected the topic "name and identity" and did some exploratory work to find a focus and narrow the topic. She eventually decided to write an essay examining the effects of the Chinese Cultural Revolution on family identity. Here is her unedited freewriting that led her initially to that idea. Her use of "#" is explained on page 23.

I have a unusual name, Zhe. My friends in China say it's a boys name. My friends in America think it has only one letter. Most of my American friends have difficulty pronouncing my name.

Some people ask me why don't I Americanize my name so it would be easier to pronounce. But I say if I change my name, it will not be me any more. What else can I write? When I was seven years old, I asked my mother what my name meant. "Ask your father," she said as she washed dishes. It was raining outside, and the room was so quiet that I could hear the rain puttering [?? Look this word up] on the #. My father's thoughts returned to another rainy day in 1967 when the Cultural Revolution just begun. Thousands of people had been banished to countryside and all the schools were closed. My grandparents fled to Hong Kong but my father and aunt stayed in China. Life was difficult. Gangs sent them to the countryside to work. It was here that my parents met.

Back to name again. My father named me Zhe. In Chinese my name means "remember" and "hope." He wanted me remember the Cultural Revolution and he wanted me to finish college. He didn't have that chance.

KEY POINTS

Freewriting Tips

1. Give yourself a time limit of five or ten minutes.

2. Write as much as you can as quickly as you can on possible subjects or on a subject you have already determined.

3. As you write, concentrate on getting some ideas on the page or screen. Don't pause to check or edit. This piece of writing is for your eyes only; no one else will ever read it, let alone judge it.

4. If you get stuck, just keep repeating a promising idea or writing about why you get stuck or why the topic is difficult. Use slang, abbreviations, and the first words you think of—in any language. Try not to stop writing.

5. At the end of the time limit, read through your freewriting, highlight the best idea that has emerged, and begin writing again with that idea as the focus.

TECHTOOLKIT   Blank Screen and Use of Symbols in Freewriting

Try this if you are a good typist. While freewriting on a computer, turn off the monitor so that you write freely without being tempted to scrutinize what you have written. Then you will keep writing and not stop to edit and make changes. In addition, as you write, if you cannot think of an appropriate word, simply put in a symbol such as #, as Zhe Chen did when she momentarily could not recall the word *windowpanes*. Use the Search command to find your symbol later, when you can spend more time thinking about the appropriate word. ■

ESL NOTE   Using Your First Language in Freewriting

Freewriting is writing for *you,* writing to discover ideas and get words down on a page or screen. If you can't think of a phrase or word, simply write it in your first language, or write a question in square brackets as Zhe Chen did, to remind yourself to get help from a dictionary or to ask a classmate or your instructor later. ■

3d   Brainstorming, listing, and mapping

Another way to generate ideas is by *brainstorming*—making a free-wheeling list of ideas as you think of them. Brainstorming is enhanced if you do it collaboratively in a group, discussing and then listing or mapping your ideas. By yourself or with the group, scrutinize the ideas, arrange them in lists or draw a map of them, and add to or eliminate them.

One group of students working collaboratively made the following brainstorming list on the topic "changing a name":

immigrants   show business
Ellis Island   criminals?
voluntary changes--hate name   escape from family and parents
George Eliot (Mary Ann Evans)
Woody Allen (Allen Stewart Konigsberg)
P. Diddy (Sean Combs aka Puff Daddy)
writers and their pseudonyms--who?
married women: some keep own name, some change, some use both
    names and hyphenate
Hillary Clinton/Hillary Rodham Clinton
forced name changes
political name changes
name changes because of racism or oppression

Once the students had made the list, they reviewed it, rejected some items, expanded on others, and grouped items. Thus, they developed a range of subcategories that led them to possibilities for new lists, further exploration, and essay organization:

Voluntary Name Changes
authors: George Eliot, Mark Twain, Isak Dinesen
show business and stage names: Woody Allen, Bob Dylan, Ringo Starr,
    P. Diddy, Eminem, Pink
ethnic and religious identification: Malcolm X, Muhammad Ali

Name Changes upon Marriage	Forced Name Changes
reasons for changing or not changing	immigrants on Ellis Island
Hillary Clinton	wartime oppression
problem of children's names	slavery
alternative: hyphenated name	

Mapping, also called *clustering,* is a visual way of brainstorming and connecting ideas. It focuses your brainstorming, organizes the ideas as you generate them, and can be done individually or in a group. Write your topic in a circle at the center of a page, think of ideas related to the topic, and write those ideas on the page around the central topic. Draw lines from the topic to the related ideas. Then add details under each of the ideas you noted. For an assignment on "current issues in education," a student created the following map and saw that it indicated several possibilities for topics, such as school vouchers, home-schooling, and the social exclusivity of private schools.

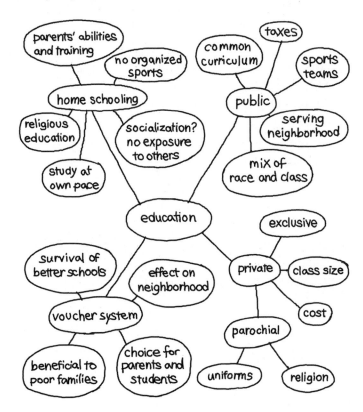

3e Journalists' questions

Journalists check the coverage of their stories by making sure that they answer six questions—Who? What? When? Where? Why? How?—though not in any set order. A report on a public transit strike, for example, would include details about the union leaders (who they were), the issue of working conditions and benefits (what the situation was), the date and time of the confrontation (when the strike occurred), the place (where it occurred), what caused the confrontation (why it happened), and how the people involved behaved and resolved the strike (how it evolved and ended). If you are telling the story of an event, either as a complete essay or as an example in an essay, asking the journalists' six questions will help you think comprehensively about your topic. (Note, though, that newspaper articles have different conventions from academic essays, such as shorter paragraphs and fewer or no source citations.)

EXERCISE 3.2   Explore a topic in several ways.
Work with a group of other students to select a broad topic (such as the environment, heroes, immigration, aging, or fast food). Each person in the group will explore the topic using **two** of the following methods:

- writing a blog to initiate an online discussion
- freewriting
- brainstorming and grouping ideas
- mapping
- writing answers to the journalists' questions

Read each other's explorations, and discuss which methods generated good ideas.

4   Find a Focus and a Structure.

After you have explored ideas both for discovery of a topic and about the chosen topic, you may end up with pages of journal writing, brainstorming, listing, freewriting, and notes from reading; with screens of discussion board postings or blogs; and with more ideas buzzing around your head. The next task is to put all those randomly generated ideas into some kind of logical order so that readers can discern in your finished piece of writing a clear focus and a recognizable structuring of ideas.

4a From topic to thesis

In college courses, you may be given any of the following types of assignments for an essay, arranged here from the broadest in scope to the narrowest:

- a free choice of subject or a broad subject area, such as "genetic engineering" or "affirmative action"
- a focused and specific topic, such as "the city's plans to build apartments on landfill" or "the treatment of welfare recipients in California"
- an actual question to answer, such as "Is age an issue in cases of driving accidents?"

Wherever you start, you need to move toward what you want to say on the issue. This process is illustrated in the Key Points box.

KEY POINTS

Subject, Topic, Question, Thesis: A Continuum

Level 1: *Broad subject area*

Level 2: *Narrowed topic* for exploration within that subject area

Level 3: *Key question* that concerns you

Level 4: Your *thesis* (your claim or statement of opinion or your main idea in answer to the question). Often you need to do a great deal of reading and writing and trying out possible theses before you settle on an appropriate one.

Your *thesis*, or *claim*, is your statement of opinion, main idea, or message that unifies your piece of writing, makes a connection between you and the subject area, lets readers know where you stand in relation to the topic, or answers the question posed. But you cannot move toward a good thesis if your topic is too broad or too narrow.

Here is one student's movement from subject to thesis over several days of reading, discussion, freewriting, and note-taking:

Subject: College admissions policies

Narrowed Topic: College admissions for athletes

Question: Should success in sports have any influence on
college admissions?

Thesis: College admissions policies should be based solely on academic
performance and potential, not on athletic ability.

If you choose a topic and a question that are too broad, you will find it difficult to generate a thesis with focused ideas and examples. Whenever you find yourself thinking, for instance, "There's so much to say about college admissions policies—their history, goals, practice, criticisms, successes—that I don't know where to start," narrow your topic. If you begin by choosing a topic and a question that are too narrow, you probably will not find enough material, so you may have to change your topic or question because of this lack of information. Whenever you feel you have enough material to fill only a page and can't imagine how you will find more ("What else *can* I say about how my cousin got into college?"), broaden your topic or change it completely. Above all, stay flexible; you may also want to change your topic or your question as you discover more information.

EXERCISE 4.1   Move from topic to thesis.
In groups of two or three, discuss the ways in which one of the following broad subject areas could be narrowed to a topic and a thesis appropriate to a seven-page essay.

small businesses	women's rights	migration
home-schooling	gambling	genetics
gun control	soap operas	the Olympics
health and	the film industry	beauty pageants
physical	advertisements	
education		

4b Formulating a working thesis—and why you need one

Suppose someone were to ask you, "What is the main idea that you want to communicate to readers in your piece of writing?" The sentence you would give in reply is your thesis, also known as a claim. Your thesis tells readers what point you are going to make about your topic, what stand you are going to take. It is not enough to say, "I am writing about bilingual education." Are you going to address bilingual education in elementary, secondary, or higher education? Which readers do you regard as your primary audience? Which geographical areas will you discuss? In short, what point do you want to make about which aspect of bilingual education—for which readers?

You don't have to know where to put your thesis statement in your essay right away, nor do you need to settle immediately on the exact wording of your thesis. However, even a preliminary idea for a topic can generate a working thesis that you can then refine as you plan, read, and write. See 6b on the thesis in an argument paper.

How to write a good thesis statement   A good thesis statement may be one or more of the following:

1. a strong, thought-provoking, or controversial statement

   ▶ **Bilingual education has not fulfilled its early promise.**

2. a call to action

   ▶ **All inner-city schools should set up transitional bilingual programs.**

3. a question preceding the thesis statement as its answer, backed up with details in the essay

   ▶ **What can bilingual education accomplish for a child? It can lead to personal as well as academic development.**

4. a preview or reflection of the structure of the essay

   ▶ **Bilingual education suffers from two main problems: a shortage of trained teachers and a lack of parental involvement.**

   ▶ **Although bilingual education suffers from a shortage of teachers and lack of parental involvement, its theoretical principles are sound.**

KEY POINTS

Thesis Checklist

You should be able to put a checkmark next to each quality as you examine your draft. Your thesis

1. is worth presenting and is the answer to a question that could be debated (is not an obvious truism or vague generalization)

2. narrows your topic to the main idea that you want to communicate

3. makes a claim or states your view about your topic

4. can be supported by details, facts, and examples within the assigned limitations of time and space

5. stimulates curiosity and interest in readers and prompts them to think "Why do you say that?" and then to read on and be convinced by what you have written

6. forecasts and unifies all that follows in your essay; does not include ideas or points that you do not intend to discuss in your essay

7. is expressed concisely in one or two complete sentences (though you will come across many variations as you read)

After you have formulated your thesis statement, write it on a self-stick note or an index card and keep it near you as you write. The note or card will remind you to stick to the point. If you still digress as you write, you may need to consider changing your thesis.

From working thesis to revision   An initial working thesis may be a tentative opinion statement that you formulate soon after you choose a topic—but try to move beyond it to something focused as soon as you can. As you think more, read more, learn more, and discover more specific ideas, you will usually find that you rework your thesis several times to make it more informative, less general, and more precise. You may even indicate in your thesis what main points of support you will discuss in your essay. Here are some examples of a preliminary working thesis later revised as a final draft thesis for a two- to three-page essay:

PERSONAL ESSAY

Preliminary working thesis: Starting college at age thirty-four was difficult for me.

Revised thesis: Starting college at age thirty-four has involved reassessing my commitments to work and family.

INFORMATIVE ESSAY

Preliminary working thesis: There are many ways to handle credit responsibly.

Revised thesis: To handle credit responsibly, students need to stick to a budget and control their shopping. [Here the "many ways" have been limited to two, named specifically. In addition, the target population has been limited to students.]

PERSUASIVE ESSAY

Preliminary working thesis: Affirmative action is a controversial policy in college admissions.

Revised thesis: Affirmative action used in the college admissions process is a good way to ensure diversity of students and equality in society. [Here readers expect a twofold argument, one addressing the ability of affirmative action to create diversity in a student body, the other broadening the concept to the idea of affirmative action also having an equalizing effect on society.]

PERSUASIVE ESSAY

Preliminary working thesis: Cell phones have many advantages.

Revised thesis: Although cell phones may cause problems when they are misused, they are a boon to working parents wanting to keep track of their children's whereabouts after school hours. [This refined thesis statement limits discussion of the advantages of cell phones to the benefits they provide to working parents; it also indicates that the writer will acknowledge some disadvantages but will evaluate these as less important than the advantages.]

Recognizing and writing a good thesis statement   A good thesis statement is a complete sentence (or, sometimes, more than one sentence), makes an interesting and debatable assertion, expresses an opinion that needs to be supported and explained, and does not simply state a fact or obvious truism. A good thesis statement also gives readers some sense of what main points will be used to support the thesis and how the essay will be organized.

INEFFECTIVE   **The desolation of shopping malls.**   [This phrase lacks a verb and so is not a sentence. It is more suitable as a title than a thesis. A thesis statement is a sentence that makes an assertion.]

INEFFECTIVE   **There are many kinds of exercise machines.**   [This statement is a sentence, but it does not make an interesting and debatable assertion. It does not express an opinion that needs to be supported and explained. Instead, it states a fact. The reader has no incentive to read on, no notion that by reading on he or she will find out useful or necessary information about exercise machines.]

INEFFECTIVE   *Death of a Salesman* **is a play by Arthur Miller.**   [This sentence states a fact. It does not make an interesting and debatable assertion. Readers, especially those who know their literature, will nod and think "Yes, I know that," and will not feel driven to read on to find out what makes you say that.]

INEFFECTIVE   **Murder is wrong.**   [Almost nobody would disagree or find this an interesting statement. This sentence states a truism, a statement so obvious that it does not merit discussion or engage readers' interest.]

EFFECTIVE   **Because so many students are older adults, colleges should allow a longer time to get a degree, provide more day-care centers, and develop more online courses.**   [This thesis statement establishes a clear focus on a topic, asserts an opinion, and gives the reader some sense of what main points will be used to support the thesis and how the essay will be organized.]

Stating your thesis in your paper   Even though it is useful to have a working thesis as you read and write drafts and to refine your thesis as you work, you will eventually need to decide if and where you will include a thesis statement in your essay. Ask your instructor about any special requirements for thesis location. In most academic writing in the humanities and social sciences, a thesis is stated clearly in the essay, usually near the beginning. See your thesis statement as a signpost—both for you as you write your draft and, later, for readers as they read your essay. A clear thesis prepares readers well for the rest of the essay.

Sometimes, though, particularly in descriptive, narrative, and informative writing, you may choose to imply your thesis and not

LANGUAGE AND CULTURE
Language, Identity, and the Thesis Statement

Often writers who have developed their writing skills in one language notice distinct differences in the conventions of writing in another, particularly with respect to the explicit statement of opinion in the thesis. A Chinese writer, Fan Shen, for example, sees the explicit thesis statement favored in Western writing as "symbolic of the values of a busy people in an industrialized society, rushing to get things done" (*College Composition and Communication* [Dec. 1989]: 462). It is difficult to determine how much of a role one's culture plays in the way one writes and to separate culture's role from the roles of gender, socioeconomic status, family background, and education. However, always consider what approaches your anticipated readers are likely to be familiar with and to value.

explicitly state it. In such a case, you make your thesis clear by the examples, details, and information you include. You may also choose to state your thesis at the end of your essay instead of the beginning. If so, you present all the evidence to build a case and then make the thesis act as a climax and logical statement about the outcome of the evidence. If you use key words from your thesis as you write, you will keep readers focused on your main idea.

On not falling in love with your working thesis   A good working thesis often takes so long to develop that you might be reluctant to change it. Be willing, however, to refine and change your thesis as you find more information and work with your material. Many writers begin with a tentative working thesis and then find that they come to a new conclusion at the end of the first draft. If that happens to you, start your second draft by focusing on the thesis that emerged during the writing of the first draft. In other words, change your thesis as you go along. Be flexible: it is easier to change a thesis statement to fit new ideas and new evidence that you discover than to find new evidence to fit a thesis. Note that your final revised thesis statement should take a firm stand on the issue. Flexibility during the writing process is not the same as indecision in the final product.

EXERCISE 4.2 Revise thesis statements.
The following thesis statements are too narrow, too broad, or too vague or are factual statements. Revise each one to make it an appropriate thesis statement for a three- to five-page essay. (**A** = See Answer Key.)

A 1. Legalizing homosexual marriage is a controversial issue.

A 2. Literacy is an important issue that must be dealt with.

A 3. Plants enhance the beauty of a home.

4. People with disabilities can face employment discrimination in several ways.

5. Alcoholism affects children.

6. Advertisers of food products use color-enhanced images to entice consumers into purchasing their products.

7. The media are responsible for causing eating disorders and encouraging unrealistic ideals of beauty.

4c Developing support

Once you have come up with a good thesis for your essay, you then have to find ways to develop and support it. Readers expect to find out why you hold a certain point of view or why you regard your information as important: What are your reasons? What is your evidence? Where does the evidence come from? Your paragraphs will develop and support your thesis one point at a time.

Let's say you are writing a paper with the following thesis:

College admissions policies should be based solely on academic performance and potential, not on athletic ability.

Your job in the paper is to show readers why you think that, to provide information that backs up your case, and to write a convincing argument. You may not be able to win over a scholarship football star to your side, but you should be able to make his team recognize that sound arguments exist. Here are some strategies you might use:

- Provide information about research studies showing low academic success rate of athletes, and report statistics of class rank at graduation.

- Give an account of an interview with a college admissions officer and an athletics coach.

- Give examples of credentials of nonathlete students who were rejected when athletes were admitted.

- Describe details of the athletic culture on a campus, showing how the athletic culture discourages academic study.
- Tell a story about an athlete's college applications.
- Provide instructions on how to highlight academic performance.
- Compare and contrast two high school students—one athlete and one nonathlete—applying to the same college.
- Define the terms *academic performance* and *athletic ability*.
- Classify athletes into types of athlete (for example, athletes who have maintained a B, C, or D average; athletes who need to practice for seven hours a week, fifteen hours, or more than fifteen).
- Explain the problem facing admissions officers, and offer a solution.

See 5c for examples of support that various writers have used within paragraphs and essays.

4d Planning and structuring your essay: Road maps, purpose statements, and outlines

Road maps   Once you have found a good topic and a working thesis, you will be ready to grapple with all the ideas you have generated. Think of organizing your ideas as preparing a road map for your readers. As MapQuest does for travelers, you can provide an analogous set of directions to take your readers along the most scenic, direct route, avoiding digressions and detours.

Understanding your thesis is the destination you want readers to reach—in fact, your thesis drives the essay and sets the course. Keep your working thesis in mind at all times.

Ask yourself these questions to help determine the best route to the destination for you and your readers:

1. *Plan of trip*   Where do I want to take my readers? What do I want them to learn about my topic and my views on the topic?
2. *Starting point*   What should readers know to make them want to get started on this journey?
3. *Major points of interest*   What major landmarks (major points of interest) should I point to as I take readers on the journey?
4. *Hazards on the route*   What do readers need to know about roads to avoid or roads that look inviting but do not go to the destination?
5. *Destination*   How do I let readers know that they have arrived at the destination? What landmark will indicate to them that they are there, where I want them to be?

Analogies aside, planning your essay means planning a beginning to capture readers' interest, clear points to validate your thesis, acknowledgment and refutation of any dissenting views, and an ending that leaves readers feeling informed and satisfied. For planning, you may find purpose statements, proposals, and outlines helpful.

Purpose statements A purpose statement is useful to focus your ideas and give yourself something to work with. Write a simple statement of purpose after you have crafted a working thesis. This statement may become more developed or later even change completely, but it will serve to guide your first steps in the process. Here is an example of a purpose statement written by Nick Sakari for a short paper in his first-year writing course. (Purpose statements can often be expanded into full-scale proposals, like the one in 38f.)

In this essay, I will try to persuade my professor and my classmates that historical novels blending fact and fiction--such as In the Time of the Butterflies by Julia Alvarez--should be included as required texts for history courses even though they go beyond historical fact. My thesis will be that history can never be the exact truth, and historical novels, along with memoirs and journals, offer valuable insight into how individual people are affected by historical events.

Scratch outlines A *scratch outline* is a rough list of numbered points that you intend to cover in your essay. A scratch outline lets you see what ideas you already have, how they connect, what you can do to support and develop them, and what further planning or research you still need to do. One student in the group that made the brainstorming list on page 24 developed the following scratch outline and formulated a working thesis:

Topic: Changing a name
Question: Why do people change their names?
Tentative working thesis: People change their names because they either have to or want to.
Types of name changes:
1. Forced name changes in a new country or a new school
2. Name changes to avoid discrimination or persecution
3. Name changes upon marriage
4. Name changes in show business
5. Voluntary name changes to avoid recognition
   a. Criminals
   b. Writers

When this student began to write his draft, however, he changed direction and unified some of his points, developing a more focused thesis (see more on formal outlines, directly following).

Formal outlines A *formal outline* spells out, in order, what points and supportive details you will use to develop your thesis and arranges them to show the overall form and structure of the essay, moving from the general to the specific, using points you have generated in brainstorming, mapping (3d), or other methods. As you formulate an outline, keep an image of readers in mind. Imagine them asking when they read your thesis, "Why do you think that? What is the evidence?" If you have explored the question in enough depth and breadth, you should be able to identify several reasons or main points of support. These will form the structural backbone of the essay. Then for each main reason or piece of support, imagine readers again asking, "Why is this point important? What is the evidence?"

You may produce a formal outline before you begin to write, but you are likely to find that making an outline with a high level of detail is more feasible after you have written a draft. Done at this later point, the outline serves as a check on the logic and completeness of what you have written, revealing any gaps, repetition, or illogical steps in the development of your essay.

KEY POINTS
Writing an Outline

1. Write a formal outline only after you have done a great deal of thinking, reading, writing, and research. Sometimes it is better to delay writing an outline until after you have a rough draft on paper; then you can outline what you have written and see if it makes sense.

2. Decide on whether items in the outline will be words and phrases (with no end punctuation) or complete sentences. If you can, go with complete sentences—you will find that doing that helps record or formulate your ideas more clearly. For a short essay, complete sentences written to indicate major points can then stand as the topic sentences of supporting paragraphs.

3. Use parallel structures for major headings—sentences or phrases, but not a mixture.

(continued on next page)

(continued)

4. Organize your outline so that it moves from larger ideas to smaller, with all ideas under a similar letter or number equal in level of generality and importance.

5. Whenever you divide a point, always have at least two parts (just like dividing a cake). So whenever you have I, you must have II. Whenever you have A, you must have B, and so on.

6. Keep outline categories separate and distinct, without confusing overlap.

7. Do not include the introduction and the conclusion in your outline.

The student who worked with the group on brainstorming (3d) and made the scratch outline finally settled on a thesis and made this formal topic outline.

Thesis: A voluntary name change is usually motivated by a desire to avoid or gain recognition.

I. The desire to avoid recognition by others is one motive for a name change.
  A. Criminals
  B. Writers
    1. Women writers adopt men's names.
      a. George Eliot (Mary Ann Evans)
      b. George Sand (Amandine Aurore Lucie Dupin)
      c. Isak Dinesen (Karen Blixen)
    2. Some writers adopt a pseudonym.
      a. Mark Twain (Samuel Clemens)
      b. Lewis Carroll (Charles Dodgson)
      c. Amanda Cross (Carolyn Heilbrun)
  C. Some change a name to avoid ethnic identification.
II. Married women and entertainers may change a name to join a group and gain recognition.
  A. Married women mark membership in a family.
    1. They want to indicate married status.
    2. They want the same name as their children.
  B. Entertainers choose eye-catching names.
    1. Marilyn Monroe (Norma Jean Baker)
    2. Woody Allen (Allen Stewart Konigsberg)

3. Ringo Starr (Richard Starkey)
4. P. Diddy (Sean Combs), Eminem (Marshall Mathers), and
   Pink (Alecia Moore)

Making this outline allowed the student to see that his draft was basically well structured but that he needed to find out more about criminals and their aliases (I.A.) and about people who change a name to avoid ethnic identification (I.C.).

4e The power of a title

You probably have in mind a useful working title as you write, but after you finish writing, brainstorm several titles and pick the one you like best. If titles occur to you as you write, make a note of them. A good title captures readers' attention, makes readers want to read on, and lets readers know what to expect in the essay.

Pay attention to the mechanics of a title. Do not italicize or underline your title, and do not enclose it in quotation marks unless your title is a quotation from a source. Capitalize all words except the following: prepositions (such as *in, on, of, for, with, without*), articles (*a, an, the*), coordinating conjunctions (*and, but, or, nor, so, for, yet*), and *to* in an infinitive phrase (*to* laugh). But capitalize those words if they occur at the beginning of the title or subtitle (after a colon).

WORKING TITLE   **Problems in the Fashion Industry**

REVISED TITLE   **Thin and Thinner: How the Fashion Industry Denigrates Women**

WORKING TITLE   **Name Changes**

REVISED TITLE   **Names to Live By**

5 Develop Paragraphs.

It is not hard to signal the beginning of a new paragraph: indent the beginning of its first sentence five spaces from the left margin or, in business and online documents, leave a one-line space. However, a good paragraph needs more than the mark of indentation or a blank line above and below it. In the body of an academic essay, a new paragraph should signal a progression in your ideas.

5a   Paragraph basics

A good paragraph advances your argument, supports your thesis, and has internal unity. It does not drift in a vague, unfocused way. Collectively, paragraphs are the building blocks of a piece of writing and should be shaped and arranged with care. They are, as Stephen King calls them, "maps of intent," letting readers know where you are heading.

Body paragraphs in an essay   How do you know when to begin a new paragraph? Use these three points as a guide.

- Begin a new paragraph to introduce a new point in support of your thesis.

- Use a new paragraph to expand on a point already made by offering a further example or evidence.

- Use a paragraph to break up a long discussion or description into manageable chunks that readers can assimilate.

Therefore, both logic and aesthetics dictate when it is time to begin a new paragraph. Think of a paragraph as something that gathers together in one place ideas that connect to each other and to the main purpose announced in the piece of writing.

KEY POINTS

Paragraph Basics

A good paragraph in the body of an academic essay should contain the following:

- one clearly discernible main idea, either explicitly stated (in a topic sentence) or implied clearly in the content of the paragraph, with that idea clearly related to the thesis of the essay

- unity of content, with no extraneous ideas or asides intruding or diverting readers' attention from the main idea

- development and support of its main idea with examples, reasons, definitions, and so on

- coherence—that is, a logical flow of ideas from one sentence to the next, with the relationships between ideas clearly indicated

See 5b–5d for more on these features.

Transitional paragraphs Some paragraphs have more to do with function than with content. They serve to take readers from one point to another, making a connection and offering a smooth transition from one idea to the next. These *transitional paragraphs* are often short.

In her autobiography, *Dust Tracks on a Road,* Zora Neale Hurston tells about meeting the man she fell in love with. One paragraph is devoted to describing how she "made a parachute jump" into love, admiring his intellect, strength, good looks, and manly resolution. The next paragraph provides a transition to the story of how they met:

> To illustrate the point, I got into trouble with him for trying to loan him a quarter. It came about this way.

For introductory and concluding paragraphs, see 7d.

5b Focus and topic sentence

When you begin to write or revise a paragraph in an essay, keep in mind what the focus of the paragraph will be and how it will support your thesis. Imagine readers asking you, "What point are you making in this paragraph, and how does it relate to your thesis?" Write a sentence that makes a clear supporting point. You can include such a sentence (known as a *topic sentence*) to guide both the writing and the reading of the paragraph. Here are questions for you to consider:

- What point do you want to make in a paragraph? Make sure the main idea is clear. Readers should be able to discern the point you want to make in a far more specific way than just noting that the paragraph is "about" a topic.

- Are you going to express that point in an actual topic sentence, or do you expect readers to infer the point from the details you provide? In academic writing, it is a common convention to express the point clearly in one sentence within the paragraph. Including such a topic sentence will help you stick to your point and limit a paragraph to discussion of that point. A topic sentence helps readers grasp the point of the paragraph.

- If you include a topic sentence, where will you position it in the paragraph? In academic writing, a topic sentence frequently begins a paragraph, letting readers know what to expect. Sometimes, though, a writer will prefer to lead up to the statement of the main idea and place it at the end of the paragraph.

KEY POINTS

Placement or Inclusion of a Topic Sentence

1. *Topic sentence at the beginning* If you state the main idea in the opening sentence, readers will then expect the rest of the paragraph to consist of specific details that illustrate and support that topic sentence. For an example, see the first paragraph example in 5d, item 1.

2. *Topic sentence at the end* You may prefer to begin with details and examples and draw more general conclusions from them in a topic sentence expressed at the end of the paragraph. This strategy is useful for building up to a climax and driving home the point you want to make. For an example, see the paragraph in 5d, item 3.

3. *Topic sentence implied* It may suit your content and purpose better to not state the main idea explicitly in a topic sentence but to use details vivid enough that readers can easily infer the main point you are making. Do this if your specific details are vivid and lead to an indisputable conclusion.

EXERCISE 5.1 Identify topic sentences in paragraphs.
Read each of the following paragraphs. Then determine whether the topic sentence is at the beginning, at the end, or implied. (**A** = See Answer Key.)

A 1.   Lisa wrote a list of all items they needed. She then went to the store, purchased essentials, and upon returning, packed the overnight bags for the family weekend getaway trip to upstate New York in the Catskills. Her husband Charlie confirmed the reservations at the resort and wrote down the directions. Their son Dave, who had recently received his driver's license, got the car washed and filled the tank with regular unleaded gas. Everyone in the family pitched in. Teamwork is essential in planning a trip.

   2.   On Wednesday, I ran for a bus and made it. The dentist said I had no cavities. The phone was ringing when I arrived home and even after I dropped my key a couple of times, I answered it and they were still on the line. The Avon lady refused me service saying I didn't need her as I already

looked terrific. My husband asked me what kind of a day I
had and didn't leave the room when I started to answer.

—Erma Bombeck, *If Life Is a Bowl of Cherries,
What Am I Doing in the Pits?*

3.   There are only three ways to make money. One is to go out
and work for it. However, few among us can work forever,
and there will likely come a time in our lives when working
for a paycheck may not be an option. The second way to make
money is to inherit it or to win the lottery. Again, not something we all can count on. The third way, and the only one that
is available to all of us for an unlimited amount of time, is to
invest what we earn during our working years wisely, so that
the money we work so hard for goes to work for us.

—Suze Orman, *The Courage to Be Rich*

5c   Unity

When you write a body paragraph in an essay, you should be able to
finish these two following sentences about it without hesitation—
and so should your readers:

1. The paragraph is about . . . (What is the topic of the paragraph?)
2. The stated or implied topic sentence of this paragraph is . . . (What
   is the one main idea the paragraph expresses?)

You should also be able to look at a well-organized expository paragraph and note that the paragraph is unified—that is, that it contains
only material that develops and supports the point of the paragraph.

In academic writing, a unified paragraph mirrors the structure of
the whole essay: it includes one main idea that the rest of the piece of
writing (paragraph or essay) explains, supports, and develops. When
you write a paragraph, imagine a reader saying, "Look, I don't have
time to read all this. Just tell me in one sentence (or two) what point
you are making here." Your reply would express your main point.
Each paragraph in an academic essay generally contains a controlling idea expressed in one or two sentences, and all the other sentences in the paragraph relate to and develop and explain that
controlling idea. A paragraph does not digress or switch topics in
midstream. Its content is unified.

The following paragraph is indeed devoted to one topic—
tennis—and the first sentence makes a promise to discuss the *trouble*
the *backhand* causes *average* players (the key words are italicized).
Some of the sentences in the paragraph do exactly that, but in the

middle the writer, while still writing about tennis, loses sight of the announced focus in the topic sentence.

> The backhand in tennis causes average weekend players more trouble than other strokes. Even though the swing is natural and free flowing, many players feel intimidated and try to avoid it. Serena Williams, however, has a great backhand, and she often wins difficult points with it. Her serve is a powerful weapon, too. When faced by a backhand coming at them across the net, mid-level players can't seem to get their feet and body in the best position. They tend to run around the ball or forget the swing and give the ball a little poke, praying that it will not only reach but also go over the net.

What is Grand Slam winner Serena Williams doing in a paragraph about average players? What relevance does her powerful serve have to the average player's problems with a backhand? The passage can be effectively revised by cutting out the two sentences about Serena Williams.

5d Strategies for developing paragraphs

Whether you are writing a paragraph or an essay, you will do well to keep in mind the image of skeptical readers always inclined to say something challenging, such as "Why on earth do you think that?" or "What could possibly lead you to that conclusion?" You have to show readers that your claim is well founded and supported by experience, knowledge, logical arguments, the work of experts, or reasoned examples. In addition, try to engage readers and provide vital, unique details.

The following passages show a range of strategies that writers use to construct and develop a paragraph. While some writers may choose to use only one method of development in a paragraph (all statistics or all examples, for instance), others may combine methods to make their point in a varied and effective way. In fact, many published nonfiction writers write perfectly clear and acceptable paragraphs containing several methods of development, often with no explicit topic sentence, and sometimes even with more than one main idea.

However, the rule of thumb that has emerged for traditional academic writing is "One main idea per paragraph, with one method of development." Take that for what it is—a helpful guide rather than a straitjacket.

1. Examples Examples make writing more interesting and informative. The paragraph that follows begins with a topic sentence that announces the controlling idea: "Ant queens . . . enjoy exceptionally long lives." The authors could have stopped there, expecting us to assume that they were right. We might wonder, however, what "exceptionally long" means about the life of an ant (a month? a year? seven years?). Instead of letting us wonder, the authors develop and support the controlling idea with five examples organized to build to a convincing climax. Beginning with a generalization and supporting it with specific illustrative details is a common method of organizing a paragraph.

> Ant queens, hidden in the fastness of well-built nests and protected by zealous daughters, enjoy exceptionally long lives. Barring accidents, those of most species last 5 years or longer. A few exceed in natural longevity anything known in the millions of species of other insects, including even the legendary 17-year-old cicadas. One mother queen of an Australian carpenter ant kept in a laboratory nest flourished for 23 years, producing thousands of offspring before she faltered in her reproduction and died, apparently of old age. Several queens of *Lasius flavus*, the little yellow mound-building ant of European meadows, have lived 18 to 22 years in captivity. The world record for ants, and hence for insects generally, is held by a queen of *Lasius niger*, the European black sidewalk ant, which also lives in forests. Lovingly attended in a laboratory nest by a Swiss entomologist, she lasted 29 years.
>
> —Bert Hölldobler and Edward O. Wilson, *Journey to the Ants*

2. Narration   Choose a pattern of organization that readers will easily grasp. Organize the events in a story chronologically so that readers can follow the sequence. In the following paragraph, the writer tells a story that leads to the point that people with disabilities often face ignorance and insensitivity. Note that she begins with background information and the specific details of the story in chronological order and ends with a generalization.

> Jonathan is an articulate, intelligent, thirty-five-year-old man who has used a wheelchair since he became a paraplegic when he was twenty years old. He recalls taking an ablebodied woman out to dinner at a nice restaurant. When the waitress came to take their order, she patronizingly asked his date, "And what would he like to eat for dinner?" At the end of the meal, the waitress presented Jonathan's date with the check and thanked her for her patronage. Although it may be hard to believe the insensitivity of the waitress, this incident is not an isolated one. Rather, such an experience is a common one for persons with disabilities.
>
> —Dawn O. Braithwaite, "Viewing Persons with Disabilities as a Culture"

Develop paragraphs: examples and narration. Imagine that you and your friends have gone to the library to work on your research papers. Everyone is there except Mary. One of your friends remarks, "Mary always delays writing a paper. She shouldn't wait until the night before." Imagine that you are all in accordance with the following statement: "Mary needs to begin working on her research paper." (**A** = See Answer Key.)

A 1. Write a paragraph that begins with that statement as the topic sentence and supplies examples showing what Mary needs to do to begin working on her research paper.

2. Write a second paragraph in which you give examples or tell a story about Mary's problems with writing. Conclude with the statement above as the topic sentence.

3. Description   To help readers see and experience what you feel and experience, describe people, places, scenes, and objects by using sensory details that re-create those people, places, scenes, or objects for your readers. In the following paragraph from a memoir about growing up to love food, Ruth Reichl tells how she spent days working at a summer camp in France and thinking about eating. However, she does much more than say, "The food was always delicious." Reichl appeals to our senses of sight, smell, touch, and taste. We get a picture of the campers, we smell the baking bread, we see and almost taste the jam, we smell and taste the coffee, and we feel the crustiness of the rolls. We feel as if we are there—and we wish we were.

> When we woke up in the morning the smell of baking bread was wafting through the trees. By the time we had gotten our campers out of bed, their faces washed and their shirts tucked in, the aroma had become maddeningly seductive. We walked into the dining room to devour hot bread slathered with country butter and topped with homemade plum jam so filled with fruit it made each slice look like a tart. We stuck our faces into the bowls of café au lait, inhaling the sweet, bitter, peculiarly French fragrance, and Georges or Jean or one of the other male counselors would say, for the hundredth time, "*On mange pas comme ça à Paris.*" Two hours later we had a "*gouter*," a snack of chocolate bars stuffed into fresh, crusty rolls. And two hours later there was lunch. The eating went on all day.

> —Ruth Reichl, *Tender at the Bone:*
> *Growing Up at the Table*

Exercise 5.3 Describe by using details.

Write a paragraph on the distractions that you experience as a college student. In the paragraph, tell a story, use descriptive details, and include sensory details that have a specific appeal to at least one of the senses (sight, hearing, smell, touch, and taste). Be creative.

4. Illustration You saw in the paragraph on page 45 how a statement about the long life of ant queens is supported by a series of examples and facts. The author of the next paragraph uses one extended illustrative example to explain the point made in the opening sentence.

> Paper enables a certain kind of thinking. Picture, for instance, the top of your desk. Chances are that you have a keyboard and a computer screen off to one side, and a clear space roughly eighteen inches square in front of your chair. What covers the rest of the desktop is probably piles—piles of paper, journals, magazines, binders, postcards, videotapes, and all the other artifacts of the knowledge economy. The piles look like a mess, but they aren't. When a group at Apple Computer studied piling behavior several years ago, they found that even the most disorderly piles usually make perfect sense to the piler, and that office workers could hold forth in great detail about the precise history and meaning of their piles. The pile closest to the cleared, eighteen-inch square working area, for example, generally represents the most urgent business, and within that pile the most important document of all is likely to be at the top. Piles are living, breathing archives. Over time they get broken down and resorted, sometimes chronologically and sometimes thematically and sometimes chronologically and thematically; clues about certain documents may be physically embedded in the files by, say, stacking a certain piece of paper at an angle or inserting dividers into the stack.
>
> —Malcolm Gladwell, "The Social Life of Paper"

5. Facts and statistics Facts and statistics provide convincing evidence to help persuade readers of your point. The following paragraph supports with facts and statistics the assertion made in its first sentence (the topic sentence) that the North grew more than the South in the years before the Civil War.

> While southerners tended their fields, the North grew. In 1800, half the nation's five million people lived in the South. By 1850, only a third lived there. Of the nine largest cities, only New Orleans was located in the lower South. Meanwhile, a tenth of the goods manufactured in America came from southern mills and factories. There were one hundred piano makers in New York alone in 1852.

In 1846, there was not a single book publisher in New Orleans; even the city guidebook was printed in Manhattan.

—Geoffrey C. Ward, *The Civil War: An Illustrated History*

6. Account of a process   Accounts of the process of doing something usually either give instructions in chronological order or describe the steps in a sequence. The following paragraph gives a list of instructions for beginning the process of making a piñata.

> Start making a piñata by covering an inflated beach ball with a thin layer of petroleum jelly. Dip newspaper strips into a prepared adhesive and apply them one at a time to the ball. Cover the entire surface of the ball, except for its mouthpiece, with about 10 layers of strips. Then let the paper dry, deflate the ball, and remove it through the mouthpiece opening. Poke two small holes through the surface of the papier-mâché and attach a long, sturdy string. Fill the sphere with candy and prizes. Seal the opening with masking tape.
>
> —Reader's Digest Association, *How to Do Just about Anything*

7. Definition of terms   Sometimes writers clarify and develop a topic by defining a key term, even if it is not an unusual term. Often they will explain what class an item fits into and how it differs from other items in its class: for example, "A duckbilled platypus is a mammal that has webbed feet and lays eggs." In his book on diaries, Thomas Mallon begins by providing an extended definition of his basic terms. He does not want readers to misunderstand him because they wonder what the differences between a diary and a journal might be.

> The first thing we should try to get straight is what to call them. "What's the difference between a diary and a journal?" is one of the questions people interested in these books ask. The two terms are in fact hopelessly muddled. They're both rooted in the idea of dailiness, but perhaps because of *journal*'s links to the newspaper trade and *diary*'s to *dear,* the latter seems more intimate than the former. (The French blur even this discrepancy by using no word recognizable like *diary;* they just say *journal intime,* which is sexy, but a bit of a mouthful.) One can go back as far as Dr. Johnson's *Dictionary* and find him making the two more or less equal. To him a diary was "an account of the transactions, accidents, and observations of every day; a journal." Well, if synonymity was good enough for Johnson, we'll let it be good enough for us.
>
> —Thomas Mallon, *A Book of One's Own: People and Their Diaries*

As necessary, define technical terms for readers, particularly if readers will need to understand the term to understand the rest of your essay. In the following paragraph, the authors establish the meaning of a filmmaking term that they will use in later discussion.

> In the original French, *mise-en-scène* (pronounced "meez-ahn-sen") means "staging an action," and it was first applied to the practice of directing plays. Film scholars, extending the term to film direction as well, use the term to signify the director's control over what appears in the film frame. As you would expect from the term's theatrical origins, mise-en-scène includes those aspects that overlap with the art of the theater: setting, lighting, costume, and the behavior of the figures. In controlling the mise-en-scène, the director *stages the event* for the camera.
>
> —David Bordwell and Kristin Thompson,
> *Film Art: An Introduction*, 3rd ed.

EXERCISE 5.4 Experiment with different methods of development. Choose a topic that interests you. First, write a paragraph about some aspect of your topic, developing your paragraph with one of the following:

1. one extended illustration
2. facts and statistics
3. an account of a process
4. definition of terms

Then write another paragraph on another aspect of your topic using a second method of development from the preceding list. In groups, discuss how different aspects of your topic worked with the two methods of development that you chose. Did one method work better or less well than the other, and if so, why?

8. Comparison and contrast When you compare people, objects, or concepts and examine similarities and differences, different types of development achieve different purposes.

BLOCK ORGANIZATION You can deal with each subject one at a time in a block style of organization. This organization works well when each section is short and readers can easily remember the points made. A paragraph or an essay comparing and contrasting writing in college and writing at work could therefore be organized as follows:

> Subject A: Writing in college
>
> > Point 1: Audience   Instructor or classmates
> >
> > Point 2: Purpose   To fulfill an assignment
> >
> > Point 3: Outcomes   Feedback, evaluation, grade

Subject B: Writing at work

Point 1: Audience   Boss, colleagues, or customers

Point 2: Purpose   To convey information

Point 3: Outcomes   Follow-up action, filing, evaluation by boss

POINT-BY-POINT ORGANIZATION   Alternatively, you can consider the important points of similarity or difference in a point-by-point style of organization, referring within each point to both subjects. The preceding material would then be presented as follows:

Point 1: Audience

College: Instructor or classmates

Work: Boss, colleagues, or customers

Point 2: Purpose

College: To fulfill an assignment

Work: To convey information or respond to a problem

Point 3: Outcomes

College: Feedback, evaluation, grade

Work: Follow-up action, filing, evaluation by supervisor

In a *New York Times* article on U.S. presidents with sons who also became president, Sean Wilentz points out first the similarities between John Quincy Adams and George W. Bush and then the differences. Here is the paragraph that details the similarities, using a point-by-point pattern of organization.

> Both Adams and George W. Bush were born to privileged New England families, though Mr. Bush went with his father to Texas and adopted the persona and politics of a down-home Western oil man. Both followed fathers whose presidencies lasted just one term: John Adams, like the elder George Bush, was rejected by the electorate after four years in office. And like the younger Bush, the younger Adams was elected president with a disputed voter mandate and under controversial circumstances.
>
> —Sean Wilentz, "The Father-and-Son Presidencies"

THE VOCABULARY OF COMPARING AND CONTRASTING   Helpful words and terms to use for comparing and contrasting are these:

although	on the contrary
both	on the other hand
however	similarly

in contrast	though
like	where (or whereas)
not . . . but rather	while

EXERCISE 5.5   Compare or contrast two people.
Write a comparison or contrast essay on two people you know well. You can compare or contrast their work habits, attitudes, styles, appearances, approaches to life, reactions to stresses or crises, clothing, and so on. Use either a block or a point-by-point organization.

9. Analysis and division   One way to approach a topic is to analyze it and divide it into its component parts for the purposes of discussion. This approach allows readers to get a better understanding of the whole from a description of the parts. In the following example, the *Columbia Encyclopedia* online helps readers understand the vast concept of *life* itself by breaking it down into six component parts (at <http://www.bartleby.com/65/li/life.html>).

> Although there is no universal agreement as to a definition of life, its biological manifestations are generally considered to be organization, metabolism, growth, irritability, adaptation, and reproduction. . . . Organization is found in the basic living unit, the cell, and in the organized groupings of cells into organs and organisms. Metabolism includes the conversion of nonliving material into cellular components (synthesis) and the decomposition of organic matter (catalysis), producing energy. Growth in living matter is an increase in size of all parts, as distinguished from simple addition of material; it results from a higher rate of synthesis than catalysis. Irritability, or response to stimuli, takes many forms, from the contraction of a unicellular organism when touched to complex reactions involving all the senses of higher animals; in plants response is usually much different than in animals but is nonetheless present. Adaptation, the accommodation of a living organism to its present or to a new environment, is fundamental to the process of evolution and is determined by the individual's heredity. The division of one cell to form two new cells is reproduction; usually the term is applied to the production of a new individual (either asexually, from a single parent organism, or sexually, from two differing parent organisms), although strictly speaking it also describes the production of new cells in the process of growth.

10. Classification   One way to examine people, objects, or concepts is to classify them, which means to split them up into groups that cover all the options. In the following paragraphs, Matthew Gilbert examines cell phone users by dividing them into three groups, each with a "different psychological need," and devoting one paragraph to each group in the classification. He assumes there are no other possible needs here, an assumption his readers might not agree with. However, he does qualify his classification by saying, "As I see it."

> Cell phone use has far exceeded practicality. For many, it's even a bit of an addiction, a prop—like a cigarette or a beer bottle—that you can hold up to your mouth. And each person is meeting a different psychological need by clinging to it.
>
> As I see it, the pack breaks down something like this: Some users can't tolerate being alone and have to register on someone, somewhere, all of the time. That walk down [the street] can be pretty lonely without a loved one shouting sweet nothings in your ear.
>
> Others are efficiency freaks and can't bear to lose ten minutes standing in line at Starbucks. They have to conduct business while their milk is being steamed, or they will implode. The dividing line between work and home has already become permeable with the growth of telecommuting; cell phones contribute significantly to that boundary breakdown.
>
> Then there are those who like to believe they are so very important to the people in their personal and professional lives that they must be in constant touch. "Puffed up" is one way to describe them; "insecure" is another.
>
> —Matthew Gilbert, "All Talk, All the Time"

EXERCISE 5.6   Consider bases for classification.
Write down a number of different ways you could classify each of the following broad topics. (**A** = See Answer Key.)

A 1. Students in your class
A 2. Buildings on your campus
3. Restaurants in your neighborhood
4. Current movies showing in the theaters

11. Cause and effect   In writing about history, art history, or social movements, an examination of the causes and effects of events and trends can work well. In the following passage, Larry McMurtry begins by identifying a situation and devotes the next two paragraphs to discussing the cause that produced this effect.

> The American West has so far produced depressingly little in the way of literature. Out of it may have come a hundred or so good books, a dozen or so very good books; but it has not, as yet, yielded up a great book. In literature it still seems to be waiting its turn. At the beginning of the century the Midwest seemed dominant, in terms of literary gifts and literary energies; then,

largely because of Faulkner, the South had a turn, after which the great concentration of American literary energy returned to where it had mainly always been, the East.

Lately, looking through the various collections of photographs by the early photographers of the West—Alexander Gardner, John Hillers, Timothy O'Sullivan, William H. Jackson, and the others—it occurred to me that one reason the West hasn't quite got a literature was in part because the camera arrived just when it did. The first photographs were taken in the West only about forty years after Lewis and Clark made their memorable trek. By the 1850s there were cameras everywhere, and the romantic landscapes of Catlin, Bodmer, Miller, Moran, and the rest gave way to photography that was almost equally romantic—the photographers, quite naturally, gravitated to the beauty spots, to the grandeur of Yosemite, Grand Canyon, Canyon de Chelly.

Writers weren't needed, in quite the same way, once the camera came. They didn't need to explain and describe the West to Easterners because the Easterners could, very soon, look at those pictures and see it for themselves. And what they saw was a West with the inconveniences—the dust, the heat, the distances—removed.

—Larry McMurtry, *Walter Benjamin at the Dairy Queen*

12. Problem and solution   Many articles and many college writing assignments pose a problem and ask for the consideration of possible solutions, leading to a recommendation for one course of action. An article in the *New York Times* presents the problem of the considerable risks involved for a donor of an organ such as a kidney or part of a liver. After a discussion of the legal and ethical issues, the author devotes the following paragraph to proposing a solution to the problem.

One way to ensure that the interests of prospective donors are recognized is to create a federal agency that would make certain that hospitals meet minimum standards when employing these new therapies and would monitor how hospital review boards screen potential donors. The boards also need to be able to shield potential donors from coercion. For example, in cases when an individual decides against becoming a donor, a board should simply inform the intended recipient that the potential donor is "not suitable" without further explanation.

—Ronald Munson, "The Donor's Right to Take a Risk"

EXERCISE 5.7   Develop paragraphs using cause/effect or problem/solution.

Write two paragraphs, one analyzing the cause and effect of excessive credit card use and the other focusing on the problem of and solutions for credit card debt.

5e Coherence with links, parallel structures, and transitions

However you develop your individual paragraphs, readers expect to move with ease from one sentence to the next and from one paragraph to the next, following a coherent flow of argument and logic. When you construct an essay or paragraph, do not cause readers to grapple with sudden jumps from one idea to another without clear links. Avoid such grasshopper prose. Instead, a piece of writing needs to be coherent, with all the parts connecting clearly to one another—and to the thesis—with links and transitions.

Context links   A new paragraph introduces a new topic, but that topic should not be entirely separate from what has gone before. Let readers know the context of the big picture. If you are writing about the expense of exploring Mars and then switch abruptly to the hazards of climbing Everest, readers will be puzzled. You need to state clearly the connection with the thesis: "Exploration on our own planet can be as hazardous and as financially risky as space exploration."

Word links, repeated phrases, and rhetorical questions   You can also provide coherence by using repeated words, or connected words, such as pronouns linked to nouns; words with the same, similar, or opposite meaning; or words linked by context. The writer of the following paragraph maintains coherence by repeating words and phrases (italicized) and using pronouns (in bold—*she* and *her* to refer to *wife*, and *they* to refer to *Greeks*) to provide a linking chain.

> Entire cultures operate on elaborate systems of *indirectness*. For example, I discovered in a small research project that most Greeks assumed that a wife who asked, "Would you like to go to the party?" was hinting that **she** *wanted to go.* **They** *felt* that **she** wouldn't bring it up if **she** didn't *want to go.* Furthermore, **they** *felt*, **she** would not state **her** *preference* outright because **that** would sound like a demand. *Indirectness* was the appropriate means for communicating **her** *preference*.
>
> —Deborah Tannen, *You Just Don't Understand*

In the following paragraph, Alice Walker, writing about the writer Zora Neale Hurston, uses the repetition of the phrase "without money" to drive her point home. She adds emphasis by including a rhetorical question (a question that readers are expected to know the answer to).

Without money, an illness, even a simple one, can undermine the will. Without money, getting into a hospital is problematic, and getting out without money to pay for the treatment is nearly impossible. Without money, one becomes dependent on other people who are likely to be—even in their kindness—erratic in their support and despotic in their expectations of return. Zora was forced to rely, like Tennessee Williams's Blanche, "on the kindness of strangers." Can anything be more dangerous, if the strangers are forever in control? Zora, who worked so hard, was never able to make a living from her work.

—Foreword to Robert E. Hemenway,
Zora Neale Hurston: A Literary Biography

Parallel structures as a linking device   Parallel structures help readers see the connection between ideas:

United, there is little we cannot do. Divided, there is little we can do.
—John F. Kennedy, Inaugural Presidential Address

The structures can be clauses or phrases, as shown in the following passages, the first four of which are from "Maintenance" by Naomi Shihab Nye. (See 12d and 12e for more on clauses and phrases, and 15g for errors arising from faulty parallelism.)

PARALLEL STRUCTURES: CLAUSES

We saw one house *where walls and windows had been sheathed in various patterns of gloomy brocade.* We visited another *where the kitchen had been removed* because the owners only ate in restaurants.

PARALLEL STRUCTURES: VERB PHRASES

Sometimes I'd come home to find her *lounging* in the bamboo chair on the back porch, *eating* melon, or *lying* on the couch with a bowl of half-melted ice cream balanced on her chest.

PARALLEL STRUCTURES: ABSOLUTE PHRASES

One day she described having grown up in west Texas in a house of twelve children, *the air jammed* with voices, crosscurrents, *the floors piled* with grocery bags, mountains of tossed-off clothes, toys, blankets, the clutter of her sisters' shoes.

PARALLEL STRUCTURES: NOUN PHRASES

Barbara has the best taste of any person I've ever known—
the best khaki-colored linen clothing, the best books, the name of the best masseuse.

Parallel Structures: prepositional phrases

> Adolescence is a tough time for parent and child alike. It is a time between: *between childhood and maturity, between parental protection and personal responsibility, between life stage-managed by grown-ups and life privately held.*

> —Anna Quindlen, "Parental Rites," *Thinking Out Loud*

Transitions Writers use transitional words and expressions to signal relationships between ideas. They can connect clauses within one sentence, one or more sentences in a paragraph, two or more paragraphs, and a paragraph and the thesis. Deborah Tannen, in the passage on page 54, uses *for example* and *furthermore* to indicate meaning connections. The Key Points box identifies the most common uses of transitional expressions and provides examples of each.

KEY POINTS

Transitional Expressions

Adding an idea   also, in addition, further, furthermore, moreover

Contrasting   however, nevertheless, nonetheless, on the other hand, in contrast, still, on the contrary, rather, conversely

Providing an alternative   instead, alternatively, otherwise

Showing similarity   similarly, likewise

Showing order of time or order of ideas   first, second, third (and so on); then; next; later; subsequently; meanwhile; previously; finally

Showing result   as a result, consequently, therefore, thus, hence, accordingly, for this reason

Affirming   of course, in fact, certainly, obviously, to be sure, undoubtedly, indeed

Giving examples   for example, for instance

Explaining   in other words, that is

Adding an aside   incidentally, by the way, besides

Summarizing   in short, generally, overall, all in all, in conclusion

For punctuation with transitional expressions, see 23e.

Transitional expressions are useful to reinforce meaning connections and connect one sentence to another or one paragraph to another. Make sure, though, that you do not overuse these expressions. Too many of them, used too often, make writing seem heavy and mechanical. To add an idea, point out a contrast, or show a result, *and, but,* or *so* may serve the purpose just as well.

EXERCISE 5.8 Identify the transitions in a paragraph.
In the following student paragraph, underline or highlight transitional words and expressions. (**A** = See Answer Key.)

A Although Julia is a returning college student, she has tried hard to blend in with the student population. **A** As a result, she doesn't let the age difference interfere with her relationships with other students. **A** Before she returned to school, however, she had concerns about whether or not she would fit in. **A** Still, after two semesters of interacting with other students, Julia has gained confidence. The younger students do not treat her differently. In fact, many of her classmates are interested in the reasons why Julia decided to return to school after her ten-year successful career as a nurse. Julia, likewise, shows interest in her classmates and enjoys the dialogue, debate, and controversies that arise during class discussion.

6 Construct an Argument.

We often associate the word *argument* with combat and confrontation, but the Latin root of the word *argue* means "to make clear." The goal of an argument, then, is to win your audience over fairly with persuasion, not coercion. In the end, the good argument is the one that has clearly and nonconfrontationally presented its position on a claim by logically considering its evidence, reasons, assumptions, and exceptions.

6a What makes a good argument?

When you are writing an argument, the goal is to persuade readers to adopt your point of view on your chosen or assigned topic. At the very least, you will want readers to acknowledge that the claim you make about your topic rests on solid, reliable evidence and that you provide a fair, unbiased approach to this evidence. Let readers discover that you have good reasons for your position.

> **KEY POINTS**
>
> ### The Features of a Good Argument
>
> A good argument
>
> - is not based solely on gut reactions or beliefs unsubstantiated by evidence (6c)
> - deals with an arguable claim (6c)
> - takes a position on and makes a clear claim about the topic (6c)
> - supports that position with detailed and specific evidence (such as reasons, facts, examples, descriptions, and stories) (6c)
> - establishes common ground with listeners or readers and avoids confrontation (6e)
> - takes opposing views into account and either refutes them or shows why they may be unimportant or irrelevant (6e)
> - presents reasons logically (6d, 6f)

TECHTOOLKIT   Useful Web Sites for Writing Arguments

Try the following sites for help with writing arguments.

- *Paradigm Online Writing Assistant,* a site that began at Boise State University, at <http://www.powa.org/argument/index.html>
- The Capital Community College site on writing arguments at <http://grammar.commnet.edu/grammar/composition/argument.htm> with a sample annotated argument paper ■

6b Topic

A good argument begins with a good topic. The topic should be significant and debatable, such as in what grade standardized testing should begin in schools rather than how many states require standardized tests. The former issue can lead to an arguable claim (see 6c), such as "Standardized testing should not begin until the fifth grade," rather than a truism (a statement that is obviously true and is not debatable), such as "Standardized testing is administered in many states."

Choose an issue that is fresh. Avoid topics such as the death penalty, prayer in schools, drug laws, and abortion; they have been written about so often that original or interesting arguments are hard to find. In general, avoid issues that are largely emotional reactions to matters of ideology or religion. Your views on these topics will tend to rest on belief rather than logical argument. Beware, also, of saying that you intend to write about "the importance of family," "the church and morality," or "racial prejudice." Such issues might mean a great deal to you personally, but unless you have a clear sense of a logical and debatable claim rather than just strong feelings, you will have difficulty structuring an argument around them and making a valid claim that you can support with evidence.

Brainstorming, reading (books, magazines, and newspapers), and browsing on the Internet in search directories, informational sites, or online discussion groups (see 3a, 3f, and 39) can help you discover novel and timely issues. When you find an interesting topic and your instructor has approved it (if necessary), begin by writing a question about it. Then make lists of the arguments on both (or all) sides.

Because her family had been plagued by a spate of intrusive telephone marketing calls, in 2002, before legislation was passed, Jennifer Hopper decided to tackle the topic of telemarketing and its impact on society. She began by thinking that she would claim that telemarketing is more harmful than beneficial. Before beginning her research, she listed her topic, her research question, and her initial brainstormed ideas on the effects of telemarketing.

TOPIC: The impact of telemarketing on our society
QUESTION: Does telemarketing have more harmful than beneficial effects on our daily lives?

Harmful effects:
  Telemarketing intrudes on our privacy.
  Some telemarketers prey on the elderly.
  Some of their offers are scams.
  Telemarketing takes business away from retail stores.

Beneficial effects:
  Telemarketing provides jobs, especially for women, students, retirees, and minorities.
  It promotes the economy in rural areas.
  It provides buying opportunities for people who are elderly, disabled, and homebound.

See 6g for a draft of Hopper's essay, in which she includes some of the points from her list and omits or changes others.

6c An arguable claim (thesis), reasons, and evidence

The position you take on a topic constitutes your claim or your thesis and needs to be bolstered and explained with reasons and evidence. When readers ask, "Why do you think that?" about your claim, the support you offer—reasons, statistics, facts, examples, and expert testimony—should answer that question in detail and in a clearly organized way.

Making an arguable claim Jennifer Hopper knew that the claim in her argument paper should be debatable, and some claims she considered were "Telemarketing provides jobs and benefits the economy" and "Telemarketers always seek out the elderly and the gullible," both of which would be arguable claims. Avoid the following types of claims, which are not arguable:

- a neutral statement, which gives no hint of the writer's position
- an announcement of the paper's broad subject
- a fact
- a truism (statement that is obviously true)
- a personal or religious conviction that cannot be logically debated
- an opinion based only on your feelings
- a sweeping generalization

Here are some examples of nondebatable claims, each with a revision.

NEUTRAL STATEMENT	**There are unstated standards of beauty in the workplace.**
REVISED	**The way we look affects the way we are treated at work and the size of our paychecks.**
TOO BROAD	**This paper is about violence on TV.**
REVISED	**TV violence has to take its share of blame for the violence in our society.**
FACT	*Plessy v. Ferguson,* **a Supreme Court case that supported racial segregation, was overturned in 1954 by** *Brown v. Board of Education.*
REVISED	**The overturning of** *Plessy v. Ferguson* **by** *Brown v. Board of Education* **has not led to significant advances in integrated education.**

TRUISM	**Bilingual education has advantages and disadvantages.**
REVISED	**A bilingual program is more effective than an immersion program at helping students grasp the basics of science and mathematics.**

PERSONAL CONVICTION	**Racism is the worst kind of prejudice.**
REVISED	**The best weapon against racism is primary and secondary education.**

OPINION	**I think water-skiing is a dumb sport.**
REVISED	**Water-skiing should be banned from public beaches.**

SWEEPING GENERALIZATION	**Women understand housework.**
REVISED	**The publication of a big new guide to housekeeping and that guide's success among both men and women suggest a renewed interest in the domestic arts.**

Avoiding loaded terms   In your claim, avoid sweeping and judgmental words: for instance, *bad, good, right, wrong, stupid, ridiculous, moral, immoral, dumb, smart.*

Modifying or changing your claim   Sometimes you will have an instant reaction to an issue and immediately decide which position you want to take. At other times, you will need to reflect and do research before you take a stand. Whenever you decide what your position is, formulate a position statement that will serve as your working thesis—for example, "Undocumented aliens should [or should not] have to pay higher college tuition fees than citizens or other immigrants." However, keep an open mind. Be prepared to find out more about an issue so that you can make an educated claim with concrete support, and be prepared to modify, qualify, or even change your original claim as you do your research.

Jennifer Hopper began her argument paper expecting to make a case for one side of the telemarketing debate (telemarketing takes trade away from retail stores, deceives the elderly, and invades everyone's privacy), only to find that her research produced enough evidence to persuade her to look at the situation from a different angle (telemarketing is a valuable source of American dollars and provider of goods and services). You can read a draft of her essay in 6g.

LANGUAGE AND CULTURE
Arguments across Cultures: Making a Claim and Staking a Position

The types of arguments described in this section are those common in academic and business settings in North America and the Western world. Writers state their views directly, arguing for their viewpoints. The success of their arguments lies in the credibility and strength of the evidence they produce in support. But such an approach is not universal. Other cultures may prefer a less direct approach, one that begins by exploring and evaluating all options rather than by issuing a direct claim. One of the basic principles of writing well—know your audience's expectations—is especially relevant to writing arguments in cultures different from your own.

Reasons   Imagine someone saying to you, "OK. I know your position on this issue, but I disagree with you. What led you to your position?" This is asking you to provide the reasons you have for your conviction. To begin to answer the question, add at least one "because" clause to your claim. (See page 68 on developing this argument.)

Claim: Colleges should stop using SAT scores to determine admissions.

Reason: (because) High school grades predict college success with more accuracy.

Once you have formulated a tentative claim, make a scratch outline (4d) listing the claim and your reasons for supporting it. As you work more on your argument, you will need to find specific and concrete evidence to explain and support each reason.

Here is an example of a scratch outline that argues against building a cement factory in a rural scenic region. The writer used the accompanying image as a visual argument in the finished text (11b). It is worth noting here that vocal community opposition over many years was effective and that the plans for the factory were eventually withdrawn.

> *Claim:* Although a large cement factory on the Hudson River would satisfy the increased demand for building materials and might help boost the local economy, it would not only pollute air and water but also threaten wildlife and the natural beauty of the area.

Reasons

1. Drilling, blasting, and mining pose dangers to the local aquifer and to the nearby city's water supply.

2. A 1,800-acre coal-burning plant with a 406-foot stack would emit just under 20 million pounds of pollution a year, including arsenic, lead, and mercury.

3. Smokestack emissions could affect birds; barge traffic and discharge into the river could affect fish.

4. Views portrayed by the Hudson River School of painters would be spoiled.

Concrete evidence   You need reasons, but reasons are not enough. You also need to include specific evidence that supports, illustrates, and explains your reasons. Imagine a reader saying after you give one of your reasons, "Tell me even more about why you say that." The details you provide are what will make your argument vivid and persuasive.

Add to the outline any items of concrete evidence you will include to illustrate and explain your reasoning. What counts as evidence? Facts, statistics, stories, examples, and testimony from experts can all be used as evidence in support of your reasons.

 ESL Note   Evidence Used to Support an Argument

The way arguments are structured, the concept of *expertise,* and the nature of evidence regarded as convincing may vary from one culture to another. In some cultures, for example, the opinions of religious or political leaders may carry more weight than the opinions of a scholar in the field. Looking at newspaper editorials written in your home language and in English will help you discern what differences, if any, exist in the types of evidence used to support an argument. Be sure to consider the readers you will be writing for and the type of evidence they will expect. ■

6d Argument structures

Two common structures used in designing an argument are derived from Aristotle's famously distinguished modes of reasoning: deductive and inductive logic. A *general to specific* structure is a deductive approach while a *specific to general* structure is inductive.

General to specific (deductive approach) If you have not had much experience with writing arguments, you may find it useful to work with and adapt the following basic structure for an argument. Used frequently in the humanities and arts, this structure moves from the thesis to support and evidence.

KEY POINTS

Basic Structure for a General-to-Specific Argument

1. *Introduction* Provide background information on the issue, why it is an issue, and what the controversies are. After you have introduced readers to the nature and importance of the issue, announce your position in a claim or thesis statement, perhaps at the end of the first paragraph or in a prominent position within the second paragraph, depending on the length and complexity of your essay.

2. *Body* Provide evidence in the form of supporting points for your thesis, with concrete and specific details. For each new point, start a new paragraph.

3. *Acknowledgment of opposing views* Use evidence and specific details to describe and logically refute the opposing views. You could also deal with opposing views one by one as you deal with your own points of support.

4. *Conclusion* Return to the issue and your claim. Without repeating whole phrases and sentences, reiterate the point you want to make. End on a strong note.

Refute specific to general (inductive approach) Alternatively, you might choose to begin with data and points of evidence and then draw a conclusion from that evidence. A basic specific-to-general argument looks like this:

Introduction: Background, statement of problem

Data:

1. Cell phone users admit to being distracted while driving.
2. Many accidents are attributable to cell phone use.
3. New York and New Jersey have passed laws against using a handheld cell phone while driving.
4. The AAA and insurance companies report that . . .

Conclusion: Discussion of data and presentation of thesis (generalization formed from analysis of the data): All states should prohibit the use of handheld cell phones while driving.

In an argument in the sciences or social sciences (see, for example, the APA-style sample paper in chapter 48), writers often begin with a hypothesis that they can test: they list their findings from experimentation, surveys, facts, and statistics, and then from the data they have collected they draw conclusions to support, modify, or reject the hypothesis.

6e Appeals, common ground, and opposing views

Ask who your readers are. Consider the readers you are writing for. Assess what they might know, what assumptions they hold, what they need to know, how they can best be convinced to accept your position, and what strategies will persuade them to respect or accept your views.

If you are writing for readers with no specific prior knowledge, biases, or expertise—a *general audience*—remember to include background information: the place, the time, the context, the issues. Do not assume that a general reader knows a great deal more than you do. For more on audience, see 1b.

Appeal to readers. Your profile of readers will help you decide what types of appeal to use in arguments. The following appeals, developed by Aristotle, have been the basis for persuasion since classical times.

Rational appeal (logos) A rational appeal bases an argument's conclusion on logical reasoning from evidence. Such an appeal is appropriate for academic readers and useful when readers are uninformed or hostile.

Ethical appeal (ethos) You make an ethical appeal to readers when you represent yourself or any experts you refer to as knowledgeable, reliable, reasonable, and evenhanded. Such an appeal is appropriate for formal situations in business and academic worlds. In advertising, ethical appeals are often adapted to include testimony from famous people, whether they are experts or not—for example, American Express uses Robert De Niro to promote its credit card.

Emotional appeal (pathos) You make an emotional appeal when you try to gain the empathy and sympathy of your readers by assessing their values and using stories and language to appeal to those values. Such an appeal is less common in academic writing than in journalism and the other media. It is appropriate when readers are regarded as either already favorable to particular ideas or apathetic toward them.

Within one extended argument, you will probably find it necessary to use all types of argument to reach the maximum number of readers, each with individual expectations, preferences, and quirks.

EXERCISE 6.1 Add an emotional appeal.
The following passage presents a rational appeal. What could the writer add to include an emotional appeal, too? Sample answers are in the Answer Key.

> Hunger is not as serious here [in the United States] as in countries where children are so nutrient-deprived that brain growth is impeded. The moderate undernutrition found in the United States affects performance, but recovery is usually possible with adequate diet. Yet if dietary deficiencies persist, learning can suffer. Iron deficiency anemia, which is twice as common in poor as in better-off children, affects cognitive ability. In experiments where people got inexpensive vitamin and mineral supplements, test scores rose from that treatment alone.
>
> —Richard Rothstein, "Lessons: Food for Thought? In Many Cases, No"

Establish common ground. Remember that readers turned off by exaggerations or extreme language have the ultimate power to stop reading and ignore what you have to say.

Opposing views It is not enough to present your own reasons and evidence for your claim. You also need to take into account any opposing arguments and the reasons and evidence that support those arguments. Examine those arguments; describe the most common or convincing ones; evaluate their validity, applicability, and limitations; and explain what motivates people to take those positions. Then discuss the ways in which your reasons and evidence are more pertinent and convincing than those in opposing arguments.

KEY POINTS

Ways to Establish Common Ground with Readers

1. Avoid extreme views or language. Do not label someone's views as *ridiculous, ignorant, immoral, fascist,* or *crooked,* for example.

2. Write to convince, not to confront. Recognize shared concerns, and consider the inclusive use of *we.*

3. Steer clear of sarcastic remarks, such as "They have come up with the amazingly splendid idea of building a gigantic cement factory right in the middle of a natural beauty spot."

4. Use clear, everyday words that sound as if you are speaking directly to your readers.

5. Acknowledge when your opponents' arguments are valid, and work to show why the arguments on your side carry more weight.

6. If possible, propose a solution with long-term benefits for everyone.

Be careful to argue logically and rationally without insulting your opponents—for instance, do not call opponents *crazy* or *stupid.* Take pains to explain rationally why your views differ from theirs. You might choose to do this by following each one of your own points with a discussion of an opposing view. Or you may prefer to devote a section of your essay to dealing with opposing views.

6f Logic and flaws in logic

As a reader of arguments, you will want to employ your critical thinking capabilities to examine the reasoning a writer uses and to ferret out the writer's assumptions, biases, and lapses in logic. Remember, too, that readers will be looking for *your* assumptions, biases, and lapses in logic as they read. Consider the following as you evaluate your argument.

Examine your logic with four questions. The four questions in the Key Points box, derived from Stephen Toulmin's *The Uses of Argument,* will provide you with a way to examine your own arguments critically.

>
>
> ### 🔑 KEY POINTS
>
> **Four Questions to Ask about Your Argument**
>
> 1. What is your point? (What are you claiming?)
>
> 2. What do you have to go on? (What support do you have for your claim, in the form of reasons, data, and evidence?)
>
> 3. How do you get there? (What assumptions—Toulmin calls them "warrants"—do you take for granted and expect readers to take for granted, too?)
>
> 4. What could prevent you from getting there? (What qualifications do you need to include, using *but, unless,* or *if* or adding words like *usually, often, several, mostly,* or *sometimes* to provide exceptions to your assumptions?)

Here is an example showing how these questions can be used:

> Claim: Colleges should stop using SAT scores in their admissions process.
>
> Support/data: (because) High school grades and recommendations predict college success with more accuracy.
>
> Assumption/warrant: Colleges use SAT scores to predict success in college.
>
> Qualifier: . . . unless colleges use the scores only to indicate the level of knowledge acquired in high school.
>
> Revised claim: Colleges that use SAT scores to predict college success should instead use high school grades and recommendations.

EXERCISE 6.2 Analyze assumptions.

Examine the following arguments. What are the assumptions that connect the claim to the data? Write a short analysis of the warrants (the assumptions). Then write a revised claim, suggesting any necessary qualifiers. Use extra paper as necessary. (**A** = See Answer Key.)

A 1. Claim: Steve is wealthy.

Support/data: Steve wears designer clothing, drives a Mercedes, and has a summer home.

Assumption/warrant: _____

Qualifier: _____

Revised claim: _____

2. Claim: Rita Fiorella is probably of Italian descent.

   Support/data: She has an Italian last name and long dark hair.

   Assumption/warrant: _____

   Qualifier: _____

   Revised claim: _____

Examine your assumptions. Pay special attention to examining assumptions that link a claim to the reasons and evidence you provide. Consider whether readers will share those assumptions or whether you need to explain, discuss, and defend them. For example, the claim "Telemarketing should be monitored because it preys on the elderly and the gullible" operates on the assumption that monitoring will catch and reduce abuses. The claim "Telemarketing should be encouraged because it benefits the economy" operates on the assumption that benefiting the economy is an important goal. These different assumptions will appeal to different readers, and some may need to be persuaded of the assumptions before they attempt to accept your claim or the reasons you give for it.

Note that if your claim is "Telemarketing should be encouraged because it is useful," you are saying little more than "Telemarketing is good because it is good." Your reader is certain to object to and reject such circular reasoning. That is why it is important to ask question 3 in the Key Points box on page 68. That question leads you to examine how you get from your evidence to your claim and what assumptions your claim is based on.

Avoid flaws in logic. Faulty logic can make readers mistrust you as a writer. Watch out for these flaws in logic (known as *logical fallacies*) as you write and check your drafts.

1. Sweeping generalization Generalizations can sometimes be so broad that they fall into stereotyping. Avoid them.

   All British people are stiff and formal.

   The only thing that concerns students is grades.

Readers will be right to wonder what leads to these conclusions. Without any explanation or evidence, these conclusions will simply be dismissed. Beware, then, of the trap of using words like *all, every, only, never,* and *always.*

2. Hasty conclusion with inadequate support To convince readers of the validity of a generalization, you need to offer enough evidence—usually more than just one personal observation. Thoughtful readers can easily spot a conclusion that is too hastily drawn from flimsy support.

> My friend Arecelis had a terrible time in a bilingual school. It is clear that bilingual education has failed.

> Bilingual education is a success story, as the school in Chinatown has clearly shown.

A conclusion that can be contradicted by any evidence is not a sound conclusion.

3. Non sequitur *Non sequitur* is Latin for "it does not follow." Supporting a claim with evidence that is illogical or irrelevant causes a non sequitur fallacy.

> Maureen Dowd writes so well that she would make a good teacher.

Here the writer needs to establish a connection between good writing and good teaching if this sentence is to work logically—and doing this may be difficult.

> Studying economics is a waste of time. Money does not make people happy.

Here the writer does not help us see any relationship between happiness and the study of a subject.

4. Causal fallacy You are guilty of a causal fallacy if you assume that one event causes another merely because the second event happens after the first. (The Latin name for this logical flaw is *post hoc, ergo propter hoc:* "after this, therefore because of this.")

> The economy collapsed because a new president was elected.

Was the election the reason? Or did the election happen to occur before the economy collapsed?

> The number of A's given in college courses has increased. This clearly shows that faculty members are inflating grades.

But does it clearly show that? Is it not possible for the cause to be that students are better prepared in high school? Examine carefully any statements you make about cause and effect.

5. Ad hominem attack   *Ad hominem* (Latin for "to the person") refers to appeals to personal considerations rather than to logic or reason. Avoid using arguments that seek to discredit an opinion through criticizing a person's character or lifestyle.

> The new curriculum should not be adopted because the administrators who favor it have never even taught a college course.

> The student who is urging the increase in student fees for social events is a partygoer and a big drinker.

Argue a point by drawing attention to the logic of the argument, or lack of it, not to flaws in character. However, personal considerations may be valid if they pertain directly to the issue, as in "The two women who favor the closing of the bar own property on the same block."

6. Circular reasoning   In an argument based on circular reasoning, the evidence and the conclusion restate each other, thus proving nothing.

> Credit card companies should be banned on campus because companies should not be allowed to solicit business from students.

> That rich man is smart because wealthy people are intelligent.

Neither of these statements moves the argument forward. They both beg the question; that is, they argue in a circular way.

7. False dichotomy or false dilemma   Either/or arguments reduce complex problems to two simplistic alternatives without exploring them in depth or considering other alternatives.

> To improve education, the board can either hire more teachers or build more schools.

Such a statement presents a false dichotomy. Those two options are not the only ways to improve education: science labs could be renovated, computer instruction could be developed, teachers could be assigned to only classroom duties, and so on.

> After September 11, the New York mayor can do one of two things: increase airport security or screen immigrants.

This proposal presents a false dichotomy. These are not the only two options for dealing with potential terrorism. Posing a false dilemma like this will not win you converts to your argument.

EXERCISE 6.3 Examine arguments.

For each of the following statements, determine whether the argument is logical or contains a logical fallacy. If it contains a logical fallacy, identify the logical fallacy and explain why it is a fallacy. (**A** = See Answer Key.)

A 1. The new vice president of sales is untrustworthy because many years ago he was arrested for civil disobedience while in college.

A 2. Married couples without children often experience societal pressure to have or adopt children.

3. Mary can either matriculate as a full-time student in the fall or wait until the following fall to attend classes.

4. Keeping a diary is cathartic because writing on a daily basis releases bottled-up emotions.

5. All men like sports.

TECHTOOLKIT Logical Fallacies on the Web

Go to *Stephen's Guide to the Logical Fallacies* at <http://datanation.com/fallacies> for lists of many more types of logical fallacies, all with explanations and examples. ■

6g A student's argument essay

Here is a draft of Jennifer Hopper's argument paper on telemarketing, developed from her brainstormed notes and further research (6b and 6c). She uses MLA style (see Part 7 for details and another student paper).

Hopper 1

Jennifer Hopper

Professor Raimes

English 120

1 May 2003

Why Telemarketing Is a Real Job:
The Ongoing War between the Right to Privacy and Telemarketing

Just a few years ago, when we wanted to shop, we had to leave our homes to go to the store or mall. The alternative was to order from catalogs. But the initiative remained with us, and for couch potatoes, that was not always easy. Now, however, we do not have to leave our house or dial a number. We can wait for goods and services to come to us. And come they will. Telemarketing involves millions of telephone calls every day from company representatives to households across America (Bacon and Roston 56). The demand for workers to make those calls and the billions of dollars' worth of goods and services sold via the calls have created a booming business for telemarketers, with revenues increasing 250% in twelve years, reaching a total of $295 billion in 2002 (Bacon and Roston 56). *Background context and statistics*

Yet every silver lining has its cloud. There has been a substantial outcry from the American public about the irritation of receiving sales calls at home, especially at meal times and during family gatherings. These objections have led to several attempts at solutions: the creation of anti-telemarketing Web sites, legislation, the proliferation of caller-ID plans, phone company services to protect telephone privacy, and court battles. Training programs remind telemarketers that if a prospective client does not need their services, no one will benefit from a forced sale (Allen 101). These developments center around the issue of Americans' right to privacy at home and whether telephone solicitations are an intrusion on that privacy. *Presentation of problem*

Hopper 2

Of course, this ugly side of telemarketing is accompanied by a bright side. Telemarketing has proven itself substantially important to both American workers and consumers. It increasingly provides millions of jobs to Americans (growing from 175,000 jobs to 5 million in ten years) and has sparked the growth and development of many declining U.S. cities (Greenwald). Therefore, if some individuals find that telephone solicitations do them more harm than good, they can address the problem without compromising the rights of the consumers and workers who benefit from the industry. In short, telemarketing cannot be *Claim (thesis)* written off as a public nuisance when it is such a valuable source of American dollars and provider of goods and services.

Support 1: importance to business (rational appeal) Although it is difficult to find a person with a listed phone number who has never received a telemarketing call, consumers are not the main target of phone solicitations. Greenwald reports that "pitches to other businesses generate more than 80% of the revenues of telemarketing and account for some 90% of its jobs." Just as *Concrete evidence* companies have found it cheaper to use phone calls rather than mail to gain customers, they have also found telemarketing to be a cheaper means of promoting business than sending sales teams (Greenwald).

Support 2: Creation of jobs in rural areas (rational and ethical appeal) In some parts of the country, the impact of telemarketing industries is especially beneficial. Omaha, Nebraska, is a prime example. In 1995, there were as few as thirty telemarketing companies located there, and yet "20,000 or so Omahans—about 5% of the resident population—work for them dialing out more *Concrete evidence* than one million quality calls per week" (Singer). Omaha proved to be a very profitable site for the industry, from the viewpoints of both company owners and Omaha residents. Located right in the middle of the United States, the town lends itself to "easy access" to all corners of the country and its four time zones (Singer). Not only that, but the majority of Omahan laborers are reasonably

Hopper 3

well educated, another advantage in the telemarketing field.
According to <u>New York Times</u> correspondent James Brooke, a
similar situation has developed in North Dakota, where Native
Americans have been able to take telemarketing jobs near their
reservations. In fact, Native Americans, usually vastly overlooked
by American employers, are catching the interest of telemarketers.
It may not be an exhibition of social consciousness on the part of
telemarketing companies, but it still provides opportunities for a
group of people not known for their earning power.

Concrete evidence

An important point to note is not just the number of jobs
that telemarketing provides but the significant economic changes
those jobs make in the lives of the people who hold them. In both
Omaha and North Dakota, farming used to be the way of life
(Brooke). As it became more and more difficult to subsist on crops
and cattle in the United States of the late twentieth century, the
need arose for another way for locals to supplement their earnings
and gain security. Telemarketing provided a means for people to
keep their homes and farms by working part-time in a booming
industry. Telemarketing also provided part-time jobs that were
stable and relatively easy. When asked about the rigors of her job,
Omahan telemarketer Erin Kline responded, "Stressful? More tiring.
But to sit here and get paid over 10, 11 bucks an hour to sit on
your butt, basically, and make phone calls . . . that's a really good
job" (qtd. in Singer). Telemarketing jobs continue to be held by
housewives, college students, and retired persons.

Support 3: economic benefit and security (emotional appeal)

Yet we can hardly forget the millions of people <u>receiving</u>
these phone calls. Many Americans express distaste for the entire
industry, united in the belief that people's homes should be a safe
haven from the rabid commercialism that has permeated all corners
of society. Some believe that telemarketing preys on so-called "nice
guys" and older people, who are loath to be rude and reject the sale

Use of we to establish common ground

Presentation of opposing view of telemarketing as a nuisance offered, which may even be a scam. Legislation is helping, too. Thirty states have initiated a "Do Not Call" list that informs companies of homes that request no more calls, with more than 15 million people signing the lists (Bacon and Roston 58). In addition, a national "Do Not Call" list was signed into law on 11 March 2003, legislating fines for violators ("House Passes"). However, even with legislation and penalties, consumers often take matters into their own hands.

Two different approaches have been used by indignant consumers to fight the telemarketing industry. One method is used most notably by a man named Robert Bulmash, of Private Citizen, Inc., whose name is practically synonymous with anti-telemarketing. Mr. Bulmash took his grievances straight to the American legal system, suing a telemarketing company that had especially plagued him (Sharkey). He has channeled his efforts into heading a group that helps cut down on unwelcome telephone solicitations. Its members' names are given to telemarketing companies, which are then informed there is a "service charge" for calling them. If calls continue, Mr. Bulmash helps members take legal action against the companies (Raisfield). Mr. Bulmash's approach was unique in that he brought his objections to the owners and operators of the company, who would have to deal with the lawsuit.

Other people use less noble tactics. Many screen calls or simply hang up. Some are rude or irritating to telemarketers in order to make them hang up and/or stop calling permanently. One proponent of this technique is Vince Nestico, who has even created a Web site to provide ideas to other exasperated people on how to "torture" telemarketers. He sells tapes that offer such extreme retorts to solicitors as, "Shhh . . . Wait a minute. I'm here robbing the house. Whoa! I think the owners just got home. Can you hold?" (qtd. in Sharkey). Unlike Mr. Bulmash, Mr. Nestico has decided that the best way to obtain phone lines free of solicitors is to take up his

Concrete evidence

Ethical and emotional appeal in opposition to telemarketing

Hopper 5

grievances with the employees, not the heads of the telemarketing companies. It is understandable that Mr. Nestico is tired of receiving telemarketing calls, but it may be more difficult to comprehend his motivations for trying to capitalize on the sale of goods like the "Telemarketer Torture Tape" he has created.

Are such tapes the mature, responsible way to handle an onslaught of telemarketing calls? Just as the consumer has a right to privacy, the telemarketer has the right to hold a job and not be tormented in the process. If people have a problem with telemarketing as a selling strategy, then they need to add their names to the "Do Not Call" lists and take up any violations with the heads of companies or the government, as many of them already have done.

Refutation of opposing views (rational appeal) with solution to problem

After learning the industry's employment numbers and sales revenues, we can no longer write off telemarketing as unnecessary and dispensable. It has become important and necessary to places like Omaha and North Dakota, where jobs were badly needed. Telemarketing industries are selling billions of dollars' worth of goods and services to American consumers every year. Not all these sales, or even a majority of them, can be the result of telemarketers supposedly deceiving consumers. Americans who may not agree with telemarketing techniques can fight the industry legally. But telemarketers have as much a right to hold down a job without interference as other Americans. Linda Scobee, an Omahan telemarketer, had this in mind when a man attacked her for doing her job. "He said, 'Why don't you get a real job?' and I wanted to say, 'If you'd like to send me a check every month to take care of my kids, I'll stop.' But I didn't. You know, company policy" (qtd. in Singer).

Conclusion

Reiteration of claim and main points of argument

Hopper 6

Works Cited

New page

Allen, Margaret. Direct Marketing. London: Kagan Page, 1997.

Bacon, Perry, Jr., and Eric Roston. "Stop Calling Us." Time
28 Apr. 2003: 56–58.

Brooke, James. "Telemarketing Finds a Ready Labor Market in
Hard-Pressed North Dakota." New York Times 3 Feb. 1997:
A10. Academic Universe: News. LexisNexis. City U of New
York Lib. 23 Apr. 2003 <http://web.lexis-nexis.com>.

Greenwald, John. "Sorry, Right Number." Time 13 Sept. 1993: 66.
Academic Search Premier. EBSCO. City U of New York Lib.
18 Apr. 2003 <http://search.epnet.com/direct.asp?an=
9309080045&db=aph>.

"House Passes 'Do Not Call' Legislation." Association Management
Apr. 2003: 7. Business Source Premier. EBSCO. City U of
New York Lib. 29 Apr. 2003 <http://search.epnet.com/
direct.asp?an+9376434&db=buh>.

Raisfield, Robin. "Telenuisances." New York Magazine 31 Jan.
1994: 31.

Sharkey, Joe. "Answering the Phone as an Act of Revenge."
New York Times 22 June 1997, sec. 4: 3. Academic
Universe: News. LexisNexis. City U of New York Lib. 24 Apr.
2003 <http://web.lexis-nexis.com>.

Singer, Barry. "It's 7 P.M. and 5 Percent of Omaha Is Calling. Want
28 Steaks and a Radio?" New York Times Magazine 3 Dec.
1995: 68– . Academic Universe: News. LexisNexis. City U of
New York Lib. 1 May 2003 <http://web.lexis-nexis.com>.

7 Draft, Revise, and Edit.

Always allow time in your writing schedule to put your draft away before looking at it with a critical eye.

Revising—making changes to improve a piece of writing—is an essential part of the writing process. It is not a punishment inflicted on inexperienced writers. Good finished products are the result of careful revision. Even Leo Tolstoy, author of the monumental Russian novel *War and Peace,* commented: "I cannot understand how anyone can write without rewriting everything over and over again."

As you revise and edit, address both "big-picture" and "little-picture" concerns. Big-picture revising involves making changes in content and organization. When you revise, you may add or delete details, sections, or paragraphs; alter your thesis statement; vary or strengthen your use of transitions; move material from one position to another; and improve clarity, logic, flow, and style. Little-picture editing involves making adjustments to improve words and sentences and to correct errors in grammar, spelling, word choice, mechanics, and punctuation. Both are necessary, but most people like to focus first on the big picture and then turn to fixing up the details.

7a Tips for writing and managing drafts

Writing provides what speech can never provide: the opportunity to revise your ideas and the way you present them without your audience's realization. The drafting process lets you make substantive changes as you progress through drafts. You can add, delete, and reorganize sections of your paper. You can rethink your thesis and support. You can change your approach to parts or all of the paper. Writing drafts allows you to work on a piece of writing until you feel you have made it meet your goals.

> **KEY POINTS**
>
> **Tips for Drafts**
>
> 1. Set a schedule. First set the deadline date; then, working backward, establish dates for completing drafts and getting feedback. See 1c and 38b for sample schedules.
>
> 2. Don't automatically begin at the beginning. Begin by writing the essay parts for which you already have some specific material.
>
> *(continued on next page)*

(continued)

3. Write in increments of twenty to thirty minutes to take advantage of momentum.

4. Write your first draft as quickly and fluently as you can. Write notes to yourself in capitals or surrounded by asterisks to remind yourself to add or change something or do further research.

5. Print out your draft triple-spaced so that you can easily write in questions, comments, and changes.

6. Keep your topic, purpose, and thesis very much in mind.

7. Avoid the obvious (such as "All people have feelings"). Be specific, and include interesting supporting details.

8. Revise for ideas, interest, and logic; don't merely fix errors. It is often tempting just to correct errors in spelling and grammar and see the result as a new draft. Revising entails more than that. You need to look at what you have written, check for the logic and development of each paragraph (5c), imagine readers' reactions, and rethink your approach to the topic.

TECHTOOLKIT   Using Comments and Auto Correct in a Word Document

Some word processing programs have a Comment function that allows you to type notes that can appear only on the screen, or on the screen and in a printout. These notes—to yourself or to your instructor—can be easily deleted from later drafts. In addition, if you use a term frequently (for example, *bilingual education*), abbreviate it (as *b.e.,* for example) and use a tool like AutoCorrect to replace the whole phrase throughout your draft as you type.

Overcoming writer's block   Most writers, however much they write or even profess to like writing, have at one time or another felt a dreaded block. They sit and stare at the blank screen and then, often, take trips to the refrigerator for comfort. Instead, consider these questions, and try the strategies.

KEY POINTS

Overcoming Writer's Block

1. Do you have a set of rules that you follow in your writing process, such as "Always begin by writing a good introduction" or "Always have a complete outline before starting to write"? If you do, consider whether your rules are too rigid or even unhelpful. As you gather ideas and do your preparatory drafting, ignore any self-imposed rules that hinder you.

2. Do you edit as soon as you write, and do you edit often? Your desire to write correctly might be preventing you from thinking about ideas and moving forward. Try blogging, freewriting, brainstorming, or mapping (3b–3d).

3. Do you feel anxious about writing, even though you have knowledge of and interest in your topic? Try using some freewriting and brainstorming strategies (3c, 3d), or begin writing as if you were talking about your topic with a friend.

4. Do you feel that you do not yet know enough about your topic to start writing, even though you may have done a great deal of research? Try freewriting or try drafting the sections you know most about. Writing will help show you what you know and what you need to know.

However, if you sit down to a writing task close to the deadline without having done the necessary preliminary work—reading, interpreting, taking notes, and generating ideas—you probably are suffering not from writer's block but from lack of preparation.

Managing drafts and files Save all your notes and drafts until your writing is completed and the course is over. Print out a copy of each new draft so that if something happens to your disk, pen drive, or computer, you still have a copy of your work. In addition, save each new draft under a new file name, just in case you want to compare versions or return to ideas in a prior draft. If you cut out substantial passages, save them in a separate file labeled "Outtakes." Then you can easily retrieve the passages if you change your mind and want to use them. Above all, do remember to make back-up copies of all your draft files.

For a ten-page essay on athletic scholarships, a student kept eight computer documents in one "Athletic Scholarships Essay" folder to handle the recording of information from sources, as well as his own notes and drafts:

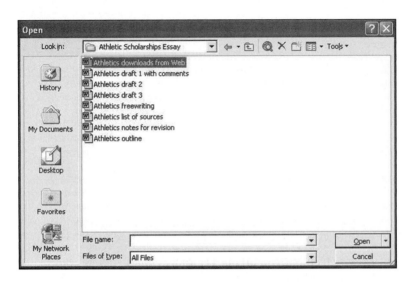

Consider the file structure you will use for every essay or report you write.

7b Writing collaboratively

Writing, as well as providing feedback, is not necessarily a solitary process. In the academic or business world, you might be expected to work in formal collaborative structures. Groups, teams, or committees might be formed to draft a proposal or report, or you might be expected to produce documents reflecting the consensus of your section or group. You will always want to be sure, however, that you work collaboratively only when doing so is expected. An instructor who assigns an essay may not expect or want you to work on it with anyone else.

In such group settings, make sure that you work out a way for every member of the group to contribute. You can do this by assigning each person a set of specific tasks, such as making lists of ideas, drafting, analyzing the draft, revising, editing, assembling visuals, and preparing the final document. Schedule regular meetings, and expect everyone to come with a completed written assignment. Build on strengths within the group. For example, for a business report, ask the member skilled in document design and computer graphics to prepare the visual features of the final document (See chapter 10).

TECHTOOLKIT   Working Collaboratively on the Computer

In networked computer labs, in distance-learning courses, and in the business world, writing collaboratively is often encouraged—and certainly the technology makes it easy. One person can post an idea or a draft and invite response; or participants can work together on an outline, research, drafting, and editing, with assigned roles. Then all the results and drafts can be posted online, with feedback from peers, the instructor, or the project leader. See 7e on computer tools for revising and collaborating.   ■

7c   Giving and getting feedback

Ask a friend, colleague, or tutor to read your draft with a pencil in hand, placing a checkmark next to the passages that work well and a question mark next to those that do not. Ask your reader to tell you what main point you made and how you supported and developed it. This process might reveal any lack of clarity or indicate gaps in the logic of your draft. Your reader does not have to be an expert English teacher to give you good feedback. If you notice worried frowns (or worse, yawns) as the person reads, you will know that something in your text is puzzling, disconcerting, or boring. Even that simple level of feedback can be valuable. See 7g for an example of student writing revised after feedback.

If you are asked to give feedback to a classmate or colleague, use the following guidelines.

KEY POINTS

Giving Feedback to Others

1. When you are asked to give feedback to a classmate, don't think of yourself as an English teacher armed with a red pen.

2. Read for positive reactions to ideas and clarity. Look for parts that make you think "I agree," "I like this," or "This is well done."

3. As you read, put a light pencil mark next to one or two passages that make you pause and send you back to reread.

4. Try to avoid comments that sound like accusations ("You were too vague in paragraph 3"). Instead, use *I* to emphasize your reaction as a reader ("I had a hard time visualizing the scene in paragraph 3").

Go to *The Open Handbook* at <http://college.hmco.com/keys.html>, and click on Forms and Checklists for a peer response form you can customize.

Draft by _____   Date _____

Response by _____   Date _____

1. What do you see as the writer's main point in this draft?

2. What part of the draft interests you the most? Why?

3. Where do you feel you would like more detail or explanation? Where do you need less?

4. Do you find any parts unclear, confusing, or undeveloped? Mark each such spot with a pencil question mark in the margin. Then write a note to the writer with questions and comments about the parts you have marked.

5. Give the writer one suggestion about one change that you think would improve the draft.

7d   Beginning and ending well

Beginnings and endings are important. Try to give readers an idea of what to expect in your essay and make them eager to read more. And once they have read your explanations and arguments, your conclusion should make it clear that you have provided substantive information and covered the important points. Readers should leave your document feeling satisfied, not turning the page and looking for more or shrugging with a "So what?" expression on their faces.

Introduction   Imagine a scene at a party. Someone you have never met before comes up to you and says, "Capital punishment should be abolished immediately." You're surprised. You wonder where this position came from and why you are being challenged with it. You probably think this person rather strange and pushy. Imagine now readers picking up a piece of your writing. Just like people at a party, readers would probably like to know something about the topic and its relevance before you pronounce on it. Think of your introduction as providing a social function between writer and reader.

Examine the following introductions.

> On the day before Memorial Day, 1983, a poet called me to describe a city he had just visited. He said that one section included mosques, built by the Islamic people who dwelled there. Attending his reading, he said, were large numbers of Hispanic people, forty thousand of whom lived in the same city. He was not talking about a fabled city located in some mysterious region of the world. The city he'd visited was Detroit.
>
> —Ishmael Reed, "America: The Multinational Society,"
> *Writin' Is Fightin'*

Reed introduces the theme of multinationalism in the United States with an anecdote that leads readers to expect that the city he describes is in an unfamiliar part of the world. He then grabs readers with a surprise in the last sentence—the city is Detroit—and prepares readers for his discussion of a multinational continent.

> As the captain of the Yale swimming team stood beside the pool, still dripping after his laps, and listened to Bob Moses, the team's second-best freestyler, he didn't know what shocked him more—the suggestion or the fact that it was Moses who was making it.
>
> —Robert A. Caro, *The Power Broker:*
> *Robert Moses and the Fall of New York*

This sentence is the first in the introductory chapter of Caro's massive biography of Robert Moses, a powerful force in New York City construction and politics for four decades. Caro does not begin with where and when Moses was born. Instead, he draws us into the story by making us want to read on to find out what the suggestion was (Moses proposed misleading a donor into giving money to the swim team) and why it was shocking.

If you find it difficult to write an introduction because you are not yet clear about your thesis or how you will support it, wait until you have written the body of your essay. You will find something concrete easier to introduce than something you have not yet written.

When you write an introduction to an essay in the humanities, keep the following points in mind.

KEY POINTS

How to Write a Good Introduction

Options

- Make sure your first sentence stands alone and does not depend on readers' being aware of the essay title or an assigned question. For instance, avoid beginning with "This story has a complex plot."
- Provide context and background information to set up the thesis.
- Indicate what claim you will make in your essay, or at least indicate the issue on which you will state a claim.
- Define any key terms that are pertinent to the discussion.
- Establish the tone of the paper: informative, persuasive, serious, humorous, personal, impersonal, formal, informal.
- Engage the interest of your readers to make them want to continue reading.

What to Avoid

- Avoid being overly general and telling readers the obvious, such as "Crime is a big problem" or "In this fast-paced world, TV is a popular form of entertainment" or "Since the beginning of time, the sexes have been in conflict."
- Do not refer to your writing intentions, such as "In this essay, I will . . ." Do not make extravagant claims, such as "This essay will prove that bilingual education works for every student."
- Do not restate the assigned essay question.

The following may help to engage readers' interest:

surprising statistics

a challenging question

a pithy quotation

interesting background details

an unusual fact

an intriguing opinion statement

a relevant anecdote

EXERCISE 7.1 Evaluate introductory paragraphs.
Read the following three paragraphs, and identify which method the author has chosen to introduce the topic. Consider whether the author's choice seems effective and why. (**A** = See Answer Key.)

A 1. "If I die first and Papi ever gets remarried," Mami used to tease when we were kids, "don't you accept a new woman in my house. Make her life impossible, you hear?" My sisters and I nodded obediently, and a filial shudder would go through us. We were Catholics, so of course, the only kind of marriage we could imagine had to involve our mother's death. We were also Dominicans, recently arrived in Jamaica, Queens, in the early 60s before waves of other Latin Americans began arriving. So, when we imagined who exactly my father might possibly ever think of remarrying, only American women came to mind. It would be bad enough having a *madrastra*, but a "stepmother" . . .

—Julia Alvarez, "Hold the Mayonnaise"

2. How far can we go in exalting Newton's scientific achievements? Not far enough. Few minds in the intellectual history of humankind have left such an imprint as Newton's. His work represents the culmination of the Scientific Revolution, a grandiose solution to the problem of motion that had haunted philosophers since pre-Socratic times. In doing so, he laid the conceptual foundations that were to dominate not only physics but also our collective worldview until the dawn of the twentieth century.

—Marcelo Gleiser, *The Dancing Universe:
From Creation Myths to the Big Bang*

3. Since 1970, the composition of households and families and the marital status and living arrangements of adults in the United States both experienced marked changes. For example, the proportion of the population made up by married couples with children decreased, and the proportion of single mothers increased, while the median age at first marriage grew over time. Much of this variety has been regularly reported in two separate Census Bureau reports—*Household and Family Characteristics* and *Marital Status and Living Arrangements*. Beginning with the March 2001 Current Population Survey, these two reports are being replaced by this new publication, *America's Families and Living Arrangements*.

—*America's Families and Living Arrangements*, U.S. Census Bureau,
<http://www.census.gov/prod/2001pubs/p20-537.pdf>

Conclusion Think of your conclusion as completing a circle. You have taken readers on a journey from presentation of the topic in your introduction, to your thesis, to supporting evidence and discussion, with specific examples and illustrations. Remind readers of the purpose of the journey. Recall the main idea of the paper, and make a strong statement about it that will stick in their minds. Don't let readers turn the page looking for more.

KEY POINTS
How to Write a Good Conclusion

Options

- Frame your essay by reminding readers of something you referred to in your introduction and by reminding readers of your thesis.
- End on a strong note: a quotation, a question, a suggestion, a reference to an anecdote in the introduction, a humorous insightful comment, a call to action, or a look to the future.

What to Avoid

- Do not use the obvious "In conclusion."
- Do not apologize for the inadequacy of your argument ("I do not know much about this problem") or for holding your opinions ("I am sorry if you do not agree with me, but . . .").
- Do not use the identical wording you used in your introduction.
- Do not introduce totally new ideas. If you raise a new point at the end, readers might expect more details.
- Do not contradict what you said previously.
- Do not be too sweeping in your conclusions. Do not condemn the whole medical profession, for example, because one person you know had a bad time in one hospital.

EXERCISE 7.2 Improve an unsatisfactory conclusion.
Read the following concluding paragraph from a paper on protecting data from computer viruses. What suggestions would you give to the student writer about how to improve it? Be specific. Then revise the paragraph according to your suggestions. A sample answer is in the Answer Key.

> This concludes my paper on dangerous computer viruses. I am not an expert, but each of the measures mentioned above, if practiced, will help you to avoid having your data destroyed. It's easy to minimize danger. First, buy an antivirus program. Second, screen unknown data. Third, back up all your files. In doing so, one will, if not eliminate all potential danger, at the very least protect valuable data. Each day more viruses are created, so since we can't know what's coming, we can, at the very least, use "an ounce of prevention."

7e Tools for content revision

For college essays and important business documents, always allow time in your writing schedule for at least a second draft—more if possible. Before writing a second draft, examine a printed copy of your first draft, assess how it measures up to the assignment, evaluate it as a response to the assignment, and plan the changes you need to make. Occasionally, a few simple changes may be enough (the Band-Aid approach); more often, however, radical surgery will be necessary, in the form of cutting, rearranging, and adding—or in extreme cases, starting all over. Do any of the following to help you with your analysis.

- Create distance and space. Put a draft away for a while and then read it again with fresher, more critical eyes. Imagine readers' reactions to your title and your thesis.

- Highlight key words in the assignment. Mark passages in your draft that address the words. If you fail to find any, it could be a clear signal that you need to revise.

- Read your draft aloud. Mark any places where you hesitate and have to struggle to understand the point. Go back to them later. Alternatively, ask somebody else to read a copy of the draft; note where the reader hesitates or seems unclear about the meaning.

- Make an outline of what you have written (4d).

- Select the first sentence of each paragraph, and use the Copy and Paste features to move the sequence of sentences into a new file. Then examine these first sentences. Do they provide a sense of logical progression of ideas? Is there any repetition? What will readers of these first sentences expect the paragraph to contain?

See 7g for a student's annotations on his first draft.

KEY POINTS

Triggers for Revision

The following should alert you to consider the need for revision:

1. a weak or boring introductory paragraph (see 7d)

2. any spot in your draft that causes a worried frown, a pause, or a thought of "Huh? Something is wrong here" as you read

3. a paragraph that never makes a point or offers support

4. a phrase, sentence, or passage that you cannot immediately and fully understand (if you have trouble grasping your own ideas, readers surely will have trouble, too)

5. excessive use of generalizations—*everyone, most people, all human beings, all students/lawyers/politicians,* and so on (better to use specific examples in their place: *the students in my political science course this semester*)

6. a feeling that you would have difficulty summarizing your draft (maybe it is too vague?)

7. an awareness that you read the same point earlier in the draft

8. a sense that you would like to turn beyond the last page in an attempt to find a definite conclusion

TECHTOOLKIT   Computer Tools for Revising

- The AutoCorrect feature in Word allows you to take shortcuts and to save time. If, for example, you are writing about "housing preservation," you can simply write "hp" whenever you want to write "housing preservation." Go to Tools/AutoCorrect Replace text and then With.

- The Find feature helps you find words and phrases that you tend to overuse. Use it to look for instances of "there is" or "there are," for example, and you will see if you are using either phrase too often.

- The Insert/Comment feature allows you to write a note in the middle of a draft. The place where a comment is inserted will be highlighted on your screen, and you can see the comment appear at the end of your document. You can then choose to print your document with or without the comments showing.

- The File/Hidden Text feature is useful when revising a document. Rather than deleting paragraphs or sections you are thinking about cutting, you can simply hide them (and reveal them) as necessary. The Help index will show you more about using the Hidden Text feature in your word processing software.

- The Tools/Track Changes feature allows you to mark and highlight additions and changes to your own document or one received via e-mail that you want to work on collaboratively and have copied into your word processing program. This feature lets you see clearly on the screen and on the printed page the changes you have made. Going to Tools/Options allows you to set the color of the inserts and to label each insert with your user name, which will appear as a pop-up with the added text. The Accept or Reject Changes option allows you to accept or reject all the changes or each change separately, and it will make the changes to your document automatically. ■

7f Tools for editing and proofreading

Examine your draft for grammar, punctuation, and spelling errors. Often, reading your essay aloud will help you find sentences that are tangled, poorly constructed, or not connected. Looking carefully at every word and its function in a sentence will alert you to grammatical problem areas. Turn to chapters 12 and 13 for help with Standard English and methods for correcting common errors.

TECHTOOLKIT Computer Tools for Editing

- A spelling checker will flag any word it does not recognize, and it is very good at catching typographical errors such as *teh* for *the* or *responsability* for *responsibility*. However, it will not identify grammatical errors that affect only spelling, such as missing plural or *-ed* endings. Nor will it flag an omitted word or find a misspelled word that forms another word, such as *then* for *than*, *their* for *there*, or *affect* for *effect*.

- An online thesaurus will prompt you with synonyms and words close in meaning to a highlighted word; check suggested words in a dictionary for their connotations.

- The Tools/Word Count feature is handy when you are given a word limit; it provides an immediate, accurate count.

- Grammar-check programs will analyze your sentences and make suggestions about what might need to be fixed, tightened, or polished. However, these programs cannot take context or meaning into account, so their capabilities are limited. For example, if you wrote "The actors were boring" but meant to write "The actors were bored," the grammar-check programs would not reveal your mistake. ■

ESL NOTE The Dangers of Grammar-Check Programs

Never make a change in your draft at the suggestion of a grammar-check program before verifying that the change is really necessary. A student from Ukraine wrote the grammatically acceptable sentence "What he has is pride." Then, at the suggestion of a grammar-check program, he changed the sentence to "What he has been pride." The program had not recognized the sequence "has is." ■

Proofreading Even after editing carefully and getting as much help from computer tools as you can, you still need to proofread your final draft to make sure no errors remain.

 EXERCISE 7.3 Try out spelling and grammar checkers.
Type these two sentences into your word processor exactly as they are written

> The economists spraedsheets were more simpler then the ones there competitors have prepared. "They was prepared quickly, said the manager.

Now run the spelling and grammar checkers. What do you find, and what conclusions can you draw? Check Settings to see what your word processor has been set to find. Do you think you need to change any of those settings? How would *you* correct the sentences? A sample answer is in the Answer Key.

 KEY POINTS

Proofreading Tips

Try any or all of the following strategies:

1. Do not try to proofread a document on the computer screen. Always print out a hard copy to make it easier to find mistakes.

2. Make an additional copy, and ask a friend to read your document aloud while you note places where he or she stumbles over an error.

3. Put a piece of paper under the first line of your text. As you read, move it down line by line to focus your attention on one line at a time. Touch each word with the end of a pencil

as you either say the word aloud or mouth it silently to yourself.

4. Read the last sentence first, and work backward through your text. This strategy will not help you check for meaning, logic, pronoun reference, fragments, or consistency of verb tenses, but it will focus your attention on the spelling, punctuation, and accuracy of one sentence at a time.

5. Put your manuscript away for a day or two after you have finished it. Proofread it when the content is not so familiar.

EXERCISE 7.4 Proofread a passage and use correction marks. Proofread this paragraph for the writer who drafted it. Use correction marks (p. 609) to indicate any problems or errors. (**A** = See Answer Key.)

>   **A** Insomnia is a sleep disorder that effects millions of people. **A** Often they turn to over-the-counter pills to relieve their insomnea. Medication, especially self-medication, should not be the first course of action. **A** Patients should seek the advice of there physician. **A** However, before taking any medication, they should seriously consider other options lifestyle changes can help including cutting back on caffeinated beverages, drinking herbal tea such as chamomile, reading a pleasant book, and writing a "to do" list before they go to bed.

7g A student's drafts

After Brad Thompson wrote the first draft of an essay describing and analyzing a magazine advertisement for the clothing company DKNY (Donna Karan New York), he read it aloud to a group of classmates and took note of their comments. He also received feedback from his instructor. Here you see Thompson's introduction and first descriptive paragraph, with his own annotations for revision. Following that is his second draft, with some small-scale revisions added by hand. Thompson then went on to write one more draft, making the changes he had indicated and fine-tuning style, sentence structure, and word choice.

FIRST DRAFT

Change title?

DKNY: An Analysis of an Ad

In the September issue of Details, page 13 to be exact,
one will find a rather strikeing advertisement for DKNY   *Begin with this?*
clothing. DKNY is power, DKNY is wealth, DKNY is women,
DKNY is stability. And to think, for the price of a mere overcoat,   *Add thesis*
you too can be all this. I will tell you how.   *Fix fragments*

frag   The city (on page one): A dull white light illuminates
the gray desolation of downtown manhattan. The picture is out   *cap*
frag   of focus. Perhaps another in the endless series of bad days at   *it shows*
the office, perhaps one too many at the bar? Well, it does look   *cap*
like it could be dawn, maybe you have just woken up to find   *Change you*
yourself on the A train going uptown. The city is a bad place.
It can't quite be seen clearly, it's crooked, like some sinister
shot out of The Third Man. The picture creates an environment,
Move   an urban Siberia. What kind of man could possibly survive in
up to   such a place?
focus ¶ ?   A DKNY kind of man enters . . . .   *Better transition?*

SECOND DRAFT

Downtown, Killer, New York: Advertising and Power
DKNY is power, DKNY is wealth, DKNY is women, DKNY is
stability. In the September issue of Details, page 13 to be exact, a
rather striking two-page advertisement for DKNY clothing says all
these things. It illustrates a nightmare world inhabited by the vast
majority of DKNY's target audience, as well as a survivor of such a   ^

world. DKNY sells the myth of rugged individualism, man against the wilderness. It offers to all everything it stands for $\wedge$ power, wealth, women, security. All this, for the price of a mere overcoat.

    The first page of the DKNY advertisement presents an image of the city as an urban Siberia. A dull white light illuminates the gray desolation of downtown Manhattan. ~~The picture is out of focus.~~ Perhaps it shows another in the endless series of bad days at the office, perhaps one too many at the bar? It could be dawn, just waking up on the A train headed uptown. The city is a bad place, *with people* ~~It can't quite be seen clearly.~~ Like some sinister shot out of <u>The Third Man</u>, with crooked streets over crooked sewers and serpentine subway tubes. What kind of man could possibly survive in such a place?

    Enter the DKNY man, the survivor . . . .

EXERCISE 7.5 Evaluate drafts.
Discuss with classmates the changes Thompson made in his second draft. In what ways has he improved on his first draft? Are there further changes you would suggest for his third draft?

8   Pay Attention to the 5 C's of Style.

Style is important to readers. It affects their response to a piece of writing and influences their willingness to continue reading. Sometimes, even when ideas are well organized, readers can suffer from the so-called MEGO reaction to a piece of writing—"My Eyes Glaze Over." Readers are bored by wordiness, flatness, inappropriate word choice, clichés, and sentences constructed without interesting variations. Working on style can help prevent that glazing over.

LANGUAGE AND CULTURE
Style across Cultures

It is impossible to identify one style as the best. What is considered good (or appropriate) style varies according to the writer's purpose and the expectations of the anticipated readers. Country, culture, region, ethnic heritage, language, gender, class—all can play a role in influencing what readers define as *style*. What may please readers in one language and culture in one setting in one part of the world may seem too flat or too adorned in another. The Japanese novelist Junichuro Tanizaki, for example, gives writers this advice: "Do not try to be too clear; leave some gaps in the meaning." Other cultures value clarity. Good style is relative.

With acknowledgment to Joseph Williams's *Style: Ten Lessons in Clarity and Grace*, 7th edition, sections 8a–8e examine five anti-MEGO strategies, called here the "Five C's of Style": cut, check for action, connect, commit, and choose the right words.

8a   The first C: Cut.

You can improve most of your writing if you focus on stating your ideas succinctly. Do not be tempted to pad your work to fill an assigned number of pages.

1. Cut wordiness.   Say something only once and in the best place.

▶ The Lilly Library ~~contains many rare books. The books in the library are~~ carefully preserved~~,~~ ^s^ ~~The library also houses~~
many rare books and manuscripts
~~a manuscript collection.~~ ^

director of
▶ Steven Spielberg, ~~who has directed~~ the movie ~~that has been~~ described as the best ^war movie ever made, ~~is someone who~~ knows many politicians.

▶ California residents voted to abolish bilingual education/
~~The main reason for their voting to abolish bilingual~~

          . because
~~education was that~~ many children were being placed
          ^

indiscriminately into programs and kept there too long.

If your draft says something like "As the first paragraph states" or "As previously stated," beware. Such phrases probably indicate that you have repeated yourself.

2. Cut formulaic phrases. Writers sometimes use formulaic phrases in a first draft to keep the writing process going. In revision, these wordy phrases should come out or be replaced with shorter or more concise expressions.

FORMULAIC	CONCISE
at the present time	now
at this point in time	
in this day and age	
in today's society	
are of the opinion that	believe
have the ability to	can
is dependent upon	depends on
last but not least	finally
prior to	before
concerning the matter of	about
because of the fact that	because
due to the fact that	
in spite of the fact that	although

3. Cut references to your intentions. Eliminate references to the organization of your text and your own planning, such as *In this essay, I intend to prove . . .* or *In the next few paragraphs, I hope to show . . .* or *In conclusion, I have demonstrated . . .* or *What I want to say here is . . .*

However, note that in writing for the social sciences or sciences, the main goal is usually to provide information. In those disciplines, therefore, you may acceptably state how you intend to structure your argument—for example, *This paper describes three approaches to treating depression.*

4. Cut redundant words and phrases.   Trim words that repeat an idea expressed by another word in the same phrase: *basic* essentials, *true* facts, circle *around,* cooperate *together, final* completion, return *again,* refer *back,* reimburse *back, advance* planning, consensus *of opinion, free* gift. Also edit redundant pairs (*various and sundry, hopes and desires, each and every*) and any redundant phrases.

▶ The task took ~~diligence and~~ perseverance.

        has
▶ His surgeon ~~is a doctor with~~ a great deal of clinical experience.
               ^

EXERCISE **8.1**   Make appropriate cuts.
Edit the following passage to eliminate any unnecessary material. Go to *The Open Handbook* at <http://college.hmco.com/keys.html>, and click on Writing Process to download this excerpt if you would like to change the line spacing or use Track Changes to make your annotations. (**A** = See Answer Key.)

    A With computer graphics imaging becoming more lifelike and realistic in today's society, filmmakers in the motion picture industry are now able to create animated characters who could conceivably take the place of human beings or people in leading roles onscreen. **A** Nonliving stars are not a completely and totally unknown quantity, of course. **A** Mickey Mouse and Bugs Bunny are cartoon characters who earned millions of fans in spite of the fact that they did not exist in the real world outside of an animation studio. **A** King Kong, who was the first stop-motion animation star, thrilled and delighted audiences beginning in the decade of the 1930s because of the fact that he was believably realistic at that point in time.

    However, modern innovations in computer graphics make cartoons and stop-motion characters look quaint and dated. At the present time, filmmakers are resolved and determined to create "synthespians" who will look, move, speak, and talk in such a realistic manner that audiences will be awed, and studios are enlisting animators with expertise and experience in computer graphics rather than traditional old-fashioned cartoonists to model the new breed of cyber-actors. Some film and movie critics are of the opinion that filmmakers are failing to grasp something vital and important, which is that audiences want genuine and honest emotion and creative storytelling rather than whiz-bang special effects and computer graphics. They argue that no computer-generated synthespian will ever really matter or be important to filmgoers unless his or her films are well written and well directed.

8b The second C: Check for action.

The parts of a sentence that carry the weight of the meaning are the subject and the verb. Don't waste them. As a general rule, write vigorous sentences with vivid, expressive verbs. Avoid overusing the verb *be* (*be, am, is, are, was, were, being, been*), and use the active voice to have the subject of your sentence perform the action.

1. Ask "Who's doing what?" about subject and verb. The subject (*approval*) and verb (*was*) in the following sentence tell readers very little:

WORDY   **The mayor's approval of the new law was due to voters' suspicion of the concealment of campaign funds by his deputy.**

This dull thud of a sentence revolves around the verb *was*. It contains three abstract nouns (*approval, suspicion,* and *concealment*) formed from verbs (*approve, suspect,* and *conceal*), as well as five prepositional phrases: *of the new law, due to voters' suspicion, of the concealment, of campaign funds,* and *by his deputy.*

WHO'S DOING WHAT?

SUBJECT	VERB
the mayor	approved
the voters	suspected
his deputy	had concealed

Always put verbs to work to make a stronger sentence.

REVISED   **The mayor approved the new law because voters suspected that his deputy had concealed campaign funds.**

2. Use caution in beginning a sentence with *there* or *it*. For a lean, direct style, rewrite sentences in which *there* or *it* occupies the subject position (as in *there is, there were, it is, it was*). Revise by using verbs that denote an action and subjects that perform the action. Asking "Who's doing what?" helps here, too.

WORDY   **There was a discussion of the health care system by the politicians.**   [Who's doing what?]

REVISED   **The politicians discussed the health care system.**

WORDY   **It is a fact that Arnold is proudly displaying a new tattoo.**

REVISED   **Arnold is proudly displaying a new tattoo.**

TECHTOOLKIT Searching for Uses of *It* and *There*

Use the Find function of your word processing program to find all instances in your draft of *it is/was, there is/are,* and *there was/were.* If you find a filler subject with little purpose, edit (see 7f). ■

3. Avoid unnecessary passive voice constructions. The *passive voice* tells what is done to the grammatical subject of a clause ("The turkey *was cooked* too long"). Extensive use of the passive voice makes your style dull and wordy. When you can, replace it with active voice verbs, especially when you mention the doer of the action.

PASSIVE   **The problem will be discussed thoroughly by the committee.**

ACTIVE   **The committee will discuss the problem thoroughly.**

If you are studying in the social sciences or sciences, disciplines in which readers are primarily interested in procedures and results rather than who developed or produced them, you will find passive voice constructions are more common and more acceptable than in the humanities. For example, in lab reports and experiments, you will read *The rats were fed* instead of *The researchers fed the rats.* For acceptable uses of the passive voice, see 16g.

TECHTOOLKIT Grammar-Check Software and the Passive Voice

Grammar checkers will point out passive voice constructions. If you have a tendency to overuse the passive voice, use a grammar checker to alert yourself to the places that you can check. However, use the grammar checker as only a guide; programs sometimes identify structures wrongly. Use the grammar checker simply to send yourself back to your sentence to reread and check it (see 7f). ■

EXERCISE 8.2 Check for action.
Revise any sentences that could be made more vigorous. Go to *The Open Handbook* at <http://college.hmco.com/keys.html>, and click on Style to download this excerpt if you would like to change the line spacing or use Track Changes to make your annotations. (**A** = See Answer Key.)

> **A** Alzheimer's disease is a terrible affliction of the elderly in the United States and around the world. **A** People are robbed by the disease of a lifetime of memories, and family members often care for patients who no longer recognize them. **A** There can be

years of round-the-clock care required to help an Alzheimer's patient, and such care is expensive. **A** A heavy toll is taken on any stricken family by this disease.

However, there is hope offered by new research to those who fear that they may develop this illness. The rate of people affected by Alzheimer's in India is the lowest in the world, and scientists have been investigating possible reasons. The Indian diet is considered by some scientists to be an answer. There is a spice called curcumin that is common in Indian curries, and it is being tested by researchers as a possible preventive medicine. In one intriguing study, a diet rich in curcumin was fed to laboratory mice bred to develop brain defects similar to those produced by Alzheimer's, and the result was the development of fewer brain defects in the mice during the aging process. It is not yet known whether curcumin or other spices will help reduce the number of people developing Alzheimer's; if curcumin does prove to be effective, it will take some time for scientists to discover the reasons. Someday, perhaps, there will be a currently unknown property of curcumin found by researchers that will reveal a solution to the puzzle of Alzheimer's.

8c The third C: Connect.

In coherent pieces of writing, information that has been mentioned before is linked to new information in a smooth flow, not in a series of grasshopper-like jumps.

1. Apply the principle of using consistent subjects.   Readers need to have a way to connect the ideas beginning a sentence with what has gone before. From one sentence to the next, avoid jarring and unnecessary shifts of subjects.

JARRING SHIFT	*Memoirs* **frequently top the bestseller list.** *Readers* **of all ages are finding them appealing.**
REVISED	*Memoirs* **frequently top the bestseller list.** *They* **appeal to readers of all ages.**

In the revised version, the subject of the second sentence, *they,* refers to the subject of the previous sentence, *memoirs;* the new information about "readers of all ages" comes at the end, where it receives more emphasis.

Keeping subjects consistent and constructing a chain of topics may mean using the passive voice, as in the last sentence of the revision that follows:

Frequent Topic Switches	*I* have lived all my life in Brooklyn, New York. *Park Slope* is a neighborhood that has many different ethnic cultures. *Harmony* exists among the people there, even though it does not in many other Brooklyn neighborhoods. *Several articles in the press* have praised the Slope for its ethnic variety.
Revised	*Many different ethnic cultures* flourish in Park Slope, Brooklyn, where I have lived all my life. *These different cultures* live together harmoniously there, even though they do not in many other Brooklyn neighborhoods. In fact, *the ethnic variety* of the Slope has often been praised in the press.

2. Let old information lead to new. If you begin with the old information of a subject you have previously mentioned, new information will come at the end of the sentence. This pattern helps sentences end on a strong and interesting note, one that you want to emphasize, which keeps your ideas flowing smoothly. Don't let a sentence trail off weakly.

Weak Ending	Women often feel silenced by men, according to one researcher.
Revised	According to one researcher, women often feel silenced by men.

Weak Ending	Odysseus encounters Calypso, who tempts him with immortality, after he has resisted the Sirens.
Revised	After resisting the Sirens, Odysseus encounters Calypso, who tempts him with immortality.

Cumulative and periodic sentences Cumulative (or loose) sentences begin with the independent clause and add on to it. Periodic sentences begin with words and phrases that lead to the independent clause, giving emphasis to the end of the sentence. The cumulative sentence is the norm in English prose. Use a periodic sentence to make a specific impact.

Cumulative	*The experienced hunter stood stock-still for at least five minutes,* sweat pouring from his brow, all senses alert, waiting to hear a twig snap.
Periodic	Sweat pouring from his brow, all senses alert, waiting to hear a twig snap, *the experienced hunter stood stock-still for at least five minutes.*

3. Explore options for connecting: Coordination, subordination, and transitions. When you write sentences containing two or more clauses, consider where you want to place the emphasis. Decide whether to give each clause equal weight or to subordinate one or more ideas in a complex sentence. See 2e and 8d, item 3.

COORDINATION You give two or more clauses equal emphasis when you connect them with a coordinating conjunction—*and, but, or, nor, so, for,* or *yet*. See 12c and 23b.

┌─── independent clause ───┐ ┌─── independent clause ───
▶ **The bus trip was long,** *and* **the seats seemed more**

└──────────────────────────┘
uncomfortable with every mile.

┌── independent clause ──┐ ┌── independent clause ──┐
▶ **The bus trip was long,** *but* **we managed to enjoy it.**

Sometimes writers choose to start a sentence with *and* or *but*, either for stylistic effect or to make a close connection to a previous, already long sentence:

▶ **You can have wealth concentrated in the hands of a few, or democracy. But you cannot have both.**

—Justice Louis Brandeis

As with any stylistic device, it is wise not to overuse *and* or *but* at the beginning of sentences. Given the difference of opinion on this usage, check with your instructor, too.

SUBORDINATION When you use subordinating conjunctions (12c) such as *when, if,* or *because* to connect clauses, you give one idea more importance by putting it in the independent clause.

┌────── dependent clause ──────┐ ┌──────────────
▶ **If we cannot now end our differences, at least we can help**

┌────── independent clause ──────┐
make the world safe for diversity. —John F. Kennedy

[Two clauses connected by *if*; emphasis on the independent clause at the end of the sentence]

TRANSITIONAL EXPRESSIONS Use words such as *however, therefore,* and *nevertheless* (known as *conjunctive adverbs*) and phrases such as *as a result, in addition,* and *on the other hand* to signal the logical connection between independent clauses. (For a list of transitional expressions, see 5e.) A transitional expression can move around in its own clause—yet another stylistic option for you to consider.

▶ He made a lot of money; however, his humble roots were always evident.

▶ He made a lot of money; his humble roots, however, were always evident.

KEY POINTS

Options for Connecting Clauses

Purpose	Coordinating Conjunction	Transitional Expression	Subordinating Conjunction
addition	and	also, further, furthermore, moreover, in addition	
contrast	but, yet	however, nevertheless, on the other hand	although, even though, whereas, while
alternative	or, nor	instead, otherwise, alternatively	unless
result	so, for	therefore, as a result, hence, consequently, thus, accordingly, then	because, as, since, so/such . . . that, now that, once

---

The following examples illustrate how the options may work.

▶ Brillo pads work well, but I don't give them as gifts.

▶ Although Brillo pads work well, I don't give them as gifts.

▶ Brillo pads work well; nevertheless, I don't give them as gifts.

▶ Brillo pads work well; I, however, don't give them as gifts.

Make your choice by deciding what you want to emphasize and seeing what structures you used in nearby sentences. If, for example, you used *however* in the immediately preceding sentence, choose some other option for expressing contrasting ideas. Notice how subordinating a different idea can change your meaning and emphasis.

▶ **Although I don't give Brillo pads as gifts, they work well.**

AVOIDING EXCESSIVE COORDINATION OR SUBORDINATION   Too much of any one stylistic feature will become tedious to readers.

EXCESSIVE
COORDINATION
WITH *AND*

I grew up in a large family, and we lived on a small farm, and every day I had to get up early and do farm work, and I would spend a lot of time cleaning out the stables, and then I would be exhausted in the evening, and I never had the energy to read.

REVISED

Because I grew up in a large family on a small farm, every day I had to get up early to do farm work, mostly cleaning out the stables. I would be so exhausted in the evening that I never had the energy to read.

EXCESSIVE
SUBORDINATION

Because the report was weak and poorly written, our boss, who wanted to impress the company president by showing her how efficient his division was, to gain prestige in the company, decided, despite the fact that work projects were piling up, that he would rewrite the report over the weekend.

REVISED

Because the report was weak and poorly written, our boss decided to rewrite it over the weekend, even though work projects were piling up. He wanted to impress the company president by showing her how efficient his division was; that was his way of gaining prestige.

4. Connect paragraphs.   Just as readers appreciate a smooth flow of information from sentence to sentence, they also look for transitions—word bridges—to move them from paragraph to paragraph. A new paragraph signals a shift in topic, but careful readers will look for transitional words and phrases that tell them *how* a new paragraph relates to the paragraph that precedes it. Provide readers with steppingstones; don't ask them to leap over chasms.

> ## 🔑 KEY POINTS
>
> ### A Checklist for Connecting Paragraphs
>
> 1. Read your draft aloud. When you finish a paragraph, make a note of the point you made in the paragraph. Then check your notes for the flow of ideas and logic.
>
> 2. Refer to the main idea of the previous paragraph as you begin a new paragraph. After a paragraph on retirement, the next paragraph could begin like this, moving from the idea of retirement to saving: *Retirement is not the only reason for saving. Saving also provides a nest egg for the unexpected and the pleasurable.*
>
> 3. Use words like *this* and *these* to provide a link. After a paragraph discussing urban planning proposals, the next paragraph might begin like this: *These proposals will help. However, . . .*
>
> 4. Use transitions such as *also, too, in addition, however, therefore,* and *as a result* to signal the logical connection between ideas (5e).

EXERCISE 8.3 Make connections.

Revise the following passage to improve connections between ideas. As necessary, improve consistency of subjects; add emphasis; include coordination, subordination, and transitions; eliminate any excessive use of coordination and subordination; and connect paragraphs. Go to *The Open Handbook* at <http://college.hmco.com/keys.html>, and click on Style to download this excerpt if you would like to change the line spacing or use Track Changes to make your annotations. (**A** = See Answer Key.)

    A The Taliban rulers of Afghanistan fell from power in the fall of 2001. **A** An interim government was formed to rule the war-torn country, and under the Taliban, the law had forbidden women to hold jobs, reveal their faces in public, or speak to men other than their relatives, and the interim government included a department devoted to women's affairs in a sign that times had changed in Afghanistan. **A** Dr. Sima Samar was chosen as the minister for women's affairs. **A** Dr. Samar earned a medical degree from Kabul University. **A** Dr. Samar had spent years working from exile and from within Afghanistan to improve the conditions for women in her native country.

    Dr. Samar had practiced medicine in refugee camps in Pakistan. She had helped to set up clinics and schools for women and girls inside Afghanistan, traveling frequently between Pakistan and her homeland. She was breaking Taliban law by giving women access to medical services and education. She believed that her work was worth the risk. "I've always been in danger, but I don't mind," she said in a BBC interview in December 2001.

Dr. Samar did not anticipate problems with any of the men who would work under her as she took her new post in the ministry for women's affairs. She told a reporter for the *New York Times* that she had goals for the ministry, and she expected the men working for her to help achieve the goals, and those goals included making sure that each woman in Afghanistan had "access to education, the right to vote, the right to go to work, to choose her spouse. All those things are the basic rights of human beings." Offering Afghan women even those basic rights after decades of war would be a difficult task for anyone. Dr. Samar did not turn away from the responsibility of ensuring women those rights when she was asked to serve her country through its interim government.

8d The fourth C: Commit.

According to E. B. White, coauthor of *The Elements of Style*, the original author William Strunk, Jr., "scorned the vague, the tame, the colorless, the irresolute. He felt it was worse to be irresolute than to be wrong." This section focuses on ways to commit to being detailed, bold, colorful, and resolute.

1. Commit to a confident presence.   Academic writing is certainly not the same as personal accounts of feelings, events, and opinions. But it is not writing from which you as the writer should fade from sight. The best academic writing reveals personal engagement with the topic, details of what the writer has observed and read, an unmistakable *you*. Always ask yourself: Where am I in this draft? What picture of me and my world do readers get from my piece of writing? Do they see clearly what I base my opinions on? If you use sources, readers should be able to perceive you in conversation with your sources; they should see not just a listing of what sources say but also your responses to and comments on those sources.

Showing a confident presence does not necessarily mean always using *I* or repeatedly saying "In my opinion." It means writing so that readers see a personal stance in what you write.

When you are trying to persuade readers to accept your point of view, avoid the ambivalence and indecisiveness evident in words and phrases like *maybe, perhaps, it could be, it might seem,* and *it would appear.*

Hedging will not heighten readers' confidence in your opinions:

> ▶ **Tough economic times did not stop me from bidding on eBay,~~but others might have had different experiences.~~**
> ☉

Aim for language that reflects accountability and commitment: *as a result, consequently, of course, believe, need, demand, should, must.* Use the language of confident commitment, however, only after thoroughly researching your topic and satisfying yourself that the evidence is convincing.

In addition, convey to readers an attitude of confidence in your own abilities and judgment. Make an ethical appeal to readers by stressing your expertise (6e). Avoid apologies. One student ended a first draft this way:

Too APOLOGETIC **I hope I have conveyed something about our cultural differences. I would like my reader to note that this is just my view, even if a unique one. Room for errors and prejudices should be provided. The lack of a total overview, which would take more time and expertise, should also be taken into account.**

If you really have not done an adequate job of making and supporting a point, try to gather more information to improve the draft instead of adding apologetic notes. The student writer revised the ending after reading 7d on how to end well.

REVISED VERSION **The stories I have told and the examples I have given come from my own experience; however, my multicultural background has emphasized that cultural differences do not have to separate people but can instead bring them closer together. A diverse, multicultural society holds many potential benefits for all its members.**

2. Commit to an appropriate and consistent tone. Readers will expect the tone of your document to fit its purpose. The tone of your piece of writing reflects your attitude toward your subject matter and is closely connected to your audience's expectations and your purpose in writing. If you were, for example, writing about a topic such as compensation for posttraumatic stress disorder suffered by families of victims of the September 11, 2001, World Trade Center attack, a serious, respectful tone would be appropriate.

For most academic writing, commit resolutely to an objective, serious tone. Avoid sarcasm, colloquial language, name-calling, or pedantic words and structures, even in the name of variety. Make sure you dedicate a special reading of a draft to examining your tone; if you are reading along and a word or sentence strikes you as unexpected and out of place, flag it for later correction. In formal college essays, watch out especially for sudden switches to a chatty and conversational tone, as in "Nutrition plays a large part in whether people *hang on to* their own teeth as they age." (You would revise *hang on to,* changing it to *retain.*) Ask a tutor or friend to read your document and note any lapses in consistency of tone. See 1d and Exercise 1.1 for more on tone.

3. Commit to sentence variety.

LENGTH   Readers appreciate variety, so revise for a mix of long and short sentences. If your editing program can print out your text in a series of single numbered sentences, you will easily be able to examine the length and structure of each sentence. Academic writing need not consist solely of long, heavyweight sentences. Short sentences interspersed among longer ones can have a dramatic effect.

This passage from a student memoir demonstrates the use of short sentences to great effect:

> When I started high school and Afros became the rage, I immediately decided to get one. Now at that time, I had a head full of long, thick, kinky hair, which my mother had cultivated for years. When she said to me, "Cut it or perm it," she never for one minute believed I would do either. I cut it. She fainted.

> —Denise Dejean, student

SENTENCE TYPES   As you revise, try to vary the structure of your sentences. Aim for a mix of simple, compound, complex, and compound-complex sentences.

A *simple sentence* contains one independent clause.

▶ **Kara raised her hand.**

A *compound sentence* contains two or more independent clauses connected with one or more coordinating conjunctions (*and, but, or, nor, so, for, yet*), or with a semicolon alone, or with a semicolon and a transitional expression (5e).

┌─ independent clause ─┐   ┌──────── independent clause ────────┐
▶ **She raised her hand, and the whole class was surprised.**

┌─ independent clause ─┐   ┌──── independent clause ────┐
▶ **She raised her hand, but nobody else responded.**

┌─ independent clause ─┐   ┌──────── independent clause ────────┐
▶ **She raised her hand; as a result, the whole class was surprised.**

A *complex sentence* contains an independent clause and one or more dependent clauses.

┌────── dependent clause ──────┐ ┌────── independent clause ──────┐
▶ **When she raised her hand, the whole class was surprised.**

┌────── independent clause ──────┐ ┌────── dependent clause ──────┐
▶ **The whole class was surprised when she raised her hand.**

A *compound-complex sentence* contains at least two independent clauses and at least one dependent clause.

┌────── dependent clause ──────┐ ┌────── independent clause ──────┐
▶ **When she raised her hand, the whole class was surprised,**

┌────── independent clause ──────┐ ┌────── dependent clause ──────┐
and the professor waited eagerly as she began to speak.

INVERTED WORD ORDER Sometimes, inverted word order—switching from the usual subject (S) + verb (V) order to verb + subject—will help you stylistically to achieve coherence, consistent subjects, emphasis, or a smooth transition:

          V   ┌──── S ────┐
▶ **Next to the river runs a superhighway.**

      V S V
▶ **Never have I been so tired.**

      V ┌─ S ─┐   V
▶ **Not only does the novel entertain, but it also raises our awareness of poverty.**

      V S
▶ **So eager was I to win that I set off before the starter's gun.**

      V ┌S┐   V
▶ **Rarely has a poem achieved such a grasp on the times.**

Using an occasional rhetorical question will also help drive a point home:

      V   S   ┌──── V ────┐
▶ **How could anyone have thought that war was the answer?**

SENTENCE BEGINNINGS Consider using some of the following variations to begin a sentence, but remember that beginning with the subject will always be clear and direct for readers. Any of these beginnings repeated too often will seem like a stylistic tic and will annoy or bore readers.

Begin with a *dependent clause* or a *condensed clause.*

────── dependent clause ──────

► **While my friends were waiting for the movie to begin, they ate three tubs of popcorn.**

────── clause condensed to a phrase ──────

► **While waiting for the movie to begin, my friends ate three tubs of popcorn.**

Begin with a *participle* or an *adjective*. A sentence can begin with a participle or an adjective only if the word is in a phrase that refers to the subject of the independent clause. If the word does not refer to the subject, the result is a *dangling modifier* error (15c).

-ing participle

► **Waiting for the movie to begin, my friends ate popcorn.**

past participle

► **Forced to work late, they ordered a pepperoni pizza.**

adjective

► **Aware of the problems, they nevertheless decided to continue.**

Begin with a *prepositional phrase.*

┌ prepositional phrase ┐

► **With immense joy, we watched our team win the pennant.**

You can also occasionally use inverted word order after a prepositional phrase for stylistic flow.

────── prepositional phrase ──────   verb   ────── subject ──────

► **At the end of my block stands a deserted building.**

EXERCISE 8.4   Identify sentence types.
Select a piece of your own writing, and in it identify the sentence types you have used: simple, compound, complex, or compound-complex.

8e   The fifth C: Choose the right words.

Word choice, or *diction,* contributes a great deal to the effect your writing has on readers. Do not give readers puzzles to solve; state clearly what you mean.

1. Use exact words and connotations.   When you write, use words that convey exactly the meaning you intend at the appropriate level of specificity and that meet readers' expectations of tone and level of formality.

CHECK FOR CONNOTATION.   Two words that have similar dictionary definitions (*denotation*) can also have additional positive or negative implications and emotional overtones (*connotation*). Readers will not get the impression you intend if you describe a person as *lazy* when you mean *relaxed*. Select words with appropriate connotations. Hurricanes *devastate* neighborhoods; construction workers *demolish* buildings. Writing "Construction workers devastated the building" would be inappropriate. Note how word choice can affect meaning:

VERSION 1   **The crowd consisted of young couples holding their children's hands, students in well-worn clothes, and activist politicians, all voicing support of their cause.**

VERSION 2   **The mob consisted of hard-faced workers dragging children by the hand, students in leather jackets and ragged jeans, and militant politicians, all howling about their cause.**

A thesaurus, which lists synonyms and often also includes antonyms and related words, can help you find the right word. However, thesaurus programs attached to word processing programs (7f) typically offer lists of synonyms but little guidance on connotation. Using a thesaurus alone is not enough. You also need to check a word in a dictionary that provides examples of usage.

CHOOSE VIVID AND SPECIFIC WORDS.   Notice the increasing concreteness and specificity in this list: *tool, cutting instrument, knife, penknife. Tool* is a general term; *penknife* is a specific term. Some words do little more than fill space because they are so abstract, general, and vague. Words such as the following signal the need for revision: *area, aspect, certain, circumstance, factor, kind, manner, nature, situation, thing.*

If you do not move away from the general and abstract, you will give readers too much imaginative leeway. "Her grandmother was shocked by the clothing she

bought" leaves a great deal to readers' imaginations. What kind of clothing do you mean: a low-necked dress, high-heeled platform shoes, and black fishnet stockings, or a conservative navy blue wool suit? Choose words that convey exact images and precise information.

CHECK THAT YOUR WORDS FIT THE TONE OF YOUR DOCUMENT.   Word choice conveys tone (see also 1d; 8e, item 2; 9e) as well as connotation and specificity. The synonyms listed here suggest different eras and attitudes and varying degrees of formality:

child: kid, offspring, progeny

friend: dog, peeps, buddy, brother/sister, comrade

jail: slammer, cooler, prison, correctional institution

angry: ticked off, furious, mad, fuming, wrathful

computer expert: geek, hacker, techie, programmer

threatening: spooky, scary, eerie, menacing

fine: rad, phat, dope, fly, cool, first-rate, excellent

Some of these words—*kid, slammer, ticked off, geek, spooky, rad*—are so informal that they would rarely, if ever, be appropriate in formal academic writing or business letters, though they would raise few eyebrows in journalism, advertising, or e-mail. Overuse of formal words—*progeny, comrade, wrathful*—on the other hand, could produce a tone that suggests a stuffy, pedantic attitude (see page 119).

2. Avoid slang, regionalisms, and jargon.

SLANG   In a formal college essay, avoid colloquial language and slang. Do not enclose a slang expression in quotation marks to signal to readers that you know it is inappropriate. Instead, revise it.

▶ The working conditions were "~~gross.~~" *inhumane.*

▶ The sound of sirens ~~gets to me.~~ *affects me powerfully*

▶ The jury returned the verdict that the ~~guy~~ was guilty. *defendant*

In formal writing, avoid the following colloquial words and expressions: *dude, folks, guy, OK or okay, pretty good, cool, hassle, kind of interesting/nice, a ways away,* and *no-brainer.* See 9e on formal and informal language in online communications.

REGIONAL AND ETHNIC LANGUAGE Use regional and ethnic dialects in your writing only when you are quoting someone directly (*"Your car needs fixed," the mechanic muttered.*) or you know that readers will understand why you are using a nonstandard phrase.

> I bought ~~me~~ a camcorder. [*myself*]

> He vowed that he wouldn't pay them ~~no never mind~~. [*any attention*]

> They~~'re~~ here three years already. [*have been*]

> She used to ~~could~~ run two miles, but now she's out of shape. [*be able to*]

LANGUAGE AND CULTURE
Dialect and Dialogue in Formal Writing

Note how Paule Marshall uses Standard English for the narrative thread of her story while reproducing the father's Barbadian dialect and idioms in the dialogue, thus combining the formal and the informal, the academic and the personal into a rich whole:

> She should have leaped up and pirouetted and joined his happiness. But a strange uneasiness kept her seated with her knees drawn tight against her chest. She asked cautiously, "You mean we're rich?"
>
> "We ain rich but we got land."
>
> "Is it a lot?"
>
> "Two acres almost. I know the piece of ground good. You could throw down I-don-know-what on it and it would grow. And we gon have a house there—just like the white people own. A house to end all house!"
>
> "Are you gonna tell Mother?"
>
> His smile faltered and failed; his eyes closed in a kind of weariness.
>
> —Paule Marshall, *Brown Girl, Brownstones*

TECHNICAL LANGUAGE AND JARGON People engaged in most areas of specialized work and study use technical words that outsiders perceive as jargon. A sportswriter writing about baseball will refer to *balks, twi-night double-headers, ERAs, brushbacks,* and *crooked numbers.* A linguist writing about language for an audience of linguists will use terms like *phonemics, sociolinguistics, semantics, kinesics,* and *suprasegmentals.* If you know that your audience is familiar with the technical vocabulary of a field, specialized language is acceptable. Avoid jargon when writing for a more general audience; if you must use technical terms, provide definitions that will make sense to your audience.

3. Use figurative language for effect, but don't overuse it. Figures of speech can enhance your writing and add to imaginative descriptions. Particularly useful are similes and metaphors. A *simile* is a comparison in which both sides are stated explicitly and linked by the words *like* or *as*. A *metaphor* is an implied comparison in which the two sides are indirectly compared. When figurative language is overused, however, it becomes tedious and contrived.

SIMILE: AN EXPLICIT COMPARISON WITH BOTH SIDES STATED

▶ America is *not like a blanket*—one piece of unbroken cloth, the same color, the same texture, the same size. America is more *like a quilt*—many pieces, many colors, many sizes, all woven and held together by a common thread.

—Rev. Jesse Jackson

METAPHOR: AN IMPLIED COMPARISON, WITHOUT *LIKE* OR *AS*

▶ Some television programs are so much chewing gum for the eyes.

—John Mason Brown

MIXED METAPHORS

Take care not to mix metaphors.

▶ As she walked onto the tennis court, she was ready to sink or swim.   [Swimming on a tennis court?]

▶ He was a whirlwind of activity, trumpeting defiance whenever anyone crossed swords with any of his ideas. [The three metaphors—*whirlwind, trumpet, crossed swords*—obscure rather than illuminate.]

For more on figurative language in literature, see 52b.

4. Avoid biased and exclusionary language.   You cannot avoid writing from perspectives and backgrounds that you know about, but you can avoid divisive terms that reinforce stereotypes or belittle other people. Be sensitive to differences. Consider the feelings of members of the opposite sex, minorities (perhaps more correctly labeled as "world majorities"), and special-interest groups. Do not emphasize differences by separating society into *we* (people like you) and *they* or *these people* (people different from you). Use *we* only to be truly inclusive of yourself and all readers. Be aware, too, of terms that are likely to offend. You don't have to be excessive in your zeal to be PC (politically correct)—using *underachieve* for *fail*, or *vertically challenged* for *short*—but do your best to avoid alienating readers.

GENDER   The writer of the following sentence edited it after a reader alerted him to gender bias in the perception of women's roles.

> ▶ ~~Mrs. John~~ Harrison, ~~married to a real estate tycoon and herself the bubbly, blonde~~ chief executive of a successful computer company, has expanded the business overseas.

(insertion: Andrea)

Choice of words can reveal gender bias, too.

AVOID	USE
actress	actor
chairman	chair *or* chairperson
female astronaut	astronaut
forefathers	ancestors
foreman	supervisor
mailman	mail carrier
male nurse	nurse
man, mankind (meaning any human being)	person, people, our species, human beings, humanity
manmade	synthetic, artificial
policeman, policewoman	police officer
salesman	sales representative, salesclerk
veterans and their wives	veterans and their spouses

When using pronouns, too, avoid the stereotyping that occurs by assigning gender roles to professions.

> ▶ Before a surgeon can operate, he *or she* must know every detail of the patient's history.

Often it is best to avoid *he or she* by recasting the sentence or using plural nouns and pronouns.

> ▶ Before operating, a surgeon must know every detail of the patient's history.

▶ **Before *surgeons* can operate, *they* must know every detail of the patient's history.**

See 18e for more on gender, the use of *he or she*, and the use of plural pronouns.

RACE Mention a person's race only when it is relevant. If you write "Attending the meeting were three doctors and an Asian computer programmer," you reveal more about your own stereotypes than you do about the participants in the meeting. In general, use the names that people prefer for their racial or ethnic affiliation. *The Columbia Guide to Standard American English* advises: "It is good manners (and therefore good usage) to call people only by the names they wish to be called." Consider, for example, that currently *African American* or *black* are preferred terms; *Asian* is preferred to *Oriental*, and *American Indian* is now preferred to *Native American*.

PLACE Avoid stereotyping people according to where they come from. Some British people may be stiff and formal, but not all are, and they certainly do not all play cricket, drink tea all day, and wear derbies (called "bowler hats" in England). Not all Germans eat sausage and drink beer; not all North Americans carry cameras and wear plaid shorts. Be careful, too, with the way you refer to countries and continents. The Americas include both North and South America, so you need to make the distinction. England, Scotland, Wales, and Northern Ireland make up the United Kingdom. In addition, shifts in world politics and national borders have resulted in the renaming of many countries. Always consult a current atlas, almanac, or Web site.

AGE Avoid derogatory or condescending terms associated with age. Refer to a person's age or condition neutrally, if at all: not "a well-preserved little old lady" but "a woman in her eighties" or just "woman."

POLITICS Words referring to politics are full of connotations. Consider the positive and negative connotations of *liberal* and *conservative* in various election campaigns. Take care when you use words like *radical, left-wing, right-wing,* and *moderate.* How do you want readers to interpret them? Are you identifying with one group and implicitly criticizing other groups?

RELIGION An older edition of an encyclopedia referred to "devout Catholics" and "fanatical Muslims." A newer edition refers to both Catholics and Muslims as "devout," thus eliminating the bias of a sweeping generalization. Examine your use of the following: words that sound derogatory or exclusionary, such as *cult* or *fundamentalist;* expressions, such as *these people,* that emphasize difference; and even the word *we* when it implies that all readers share your beliefs.

HEALTH AND ABILITIES Avoid expressions such as *confined to a wheelchair* and *AIDS victim* so as not to focus on difference and disability. Instead, write *someone who uses a wheelchair* and *person with AIDS,* but only if the context makes it necessary to include the information. Do not unnecessarily draw attention to a disability or an illness. If the CEO of a huge fashion chain has Parkinson's disease, how relevant is that information to your account of the rise of the company in the stock market?

SEXUAL ORIENTATION Mention a person's sexual orientation only if the information is relevant in context. To write that someone accused of stock market fraud was "defended by a homosexual lawyer" would be to provide gratuitous information. The sexual orientation of the attorney might be more relevant in a case involving discrimination against homosexuals. Since you may not know the sexual orientations of readers, do not assume it is the same as your own.

THE WORD *NORMAL* Be especially careful about using the word *normal* when referring to your own health, ability, or sexual orientation. Some readers might justifiably find that usage offensive.

EXERCISE 8.5 Avoid biased language.
In each of the following sentences, revise any biased or exclusionary language. (**A** = See Answer Key.)

EXAMPLE:

~~The radical leftist~~ Aaron McGruder's comic strip offended some readers with its claim that the United States had helped to arm and train Osama bin Laden.

A 1. Some comic strips, such as *Doonesbury,* written by Garry Trudeau, and *The Boondocks,* created by the African American Aaron McGruder, can be considered political satires.

A 2. Many normal people have found *Doonesbury* offensive throughout its long history, for Trudeau has depicted premarital sex and drug use, championed women's libbers and peaceniks, and criticized politicians from Richard Nixon to George W. Bush.

3. In the fall of 2001, the main character in McGruder's comic strip argued that the ultra-conservative Reagan administra-

tion had aided Osama bin Laden and other fanatical Muslims fighting against the Soviet Union.

4. Many newspapers refused to carry McGruder's comic that day, and one female editor who claimed to be a fan of *The Boondocks* argued that the strip was inappropriate.

5. As newspaper comics have become more modern, comic strips feature single girls and dysfunctional families, but political issues that upset Midwestern readers are apparently still out of bounds.

5. Avoid pretentious language, clichés, and euphemisms.

MAKE FORMAL ACADEMIC WRITING CLEAR. Don't think that a formal college essay has to be filled with big words and long, complicated sentences. It certainly does not. In fact, the journal *Philosophy and Literature* sponsors an annual Bad Writing Contest, often "won" by renowned college professors. Convoluted writing is not necessarily a sign of brilliance or of an astonishingly powerful mind. It is usually a sign of bad writing.

DISTINGUISH THE FORMAL FROM THE STUFFY. Formal does not mean stuffy and pretentious. Writing in a formal situation does not require you to use obscure words and long sentences. Clear, direct expression works well in formal prose. Pretentious language makes reading difficult.

Here are some words to watch out for:

STUFFY	DIRECT	STUFFY	DIRECT
ascertain	find out	optimal	best
commence	begin	prior to	before
deceased	dead	purchase	buy
endeavor	try	reside	live
finalize	finish	terminate	end
implement	carry out	utilize	use

AVOID CLICHÉS. *Clichés* are tired, overly familiar expressions such as *hit the nail on the head, crystal clear, better late than never,* and *easier said than done.* They never contribute anything fresh or original. Avoid or eliminate them as you revise your early drafts.

> Finally,
> ▶ ~~Last but not least,~~ the article recommends the TeleZapper.
> ^

▶ My main ambition in life is not to make a fortune since I

know that/ ~~as they say, "money is the root of all evil."~~

having
~~Having~~ money does not lead automatically to a good life.
⌃

arose
▶ For Baldwin, the problem never ~~reared its ugly head~~ until
⌃

one dreadful night in New Jersey.

AVOID EUPHEMISMS. *Euphemisms* are expressions that try to conceal a forthright meaning and make the concept seem more delicate, such as *change of life* for *menopause* or *downsized* for *fired*. Because euphemisms often sound evasive or are unclear, avoid them in favor of direct language. Similarly, avoid *doublespeak* (evasive expressions that seek to conceal the truth, such as *incendiary device* for *bomb*). Examples of such language are easy to find in advertising, business, politics, and some reporting. Do not equate formality with these roundabout expressions.

Go to *The Open Handbook* at <http://college.hmco.com/keys.html>, and click on Style for exercises on using correct words.

8f Put it all together: Delight your readers.

As you write and revise, keep in mind the five C's of style. For a final quick review of your style, read your draft aloud and use these tips.

KEY POINTS

Style Tips

1. *Be adaptable.* Consider the style your readers will expect. Don't work on developing a figurative style for short stories and then continue to use it in business communications or e-mail. Choose a style as you choose your clothes: the right outfit for the occasion.

2. *When in doubt, favor a plain style.* Be clear and straightforward. Don't search for the big words or the obscure turn of phrase. The following sentences, part of an e-mail message from an AOL technical adviser in response to a question about send-

ing an e-mail message, are decidedly overdressed and stuffed with bureaucratic nothings: "It has been a pleasure assisting you. It is my hope that the information provided would be of great help with regards to your concern."

3. *Less is often better.* Details and descriptions are interesting, but don't overload your writing with adjectives and adverbs: *The perky little redheaded twin sat languidly in the comfortable overstuffed green-striped armchair and bit enthusiastically into a red and yellow fleshy, overripe peach.* Such prose is as overripe as the peach. Also avoid intensifying adverbs such as *very, really, extremely, terribly,* and *enormously.* Find a stronger word to use in place of the two words, such as *terrified* in place of *extremely scared.*

4. *Place your emphasis.* Use to best advantage the parts of a sentence that carry the most weight: the subject, the verb, the ending.

   NOT **Speed is a feature of the new Jaguar manufactured in Germany.**

   BUT **The new Jaguar manufactured in Germany roars past other cars.**

5. *Be adventurous.* Provide nuance in your writing with stylistic highlights such as parallel structures (5e), rhetorical questions (5e), inverted word order (8d), figures of speech (8e), and distinctive word choice (8e).

EXERCISE 8.6 Revise a draft for style.
Here is a student's draft of a paragraph:

A I think smoking is not a good idea in bars and restaurants, so it should be banned in New York. Some people may disagree with this, but it is not fair to people that they should have to breathe in the smoke that other people breathe out. Bars and restaurants are public places. They are crowded, and there are always some people among all the people there who smoke and do not go outside to smoke. I think those people should be made to go outside. If they stay inside, they should not be allowed to smoke. All people should be allowed to be healthy. Smoking can kill you, even if you are not doing the smoking yourself, and should be banned.

Extensive discussion of style ensued in a peer group discussion in her class, during which her group members read and discussed her paragraph and wrote the following feedback:

> You make a point, but I wonder if you need to make it so often. There's a lot of repetition.
>
> Remember what the prof said about cutting.
>
> It is all a bit general. I don't get any sense that you have a real place in mind. Could you tell about a restaurant or bar that *you* go to? Include real people, too, if you can.
>
> Play up the point about secondhand smoke.
>
> Are there too many instances of "should" and "I think"?
>
> Try to paint a picture of a place. I can't see a time, a place, or *you* here anywhere. Make it more lively.
>
> Remember what the book says about being confident. I'd cut out "Some people may disagree with this."

What should the student do to revise the paragraph? Write a revision. The student's actual revision is in the Answer Key.

When you think about preparing your document for readers, consider the following questions:

- What will readers expect the document to look like? What are the conventions for this type of writing?
- What features does your word processing software provide for designing a document?
- How can you present a clear, clean design that displays your content to its best advantage and with maximum impact?
- What visual elements—such as color, headings, tables, graphs, and images—can you use to help make a point in writing and in oral presentations?

9 Academic Documents: Page and Screen

9a Formats for academic essays—hard copy

Various organizations that offer guidelines for manuscript preparation (as found in the MLA, APA, and other style manuals) provide different sets of recommendations, and individual instructors may have their own preferences. Whichever format you choose, use your word processor's functions to help with your design.

Formatting guidelines   Here are basic guidelines for preparing your essay on paper, whichever style guide you follow. See 9d for more on the formatting tools on a word processor, and see 9e for posting an essay online.

KEY POINTS

Formatting a College Essay

Paper   White bond, unlined, $8^1/_2$" × 11"; not erasable or onion-skin paper. Clip or staple the pages.

Print   Dark black printing ink—an inkjet or laser printer if possible.

Margins   One inch all around. In some styles, one and one-half inches may be acceptable. Lines should not be justified (aligned on the right). In Microsoft Word, go to Format/Paragraph to adjust alignment.

Space between lines   Uniformly double-spaced for the whole paper, including any list of works cited.

Spaces after a period, question mark, or exclamation point   One space, as suggested by most style manuals. Your instructor may prefer two in the text of your essay.

Type font and size   Standard type font (such as Times New Roman or Arial), not a font that looks like handwriting. Select a regular size of 10 to 12 points.

Page numbers   In the top right margin. (In MLA style, put your last name before the page number. In APA style, put a short version of the running head before the page number.) Use Arabic numerals with no period. See 9d for the header formatting tools available in Word.

Paragraphing   Indent one-half inch (5 spaces) from the left.

Title and identification   On the first page or on a separate title page. See the examples on pages 125 and 126.

Parentheses around a source citation   MLA and APA style, for any written source you refer to or quote, including the textbook for your course (for an electronic source, give author only); then add at the end an alphabetical list of works cited. See examples in chapters 44 and 47.

Your instructor may prefer a separate title page or ask you to include the identification material on the first page of the essay.

9b Title and identification on the first page

The following sample of part of a first page shows one format for identifying a paper and giving it a title. The MLA recommends this format for papers in the humanities. However, the MLA format does not show a clear distinction between title and text, so your instructor may give you different guidelines.

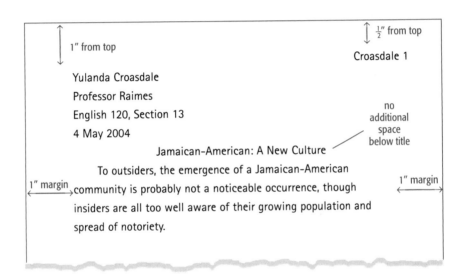

At the top of subsequent pages, write the page number in the upper right corner, preceded by your last name (9d explains how to make this header). Do not use a period or parentheses with the page number.

9c Separate title page

In the humanities, include a title page only if your instructor requires one or if you include an outline.

If you include a title page, do not also include the title and identification on your first page. For an example of a title page in APA style, see chapter 48.

Title centered, about 1/3 of way down page
No quotation marks, no underlining, no period

Jamaican-American: A New Culture

Name, centered   By Yulanda Croasdale

Course information, centered English 120, Section 13

Professor Ann Raimes

Date, centered   4 May 2004

9d Formatting with MS Word

The following functions are useful for college essays as well as for community and work-related documents. Other word processing programs, such as Corel WordPerfect, provide similar functions.

Microsoft Word is a trademark of Microsoft.

1. Previewing the page before printing   When you have written your document, Print Preview shows what each page will look like, before you actually print. The screenshot shows Word 2003; other versions of Word may vary, as will individual settings.

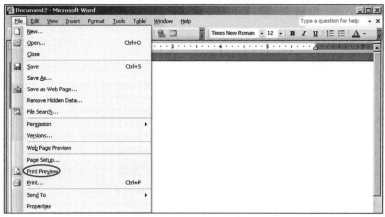

—Screenshot reprinted with permission of Microsoft.

2. Adding a header or footer on every page   When you open the View menu (see below), you will see the Header/Footer option. The toolbar allows you to (a) include a page number along with any text, such as your name or a short running head; (b) include the date and time; (c) toggle between the choice of headers or footers. Headers and footers will adjust automatically to any changes in the pagination of your document. You type the information once only, and it appears in the place you specify on every page, however much material you add or delete.

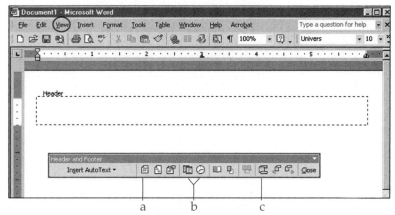

—Screenshot reprinted with permission of Microsoft.

3. Inserting a page number, a comment, a footnote, a caption, a file, a chart, a bookmark, or a hyperlink to a URL   The Insert menu gives you access to all the functions above. The Insert/Comments feature is especially useful in collaborative writing. The Insert/Chart feature creates bar graphs, line graphs, pie charts, and other types of charts from data that you insert.

4. Applying text features   The Format menu takes you to the following features:

- Font: for changing typeface, style, and size as well as for using superscripts (see also 10a)
- Paragraph: options for line spacing and indenting (see the screen capture below for how to set the special command for the hanging indents used in an MLA list of works cited)
- Bullets and Numbering for lists, Borders and Shading, Columns, Tabs, Dropped Capitals (just highlight the text to be formatted)
- Change Case: for changing your text from capital letters to lowercase or vice versa

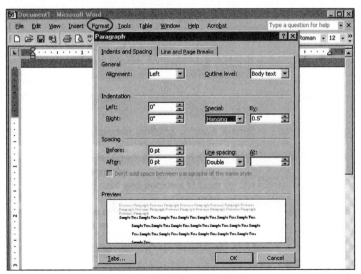

—Screenshot reprinted with permission of Microsoft.

5. Formats for URLs   The Tools menu enables you to turn off automatic hyperlinks when you do not need them underlined for an MLA list of works cited. Go to Tools/AutoCorrect/AutoFormat as You Type, and uncheck the box to replace Internet paths with hyperlinks.

6. Inserting a table When you click on Table/Insert Table, you can then select the numbers of columns and rows you want.

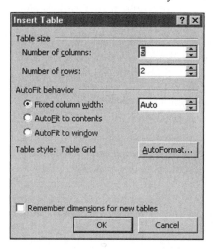

 Go to *The Open Handbook* at <http://college.hmco.com/keys.html>, and click on Design and Visuals for online exercises in formatting and document design.

9e Posting academic writing online

You may be required to submit an essay for a course online rather than in hard copy. Your instructor may ask you to e-mail him or her an attachment, or, in a hybrid or asynchronous distance-learning course, you may be required to submit your essays in a drop box or post them on a class bulletin board for the instructor and other students to read and comment on. In either case, keep in mind the following general guidelines, and ask your instructor for instructions specific to the course, format, and type of posting.

KEY POINTS

Posting an Essay or Research Paper Online

Structure Set up a structure with sections and subsections (called "fragments"), all with headings.

Links to sections from a table of contents Provide a table of contents, with an internal link anchored to each fragment,

(continued on next page)

(continued)

marked with a "bookmark" or "target," and give each bookmark or target a name. Readers can then click on and go directly to any section they are interested in.

Internal hyperlinks   Use internal hyperlinks (Insert/Hyperlink) to connect readers directly to relevant sections of your text, content notes, and visuals. Also provide a link from a hard-copy source cited in the body of your paper to the entry in your list of works cited.

External hyperlinks   Use external hyperlinks to connect to Web documents from references in the body of your paper and from your list of works cited. Word has a function that will automatically convert any string starting with <http://> into a hyperlink (go to Tools/AutoCorrect/ AutoFormat, and then check Replace Internet And Network Paths With Hyperlinks).

No paragraph indentation   Do not indent for a new paragraph. Instead, leave a line of space between paragraphs.

Attribution of sources   Make sure that the link you give to an online article in a database is a persistent link and not one that works only for a few hours or days. For more information on finding persistent links and on evaluating and citing online sources and authors, see <http://www.lehigh.edu/~inref/ guides/persistentlinks2.htm>.

List of works cited or list of references   Give a complete list, with URLs, even if you provide external links to the sources from the body of your paper. If a reader prints your paper, the exact references will then still be available.

Zip files   If your online document contains some images that you have created or modified, these images are stored in separate files, so use software to "zip" all the text and graphics files together in one folder, making sure that you include path information where necessary for the location of the images. Then you can send one zip file to your instructor for posting on a course Web site.

 Go to *The Open Handbook* at <http://college.hmco.com/keys.html>, and click on Student Papers for a sample online paper.

10 Visual Presentation of Text and Data

Everywhere we look, we see images—on billboards, on television, and flashing at us constantly from the Web. With so many visuals and images all around us, it is hardly surprising that many writers today include tables, charts, and graphs in their texts because these devices are functional, not just decorative or amusing. With them, writers can make data and statistics clearer and more accessible to their readers.

10a Typefaces

What's in a typeface? A lot. It's not just what you write but how it looks when it's read. Fitting the typeface to the content of a public document can be seen as an aesthetic challenge, as it was for the choice of the simple and legible Gotham typeface for the Freedom Tower cornerstone at the site of the former World Trade Center. The silver-leaf letters, with strokes of uniform width with no decorative touches, have been described by David Dunlap in the *New York Times* as conjuring "the exuberant, modernist, midcentury optimism of New York even as they augur the glass and stainless-steel tower to come." That's what's in a typeface. The cornerstone, according to Dunlap, looks "neutral enough so that viewers could impose their own meanings" on a site of profound historical and emotional impact.

Of course, you are designing the presentation of an essay, not of a historic monument. However, you can still make a choice that emphasizes simplicity and legibility.

The business text *Contemporary Business Communication,* 6th edition, by Scot Ober (Boston: Houghton, 2006) recommends the following typefaces in business correspondence, and the advice extends to college essays in hard copy:

> Times Roman for the body of the text (This is a *serif* font, with little strokes—serifs—at the top and bottom of individual characters: Times Roman.)

> Arial or some other *sans serif* font for captions and headings (The word *sans* is French for "without"; a sans serif font does not have the little strokes at the top and bottom of the characters.)

Avoid ornamental fonts such as **Dom Casual** and *Brush Script.* They are distracting and hard to read.

Note that if you are designing a Web page or an online communication, readers' settings and their browser configurations determine which fonts can be displayed. The simpler the font you choose, the more likely readers are to see the font of your choice.

For the body of your text in a college essay or a business communication, stick to 10- to 12-point type. Use larger type only for headings and subheadings in business, technical, or Web documents. Never increase or decrease font size in order to achieve a required page length. You will convey desperation, and you will certainly not fool your instructor.

Note: MLA and APA guidelines do not recommend typeface changes or bold type for titles and headings.

10b Color

Color printers and online publication have made the production of documents an exciting enterprise for both writers and readers. You can include graphs and illustrations in color, and you can highlight headings or parts of your text by using a different color typeface. However, simplicity and readability should prevail. Use color only when its use will enhance your message. Certainly, in the design of business reports, newsletters, brochures, and Web pages, color can play an important and eye-catching role. But for college essays, the leading style manuals ignore and implicitly discourage the use of color. Also keep in mind that many people do not have a color printer, and printing a color page on a black-and-white printer may lead to parts that are difficult to read or do not print at all.

10c Headings and columns

Headings Headings divide text into helpful chunks and give readers a sense of your document's structure. Main divisions are marked by first-level headings, subdivisions by second-level and third-level headings. In the heading structure of chapter 10, for example, the main heading is "Visual Presentation of Text and Data," and the subheadings include "Typefaces," "Color," "Headings and Columns," "Lists," and "Presenting Data Visually: Tables and Charts (Graphs)."

For headings, bear in mind the following recommendations:

- If you use subheadings, use at least two—not just one.
- Whenever possible, use the Style feature from the Format menu to determine the level of heading you need: heading 1, 2, 3, and so on.
- Style manuals, such as the one for APA style, recommend specific formats for typeface and position on the page for levels of headings. Follow these recommended formats. See chapter 48 for an APA paper with headings.
- Keep headings clear, brief, and parallel in grammatical form (for instance, all commands: "Set Up Sales Strategies"; all beginning with -*ing* words: "Setting Up Sales Strategies"; or all noun-plus-modifier phrases: "Sales Strategies").

TECHTOOLKIT Using Outline View on Your Word Processor

Note that if you are careful in applying the correct levels of headings, you can then switch to the Outline View of your document, which will collapse the body text for you and let you view only the headings above a certain level—only first-level and second-level headings, for example. This view omits all the text except for the headings you specify, so it lets you see how you have structured the organization of your document. It also helps you create an accurate table of contents for longer papers. ■

Columns Columns are useful for preparing newsletters and brochures. In Word, go to Format/Columns to choose the number of columns and the width. Your text will be automatically formatted. This feature is especially useful for creating brochures and newsletters.

10d Lists

Lists are particularly useful in business reports, proposals, and memos. They direct readers' attention to the outlined points or steps. Decide whether to use numbers, dashes, or bullets to set off the items in a list (see 9d, item 4). Introduce the list with a sentence ending in a colon (see 10c for an example). Items in the list should be parallel in grammatical form: all commands, all *-ing* phrases, or all noun phrases, for example (see 15j). Listed items should not end with a period unless they are complete sentences.

10e Presenting data visually: Tables and charts (graphs)

The technology of scanners, photocopiers, digital cameras, and downloaded Web images provides the means of making documents more functional and more attractive by allowing the inclusion of visual material. Frequently, when you are dealing with complicated data, the best way to get information across to readers is to display it visually.

KEY POINTS

On Using Visuals

1. Decide which type of visual presentation best fits your data, and determine where to place your visuals—within your text or in an appendix. See 11d and 11e on using PowerPoint for an oral presentation.

2. Whenever you place a visual in your text, introduce it and discuss it fully before readers come across it. Do not just make a perfunctory comment like "The results are significant, as seen in Figure 1." Rather, say something like "Figure 1 shows an increase in the number of accidents since 1997." In your discussion, indicate where the visual appears ("In the table below" or "In the pie chart on page 8"), and carefully interpret or analyze the visual for readers, using it as an aid that supports your points, not as something that can stand alone.

3. When you include a visual from the Web in your own online document, make sure the image file is not so large that it will take a long time for readers to download.

4. Give each visual a title, number each visual if you use more than one of the same type, and credit the source.

5. Do not include visuals simply to fill space or make your document look colorful. Every visual addition should enhance your content and provide an interesting and relevant illustration.

Computer software and word processing programs make it easy for you to create your own tables and charts to accompany your written text. For detailed information on using and creating visual material, Edward Tufte provides valuable resources: <http://www.edwardtufte.com/tufte>.

Tables Tables are useful for presenting data in columns and rows. They can be created easily with word processing programs using figures from large sets of data, as the table below was (see 9d, item 6).

TABLE 1 **Internet Use from Any Location by Individuals Age 3 and Older, September 2001 and October 2003, and Living in a Home with Internet Broadband, Age 3 and Older, October 2003**

Educational Attainment	Internet Users (Percent)		Lives in a Broadband Household (Percent)
	Sept. 2001	Oct. 2003	Oct. 2003
Less than high school	13.7	15.5	5.9
High school diploma/GED	41.1	44.5	14.5
Some college	63.5	68.6	23.7
Bachelor's degree	82.2	84.9	34.9
Beyond bachelor's degree	85.0	88.0	38.0

Source: *A Nation Online: Entering the Broadband Age,* September 2004. From Appendix, Table 1. U.S. Dept. of Commerce, National Telecommunications and Information Administration. Data from *U.S. Bureau of the Census, Current Population Survey* supplements, September 2001, and October 2003, based on a survey of 57,000 households.

Graphs and charts Graphs and charts (the terms are used interchangeably in many cases) are useful for presenting data and comparisons of data. Many software products allow you to produce graphs easily, and even standard word processing software gives you several ways to present your numbers in visual form. In Microsoft Office you can create graphs and charts in Word or Excel. In Word, for example, go to Insert/Picture/Chart, and in the Chart screen go to Chart/Chart Type. You will be able to select a type of chart, such as a pie chart or a bar chart, and enter your own details, such as title, labels for the vertical and horizontal axes of a bar graph, numbers, and data labels.

> ### KEY POINTS
>
> ## Using Graphs and Charts
>
> - Use a graph or chart only to help make a point.
> - Set up a graph or chart so that it is self-contained and self-explanatory.
> - Make sure that the items on the time axis of a line graph are proportionately spaced.
> - Always provide a clear caption.
> - Use precise wording for labels.
> - Always give details about the source of the data or information.

LINE GRAPHS   Use a line graph to show changes over time. Figure 1 shows changes over time for households with computers and Internet connections. Figure 2 shows grade inflation from 1966 to 2003.

FIGURE 1   Percentage of U.S. Households with Computers and Internet Connections

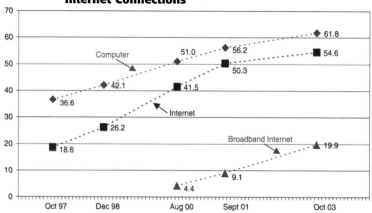

Note: 2001 and 2003 reflect 2000 Census-based weights and earlier years use 1990 Census-based weights.

Source: *A Nation Online: Entering the Broadband Age,* September 2004, U.S. Dept. of Commerce, Economics and Statistics Administration, National Telecommunications and Information Administration, page 4 <http://www.ntia.doc.gov/reports/anol2004/NationOnlineBroadband04.pdf>. Data are based on supplements to the U.S. Census Bureau's *Current Population Survey* of 57,000 households.

FIGURE 2   Grade Inflation, 1966–2003

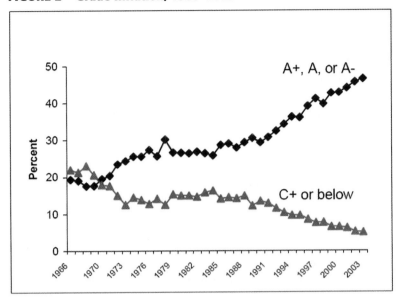

Source: Linda J. Sax et al., *The American Freshman: National Norms for Fall 2003,* Los Angeles, Higher Education Research Institute, UCLA, 2003 <http://www.gseis.ucla.edu/heri/03_norms_charts.pdf>. Data are from weighted responses of 276,449 students at 413 higher education institutions.

 TECHTOOLKIT   Using Word to Save/Download Visuals

Here are some tips for saving visuals that you find rather than create yourself:

- On a Web page, right-click the image and go to Save Image (Picture) as. . . . For the file format, use *.jpg* for photos and *.gif* for charts and graphs.

- The easiest way to save an image in a PDF document is to take a screenshot (Print Scrn on your keyboard). You can then save the screen to MS Word and use the picture toolbar to crop or adjust the image.

- Alternatively, if the PDF document is not restricted against this activity, you can use the "snapshot tool" with Adobe Reader 6 and 7. Just click on the "camera" icon in the toolbar, mark the region that you want to capture by dragging your mouse, and copy (Ctrl+C) and then paste (Ctrl+V).

- If the PDF document is in a restricted format, use a program such as SnagIt, available from Techsmith, or the freeware ScreenShotWizard to capture a specific region of the screen or a region that scrolls beyond the screen. This method allows you the most flexibility.

- When saving an image from an Adobe .pdf document, use the viewing scale to increase or decrease the image size to present the image clearly before you save it.

- To get a clear shot, you may need to temporarily change your screen resolution to increase the pixel size: Right-click on an empty spot on your desktop, select Properties/Settings, and then select the highest resolution.

For more detailed advice written for students in a college course, go to <http://urban.hunter.cuny.edu/~mkuechle/Tech_Advice/saving_images.html>. ■

PIE CHARTS   A pie chart is useful to show how fractions and percentages relate to one another and make up a whole. Figure 3 shows reasons people offer for not having high-speed Internet access.

FIGURE 3   Main Reasons for No High-Speed Internet Use at Home, 2003

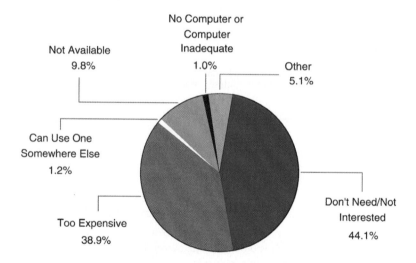

Source: *A Nation Online: Entering the Broadband Age,* September 2004, U.S. Dept. of Commerce, Economics and Statistics Administration, National Telecommunications and Information Administration, page 14 <http://www.ntia.doc.gov/reports/anol2004/NationOnlineBroadband04.pdf>. Data are based on 57,000 households.

BAR CHARTS   A bar chart shows comparisons and correlations and highlights differences among groups. The bar chart in Figure 4, available on a Web site for downloading, presents clear data for grade inflation over time at a variety of institutions.

FIGURE 4 Grade Inflation among Students Entering Different Types of Institutions (Percentage Earning A Averages)

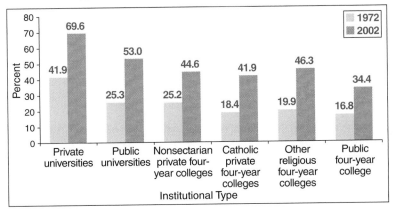

Source: L. J. Sax et al., *The American Freshman: National Norms for Fall 2002,* Los Angeles, Higher Education Research Institute, UCLA, 2003 at <http://www.gseis .ucla.edu/heri/norms.charts.pdf>. Data are from 282,549 students at 437 higher education institutions.

Instead of downloading data charts, you can make your own. See the bar charts that student Emily Luo included in her PowerPoint presentation on genetically modified crops (11e).

A bar chart can also be presented horizontally, a configuration that makes it easier to attach labels to the bars. Figure 5 was produced in MS Office using the data from Table 1.

FIGURE 5 Internet Use by Percentage from Any Location by Individuals Age 3 and Older, September 2001 and October 2003, and Living in a Home with Internet Broadband, Age 3 and Older, October 2003

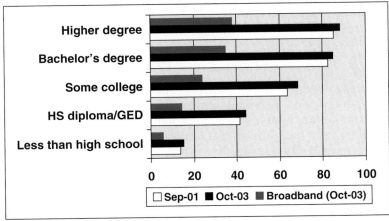

Exercise 10.1 Create a pie chart and a bar chart.

Suppose that at a college 43 percent of the students live on campus, 29 percent commute by car, 18 percent commute by bicycle, and 10 percent live near enough to walk to the campus. Using your word processing program, create a pie chart to display these data. Then create a bar chart using the same data. A sample answer is in the Answer Key.

11 Visuals: Analysis and Preparation

Words are often used to generate images in our minds. When we say, "Picture this," we want our listeners to *see* what we see in our mind's eye. We want them to understand what we understand. Often, *I see* is synonymous with *I understand.* To make sure, we often ask, "Do you see what I am saying?"

Although words might seem to carry the ultimate authority (we speak of someone having "the last word"), images—alone and in collaboration with words—are increasingly becoming more a part of how we come to know our world and how we convey our world to others.

Whereas *rhetoric* is the art of using words effectively and persuasively, *visual rhetoric* is the art of using images effectively and persuasively. More and more, your instructors may require you to call on your critical skills to consider images as texts to read and as evidence and support when you write. Images do not necessarily stand in place of what you write; rather, they focus and direct your readers' attention. Remember that your images need to be powerful enough to withstand a critical reading and clear enough to make the argument you want them to make.

11a How to read visual images critically

All images—charts, graphs, maps, cartoons, photographs, graffiti, illustrations, and paintings—contain information and ideas that need to be interpreted. When considering a written text critically, readers examine it from beginning to end, in a linear way. Confronted with an image, however, we lose the traditional structure of linear progression. The idea of discerning purpose and audience stays with us from the analysis of written texts, but now we include a close look at the following features:

- the effect of spatial organization, in which elements of the image appear in relation to each other
- the visual focus, the part of the image that speaks to us most directly and expresses the main idea of the image
- the juxtaposition of image and written text: what does one do to and for the other?
- the connections we (along with the originator of the image) make with other visual images in our experience and memory
- our response to color, to alignment, and (with multimedia images) to the sequence and progression of the images

Think, for example, of films that reverse chronology, use fade-outs and flashbacks, and cut rapidly from one image to another. We "read" such visual texts differently from the way we read a print article or a piece of fiction.

The following photograph, used in an article exploring the causes of obesity in children in Starr County, Texas, makes a strong visual argument. Three children look trustingly into the camera—at us—as they sit in front of their hamburger lunches in a school cafeteria. The child on the left is obese; the other two appear small, even frail. A cut-out painting of a hamburger hangs emblematically on the gray cinderblock wall behind them. To its left, a poster displays a cartoon wizard waving a wand (the word *magic* can be discerned) over a loaf of sliced white bread. Are we to believe that bland foods can

Heavy Questions

magically be transformed into something nutritious and wholesome? The image suggests that nutritional planning at the institutional level—no matter how well-meaning—has serious consequences for individual children. In Starr County, children are just as likely to be obese as they are to be underweight.

EXERCISE **11.1**   Read an image critically.

Consider the advertisement for the American Indian College Fund. As it appears in a magazine, the print along its bottom and side borders reads: "Carly Kipp, Blackfeet. Biology major, tutor, mom, pursuing a doctorate in veterinary medicine, specializing in large-animal surgery. Many of our graduates stay on the reservation. Economists project every dollar of their incomes will turn over two and a half times." Considering the aspects of critical reading of images discussed on pages 140 to 141, analyze how the advertisers have used the image of Carly Kipp effectively to persuade viewers to donate to the fund. A sample answer is in the Answer Key.

11b   Visuals to make or strengthen an argument

We commonly think of arguments as being spoken or written. However, it is worth noting that another type of argument is widespread—an argument that is presented visually. Think, for example, of arguments made in cartoons, advertisements, drawings, and works of art. The famous 1976 *New Yorker* magazine cover by Saul Steinberg called "View of the World from Ninth Avenue" shows New York City in the foreground, with cars on Ninth Avenue, gradually giving way to New Jersey, Kansas, the Pacific Ocean, and Japan in the background. The argument? That New York City is the center of the world to New Yorkers.

You can supplement your written arguments with visual arguments: maps, superimposed images, photographs, charts and graphs, political cartoons—vivid images that will say more than many words to your readers. An argument essay on the media, for example, would make a strong visual impact if its argument included this Adbusters image, which itself makes an argument.

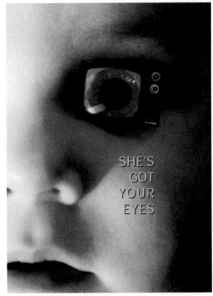

It says that children see what their parents watch, and it challenges us to consider how much the media dictate what we see.

Visual arguments make their appeals in ways similar to written arguments, appealing to logic, showcasing the character and credentials of the author, or appealing to viewers' emotions. When you write an argument, consider adding to the impact of your thesis by including a visual argument.

EXERCISE 11.2 Analyze a visual argument.

Write about one of the following images. What compelling argument could you make based on the image and how effective it is as a visual? (**A** = See Answer Key.)

A a.

b.

TECHTOOLKIT Finding Images on the World Wide Web

This comprehensive Web site, <http://www.lib.uconn.edu/~habbey/images/>, constructed by librarian Heidi Abbey of the University of Connecticut Libraries, provides demystifying information on digital image formats; a primer on basic copyright issues; links to search engines; and best of all, links to several annotated image Web sites, including image resources for specific subjects. ■

11c Presentations with multimedia

Today writers are no longer limited to using type or visuals printed on a page. Thanks to multimedia technology, they can use screens to present an interaction of words, drawings, photographs, animation, film, video, and audio to make a point.

In preparing a live or online multimedia presentation, consider the effectiveness of positioning images near your words and of conveying emotion and meaning through pictures. Imagine, for instance, how you might present an argument against genetic engineering of food crops to classmates or colleagues. In addition to your well-formed argument, you could show graphs of public opinion data on the issue, pictures of chemicals that are used on crops and of the way they are applied, and a movie clip of interviews with shoppers as they read labels and buy produce. If you use media imaginatively, you can do what writing teachers have long advised for printed essays: Show; don't just tell.

TECHTOOLKIT A Multimedia Project

For an example of a multimedia visual argument created by students, go to <http://www.iml.annenberg.edu/projects/>. "The City of Troy" project was created by undergraduates at the University of Southern California for a course in Near Eastern and Mediterranean Archeology. ■

11d PowerPoint

Using a multimedia tool like PowerPoint to prepare a presentation gives you access to organizing tools. As the name suggests, PowerPoint forces you to think of your main points and organize them. Preparing slides that illustrate the logic of your presentation helps you separate the main points from the supporting details, and the slides keep you focused as you give your presentation. Your audience follows your ideas not only because you have established a clear principle of organization but also because the slide on the presentation screen reminds people of where you are in your talk, what point you are addressing, and how that point fits into your total scheme. Presentation software also allows you to include sound, music, and movie clips to illustrate and drive home the points you want to make. However, be careful not to overdo these effects. PowerPoint features can easily become distracting "bells and whistles" to make up for lack of content. They should enhance your work, not replace it.

A PowerPoint specialist has advised, "If you have something to show, use PowerPoint." *Show* is the important word. Do not expect your audience to read a lot of text. PowerPoint is not for writing paragraphs and essays for readers to digest. It's for getting and keeping the audience's attention with the main points and illustrative details. Outlines, bulleted lists, tables, pie charts, and graphs are what PowerPoint does well.

Peter Norvig, a computer scientist and director of search quality at Google, cautions PowerPoint users to "use visual aids to convey visual information: photographs, charts, or diagrams. But do not use them to give the impression that the matter is solved, wrapped up in a few bullet points." For a wonderful object lesson of PowerPoint gone wrong, see Norvig's Web site at <http://www.norvig.com/Gettysburg>.

11e A student's PowerPoint slides

The PowerPoint slides shown here were prepared by student Emily Luo for a project in a course called "Empirical Research Using the Internet." The assignment was to find public-opinion data and documents to present a "fact-based and balanced summary of the public debate" surrounding an issue. The students each wrote a paper to be posted on the course Web site, with links to all sources. Each student also prepared a classroom presentation of his or her research, using PowerPoint slides. Luo chose the assigned topic "Genetic Engineering" and narrowed the focus to "Genetically Modified Crops." For her presentation, she prepared several slides. Shown here are her outline slide and a slide showing public-opinion data. She prepared the bar charts herself with Microsoft Word (see 10e), using data from three polling organizations.

The Debate over Genetically Modified Crops

- An Overview
- Governmental Agencies
- The Proponents
- The Opponents
- Public Opinion

Presenter: Emily Luo

Public Opinion

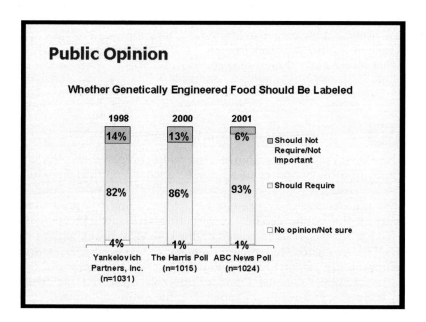

Whether Genetically Engineered Food Should Be Labeled

Science fiction writer and editor Teresa Neilson Hayden, in *Making Book*, characterizes English as "a generous, expansive, and flexible language" but adds, "a less charitable description would characterize it as drunk and disorderly." The task of editing, she claims, is to try to impose "a degree of regularity on something that is inherently irregular." What exists to help you move away from irregularities that appear in your writing is a set of conventions that go under the label of Standard English (1e). Its practices are what readers expect in the academic world. Writing instructors often hear students complain that making changes in their writing to conform to Standard English hinders their creativity. However, being creative and meeting readers' expectations are not mutually exclusive aims.

Attention to accuracy is important in the business world as well as in college. A recent study of 120 corporations found that one third of the employees of major companies had poor writing skills, leading an executive to say, "It's not that companies want to hire Tolstoy. But they need people who can write clearly."

The chapters in Part 3 provide help with editing for accuracy. Chapters 32–36 provide additional editing assistance for students who grew up surrounded by languages or dialects other than Standard English.

12 How a Sentence Works (Review)

This chapter reviews the basic elements of a sentence and the terms used to describe those elements. Knowing how sentences work helps you edit those that don't work well.

12a What a sentence is and does

What a sentence is   You have probably heard various definitions of a sentence, the common one being that "a sentence is a complete thought." Sometimes it is. Sometimes it is not, depending on what one expects by "complete." In fact, that definition is not particularly helpful. How complete is this thought?

▶ **He did not.**

You probably do not regard it as complete because it relies on text around it, on other sentences, to tell what it was he did not do, as in the following example.

▶ **She always made an effort to be punctual. He did not.**

Both sentences are grammatically complete, displaying the features listed in the Key Points box.

Read more about writing complete sentences and avoiding sentence fragments in chapter 14.

KEY POINTS

Features of a Written English Sentence

1. It begins with a capital letter.

2. It ends with a period (a "full stop" in British English), question mark, or exclamation point. A semicolon can provide a partial ending, taking readers on to the next idea without a full stop.

3. It must contain at the very least a subject (or an implied *you* subject, as in "Run!") and a predicate (12e) that provides information about the subject and both must form an independent clause. The predicate must contain a complete verb, as indicated here in italics:

<u>INDEPENDENT CLAUSE</u>

<u>SUBJECT</u>	<u>VERB + REST OF PREDICATE</u>
Birds	*sing.*
Max	*was* tired.
Everyone	*wants* security.
The driver	*had forgotten* to signal.
His three sisters	*sent* him a hammock.
Bills and mortgage payments	*must have consumed* most of his salary.
Skating	*can be* wonderful exercise.
What you wrote	*should have been edited.*

Sentences like these, with no attachments to the basic subject + predicate frameword, are called *simple sentences* (see 8d, item 3).

4. Words, phrases, and clauses can be attached to the frameword of the simple sentence.

—————————— independent clause ——————————

S   V

▶ **The birds on the branch outside my window sing loudly whenever I fill the feeder with seeds.**

What a sentence does A sentence can function as a statement, question, command, or exclamation. Most of the sentences in exposi-

Sentence Functions

Sentence function	What it does	Example
Declarative	Makes a statement	*Lower interest rates help home buyers.*
Interrogative	Asks a question	*Who can afford to buy a house on the beach?*
Imperative	Gives a command	*Watch this space.*
Exclamatory	Expresses surprise or emotion	*This expensive restaurant has had no fewer than fifteen violations!*

tory and academic writing are declarative statements, though a question can be useful to draw readers into thinking about a topic. An occasional exclamatory sentence can be powerful, too, but bear in mind that, according to *The New York Times Manual of Style and Usage*, "When overused, the exclamation point loses impact, as advertising demonstrates continually." (See 22c.)

ESL NOTE Language and Sentence Structure

The shape of a sentence varies from language to language; in German, for instance, the verb does not necessarily follow the subject (*Gestern habe ich ihm einen Brief geschrieben* is literally translated as "Yesterday have I him a letter written"). In other words, the structure of a sentence is not fixed across languages. If English is not your first language, keep its basic structures in mind as you write and revise, especially when you grapple with new and challenging subject matter. Use your first language to help you with ideas, but avoid transferring sentences from one language to another without first reminding yourself of the features of words and sentences in English. See 32e for more on language transfer. ■

12b Sentence essentials: Subject and verb

A sentence in English minimally consists of a *subject* (person, place, thing, or concept) that is doing an action, is being something, or is being acted upon, and a *verb*. The verb shows the action or state and tells about the subject.

            S   V
▶ A huge *storm rattled* the windows.

      S   V
▶ *Physics is* a challenging subject.

       S   ┌────V────┐
▶ The *president was impeached.*

A simple subject is one word (*storm, physics, president*); a complete subject includes the simple subject and all its modifiers (*a huge storm, the president*). A verb can be a main verb or auxiliaries (forms of *do, have, be,* and modals) with a main verb, such as *sit, sat, will sit, persuades, persuaded, might persuade, should be working, must have been built.* Finding the subject and verb is a basic tool for many strategies in the editing process.

Finding the subject   To test what the subject of a sentence is, ask a question about the verb. This questioning is easy with a short simple sentence:

> verb
> ▶ **Henry smiled.**   [Who smiled? Henry. *Henry* is the subject of the sentence.]

> verb
> ▶ **The ball was thrown.**   [What was thrown? The ball. *The ball* is the complete subject.]

These sentences have simple subjects, just one or two words. Often, though, a subject consists of more than just the simple subject of one word. Again, to determine what the simple subject is, ask a question about the verb and shrink the answer down to one word.

> ▶ **His new boss left.**   [Who left? His new *boss.* The complete subject is *His new boss.*]

When you ask the same question about the much longer simple sentence that follows, the answer is still the same simple subject:

> simple subject ———— complete subject ———— verb
> ▶ **The *boss* of the successful new computer company *left* the elegantly furnished conference room.**

Compound subjects and compound predicates   A subject may consist of two or more items usually joined by *and.*

> ┌ compound subject ┐
> ▶ ***Juan and Rafael* fell asleep.**

> compound
> ┌—— subject ——┐
> ▶ ***Li Chen and I* waded in the ocean.**

Similarly, a predicate may consist of two or more verbs, known as a *compound predicate:*

> ┌———— compound predicate ————┐
> ▶ **Li Chen and I *waded in the ocean and collected shells.***

ESL NOTE   Subject and Verb across Languages

Not all languages require a subject and a verb. English requires both, except in a command. See 35a. ■

EXERCISE 12.1   Identify the subject and verb in a simple sentence.

In the following sentences, underline the complete subject and write *S* over the simple subject. Then underline the complete verb and write *V* above it. Remember that the verb may consist of more than one word and that a clause may have more than one subject or verb. (**A** = See Answer Key.)

EXAMPLE:

S   V

Many people in the United States carry too much credit-card debt.

A 1. Most experts consider some types of debt, such as a mortgage, financially necessary.

A 2. However, credit-card debt never benefits an individual's long-term financial goals.

3. Today even college students without jobs or credit records can usually acquire credit cards easily.

4. Unfortunately, many young people and many students charge expensive purchases and pay only the minimum balance on their cards every month.

5. Graduating from college with a large credit-card debt can severely limit a person's opportunities.

12c   Parts of speech

To think about and discuss how sentences work and how to edit them, a shared vocabulary is useful. Words are traditionally classified into eight categories called *parts of speech*. Note that the part of speech refers not to the word itself but to its function in a sentence. Some words can function as different parts of speech.

verb

▶ **They respect the orchestra manager.**

noun

▶ **Respect is a large part of a business relationship.**

Nouns Words that name a person, place, thing, or concept—*teacher, valley, furniture, Hinduism*—are called *nouns*. When you use a noun, determine the following: Is it a proper noun, requiring a capital letter? Does it have a plural form? If so, are you using the singular or plural form? See 29a and 33a for more on countable, collective, proper, and compound nouns.

Pronouns A pronoun represents a noun or a noun phrase. In writing, a pronoun refers to its antecedent—that is, a noun or noun phrase appearing just before it in the text.

▶ My sister loves *her* new car, but *she* dented *it* last week.

Pronouns fall into seven types: personal (18a), possessive (18b), demonstrative (18d), intensive or reflexive (18h), relative (20a), interrogative (18i), and indefinite (17h). When you use a pronoun, determine the following: What word or words in the sentence does the pronoun refer to? Does the pronoun refer to a noun or pronoun that is singular or plural?

Verbs Words that tell what a person, place, thing, or concept does or is—*smile, throw, think, seem, become, be*—are called *verbs*. Verbs change form, so when you use a verb, determine the following: What time does the verb refer to? What auxiliary verbs are needed for an appropriate tense or meaning? Is the subject of the verb singular or plural? Is the subject of the verb doing or receiving the action (active or passive voice)? What are the five forms of the verb (*sing, sings, singing, sang, sung*), and are you using the correct form?

Main verbs often need auxiliary verbs (*be, do, have*) or modal auxiliaries (*will, would, can, could, shall, should, may, might, must*) to complete the meaning. For more on verbs, see chapters 16 and 17.

Adjectives Words that describe nouns—*purple, beautiful, big*—are called *adjectives*. An adjective can precede a noun or follow a linking verb:

▶ Samantha is wearing *purple* boots.

▶ Her boots are *purple*.

Descriptive adjectives have comparative and superlative forms: *short, shorter, shortest*. Also functioning as adjectives (before a noun) are *a*, *an*, and *the*, as well as possessives and demonstratives: *a* cabbage, *an* allegory, *their* poems, *this* book. For more on adjectives, see chapter 19.

Adverbs Words that provide information about verbs, adjectives, adverbs, or clauses are called *adverbs*. Many, but not all, adverbs end in *-ly: quickly, efficiently*. Adverbs also provide information about how or when: *very, well, sometimes, often, soon, never*. Adverbs modify verbs, adjectives, other adverbs, or clauses.

▶ Rafael dunked brilliantly.
modifies verb

▶ He played spectacularly well.
modifies adverb

▶ He is a very energetic player.
modifies adjective

▶ Undoubtedly, he is a genius.
modifies whole clause

Conjunctive adverbs—such as *however, therefore, furthermore*—make connections between independent clauses. For a list of conjunctive adverbs and other transitional expressions, see 5e and 8c, item 3.

Conjunctions Words that connect words, phrases, and clauses are called *conjunctions*.

▶ Asa loves ham *and* eggs.

▶ We bought a red table, a blue chair, *and* a gold mirror.

▶ The magazine was published, *and* his article won acclaim.

The seven coordinating conjunctions—*and, but, or, nor, so, for, yet*—connect ideas of equal importance. Subordinating conjunctions—*because, if, when, although*, for instance (see 12e and 8c, item 3, for lists)—make one clause dependent on another. Consider the meaning before using a conjunction.

Prepositions Words used before nouns and pronouns to form phrases that usually do the work of an adjective or adverb are called *prepositions*.

▶ A bird with a red crest flew onto the feeder.
preposition   *preposition*

Some common prepositions are *against, around, at, behind, between, except, for, from, in, into, like, on, over, regarding, to,* and *without*. For language learners, prepositions are difficult because they are so often idiomatic: *on occasion, in love*. To understand their use and meaning, consult a good dictionary. See also 36a.

Interjections Words that express emotion and can stand alone—*Ha! Wow! Ugh! Ouch! Say!*—are called *interjections*. Interjections are not used frequently in academic writing. The more formal ones (such as *alas, oh*) are sometimes used in poetry:

> But she is in her grave, and, oh,
> The difference to me!

—William Wordsworth

EXERCISE 12.2 Identify parts of speech.

On the lines after each sentence, identify the two parts of speech that are underlined in the sentence. (**A** = See Answer Key.)

EXAMPLE:

Nelson <u>Mandela</u>, the former president of South Africa, spent nearly thirty years in prison <u>for</u> his work to end apartheid.

Mandela   _noun_

for   _preposition_

A 1. <u>He</u> <u>wrote</u> an autobiography called *Long Walk to Freedom*.

He   _____

wrote   _____

A 2. In his book, Mandela says, "I am not <u>truly</u> free if I am taking away someone else's freedom, just as surely as I am not free when my freedom is taken away from <u>me</u>."

truly   _____

me   _____

3. <u>Many</u> additional writers have also used their talents to fight for <u>freedom</u> for themselves and others.

Many   _____

freedom _____

4. Writers such as Frederick Douglass, Aleksandr Solzhenitsyn, <u>and</u> Mary Wollstonecraft called attention <u>to</u> injustices that they saw around them.

and   _____

to   _____

5. The Lithuanian poet Czeslaw Milosz <u>once</u> asked, "What <u>is</u> poetry which does not save nations and peoples?"

once   _____

is   _____

12d Phrases

A phrase is a group of words that lacks a subject, a verb, or both. A phrase is only a part of a sentence. It cannot be punctuated as a sentence. (See 14c for more on phrase fragments.)

an elegant evening gown	worried by the news
singing in the rain	with her thoughts in turmoil
on the corner	to travel around the world

12e Clauses

Clauses can be independent or dependent. A sentence must contain an *independent clause*, one that can stand alone. A clause introduced by a word such as *because, when, if,* or *although* is a *dependent clause*. Every independent clause and dependent clause needs a subject and predicate. See 14b for more on dependent clause fragments.

▶ The XM radio had poor indoor reception. [independent clause]

▶ Because the XM radio had poor indoor reception, Juana [dependent (subordinate) clause] decided to return it. [independent clause]

> ### KEY POINTS
>
> #### Subordinating Conjunctions
>
> **time:** when, whenever, until, till, before, after, while, once, since, as soon as, as long as
>
> **place:** where, wherever
>
> **reason/cause:** because, as, since
>
> **condition:** if, even if, unless, provided that
>
> **contrast:** although, though, even though, whereas, while
>
> **comparison:** than, as, as if, as though
>
> **purpose:** so that, in order that
>
> **result:** so . . . that, such . . . that

Dependent clauses can function as adjectives or nouns as well as adverbs.

▶ *When the sun shines,* the strawberries ripen.   [Adverb clause expressing time]

▶ The berries *that we picked yesterday* were delicious. [Adjective relative clause modifying *berries;* see chapter 20]

▶ The farmers know *what they should do.*   [Noun clause functioning as a direct object]

EXERCISE 12.3 Identify dependent clauses.

In the following sentences underline any dependent clauses. Note that some sentences may contain only independent clauses. (**A** = See Answer Key.)

EXAMPLE:

> **Scientists who study the brain disagree about the nature of dreams. Because dreams cannot be examined by direct observation, scientists have to rely on the dreamers' descriptions of their dreams.**

A 1. In 1900, Sigmund Freud, a former neurologist, published a book called *The Interpretation of Dreams*, which discussed the purpose of dreams.

A 2. Freud believed that dreams reveal the sleeper's unconscious desires in a disguised form.

A 3. Today modern psychoanalysts are less interested in dream interpretation, and some disagree with Freud's theories.

A 4. One of these is Dr. J. Allan Hobson, a psychiatrist at Harvard Medical School, who considers dreams simply a byproduct of the sleeping brain.

A 5. The activity of the brain stem produces dream images, but according to Dr. Hobson, this activity is random.

6. However, Mark Solms of the Royal London School of Medicine, a neuropsychologist, holds a different view and maintains that dreams help to motivate people to pursue goals.

7. Dr. Solms's opinion is more in line with Freud's century-old theory because Freud saw providing motivation as one purpose of dreams.

8. Although everyone without brain damage appears to dream, dreams may serve different functions for people in different societies.

9. For example, according to a Finnish researcher, when people in hunter-gatherer societies dream about threatening events, they apparently unconsciously use these dreams to prepare responses to the threats.

10. Freud abandoned the physical study of the brain, neurology, to study the workings of the mind, but neurologists today use dreams to understand how the brain and the mind work together.

13 Sentence Troublespots

13a Students' FAQs

Questions	Short Answer	Long Answer
Can I begin a sentence with *and* or *but*?	Occasionally, yes	8c, item 3
Can I begin a sentence with *because*?	Yes	14b
How do I know whether to use *I* or *me* with *and*?	Use the "Drop the noun in the *and* phrase" test.	18a
What is the difference between *who* and *whom*?	Use *whom* in formal writing as an object form.	18i, 20a
When do I use *who*, *which*, or *that*?	Ask: person or thing? Consider *restrictive* vs. *nonrestrictive*.	20a, 20d
When is it OK to use the phrase *he or she*?	To refer to a singular noun phrase—but limit the use, or use plural throughout.	18e
Can I interchange *but* and *however*?	No. Meanings are similar; usage and punctuation differ.	23b, 23e
When do I use *good* or *well*, *bad* or *badly*?	*Good* and *bad* modify nouns, not verbs, but can follow linking verbs.	19a, 19b
What is the difference between		
a. *its* and *it's*?	*It's* stands for *it is* or *it has*.	25e
b. *whose* and *who's*?	*Who's* stands for *who is* or *who has*.	Glossary of Usage
c. *lie* and *lay*?	Use *lay* with a direct object. Learn all the forms.	16b

13b Teachers' top ten sentence troublespots

Here are the problems that teachers often find and mark in their students' writing. Try to find these in your own writing before your instructor does. If you cannot immediately identify and correct an error in the middle column, read the section listed in the right column for more explanation and examples.

Type of Error	Example of Error	More Details and Examples
1. Fragment	She had an ambitious dream. *To become a CEO.*	14a–14f
2. Run-on sentence or comma splice	The city is *lively the clubs* are open late. The city is *lively, the clubs* are open late.	14g–14h
3. Tangled sentence	In the essay "Notes of a Native Son" by James Baldwin discusses his feelings about his father.	15a
4. Wrong verb form or tense	They have never *drank* Coke.	16a, 16c
5. Tense shift	Foote *wrote* about Shiloh and *describes* its aftermath.	15d
6. Lack of subject-verb agreement	The *owner have* gone bankrupt.	17a–17i
7. Pronoun error	The coach rebuked my teammates and *I.* Nobody knows *whom* will be fired.	18a, 18d, 18i
8. Unclear pronoun reference	When I crossed the border, *they* searched my backpack.	18c
9. Adjective/adverb confusion	The Diamondbacks played *good* in spring training.	19a–19c
10. Double negative	They do*n't* have *no* luck.	19e

Page 609 shows you some of the editing and correction marks that your instructor is likely to use.

KEY POINTS

Keep a Troublespot Log

1. Keep a written log of any of the top ten troublespots you or your tutor, instructor or classmates identify in your writing.

2. Write down each troublespot sentence and one way to revise it.

3. Identify the nature of each problem.

4. Write down which handbook sections may help you deal with those troublespots and how you intend to work on identifying and correcting those types of errors. As time goes on, you should find yourself adding fewer and fewer examples to the list.

Go to *The Open Handbook* at <http://college.hmco.com/keys.html>, and click on Forms and Checklists to find a sample Troublespot Log form that you can download.

Exercise 13.1   Identify troublespots.
Find and correct the troublespot in each sentence. Then write the name of the error on the line following the sentence. (**A** = See Answer Key.)

Example:

When an ecosystem becomes less diverse. ∧ A disease that strikes one kind of plant or animal can affect every creature in the food chain. _____fragment_____

A 1. In 1983, a mysterious disease attacks sea urchins in the Caribbean and killed most of the species known as *Diadema*. _____

A 2. According to the Smithsonian Tropical Research Institute, they reported the biggest die-off ever for a marine animal. _____

A 3. In a 3.5-million-square-kilometer area of the Caribbean had once been home to millions of *Diadema* sea urchins. _____

A 4. Algae began to spread quickly in this vast ocean area. After 97 percent of the *Diadema* urchins that had once controlled the algae's growth by eating them died. _____

A 5. Soon, the algae had grew over many of the coral reefs, preventing young coral from attaching and building on top of older coral. _____

6. Consequently, the coral reefs of the Caribbean have been dying off since 1983 scientists now know that their survival depends on the algae-eating services of the *Diadema* sea urchins. _____

7. *Diadema* sea urchins had not always been the only algae-controlling species in this part of the Caribbean; several species of fish and them had once competed to eat the aquatic plants. _____

8. Then overfishing removed most of the other algae eaters of the coral reefs so that for a time the sea urchins could dine real well on the algae until they, too, began to disappear. _____

9. Scientists from a Florida laboratory has a plan to reintroduce *Diadema* sea urchins to the algae-choked waters. _____

10. Marine biologists do not have no illusions that simply bringing sea urchins back to the Caribbean can save the reefs, but the experiment is a hopeful start. _____

14 The Boundaries of a Sentence: Fragments, Run-ons, and Comma Splices

The boundaries of a sentence are important in Standard English. Readers expect the beginnings and endings of sentences to occur at anticipated points and with appropriate signals in the form of punctuation marks. Misleading signals mislead readers. Do not use a comma to mark the end of a sentence, and never use a period if a group of words is not a complete sentence. Indicate the end of a sentence with a period, question mark, or exclamation point (chapter 22).

14a What is a fragment?

A complete sentence (12a) needs at least the following:

1. a capital letter at the beginning
2. an independent clause containing a subject and a complete verb
3. appropriate end punctuation: a period, question mark, or exclamation point

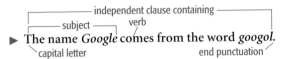

The name *Google* comes from the word *googol.*

A fragment is an incomplete sentence incorrectly punctuated as if it were a complete sentence. The following is a fragment with no independent clause:

FRAGMENT | **Which is the mathematical term for a one followed by a hundred zeros.**

You can often make a fragment into a complete sentence by adding or changing words or by connecting the fragment to an independent clause.

POSSIBLE REVISION | **The name *Google* comes from the word *googol*, which is the mathematical term for a one followed by a hundred zeros.**

14b Correcting a dependent clause fragment

A dependent clause cannot stand alone. The subordinating words that introduce dependent adverb clauses include *because, if, unless, when, whenever, while, although,* and *after* (see 12e for a list). Words introducing dependent adjective or noun clauses include *who, whom, whose, which, that, what, when,* and *whoever.* A clause introduced with any subordinating word must always be attached to an independent clause.

Methods of correcting a dependent clause fragment

1. Connect the dependent clause to an independent clause.

   ▶ Lars wants to be a stand-up comedian/ ~~Because~~ because he likes to make people laugh.
   ▶ The family set out for a new country/ ~~In~~ in which they could practice their culture and religion.
   ▶ She made many promises to her sisters/ ~~That~~ that she would write to them every day.

2. Delete the subordinating conjunction. The dependent clause then becomes an independent clause, which can stand alone.

   ▶ Lars wants to be a stand-up comedian. ~~Because~~ He ~~he~~ likes to make people laugh.

Beginning a sentence with a dependent clause A subordinating conjunction at the beginning of a sentence does not always signal a fragment. A correctly punctuated sentence may begin with a subordinating conjunction introducing a dependent clause, as long as the sentence also contains an independent clause.

If you begin your sentence with an adverb clause, always make sure that you put a comma rather than a period at the end of that clause. A period at the end of an adverb clause at the beginning of a sentence creates a sentence fragment as in *Because he likes to make people laugh.*

Look for the following pattern whenever you begin a sentence with a capitalized subordinating conjunction:

Because (When, Although, Since, etc.)..., subject + verb in independent clause.

▶ **Because Lars likes to make people laugh, he wants to be a stand-up comedian.**

(labels above the example sentence: comma, subject, verb)

EXERCISE 14.1 Identify and correct dependent clause fragments. Identify and correct any dependent clause fragments either by connecting the dependent clause to an independent clause (deleting any unnecessary repetition) or by deleting the subordinating conjunction. Some sentences may be correct. (**A** = See Answer Key.)

EXAMPLE:

A study by psychologists at the University of Kentucky

in Lexington offers interesting results. That support a

that (inserted, with "That" struck through)

relationship between thinking positively and living a

long life.

A 1. A group of nuns wrote autobiographies sixty years ago. When they were young women.

A 2. Because the nuns all had similar lifestyles and social status. Psychologists have looked closely at the autobiographies and compared the lives of the writers.

A 3. Not surprisingly, few nuns reported negative emotions. Since they knew that their Mother Superior would read the autobiographies.

A 4. However, some reported having "very happy" experiences and a positive attitude about the future. Others were more neutral.

A 5. Psychologists discovered that the nuns who had expressed positive views lived an average of seven years longer than the other nuns. A conclusion that indicates that looking on the bright side may be good for a person's health.

6. The nuns' autobiographies have also been studied by experts in Alzheimer's disease. Who were hoping to discover clues about the illness.

7. Researchers examined the autobiographies to find out. If the nuns who later developed the disorder had provided hints in their writing.

8. After they had analyzed the autobiographies. The researchers found an interesting difference between the nuns who had developed Alzheimer's disease and the nuns who had not.

9. The nuns whose memories had remained intact throughout their lives had used more complicated syntax. When they had written about their experiences.

10. Although the research findings are fascinating, no one knows how syntax and Alzheimer's are linked. Using complicated syntax may not cause any changes in a person's brain.

14c Correcting a phrase fragment

A phrase is a group of words that lacks a subject, a complete verb, or both. Do not punctuate a phrase as a complete sentence.

┌─────── phrase fragment ───────┐
▶ **He wanted to make a point. To prove his competence.**

Methods of correcting a phrase fragment

1. Attach the phrase to a nearby independent clause. Remove the period and the capital letter.

                       to
▶ **He wanted to make a point,** ~~To~~ **prove his competence.**

                       on
▶ **The officer parked illegally,** ~~On~~ **the corner, right in front of a hydrant.**

                     the
▶ **A prize was awarded to Ed,** ~~The~~ **best worker in the company.**

[Use a comma before an appositive phrase describing a noun.]

2. Change the phrase to an independent clause with its own subject and verb.

▶ Althea works every evening. ~~Just~~ trying to keep up with her boss's demands.

She is just (above "Just")

▶ Nature held many attractions for Thoreau. First, the solitude.

he valued (inserted before "the solitude")

3. Rewrite the passage.

▶ Ralph ~~talked for hours. Elated~~ by the company's success.

was so (above "talked for hours") *elated* (above "Elated") *that he talked for hours.* (after "success")

EXERCISE 14.2   Identify and correct phrase fragments.
In the following items, identify any phrase fragment and correct it either by attaching it to a nearby independent clause or by changing it to an independent clause. Some sentences may be correct. (**A** = See Answer Key.)

EXAMPLE:

American popular music has had an enthusiastic following around the world, ~~Since~~ the early days of rock-and-roll.

since (above "Since")

A 1. Every country has its own musical styles. Based on the traditional music of its people.

A 2. Having its own tradition as the birthplace of jazz, blues, and rock music. The United States has long been one of the world's leading exporters of popular music.

A 3. In spite of enjoying enormous popularity in their own countries. Many performers from Europe, South America, Africa, and Asia have had a hard time attracting American fans.

A 4. Some American musicians have championed their favorite artists from abroad. Examples include the hip-hop artist Jay-Z's collaboration with South Asian artist Punjabi MC on the hit song "Beware of the Boys" and Beck's tribute to the late French singer-songwriter Serge Gainsbourg.

A 5. Although some U.S. music fans pay attention to foreign musical styles, most Americans download the music they know from American top-40 radio and MTV. Songs also loved by fans around the world for sounding typically American.

6. However, not all Americans are native English speakers. Listening exclusively to English-language music.

7. Latin music has had some crossover success in the United States. Propelled, at least at first, by the high percentage of Spanish-speaking people in this country.

8. On American radio and television, some of the most popular male acts have been Latin pop stars. Singing sensations such as Marc Anthony, Ricky Martin, and Enrique Iglesias.

9. These singers are considered crossover artists because they achieved mainstream success by singing in English. After making earlier recordings in Spanish.

10. Perhaps there will be a time when artists can have big hits with songs sung in a foreign language. At present, however, singing in English is almost always required for being successful in America.

14d Correcting a fragment with a missing subject, verb, or verb part

Every sentence must contain a subject and a complete verb in an independent clause. A word group that is punctuated like a sentence but lacks a subject or a verb or has a verbal (a verbal is an incomplete verb that does not show tense) in place of a verb is a fragment.

▶ I sent out a memo yesterday. <u>Just wanted everyone to know</u> the plan.
— fragment: missing subject —

▶ Overcrowding is a problem. <u>Too many people living in one area.</u>
— fragment: no complete verb —

▶ The candidate explained his proposal. <u>A plan for off-street parking.</u>
— fragment: missing verb —

Methods of correcting

1. Add a subject to the fragment.

▶ I sent out a memo yesterday. ~~Just~~ I just wanted everyone to know the plan.

2. Add a complete verb.

> Overcrowding is a problem. Too many people _{are} living in one area.

3. Revise the sentence.

> Overcrowding is a problem_{with too} ~~Too~~ many people living in one area.

> The candidate explained his ~~proposal. A~~ plan for off-street parking.

EXERCISE 14.3 Identify and correct fragments resulting from missing subjects, verbs, or verb parts.

In the following items, identify and correct any fragment resulting from a missing subject, verb, or verb part either by adding the necessary subject, verb, or verb part or by rewriting. Some items may be correct. (**A** = See Answer Key.)

EXAMPLE:

Many parts of the United States now face a shortage of

teachers. ~~People~~ _{Few people are} willing to put up with evening and

weekend work, unruly classes, and a smaller paycheck

than other professions offer.

A 1. Teachers were once regarded as committed, admirable professionals. People earning more respect than money.

A 2. Today, many teachers feel that they do not command respect. Instead seem to get blamed when students do not do well.

3. Most people enter teaching with high ideals. Young graduates hoping to make a difference in a child's life.

4. To many young people today, however, teaching seems less attractive than ever. Trying to remain idealistic is difficult in the face of low pay, large classes, and disrespect from politicians and parents who accuse teachers of performing their jobs badly.

5. Better training, higher pay, and more respect from political figures might help attract bright, motivated young people to the teaching profession. Might make them choose the classroom over a business or legal career.

14e Correcting a fragment with a missing subject
after *and*, *but*, or *or*

If you use a word such as *and*, *but*, or *or* to begin a sentence, make
sure that the sentence includes a subject and does not rely on the subject of the previous sentence. One subject cannot do the work of a
subject across two sentences.

▶ After an hour, the dancers changed partners. **And adapted to a** ⎤── fragment ──⎤

different type of music.

Methods of correcting

1. Correct the fragment by removing the period and capital letter.

   ▶ After an hour, the dancers changed partners, ~~And~~ *and* adapted to
   a different type of music.   [This forms what is known as a
   compound predicate. The subject of *changed* and *adapted* is
   dancers.]

2. Include an appropriate subject to form an independent clause.

   ▶ After an hour, the dancers changed partners. ~~And~~ *They* adapted
   to a different type of music.

3. Turn the fragment into an *-ing* participle phrase, and attach it to
   the independent clause.

   ▶ After an hour, the dancers changed partners. ~~And adapted~~ *adapting*
   to a different type of music.

EXERCISE 14.4 Identify and correct fragments with no
subject after *and*, *but*, or *or*.
In the following items, identify and correct any fragment containing part of a compound predicate beginning with *and*, *but*, or *or*.
(**A** = See Answer Key.)

EXAMPLE:

Carl Linnaeus, an eighteenth-century Swedish botanist,

placed all living things into carefully defined categories,/
and
~~And~~ **created a system for naming every creature and plant.**

A 1. Entomologists, scientists who study insects, often discover new species. And get the opportunity to name the creatures that they find.

A 2. Most people who name a new species either choose a name in honor of someone who assisted with the discovery. Or describe the species—often in Latin—with the new name.

3. However, the discoverer of a new wasp in the genus *Heerz* wanted to add humor to the new discovery. And called the wasp *Heerz tooya*.

4. One entomologist wanted to compliment "Far Side" cartoonist Gary Larson. And named a newly discovered owl louse *Strigiphilus garylarsoni* in 1989.

5. Entomologists do serious work with insects, but many of them also appear to have a sense of humor about their discoveries.

14f Using fragments intentionally

Advertisers and writers occasionally use fragments deliberately for a crisp, immediate effect: "What a luxury should be." "Sleek lines." "Efficient in rain, sleet, and snow." "A magnificent film." Novelists and short story writers use fragments in dialogue to simulate the immediacy and fragmentary nature of colloquial speech. Journalists and nonfiction writers often use a fragment for a stylistic effect, to make a point. In academic writing, too, writers sometimes use a fragment intentionally to make an emphatic point.

> He [Dylan Thomas] lived twenty-four years after he began to be a poet. Twenty-four years of poetry, dwindling rapidly in the last decade.
>
> —Donald Hall, *Remembering Poets*

You will also find fragments used intentionally in question form. This use is quite common in academic writing.

> The point of the expedition is to bring them back alive. But what then?
>
> —Carl Sagan, *Cosmos*

By all means, use fragments to achieve a specific effect. However, edit fragments that readers may perceive as errors.

14g What are run-ons and comma splices?

A writer who takes two independent clauses and rams them up against each other, end to end, creates the error of a *run-on sentence*, also known as a *fused sentence*.

RUN-ON ERROR

———————————— independent clause ————————————
▶ **Blue jeans were originally made as tough work clothes**
———————— independent clause ————————
they became a fashion statement in the 1970s.

Inserting a comma between the two clauses adds a little more separation, but not enough. The result is a comma splice—another error.

COMMA SPLICE ERROR

▶ **Blue jeans were originally made as tough work clothes, they became a fashion statement in the 1970s.**

VARIATION As with fragments, you will find comma splices and run-ons used in advertising, journalism, and other writing for stylistic effect, often for emphasizing a contrast.

▶ **W. [George W. Bush] and Hillary [Clinton] took radically**

comma splice emphasizing contrast

different paths. She clutched her husband's coattails, he

clutched his father's.   —Maureen Dowd, "From A to Y at Yale"

Readers of academic expository writing may prefer a period or semicolon or a recasting of the sentence instead of such use of a comma. Take the stylistic risk of using an intentional comma splice only if you are sure what effect you want to achieve and if you are sure readers will realize your intentions. ■

14h Correcting run-on sentences and comma splices

Often several options will work grammatically. To choose the most desirable option, consider the nature of the sentence, the clause you want to emphasize, and the structure of surrounding sentences, as in the following examples.

KEY POINTS

Options for Editing a Run-on or a Comma Splice

1. Separate the sentences. (Create two complete and separate sentences by adding either a period or a semicolon between the two or by adding a question mark, if appropriate.)

   ▶ **Blue jeans were originally made as tough work clothes.** *They* **became a fashion statement in the 1970s.**

   ▶ **Blue jeans were originally made as tough work clothes;** *they* **became a fashion statement in the 1970s.**

2. Include a comma, but make sure it is followed by one of the seven coordinating conjunctions: **and, but, or, nor, so, for,** or **yet.**

   ▶ **Blue jeans were originally made as tough work clothes,** *but* **they became a fashion statement in the 1970s.**

3. Separate the sentences with a period or a semicolon, followed by a transitional expression such as *however* or *therefore*, followed by a comma.

   ▶ **Blue jeans were originally made as tough work clothes;** *however*, **they became a fashion statement in the 1970s.**

4. Rewrite the sentences as one sentence by using a subordinating conjunction to make one clause dependent on the other.

   ▶ *Although* **blue jeans were originally made as tough work clothes, they became a fashion statement in the 1970s.**

5. Condense or restructure the sentence.

   ▶ **Blue jeans,** *originally made* **as tough work clothes, became a fashion statement in the 1970s.**

Option 1   Separate the sentences.

- Insert a period when the two independent clauses are long.

▶ **Sheep Meadow in Central Park actually had sheep**
  _{. The}
  grazing on it until 1934 ~~the~~ **sheep saved the city the expense of mowing and fertilizing.**

- Use a semicolon to separate independent clauses closely connected in meaning or indicating a contrast.

    ▶ **Documentaries show us history in action;Hollywood movies force us to sort out fact from fiction.**

- Use a question mark to end a clause that asks a question.

    ▶ **Why do more and more new diet fads appear? People people should realize the value of exercise instead.**

Note: If the second clause offers an explanation of the first, consider using a colon or a dash.

    ▶ **Students frequently comment on older people's choice of words: Their their grandmothers say "dungarees" and "slacks" instead of "jeans" and "pants."**

Option 2 Include a comma, but make sure it is followed by *and*, *but*, *or*, *nor*, *so*, *for*, or *yet*. This option is appropriate when the two independent clauses are not excessively long and can logically be linked to each other with one of the coordinating conjunctions.

    ▶ **A pickup truck is good for country living, but a sports car will get stuck in the mud.**

Option 3 Separate the sentences with a period or a semicolon, followed by a transitional expression (such as *however*, *in addition*, or *therefore*), and then a comma. This option is appropriate when you are switching direction and want to stress the second of the two clauses.

    ▶ **Ambiguity can be an effective literary device; however, however sometimes ambiguity is unintentionally funny.**

Option 4 Rewrite the sentences as one sentence by using a subordinating conjunction to make one clause dependent on the other. This option is appropriate when one clause can be used effectively to introduce, establish a context for, or otherwise "set up" the clause containing the more notable point.

    ▶ **When monarch Monarch butterflies migrate south, they sometimes travel as many as 2,000 miles.**

Note: Do not include a comma between the two clauses if the dependent clause occurs after the independent clause.

▶ **Monarch butterflies sometimes travel as many as 2,000 miles when they migrate south.**

Option 5 Condense or restructure the sentence. This option is a good way to eliminate wordiness and repetition and to make your prose flow more smoothly. A useful way to restructure a run-on or a comma splice is to make a clause into a phrase using an *-ing* form of a verb.

                                    making
▶ **Engineers worked on the plans, ~~they made~~ the bridge less vulnerable to an earthquake.**

EXERCISE 14.5   Correct run-on sentences and comma splices. For each of the following items, write *CS* on the line if the item is a comma splice or write *RO* if it is a run-on sentence. Then correct the error by using one of the five methods described in 14h. (**A** = See Answer Key.)

EXAMPLE:

_____CS_____ **Pierre de Fermat, who was a brilliant**

                                                        but
mathematician, left a puzzle in the margin of a book, he

died without providing its solution.

A 1. _____ Pierre de Fermat was a lawyer by trade his passion was mathematics.

A 2. _____ Fermat discussed his ideas in correspondence with other mathematicians nevertheless, as a modest man, he refused to have his name attached to any published work on mathematics.

A 3. _____ Fermat regarded prime numbers with a special fascination, he formulated a theory about prime numbers in 1640 that later became famous as Fermat's Last Theorem.

A 4. _____ In his notes, Fermat said that the theorem had a "marvelous" proof however, he claimed that he did not have enough room in the margin to write it down.

A 5. _____ Some mathematicians believed that a short, elegant answer existed, they struggled to find the proof of Fermat's Last Theorem.

6. _____ No one has ever found a short proof of the theorem most mathematicians now think that Fermat did not have one, either.

7. _____ Mathematician Andrew Wiles, who had been intrigued by Fermat's theorem since childhood, spent seven years working on the problem, in 1993, he announced that he had solved it.

8. _____ His proof was 150 pages long, a month after his announcement, other mathematicians discovered an error in Wiles's calculations.

9. _____ Wiles worked with another mathematician, Richard Taylor, he repaired the proof a year later.

10. _____ The proof of Fermat's Last Theorem was finally complete Wiles now says that successfully solving the problem that had occupied his mind for so many years was a bittersweet experience.

15 Sentence Snarls

Snarls, tangles, and knots are as difficult to deal with on a bad writing day as on a bad hair day, though they may not be as painful. Sentences with structural inconsistencies give readers trouble. They make readers work to untangle the meaning. This section points out how to avoid or edit common sentence snarls.

15a Tangles: Mixed constructions, faulty comparisons, and convoluted syntax

Revise sentences that begin in one way and then veer off the track, departing from the original structure. When you mix constructions, make faulty comparisons, or tangle your syntax (sentence structure), you confuse readers.

Mixed constructions   A mixed construction is a sentence with parts incompatible in grammar and meaning. The sentence starts in one style and then goes off in an unexpected direction. Check to ensure that the subject and verb in your sentence are clear and work together. Do not use a pronoun to restate the subject (15f, 35f).

▶ ~~In the~~ The excerpt by Heilbrun and the story by Gould are similar.

▶ ~~By working~~ ^{Working} at night can create tension with family members.

When you start a sentence with a dependent clause (beginning with a word like *when*, *if*, *because*, and *since*), make sure you follow that clause with an independent clause. A dependent clause cannot serve as the subject of a verb.

MIXED   **When a baseball player is traded often causes family problems.**

POSSIBLE REVISIONS   **Trading a baseball player often causes family problems.**

      When a baseball player is traded, the move often causes family problems.

Faulty comparisons When you make comparisons, readers need to know clearly what you are comparing. See also 18a for faulty comparisons with personal pronouns.

FAULTY COMPARISON   **Like Wallace Stevens, her job strikes readers as unexpected for a poet.**   [It is not her job that is like the poet Wallace Stevens; her job is like his job.]

POSSIBLE REVISION   **Like Wallace Stevens, she holds a job that strikes readers as unexpected for a poet.**

Convoluted syntax Revise sentences that ramble on to such an extent that they become tangled. Make sure they have clear subjects, verbs, and connections between clauses.

TANGLED   **The way I feel about getting what you want is that when there is a particular position or item that you want to try to get to do your best and not give up because if you give up you have probably missed your chance of succeeding.**

POSSIBLE REVISION   **To get what you want, keep trying.**

EXERCISE 15.1   Correct tangled syntax: Mixed constructions and faulty comparisons.

In the following items, suggest corrections for any mixed constructions or faulty comparisons. (**A** = See Answer Key.)

EXAMPLE:

> Adopting
> ~~By adopting~~ the poetic techniques popular in colonial America
> enabled Phillis Wheatley to find an audience for her writings.

A 1. Phillis Wheatley's education, which was remarkable mainly because she received one, a rare luxury for a slave girl in the American colonies.

A 2. Wheatley, kidnapped from her homeland and sold into slavery when she was about seven, an experience that must have been traumatic.

A 3. By learning to read and write gave Phillis an opportunity to demonstrate her aptitude for poetry.

Book of poems by Phillis Wheatley, 1773

A 4. Like Alexander Pope, iambic pentameter couplets were Phillis Wheatley's preferred poetic form.

5. Publishing a book of poems, Phillis Wheatley, becoming famous partly because she was an African slave who could compete as a poet with well-educated white men.

6. Her work, poems in a very formal eighteenth-century style that found aristocratic admirers in America and England.

7. With the deaths of Mr. and Mrs. Wheatley, when Phillis was in her twenties, left her free but also penniless.

8. Like Zora Neale Hurston in the twentieth century, an impoverished, lonely death followed a loss of public interest in Wheatley's writings, but scholars discovered her work posthumously and realized her contribution to American literature.

15b Misplaced modifiers: Words, phrases, clauses, *only*, and split infinitives

A modifier is a word, phrase, or clause that describes or limits another word or phrase. Keep single words, phrases, and clauses next to or close to the sentence elements that they modify. That is, avoid *misplaced modifiers*.

> *not*
> ▶ Next year, everyone in the company will ~~not~~ get a raise.
> [The unrevised sentence says that nobody at all will get a
> raise. If you move *not*, the sentence now says that although
> not all workers will get a raise, some will.]

Take care with words such as *only*.   Place a word such as *only*, *even*, *just*, *nearly*, *not*, *merely*, or *simply* immediately before the word it modifies. The meaning of a sentence can change significantly as the position of a modifier changes, so careful placement is important.

> ▶ *Only* the journalist began to investigate the incident.
> [no one else]

> ▶ The journalist *only* began to investigate the incident.
> [but didn't finish]

> ▶ The journalist began to investigate *only* the incident.
> [nothing else]

Place a phrase or clause close to the word it modifies.

MISPLACED   **Sidel argues that young women's dreams will not always come true in her essay.**

REVISED   **In her essay, Sidel argues that young women's dreams will not always come true.**

Consider the case for splitting an infinitive.   You split an infinitive when you place a word or phrase between *to* and the verb. Avoid splitting an infinitive when the split is unnecessary or the result is clumsy, as in the following:

> *to shine brightly.*
> ▶ They waited for the sun ~~to brightly shine.~~

> *to inform*
> ▶ We want ~~to honestly and in confidence inform~~ you of
> *honestly and in confidence.*
> **our plans/**

Traditionally, a split infinitive was frowned upon, but it is now much more acceptable, as in the *Star Trek* motto "To boldly go where no man has gone before. . . ." Sometimes, splitting is necessary to avoid ambiguity.

▶ We had *to stop* them from talking *quickly.*   [Were they talking too quickly? Did we have to stop them quickly? The meaning is ambiguous.]

▶ We had *to quickly stop* them from talking.   [The split infinitive clearly says that we were the ones who had to do something quickly.]

EXERCISE 15.2 Change meaning by changing the position of a modifier.
How many meanings can you get from the following sentence about a bus accident by placing the word *only* in a variety of positions within the sentence? What are the positions, and what are the meanings that result from each position? Sample answers are in the Answer Key.

The passenger hurt his arm.

15c Dangling modifiers

A modifier that is not grammatically linked to the noun or phrase it is intended to describe is said to be dangling. An *-ing* or *-ed* modifier at the beginning of a sentence must provide information about the subject of the sentence.

DANGLING   *Driving* across the desert, the saguaro *cactus* appeared eerily human.   [Who or what was driving? The cactus?]

You can fix a dangling modifier in the following ways:

Method 1 Retain the modifier, but make it modify the subject of the independent clause.

REVISED   **Driving across the desert, the naturalists thought the saguaro cactus appeared eerily human.**

Method 2 Change the modifier phrase into a clause with its own subject and verb.

REVISED   **When the naturalists were driving across the desert, the saguaro cactus appeared eerily human.**

VARIATION Not all dangling modifiers are equal. Some are awkward and may make readers laugh (*After boiling for five hours, Granny May turned off the cabbage*), while others, particularly those with *it* used as a filler subject, are barely noticeable: *Looking at the house, it occurred to me that I had seen it before.* Readers can easily adjust to that usage and will not always feel confused. Still, it ultimately may please readers more (especially English instructors) if you are consistent and do not let your modifiers dangle. ■

EXERCISE 15.3 Identify dangling modifiers.
Classify each of the following sentences as *No DM* (if the sentence contains no dangling modifier), *DM* (if the sentence contains a dangling modifier that is a clear error), or *DM?* (if the sentence contains a dangling modifier that might not offend the average reader). Then revise any sentences classified as *DM* or *DM?* (**A** = See Answer Key.)

EXAMPLE:

                                 I spotted
_____DM_____ **Browsing at the bookstore, a copy of the new translation of the *Iliad* caught my eye.**

A 1. _____ Translating literature from one language into another, it is important to strive for both literal accuracy and a similar effect to that of the original work.

A 2. _____ Turning the Greek of the *Iliad* into English in 1997, Robert Fagles managed to translate the words accurately while keeping the poetry lyrical and muscular.

3. _____ Awarded several prizes for his translation of the *Iliad*, many educators delighted in using Fagles's book to show their students the difference that a good translation can make.

4. _____ Turning a lively, intelligent book from another culture into a dry, dull, or inaccurate English-language text, a reader's perspective can be distorted by a bad translation.

5. _____ Helping people everywhere appreciate the beauty and power of literature from around the world, cultural awareness improves with every great translation.

15d Shifts: Statements/commands, indirect/direct quotation, point of view, tense

Sudden shifts in your sentences can disconcert readers.

Do not shift abruptly from statements to commands.

▶ The students in this university should do more to keep the

        They should pick
place clean. ~~Pick~~ up the litter and treat the dorms like home.

Do not shift from indirect to direct quotation. (See 35d for more on tenses in indirect quotations.)

SHIFT   The client told us that he wanted to sign the lease and would we prepare the papers.

REVISED   The client told us that he wanted to sign the lease and asked us to prepare the papers.

SHIFT   She wanted to find out whether any interest had accumulated on her account and was she receiving any money.

REVISED   She wanted to find out whether any interest had accumulated on her account and whether she was receiving any money.

Do not shift point of view in pronouns. Be consistent in using first, second, or third person pronouns. For example, if you begin by referring to *one*, do not switch to *you* or *we*. Also avoid shifting unnecessarily between third person singular and plural forms as well as using *you* to refer to people generally (18g).

SHIFT   *One* needs a high salary to live in a city because *you* have to spend so much on rent and transportation.

POSSIBLE *One* needs a high salary to live in a city because *one*
REVISIONS has to spend so much on rent and transportation.

          People need a high salary to live in a city because *they* have to spend so much on rent and transportation.

          A high salary is necessary in a city because rent and transportation are expensive.

Do not shift tenses. If you use tenses consistently throughout a piece of writing, you help readers understand what is happening and when. Check that your verbs consistently express present or past time, both within a sentence and from one sentence to the next.

TENSE   Selecting a jury *was* very difficult. The lawyers *ask*
SHIFTS   many questions to discover bias and prejudice; some-
          times the prospective jurors *had* the idea they *are*
          acting in a play.

REVISED   Selecting a jury *was* very difficult. The lawyers *asked*
          many questions to discover bias and prejudice; some-
          times the prospective jurors *had* the idea they *were*
          acting in a play.

When you write about events or ideas presented by another writer, use the literary present tense consistently (see 16d).

> *illustrates*
> ▶ The author ~~illustrated~~ the images of women in two ways, using advertisements and dramas on TV. One way shows women who advanced their careers by themselves, and the other shows those who used beauty to gain recognition.

Tense shifts are appropriate in the following instances:

1. When you signal a time change with a time word or phrase

> *signal for switch from past to present*
> ▶ Harold *was* my late grandfather's name, and *now* it *is* mine.

2. When you follow a generalization (present tense) with a specific example of a past incident

> ┌──────────── generalization ────────────┐
> ▶ Some bilingual schools *offer* intensive instruction in English.
> ┌──────────── specific example ────────────┐
> My sister, for example, *went* to a bilingual school where she *studied* English for two hours every day.

EXERCISE 15.4 Correct inappropriate shifts: statement and command, pronoun person and number, direct and indirect quotations, and tense shifts.

On the line after each of the following sentences, use the following abbreviations to identify shifts: shift in statement/command: *SC*; shift in pronoun person: *PP*; shift in pronoun number: *PN*; shift in direct/indirect quotation: *Q*; shift in tense: *T*. Then revise each inappropriate shift. (**A** = See Answer Key.)

EXAMPLE:

> *people*
> Sharks do occasionally attack swimmers, but ~~you~~ are more likely to be killed by a falling television than by a shark bite. ___PP___

A 1. When a tourist in Florida wants an underwater adventure, you can swim in the ocean with sharks. _____

A 2. In 2001, a series of shark attacks on the east coast of the United States made Florida Fish and Wildlife Conservation commissioners ask whether swimmers are being too careless or were tourist attractions that feature swimming with sharks the cause of the problem? _____

A 3. When a tour operator puts bait in the water before a shark swim, they may be teaching sharks to associate people with food. _____

A 4. If sharks were fed too frequently by human beings, the commissioners wondered, will the big fish be more likely to endanger swimmers? _____

A 5. The curator of the International Shark Attack File told commissioners that the feeding probably didn't contribute to the attacks and would they tell people more about the good behavior of sharks. _____

6. The shark attacks shocked people around the country, and you heard about the attacks constantly in the late summer of 2001. _____

7. A shark can seem ferocious, but they are often in more danger from humans than humans are from the sharks. _____

8. People should not be frightened by the shark's torpedolike body, scaly skin, and sharp teeth. Try to learn about the shark's habits instead. _____

9. Some scientists believe that if a person studies sharks, they will understand ocean ecosystems better. _____

10. Some species of sharks had become endangered because so many people like the taste of them. _____

15e Logical sequence after the subject

Logic of subject and verb   Do not use a subject and verb that do not make logical sense together. (This error is known as *faulty predication*.)

> ~~The decision to build~~ _Building_ an elaborate extension onto the train station made all the trains arrive late.   [It was not the decision that delayed the trains; building the extension did.]

> According to the guidelines, ~~people in~~ dilapidated public housing will be demolished this year.   [The housing, not people, will be demolished.]

Logical sequence with definitions and reasons   When you write a definition of a term, use parallel structures on either side of the verb *be*. In formal writing, avoid defining a term by using *is when* or *is where* (or *was when, was where*).

No   **A tiebreaker in tennis *is where* they play one final game to decide the set.**

Yes   **A tiebreaker in tennis is the final deciding game of a tied set.**

Writing about reasons, like writing definitions, has pitfalls. Avoid *the reason is because* in Standard English. Grammatically, an adverb clause beginning with *because* cannot follow the verb *be*. Instead, use *the reason is that,* or recast the sentence.

No   **The *reason* Tiger Woods lost *is because* he could not handle the weather in Scotland.**

Yes   **The *reason* Tiger Woods lost *is that* he could not handle the weather in Scotland.**

Yes   **Tiger Woods lost *because* he could not handle the weather in Scotland.**

VARIATION   In speech, *the reason is because* is common and would probably hardly be noticed or tagged as an error. In writing, though, consider the audience and your writing situation. If formality and correctness are important to readers, avoid using *the reason is because.* Similarly, you may hear and see in print *the reason why.* Use *the reason that* in formal contexts.

▶ **The TV commentator explained the reason ~~why~~ Tiger Woods lost.**
                                 that

Another possibility is to omit *that* if the meaning is clear without it.

▶ **The TV commentator explained the reason Tiger Woods lost.** ■

EXERCISE 15.5   Avoid errors with logical sequence of subject and verb and with definitions and reasons.
In the following sentences, identify and revise any errors. Some sentences may be correct. (**A** = See Answer Key.)

EXAMPLE:
                 cash grants
Farm subsidies are ~~where~~ the government gives farmers ~~money~~ to help them grow certain crops.

A 1. One reason for farmers to receive subsidies is because they set aside part of their land for wildlife conservation.

A 2. Conservation, which is where the land is preserved in the most natural state possible, accounts for about 9 percent of farm subsidies in the United States.

3. Farmers stop draining swampy land preserve wetlands for ducks.

4. The main reason why the duck population is rebounding after ten years of decline is that a large percentage of farmers in North Dakota accepted subsidies to preserve wetlands on their property.

5. Providing federal subsidies for conservation was originally proposed by environmental groups but are now supported enthusiastically by organizations such as the National Rifle Association because the subsidies also benefit hunters.

15f Necessary and unnecessary words

Include necessary words in compound structures. If you use only one main verb form in a compound verb, the form must fit into each part of the compound; otherwise, you must use the complete verb in each part (see 15g on parallelism).

> tried
> ▶ He has always and will always try to preserve his father's
>   good name in the community. [*Try* fits only with *will*, not with *has*.]

Include necessary words in comparisons. (See also 19g.)

> as
> ▶ The volleyball captain is as competitive or even more
>   competitive than her teammates. [The comparative
>   structures are *as competitive as* and *more competitive than*.
>   Do not merge them.]

If you omit the verb in the second part of a comparison, ambiguity may occur.

> did
> ▶ He liked baseball more than his son. [Omitting *did* implies
>   that he liked baseball more than he liked his son.]

Also include apostrophes with words that need them.

> 's
> ▶ My mother's expectations differed from Jing-Mei's mother.

State the grammatical subject only once. Even when a phrase or clause separates the subject and main verb of a sentence, do not restate the subject in pronoun form. See also 35a.

> restated subject
> ► The nurse who took care of my father for many years ~~she~~ gave him comfort and advice.

When the subject is a whole clause functioning as a noun, do not add an *it* subject.

> ► What may seem moral to some ~~it~~ is immoral to others.

EXERCISE 15.6 Identify omitted words and apostrophes.
In the following sentences, find and correct any errors of missing words or apostrophes. (**A** = See Answer Key.)

EXAMPLE:

> at
> Quantum mechanics inspires new ways of looking ˄and thinking about the universe.

A 1. One physicist seriously claims that there are as many universes or even more universes than the human mind can imagine.

A 2. This theory, known as the Many Worlds Interpretation, has always and may always be considered by many other physicists to be nothing more than a poetic way of thinking about quantum mechanics.

3. However, their basically metaphorical view of the Many Worlds Interpretation differs from David Deutsch.

4. Deutsch, an Oxford physicist, regards the Many Worlds Interpretation as more realistic than, for example, Stephen Hawking.

5. Deutsch's book *The Fabric of Reality* argues for the existence of infinite parallel universes populated by people who are similar but not quite the same as the individuals existing in our own universe.

15g Faulty parallelism

The use of parallel structures helps produce cohesion and coherence in a text. Aim for parallelism in sentences and in longer passages. The structures can be clauses or phrases, as shown in the following passages.

PARALLEL STRUCTURES: CLAUSES	**Hiram lived in a town** *where houses and storefronts had been adorned with bouquets of flowers every first of the month.* **He stayed in another** *where public gardens had been replaced by asphalt playgrounds* **after the elimination of the Parks Department.**
PARALLEL STRUCTURES: PHRASES	**Sometimes she'd come home to find the boy** *sitting* **at the table,** *listening* **to stories on his tape player, and** *making* **the drawings that became the inspiration for his father's strongest work.**

Sentences become confusing when you string together phrases or clauses that are not parallel in form.

NOT PARALLEL **He wants a new girlfriend, to get a house, and find a good job.**

PARALLEL **He wants a new girlfriend, a house, and a good job.**

Parallel structures with paired (correlative) conjunctions When your sentence contains pairs such as *either . . . or, neither . . . nor, not only . . . but also, both . . . and, whether . . . or,* and *as . . . as,* the structure after the second part of the pair should be exactly parallel in form to the structure after the first part.

▶ **He made up his mind** *either* **to paint the van** *or* ^to^ sell **it to another buyer.** [*To paint* follows *either*; therefore, *to sell* should follow *or*.]

▶ **She loves** *both* **swimming competitively** *and* ^playing^ ~~to play~~ **golf.**
[An *-ing* form follows *both*; therefore, an *-ing* form should also follow *and*.]

▶ **The drive to Cuernavaca was** *not only* **too expensive** *but also* ~~was~~ **too tiring to do alone.** [*Too expensive* follows *not only*; therefore, *too tiring* should follow *but also*.]

Parallel structures in comparisons When making comparisons with *as* or *than,* use parallel structures. In the following examples, the revisions could have used either the infinitive form *(to drive, to take)* in both parts of the sentence, or the *-ing* form.

▶ ^To drive^ ~~Driving~~ **to Cuernavaca is** *as* **expensive** *as* **to take the bus.**
▶ ^Taking^ ~~To take~~ **the bus is less comfortable** *than* **driving.**

EXERCISE 15.7 Revise for parallelism.
Revise the following sentences to make structures parallel. Some sentences may be correct. (**A** = See Answer Key.)

EXAMPLE:

Evangelist Aimee Semple McPherson made news in 1926 for

running a successful radio ministry, preaching in a Los Angeles

            disappearing
temple, and ~~her disappearance~~ during an ocean swim.

A 1. Aimee Semple McPherson was not only the founder of a phenomenally successful ministry but became the first female evangelist to preach on the radio.

A 2. McPherson's thousands of followers reacted with shock and horror in May 1926 when the evangelist either staged her own disappearance or kidnappers captured her.

3. Resurfacing in Mexico, McPherson claimed to have escaped from kidnappers by walking through the desert for seventeen hours, but she showed no signs of dehydration, heavy sweating, or that she had been sunburned.

4. Was McPherson having an affair with her married radio engineer, telling the truth about the kidnapping, or did she simply need a break from the pressures of celebrity?

5. Not knowing the truth about her disappearance is perhaps more fascinating than to be sure of what happened to Aimee Semple McPherson.

16 Verbs

A verb tells what a person, thing, or concept does or is.

▶ **The community college in my county *provides* opportunities for disadvantaged students.**

Ask the following question about a clause to determine the verb: *Who* (or *what*) *does* (or *is*) (*what*)?   [Answer: The community college *provides* opportunities.]

The base form of a verb (the form with no endings or vowel changes) will fit into one or both of the following slots:

▶ **They will _____.**   [They will provide.]

▶ **It might _____.**   [It might provide.]

16a Verb forms

Although you might use a variety of verb forms when you speak, readers generally expect formal writing to conform to Standard English usage. All verbs except *be* have five forms.

Regular verbs The five forms of *regular verbs* follow a predictable pattern: approach, approaches, approaching, approached, approached. Once you know the base form, you can construct all the others:

1. base form: the form listed in a dictionary (*paint, help*)
2. -*s* form: the third person singular form of the present tense (*paints, helps*)
3. -*ing* form (the *present participle*): needs an auxiliary verb to function as a complete verb; can appear in a verbal phrase and as a noun (gerund) (*painting, helping*)
4. past tense form: functions as a complete verb, without any auxiliary verbs (*painted, helped*)
5. past participle: sometimes called the -*ed* form; needs an auxiliary verb to function as a complete verb (*has painted, was helped*); can appear as an adjective in a phrase (*the painted wall*)

Irregular verbs *Irregular verbs* do not use -*ed* to form the past tense and the past participle. Here are the forms of some common irregular verbs.

Irregular Verbs

Base Form	Past Tense	Past Participle
arise	arose	arisen
be	was/were	been
bear	bore	born, borne
beat	beat	beaten
become	became	become
begin	began	begun
bend	bent	bent
bet	bet	bet, betted
bind	bound	bound
bite	bit	bitten
bleed	bled	bled
blow	blew	blown
break	broke	broken
bring	brought	brought
build	built	built

Base Form	Past Tense	Past Participle
burst	burst	burst
buy	bought	bought
catch	caught	caught
choose	chose	chosen
cling	clung	clung
come	came	come
cost	cost	cost
creep	crept	crept
cut	cut	cut
deal	dealt	dealt
dig	dug	dug
do	did	done
draw	drew	drawn
drink	drank	drunk
drive	drove	driven
eat	ate	eaten
fall	fell	fallen
feed	fed	fed
feel	felt	felt
fight	fought	fought
find	found	found
flee	fled	fled
fly	flew	flown
forbid	forbad(e)	forbidden
forget	forgot	forgotten
forgive	forgave	forgiven
freeze	froze	frozen
get	got	gotten, got
give	gave	given
go	went	gone
grind	ground	ground
grow	grew	grown
hang*	hung	hung
have	had	had
hear	heard	heard
hide	hid	hidden
hit	hit	hit
hold	held	held
hurt	hurt	hurt
keep	kept	kept
know	knew	known
lay	laid	laid (16b)

Hang meaning "put to death" is regular: *hang, hanged, hanged.*

Base Form	Past Tense	Past Participle
lead	led	led
leave	left	left
lend	lent	lent
let	let	let
lie	lay	lain (16b)
light	lit, lighted	lit, lighted
lose	lost	lost
make	made	made
mean	meant	meant
meet	met	met
put	put	put
quit	quit	quit
read	read	read
ride	rode	ridden
ring	rang	rung
rise	rose	risen (16b)
run	ran	run
say	said	said
see	saw	seen
seek	sought	sought
sell	sold	sold
send	sent	sent
set	set	set (16b)
shake	shook	shaken
shine	shone	shone
shoot	shot	shot
shrink	shrank	shrunk
shut	shut	shut
sing	sang	sung
sink	sank	sunk
sit	sat	sat (16b)
sleep	slept	slept
slide	slid	slid
slit	slit	slit
speak	spoke	spoken
spend	spent	spent
spin	spun	spun
spit	spit, spat	spit
split	split	split
spread	spread	spread
spring	sprang	sprung
stand	stood	stood
steal	stole	stolen

Base Form	Past Tense	Past Participle
stick	stuck	stuck
sting	stung	stung
stink	stank, stunk	stunk
strike	struck	struck, stricken
swear	swore	sworn
sweep	swept	swept
swim	swam	swum
swing	swung	swung
take	took	taken
teach	taught	taught
tear	tore	torn
tell	told	told
think	thought	thought
throw	threw	thrown
tread	trod	trodden, trod
understand	understood	understood
upset	upset	upset
wake	woke	waked, woken
wear	wore	worn
weave	wove	woven
weep	wept	wept
win	won	won
wind	wound	wound
wring	wrung	wrung
write	wrote	written

The verbs *be*, *do*, and *have* and the nine modal verbs (*will*, *would*, *can*, *could*, *shall*, *should*, *may*, *might*, and *must*) are also used as auxiliary verbs along with a main verb to help provide information about tense, voice, mood, the concepts of progressive or perfected action, and other meanings. (See 17a for present tense forms and agreement with *be*, *do*, and *have*; see 34a and 34b for the conventions of use and of verb sequence after an auxiliary.)

16b Verbs commonly confused

Give special attention to verbs that are similar in form but differ in meaning. Some of them can take a direct object; these are called *transitive verbs*. Others never take a direct object; these are called *intransitive verbs* (35c).

1. *rise:* to get up, to ascend (intransitive; irregular)

   raise: to lift, to rear (a child) (transitive; regular)

BASE	–s	–ing	PAST TENSE	PAST PARTICIPLE
rise	rises	rising	rose	risen
raise	raises	raising	raised	raised

▶ **The bread *rose* as soon as she put it in the oven.**

▶ **She *raised* three sons by herself.**

2. *sit:* to occupy a seat (intransitive; irregular)
   set: to put or place (transitive; irregular)

BASE	–s	–ing	PAST TENSE	PAST PARTICIPLE
sit	sits	sitting	sat	sat
set	sets	setting	set	set

▶ **He *sat* on the wooden chair.**

▶ **She *set* the vase on the middle shelf.**

3. *lie:* to recline (intransitive; irregular)
   lay: to put or place (transitive; regular)

BASE	–s	–ing	PAST TENSE	PAST PARTICIPLE
lie	lies	lying	lay	lain
lay	lays	laying	laid	laid

Note the possibility for confusion especially with the form *lay* being both the base form of the transitive verb and the past tense form of the intransitive verb. (But, then, whoever said language was logical?)

>   lay
> ▶ I ~~laid~~ down for half an hour.
>   lying
> ▶ I was ~~laying~~ down when you called.
>   Lay
> ▶ ~~Lie~~ the map on the floor.

VARIATION   You are likely to come across many variations of the *lie/lay* distinction. Confusion is commonplace. You will certainly hear people say things like "Grandma laid down for a nap" or "She lay the dress out on the bed." You will also come across confusion of the forms in (presumably) edited writing: "Do you want a comfortable mattress to lay down on?" and "He just laid there, asking for help." Yes, people will understand you, but they may also notice that you do not seem to be aware of the difference between the two forms and regard that negatively. So avoid falling into the common trap. Make a point of showing you *are* aware of the distinction between *lie* and *lay*. ■

In addition, note the verb *lie* ("to say something untrue"), which is intransitive.

BASE	–s	–ing	PAST TENSE	PAST PARTICIPLE
lie	lies	lying	lied	lied

▶ **He *lied* when he said he had won three trophies.**

EXERCISE 16.1 Use commonly confused verbs correctly.
In the following sentences, choose the verb needed in the sentence from the choices in parentheses and underline it. Then write the correct form of the verb in the blank. (**A** = See Answer Key.)

EXAMPLE:

Most children who are raised (raise/rise) in the United States learn the Pledge of Allegiance in elementary school.

A 1. Francis Bellamy, the author of the Pledge of Allegiance, wanted to add the word *equality* when he _____ (set/sit) down the line *with liberty and justice for all* in 1892.

A 2. He knew, however, that many Americans at that time would _____ (raise/rise) objections because equality for women and African Americans was not a widely accepted idea a hundred years ago.

3. Although Bellamy was a Baptist minister, he did not _____ (set/sit) down to write a prayer; the original version of the Pledge of Allegiance does not contain the phrase *under God*.

4. Responsibility for adding *under God* to the Pledge must _____ (lay/lie) with Congress, which voted to include those words in 1954.

5. Bellamy _____ (lay/lie) plans to incorporate the Pledge into a flag-raising ceremony in honor of the 400th anniversary of the discovery of America, and since then, his pledge has been a popular addition to American ceremonies of all kinds.

16c Verb tenses

Tenses indicate time as perceived by the speaker or writer. Verbs change form to indicate present or past time: *We play. We played.* To indicate future time, English uses the modal auxiliary *will* (*We will play*) as well as expressions such as *be + going to* (*We are going to play when our work is finished*). For each time (present, past, and future), we can use auxiliary verbs with the main verb to convey completed actions (perfect forms), actions in progress (progressive forms), and actions that are completed by some specified time or event or emphasize the length of time in progress (perfect progressive forms).

The following examples illustrate active voice verbs referring to past, present, and future time. For passive voice verbs, see 16g.

PAST TIME

Simple past	They *arrived* yesterday.
	They *did* not *arrive* today.
Past progressive	They *were leaving* when the phone rang.
	She *was sleeping* when he called.
Past perfect	Everyone *had left* when I called.
Past perfect progressive	We *had been sleeping* for an hour before you arrived.

PRESENT TIME

Simple present	They *eat* oatmeal every morning.
	He *eats* Wheaties.
	He *does* not *eat* eggs.
Present progressive	They *are working* today.
	He *is playing* hooky.
Present perfect	She *has* never *read* Melville.
	We *have read* several recent novels.
Present perfect progressive	He *has been living* here for five years.
	They *have* never *lived* in the suburbs.

FUTURE TIME (USING *WILL*)

Simple future	She *will arrive* soon.
	She *will* not (*won't*) *be* late.
Future progressive	They *will be playing* baseball at noon tomorrow.
Future perfect	He *will have finished* the project by Friday.
Future perfect progressive	By the year 2009, they *will have been running* the company for twenty-five years.

Other modal auxiliaries can substitute for *will* and thus change the meaning: *must arrive, might be playing, may have finished, should have been running* (see 34c).

ESL Note　Verbs Not Using *-ing* Forms for Progressive Tenses

Use simple tenses, not progressive forms, with verbs expressing not action but mental activity referring to the senses, preference, or thought, as well as with verbs of possession, appearance, and inclusion (for example, *smell, prefer, understand, own, seem, contain*).

> *smells*
> The fish in the showcase ~~is smelling~~ bad.

> *possess*
> They ~~are possessing~~ different behavior patterns.

However, see also 19b for *smell* used as an action verb. ■

Present tenses

Simple present　Use the simple present tense for the following purposes:

1. To make a generalization

  > **Gardening *nourishes* the spirit.**

2. To indicate an activity that is permanent or happens habitually

  > **He *works* for Sony.**

  > **The directors *distribute* a financial report every six months.**

3. To discuss literature and the arts—even if the work was written in the past or the author is no longer alive

  > **In *Zami,* Audre Lorde *describes* how a librarian *introduces* her to the joys of reading.**

When used in this way, the present tense is called the *literary present*. However, when you write a narrative of your own, use past tenses to tell about past actions.

> *walked*　　　　　　　　　　*kissed*
> **Then the candidate ~~walks~~ up to the crowd and ~~kisses~~ all the babies.**

 ESL Note　No *Will* in Time Clause

In a dependent clause beginning with a conjunction such as *if, when, before, after, until,* or *as soon as,* do not use *will* to express future time. Use *will* only in the independent clause. Use the simple present in the subordinate clause.

> When they ~~will~~ arrive, the meeting will begin. ■

PRESENT PROGRESSIVE Use the present progressive to indicate an action in progress at the moment of speaking or writing.

▶ Publishers *are getting* nervous about plagiarism.

LANGUAGE AND CULTURE
Language and Dialect Variation with Present Tense Forms of *Be*

In some languages (Chinese and Russian, for example), forms of *be* used as a present tense auxiliary ("She *is* singing") or as a linking verb ("He *is* happy") can be omitted. In some spoken dialects of English (African American Vernacular, for example), subtle linguistic distinctions not possible in Standard English can be achieved: the omission of a form of *be* and the use of the base form in place of an inflected form (a form that shows number, person, mood, or tense) signal entirely different meanings.

VERNACULAR		STANDARD
He busy.	(temporarily)	He is busy now.
She be busy.	(habitually)	She is busy all the time.

Standard English always requires the inclusion of a form of *be*.

▶ Latecomers _∧always at a disadvantage.
               are

PRESENT PERFECT AND PRESENT PERFECT PROGRESSIVE Use the present perfect in the following instances:

1. To indicate that an action occurring at some unstated time in the past is related to present time

   ▶ They *have worked* in New Mexico, so they know its laws.

2. To indicate that an action beginning in the past continues to the present

   ▶ She *has worked* as a paralegal for three years.

   However, if you state the exact time when something occurred, use the simple past tense, not the present perfect.

   ▶ They ~~have worked~~ in Arizona three years ago.
          worked

3. To report research results in APA style

▶ Feynmann *has shown* that science can be fun.

Use the present perfect progressive when you indicate the length of time an action has been in progress up to the present time.

▶ **Researchers have been searching for a cure for arthritis for many years.** [This implies that they are still searching.]

EXERCISE **16.2** Use present tenses correctly.
In the following sentences, correct any errors in the use of present tense verb forms. Some sentences may be correct. (**A** = See Answer Key.)

EXAMPLE:

do   *observe*
What ~~did~~ babies ~~observed~~ when they look at faces?
        ^   ^

A 1. Within a few hours of birth, newborn babies are showing a preference for looking at human faces.

A 2. Cognitive psychologists determine what has interested babies by measuring how long they look at certain patterns or objects.

3. Recent studies have shown that babies' brains have been forming the ability to differentiate faces by the time the babies are a few months old.

4. Scientists have not yet come to an agreement on whether babies are born with the ability to recognize faces or whether they are simply born with a preference for certain shapes and contours.

5. Scientific debate on the subject is raging, but as further studies will be completed, our understanding of how humans learn face recognition will continue to grow.

Past tenses   Use past tenses consistently. Do not switch to present or future for no reason. See 15d for more on avoiding tense shifts.

SIMPLE PAST   Use the simple past tense as follows:

1. To specify exactly when an event occurred or to illustrate a general principle with a specific incident in the past

▶ **World War I soldiers** *suffered* **in the trenches.**

▶ **Some bilingual schools offer intensive instruction in English. My sister** *went* **to a bilingual school where she** *studied* **English for two hours every day.**

When the sequence of past events is indicated with words like *before* or *after,* use the simple past for both events.

▶ She *knew* how to write her name before she *went* to school.

2. To indicate past time in an indirect quotation introduced by a past tense verb

▶ His chiropractor *told* him that the adjustments *were* over.

PAST PROGRESSIVE Use the past progressive for an activity in progress over time or at a specified point in the past.

▶ Abraham Lincoln *was attending* the theater when he was assassinated.

PAST PERFECT AND PAST PERFECT PROGRESSIVE Use the past perfect or the past perfect progressive only when one past event was completed before another past event or stated past time.

▶ Ben *had cooked* the whole meal by the time Sam arrived. [Two events occurred: Ben cooked the meal; then Sam arrived.]

▶ He *had been cooking* for three hours when his sister finally offered to help. [An event in progress—cooking—was interrupted in the past.]

Make sure that the past tense form you choose expresses your exact meaning.

▶ When the student protesters marched into the building at noon, the administrators *were leaving.* [The administrators were in the process of leaving. They began to leave at, say, 11:57 a.m.]

▶ When the student protesters marched into the building at noon, the administrators *had left.* [There was no sign of the administrators. They had left at 11 a.m.]

▶ When the student protesters marched into the building at noon, the administrators *left.* [The administrators saw the protesters and then left at 12:01 p.m.]

EXERCISE 16.3 Use past tenses correctly.
In the following passage, correct any errors in the use of past tense forms. Some sentences may be correct. (**A** = See Answer Key.)

EXAMPLE:

have been

Since the late 1970s, teenagers ~~were~~ buying every hip-hop record they can find.

A In 1973, Clive Campbell, a Jamaican immigrant who was living in the Bronx, New York, since 1967, christened himself "DJ Kool Herc" and begun to work as a neighborhood disc jockey. **A** During his childhood in Jamaica, Campbell saw performers known as *toasters* talking rhythmically over reggae music. **A** At dance parties in the Bronx, DJ Kool Herc had chanted rhymes while he played popular records. His favorite parts of the records, the parts that had made the crowds dance, were the instrumental breaks, some of which were lasting only fifteen seconds. Kool Herc began

DJ Kool Herc

buying two copies of the records with the best breaks and performing with two turntables, which he manipulated by hand so that the fifteen-second break could last as long as the crowd enjoyed it. DJ Kool Herc's innovation had been creating the music now known as hip-hop.

16d *-ed* endings: Past tense and past participle forms

Both the past tense form and the past participle of regular verbs end in *-ed*. This ending causes writers trouble because in speech the ending is often dropped—particularly when it blends into the next sound.

> *ed*
> ► They wash two baskets of laundry last night.
>   ^

Standard English requires the *-ed* ending in the following instances:

1. To form the past tense of a regular verb

> *ed*
> ► He ask to leave early.
>   ^

2. To form the expression *used to,* indicating past habit

> *d*
> ► Computers use to be more expensive than they are now.
>   ^

3. To form the past participle of a regular verb after the auxiliary *has, have,* or *had* in the active voice or after a form of *be* (*am, is, are, was, were, be, being, been*) in the passive voice (see 16g).

> *ed*
> ► The Kennedy family has work in politics for a long time.
>   ^
> [Active]

> Their work will not soon be finish^{ed}. [Passive]

4. To form a past participle to serve as an adjective

> The recipe calls for lean chop^{ped} meat.

> The frighten^{ed} soldier yelled to his commanding officer.

Note: The following *-ed* forms are used with *be*. Some can also be used with *get, seem, appear,* and *look.*

concerned	married	supposed (to)
confused	prejudiced	surprised
depressed	satisfied	used (to)
divorced	scared	worried
embarrassed		

Do not omit the *-ed* or *-d* ending.

> I was surprise^d to see how many awards they won.

> The general was suppose^d to be in charge.

> Parents get worr^{ied} when their children are depress^{ed}.

Do not confuse the past tense form and the past participle of an irregular verb. A past tense form always stands alone as a complete verb, but a past participle does not.

> They ~~done~~ ^{did} well.

> The skiers should not have ~~went~~ ^{gone} alone.

> The students ~~drunk~~ ^{drank} too much at the game.

EXERCISE 16.4 Use *-ed* endings correctly.
In the following sentences, edit errors in *-ed* forms of verbs. Some sentences may be correct. (**A** = See Answer Key.)

EXAMPLE:

Technology has ~~change~~ ^{changed} the classroom experience for many students.

A 1. College classrooms use to be seen as places where professors lectured to passive students, with only the most verbal students participating in discussions of the material.

A 2. Today, however, many professors have noticed the difference computers can make in their students' ability to join in class discussions.

3. For some courses, students are expose to Web sites filled with multimedia materials as well as to more typical readings on a given subject.

4. Before attending class, students are often ask to participate in e-mail discussions on a topic related to what they are studying; the discussions usually continue in the classroom.

5. Professors who once notice the same students doing all the talking in every class maintain that starting discussions in writing on a listserv is more likely to enable all students to participate.

16e Tenses in indirect quotations

An indirect quotation reports what someone said. It does not use quotation marks. When the verb introducing an indirect quotation is in a present tense, the indirect quotation should preserve the tense of the original direct quotation. See also 15d and 35d.

DIRECT **"The client *has signed* the contract."**

INDIRECT **The lawyer *tells* us that the client *has signed* the contract.**

When the introductory verb is in a past tense, use forms that express past time in the indirect quotation.

DIRECT **"The meetings are over and the buyer has signed the contract."**

INDIRECT **Our lawyer *told* us that the meetings *were* over and the buyer *had signed* the contract.**

In a passage of more than one sentence, preserve the sequence of tenses showing past time throughout the whole indirect quotation.

▶ **Our lawyer, Larraine, told us that the meetings *were* over and the buyer *had signed* the contract. Larraine's firm *had reassigned* her to another case, so she *was leaving* the next day.**

Note: Use a present tense after a past tense introductory verb only if the statement is a general statement that holds true in present time.

▶ Our lawyer *told* us she *is* happy with the progress of the case.

EXERCISE 16.5 Use the correct tense in indirect quotations. In the following sentences, correct any errors in verb tense. Some sentences may be correct. (**A** = See Answer Key.)

EXAMPLE:

                                 had

In 1996, two sportsmen reported that they ~~have~~ found a human skeleton in a riverbank in Kennewick, Washington.

A 1. James Chatters, the forensic anthropologist who examined the bones, at first believed that the skeleton is a modern murder victim.

A 2. He then told authorities that he had noticed a prehistoric arrowhead embedded in the skeleton's pelvic bone.

3. After the skeleton had been determined to be over 9,000 years old, Native American groups announced that they want to rebury the bones.

4. Tribal leaders claim that the bones were those of an ancient tribal ancestor.

5. Many scientists argue that the skull's features did not resemble a Native American's face and that researchers needed to study the bones to find out all they could about the history of ancient peoples in this country.

16f Verbs in conditional sentences, wishes, requests, demands, and recommendations

Conditions When *if* or *unless* is used to introduce a dependent clause, the sentence expresses a condition. Four types of conditional sentences are used: two refer to actual or possible situations, and two refer to speculative or hypothetical situations.

USE OF SUBJUNCTIVE *WERE* IN PLACE OF *WAS* With speculative conditions (item 3 in the Key Points box) about the present and future using the verb *be*, *were* is used in place of *was* in the dependent *if* clause. This use of *were* to indicate hypothetical situations involves what is called the *subjunctive mood*.

▶ If my aunt *were* sixty-five, she *could get* a discount air fare. [My aunt is sixty.]

KEY POINTS

Verb Tenses in Conditional Sentences

Meaning Expressed	*If* Clause	Independent Clause
1. Fact	Simple present	Simple present

▶ If people *earn* more, they *spend* more.

▶ If mortgage rates *go* down, house sales *increase*.

2. Prediction/ possibility	Simple present	*will, can, should, might* + base form

▶ If you *turn* left here, you *will end up* in Mississippi.

▶ If you *continue* making progress, you *can get* an A.

3. Speculation about present or future	Simple past *or* subjunctive *were*	*would, could, should, might* + base form

▶ If he *had* a cell phone, he *would* use it.   [But he does not have one.]

▶ If she *were* my lawyer, I *might win* the case.   [But she is not.]

4. Speculation about past	Past perfect (*had* + past participle)	*would have could have should have might have* } + past participle

▶ If they *had saved* the diaries, they *could have sold* them. [But they did not save them.]

BLENDING   Some blending of time and tenses can occur, as in the case of a condition that speculates about the past in relation to the effect on the present.

▶ If I *had bought* a new car instead of this old wreck, I *would feel* a lot safer today.

USE OF *WOULD*   When writing Standard English, use *would* only in the independent clause, not in the conditional clause. However, *would* occurs frequently in the conditional clause in speech and in informal writing.

> If the fish fry committee ~~would show~~ ^{showed} more initiative, people might attend their events more regularly.

> If the driver ~~would have~~ ^{had} heard what the pedestrian said, he would have been angry.

***WOULD, COULD,* AND *MIGHT* WITH CONDITIONAL CLAUSE UNDERSTOOD** *Would, could,* and *might* are used in independent clauses when no conditional clause is present. These are situations that are contrary to fact, and the conditional clause is understood.

> I *would* never *advise* her to leave college without a degree. She *might come back* later and blame me for her lack of direction.

Wishes Like some conditions, wishes deal with speculation. For a present wish—about something that has not happened and is therefore hypothetical and imaginary—use the past tense or subjunctive *were* in the dependent clause. For a wish about the past, use the past perfect: *had* + past participle.

A WISH ABOUT THE PRESENT

> I wish I *had* your attitude.

> I wish that Shakespeare *were* still alive.

A WISH ABOUT THE PAST

> Some union members wish that the strike *had* never *occurred.*

> He wishes that he *had bought* a lottery ticket.

Requests, demands, and recommendations The subjunctive also appears after verbs such as *request, command, insist, demand, move* (meaning "propose"), *propose,* and *urge.* In these cases, the verb in the dependent clause is the base form, regardless of the person and number of the subject.

> The dean suggested that students *be* allowed to vote.

> He insisted that she *submit* the report.

> I move that the treasurer *revise* the budget.

Some idiomatic expressions preserve the subjunctive in standard English—for example, *far* be *it from me, if need* be, *as it* were.

EXERCISE 16.6 Use correct verb tenses in conditional sentences. In the following sentences, correct any errors in the use of verb tenses. Then identify which of the four types of conditional sentences the item represents. (**A** = See Answer Key.)

EXAMPLE:

ate

If domestic dogs ~~would eat~~ **the same diet that their wild ancestors ate, they might not have tooth and gum problems.**

#3 Speculation about the present (hypothetical situation)

A 1. If prehistoric canines would have eaten crunchy, bite-sized food, they would probably have lost most of their teeth at an early age.

A 2. If dogs eat commercial dog food, plaque will tend to collect on their teeth.

3. If people would allow their pet dogs to forage for their own food, the canines might develop stronger teeth.

4. Unless pet owners managed to brush their dogs' teeth daily—which is difficult to do, even with a cooperative dog—their pets will develop gum diseases and lose their teeth, just as humans do.

5. Veterinarians believe that if commercial kibble was made with larger pieces and a chewier texture, it could clean dogs' teeth effectively.

16g Active and passive voice

In the active voice, the grammatical subject is the doer of the action, and the sentence tells "who's doing what." The passive voice, on the other hand, tells what "is done" to the subject of the sentence. The person or thing doing the action may or may not be mentioned but is always implied: "My car has been repaired [by somebody at the garage]."

ACTIVE

┌── subject ──┐ active voice verb ┌── direct object ──┐
▶ **Alice Walker** **wrote** *The Color Purple.*

PASSIVE

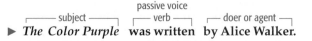

┌──── subject ────┐ passive voice verb ┌── doer or agent ──┐
▶ *The Color Purple* **was written** **by Alice Walker.**

ESL Note Passive Voice with Transitive Verbs

Use the passive voice only with verbs that are transitive in English. Intransitive verbs such as *happen, occur,* and *try (to)* are not used in the passive voice.

▶ The accident ~~was~~ happened yesterday.

                 have

▶ Morality is an issue that ~~was~~ tried to explain ~~by~~ many philosophers.

When to use the passive voice Use the passive voice sparingly. However, do use it specifically in two cases.

1. Use the passive voice when the doer or agent in your sentence (the person or thing acting) is unknown or is unimportant. This use is common in scientific writing.

   ▶ **The pandas are rare. Two of them will be returned to the wild.** [It is not important to mention who will return the pandas to the wild.]

2. Use the passive voice to establish a topic chain from one clause or sentence to another.

   ▶ **He had a lot of people working for him, maybe sixty, and most of them liked him most of the time. Three of them** *will be* **seriously** *considered* **for his job.**

                  —Ellen Goodman, "The Company Man"

   [The idea of *people* in the first sentence sets up the need for the subject *three of them,* which necessitates the passive voice verb.]

   ▶ **I remember to start with that day in Sacramento . . . when I first entered a classroom, able to understand some fifty stray English words. The third of four children, I** *had been preceded* **to a Roman Catholic school by an older brother and sister.**

                  —Richard Rodriguez, *Hunger of Memory*

   [The passive voice preserves the chain of *I* subjects.]

For more on using the passive voice to make old and new information connect well, see 8c, item 1.

How to form the passive voice The complete verb of a passive voice sentence consists of a form of the verb *be* followed by a past participle.

               verb: *be* +

    receiver   past participle   doer omitted or named after *by*

  ┌— as subject —┐ ┌—————┐

▶ **The windows are cleaned (by someone) every month.**

With different tenses, note the forms of the verb in the passive transformations:

Tenses: Active and Passive

Tense	Active Voice	Passive Voice
Simple present	Someone *cleans* the windows every month.	The windows *are cleaned* every month.
Present progressive	Someone *is cleaning* the windows right now.	The windows *are being cleaned* right now.
Present perfect	Someone *has* just *cleaned* the windows.	The windows *have* just *been cleaned*.
Present perfect progressive	Someone *has been cleaning* the windows for hours now.	[rare]
Simple past	Someone *cleaned* the windows yesterday.	The windows *were cleaned* yesterday.
Past progressive	Someone *was cleaning* the windows all yesterday afternoon.	The windows *were being cleaned* all yesterday afternoon.
Past perfect	Someone *had cleaned* the windows before the family moved in.	The windows *had been cleaned* before the family moved in.
Past perfect progressive	Someone *had been cleaning* the windows for several hours when the wedding began.	[rare]
Simple future	Someone *will clean* the windows tomorrow.	The windows *will be cleaned* tomorrow.
Future progressive	Someone *will be cleaning* the windows during the meeting this afternoon.	[rare]
Future perfect	Someone *will have cleaned* the windows by the end of the workday.	The windows *will have been cleaned* by the end of the workday.

Tense	Active Voice	Passive Voice
Future perfect progressive	Someone *will have been cleaning* the windows for eight hours by the time the caterers arrive.	[rare]

Auxiliaries such as *would, can, could, should, may, might,* and *must* can also replace *will* when the meaning demands it.

▶ The windows *might be cleaned* next month.

▶ The windows *should have been cleaned* already.

Caution with the passive voice In the humanities especially, your writing will be stronger if you name the subject and use verbs in the active voice to tell "who's doing what." If you overuse the passive voice, the effect will be heavy and impersonal (see also 8b, item 3).

UNNECESSARY PASSIVE
He *was alerted* to the danger of drugs by his doctor and *was persuaded* by her to enroll in a treatment program.

REVISED
His doctor *alerted* him to the danger of drugs and *persuaded* him to enroll in a treatment program.

EXERCISE 16.7 Identify active and passive voices.
In the following sentences, write *P* on the line before each sentence that uses the passive voice and *A* before each sentence that is in the active voice. Then rewrite each passive voice sentence as active whenever it is advisable to do so and underline the verb that you changed. (**A** = See Answer Key.)

EXAMPLE:

Each acre of the fertile rice fields
of southern China yields more
___P___ ~~More~~ than a thousand pounds of rice ~~is yielded by each acre of the fertile rice fields of southern China.~~

A 1. _____ The sticky rice that brings the highest prices in China is often attacked by rice blast, a fungus that destroys the rice crop.

A 2. _____ A farmer in Yunnan province discovered that he could nearly eliminate rice blast by planting alternating rows of sticky rice and long-grain rice.

3. _____ The technique of alternating rows of rice was then adopted widely.

4. _____ The application of expensive and toxic fungicides that had been used to fight the rice blast was discontinued by most farmers.

5. _____ Healthier fields, bigger rice yields, and more money for the farmers were subsequently produced by this low-tech, environmentally sound agricultural method.

17 Subject-Verb Agreement

A third person singular subject (*he, she, it*) in some tenses will need a specific third person form of the verb.

17a Basic principles for an -s ending

When you use the present tense, subject and verb must agree in person (first, second, or third) and number (singular or plural). In English, the ending -*s* is added to both nouns and verbs, but for very different reasons.

KEY POINTS

Two Key Points about Agreement

1. Follow the "one -*s* rule." Generally, you can put an -*s* on a noun to make it plural, or you can put an -*s* on a verb to make it singular. (But see the irregular forms *is* and *has*, on p. 211.) An -*s* added to both subject and verb is not Standard English.

FAULTY AGREEMENT	**My friends comes over every Saturday.** [Violates the "one -*s* rule"]
POSSIBLE REVISIONS	**My friend comes over every Saturday.**
	My friends come over every Saturday.

2. Do not omit a necessary -*s*.

   ▶ His supervisor want him to work the night shift.
   (s)

   ▶ The book on my desk describe life in Tahiti.
   (s)

   ▶ She *uses* her experience, *speaks* to the crowds, and *win* their confidence.
   (s)

Most simple present verbs add an -s ending for a third person singular subject. The verb *be* has three instead of two present tense forms (*am, is,* and *are*) and is the only verb to show agreement in the past tense, where it has two forms: *were* and the first and third person singular *was.*

Subject-Verb Agreement

BASE FORM	like (regular)	have	be	do
SIMPLE PRESENT: SINGULAR				
First person: I	like	have	am	do
Second person: you	like	have	are	do
Third person: he, she, it	likes	has	is	does
SIMPLE PRESENT: PLURAL				
First person: we	like	have	are	do
Second person: you	like	have	are	do
Third person: they	like	have	are	do

17b Subject separated from verb

When words separate the subject and verb, find the verb and ask "Who?" or "What?" about it to determine if the subject is singular or plural. Ignore the intervening words. See also 12b.

▶ **The child picking flowers looks tired.** [Who looks tired? The subject, *child*, is singular.]

▶ **Her collection of baseball cards is valuable.** [What is valuable? The subject, *collection*, is singular.]

▶ **The government's proposals about preserving the environment cause controversy.** [What things cause controversy? The subject, *proposals*, is plural.]

Do not be confused by intervening words ending in -s, such as *always* and *sometimes.* The -s ending still must appear on a present tense verb if the subject is singular.

▶ His assistant always make mistakes.
           s

Phrases introduced by *as well as, along with,* and *in addition to* that come between the subject and the verb do not change the number of the verb.

▶ His daughter, as well as his two sons, want him to move nearby.
                                         s

LANGUAGE AND CULTURE
Issues of Subject-Verb Agreement

Many languages make no change in the verb form to indicate number and person, and several spoken versions of English, such as African American Vernacular (AAV), Caribbean Creole, and London Cockney, do not observe the standard rules of agreement.

▶ AAV: She *have* a lot of work experience.

▶ Cockney: He *don't* never wear that brown whistle.   [The standard form is *doesn't*; other nonstandard forms in this sentence are *don't never* (a double negative) and *whistle*— short for *whistle and flute*, rhyming slang for *suit*.]

Use authentic forms like these when quoting direct speech; for formal academic writing, though, follow the subject-verb agreement conventions of Standard English.

EXERCISE 17.1   Ignore words between the subject and verb.
In the following sentences, underline the simple subject. Then correct any errors in subject-verb agreement. (**A** = See Answer Key.)

EXAMPLE:

Environmentalists in the United States and Canada

                    have
finally h̶a̶s̶ some good news about the pollution in the
                    ^

Great Lakes.

A 1. An international agency monitoring the air and water quality around the Great Lakes have discovered a previously unknown ecological process.

A 2. Toxic chemicals banned for at least a quarter of a century is dispersing from the lakes into the air.

3. Since 1992, Lake Ontario, along with the other lakes, have released tons of PCBs and other dangerous chemicals in a self-cleaning process.

4. Massive pollution in the enormous lakes were first brought to public attention thirty years ago, and pollution remains a serious problem there.

5. The lakes' "exhaling," according to researchers, help to clean the water without posing any danger to human beings.

17c Subject after verb

When the subject follows the verb in the sentence, make the subject and verb agree.

1. Questions In a question, the auxiliary verb agrees with the subject.

singular
subject
► *Does* the editor agree to the changes?

plural
subject
► *Do* the editors approve?

plural subject
► *Do* the editor and the production manager agree to them?

2. Initial *here* or *there* When a sentence begins with *here* or *there,* the verb agrees with the subject.

singular
subject
► There *is* a reason to rejoice.

plural subject
► There *are* many reasons to rejoice.

However, avoid excessive use of initial *there* (see 8b): *We have a reason to rejoice.*

ESL Note Agreement with Subject *It*

It does not follow the same pattern as *here* and *there.* The verb in a sentence beginning with *it* is always singular.

► It *looks* like a good match.

► It *is* hundreds of miles away. ■

3. Inverted word order When a sentence begins not with the subject but with a phrase preceding the verb, the verb still agrees with the subject.

plural
prepositional phrase — verb — plural subject
► **In front of the library sit two stone lions.** [Who or what performs the action of the verb? Two stone lions do.]

17d Agreement with a linking verb

Linking verbs such as *be, seem, look,* and *appear* agree with the subject, not with the complement that follows.

plural
┌── subject ──┐
▶ **Rare books are her passion.**
plural verb

singular
┌── subject ──┐
▶ **Her passion is rare books.**
singular verb

▶ **My favorite part of city life *is* the many parties.**

▶ **The many parties *are* my favorite part of city life.**

EXERCISE 17.2 Make subjects and verbs agree.
In the following passage, underline the simple subject in each clause. Then correct any errors in subject-verb agreement. (**A** = See Answer Key.)

EXAMPLE:

    are
There ~~is~~ many security <u>questions</u> involved in cryptography.
     ^

    A Do the government have the right to keep certain kinds of information out of the hands of the public? **A** There is no easy answers to this question. **A** When the science of cryptography was being developed, the National Security Agency wanted to restrict access to powerful, unbreakable codes. **A** After all, using codes are one way that a government keeps information from its enemies, and breaking codes allows a government to find out what its enemies are planning. **A** NSA agents worried that unbreakable codes would allow enemies of the United States to conceal their activities from U.S. intelligence. Cryptographers won the right to develop and distribute their new codes to the general public, and unbreakable codes have certainly been a boon to the computer science and communications industries. Does these codes also hamper efforts to discover what terrorists are doing? Probably, say cryptographers. However, technologies that scientists decide not to develop out of fear of the results is a potential danger: If someone else develops these technologies, they can be used against anyone who has not considered their potential. There is dangers in cryptography, but perhaps there is even more problems in avoiding the issue. Somewhere in the future is the answers to these and other urgent security questions.

17e Tricky subjects

1. *Each* and *every* *Each* and *every* may seem to indicate more than one, but grammatically they are singular words. Use them with a singular verb.

▶ Each of the cakes *has* a different frosting.

▶ Every change in procedures *causes* problems.

2. *-ing* verb form as subject With a subject beginning with the *-ing* verb form used as a noun (called a *gerund,* see 12d), always use a singular verb form.

singular
┌ subject ┐
▶ Playing the piano in front of a crowd *causes* anxiety.

3. Singular nouns ending in *-s* Some nouns that end in *-s* (*news, economics, physics, politics, mathematics, statistics*) are not plural. Use them with a singular verb.

▶ The news *has* been bad lately.   ▶ Politics *is* dirty business.

4. Phrases of time, money, and weight When the subject is regarded as one unit, use a singular verb.

▶ Five hundred dollars *seems* too much to pay.

▶ Seven years *was* a long time to spend at college.

But

▶ Seven years *have* passed.

5. Uncountable nouns An uncountable noun (*furniture, jewelry, equipment, advice, happiness, honesty, information, knowledge*) encompasses all the items in its class. An uncountable noun does not have a plural form and is always followed by a singular verb (33b).

▶ That advice *makes* me nervous.

▶ The information found in the press *is* not always accurate.

6. *One of* *One of* is followed by a plural noun (the object of the preposition *of*) and a singular verb form. The verb agrees with the subject *one,* not with the object of the preposition *of.*

▶ *One* of her friends *loves* to tango.

▶ *One* of the reasons for his difficulties *is* that he spends too much money.

For agreement with *one of … who* and *the only one of … who,* see 20b.

7. The number of/a number of The phrase *the number of* is followed by a plural noun (the object of the preposition *of*) and a singular verb form.

▶ The number of reasons *is* growing.

However, with the phrase *a number of,* meaning "several," use a plural verb.

▶ A number of reasons *are* listed in the letter.

8. The title of a work or a word referred to as the word itself Use a singular verb with the title of a work or a word referred to as the word itself. Use a singular verb even if the title or word is plural in form.

▶ *Cats has* finally ended its long run on Broadway.

▶ In her story, the word *dudes appears* five times.

9. Percent Use a singular or plural verb, according to how the quantity is perceived.

▶ Forty percent of available housing *is* owned by the city.

▶ Polls report that 10 percent of the voters *are* undecided.

10. Possessive pronoun as subject Possessive pronouns such as *mine, his, hers, ours, yours,* and *theirs* can refer to either singular or plural antecedents (see 18b).

singular
subject singular verb
▶ Her average *is* good, but *mine is* better.

plural
subject plural verb
▶ His grades are good, but *mine are* better.

11. Clauses beginning with what When a whole clause introduced by *what* functions as the subject of the independent clause, its verb should be singular.

subject
▶ What they are proposing *concerns* us all.

When the verb is followed by the linking verb *be* and a plural complement, some writers use a plural verb: *What I need* are *black pants and an orange shirt*. However, some readers may find this strange. You can avoid the issue by revising the sentence to eliminate the *what* clause: *I need black pants and an orange shirt*.

17f Collective nouns

Generally, use a singular verb with a collective noun (*class, government, family, jury, committee, group, couple, team*) if you are referring to the group as a whole.

▶ **My family *goes* on vacation every year.**

Use a plural verb if you wish to emphasize differences among individuals or if members of the group are thought of as individuals.

▶ **His family *are* mostly artists and musicians.**

▶ **The jury *are* from every walk of life.**

If that usage seems awkward, revise the sentence.

▶ **His close relatives *are* mostly artists and musicians.**

▶ **The members of the jury *are* from every walk of life.**

Some collective nouns, such as *police, poor, elderly*, and *young*, always take plural verbs.

▶ **The elderly *deserve* our respect.**

EXERCISE 17.3 Make verbs agree with tricky subjects and collective nouns.

In the following sentences, underline the simple subject of each independent clause and correct any errors in subject-verb agreement. (**A** = See Answer Key.)

EXAMPLE:

Every possible <u>complaint</u> about the violence of soccer

  has
players and their fans ~~have~~ been made at one time or
                    ^

another since the sport began around 1100 C.E.

A 1. To play soccer, a team need few things other than a ball, a field, and a group of opponents.

A 2. When medieval British warriors defeated a Danish chieftain on the battlefield a millennium ago, their kicking the loser's head around the bloody fields were the origin of soccer, according to a hard-to-prove legend.

3. There was still violent aspects of the game in the 1100s when whole towns, each with hundreds of players, competed against each other on fields several miles long.

4. One of the signs that soccer would eventually be the world's most popular sport were that soccer was banned repeatedly in fourteenth- and fifteenth-century England; a number of kings was worried that soldiers who played soccer would not spend enough time at archery practice.

5. Modern soccer follows rules drawn up at Cambridge University in 1863, but the sport's following among some devoted but aggressive fans have ensured that soccer's bloody reputation does not disappear entirely.

17g Subjects with *and, or,* and *nor*

With *and* When a subject consists of two or more parts joined by *and*, treat the subject as plural and use a plural verb.

▶ His instructor and his adviser *want* him to change his major.

plural subject — plural verb

However, if the parts of the compound subject refer to a single person or thing, use a singular verb.

▶ The restaurant's chef and owner *makes* good fajitas.

singular subject (one person) — singular verb

▶ Fish and chips *is* a popular dish in England, but it is no longer served wrapped in newspaper.

singular subject — singular verb

With *each* or *every* When *each* or *every* is part of a compound subject, the verb is singular.

▶ Every toy and game *has* to be put away.

▶ Each plate and glass *looks* new.

With *or* or *nor* When the parts of a compound subject are joined by *or* or *nor*, the verb agrees with the part nearer to it.

▶ Her sister or her parents *plan* to visit her next week.

▶ Neither her parents nor her sister *drives* a station wagon.

EXERCISE 17.4 Use correct subject-verb agreement with compound subjects.

In the following sentences, underline the subject or subjects of each independent clause, and correct any errors in subject-verb agreement. Some sentences may be correct. (**A** = See Answer Key.)

EXAMPLE:

Every statue, painting, and photograph of human beings

is
~~are~~ **forbidden by fundamentalist factions of Islam.**

A 1. In the Bamiyan valley of eastern Afghanistan, a 150-foot Buddha, believed to have been the largest standing Buddha in the world, and a 120-foot Buddha was carved out of sandstone cliffs in the fourth or fifth century.

A 2. During that period, when the Silk Route wound through the mountains of Afghanistan, wandering Buddhist monks or a caravan of silk or ivory merchants was a common sight in the Bamiyan valley, which was home to Buddhist monasteries until the arrival of Islam in the ninth century.

Bamiyan Buddha

3. The Buddhas of Bamiyan and other art from Afghanistan's non-Islamic past was destroyed by order of Taliban leaders in March 2001.

4. A Taliban commander and leader of the operation to destroy the statues were reported to have said that the statues represented a woman and her husband.

5. Neither the protests before the destruction of the Buddhas nor the global outrage expressed afterward were enough to convince Taliban leaders that the Buddhas had been an important part of Afghan history.

17h Indefinite pronouns

Words that refer to nonspecific people or things (indefinite pronouns) can be tricky. Most of them take a singular verb. Usage may differ in speech and writing, so when you write, it is important to pay attention to Standard English usage.

Indefinite pronouns used with a singular verb

anybody	everybody	nothing
anyone	everyone	somebody
anything	everything	someone
each	nobody	something
either	no one	

▶ Nobody *knows* the answer.

▶ Someone *has* been sitting on my chair.

▶ Everyone *agrees* on the author's intention.

▶ Everything about the results *was* questioned in the review.

▶ Each of the chairs *costs* more than $300.

See 18d on personal pronouns to use (*he? she? they?*) to refer to indefinite pronouns.

A note on *none* and *neither*

NONE Some writers prefer to use a singular verb after *none (of)*, because *none* means "not one": *None of the contestants has smiled.* However, as *The American Heritage Dictionary* (4th ed.) points out, a singular or a plural verb is technically acceptable: *None of the authorities has (or have) greater tolerance on this point than H. W. Fowler.* Check to see if your instructor prefers the literal singular usage.

NEITHER The pronoun *neither* is, like *none*, technically singular: *The partners have made a decision; neither wants to change the product.* In informal writing, however, *neither* may occur with a plural verb, especially when followed by an *of* phrase: *Neither of the novels reveal a polished style.*

17i Quantity words

Some quantity words are singular; some are plural; some can be used to indicate either singular or plural, depending on the noun they refer to.

Words Expressing Quantity

With Singular Nouns and Verbs	With Plural Nouns and Verbs
much	many
(a) little	(a) few
a great deal (of)	several
less	fewer
another	both
every	all

See the Glossary of Usage for the difference between *few* and *a few*.

▶ Much *has* been accomplished.

▶ Much of the machinery *needs* to be repaired.

▶ Many *have* gained from the recent stock market rise.

▶ Few of his fans *are* buying his recent book.

You will see and hear *less* used in place of *fewer,* but in formal writing, use only *fewer* to refer to a plural word.

▶ More *movies* have been made this year than last, but *fewer have* made money.

The following quantity words can be used with either singular or plural nouns and verbs: *all, any, half (of), more, most, no, other, part (of), some.*

▶ You gave me *some information. More* is necessary.

▶ You gave me *some facts. More are* needed.

▶ *All the furniture is* old.

▶ *All the students look* healthy.

EXERCISE 17.5 Use correct subject-verb agreement with indefinite pronouns and quantity words.
In the following sentences, choose the verb that agrees with the subject, and underline the subject. (**A** = See Answer Key.)

EXAMPLE:

<u>Nothing</u> (was / ~~were~~) dearer to Edward Gorey than the New York City Ballet, except perhaps his six cats.

A 1. Many of the small, hand-lettered, meticulously illustrated books by Edward Gorey (concerns / concern) macabre events, yet most of Gorey's stories (is / are) hilarious.

A 2. In the story "The Wuggly Ump," for example, every human character (ends up / end up) being eaten by the title monster, yet the tale itself looks and sounds like a Victorian nursery rhyme.

3. Anyone who saw Gorey in person (is / are) sure to remember the tall, bearded man in a floor-length fur coat and sneakers, dressed like one of the odd characters that he drew.

4. Several interviewers and critics (was / were) able to talk to the eccentric writer, illustrator, and designer before his death in 2000, and a great deal (has been / have been) written about the intersections of his life and his art.

5. Gorey admitted that some of his eccentricity (was / were) genuine although some of his behaviors (was / were) deliberately cultivated for shock value.

It would carry off objects of which it grew fond,
And protect them by dropping them into the pond.

Illustration from *The Doubtful Guest* by Edward Gorey

Illustration © 1957 Edward Gorey. Used with permission of the Estate of Edward Gorey.

18　Pronouns

A pronoun is a word that substitutes for a noun, a noun phrase, or another pronoun (see 12c).

▶ Jack's hair is so long that *it* hangs over *his* collar.

18a　Personal pronouns (*I* or *me*, *he* or *him*)

Personal pronouns change form to indicate person (first, second, or third), number (singular or plural), and function in a clause.

In a compound subject or compound object with *and*: *I* or *me*; *he* or *him*?　To decide which pronoun form to use with a compound subject or compound object, mentally recast the sentence with only the pronoun in the subject or object position.

He
┌──── subject ────┐   ┌──── object ────┐ me

▶ ~~Him~~ and his sister invited my cousin and ~~I~~ to their party.
         ^   ^

[He invited me.]

KEY POINTS

Summary of Forms of Personal Pronouns

Person	Subject	Object	Possessive (+ Noun)	Possessive (Stands Alone)	Intensive and Reflexive
1st person singular	I	me	my	mine	myself
2nd person singular and plural	you	you	your	yours	yourself/ yourselves
3rd person singular	he she it	him her it	his her its	his hers its [rare]	himself herself itself
1st person plural	we	us	our	ours	ourselves
3rd person plural	they	them	their	theirs	themselves

                I

▶ **Jenny and ~~me~~ went to the movies.** [If *Jenny* is dropped, you
would say *I went to the movies*, not *me went to the movies*. Here
you need the subject form, *I*.]

     She   I

▶ **~~Her~~ and ~~me~~ have solved the problem.** [She has solved the
problem. I have solved the problem.]

Sometimes people who are not sure of the use of *I* or *me* in the subject position get anxious and overcorrect from *me* to *I* in the object
position, too—and make another error.

                        me

▶ **They told my brother and ~~I~~ to wait in line.** [If *my brother* is
dropped, you would say, *They told me to wait in line*. Here you
need the object form, *me*.]

After a preposition After a preposition, you need an object form.

         me
▶ Between you and ~~I~~, the company is in serious trouble.

                      me
▶ Rachid stared at my colleague and ~~I~~.   [He stared at my colleague. He stared at me.]

After a linking verb In formal academic writing, use the subject form of a personal pronoun after a linking verb such as *be, seem, look,* or *appear.*

▶ Was that Toni Morrison? It was *she.*   [Informal: "It was her."]

▶ It was *she* who sent the flowers.   [Many writers would revise this sentence to sound less formal: "She was the one who sent the flowers."]

After a verb and before an infinitive Use the object form of a personal pronoun after a verb and before an infinitive. When a sentence has only one object, this principle is easy to apply.

▶ The dean wanted *him* to lead the procession.

Difficulties occur with compound objects.

                  him and me
▶ The dean wanted ~~he and I~~ to lead the procession.

In appositive phrases and with *we* or *us* before a noun When using a personal pronoun in an appositive phrase (a phrase that gives additional information about a preceding noun), determine whether the noun that the pronoun refers to functions as subject or as object in its own clause.

               — direct object   appositive phrase
▶ The supervisor praised only two employees, Ramon and me.

      — subject   appositive phrase
▶ Only two employees, Ramon and I, received a bonus.

Similarly, when you consider whether to use *we* or *us* before a noun, use *us* when the pronoun is the direct object of a verb or the object of a preposition, *we* when it is the subject.

          object of preposition
▶ LL Cool J waved to us fans.
   subject
▶ We fans have decided to form a club.

In comparisons When writing comparisons with *than* and *as,* decide on the subject or object form of the personal pronoun by mentally completing the meaning of the comparison. See also 19g.

▶ **She is certainly not more intelligent than I.** [. . . than I am]

▶ **Jack and Sally work in the same office; Jack criticizes his boss more than she.** [. . . more than Sally does.]

▶ **Jack and Sally work in the same office; Jack criticizes his boss more than her.** [. . . more than he criticizes Sally.]

EXERCISE 18.1 Use the correct form of personal pronouns. In the following passage, correct any errors in the form of personal pronouns. (**A** = See Answer Key.)

EXAMPLE:

Although Marie and Pierre Curie made important scientific

discoveries, both ~~her~~ and ~~him~~ spent years being unable to
       she   *he*

afford a decent laboratory to work in.

A Marie Curie, born Maria Sklodowska in Poland in 1867, devoted her life to pure science in the hope that humans would benefit from what she discovered. **A** Her parents, poor teachers, wanted she and her siblings to get an education. **A** Marie went to Paris to study at the Sorbonne when she was twenty-four; her work as a governess had earned her enough money to educate she and her older sister. **A** Marie struggled to learn French and overcome her deficient early education in physics and mathematics—subjects that girls in Poland such as her and her sister had not been

Marie and Pierre Curie

allowed to study. ▲When she completed her master's degree in physics in 1894, she placed first in her class. ▲Pierre Curie, who was doing research on magnetism, and her met when Marie was searching for a laboratory she could use. ▲Although Pierre did not have space for Marie in his lab, him and her fell in love and married.

The Curies did much of their innovative research in a small lab set up in an abandoned shed because both she and him believed that scientists should not waste valuable research time trying to make money. Marie did work on uranium and thorium, and it was her who invented the term *radioactivity*. In 1903, three scientists, Pierre and her, along with Henri Becquerel, shared the Nobel Prize in Physics. At around the same time, Pierre and Marie discovered the elements polonium (named after Marie's homeland) and radium. In 1911, after her husband's death, an unprecedented second Nobel Prize, this time in chemistry, was awarded to she alone. Marie Curie died in 1934 as a result of years of exposure to radiation, but her legacy continued. The Curies' daughter Irene, who had learned physics and chemistry from Marie and was nearly as skilled in scientific research as her, shared a Nobel Prize in Chemistry with her husband, Frederic Joliot-Curie, in 1935.

18b Possessive forms (*my* or *mine, her* or *hers*)

Distinguish between the adjective form of the possessive personal pronoun and the pronoun itself, standing alone.

▶ **The large room with three windows is *her* office.**   [*Her* is an adjective.]

▶ **The office is *hers*.**   [*Hers*, the possessive pronoun, can stand alone.]

Note: The word *mine* does not follow the pattern of *hers, theirs, yours,* and *ours*. The form *mines* is not Standard English.

mine.
▶ **The little room on the left is ~~mines.~~**
⌃

When a possessive pronoun functions as a subject, its antecedent determines singular or plural agreement for the verb. See 17e, item 10.

▶ **My shirt is cotton; hers *is* silk.**   [Singular antecedent and singular verb]

▶ **My gloves are black; hers *are* yellow.** [Plural antecedent and plural verb]

Possessive pronoun before an *-ing* form Generally, use a possessive personal pronoun before an *-ing* verb form used as a noun (a gerund).

▶ **We would appreciate *your* participating in the auction.**

▶ **We were surprised at *their* winning the marathon.**

Sometimes, though, the *-ing* form is a participle functioning as an adjective. In that case, the pronoun preceding the *-ing* form should be the object form.

▶ **We saw *them* giving the runners foil wraps.**

No apostrophe with possessive personal pronouns Even though possessive in meaning, the pronouns *yours, ours, theirs, his,* and *hers* should never be spelled with an apostrophe. Use an apostrophe only with the possessive form of a noun (25b).

▶ **That coat is *Maria's*.**   ▶ **These books are the *twins'*.**

▶ **That is *her* coat.**   ▶ **These are *their* books.**

▶ **That coat is *hers*.**   ▶ **These books are *theirs*.**

No apostrophe with *its* as a possessive pronoun An apostrophe is never used with *its,* the possessive form of the pronoun *it* (see also 25e). The word *it's* is not a pronoun; it is the contraction of *it is* or *it has.*

▶ **The paint has lost *its* gloss.**

▶ **It's not as glossy as it used to be.** [It is not as glossy . . .]

Comparisons using possessive forms Note how using *them* in place of *theirs* in the following sentence would change the meaning by comparing suitcases to roommates, not suitcases to suitcases.

▶ **It's really hard to be roommates with people if your suitcases are much better than *theirs*.**

—J. D. Salinger, *The Catcher in the Rye*

Forgetting to use the appropriate possessive form in the next example, too, could create a misunderstanding: Are you comparing a house to a person, or his house to her house?

▶ **I like his house more than I like her.**

EXERCISE 18.2 Use the correct possessive pronoun form.
In the following sentences, correct any errors in the use of possessive forms of pronouns. Some sentences may be correct. (**A** = See Answer Key.)

EXAMPLE:

Bonhoeffer tried to convince other Germans to oppose Nazi

views of racial purity, and ~~him~~ his playing gospel records in
Nazi Germany required courage.

A 1. When Dietrich Bonhoeffer was a visiting pastor at Harlem's Abyssinian Baptist Church in 1931, the congregation was pleased with him learning to love gospel music.

A 2. As a white German Protestant among African American worshippers, Bonhoeffer at first worried that his life was too different from them.

3. When Bonhoeffer returned to Germany, something of their's went with him: members of the church gave him several gospel records.

4. Dietrich Bonhoeffer's opposition to the Nazi regime led to him putting his life on the line by participating in the plot to assassinate Hitler in 1944; it's failure resulted in his imprisonment and execution.

5. Bonhoeffer's influence still appears in today's Germany, where the popularity of gospel music is still growing as a result of his championing of it decades ago.

18c Clear reference

The word or phrase that a pronoun refers to is known as the pronoun's *antecedent*. Antecedents should always be clear and explicit.

▶ Although the Canadian skater practiced daily with *her* trainers,

she didn't win the championship.

State a specific antecedent. Be sure to give a pronoun such as *they* or *it* an explicit antecedent.

NO SPECIFIC ANTECEDENT **When Mr. Rivera applied for a loan, *they* outlined the procedures for him.** [The pronoun *they* lacks an explicit antecedent.]

REVISED

> When Mr. Rivera applied to bank officials for a loan, *they* outlined the procedures for him.

When you use a pronoun, make sure it does not refer to a possessive noun or to a noun within a prepositional phrase.

George Orwell

▶ In ~~George Orwell's~~ "Shooting an Elephant," ~~he~~ reports an incident that shows the evil effects of imperialism. [The pronoun *he* cannot refer to the possessive noun *Orwell's*.]

Lance Morrow's essay

▶ ~~In the essay by Lance Morrow, it~~ points out the problems of choosing a name. [*It* refers to *essay*, which functions as the object of the preposition *in* and therefore cannot function as an antecedent.]

Avoid ambiguous pronoun reference.   Readers should never wonder what your pronouns refer to.

AMBIGUOUS   **My husband told my father that *he* should choose the baby's name.**   [Does *he* refer to *husband* or *father*?]

POSSIBLE
REVISION   **My husband told my father to choose the baby's name.**

POSSIBLE
REVISION   **My husband wanted to choose the baby's name and told my father so.**

AMBIGUOUS   **He had to decide whether to move to California.**

This was not what he wanted to do.   [Does *This* refer to making the decision or to moving to California?]

POSSIBLE
REVISION   **He had to decide whether to move to California. The decision was not one he wanted to make.**

POSSIBLE
REVISION   **He had to decide whether to move to California. Moving there was not something he wanted to do.**

EXERCISE 18.3   Use clear pronoun reference.
In the following sentences, rewrite any sentence in which a pronoun lacks a clear reference (antecedent). (**A** = See Answer Key.)

EXAMPLE:

officials

At the U.S. Patent and Trademark Office, ~~they~~ do not endorse health claims made by any product.

A 1. Any food supplement or vitamin can obtain a patent, but it may not be effective.

A 2. The U.S. Patent Office's purpose is to help inventors lay claim to their unique creations, but it does not investigate whether a creation actually does what its inventor claims.

3. Consumers want products to perform miracles, but they are frequently disappointing.

4. If a food supplement or vitamin has questionable value, they may try to sell the product by advertising the fact that it is patented.

5. When a product label implies that its being patented proves a health claim, consumer advocates advise buyers to beware.

18d Pronoun agreement with an antecedent

A plural antecedent needs a plural pronoun; a singular antecedent needs a singular pronoun.

Make a demonstrative pronoun agree with its antecedent. The demonstrative pronouns *this* and *that* refer to singular nouns; *these* and *those* refer to plural nouns: *this/that house, these/those houses.*

singular antecedent

▶ **He published his autobiography two years ago. This was his first book.**

plural antecedent

▶ **One reviewer praised his honesty and directness. Those were qualities he had worked hard to develop.**

Make a pronoun agree with a generalized (generic) antecedent. Generic nouns name a class or type of person or object, such as *a student* meaning "all students" or *a company* meaning "any company" or "all companies." In formal usage, do not use *they* to refer to a singular generic noun.

singular antecedent   plural pronoun

FAULTY
AGREEMENT
When a student is educated, they can go far in the world.

singular antecedent   singular pronoun

REVISED
When a student is educated, he or she can go far in the world.

REVISED

plural antecedent   plural pronoun

When students are educated, they can go far in the world.

Increasingly, advertising, journalism, and informal writing will use a plural pronoun referring to a singular antecedent, as in the following station wagon advertisement:

▶ **One day *your child* turns sixteen and you let *them* borrow the keys to the wagon.**

However, in formal academic writing, many readers may still expect a pronoun to agree with its antecedent. Often the best solution is to make the antecedent plural.

▶ **We should judge a~~person~~ by who *they* are, not by the color of *their* skin.**

(with *people* written above *a person*)

Make a pronoun agree with an indefinite pronoun. Indefinite pronouns, such as *everyone, somebody,* and *nothing* (17h), are singular in form and used with a singular verb. A singular antecedent needs a singular pronoun to refer to it. But which singular pronoun should be used—*he, she,* or both? To avoid gender bias (8e, item 4, and 18e) and possible clumsiness, some writers use the plural *they* to refer to a singular indefinite pronoun. Some readers, however, may object to this usage, so revising the sentence is a good idea.

SINGULAR PRONOUN/ GENDER BIAS

Everyone picked up *his* marbles and ran home to do *his* homework.

REVISED BUT CLUMSY

Everyone picked up *his or her* marbles and ran home to do *his or her* homework.

REVISED BUT INFORMAL

Everyone picked up *their* marbles and ran home to do *their* homework. [The plural pronoun *their* refers to a singular antecedent.]

You will probably often hear and read sentences like the previous example, but readers of informal academic prose may object to the fact that grammatically the plural pronoun their refers to a singular antecedent. Unless you know your audience well, play it safe and revise.

PROBABLY BEST

The *children* all picked up *their* marbles and ran home to do *their* homework.

Make a pronoun agree with the nearer antecedent when *or* or *nor* is used. When the elements of a compound antecedent are connected by *or* or *nor*, a pronoun agrees with the element that is nearer to it. If one part of the compound is singular and the other part is plural, put the plural antecedent closer to the pronoun and have the pronoun agree with it.

▶ Either my tutor or my professor has left *his* book on the shelf.

▶ Neither the manager nor the assistants could find *their* keys.

Make a pronoun agree with a collective noun. Use a singular pronoun to refer to a collective noun (*class, family, jury, committee, couple, team*) if you are referring to the group as a whole.

▶ The class revised *its* examination schedule.

▶ The technology committee has not yet completed *its* report.

Use a plural pronoun if members of the group named by the collective noun are considered to be acting individually.

▶ The technology committee began to cast *their* ballots in a formal vote.

EXERCISE 18.4   Use correct pronoun-antecedent agreement. In the following sentences, correct any errors in pronoun-antecedent agreement, revising sentences as necessary. Some sentences may be correct (**A** = See Answer Key.)

EXAMPLE:

    In wartime, a country's intelligence community finds that
its
ʌt̶h̶e̶i̶r̶ work has tremendous importance and urgency.

A 1. If a historian studies World War II, they will learn how important intelligence was for the Allied victory.

A 2. At first, however, U.S. intelligence was unable to identify the risk of a Japanese attack, and their failure brought the country into the war.

   3. Neither the head of the FBI nor his counterparts at the State Department, Army, and Navy allowed other government officials access to secrets their agents had discovered, and the result was American unpreparedness for the attack on Pearl Harbor.

4. In December 1941, an American could easily have felt that his country might lose the war against the Japanese military and the still-undefeated German army.

5. Everyone involved in decoding German and Japanese messages deserves their share of the credit for the ultimate defeat of the Axis powers in 1945.

18e Gender bias

Personal pronouns For many years, the pronoun *he* was used routinely in generic references to unspecified individuals in certain roles or professions, such as student, teacher, doctor, lawyer, and banker; and *she* was used routinely in generic references to individuals in roles such as nurse, secretary, and typist. This usage is now considered biased language.

NOT
APPROPRIATE   **When an accountant learns a foreign language, *he* gains access to an expanded job market.**

To revise such sentences that make general statements about people, roles, and professions, use one of the following methods:

1. Use a plural antecedent plus *they* (see also 18d and 8e, item 4).

   ▶ **When accountants learn a foreign language, *they* gain access to an expanded job market.**

2. Rewrite the sentence to eliminate the pronoun.

   ▶ **An accountant who learns a foreign language gains access to an expanded job market.**

3. Use a singular antecedent and the phrase *he or she.*

   ▶ **When an accountant learns a foreign language, *he or she* gains access to an expanded job market.**

The problem with option 3 is that awkward and repetitive structures can result when such a sentence is continued.

   ▶ **When an accountant learns a foreign language, *he or she* gains access to an expanded job market once *he or she* has decided on *his or her* specialty.**

Use the *he or she* option only when a sentence is relatively short and does not repeat the pronouns.

See also agreement with indefinite pronouns, 17h and 18d.

Rewrite the following sentences as necessary to remove any gender-biased pronouns. Some sentences may not need revision. (**A** = See Answer Key.)

EXAMPLE:

All   parents want their
~~Every~~ concerned ~~parent wants her~~ children to have the best possible education.

A 1. In the past, a first-grade teacher might teach her students to read by asking them to sound out letters.

A 2. In the last two decades of the twentieth century, many a principal asked his school to teach reading using new theories.

3. Advocates of whole language theory hoped that a student who might otherwise have fallen behind his peers in reading would be encouraged by a method that eliminated lesson-based primers and spelling tests.

4. However, many parents were concerned to discover that their children were not reading or spelling well by the third grade.

5. By the end of the century, any lawmaker who advocated whole language theory in schools in his constituency was likely to face angry parents who wanted a return to spelling and reading basics.

18f Consistent point of view

Always have a consistent perspective from which you are writing. Pronouns can help maintain consistency. Consider the person and number of the pronouns you use:

- Are you emphasizing the perspective of the first person (*I* or *we*)?

- Are you primarily addressing the reader as the second person (*you*)?

- Are you, as is most common in formal academic writing, writing about the third person (*he, she, it, one,* or *they*)?

Avoid confusing readers by switching from one perspective to another.

INCONSISTENT   *The company* decided to promote only three mid-level managers. *You* had to have worked there for ten years to qualify.

REVISED   *The company* **decided to promote only three mid-level managers.** *The employees* **had to have worked there for ten years to qualify.**

18g   Appropriate use of *you*

In formal writing, do not use the pronoun *you* when you mean "people generally." Use *you* only to address readers directly and to give instructions.

No   **Credit card companies should educate students about how to handle credit.** *You* **should not have to find out the problems the hard way.**   [This usage assumes readers are all students and addresses them directly. Some readers will not feel included in the group addressed as "you." A reader addressed directly in this way might think, "Who, me? I don't need to be educated about credit, and I have no problems."]

YES   **Turn to the next page, where** *you* **will find an excerpt from Edith Wharton's novel that will help** *you* **appreciate the accuracy of the details in this film.**

Edit uses of *you* if you are making a generalization about a group or if using *you* entails a switch from the third person.

▶ **It doesn't matter if young professionals are avid music**

                               they   they

admirers or comedy fans; ~~you~~ **can find anything** ~~you~~ **want**

in the city.

EXERCISE 18.6   Maintain a consistent point of view, and use *you* appropriately.

Revise the following passage as needed so that it maintains a consistent point of view. (**A** = See Answer Key.)

EXAMPLE:

Residents   their

~~You~~ **do not always see eye to eye with others in** ~~your~~

community; talking about a novel might be a way to bring

people together.

A Several municipalities around the United States—from small towns to the city of Chicago—have been trying a new method to establish a sense of community: all residents are being encouraged to read the same book at the same time. **A** When we read a book that you can discuss with your neighbors, we have a common ground for discussion. **A** In the summer of 2001, ten thousand or more Chicagoans were reading Harper Lee's classic novel, *To Kill a Mockingbird.* You did not have to be a promoter of the reading program to hope that the novel's powerful portrayal of racism in the rural South could inspire discussions among all facets of the city's diverse population. Can reading books help us unite? Many around the country hope that book discussion groups held on a large scale can prove to people that they really are part of a community. Even if you don't agree with other readers about a book, the fact that you have read it means that you have something in common.

18h Intensive and reflexive pronouns

Intensive pronouns emphasize a previously mentioned noun or pronoun. Reflexive pronouns identify a previously mentioned noun or pronoun as the person or thing receiving the action. See the Key Points box in 18a.

INTENSIVE **The president *himself* appeared at the gates.**

REFLEXIVE **He introduced *himself*.**

Do not use an intensive pronoun in place of a personal pronoun in a compound subject:

> ▶ Joe and ~~myself~~ will design the brochure.
> ^I^

Forms such as *hisself, theirself,* and *theirselves* occur in spoken dialects but are not Standard English.

18i *Who/whom, whoever/whomever*

In all formal writing situations, distinguish between the subject and object forms of pronouns used in questions or dependent noun clauses.

SUBJECT	OBJECT
who	whom (or, informally, who)
whoever	whomever

Ask yourself whether the pronoun is the subject of its clause or the object of a verb or preposition. Test the pronoun's function by rephrasing a question as a statement, substituting a personal pronoun for *who* or *whom, whoever* or *whomever.*

▶ **Who wrote that enthusiastic letter?** [*He* wrote that enthusiastic letter. Subject: use *who.*]

▶ **Whoever could have written it?** [*She* could have written it. Subject: use *whoever.*]

▶ **Who[m] were they describing?** [*They* were describing *him.* Object: *whom* (formal), though *who* is common in such contexts both in speech and in writing.]

When introducing a dependent noun clause with a pronoun, determine whether to use the subject or object form by examining the pronoun's function in its own clause. Ignore expressions such as *I think* or *I know* when they follow the pronoun; they have no effect on the form of the pronoun.

subject of dependent clause
▶ **They want to know who runs the business.**

subject of dependent clause (who runs the business)
▶ **They want to know who I think runs the business.**

object of preposition *to* [the manager reports to him or her]
▶ **They want to know whom the manager reports to.**

subject of dependent clause
▶ **The manager will hire whoever is qualified.**

direct object of verb *recommends*
▶ **I will hire whomever my boss recommends.**

For related uses of *who* and *whom* in relative clauses, see 20a.

EXERCISE 18.7 Correct errors in pronoun use.
In the following passage, revise any errors in pronoun use. Remember to make all necessary changes to the sentence if you change a pronoun. (**A** = See Answer Key.)

A By some estimates, 70 percent of all of the antibiotics produced in the United States are used to promote growth in healthy livestock. **A** In 1998, in a report by the National Research Council and the Institute of Medicine, they said that feeding antibiotics to farm animals contributed to the rise of some antibiotic-resistant bacteria and that this could make human beings sick. **A** Papers published in a 2001 issue of the *New England Journal of Medicine* also concluded that you should be concerned about the use of antibiotics to make livestock grow more quickly and about the bacteria that are becoming harder to kill as a result.

When David G. White and a team of researchers from the Food and Drug Administration tested two hundred packages of supermarket chicken for salmonella, his researchers and himself discovered thirty-five samples of bacteria that were resistant to at least one antibiotic. L. Clifford McDonald and other scientists from the Centers for Disease Control and Prevention also tested supermarket chicken for an even more frightening study; their's found that 350 of 407 samples contained *Enterococcus faecium,* 250 samples of which were resistant to a potent new antibiotic cocktail called Synercid. You carry *E. faecium* in your intestines naturally, but it can cause illness if you get sick from something else. Today, a doctor usually prescribes Synercid if his patient's illness is caused by *E. faecium* because the bacteria have grown resistant to the antibiotic that was previously used.

19　Adjectives and Adverbs

Adjectives describe, or modify, nouns or pronouns. They do not add a plural *-s* or change form to reflect gender. For the order of adjectives, see 35g.

▶ Analysts acknowledge the *beneficial* effects of TV.

▶ The lawyer tried a *different* approach.

▶ The depiction of rural life is *accurate.*

▶ The novelist keeps her desk *tidy.*

 ESL Note　No Plural Form of an Adjective

Never add a plural *-s* ending to an adjective that modifies a plural noun.

▶ Mr. Lee tried three *different̶s* approaches.　■

Adverbs modify verbs, adjectives, and other adverbs, as well as whole clauses.

▶ His new assistant settled down *comfortably.*

▶ The patient is demanding a *theoretically* impossible treatment.

▶ *Apparently,* the experiment was a success.

19a Forms of adjectives and adverbs

No single rule indicates the correct form of all adjectives and adverbs.

Adverb: adjective + -ly Many adverbs are formed by adding *-ly* to an adjective: *soft/softly; intelligent/intelligently.* Sometimes when *-ly* is added, a spelling change occurs: *easy/easily; terrible/terribly.*

Adjectives ending in -ic To form an adverb from an adjective ending in *-ic,* add *-ally* (*basic/basically; artistic/artistically*), except for *public,* whose adverb form is *publicly.*

Adjectives ending in -ly Some adjectives, such as *friendly, lovely, timely,* and *masterly,* already end in *-ly* and have no distinctive adverb form.

adjective
▶ She is a friendly person.

┌─ adverbial phrase ─┐
▶ She spoke to me in a friendly way.
adjective

Irregular adverb forms Certain adjectives do not add *-ly* to form an adverb.

ADJECTIVE	ADVERB
good	well
fast	fast
hard	hard

adjective   adverb
▶ He is a good cook.   He cooks well.

adjective   adverb
▶ She is a hard worker.   She works hard.   [*Hardly* is not the adverb form of *hard.* Rather, it means "barely," "scarcely," or "almost not at all": *I could* hardly *breathe in that stuffy room.*]

Well can also function as an adjective, meaning "healthy" or "satisfactory": *A well baby smiles often. She feels well.*

Note: In speech, adjectives (particularly *good, bad,* and *real*) are often used to modify verbs, adjectives, or adverbs. This is nonstandard usage. Use an adverb to modify a verb or an adverb.

▶ The webmaster fixed the

well ──→
link ~~good~~.
^

▶ The chorus sings ~~real good~~.
really well
^

▶ The guide speaks very ~~clear~~.
clearly
^

▶ They dance ~~bad~~.
badly
^

EXERCISE 19.1 Use adjectives and adverbs appropriately.
In the following passage, correct any errors in adjective or adverb use. (**A** = See Answer Key.)

EXAMPLE:

really
High school sports are ~~real~~ important to many
^
communities.

A Participating in a team sport can teach many good lessons to high school students. **A** They can learn sportsmanship, the value of practicing to improve skills, and the strength that comes from working good together. **A** However, many administrators, teachers, alumni, and students take high school athletics too serious. **A** When students are forced to practice football in full uniforms in real hot weather at the beginning of the school year, the coaches' priorities are misplaced. When communities rally around champion high school athletes who have behaved extremely bad or even committed crimes, the communities are sending a terrible message to both athletes and nonathletes about the importance of a winning team. Sports should be fun, and although winning is important, playing good and honorable should be the most important goal of a high school team.

19b Adjectives after linking verbs

After linking verbs (*be, seem, appear, become*), use an adjective to modify the subject.

▶ Sharon Olds's poems are *lyrical.*

▶ The book seems *repetitive.*

Some verbs (*appear, look, feel, smell, taste*) are sometimes used as linking verbs, sometimes as action verbs. If the modifier tells about the subject, use an adjective. If the modifier tells about the action of the verb, use an adverb.

ADJECTIVE   **The analyst looks *confident* in her new job.**

ADVERB   **The lawyer looks *confidently* at all the assembled partners.**

ADJECTIVE   **The waiter feels *bad*.**

The steak smells *bad*.

ADVERB   **The chef smelled the lobster *appreciatively*.**

Note: Use a hyphen to connect two words used as an adjective when they appear before a noun. Do not use a hyphen when the words follow a linking verb with no noun complement.

▶ **Sonny Rollins is a *well-known* saxophonist.**

▶ **Sonny Rollins is *well known*.**

19c Compound adjectives

A compound adjective consists of two or more words used as a unit to describe a noun. Many compound adjectives contain the past participle *-ed* verb form: *flat-footed, barrel-chested, broad-shouldered, old-fashioned, well-dressed, left-handed*. Note the form when a compound adjective is used before a noun: hyphen, past participle (*-ed*) form where necessary, and no noun plural (*-s*) ending.

▶ **They have a *five-year-old* daughter.**   [Their daughter is five years old.]

▶ **She gave me a *five-dollar* bill.**   [She gave me five dollars.]

▶ **He is a *left-handed* pitcher.**   [He pitches with his left hand.]

For more on hyphenation with compound adjectives, see 30h.

EXERCISE 19.2   Use compound adjectives correctly.

In the following sentences, correct any errors in the use of compound adjectives. (**A** = See Answer Key.)

EXAMPLE:

Augusta Persse was twenty-eight years old when she

                                sixty-three-year-old
married her ~~sixty three years old~~ **neighbor, Sir William**
                            ^

Gregory, owner of Coole Park in Galway, Ireland.

A 1. Lady Gregory's twelve years marriage ended with her husband's death, and afterward she began to finish her husband's incomplete autobiography.

A 2. Her friendship with the well known poet W. B. Yeats was profitable for both of them: they inspired each other and collaborated on one act plays.

3. One play, *Cathleen ni Houlihan*, was an enormous success; although Yeats took credit for it, the manuscript contains pencil written notes that prove how much Lady Gregory had contributed.

4. Lady Gregory became the director of Dublin's famous Abbey Theatre; she won several hard fought battles over the theater's right to present plays such as John Millington Synge's *The Playboy of the Western World* and Sean O'Casey's *The Plough and the Stars.*

5. Many of the hand-pick plays that Lady Gregory championed are still considered masterpieces of Irish literature.

19d   Position of adverbs

An adverb can be placed in various positions in a sentence.

▶ *Enthusiastically,* **she ate the sushi.**

▶ **She** *enthusiastically* **ate the sushi.**

▶ **She ate the sushi** *enthusiastically.*

 ESL NOTE   Adverb Placement

Do not place an adverb between a verb and a short direct object (35b).

▶ She ate enthusiastically the sushi.   ▪

Put adverbs that show frequency (*always, usually, frequently, often, sometimes, seldom, rarely, never*) in one of four positions:

1. At the beginning of a sentence

 ▶ *Sometimes* **I just sit and daydream instead of writing.**

When *never, seldom,* or *rarely* occurs at the beginning of the sentence, word order is inverted (see also 8d, page 110).

 ▶ *Never will* **I let that happen.**

2. Between the subject and the main verb

 ▶ **They** *always* **arrive half an hour late.**

3. After a form of *be* or any auxiliary verb (such as *do, have, can, will, must*)

 ▶ **The writing center is** *always* **open in the evening.**

 ▶ **The tutors are** *seldom* **late for training.**

 ▶ **There is** *never* **an available computer when I go to the lab.**

4. In the final position

 ▶ **Amira checks her e-mail** *frequently.*

Note: Never place the adverb *never* in the final position.

EXERCISE 19.3   Position adverbs correctly.
In the following passage, revise any sentence containing a misplaced adverb. (**A** = See Answer Key.)

EXAMPLE:

>   often
> **He has read** ~~often~~ **the century-old diaries of Antarctic explorers.**

   A In the nineteenth and twentieth centuries, polar exploration attracted usually courageous and foolhardy explorers. **A** Many of these explorers kept journals or wrote books, and even today their writings are popular. **A** Why would modern people want to read them? **A** Perhaps the charm of these tales for modern readers lies in the strangeness of the quests. **A** Seldom the early polar explorers gave satisfying reasons for their journeys: on one British expedition to the South Pole, biologists endured weeks of the coldest weather ever recorded in order to collect specimens that scientists at home did not want. **A** Another fascinating feature of polar exploration adventures is that they frequently were fatal: the most celebrated heroes of polar exploration have been those often who failed. Captain Robert Scott, who lost the race to the South Pole and then died in the attempt to return home, is always almost portrayed sympathetically. Rarely Roald Amundsen, the man who beat Scott to the Pole, is mentioned unless his name comes up in discussions of Scott's doomed journey. The romance of failure and of fools' errands entices readers today; modern writers about polar exploration try to find frequently explanations of why these people took such risks. Never the answers can be known with certainty. However, generations of readers will be grateful always that the explorers preserved records of their astonishing journeys to the Poles.

19e Double negatives

Adverbs like *hardly, scarcely,* and *barely* are considered negatives, and the contraction *-n't* stands for the adverb *not.* Some languages and dialects allow the use of more than one negative to emphasize an idea (see 32d), but Standard English allows only one negative in a clause. Avoid double negatives.

DOUBLE NEGATIVE	We do*n't* have *no* excuses.
REVISED	We do*n't* have *any* excuses. [Or] We have *no* excuses.
DOUBLE NEGATIVE	She did*n't* say *nothing.*
REVISED	She did*n't* say *anything.* [Or] She said *nothing.*
DOUBLE NEGATIVE	City residents ca*n't hardly* afford the sales tax.
REVISED	City residents can *hardly* afford the sales tax.

19f Comparative and superlative forms

Adjectives and adverbs have three forms: positive, comparative, and superlative. Use the comparative form to compare two people, places, things, or ideas; use the superlative to compare more than two.

Regular forms Add the ending *-er* to form the comparative and *-est* to form the superlative of both short adjectives (those that have one syllable or those that have two syllables and end in *-y* or *-le*) and one-syllable adverbs. (Change *-y* to *-i* if *-y* is preceded by a consonant: *icy, icier, iciest.*) Generally, a superlative form is preceded by *the* (*the shortest distance*).

Positive	Comparative (Comparing two)	Superlative (Comparing more than two)
short	shorter	shortest
pretty	prettier	prettiest
simple	simpler	simplest
fast	faster	fastest

With longer adjectives and with adverbs ending in *-ly*, use *more* (for the comparative) and *most* (for the superlative). Note that *less* (comparative) and *least* (superlative) are used with adjectives of any length (*less bright, least bright; less effective, least effective*).

Positive	Comparative	Superlative
intelligent	more intelligent	most intelligent
carefully	more carefully	most carefully
dangerous	less dangerous	least dangerous

If you cannot decide whether to use *-er/-est* or *more/most*, consult a dictionary. If there is an *-er/-est* form, the dictionary will say so.

Note: Do not use the *-er* form along with *more* or the *-est* form along with *most*.

▶ The first poem was ~~more~~ better than the second.

▶ Boris is the ~~most~~ fittest person I know.

Irregular forms The following common adjectives and adverbs have irregular comparative and superlative forms:

Positive	Comparative	Superlative
good	better	best
bad	worse	worst
much/many	more	most
little	less	least
well	better	best
badly	worse	worst

***Than* with comparative forms** To compare two people, places, things, or ideas, use the comparative form and the word *than*. If you use a comparative form in your sentence, you need *than* to let readers know what you are comparing with what.

> than the previous one
> ► This course of action is more efficient.

Comparative forms are also used without *than* in an idiomatic way.

> ► The *harder* he tries, the *more satisfied* he feels.

> ► The *more,* the *merrier.*

Absolute adjectives Do not use comparative and superlative forms of adjectives that imply absolutes: *complete, empty, full, equal, perfect, priceless,* or *unique.* In addition, do not add intensifying adverbs such as *very, totally, completely,* or *absolutely* to these adjectives. To say that something is "perfect" implies an absolute rather than something measured in degrees.

>   a
> ► He has ~~the most~~ perfect view of the ocean.

> ► They bought a ~~totally~~ unique quilt at an auction.

EXERCISE 19.4 Use comparative and superlative forms correctly. In the following passage, correct any errors in comparative and superlative forms of adjectives and adverbs. (**A** = See Answer Key.)

EXAMPLE:

Before farmers and fishermen in India had access to cell

>   worse
> **phones, they fared ~~worst~~ when marketing their goods**

than they do today.

   A In the United States, the first people to have cellular telephones were the most rich members of the population. **A** In India, in contrast, many poor and working-class people have been among the people who have adopted cell phone technology most fast. **A** Many of these people live and work in areas that are not served by traditional land telephones, and they are finding that cell phones are one of the usefullest inventions for improving a small business. ▲Fishermen in western India, for example, have no other access to telephones from their boats, and calling the markets before heading to shore with the day's catch allows them to find the most high prices. ▲Growers of produce in rural areas are also beginning to rely on cell phones to find the most high prices for their wares.

Indian cellular companies are responding to a real need in the country—there are far more few telephones per household in India than in the industrialized world—but they are also creating more greater demand. The cell phone marketers have made a tremendous effort to increase the numbers of cellular telephones in the country, offering new customers efficienter service than land lines provide while also making cell phone calls widelier available and most affordable. For the time being, at least, the introduction of cell phone technology has created totally unique opportunities for both cell phone marketers and consumers in India.

19g Faulty or incomplete comparisons

Make sure that you state clearly what items you are comparing. Some faulty comparisons can give readers the wrong idea. See also 15f, 18a, and 18b.

INCOMPLETE   **He likes the parrot better than his wife.**

To avoid suggesting that he prefers the parrot to his wife, clarify the comparison by completing the second clause.

REVISED   **He likes the parrot better *than his wife does.***

Edit sentences like the following:

▶ **My essay got a higher grade than Maria's.** [Compare the two

essays, not your essay and Maria.]

▶ **Williams's poem gives a more objective depiction of the**

painting than Auden's. [To compare Williams's poem with Auden's poem, you need to include an apostrophe; otherwise, you compare a poem to the poet W. H. Auden.]

Comparisons must also be complete. If you say that something is "more efficient," your reader wonders, "More efficient than what?"

▶ **Didion shows us a home that makes her feel more tied to her**
than her home in Los Angeles does
roots. [Include the other part of the comparison.]

20   Relative Clauses and Relative Pronouns

Relative clauses are introduced by relative pronouns: *who, whom, whose, which,* and *that.* A relative pronoun in the dependent clause refers to a word or words (its *antecedent*) in the independent clause. See 12e for more on clauses.

relative clause
▶ **The girl *who* can't dance says the band can't play.**

—Yiddish proverb

20a   Relative pronouns (*who, whom, whose, which,* and *that*)

The forms of relative pronouns vary in speech and writing and in informal and formal usage. In academic writing, use the relative pronouns designated *formal* in the discussion that follows.

 ESL Note   Relative Pronouns

Languages such as Spanish, Arabic, and Thai use the same relative pronouns for human and for nonhuman antecedents. In writing Standard English, pay attention to whether the antecedent is human or not. ■

Human antecedents   In formal writing, use *who, whom,* and *whose* to refer to people.

RELATIVE PRONOUNS: HUMAN ANTECEDENTS

SUBJECT	OBJECT	POSSESSIVE
who	whom (sometimes omitted)	whose
	that (informal)	

For *who* and *whom* as question words, see 18i.

The form of the relative pronoun depends on the pronoun's grammatical function in its own clause. To identify the correct form, restate the clause, using a personal pronoun.

subject of dependent clause

▶ **The teachers who challenge us are the ones we remember.**

[*They* challenge us. *They* is the subject.]

object of dependent clause

▶ **The teachers [whom] the students honored felt proud.**   [The students honored *them*. (*Whom* may be omitted.)]

possessive

▶ **The teachers whose student evaluations were high won an award.**   [*Their* student evaluations were high—possessive.]

Do not rename the subject of the independent clause.

▶ **The teachers who challenge us ~~they~~ are the ones we remember.**

VARIATION   *Whom* is the grammatically correct form of the relative pronoun in the direct object position in its own clause. However, in speech and informal writing, it often tends to be replaced by *who*. When in doubt as to whether to use *who* or *whom*, and if you cannot work out which is grammatically appropriate, opt for *who*. Readers are far less likely to accept *whom* in place of *who* than the other way around. See also 18i.   ■

Phrases such as *I know, he thinks,* and *they realize* inserted into a relative clause do not affect the form of the pronoun.

subject of dependent clause

▶ **We should help children who we realize cannot defend**

themselves.   [*They* cannot defend themselves.]

Nonhuman antecedents: animals, things, and concepts   Use *that* or *which* to refer to nonhuman antecedents. Do not use *which* for human beings.

who

▶ **The teacher ~~which~~ taught me math in high school was strict.**
          ^

that

▶ **The dog ~~who~~ barked was fearful.**
        ^

RELATIVE PRONOUNS: NONHUMAN ANTECEDENTS

SUBJECT	OBJECT	POSSESSIVE
that	that (sometimes omitted)	of which (formal)
which	which (sometimes omitted)	whose (informal)

Use the relative pronoun *that* to refer to an antecedent naming an animal, a thing, or a concept (such as *success* or *information*). When the relative pronoun *that* functions as the direct object in its clause, it can be omitted.

▶ **They stayed at a hotel [that] their friends had recommended.**
[*That* as direct object in the relative clause can be omitted.]

See 20c for the use of *that* and *which* in restrictive and nonrestrictive clauses.

Note: When you refer to places and times, you can use *where* to replace *in which, at which,* or *to which,* and you can use *when* to replace *at which, in which,* or *on which.* Do not use a preposition with *where* or *when.*

▶ **The morning on which she graduated was warm and sunny.**

▶ **The morning *when* she graduated was warm and sunny.**

▶ **The village in which he was born honored him last year.**

▶ **The village *where* he was born honored him last year.**

However, use *where* or *when* only if actual time or physical location is involved.

▶ **The influence of the Sapir-Whorf hypothesis, ~~where~~ behavior** according to which

is regarded as influenced by language, has declined.

Do not use *what* as a relative pronoun.

that
▶ **The deal ~~what~~ she was trying to make fell through.**

EXERCISE 20.1 Use relative pronouns correctly.
In the following passage, revise any incorrect or informal use of relative pronouns. (**A** = See Answer Key.)

EXAMPLE:

who
No one could dispute the fact that George Lucas, ~~which~~
created the *Star Wars* films, is a marketing genius.

A When George Lucas made the movie *Star Wars* in 1977, he told people whom asked about the film's box-office prospects that it would make sixteen million dollars. **A** In fact, the original *Star Wars*, the story of which was based on old movie serials and comic book adventures, went on to become the second-highest-grossing film of all time. **A** However, the real money-making potential of the *Star Wars* films lies in the merchandise accompanies them. Lucas, that owns the licenses for all of the merchandise, was said to have earned about four billion dollars from sales of those products even before the release of *Star Wars: Episode I—The Phantom Menace* in 1999. Before that film appeared, reporters who newspapers assigned to write *Phantom Menace* stories were typically business journalists rather than film reviewers. Many of the stories they wrote estimated that *The Phantom Menace* would make a profit even if no tickets to the film were ever sold. Not surprisingly, some film reviewers and moviegoers that saw *The Phantom Menace* were disappointed; even less surprisingly, the film was a hit, and fans continue to buy the merchandise.

20b Agreement of verbs with relative pronouns

Agreement of verbs   Determine subject-verb agreement within a relative clause by asking whether the antecedent of a subject relative pronoun is singular or plural.

▶ **The book that *is* at the top of the bestseller list gives advice about health.**   [The singular noun *book* is the antecedent of *that*, the subject of the singular verb *is* in the relative clause.]

▶ **The books that *are* at the top of the bestseller list give advice about health, success, and making money.**   [The plural noun *books* is the antecedent of *that*, the subject of the plural verb *are* in the relative clause.]

Agreement after *one of* and *the only one of*   The phrase *one of* is followed by a plural noun phrase in the independent clause. However, the verb in the relative clause can be singular or plural, depending on the meaning intended.

▶ **Juan is one of the employees who *work* long hours.**
[Several employees work long hours. Juan is one of them.
The plural word *employees* is the antecedent of *who*, so the
verb is plural.]

singular verb
▶ **Juan is the only one of the employees who *works* long hours.**
[Only Juan works long hours.]

EXERCISE 20.2 Make the verb and antecedent of a relative
pronoun agree.

In the following sentences, correct any agreement errors or relative
pronoun errors. Then draw an arrow from any relative pronoun to
its antecedent. Some sentences may be correct. (**A** = See Answer
Key.)

EXAMPLE:

make
**Keeping costs down is one of the reasons that ~~makes~~ most
health maintenance organizations require approval for
certain treatments.**

A 1. Most people whom participate in group insurance plans now
use some form of managed care.

A 2. Many insurance companies require any patients who partici-
pates in managed care plans to get a referral from their primary care physician before seeing an expensive specialist.

A 3. This practice, which are known as "gatekeeping," often infuriates both patients and physicians.

4. In some cases, patients may believe that a particular specialist
is the only one of the doctors in the group who know how to
treat a particular condition.

5. Everyone in the plan who need to see a specialist must first
make an appointment with a primary care physician to get his
or her referral; many patients resent having to make this extra
visit.

6. In addition, many insurance companies pay lower fees to any
doctor in a managed care plan who refer patients to a specialist for treatment, so doctors are often reluctant to make
referrals.

20c Restrictive and nonrestrictive clauses

The two types of relative clauses, restrictive and nonrestrictive, fulfill different functions and need different punctuation (see also 23d).

RESTRICTIVE **The people *who live in the apartment above mine* make a lot of noise at night.**

NONRESTRICTIVE **The Sullivans, *who live in the apartment above mine*, make a lot of noise at night.**

Restrictive relative clause A restrictive relative clause provides information essential for understanding the independent clause: *The people make a lot of noise at night*. Which people? The ones who live in the apartment above mine.

The clause is not set off with commas, and *that* (not *which*) is preferred for reference to nonhuman antecedents.

▶ **The book [that] you gave me is exciting.**

Nonrestrictive relative clause A nonrestrictive relative clause provides information that is not essential for understanding the independent clause. The antecedent is a unique, designated person or thing, often a proper noun.

The clause is set off by commas, and *which* (not *that*) is used to refer to a nonhuman antecedent.

▶ ***War and Peace*, which you gave me, is a fascinating novel.**
[The independent clause—"*War and Peace* is a fascinating novel"—does not promote further questions, such as "Which *War and Peace* do you mean?" The information in the relative clause ("which you gave me") is almost an aside and not essential for understanding the independent clause.]

Relative clauses beginning with a quantity word such as *some, none, many, much, most,* or *one* followed by *of which* or *of whom* are always nonrestrictive. Use a comma to set off such a clause.

▶ **They selected five candidates, one of whom would get the job.**

▶ **The report mentioned five names, none of which I recognized.**

 ESL NOTE Relative vs. Personal Pronouns

Do not use a personal pronoun along with a relative pronoun.

                most of whom
▶ I tutored some students, ~~which most of them~~ were my classmates. ■
                 ^

EXERCISE 20.3 Identify restrictive and nonrestrictive clauses.
In the following sentences, underline each relative clause and write *R* or *NR* (*restrictive* or *nonrestrictive*) on the line before the sentence. There may be more than one relative clause in a sentence. Then make sure that each clause is punctuated correctly and that the correct form of the relative pronoun is used. (**A** = See Answer Key.)

EXAMPLE:

____R____ People/who speak a pidgin language/are finding a way to bridge the communication gap.

A 1. _____ When a person who speaks only English and a person, who speaks only Spanish, must communicate, they will find common ground by using the simple grammar and vocabulary of pidgin.

A 2. _____ Pidgin which is not spoken as a native tongue by anyone is different from creolized language.

3. _____ When a language, that started out as pidgin, becomes the common speech of a community, that language has been creolized.

4. _____ For example, Haitian Creole that is a language with its own complex grammar and vocabulary came from the pidgin speech created by slaves from many cultures, who were forced to live and work together.

5. _____ Creolized languages who many of them develop when pidgin speakers raise children in a multicultural community demonstrate both the creativity of human beings— even in terrible hardship—and the depth of the human need to communicate with other people.

20d Relative clauses with prepositions

When a relative clause contains a relative pronoun within a prepositional phrase, do not omit the preposition. Keep in mind these three points:

1. Directly after the preposition, use *whom* or *which*, never *that*.

┌─────── relative clause ───────┐
▶ The man *for whom* we worked last year has just retired.

2. If you place the preposition after the verb, use *that* (or you can omit *that*), but do not use *whom* or *which*.

> The security measures ~~which~~ [that] the mayor had insisted on made him unpopular.

3. Do not add an extra personal pronoun object after the preposition at the end of the relative clause.

> The theater company [that] they are devoted to ~~it~~ has produced six new plays this season.

EXERCISE 20.4 Correct errors in relative clauses and relative pronouns.

In the following passage, correct any errors in the use of relative pronouns and relative clauses. (**A** = See Answer Key.)

A The QWERTY typewriter and computer keyboard, that is named for the first six letters on the left-hand side, was invented in the late nineteenth century. **A** That keyboard came into common use precisely because it prevented typists which used it from typing fast. **A** The typewriter keys which were used in those days became tangled if they moved too quickly, so slow typing was actually beneficial. **A** However, the situation soon changed. **A** The typewriters, which were in use by the 1920s, were more mechanically sophisticated and faster, so the QWERTY system was holding typists back instead of allowing them to type their fastest. **A** At that time Dr. August Dvorak, whom taught at the University of Washington, began to research keyboard layouts.

Dr. Dvorak, of which his original plan was to create a keyboard that could be used by a one-handed typist, studied both the most common letters used in several languages and the physiology of the human hand. He applied this research to create a new layout for the keyboard. The Dvorak keyboard, which it has all of the most frequently used letters in the home row, increased typing speeds for experienced typists and was easy for beginners to learn. The time at when Dr. Dvorak completed his design was shortly before World War II, and a planned change from the QWERTY system to the Dvorak was put aside during the war. In the meantime, the QWERTY keyboard had become a tradition. However, users who the QWERTY system is troublesome for today have an option if they use modern computers, most of that allow users to shift to the Dvorak system if they prefer it. Some Dvorak keyboard advocates believe that beginning typists should learn the Dvorak system, where common words are learned quickly, instead of the QWERTY system. Perhaps Dr. Dvorak's keyboard may yet become the standard of the future.

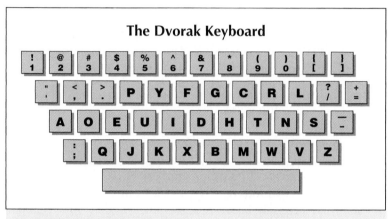

The Dvorak Keyboard

An alternative to the traditional keyboard

Adapted from *The Dvorak Keyboard* by Randy Cassingham (1986), <www.Dvorak-keyboard.com>. Used with permission of the author.

Why do punctuation and mechanics matter? They matter because they chunk words into meaningful groups for readers. Try reading the following without the benefit of the signals a reader usually expects.

> When active viruses especially those transmitted by contact can spread easily within the world health organization hard working doctors are continually collaborating to find treatments for several infectious diseases sars avian flu and hepatitis.

Conventional punctuation and mechanics clarify the meaning:

> When active, viruses—especially those transmitted by contact—can spread easily; within the World Health Organization, hard-working doctors are continually collaborating to find treatments for several infectious diseases: SARS, avian flu, and hepatitis.

21 Punctuation and Meaning

The following table summarizes what punctuation marks to use for specific purposes as you write. Turn to the sections indicated for more detailed information and examples.

How Punctuation Shows Meaning

What Do You Want to Do?	Options
Overall purpose: To end a sentence	
• To mark where a sentence ends	Period, question mark, or exclamation point (.?!), chapter 22
• To indicate the end of a sentence with a close connection to the next sentence	Semicolon (;), 24a
Overall purpose: To separate	
• To separate introductory words, a phrase, or a clause from a following independent clause	Comma (,), 23c
• To separate independent clauses only when a connecting word (*and, but, or, nor, so, for,* or *yet*) is used	Comma (,), 23b
• To separate items (words, phrases, clauses) in a list (*x, y,* and *z*)	Comma (,), 23f
• To separate coordinate adjectives	Comma (,), 23g
• To separate items in a list that contains internal commas (*x, x; y, y;* and *z*)	Semicolon (;), 24a
• To separate a verb from a quoted statement that follows or precedes it	Comma (,), 23h
• To separate lines of poetry written as running text	Slash (/), 27d
Overall purpose: To insert	
• To insert a word, words, or an "extra information" (nonrestrictive) phrase or clause into a sentence	Commas (,,), 23d
• To give more emphasis to the insert	Dashes (—), 27a
• To insert a change within a quotation	Square brackets [ ], 27c
• To insert explanatory information	Parentheses ( ), 27b

What Do You Want to Do?	Options
Overall purpose: To anticipate an explanation or a list	Colon (:), 24b
Overall purpose: To quote • To quote exact words or give the title of a story, a poem, or an article	Double quotation marks (" "), 26b
• To enclose a quotation within another quotation	Single quotation marks (' '), 26d
Overall purpose: To delete from a quotation	Ellipsis dots (. . .), 27e
Overall purpose: To indicate possession • For most words	Apostrophe + s ('s), 25a, 25b
• For nouns forming the plural with s	Apostrophe after the s (s'), 25a, 25b

22 End Punctuation

Periods, question marks, and exclamation points often function to signal the end of a sentence.

▶ I have lost my pencil.

▶ Have you taken it?

▶ It's behind your ear!

By convention, one or two spaces then follow the end punctuation and another sentence begins. The Modern Language Association (MLA), in its list of Frequently Asked Questions at <http://www.mla.org>, recommends leaving one space after a punctuation mark at the end of a sentence but sees "nothing wrong with using two spaces after concluding punctuation marks." Ask your instructor for her or his preference.

22a Period (.)

A period in British English is descriptively called a "full stop." The stop at the end of a sentence is indeed full—much more of a stop than a comma provides. Periods are also used, though, with abbreviations, decimals, and amounts of money, as in the following examples.

1. Use a period to end a declarative sentence—a sentence that makes a statement.

▶ The interviewer asked the CEO about the company's finances.

2. Use a period to end a sentence concluding with an indirect question.

No   **The interviewer asked the CEO how much did the company make last year?**

No   **The interviewer asked the CEO how much the company made last year?**

Yes   **The interviewer asked the CEO how much the company made last year.** [For more on verbs and word order in indirect questions, see also 15d, 16e, and 35d.]

3. Use a period to end an imperative sentence—a command—that does not express strong emotion.

▶ Note the use of metaphor in the last paragraph.

▶ Turn left at the iron sculpture.

4. Use a period to signal an abbreviation. In these instances, use only one space after the period:

▶ **Mr. Mrs. Dr. Rev. Tues. etc.** [The abbreviation *etc.* is short for *et cetera*, Latin for "and so on," "and the others."]

Some abbreviations contain internal periods. Do not include a space after these internal periods:

▶ **a.m. p.m.** (*or* **A.M. P.M.**) **i.e. e.g.** [The abbreviation *i.e.* is short for *id est*, Latin for "that is"; *e.g.* is short for *exempla gratia*, Latin for "for example."]

See also 29b.

5. For some abbreviations with capital letters, use or omit periods. Just be consistent.

▶ **A.M.** or   AM

▶ **P.M.** or   PM

▶ **U.S.A.** or   USA

When ending a sentence with an abbreviation, do not use two periods:

▶ **The plane left at 7 A.M.** [not 7 A.M..]

Note: In MLA style, do not use periods in uppercase initials of names of government agencies or other organizations, acronyms (abbreviations pronounced as words), Internet abbreviations, or common time indicators. See 29b.

ACLU	BC	HUD	NAACP	NPR
AD	FAQ	IBM	NASA	URL
AIDS	HTML	IRS	NOW	USC

6. Use a period at the end of each entry in a list of works cited.
Note, though, that an APA entry ending with a URL does not conclude with a period. See page 489.

7. Use a period in writing figures with decimals and amounts of money greater than a dollar.

▶ 3.7 $7.50

22b Question mark (?)

Questions are useful devices to engage readers' attention. A question will draw readers into thinking about an issue, to which you can then provide the answer. Such questions are known as *rhetorical questions.*

▶ **Many cooks nowadays are making healthier dishes. How do they do this? For the most part, they use unsaturated oil.**

Use the following guidelines with questions.

1. Use a question mark at the end of a sentence to signal a direct question. Do not use a period in addition to a question mark.

No   **What is he writing?.**

Yes   **What is he writing?**

2. Use a question mark at the end of each question in a series of questions.

▶ **In "A Rose for Emily," how does Emily relate to the town? How does the town relate to her?**

If the questions in a series are not complete sentences, you still need question marks. A question fragment may begin with a capital letter or not. Just make your usage consistent.

▶ **Are the characters in the play involved in the disaster? Indifferent to it? Unaware of it?**

▶ **Are the characters in the play involved in the disaster? indifferent to it? unaware of it?**

3. Use a question mark at the end of a direct question but not at the end of an indirect question (15d, 16e, and 35d).

DIRECT **The interviewer asked, "When is the recession going to end?"**

INDIRECT **The interviewer asked when the recession was going to end.**

4. In MLA style, do not use a comma with a question mark.

▶ **"What is the meaning of life?" the writer asks.**

VARIATION You will find, however, that many writers use both a comma and a question mark. The following example is from a book review by Elizabeth Spires in the *New York Times Book Review*.

▶ **In answer to "Who is the most important one?," Sonja declares it is "those who are closest to heaven. . . ."**

Such usage may help make it clear to readers that the sentence continues after the question mark. ∎

5. Do not use a question mark or an exclamation point enclosed in parentheses to convey irony or sarcasm.

No **The principal, that great historian (?), proposed a new plan for the history curriculum.**

YES **The principal, who does not seem to know much about history, proposed a new plan for the history curriculum.**

Note: You may occasionally come across a question mark used to express uncertainty in a statement or used within parentheses to express uncertainty about the information offered.

▶ **"She jumped in?" he wondered.**

▶ **Plato (427?–347 BC) founded the Academy at Athens.**

Use the question mark with a date only if the date is generally not established, and even then it is often better to rephrase the sentence using *about* or *approximately*. In addition, if the uncertainty is a result of your not knowing an exact date, find it out. Don't announce that you do not know by using a question mark.

REVISED   **He wondered if she had jumped in.**

REVISED   **Plato, who lived from approximately 427 to 347 BC, founded the Academy at Athens.**

See 29b for more on the use of *BC* and its alternative, *BCE*.

22c   Exclamation point (!)

An exclamation point at the end of a sentence indicates that the writer considers the statement amazing, surprising, or extraordinary. Science writer Lewis Thomas comments in "Notes on Punctuation":

> Exclamation points are the most irritating of all. Look! They say, look at what I just said! How amazing is my thought! It is like being forced to watch someone else's small child jumping up and down crazily in the center of the living room shouting to attract attention. If a sentence really has something of importance to say, something quite remarkable, it doesn't need a mark to point it out.

Try to avoid exclamation points. Let your words and ideas carry the force of any emphasis you want to communicate.

No   **The last act of her play is really impressive!**

YES   **The last act resolves the crisis in an unexpected and dramatic way.**

If you feel you absolutely have to include an exclamation point to get your point across in dialogue or with an emphatic command or statement, do not use it along with a comma, a question mark, or a period indicating the end of a sentence.

▶ **"Just watch the ball!" the coach yelled.**

▶ **How is it possible that the New York Yankees came back to tie and then win a World Series game in the bottom of the ninth inning and not just once, but twice?**

Note, however, that an exclamation point or a question mark can be used with a period that signals an abbreviation:

▶ **Where were you at 11 p.m.?**

EXERCISE 22.1 Use end punctuation correctly.

Mark with "X" the sentence (A or B) that uses more appropriate end punctuation. Explain your choice to your classmates. (**A** = See Answer Key.)

EXAMPLE:

_____ A. The Web site asks users whether they are so afraid of flying that they avoid airplanes in all circumstances?

___X___ B. The Web site asks users whether they are so afraid of flying that they avoid airplanes in all circumstances.

A 1. _____ A. With modern technology come modern fears, and thousands of people in industrial societies are terrified of air travel.

_____ B. With modern technology come modern fears, and thousands of people in industrial societies are terrified of air travel!

A 2. _____ A. If people who must fly for business or family reasons are too frightened to board an airplane, where can they turn for help.

_____ B. If people who must fly for business or family reasons are too frightened to board an airplane, where can they turn for help?

3. _____ A. Although most fearful fliers know that flying is statistically safer than driving a car, many of them cannot overcome the part of the mind that says, "What if the plane crashes?"

_____ B. Although most fearful fliers know that flying is statistically safer than driving a car, many of them cannot overcome the part of the mind that says, "What if the plane crashes?".

4. _____ A. Self-help classes and Web sites help fearful fliers to become more familiar with airplanes; the idea is that familiar things are less frightening.

_____ B. Self-help classes and Web sites help fearful fliers to become more familiar with airplanes; the idea is that familiar things are less frightening!

5. _____ A. After a plane crash has been in the news, enrollment in self-help classes for fearful fliers tends to decline; psychologists believe that such events convince people that their irrational fears are based in reality, so they say to themselves, "See. I was right to avoid airplanes at all costs."

_____ B. After a plane crash has been in the news, enrollment in self-help classes for fearful fliers tends to decline; psychologists believe that such events convince people that their irrational fears are based in reality, so they say to themselves, "See? I was right to avoid airplanes at all costs!"

23 Commas

A comma separates parts of a sentence; a comma alone does not separate one sentence from another. When readers see a comma, they think, "These parts of the sentence are being separated for a reason." Readers have expectations as to how a sentence will progress, and a misplaced or missing comma can throw off their understanding. Look at the following sentence, which misuses the comma:

▶ **The rain fell, the roof fell in.**

Here the comma is an error, forming a comma splice (see 14g). Readers reading this and seeing the comma would then expect a third item in a series, something like the following:

▶ **The rain fell, the roof fell in, and Jake fell into a depression.**

But when the sentence does not continue in the expected way because a comma is misused, readers feel thwarted and have to backtrack to make sense of the writer's intention. Readers would have no difficulties with any of the following revisions:

▶ **The rain fell. The roof fell in.**

▶ **The rain fell; the roof fell in.**

▶ **The rain fell, and the roof fell in.**

Use the guidelines in this chapter to determine when to use a comma. If you absolutely cannot decide whether commas are appropriate, follow this general principle: _When in doubt, leave them out._ Readers find excessive use of commas more distracting than a few missing ones.

23a Two checklists—comma: yes, comma: no

The two checklists provide general rules of thumb. Details and more examples of each rule follow in the rest of chapter 23.

KEY POINTS

Comma: Yes

1. Before a coordinating conjunction (*and, but, or, nor, so, for, yet*) to connect independent clauses, including commands, but optional if the clauses are short (*Wharton entertained and James visited*) and optional in British English usage (23b)

   ▶ **The producer of the drama wanted to change the ending, but the author refused.**

   ▶ **Accept your fate, and learn to accept it cheerfully.**

2. After most introductory words, phrases, or clauses (23c)

   ▶ **During the noisy party, the neighbors complained.**

   ▶ **While the guests were eating, a mouse ran across the floor.**

   Note how omitting the comma can lead to a misreading.

3. To set off any extra (nonrestrictive) information included in a sentence ("extra commas with extra information") (23d)

   ▶ **Her father, a computer programmer, works late at night.**

   ▶ **The Federalists sought help from their leader, the diminutive James Madison.**

4. To set off transitional expressions and explanatory inserts (23e)

   ▶ **The ending, however, is disappointing.**

   ▶ **On the other hand, little girls talk to maintain community and contact.**

   ▶ **And girls, I hasten to add, will often emulate their mothers.**

5. To separate three or more items in a series (23f)

   ▶ **They ordered eggs, bacon, and potatoes.**

   ▶ **Kazan used music ingeniously, let his actors interpret crucial scenes, and constantly choreographed scenes with geometric precision.**

   See also 24a for the use of semicolons in a series.

(continued)

(continued)

6. Between coordinate adjectives that can be reversed and connected with *and* (20f and 23g)

   ▶ We ate a delicious, well-prepared, and inexpensive meal.

7. After a verb that introduces a quotation (23h)

   ▶ She gasped, "We haven't a moment to lose!"

KEY POINTS

Comma: No

See 23j for additional details and examples.

1. Not between subject and verb

   ▶ The actor we saw in *Get Shorty* plays Tony in *The Sopranos.*

   However, use two commas to set off any extra information inserted between subject and verb (see 23d):

   ▶ The actor we saw in *Get Shorty,* directed by Barry Sonnenfeld, plays Tony in *The Sopranos.*

2. Not before part of a compound structure that is not an independent clause

   ▶ She won the trophy and accepted it graciously.

   ▶ Poet Marie Ponsot has published only five books of poetry but has discarded many poems during her lifetime.

3. Not *after* a coordinating conjunction connecting two independent clauses, but *before* it

   ▶ The movie tried to be engaging, but it failed miserably.

4. Not between two independent clauses without a coordinating conjunction (use either a period and a capital letter or a semicolon instead)

   ▶ He won; she was delighted.

5. Not between an independent clause and a following dependent clause introduced by *after, before, because, if, since, unless, until,* or *when* (neither before nor after the subordinating conjunction)

   ▶ **She will continue working for the city until she has saved enough for graduate school.**

   ▶ **His prose comes alive when he describes the battle scenes.**

6. Not before a clause beginning with *that*

   ▶ **They warned us that the meeting would be difficult.**

7. Not before and after essential, restrictive information (see also 23d)

   ▶ **The player who scored the goal became a hero.**

8. Not between a verb and its object or complement

   ▶ **The best gifts are food and clothes.**

   ▶ **The task was to feed and clothe all the survivors.**

9. Not after *such as*

   ▶ **Popular fast-food items, such as hamburgers and hot dogs, tend to be high in fat.**

EXERCISE 23.1   Identify commas: yes or no.

In the passage, identify commas that are used correctly with a checkmark and commas that are used incorrectly with an X. For those marked as correct, give the number of the item in the *Comma: Yes* Key Points box that explains why the comma is correct. (**A** = See Answer Key.)

EXAMPLE:

                                        √(2)

Since the first computers were invented, people have tried

                        ×

to find out if computers, can actually learn to think.

   A The notion of artificial intelligence, is one of the most intriguing, controversial ideas in computer programming today. **A** Anyone, who studies computers, has probably wondered whether modern computers are learning to think. ▲ Alan Turing, who helped to develop computers during and after World War II, believed that the only way to tell if a computer could think was to ask it questions. ▲ According to him, if the computer gave answers that were indistinguishable from those of a human, the computer could be considered intelligent. ▲ John Searle, a philosopher at the University of California at Berkeley, argued that a computer that was able to create intelligent-sounding answers to questions need not actually understand anything, it might simply be popping out replies based on the rules it had absorbed. Does a machine such as, the chess-playing computer Big Blue qualify as a thinking mechanism, or, has it simply learned the rules of chess well enough to simulate thought? One reason, that this question is difficult to answer is that human thought is difficult to define and quantify. No one, apparently, has yet figured out exactly what causes consciousness, and no one understands exactly how human brains think. As Searle points out, "I think we could build a thinking machine; it's just that we don't have the faintest idea how to go about it, because we don't know how the brain goes about it."

23b Comma before a coordinating conjunction (e.g., *and*, *but*) between independent clauses

To connect independent clauses with a coordinating conjunction (*and, but, or, nor, so, for,* or *yet*), place a comma before the conjunction.

comma + coordinating conjunction

├─── independent clause ───┤ ├─── independent clause ───┤

► The managers are efficient, but personnel turnover is high.

► The juggler juggled seven plates, and we all cheered.

► Teachers can ask for a specific assignment, or their supervisors can make plans for the whole school.

► The novel did not sell well, nor was it favorably reviewed.

► The soldiers had been well trained, so they knew exactly what to do.

► The Canadian geese are heading south, for winter is clearly on the way.

► Drugs are available for heart disease, yet many have unpleasant side effects.

VARIATIONS

1. If the two independent clauses are short, some writers omit the comma before the conjunction.

   ▶ **He offered to help and he meant it.**

   But if you always include it, you will never be wrong.

   ▶ **He offered to help, and he meant it.**

2. If the second clause presents a contrast, particularly after a negative, some writers use just a comma without a coordinating conjunction. See 14g.

   ▶ **Chicano Spanish is not correct, it is a living language.**

   —Gloria Anzaldúa, "How to Tame a Wild Tongue"

   ▶ **His dog doesn't just bark, it bites.**

   Readers of academic prose, however, may regard this as a comma splice error and may prefer a semicolon, a period, or a dash in place of the comma.

   ▶ **His dog doesn't just bark—it bites.**

3. If the two independent clauses contain internal commas, you can use a semicolon in place of a comma between the two clauses.

   ▶ **When he was awarded the prize, the actor praised his director, who had first offered him the part; but he refused to acknowledge the author.** ■

EXERCISE 23.2   Use commas before coordinating conjunctions connecting independent clauses.
Combine each of the sentence pairs into a single sentence, using a coordinating conjunction and a comma. (**A** = See Answer Key.)

EXAMPLE:

Patrick O'Brian wrote twenty novels about the voyages of a
                                        Wars, but O'Brian
sea captain and a naval doctor during the Napoleonic ~~Wars.~~

~~O'Brian~~ died after beginning to write their twenty-first

adventure.

A 1. Patrick O'Brian once said that he was a derivative writer. All of his information came from "log books, dispatches, letters, memoirs, and contemporary reports" from two centuries ago.

A 2. O'Brian wrote about adventure on the high seas and naval battles. He also brought the manners and customs of naval society to life.

3. O'Brian's books are filled with obscure naval terminology. Many readers who have little interest in sailing ships have become devoted fans of Jack Aubrey and Stephen Maturin, the main characters in his twenty-volume series.

4. A *New York Times* book review once called O'Brian's books "the best historical novels ever written." Readers recognize that the characters are every bit as realistic as the descriptions of life on a British naval ship.

5. O'Brian's fans can simply keep rereading the twenty novels about Aubrey and Maturin. They can help support the cookbooks, glossaries, and Web sites devoted to exploring every detail of O'Brian's texts.

23c Comma after an introductory word, phrase, or dependent clause

1. Use a comma to signal to readers that the introductory part of the sentence has ended.   It says, in effect, "Now wait for the independent clause."

introductory word ⌐———— independent clause ————⌐
▶ **However, many researchers disagree.**

⌐— introductory phrase —⌐ ⌐———— independent clause ————⌐
▶ **Seventeen years ago, Burma was renamed Myanmar.**

⌐———— dependent clause ————⌐ ⌐———— independent clause ————⌐
▶ **If you blow out all the candles, your wishes will come true.**

VARIATION   If the introductory element is only one word or a short phrase establishing the time frame, many writers omit the comma.

▶ **Soon the climate will change.**

▶ **In a few months children learn to crawl, walk, and talk.**

However, if you want to apply a rule consistently, it will never be wrong to include a comma:

▶ **Soon, the climate will change.**

▶ **In a few months, children learn to crawl, walk, and talk.** ■

2. Never omit the comma after an introductory phrase or clause if a misreading could result.

| MISREADING POSSIBLE | When active viruses can spread easily. |
| REVISED | When active, viruses can spread easily. |

| MISREADING POSSIBLE | While she was cooking her cat ran off with a lamb chop. |
| REVISED | While she was cooking, her cat ran off with a lamb chop. |

| MISREADING POSSIBLE | Until this spring fever was the most serious symptom treated at the health center. |
| REVISED | Until this spring, fever was the most serious symptom treated at the health center. |

3. Take special care with an *-ing* phrase at the beginning of a sentence. An *-ing* word can begin an introductory phrase modifying the sentence subject (and the phrase will end with a comma), or it can be the subject of the sentence, in which case use no comma between the subject and the verb.

INTRODUCTORY PHRASE

subject
Investigating the DNA evidence, the detectives
verb
found the attacker.

SUBJECT

├─────── subject ───────┤ verb
Investigating the DNA evidence led detectives to the attacker.

23d Commas to set off an extra (nonrestrictive) phrase or clause

Commas signal that the extra, nonessential information they set off (useful and interesting as it may be) can be removed without radically altering or limiting the meaning of the independent clause. Think of paired commas as handles that can lift the enclosed information out of the sentence without making the sentence's meaning confusing.

├───── nonrestrictive ─────┤
▶ The Colosseum, Rome's most famous landmark, once held crowds of more than fifty thousand people.

─────────── nonrestrictive ───────────

▶ The American diner, a narrow restaurant with booths and

a counter, frequently features wall-mounted juke boxes.

Note: A phrase or clause that limits or restricts the meaning of the independent clause is said to be restrictive (essential). A restrictive phrase or clause cannot be removed without changing the meaning of the sentence. Do not use commas to set off restrictive information.

─────────── restrictive ───────────

▶ The players who practice often and keep fit are usually the ones who succeed.

The restrictive element is essential. If it were removed, the sentence would be "The players are usually the ones who succeed." A reader would wonder, "Which players?" The clause "who practice often and keep fit" restricts the meaning of "the players" to a subgroup.

In the following example, the same clause "who practice often and keep fit" does not restrict the subject to a subgroup of teammates. Readers can grasp fully the meaning of "His daughter's Little League teammates win every game." Rather, the clause adds additional, nonessential information, which is nonrestrictive and therefore set off with commas.

─ nonrestrictive element ─

▶ His daughter's Little League teammates, who practice often

and keep fit, win every game.

See 20c for more on restrictive and nonrestrictive relative clauses.

Nonrestrictive phrases   In the following examples, if the phrase were omitted, readers might lose some interesting details but would still be able to understand the message.

─────── nonrestrictive ───────

▶ A collector since childhood, the gallery owner decided to leave his sculptures to a museum.

▶ His dog, a big Labrador retriever, is afraid of mice.   [If you read "His dog is afraid of mice," you would not necessarily need to know what type of dog he owns.]

▶ Salinger's first novel, *The Catcher in the Rye,* captures the language and thoughts of teenagers.   [The commas are used because Salinger obviously wrote only one *first* novel, and the title provides supplementary information, not information that identifies which novel the writer means.]

▶ **My boss, wearing a red tie and a green shirt, radiated the holiday spirit.**

Nonrestrictive clauses

┌─────── nonrestrictive ───────┐
▶ **My boss, who wears bright colors, is a cheerful person.** [The independent clause "My boss is a cheerful person" does not lead readers to ask "Which boss?" The relative clause does not restrict the meaning of *boss*.]

Do not use commas with relative clauses providing essential, restrictive information.

┌ restricts *people* to a subgroup ┐
▶ **People who wear bright colors send an optimistic message.** [The clause beginning with *who* restricts "people" to a subgroup: not all people send an optimistic message; those who wear bright colors do.]

EXERCISE 23.3   Use commas after introductory material or with nonrestrictive elements.

Add any necessary commas. Some sentences may be correct. (**A** = See Answer Key.)

EXAMPLE:

Working for a major chemical manufacturer ˌCharles

Baldwin ˌan engineer ˌhelped to develop the symbol that

identifies biohazards.

A 1. Realizing that laboratories and medical facilities around the world all needed to dispose of biohazards researchers wanted a symbol that would indicate to everyone which material was infectious.

A 2. Designers who create symbols want them to be memorable.

3. However the biohazard symbol needed to be unlike any other symbol.

4. In 1966 the symbol which is three-sided so that it looks the same if seen upside-down or sideways was chosen.

5. With its vivid orange color, a shade determined to be the most visible of all colors under most conditions the symbol was soon accepted by the Centers for Disease Control, the Occupational Safety and Health Administration, and the National Institutes of Health.

23e Commas with transitional expressions and explanatory insertions

1. Transitional expressions Transitional expressions such as *on the other hand* and words such as *therefore* and *however* (conjunctive adverbs) connect or weave together the ideas in your writing and act as signposts for readers. (See 5e for a list of these expressions.) Use commas to set off a transitional expression from the rest of the sentence. If the transitional expression is at the end of a sentence, introduce it with a comma and follow it with a period.

▶ My dog is afraid of mice. However, most Labrador retrievers are courageous.

▶ Most Labrador retrievers, however, are courageous.

▶ Most Labrador retrievers are courageous, however.

Note: When you use a transitional word or expression such as *however, therefore, nevertheless, above all, of course,* or *in fact* at the beginning of an independent clause, end the previous clause with a period or a semicolon. Then place a comma after the transitional expression.

▶ My dog is afraid of mice; however, most Labrador retrievers are courageous.

▶ The party was a success. In fact, it was still going on at 2 a.m.

See also 23c.

2. Explanatory insertions Sometimes writers insert a phrase or a clause to make a comment, to offer an example, or to point out a contrast. Insertions used for these purposes are set off by commas.

▶ The consequences will be dire, I think.

▶ Seasonal allergies, such as those caused by ragweed, are a common affliction.

▶ The best, if not the only, solution is to apologize and start over.

▶ His assets, not his earnings, are being scrutinized.

23f Commas separating three or more items in a series

Readers see commas between items in a series and think, "This is a list." If you said a series aloud, you would probably pause between items; in writing, you use commas to separate them. The items can be words, phrases, or clauses.

WORDS ▶ The performance was tasteful, emotional, and dramatic.

However, do not insert a comma between the last adjective of a series and the noun the adjectives modify (23g):

▶ The long, thorough, tireless/ investigation yielded the expected results.

PHRASES Searching through the drawer, the detective found a key, a stamp, three coins, and a photograph.

VARIATION In a series of words or phrases, some writers, particularly journalists or those using British English, will omit the comma separating the last item from the one before it—*snow, sleet and freezing rain*. Though you will see this usage, it is better to use a comma between each item in a list so that your meaning is always clear, as in the following example:

▶ The director achieved a romantic atmosphere with soft music, soothing dialogue about love and happy couples. [Without the comma after *love*, readers could think that the dialogue was about happy couples.] ∎

CLAUSES The report questioned why the collapse occurred, what could have been done to prevent it, and who was responsible.

Note: Use commas only *between* each of the items in a series. Do not insert a comma to signify the beginning or end of the series.

▶ Some basic terms in economics are/ supply, demand, and *consumption.*

▶ France, Dorset, and the Lake District/ exerted a significant influence on Wordsworth's poems.

23g Commas between coordinate adjectives

Adjectives are *coordinate* when their order can be reversed and the word *and* can be inserted between them without any change in meaning. Coordinate adjectives (such as *beautiful, delicious, exciting, noisy*) make subjective and evaluative judgments. Separate coordinate adjectives with commas. See 35g.

▶ Energetic, efficient people are the ones he likes to hire.

▶ Efficient, energetic people are the ones he likes to hire.

Do not, however, put a comma between the final adjective of a series and the noun it modifies.

▶ **Energetic, efficient, and polite salespeople are in demand.**

When each adjective in a series modifies all the adjectives that follow it and gives objectively verifiable information about, for instance, number, size, shape, color, or nationality, the adjectives are said to be *cumulative,* not coordinate. Do not separate cumulative adjectives with commas.

▶ **Entering the little old stone house brought back memories of her childhood.**   [The house is made of stone. The stone house is old. The old stone house is little.]

For the order of cumulative adjectives, see 35g.

23h Comma with a direct quotation

Use a comma to separate the verb from the direct quotation. The verb may come either before or after the quotation.

▶ **When asked what she wanted to be later in life, she replied, "An Olympic swimmer."**

▶ **"I want to be an Olympic swimmer," she announced confidently.**   [The comma is inside the quotation marks.]

However, do not add a comma to a quotation that ends with a question mark or an exclamation point (but see p. 263 for a variation).

No   **"What do you want to be?," she asked.**

Yes   **"What do you want to be?" she asked.**

In addition, do not insert a comma before a quotation that is integrated into your sentence:

No   **The advertisers are promoting, "a healthier lifestyle."**

Yes   **The advertisers are promoting "a healthier lifestyle."**

Exercise 23.4   Use commas with transitional expressions, items in a series, coordinate adjectives, and direct quotations.

Add any necessary commas; delete any that are unnecessary. (**A** = See Answer Key.)

EXAMPLE:

A surprising perplexing proposal from the U.S.

Department of Energy would allow the recycling of

steel that is slightly radioactive.

A The Department of Energy has proposed to recycle scrap metal from weapons and research plants that are going to be demolished in Tennessee, Kentucky, Ohio, South Carolina and Colorado. **A** Radiation has, unfortunately contaminated the surface of the metals that the DOE plans to recycle. **A** Over a million tons of the contaminated metal will be available for recycling in the next fifteen years if the proposal is accepted.

A First however, the DOE is, funding an environmental study of the plan analyzing the feasibility of recycling and reusing only those metals that meet lower radiation standards, and scheduling public hearings around the country. **A** On one side scrap metal dealers have expressed preliminary support for the proposal. **A** Citizens who live near steel-recycling plants on the other hand have asked the DOE to reject the proposal as an irresponsible environmentally unsound, idea. In Minnesota, which has steel-recycling plants, a public hearing drew many concerned, outspoken, citizens who testified that they did not want radioactive material trucked through their neighborhoods. In addition many noted that they would not want the government to allow scrap metal plants to add radioactive steel to the items that the plants manufacture, such as, snow shovels eyeglasses forks, and, cars. One woman announced "I propose that our federal government have a zero tolerance for any release of radioactive materials because I'm scared." Minnesota's largest steel-recycling plant has in fact already announced that it has rejected the DOE plan. The manager of the DOE environmental study said that the department would abide by the study's results.

23i Special uses of commas

1. To make the meaning clear and prevent misreading   Use a comma to separate elements in a sentence that may otherwise be confusing.

▶ **He who can, does. He who cannot, teaches.**

—George Bernard Shaw, *Man and Superman*

[Usually a comma is not used to separate a subject from the verb. Here the comma is necessary to prevent confusing the readers.]

2. With an absolute phrase Use a comma to set off a phrase that modifies the whole sentence (an absolute phrase).

> ┌──────────── absolute phrase ────────────┐
> ▶ The audience looking on in amusement, the valedictorian blew kisses to all her favorite instructors.

3. With a date Use a comma to separate the date from the year and the day from the date:

> ▶ On May 14, 1998, the legendary singer Frank Sinatra died.

> ▶ The poet laureate is reading in San Francisco on Wednesday, May 1.

Do not use a comma when you mention only the month and date (May 14) or month and year (May 1998).

4. With numbers Use a comma (never a period) to divide numbers into thousands.

> ▶ 1,200   ▶ 515,000   ▶ 34,000,000

No commas are necessary in years (*2004*), numbers in addresses (*3501 East 10th Street*), or page numbers (*page 1008*).

5. With scene or line references In the body of your text (not in a parenthetical reference) use a comma between act and scene and between page and line: act 3, scene 4; page 14, line 9.

6. With titles Use commas to set off a person's title or degree.

> ▶ Stephen L. Carter, PhD, gave the commencement speech.

7. With an inverted name Use a comma between the last name and the first:

> ▶ Dillard, Annie

8. With the parts of an address

> ▶ Alice Walker was born in Eatonton, Georgia, in 1944.

However, do not use a comma before a ZIP code: Newton, MA 02459.

9. With a conversational tag or tag question

> ▶ Yes, Salinger's daughter, like others before her, has produced a memoir.

> ▶ She has not won a Pulitzer Prize, has she?

10. With a direct address or salutation

▶ Whatever you build next, Mr. Trump, will cause controversy.

23j When not to use commas:
Nine rules of thumb

1. Do not use a comma to separate a verb from its subject.

▶ The gifts she received from her colleagues made her realize her value to the company.

▶ Interviewing so many women in the United States helped the researcher understand the "American dream."

Between a subject and verb, you may need to put two commas around inserted material, but never use just one comma.

```
         ┌──── subject ────┐
```
▶ The engraved plaque, given to her by her colleagues on her

```
                              verb
```
last day of work, made her feel respected.

2. Do not use a comma within a compound structure when the second part of the compound is not an independent clause.

▶ Amy Tan has written novels and adapted them for the screen.

▶ Tan has written about her mother and the rest of her family.

3. Do not use a comma after a coordinating conjunction that connects two sentences. The comma goes before the conjunction, not after it.

▶ *Mad Hot Ballroom* is supposed to be good, but I missed it when it came to my local movie theater.

4. Do not use a comma to join two independent clauses when no coordinating conjunction is present. Instead, end the first clause with a period and make the second clause a new sentence, or insert a semicolon between the clauses. Use a comma only if you connect the clauses with a coordinating conjunction. (See 14h for ways to correct a comma splice, the error that results when two independent clauses are incorrectly joined with a comma.)

▶ Amy Tan has written novels; they have been adapted for the screen.

VARIATION Some writers, however, do use a comma between two independent clauses when the clauses use parallel structures to point out a contrast (see also 14g and 23b).

▶ **She never insults, she just criticizes.**

If you do not know readers' expectations on this point, play it safe and separate the clauses with a period or a semicolon. ∎

5. Do not use a comma to separate an independent clause from a following dependent clause introduced by *after, before, because, if, since, unless, until,* or *when.*

▶ **The test results were good because all the students had studied in groups.**

▶ **The audience broke into wild applause when the young poet finished his reading.**

6. Do not use a comma to separate a clause beginning with *that* from the rest of the sentence.

▶ **The girl in Tan's story tried to convey to her mother that she did not have to be a child prodigy.**

Note: A comma can appear before a *that* clause when it is the second comma of a pair before and after extra information inserted as a nonrestrictive phrase.

▶ **He skates so fast, despite his size, that he will probably break the world record.**

7. Do not use commas around a phrase or clause that provides essential, restrictive information.

▶ **Alice Walker's essay "Beauty: When the Other Dancer Is the Self" discusses coping with a physical disfigurement.**
[Walker has written more than one essay. The title restricts the noun *essay* to one specific essay.]

Similarly, a restrictive relative clause introduced by *who, whom, whose, which,* or *that* is never set off by commas. The clause provides essential, identifying information (see also 20c and 23d).

▶ **The teachers praised the children who finished on time.**
[The teachers didn't praise all the children; they praised only the ones who finished on time.]

8. Do not use a comma to separate a verb from its object or complement.

▶ The qualities required for the job are punctuality, efficiency, and the ability to work long hours.

9. Do not use a comma after *such as*.

▶ They bought kitchen supplies such as detergent, paper towels, and garbage bags.

EXERCISE **23.5**   Use commas correctly.
Add any necessary commas, delete any that are unnecessary, and replace commas with periods or semicolons as needed. (**A** = See Answer Key.)

A "All men are created equal" wrote Thomas Jefferson but his deeds did not always match his eloquent words. **A** Like most of the other aristocratic landowners in Virginia, Jefferson the author of the Declaration of Independence founder of the University of Virginia and third president of the United States, owned slaves. **A** One of them was a woman named, Sally Hemings who was one-quarter African, and was probably the daughter of Jefferson's father-in-law and a half-African slave, if this genealogy is correct Hemings was the half-sister of Jefferson's late wife, Martha. **A** Indeed observers at the time noted that, Hemings looked remarkably like Martha Jefferson, who had died on September 6 1782, when Jefferson was thirty-nine.

A In 1802 a disgruntled former employee reported that President Jefferson, was the father of Hemings's three children. **A** Jefferson never responded publicly to the charge but, many people noticed the resemblance between him and the Hemings children. The believable scandalous rumors continued to circulate for years after Jefferson's death in 1826. A few historians speculated, that Jefferson's nephews might have fathered the Hemings children but, most ignored the story altogether. Yes it was true that slaveholders had often been known to impregnate slave women, yet such an act was difficult for many white Americans to reconcile with their views of one of the country's founders.

In the 1990s DNA tests were used to determine whether Jefferson could have been the father of Sally Hemings's children. The tests showed a match between the DNA of Jefferson's closest male relative's descendants, and the descendants of Hemings's youngest son, Eston. Clearly either Jefferson or a close relative was Eston's father. Most historians are now convinced that, Jefferson did father at least one of the Hemings children. A recent biography of Jefferson was called *American Sphinx* and the third president does, indeed seem to have hidden many secrets. Whether the revelations about his relationship with Hemings will change the way Americans feel about this Founding Father, remains to be seen.

24 Semicolons and Colons

A colon (:) may look like a semicolon (;). A colon is two dots; the semicolon, a dot above a comma. However, they are used in different ways, and they are not interchangeable. Note the use of the semicolon and colon in the following passage discussing the musical number "Cheek to Cheek" in the Astaire and Rogers film *Top Hat:*

[Ginger] Rogers is perhaps never more beautiful than when she's just listening; she never takes her eyes off him and throughout this scene I don't think she changes her expression once. The modesty of the effect makes her look like an angel: such a compliant, unasking attitude, handsome beyond expectation in such a fierce woman.

—Arlene Croce,
The Fred Astaire and Ginger Rogers Book

Ginger Rogers and Fred Astaire

24a Two checklists—semicolon: yes, semicolon: no

A period separates independent clauses with finality; a semicolon, such as the one you have just seen in this sentence, provides a less distinct separation and indicates that an additional related thought or item will follow immediately. Use one space after a semicolon.

KEY POINTS

Semicolon: Yes

1. Between closely connected independent clauses when no coordinating conjunction (*and, but, or, nor, so, for, yet*) is used

   ▶ **Biography tells us about the subject; biographers also tell us about themselves.**

   A comma between the two independent clauses would produce a comma splice, and no punctuation at all would produce a run-on sentence (see 14g). Do not use a capital letter to begin a clause after a semicolon.

2. Between independent clauses connected with a transitional expression like *however, moreover, in fact, nevertheless, above all,* or *therefore* (see the list in 5e)

   ▶ **The results of the study support the hypothesis; however, further research with a variety of tasks is necessary.**

   (If the transitional expression is in the middle or at the end of its clause, the semicolon still appears between the clauses: *The results support the hypothesis; further research, however, is necessary.*)

3. To separate items in a list containing internal commas (see also 23f)

   ▶ **When I cleaned out the refrigerator, I found a chocolate cake, half-eaten; some canned tomato paste, which had a blue fungus growing on the top; and some possibly edible meat loaf.**

KEY POINTS

Semicolon: No

1. Not in place of a colon to introduce a list or an explanation

   ▶ **Ellsworth Kelly has produced a variety of works of art: drawings, paintings, prints, and sculptures.**

(continued)

(continued)

2. Not after an introductory phrase or dependent clause, even if the phrase or clause is long. Using a semicolon would produce a fragment. Use a comma instead.

   ▶ **Because the training period was so long and arduous for all the players, the manager allowed one visit by family and friends.**

3. Not before an appositive phrase

   ▶ **The audience cheered the Oscar winner, Clint Eastwood.**

4. Not in place of a comma before *and, but, or, nor, so, for,* or *yet* joining independent clauses

   ▶ **The thrift shop in the church basement needed a name, and the volunteers chose Attic Treasures.**

24b Two checklists—colon: yes, colon: no

A colon signals anticipation. It follows an independent clause and introduces information that readers will need. A colon tells readers, "What comes next will define, illustrate, or explain what you have just read." Use one space after a colon.

KEY POINTS

Colon: Yes

1. After an independent clause to introduce a list

   ▶ **The students included three pieces of writing in their portfolios: a narrative, an argument, and a documented paper.**

2. After an independent clause to introduce an explanation, expansion, or elaboration

   ▶ **After an alarming cancer diagnosis and treatment in 1996, Lance Armstrong was victorious: he won the Tour de France seven times.**

   Some writers prefer to use a capital letter after a colon introducing an independent clause. Whatever you choose to do, be consistent in your usage.

3. To introduce a rule or principle, which may begin with a capital letter

  ▶ **The main principle of public speaking is simple: Look at the audience.**

4. To introduce a quotation not integrated into your sentence and not introduced by a verb such as *say*

  ▶ **Emily Post has provided an alternative to attempting to outdo others: "To do *exactly as your neighbors do* is the only sensible rule."**

  A colon also introduces a long quotation set off from your text (40g).

5. In salutations, precise time notations, titles, and biblical citations

  ▶ **Dear Chancellor Witkin:**

  ▶ **To: The Chancellor**

  ▶ **7:20 p.m.**

  ▶ *Backlash: The Undeclared War against American Women*

  ▶ **Genesis 37:31–35** [In MLA style, use a period with no space in place of the colon.]

KEY POINTS

Colon: No

1. Not directly after a verb (such as a form of *be* or *include*)

  ▶ **The two main effects were the improvement of registration and an increase in the number of advisers.**

  ▶ **The book includes a preface, an introduction, an appendix, and an index.**

2. Not after a preposition (such as *of, except,* and *regarding*) or the phrase *such as*

  ▶ **The essay consisted of a clear beginning, middle, and end.**

  ▶ **The novel will please many readers except linguists and lawyers.**

(continued)

(continued)

> ▶ They packed many different items for the picnic, such as taco chips, salsa, bean salad, pita bread, and egg rolls.

3. Not after *for example, especially,* or *including*

> ▶ His varied taste is shown by his living room furnishings, including antiques, modern art, and art deco lighting fixtures.

EXERCISE 24.1   Use semicolons and colons correctly.
Correct any errors in the use of semicolons and colons. (**A** = See Answer Key.)

A Japan has long been one of the most homogeneous of the modern industrial nations, many Japanese protect their cultural identity so strongly that foreigners are rarely allowed to feel a part of Japan, no matter how long they and their families remain in the country. **A** Foreign nationals who make Japan their home are not required to send their children to school as Japanese parents must, in addition, non-Japanese are not covered by Japan's national health insurance. **A** Many foreign nationals, consequently; consider Japan only a temporary home. **A** However, the Japanese population is: getting older, with more retirees than new babies throughout the country, currently, the Japanese birthrate is one of the lowest in the world. **A** To keep the economy alive and pay for pensions for retired workers and their families; Japan must find more workers. **A** The United Nations now recommends that Japan begin to encourage immigration.

Many Japanese emigrants in the early nineteenth century went to Brazil to work. In the 1990s, Japan began to allow Brazilians of Japanese descent to return to Japan on temporary work visas today, there are a quarter of a million Brazilians in Japan, and many of them now hold permanent visas. Japan has: two Brazilian television channels, four Brazilian newspapers, and forty-one Brazilian schools. Although many of these Brazilians have Japanese ancestors; they are culturally Brazilian, and the Brazilian and Japanese cultures occasionally clash. Some Japanese in cities with large Brazilian populations complain that Brazilians do not comply with Japanese regulations, some Brazilians say that the Japanese make them feel unwelcome. One thing, however, is certain; Japan must accommodate foreign workers if the nation's economy is to survive the population slump.

25 Apostrophes

An apostrophe indicates ownership or possession: *Fred's books; the government's plans* (the books belonging to Fred; the plans of the government). It is used in time phrases (*today's news, a year's pay*), and it also signals omitted letters (*who's, can't*).

25a Two checklists—apostrophe: yes, apostrophe: no

KEY POINTS

Apostrophe: Yes

1. Use *-'s* for the possessive form of all nouns except plural nouns that end with *-s*: *the hero's misfortune, the actress's Academy Award.*

2. Use an apostrophe alone for the possessive form of plural nouns that end with *-s*: *many politicians' lives, the heroes' misfortunes.*

3. Use an apostrophe to indicate the omission of letters in contracted forms such as *didn't, they're,* and *let's.*

4. Use *it's* only for "it is" or "it has": *It's a good idea; it's been a long time.* (The possessive form of the pronoun *it* is spelled with no apostrophe: *The house lost* its *roof.*)

KEY POINTS

Apostrophe: No

1. Generally, do not use an apostrophe to form the plurals of nouns. (See 25d for rare exceptions.)

2. Never use an apostrophe before an *-s* ending on a verb. Note that *let's* is a contracted form for *let us;* the *-s* is not a verb ending.

(continued)

(continued)

3. Do not write possessive pronouns (*hers, its, ours, yours, theirs*) with an apostrophe: *The tree lost its leaves.*

4. Do not use an apostrophe to form the plural of names: *the Browns.*

5. Do not use an apostrophe to indicate possession by objects such as buildings and items of furniture. Instead, use no apostrophe: *the hotel lobby;* or use *of: the lobby of the hotel.*

25b Apostrophe to signal possession

As a general rule, to signal possession, use -*'s* with singular nouns, with indefinite pronouns, and with plural nouns that do not form the plural with -*s.*

the child's books	anybody's opinion
the children's toys	today's world
this month's budget	Mr. Jackson's voice
someone else's idea	their money's worth

Individual and joint ownership To indicate individual ownership, make each owner possessive.

▶ **Updike's and Roth's recent works received glowing reviews.**

To show joint ownership, make only the last owner possessive: *Sam, Sue, and Pat's house.*

Compound nouns Add -*'s* to the last word in a compound noun.

▶ **my brother-in-law's car**

Singular nouns ending in -s When a singular noun ends in -*s*, add -*'s* as usual for the possessive.

▶ **Dylan Thomas's imagery**   ▶ **my boss's instructions**

However, when a singular noun ending in -*s* is a long word or ends with a *z* or *eez* sound, an apostrophe alone is sometimes used: *Charles' theories, Erasmus' rhetoric, Euripides' dramas.*

Plural nouns   If a plural noun does not end in -s, add -'s to form the possessive: *the women's tasks.*

Plural nouns already ending in -s   Add only an apostrophe when a plural noun already ends in -s.

▶ **the students' suggestions**   [more than one student]

▶ **my friends' ambitions**   [more than one friend]

Remember to include an apostrophe in comparisons with a noun understood (15f and 19g).

▶ **His views are different from other professors'.**
   [. . . from other professors' views]

EXERCISE **25.1**   Use apostrophes to signal possession. Correct any errors in the use of apostrophes.   (**A** = See Answer Key.)

EXAMPLE:

In parts of Africa that have been devastated by AIDS,

doctors who practice Western-style medicine are looking
                                            healers'
at traditional ~~healer's~~ roles in treating the sick.

A 1. Doctors and healers' ideas about useful treatments for people infected with the AIDS virus sometimes conflict with each other.

A 2. For example, traditional healers often prescribe emetics to cause vomiting, and if a patients' treatment also includes retroviral drugs, the patient may expel the drugs before they take effect.

3. Because many doctors in Africa understand their patients faith in traditional healing, some doctors are trying to work with healers rather than fighting them.

4. Some healers have agreed to attend conferences' at hospitals, where they learn to wear latex gloves when treating patients and to use alcohol to clean razor blades' edges and porcupine quills that have contacted any patients' body fluids.

5. Many patients trust healer's more than they trust doctor's, so hospitals in some areas have deputized traditional healers to monitor their patients intake of AIDS drugs and their mental well-being.

25c Apostrophe with plurals: Specific Cases

In a contraction (*shouldn't, don't, haven't*), the apostrophe appears where letters have been omitted. To test whether an apostrophe is in the correct place, mentally replace the missing letters. The replacement test, however, will not help with the following:

> won't   will not

Note: Some readers object to contractions in formal academic writing because they view them as colloquial and informal. It is safer not to use contractions unless you know your readers' preferences.

can't	cannot	they'd	they had *or* they would
didn't	did not	they're	they are
he's	he is *or* he has	it's	it is *or* it has
's	is, has, *or* does (How's it taste?)	let's	let us (Let's go.)

Never place an apostrophe before the *-s* ending of a verb:

▶ **The author let⁀s his characters take over.**

An apostrophe can also take the place of the first part of a year or decade.

▶ **the greed of the '80s**   [the 1980s]

▶ **the Spirit of '76**   [the year 1776]

Note: Fixed forms spelled with an apostrophe, such as *o'clock* and the poetic *o'er*, are contractions ("of the clock," "over").

25d Apostrophe with plurals: Special cases

A general rule is never to use an apostrophe to form a plural. However, in the following instances an apostrophe is commonly used.

1. Use -'s for the plural form of letters of the alphabet.   Italicize only the letter, not the plural ending (28c).

▶ **Maria picked all the *M*'s out of her alphabet soup.**

▶ **Georges Perec's novel called *A Void* has no *e*'s in it at all.**

2. Use -'s for the plural form of a word referred to as the word itself. Italicize the word named as a word, but do not italicize the -'s ending (28c).

▶ **You have too many *but*'s in that sentence.**

Note: MLA and APA prefer no apostrophe in the plural form of numbers, acronyms, and abbreviations (29b).

the 1900s   CDs   FAQs   BAs

However, you will frequently see such plurals spelled with *-'s*. In all cases, be consistent in your usage.

Never use an apostrophe to signal the plural of common nouns or personal names: *big bargains, the Jacksons.*

25e *It's* versus *its*

When deciding whether to use *its* or *it's*, think about meaning. *It's* is a contraction meaning "it is" or "it has." *Its* is the possessive form of the pronoun *it* and means "belonging to it." See also 18b.

▶ **It's a good idea.**   ▶ **The committee took its time.**

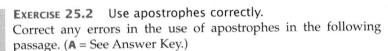

EXERCISE 25.2   Use apostrophes correctly.
Correct any errors in the use of apostrophes in the following passage. (**A** = See Answer Key.)

    A Vermonts legislature passed a law in 2000 that recognizes gay and lesbian civil unions in its state as the equivalent of marriage. **A** Since it's passage, the law has attracted gay tourists to Vermont, which along with Massachusetts is currently one of the few states that grant's gay and lesbian couples the right to all of the benefits of marriage. **A** In the first year of the new laws' existence in Vermont, two thousand gay and lesbian couples got civil-union licenses (in the same period, about five thousand heterosexual couples got traditional marriage licenses). Eighty percent of the gay and lesbian couples werent Vermont residents; the great majority of them celebrated civil unions' and then went home to states that didn't recognize their new status under the law. Most took vows for symbolic reasons, aware that they probably would'nt gain any legal rights' from the civil union. However, many of the gay and lesbian couple's trips to Vermont and now to Massachusetts seem to them, at least, to be rewarding. Most feel that its important to have official recognition of the two partners commitment to each other.

26 Quotation Marks

In American English, double quotation marks indicate where someone's exact words begin and end. However, for long quotations, see 26f.

26a Guidelines for using quotation marks

KEY POINTS

Quotation Marks: Basic Guidelines

1. Quote exactly the words used by the original speaker or writer.

2. Pair opening quotation marks with closing quotation marks to indicate where the quotation ends and your ideas begin.

3. Use correct punctuation to introduce and end a quotation, and place other marks of punctuation carefully in relation to the quotation marks.

4. Enclose the titles of articles, short stories, songs, and poems in quotation marks.

5. Enclose any added or changed material in square brackets (27c); indicate omitted material with ellipsis dots (27e).

26b Punctuation introducing and ending a quotation

After an introductory verb, such as *say, state,* or *write,* use a comma followed by a capital letter to introduce a direct quotation.

▶ Calvin Trillin says, "As far as I'm concerned, *whom* is a word that was invented to make everyone sound like a butler."

—"Whom Says So?"

Use a colon after a complete sentence introducing a quotation, and begin the quotation with a capital letter.

▶ Woody Allen always tries to make us laugh even about serious issues like wealth and poverty: "Money is better than poverty, if only for financial reasons." —*Without Feathers*

When a quotation is integrated into the structure of your own sentence, use no special introductory punctuation other than the quotation marks.

▶ Phyllis Grosskurth comments that "anxiety over money was driving him [Byron] over the brink." —*Byron*

Put periods and commas inside quotation marks, even if these punctuation marks do not appear in the original quotation.

▶ When Henry Rosovsky characterizes Bloom's ideas as "mind-boggling," he is not offering praise.　　*—The University*

In a documented paper, when you use parenthetical citations after a short quotation at the end of a sentence, put the period at the end of the citation, not within the quotation. See 26f and 40g for long quotations.

▶ Geoffrey Wolff observes that when his father died, there was nothing to indicate "that he had ever known another human being" (11).　　*—The Duke of Deception*

Put question marks and exclamation points inside the quotation marks if they are part of the original source, with no additional period.　　When your sentence is a statement, do not use a comma or period in addition to a question mark or exclamation point.

▶ She asked, "Where's my mama?"

Put a question mark, exclamation point, semicolon, or colon outside the closing quotation marks.　　If your sentence contains punctuation that is your own, not part of the original quotation, do not include it within the quotation marks.

▶ The chapter focuses on this question: Who are "the new American dreamers"?

26c Quotation marks in dialogue

Do not add closing quotation marks until the speaker changes or you interrupt the quotation. Begin each new speaker's words with a new paragraph.

interruption
⌐ of quotation ¬
▶　　"I'm not going to work today," he announced. "Why should I? I worked all weekend. My boss is away on vacation. And I have a headache."

┌——————— change of speaker ———————┐
"Honey, your boss is on the phone," his wife called from the bedroom.

If a quotation from one speaker continues for more than one paragraph, place *closing* quotation marks at the end of only the *final* paragraph of the quotation. However, place *opening* quotation marks at the beginning of every paragraph so that readers realize that the quotation is continuing.

26d   Double and single quotation marks

Enclose quotations in double quotation marks. Use single quotation marks to enclose a quotation or a title of a short work within a quotation. (British English reverses this usage.)

▶ **Margaret announced, "I have read 'The Lottery' already."**

▶ **The comedian Steven Wright once said, "I have an existential map. It has 'You are here' written all over it."**

26e   Quotation marks with titles, definitions, and translations

> **KEY POINTS**
>
> ### Titles: Quotation Marks or Italics/Underlining?
>
> 1. Quotation marks with the title of an article, short story, poem, song, or chapter: "Kubla Khan"; "Lucy in the Sky with Diamonds"; "The Yellow Wallpaper"; "America: The Multinational Society"
>
> 2. Italics or underlining with the title of a book, journal, magazine, newspaper, film, play, long poem published alone: The Tipping Point, *Newsweek, The Hours,* Beowulf (28a)
>
> 3. No quotation marks and no italics or underlining with the title of your own essay (26f): Why Telemarketing Is a Real Job
>
> For more on capital letters with titles, see 29a

For a translation or definition, use quotation marks:

▶ **The abbreviation *p.m.* means "after midday."**

26f   When not to use quotation marks

Pay attention not only to where you need quotation marks but also to where they are incorrect.

Do not put quotation marks around indirect quotations.

▶ One woman I interviewed said that ~~"~~ her husband argued like a lawyer. ~~"~~

Do not put quotation marks around clichés, slang, or trite expressions. Instead, revise to eliminate the cliché, slang, or trite expression. See also 8e, item 2, and 8e, item 5.

> *involvement.*
▶ All they want is ~~"a piece of the action."~~

Do not put quotation marks at the beginning and end of long indented quotations. When you use MLA style to quote more than three lines of poetry or four typed lines of prose, indent the whole passage one inch (or ten spaces) from the left margin. Do not enclose the quoted passage in quotation marks, but retain any internal quotation marks. See 40g for an illustration.

On the title page of your own paper, do not put quotation marks around your essay title. Use quotation marks in your title only when your title contains a quotation or the title of a short work.

▶ Charles Baxter's "Gryphon" as an Educational Warning

EXERCISE 26.1   Use quotation marks correctly.
Correct any errors in the use of quotation marks and related punctuation. (**A** = See Answer Key.)

A Child psychologist Bruno Bettelheim wrote that fairy tales, with their archetypal evil characters, terrifying situations, and improbable happy endings, could tell children a great deal, "about the inner problems of human beings and of the right solutions to their predicaments in any society". **A** In a newspaper article called Old Theory Could Explain Love of Harry Potter, Richard Bernstein argues that Bettelheim's analysis of fairy tales reveals the reasons for the staggering popularity of J. K. Rowling's books. **A** Although Bernstein sees the book *Harry Potter and the Sorcerer's Stone* as "a fairly conventional supernatural adventure story", he admits that children find the books "as powerful as the witch of "Hansel and Gretel." **A** Bernstein analyzes the narrative and concludes that, "Harry's story, . . . with its early images of alienation, rejection, loneliness and powerlessness leading to its classically fairy tale ending, contains the same basic message that Bettelheim described."

Bernstein is not alone in writing for adults about the Harry Potter "phenomenon." Academic conferences call for papers on Rowling's books; one asked graduate students and professors to ponder the ways that the books "embody, extend, exploit, or enfeeble the fantasy genre". Although children helped the Rowling books to reach "number one" on the bestseller lists, it is clear—in spite of the reservations of adults like Bernstein—that many adults are equally captivated by Harry Potter.

27   Other Punctuation Marks

27a   Dashes

A dash (—) alerts readers to an explanation, to something unexpected, or to an interruption. Form a dash by typing two hyphens, putting no extra space before, between, or after them. Recent software will transform the two hyphens into one continuous dash. A dash should be followed by a phrase, not a clause.

▶ **Armed with one weapon—his wit—he faced the crowd.**

▶ **The accused gasped, "But I never—" and fainted.**

▶ **In America there are two classes of travel—first class and with children.**   —Robert Benchley, in Robert E. Drennan, *The Algonquin Wits*

Commas can be used to set off an appositive phrase, but a pair of dashes is preferable when appositive phrases appear in a list containing commas.

▶ **The contents of his closet—torn jeans, frayed jackets, and suits shiny on the seat and elbows—made him reassess his priorities.**

Overusing the dash may produce a staccato effect. Use it sparingly.

27b   Parentheses

Use parentheses to mark an aside or provide additional information.

▶ **Everyone admired Chuck Yeager's feat (breaking the sound barrier).**

Also use parentheses to enclose citations in a documented paper and to enclose numbers or letters preceding items in a list.

▶ **(3) A journalist reports that in the course of many interviews, he met very few people who were cynical about the future of the country (Lamb 5).**

At the end of a sentence, place the period inside the last parenthesis only when a separate new sentence is enclosed (see also 29a).

▶ **Chuck Yeager's feat led to more competition in the space industry. (He broke the sound barrier.)**

27c Brackets

Square brackets ([ ]) When you insert words or comments or make changes to words within a quotation, enclose the inserted or changed material in square brackets. Be careful to insert only words that help the quotation fit into your sentence grammatically or that offer necessary explanation. Do not insert words that substantially change the meaning.

▶ **According to Ridley, "the key to both of these features of life [the ability to reproduce and to create order] is information."**

On occasion, you may need to use brackets to insert the Latin word *sic* (meaning "thus") into a quoted passage in which an error occurs. Using *sic* tells readers that the word or words that it follows were present in the original source and are not your own.

▶ **Richard Lederer tells of a man who did "exercises to strengthen his abominable [sic] muscles."**

Square brackets are also used in MLA style around ellipsis dots signaling an omission from a source itself containing ellipsis dots (see 27e).

Angle brackets (< >) Use angle brackets to enclose e-mail addresses and URLs, particularly in an MLA-style works-cited list. See chapter 31 and 43c.

27d Slashes

Use a slash (/) to separate two or three lines of poetry quoted within your own text. For quoting more than three lines of poetry, see 40g.

▶ **Philip Larkin asks a question that many of us relate to: "Why should I let the toad *work* / Squat on my life?"**

Slashes are also used in expressions such as *and/or* and *he/she* to indicate options. However, be careful not to overuse these expressions.

27e Ellipsis dots

When you omit material from a quotation, indicate the omission—the ellipsis—by using spaced dots (. . .). (MLA style recommends using square brackets around your inserted ellipsis dots if the passage you quote itself contains an ellipsis.) The following passage by Ruth Sidel, on page 27 of *On Her Own,* is used in the examples that follow.

> These women have a commitment to career, to material well-being, to success, and to independence. To many of them, an affluent lifestyle is central to their dreams; they often describe their goals in terms of cars, homes, travel to Europe. In short, they want their piece of the American Dream.

Words omitted from the middle of a quotation   Use three ellipsis dots when you omit material from the middle of a quotation, not from the beginning.

> ▶ **Ruth Sidel reports that the women in her interviews "have a commitment to career . . . and to independence" (27).**

Words omitted at the end of your sentence   When you omit part of a quotation, and the omission occurs at the end of your own sentence, insert ellipsis dots after the sentence period, followed by the closing quotation marks, making four dots in all.

> ▶ **Ruth Sidel presents interesting findings about jobs and money: "These women have a commitment to career, to material well-being. . . ."**

When a parenthetical reference follows the quoted passage, put the final sentence period after the parenthetical reference:

> ▶ **Ruth Sidel presents interesting findings about jobs and money: "These women have a commitment to career, to material well-being . . ." (27).**

Complete sentence omitted   When you omit a complete sentence or more, insert three ellipsis dots.

> ▶ **Sidel tells us how "an affluent life-style is central to their dreams; . . . they want their piece of the American Dream" (27).**

Line of poetry omitted   When you omit one or more lines of poetry from a long, indented quotation, indicate the omission with a line of dots.

> ▶ **This poem is for the hunger of my mother**
>
> . . . .
>
> **who read the Blackwell's catalogue**
> **like a menu of delights**
> **and when we moved from Puerto Rico to the States**
> **we packed 100 boxes of books and 40 of everything else.**
>
> —Aurora Levins Morales, *Class Poem*

When not to use ellipsis dots   Do not use ellipsis dots when you quote only a word or a phrase because it will be obvious that material has been omitted:

> ▶ **The women Sidel interviewed see an "affluent life-style" in their future.**

Note: Use three dots to indicate a pause in speech or an interruption.

> ▶ **The doctor said, "The good news is . . ." and then turned to take a phone call.**

For more on quoting, see 40g.

EXERCISE 27.1   Use other punctuation marks correctly.
Correct any errors in the use of dashes, parentheses, brackets, slashes, and ellipsis dots. (Citations should conform to MLA style.) (**A** = See Answer Key.)

A 1. George Harrison—the most reclusive member of the Beatles and the one who urged most strongly that the band stop playing live shows, died on November 29, 2001.

A 2. Beatles fans from all over the world mourned the death of the second member of the most famous rock band in history [John Lennon had been murdered more than twenty years before Harrison died of cancer].

A 3. Harrison (known to fans everywhere simply as "George," whose songwriting took a back seat to that of Lennon and McCartney, still wrote some of the Beatles' biggest hits, including "Something," "While My Guitar Gently Weeps," and "Here Comes the Sun."

A 4. Obituaries noted Harrison's interest in Eastern music and religion (at the time of his death, he remained a follower of a form of Hinduism he called Krishna Consciousness.

5. In many of the films in which Harrison either had a starring role or made a cameo appearance, *A Hard Day's Night, Help!,* a Beatles parody called *All You Need Is Cash* starring members of Monty Python (and produced by Harrison), *Monty Python's Life of Brian,* his sly sense of humor was apparent.

6. In *The Beatles Anthology,* Harrison noted, "As a band, we were tight . . . We could argue a lot among ourselves, but we were very, very close". . . . [83]

7. For most music lovers, Harrison will be forever associated with a band that broke up in 1970, but his 1987 album, *Cloud Nine,* "[won] over a new generation of fans (. . .) born after the Beatles' demise." (Rees and Crampton 256)

8. Expressing sorrow at Harrison's death, Paul McCartney said, "He (was) really just my baby brother" (Kozinn A1).

28   Italics and Underlining

Use italic type or underlining to highlight a word, phrase, or title in your own writing. Word processing programs offer italic type. Usually, though, in manuscript form, underlining is more distinctive and therefore preferred, particularly in MLA bibliographical lists and in material to be graded or typeset. Ask your instructor which to use.

28a   Titles of long works

In the body of an essay, italicize or underline the titles of books, journals, magazines, newspapers, plays, films, TV series, long poems, musical compositions, Web sites, online databases, and works of art.

▶ **The Sun Also Rises**   ▶ *The Daily Show*   ▶ **Newsweek**

▶ *Nickel and Dimed*   ▶ **Mona Lisa**   ▶ *Wikipedia*

Do not italicize or underline the names of sacred works such as the Bible, books of the Bible (Genesis, Psalms), and the Koran (Qur'an). Also do not italicize or underline the titles of documents and laws, such as the Declaration of Independence, the Constitution, and the Americans with Disabilities Act.

Do not italicize or underline the titles of short works, such as poems, short stories, essays, and articles; use quotation marks (26e). Do not italicize or underline the title of your own essay on your title page.

28b Transportation

Italicize or underline names of specific ships, trains, airplanes, and spacecraft.

▶ **<u>Mayflower</u>** ▶ *Silver Meteor* ▶ *Mir* ▶ **<u>Columbia</u>**

Do not underline or italicize the abbreviations sometimes preceding them: USS *Constitution.*

28c Letters, numerals, and words referring to the words themselves

Italicize or underline letters, numerals, and words referring to the items themselves, not to what they represent.

▶ **The sign had a large <u>P</u> in black marker and a <u>3</u> in red.**

▶ *Zarf* **is a useful word for some board games.**

28d Words from other languages

Expressions not commonly used in English should be italicized or underlined. Do not overuse such expressions because they tend to sound pretentious.

▶ **The author's** *Weltanschauung* **promotes gloom.**

Do not italicize common expressions: et al., croissant, film noir, etc.

28e When not to use italics

Do not use italics or underlining for emphasis.

hair-raising

▶ **The climb was ~~so scary.~~**

Select a word that conveys the emphasis you want to express.

EXERCISE 28.1 Use italics and underlining correctly.
Underline any words that need italicizing or underlining, and remove any unnecessary underlining or quotation marks. (**A** = See Answer Key.)

A In the nineteenth century, phrenology—the study of bumps on the skull and their relation to the personality—was a popular pseudoscientific practice, and one of the best-known phrenologists was Lorenzo Fowler. **A** Along with his brother Orson,

Lorenzo Fowler headed the Phrenological Institute in New York City, where the two trained other phrenologists, and Lorenzo gave readings to celebrities such as Julia Ward Howe, author of The Battle Hymn of the Republic. **A** The Fowler brothers saw themselves as leaders of a progressive movement; they ran the publishing company that put out the first edition of Walt Whitman's "Leaves of Grass." **A** They also published the Phrenological Journal, hoping that phrenological analysis could lead people to correct defects of character that had been revealed by their cranial protrusions.

A In 1872, Samuel Clemens, who had written Huckleberry Finn and many other works under the nom de plume Mark Twain, visited Fowler under an assumed name and obtained a reading and a phrenological chart. Clemens, who was an early champion both of scientific innovations like fingerprinting (which is featured in his novel "Pudd'nhead Wilson") and of inventions that proved to be dismal failures, wanted to put phrenology to the test. The results amused him: in "The Autobiography of Mark Twain," Clemens notes that Fowler found a spot on his skull that "represented the total absence of the sense of humor."

Clemens remained convinced that phrenology was quackery, and others soon agreed. By 1900, phrenology had fallen out of favor. Even in the twenty-first century, however, the use of terms such as highbrow and lowbrow, which came from phrenology, demonstrates the influence that this idea once had.

29   Capital Letters, Abbreviations, and Numbers

29a   Capital letters

Always consult a dictionary if you are not sure whether to capitalize a word. A dictionary will indicate if a noun is a proper noun demanding a capital letter:

▶ **King James Bible**

▶ **King Charles spaniel**

Use the following guidelines for capitalization.

1. Always capitalize *I*, even in e-mail communications.

▶ They announced that **I** had won the prize.

2. Capitalize the first word of a sentence, after a period, question mark, or exclamation point.

> ▶ Why do the wealthy send their children to residential colleges? They want the benefits of a liberal-arts education.

3. Capitalize the first word of a sentence quotation—if it is capitalized in the original passage.

> ▶ Quindlen says, "This is a story about a name," and thus tells us the topic of her article.

However, when you quote part of a sentence, do not begin the quotation with a capital letter.

> ▶ When Quindlen says that she is writing "a story about a name," she is telling us the topic of her article.

4. Capitalize proper nouns and proper adjectives. Begin the names of specific people, places, and things with a capital letter.

Types of Proper Nouns and Adjectives	Examples
Names of people	Albert Einstein, Madonna, T. S. Eliot, Bill Gates (but bell hooks, e.e. cummings)
Names of nations, continents, planets, stars, and galaxies	Hungary, Asia, Mercury, the North Star, the Milky Way
Names of mountains, rivers, and oceans	Mount Everest, the Thames, the Pacific Ocean
Names of public places and regions	Golden Gate Park, the Great Plains, the Midwest
Names of streets, buildings, and monuments	Rodeo Drive, the Empire State Building, the Roosevelt Memorial
Names of cities, states, and provinces	Toledo, Kansas, Nova Scotia
Days of the week and months	Wednesday, March
Holidays	Labor Day, the Fourth of July
Organizations and companies	the Red Cross, Microsoft Corporation

Types of Proper Nouns and Adjectives	Examples
Institutions (including colleges, departments, schools, government offices, and courts of law)	University of Texas, Department of English, School of Business, Defense Department, Florida Supreme Court
Historical events, named periods, and documents	the Civil War, the Renaissance, the Declaration of Independence
Religions, deities, revered persons, and sacred texts	Buddhism, Islam, Jehovah, the Torah
Races, tribes, nations, nationalities, and languages	the Navajo, Tibet, Spain, Spanish
Registered trademarks	Kleenex, Apple, Bic, Nike, Xerox
Names of ships, planes, and spacecraft	the USS *Kearsarge,* the *Spirit of St. Louis,* the *Challenger*

Note: Do not capitalize nouns naming general classes or types of people, places, things, or ideas: *government, jury, mall, prairie, utopia, traffic court, the twentieth century, goodness, reason.* For the use of capital letters in online writing, see chapter 31.

5. Capitalize a title before a person's name.

▶ The reporter interviewed Senator Thompson.

▶ The residents cheered Grandma Jones.

However, do not use a capital letter when a title is not attached to a person's name.

▶ Each state elects two senators.

▶ My grandmother is ninety years old.

When a title substitutes for the name of a known person, a capital letter is often used.

▶ Have you spoken with the Senator [senator] yet?

6. Capitalize major words in a title. In titles of published books, journals, magazines, essays, articles, films, poems, and songs, use a capital letter at the beginning of all words except articles (*the, a, an*), coordinating conjunctions (*and, but, or, nor, so, for, yet*), *to* in an infinitive (*to stay*), and prepositions unless they begin a title or subtitle.

> "A Matter of Identity"
>
> "Wrestling with the Angel: A Memoir"

7. Capitalize the first word of a subtitle, even if it is an article, a coordinating conjunction, *to*, or a preposition.

> ▶ *Reflections from the Keyboard: The World of the Concert Pianist*

8. Be consistent with using a capital or lowercase letter after a colon. Usage varies. Usually a capital letter is used with a clause that states a rule or principle (24b) or with any clause after the colon. Make your usage consistent.

EXERCISE 29.1 Use capital letters correctly.
Capitalize any letters that are incorrectly lowercase, and change any incorrect capital letters to lowercase letters. (**A** = See Answer Key.)

EXAMPLE:

       Civil War   *doctor*
During the ~~civil war~~, a ~~Doctor~~ from Kentucky tried to

      virus   North
spread a ~~Virus~~ to cities in the ~~north~~.

A 1. Biological warfare may strike modern Americans as Barbaric, but during the French and Indian war, smallpox-infected blankets given to Native Americans helped to decimate their numbers.

A 2. in the 1860s, Dr. Luke blackburn tried the same tactic, giving or selling clothing from patients with Yellow fever to Soldiers in the Union Army.

    3. According to some historians, the Doctor hoped to spread Yellow Fever in washington and new York; president Jefferson Davis of the confederate States of America probably knew about and approved of the plan.

    4. Fortunately for citizens of the north, yellow fever cannot be passed from one person to another by skin contact. although Dr. Blackburn's plot was discovered on the day of Lincoln's Assassination, the Doctor was never prosecuted in a Court of Law.

5. Blackburn eventually became the Governor of Kentucky, where he worked for penal and educational reform. A statue of the good samaritan marks his grave in frankfort cemetery.

29b Abbreviations and acronyms

The list below shows you when and how to use abbreviations.

1. Abbreviate titles used with people's names.   Use an abbreviation, followed by a period, for titles before or after names. The following abbreviated titles precede names: *Mr., Mrs., Ms., Prof., Dr., Gen.,* and *Sen.* The following abbreviated titles follow names: *Sr., Jr., PhD, MD, BA,* and *DDS.* Do not use a title both before and after a name: *Dr. Benjamin Spock* or *Benjamin Spock, MD.* Do not abbreviate a title if it is not attached to a specific name.

> ► Pat Murphy Sr. went to the ~~dr.~~ twice last week.
> doctor

2. Abbreviate the names of familiar institutions, countries, tests, diplomas, individuals, and objects.   Use abbreviations of the names of well-known institutions (*UCLA, YWCA, FBI, IBM*), countries (*USA* or *U.S.A.*), tests and diplomas (*SAT, GED*), individuals (*FDR*), and objects (*DVD*). If you use a specialized abbreviation, first use the term in full followed by the abbreviation in parentheses; then use the abbreviation.

> ► **The Graduate Record Examination (GRE) is required by many graduate schools. GRE preparation is therefore big business.**

3. Abbreviate terms used with numbers.   Use the abbreviations such as *BC, AD, a.m., p.m., $, mph, wpm, mg, kg,* and other units of measure only when they occur with specific numbers.

> ► **35 BC**   [meaning "before Christ," now often replaced with BCE, "before the common era," to avoid reference to one religion: 35 BCE]

> ► **AD 1776**   [*anno domini,* "in the year of the Lord," now often replaced with *CE,* "common era," used after the date: 1776 CE]

> ► **2:00 a.m./p.m.**   [*ante* or *post meridiem,* Latin for "before" or "after midday"]

Alternatives are A.M./P.M. or AM/PM. Be consistent. But do not use these abbreviations and other units of measure when no number is attached to them.

money
▶ His family gave him a wallet full of $ to spend on vacation.
                                        ^

afternoon.
▶ They arrived late in the ~~p.m.~~
                            ^

4. Abbreviate common Latin terms. In notes, parentheses, and source citations, use abbreviations for common Latin terms. In the body of your text, use the English meaning.

ABBREVIATION	LATIN	ENGLISH MEANING
etc.	et cetera	and so on
i.e.	id est	that is
e.g.	exempli gratia	for example
cf.	confer	compare
N.B.	nota bene	note well
et al.	et alii	and others

5. With the plural form of an abbreviation, use *-s* (not *-'s*). Do not use an apostrophe to make an abbreviation plural (see 25d).

▶ She has over a thousand CDs.

▶ Both his VCRs are broken.

6. Do not abbreviate familiar words to save time and space. In formal writing, write in full expressions such as the following:

&	and
bros.	brothers [Use "Bros." only if it is part of the official name of the business.]
chap.	chapter
Mon.	Monday
nite	night
NJ	New Jersey [Abbreviate the name of the state only in an address, a note, or a reference.]
no.	number [Use the abbreviation only with a specific number: "No. 17 on the list was deleted."]
Oct.	October [Write names of days and months in full, except in some works-cited lists.]
soc.	sociology [Write names of academic subjects in full.]
thru	through
w/	with

EXERCISE 29.2   Use abbreviations and acronyms correctly.
Correct any errors in the use of abbreviations or acronyms. (**A** =
See Answer Key.)

EXAMPLE:

> history
> Mr.   high school
> According to ~~Mister~~ Sid Green, who teaches ~~H.S.~~ ~~hist.~~ in
>   ^   ^   ^
> California
> ~~CA,~~ some U.S. colleges and universities no longer require
>   ^
>
> students to take the SAT.

A 1. An early adopter—someone who buys new devices and gadgets as soon as they are available—probably owned CD's when
most people still bought records, rented DVD's while others
still watched videos on their VCR's, and picked out iPods as
holiday gifts.

A 2. The acupuncturist's receptionist referred to him as Doctor
Loren Selwyn, but I later discovered that he was Loren Selwyn,
doctor of philosophy, not Loren Selwyn, medical doctor.

3. Ms Krebs could type so many w.p.m. that the computer
printer was spewing out pp. long after she had stopped working for the eve.

4. Sen Hammond helpfully told us that the New Year's Eve
party would be held on Dec. 31, but he neglected to say what
time we should arrive.

5. Akhenaton, orig. known as Amenhotep, ruled ancient Egypt
until his death in about 1358 before the Common Era.

29c Numbers

Conventions for using numerals (actual figures) or words vary across
the disciplines.

1. Numbers in the humanities and in business letters

> Use words for numbers expressible in one or two words and for
> fractions (*nineteen, fifty-six, two hundred, one-half*).
>
> Use numerals for longer numbers (*326; 5,625; 7,642,000*).
>
> Use a combination of words and numerals for whole millions,
> billions, and so on (*45 million, 1 billion*).

2. Numbers in scientific and technical writing

> Use numerals for all numbers above nine.
>
> Use numerals for numbers below ten only when they show pre-
> cise measurement, as when they are grouped and compared

with other larger numbers (*5 of the 39 participants*) or when they precede a unit of measurement (*6 cm*), indicate a mathematical function (*8%; 0.4*), or represent a specific time, date, age, score, or number in a series.

Use words for fractions: *two-thirds.*

3. Numbers beginning a sentence In both the humanities and the sciences, spell out numbers that begin a sentence.

▶ **One hundred twenty-five members voted for the new bylaws.**

▶ **Six thousand fans have already bought tickets.**

 ESL Note Singular and Plural Forms of *Hundred, Thousand,* and *Million*

Even after plural numbers, use the singular form of *hundred, thousand,* and *million.* Add *-s* only when there is no preceding number.

▶ Five *hundred* books were damaged in the flood. [not five hundreds]

▶ *Hundreds* of books were damaged in the flood. ■

4. Special uses of figures (numerals) In nonscientific writing, use numerals for the following:

Time and dates	6 p.m. on 31 May 2003
Decimals	20.89
Statistics	median score 35
Addresses	16 East 93rd Street
Chapter, page, scene, and line numbers	chapter 5; page 97; scene 2, line 44
Quantities appearing with abbreviations or symbols	6°C (for temperature Celsius), $21, 6'7"
Scores	The Knicks won 89–85.

For percentages and money, numerals and the symbol (*75%, $24.67*) are usually acceptable, or you can spell out the expression if it is fewer than four words (*seventy-five percent, twenty-four dollars*).

5. Plural forms of figures Be consistent in your usage. MLA style prefers no apostrophe to form the plural of a numeral.

▶ **in the 1980s**   ▶ **They scored in the 700s on the SATs.**

30 Spelling and Hyphenation

This chapter provides you with some of the basic hyphenation and spelling rules, which are worth learning, along with some lists of troublesome words for you to refer to, learn, and add to.

30a Checking spelling

A spelling checker is of limited use. Even if you check your spelling with computer software, you still need to proofread. A program will not alert you to a word used in place of a similar word (a homonym, such as *cite* used in place of *sight* or *site*). Nor will it alert you to a typographical slip if the word you mistakenly type is actually a word, such as if you write *form* in place of *from*. It also will not alert you to variant spellings across dialects of English. So using a spelling checker is only a beginning (7e, 7f).

One of the best tools at your disposal is a dictionary, for here you can check spelling, find the various word forms associated with a word (*benefit/benefited,* for example), or discover when a silent *-e* is retained or dropped before a suffix (as in *likable* or *likeness*). If you feel insecure about your spelling, be sure to keep your own list of "My Spelling Words" and add to it whenever you make an error, are surprised by the spelling of a word, or look up a word for confirmation.

30b Plurals of nouns

1. Regular plural forms   The regular plural of nouns is formed by adding *-s* or *-es* to the singular word.

essay, essays   match, matches

To form the plural of a compound noun, attach the *-s* to the main noun in the phrase.

mothers-in-law   passersby

Proofread carefully for plural forms that form the plural with *-s* but make other changes, too, such as the following:

-f OR *-fe* → *-ves*
thief, thieves   (*Exceptions:* beliefs, roofs, chiefs)
wife, wives

-o → *-oes*   *-o* → *-os*
potato, potatoes   hero (sandwich), heros
tomato, tomatoes   photo, photos
hero (man), heroes   piano, pianos

CONSONANT + -y → -ies	VOWEL + -y → -ys
family, families	toy, toys
party, parties	monkey, monkeys

2. Irregular plural forms (no -s ending)

man, men	foot, feet
woman, women	tooth, teeth
child, children	mouse, mice

3. Plural forms borrowed from other languages

Words borrowed from other languages, particularly Greek and Latin words, frequently borrow the plural form of the language, too.

basis, bases	nucleus, nuclei
thesis, theses	vertebra, vertebrae
hypothesis, hypotheses	alumnus (m.), alumni
criterion, criteria	alumna (f.), alumnae

4. Plural forms with no change

Some words have the same form in singular and plural: moose, deer, sheep, species.

30c Doubling consonants

Doubled consonants form a link between spelling and pronunciation because the doubling of a consonant signals a short vowel sound.

1. Double the consonant when the verb stem contains one vowel plus one consonant in one syllable.

slip, slipping, slipped   hop, hopping, hopped

The doubled consonant preserves the short vowel sound. Compare the pronunciation of *hop, hopping, hopped* with *hope, hoping, hoped.* Say the words aloud and compare the vowel sounds in *write, writing,* and *written.*

2. Double the consonant when the verb stem contains two or more syllables with one vowel plus one consonant in the final stressed syllable.

refer, referring, referred   control, controlling, controlled

Compare *travel, traveling, traveled* and *cancel, canceling, canceled,* which have the stress on the first syllable. (Note that British English prefers the spellings *travelling, travelled; cancelling, cancelled.*)

3. Double the consonant when the suffix -er or -est is added to one-syllable adjectives ending in one vowel plus one consonant.

big, bigger, biggest   hot, hotter, hottest

4. Double the *l* when adding *-ly* to an adjective that ends in one *-l*.

careful, carefully   successful, successfully

30d Spelling with *-y* or *-i*

VERB ENDS IN CONSONANT + -*y*	*-ies*	*-ying*	*-ied*
cry	cries	crying	cried
study	studies	studying	studied

VERB ENDS IN VOWEL + -*y*	*-ys*	*-ying*	*-yed*
play	plays	playing	played

Exceptions: pay/paid, say/said, lay/laid

VERB ENDS IN VOWEL + -*e*	*-ies*	*-ying*	*-ied*
die	dies	dying	died

TWO-SYLLABLE ADJECTIVE ENDS IN -*y*	-*i* WITH A SUFFIX
happy	happier, happily, happiness

TWO-SYLLABLE ADJECTIVE ENDS IN -*ly*	*-lier*	*-liest*
friendly	friendlier	friendliest

30e Internal *ie* or *ei*

This traditional rhyme helps with the decision about whether to use *ie* or *ei*:

> I before *e*
> Except after *c*
> Or when sounded like *ay*
> As in *neighbor* and *weigh*.

The following examples illustrate those guidelines:

i BEFORE *e*	*e* BEFORE *i* AFTER *c*	*e* BEFORE *i* WHEN SOUNDED LIKE *ay*
believe	receive	vein
relief	ceiling	reign
niece	deceive	sleigh

Exceptions:

i BEFORE *e* EVEN AFTER *c*	*e* BEFORE *i*, NOT AFTER *c*	
conscience	height	seize
science	either/neither	foreign
species	leisure	weird

30f Adding a suffix

1. Keep a silent -e before an -ly suffix.

immediate, immediately   sure, surely

Exceptions: true, truly; whole, wholly; due, duly

2. Keep a silent -e before a suffix beginning with a consonant.

state, statement   force, forceful   rude, rudeness

Exceptions: acknowledge, acknowledgment; judge, judgment; argue, argument

3. Drop a silent -e before a suffix beginning with a vowel.

hope, hoping   observe, observant

write, writing   remove, removable

Exceptions: enforce, enforceable; change, changeable. Retaining the *-e* preserves the soft sound of the preceding consonant.

4. With adjectives ending in -le, drop the -le when adding -ly.

sensible, sensibly

5. With adjectives ending in -ic, add -ally to form the adverb.

basic, basically   characteristic, characteristically

Exception: public, publicly

6. Pay attention to the suffixes -able, -ible, -ant, -ent, -ify, and -efy.
More words end in *-able* than in *-ible*. Learn the most common *-ible* words:

eligible	incredible	irresistible	legible
permissible	responsible	terrible	visible

Unfortunately, there are no rules of thumb to help you decide whether to use the suffix *-ant* or *-ent*. Learn common words with these suffixes, and have your dictionary handy for others.

-ANT	-ENT
defiant	confident
observant	convenient
relevant	existent
reluctant	imminent
resistant	independent

The suffix *-ify* is more common than *-efy*. Learn the four *-efy* words:

liquefy   putrefy   rarefy   stupefy

 Go to *The Open Handbook* at <http://college.hmco.com/keys .html> and click on Forms and Checklists for a list of commonly misspelled words and spelling exercises.

30g Multinational characters: Accents, umlauts, tildes, and cedillas

Words and names in languages other than English may be spelled with special marks above or under a letter, such as an accent (è or é), an umlaut or dieresis (ö), a tilde (ñ), or a cedilla (ç). Microsoft Word provides ways of producing multinational characters. The basic principle is that you press CTRL and the punctuation key most similar to the mark you need, release the keys, and press the letter. The letter then appears with its mark.

 TECHTOOLKIT   A Useful Web Site for Writing in Other Languages

Go to <http://www.starr.net/is/type/kbh.html> for a site titled *International Accents and Diacriticals: Theory, Charts, and Tips.* This site, prepared by Irene Starr of the Foreign Language Resource Center at the University of Massachusetts, provides charts of how to use Word, Wordperfect, or a Macintosh computer to produce the multinational characters, instructions on accessing and using the International English keyboard, and links to sites useful for those writing non-Roman alphabets. ■

30h Hyphens

Use hyphens to divide a word or to form a compound. For the use of hyphens in URLs, see chapter 31.

1. Hyphens with prefixes   Many words with prefixes are spelled without hyphens: *cooperate, nonrestrictive, unnatural.* Others are hyphenated: *all-inclusive, anti-intellectual.* Always use a hyphen when the main word is a number or a proper noun: *all-American, post-1990.* If you are unsure about whether to insert a hyphen before a prefix, check a dictionary.

2. Hyphens in compound nouns and adjectives Some compound nouns are written as one word (*toothbrush*), others as two words (*coffee shop*), and still others with one or more hyphens (*role-playing, father-in-law*). Always check an up-to-date dictionary.

Hyphenate compound adjectives preceding a noun: a *ten-page essay*, a *well-organized party*, a *law-abiding citizen.* When the modifier follows the noun, no hyphen is necessary: *The essay was ten pages long. The party was well organized. Most citizens try to be law abiding.*

Do not insert a hyphen between an *-ly* adverb and an adjective or after an adjective in its comparative (*-er*) or superlative (*-est*) form: *a tightly fitting suit, a sweeter sounding melody.*

3. Hyphens in spelled-out numbers Use hyphens when spelling out two-word numbers from twenty-one to ninety-nine. (See 29c for more on spelling out numbers.)

▶ **Twenty-two applicants arrived early in the morning.**

Also use a hyphen in spelled-out fractions: *two-thirds of a cup.*

4. End-of-line hyphens Most word processors either automatically hyphenate words or automatically wrap words around to the next line. Choose the latter option to avoid the strange and unacceptable word division that sometimes appears with automatic hyphenation.

EXERCISE 30.1 Use correct spelling and hyphenation.
Correct any misspellings and hyphenation errors. (**A** = See Answer Key.)

A Recently, researchers who study chimpanzees have come to the suprising conclusion that groups of chimpanzees have their own traditions that can be past on to new generations of chimps. **A** The chimps do not aquire these traditions by instinct; instead, they learn them from other chimps. **A** When a scientific journal published analysises of chimpanzee behavior, the author revealed that the every day actions of chimpanzees in seperate areas differ in significant ways, even when the groups belong to the same subspecies. **A** For instance, in one West African group, the chimps are often seen puting a nut on a stone and using another peice of stone to crack the nut open, a kind of behavior never observed in other groups of chimpanzees. **A** Sceintists have also observed the chimps teaching there young the nut opening method, and chimps in other places that crack nuts differentally teach their young they're own way. **A** Researchers have therefor concluded that chimpanzees have local traditions.

Frans de Waal, who has been studing primates, wrote a book makeing the arguement that these learned behaviors should be considered kinds of culture. The word culture has traditionly been used to describe human behavier, but may be, he says, a new definition is needed. Considering this startlingly-new theory of chimpanzee "culture," some researchers think that humans now have an un-deniable obligation to protect the lives of all remaining wild chimpanzees rather than zeroeing in on just a few of the threatenned animals. The lost of a single group of wild chimpanzees would, they say, destroy something irreplacable, a unique culture with its own traditions and way of life.

31 Online Punctuation

When writing online, pay attention to URLs and to your use of capital letters and hyphens.

Punctuation marks communicate essential information in Web site addresses—Uniform Resource Locators—and in e-mail addresses. Be sure to include all marks when you write an address, and if you need to spread a URL over more than one line, split it after a slash (MLA style) or before a punctuation mark. Do not split the protocol <http://>. Use angle brackets to enclose e-mail and Web addresses. Do not include any additional punctuation within the angle brackets.

> ▶ **The Modern Language Association, whose Web site is at <http://www.mla.org>, provides examples of documenting Web sources.**

Avoid using capitalized text (the whole text, not just initial letters) in e-mail communications and electronic discussion groups. In both places, the prolonged use of capital letters is regarded as "shouting" and may offend readers (51a).

Some e-mail addresses include hyphens, so never add a hyphen to indicate that you have split an address between lines. When an e-mail address includes a hyphen, do not break the line at a hyphen because readers will not know whether the hyphen is part of the address.

Part 5 focuses on what student writers need to know about the type of English commonly expected in academic settings in North America and known as *Standard English.* If you learned English as a second language (ESL) or even as a third or fourth language, or if you grew up speaking a variety of English with features different from those of Standard English, this Part Five is for you. Throughout this book, too, you will find ESL Notes that address linguistic troublespots.

32 Culture, Language, and Writing

32a Englishes around the world

At the same time as travel and the Internet make us more aware of diversity and other countries' languages and cultures, we are also experiencing an increase in the use of English. More than 350 million people speak English as their native language, and many more (estimated at more than a billion) use English as a common language spanning local dialects. They use it for special communicative, educational, and business purposes within their own communities. However, languages are not fixed and static, and the users of English in their various locations adapt the language for their own uses. See, for example, the Circle of World English in 1e.

Varieties of English spoken in different geographical locations around the world are perceived as "Englishes," and some even have their own names. Spanglish (Spanish English), Singlish (Singaporean English), and Taglish (Tagalog English, spoken in the Philippines) are just a few examples of language varieties that have developed among multiethnic populations. English is thus being reinvented around the world, sometimes to the dismay of academics and government officials, sometimes with the approval of citizens, who see the adaptation as an act of freedom, even rebellion. The Filipino poet Gemino Abad claims: "The English language is now ours. We have colonized it."

However, even while colloquial speech is being adapted and other Englishes, including the English of the Internet, provide colorful global variations, the academic world of writing inevitably retains links to the concept of a standard language. To reach the expectations of the largest number of academic readers, standard vocabulary, syntax, and grammar still prevail.

32b Difference, not deficit

Students in colleges in North America who grew up speaking another language are often called students of English as a Second Language (ESL), and the abbreviation is commonly used in college curricula, professional literature, and the press. However, this term is not broad enough. Many so-called second-language students speak three or four languages besides English, depending on their life and educational circumstances and the languages spoken at home. Along with being bilingual or multilingual, such students are frequently multicultural, equipped with all the knowledge and experience that those terms imply.

It is not only students from other countries who have to address language differences. If you are a student who speaks a local variety of English at home, you may still have to learn the conventions of academic English. As you enter this academic world, though, your background knowledge can be an advantage. Unlike many writers who know only one language or one variety of English, you can know different cultures in an in-depth way and switch among varied linguistic and rhetorical codes. You have a broader perspective—more to think about, more to write about, more resources to draw on as you write, and far more comparisons to make among languages, writers, writing, and culture. You bring your culture with you into your writing, and as you do so, you help shape and reshape the culture of North America.

32c Learning from errors

Even for students who have been learning a new language or the conventions of a standard dialect for a while, errors are inevitable. They are not a sign of laziness or stupidity. Welcome and embrace your errors; study them; learn from them. Errors show language learning in progress. If you make no errors while you are learning to write a new language, perhaps you are being too careful and using only what you know is correct. Be willing to take risks and try new words, new expressions, new combinations. That is the way to expand your repertoire.

When you make an error, write a note about it. Consider why you made the error—was it, for example, transfer from your first language or spoken dialect, a guess, a careless mistake? Or was it the employment of an erroneous hypothesis about Standard English (such as "Many verbs form the past tense with -*ed*; therefore, the past tense form of *swear* is probably *sweared*")? Analyzing the causes of errors will help you understand how to edit them and avoid them in the future. (The past tense form of *swear* is *swore*.)

EXERCISE 32.1 Examine troublespots.
List three linguistic features of Standard English that cause you difficulty when you write. Consider why those features cause you problems: Does your home language influence what you write? Or do mistakes occur because you make generalizations about Standard forms that don't always hold (such as writing "*Restaurants* in the park *is* always crowded," thinking that the subject that determines agreement is *park*)?

TECHTOOLKIT   Web Sites on Language and Writing

The Web sites listed here provide useful information.

- ESL Resources, Handouts, and Exercises from Purdue University's Online Writing Lab at <http://owl.english.purdue.edu/handouts/esl/index.html>.
- Guide to Grammar and Writing at <http://www.ccc.commnet.edu/grammar/index.htm>.

At this Capital Community College site, you will find information and quizzes on words, paragraphs, and essays. In addition, you can send in a question to "Ask Grammar" and someone will answer it. The Grammar Logs contain people's questions and answers and thus cover interesting points.   ■

32d   Editing guide to vernacular Englishes

Many of the varieties of English shown in the Circle of English on page 11 differ from Standard American English in their use of words and grammatical conventions. Speakers of these Englishes have to do a kind of translating, called *code switching*, when they speak or write in Standard English, just as we all switch codes between levels of formality when we interact with different audiences. Consider, for example, situations when you might say "'Sup?" ("What's up?") rather than "Good morning." As David Crystal, author of *The Stories of English*, points out, "We need to be very sure of our ground (or very drunk) before we say, 'Yo, Officer.'"

The following table shows some of the common features that confront speakers of African American Vernacular (AAV), Creole, and other varieties of English in North America when they move back and forth between their home culture and academia.

Vernaculars and Standard English

Linguistic Feature of Vernacular	Example (Nonstandard)	Edited for Standard English
Omitted form of *be*	*Maxine studying.*	*Maxine is studying.*
Use of *be* for habitual action	*Ray be working at home.*	*Ray usually works at home.*
Use of *been* without *have*	*I been sleeping all day.*	*I have (I've) been sleeping all day.*
Omitted -ed	*The books arrive this morning.*	*The books arrived this morning.*

Linguistic Feature of Vernacular	Example (Nonstandard)	Edited for Standard English
No -s ending for third person singular present tense verb	*That model have a big smile.*	*That model* **has** *a big smile.*
No plural form after a plural number	*Jake own two dog.*	*Jake* **owns** *two* **dogs.**
Verb inversion before indefinite pronoun subject	*Can't nobody do that.*	**Nobody can** *do that.*
They instead of possessive *their*	*The players grabbed they gear.*	*The players grabbed* **their** *gear.*
Hisself instead of *himself*	*That musician promote hisself too much.*	*That musician* **promotes** **himself** *too much.*
Personal pronoun restates subject	*His instructor, she strict.*	*His instructor* **is** *strict.*
No apostrophe + -s for possessive	*She my brother wife.*	*She* **is** *my* **brother's** *wife.*
It used in place of *there*	*It's a gate at the entrance.*	**There is (There's)** *a gate at the entrance.*
Double negative	*You don't know nothing.*	*You don't know* **anything./***You* **know** *nothing.*

32e Editing guide to multilingual transfer errors

Errors in writing in a new language can occur when you are grappling with new subject matter and difficult subjects. You concentrate on ideas and clarity, but because no writer can do everything at once, you fail to concentrate on editing.

The language guide on pages 324–328 identifies several problem areas for multilingual/ESL writers. It shows grammatical features (column 1) of specific languages (column 2), features that lead to an error when transferred to English (column 3). An edited Standard English version appears in column 4. Of course, the guide covers neither all linguistic problem areas nor all languages. Rather, it lists a selection, with the goal of being useful and practical. Use the guide to raise your awareness about your own language and Standard English.

Language Guide

Language Features	Languages	Sample Transfer Errors in English	Edited Version
ARTICLES (33)			
No articles	Chinese, Japanese, Russian, Swahili, Thai, Urdu	*Sun is hot.* *I bought book.* *Computer has changed our lives.*	*The sun is hot.* *I bought a book.* *The computer has changed our lives.*
No indefinite article with profession	Arabic, French, Japanese, Korean, Vietnamese	*He is student.* *She lawyer.*	*He is a student.* *She is a lawyer.*
Definite article with days, months, places, idioms	Arabic	*She is in the bed.* *He lives in the Peru.*	*She is in bed.* *He lives in Peru.*
Definite article used for generalization	Farsi, French, German, Greek, Portuguese, Spanish	*The photography is an art.* *The books are more expensive than the disks.*	*Photography is an art.* *Books are more expensive than disks.*
Definite article used with proper noun	French, German, Portuguese, Spanish	*The Professor Brackert teaches in Frankfurt.*	*Professor Brackert teaches in Frankfurt.*
No definite article	Hindi, Turkish	*Store on corner is closed.*	*The store on the corner is closed.*
No indefinite article	Korean (uses *one* for *a*; depends on context)	*He ran into one tree.*	*He ran into a tree.*
VERBS AND VERB FORMS (34)			
Be can be omitted.	Arabic, Chinese, Greek, Russian	*India hotter than Britain.* *She working now.* *He cheerful.*	*India is hotter than Britain.* *She is working now.* *He is cheerful.*

Language Features	Languages	Sample Transfer Errors in English	Edited Version
No progressive forms	French, German, Greek, Russian	*They still discuss the problem.*	*They are still discussing the problem.*
		When I walked in, she slept.	*When I walked in, she was sleeping.*
No tense inflections	Chinese, Thai, Vietnamese	*He arrive yesterday.*	*He arrived yesterday.*
		When I was little, I always walk to school.	*When I was little, I always walked to school.*
No inflection for third person singular	Chinese, Japanese, Korean, Russian, Thai	*The singer have a big band.*	*The singer has a big band.*
		She work hard.	*She works hard.*
Past perfect formed with *be*	Arabic	*They were arrived when I called.*	*They had arrived when I called.*
Different tense boundaries from English	Arabic, Chinese, Farsi, French	*I study here for a year.*	*I have been studying here for a year.*
		He has left yesterday.	*He left yesterday.*
Different limits for passive voice	Japanese, Korean, Russian, Thai, Vietnamese	*They were stolen their luggage.*	*Their luggage was stolen.*
		My name base on Chinese characters.	*My name is based on Chinese characters.*
		The mess clean up quick.	*The mess was cleaned up quickly.*
		A miracle was happened.	*A miracle (has) happened.*
No -*ing* (gerund) /infinitive distinction	Arabic, Chinese, Farsi, French, Greek, Portuguese, Spanish, Vietnamese	*She avoids to go.*	*She avoids going.*
		I enjoy to play tennis.	*I enjoy playing tennis.*

Language Features	Languages	Sample Transfer Errors in English	Edited Version
Infinitive not used to express purpose	Korean	*People exercise for losing weight.*	*People exercise to lose weight.*
Overuse of progressive forms	Hindi, Urdu	*I am wanting to leave now.*	*I want to leave now.*

WORD ORDER AND SENTENCE STRUCTURE (35)

Language Features	Languages	Sample Transfer Errors in English	Edited Version
Verb precedes subject.	Arabic, Hebrew, Russian, Spanish (optional), Tagalog	*Good grades received every student in the class.*	*Every student in the class received good grades.*
Verb-subject order in dependent clause	French	*I knew what would propose the committee.*	*I knew what the committee would propose.*
Verb after subject and object	Bengali, German (in dependent clause), Hindi, Japanese, Korean, Turkish	*. . . (when) the teacher the money collected.*	*. . . (when) the teacher collected the money.*
Coordination favored over subordination	Arabic	Frequent use of *and* and *so*	
Relative clause or restrictive phrase precedes noun it modifies.	Chinese, Japanese, Korean, Russian	*The enrolled in college student . . .*	*The student (who was) enrolled in college . . .*
		A nine-meter-high impressive monument . . .	*An impressive monument that is nine meters high . . .*
		He gave me a too difficult for me book.	*He gave me a book that was too difficult for me.*
Adverb can occur between verb and object or before verb.	French, Spanish, Urdu (before verb)	*I like very much clam chowder.*	*I like clam chowder very much.*
		They efficiently organized the work.	*They organized the work efficiently.*

Language Features	Languages	Sample Transfer Errors in English	Edited Version
That clause rather than an infinitive	Arabic, French, Hindi, Russian, Spanish	*I want that you stay.* *I want that they try harder.*	*I want you to stay.* *I want them to try harder.*
Inversion of subject and verb rare	Chinese	*She is leaving and so I am.*	*She is leaving, and so am I.*
Conjunctions occur in pairs.	Chinese, Farsi, Vietnamese	*Although she is rich, but she wears simple clothes.* *Even if I had money, I would also not buy that car.*	*Although she is rich, she wears simple clothes.* *Even if I had money, I would not buy that car.*
Subject (especially *it* pronoun) can be omitted.	Chinese, Italian, Japanese, Portuguese, Spanish, Thai	*Is raining.*	*It is raining.*
Commas set off a dependent clause.	German, Russian	*He knows, that we are right.*	*He knows that we are right.*
No exact equivalent of *there is*/*there are*	Japanese, Korean, Portuguese, Russian, Thai (adverb of place and *have*)	*This article says four reasons to eat beans.* *In the garden has many trees.*	*This article says [that] there are four reasons to eat beans.* *There are many trees in the garden.*

NOUNS, PRONOUNS, ADJECTIVES, ADVERBS (18, 19, 33)

Personal pronouns restate subject.	Arabic, Gujarati, Spanish (optional)	*My father he lives in California.*	*My father lives in California.*
No human/ nonhuman distinction for relative pronoun (*who/which*)	Arabic, Farsi, French, Russian, Spanish, Thai	*Here is the student which you met her last week.* *The people which arrived . . .*	*Here is the student [whom] you met last week.* *The people who arrived . . .*

Language Features	Languages	Sample Transfer Errors in English	Edited Version
Pronoun object included in relative clause	Arabic, Chinese, Farsi, Hebrew	*The house [that] I used to live in it is big.*	*The house that I used to live in is big.*
No distinction between subject and object forms of some pronouns	Chinese, Gujarati, Korean, Thai	*I gave the forms to she.*	*I gave the forms to her. Or I gave her the forms.*
Nouns and adjectives have same form.	Chinese, Japanese	*She is beauty woman.* *They felt very safety on the train.*	*She is a beautiful woman.* *They felt very safe on the train.*
No distinction between *he* and *she*, *his* and *her*	Bengali, Farsi, Gujarati, Spanish (*his* and *her* only), Thai	*My sister dropped his purse.*	*My sister dropped her purse.*
No plural form after a number	Creole, Farsi	*He has two dog.*	*He has two dogs.*
No plural (or optional) forms of nouns	Chinese, Japanese, Korean, Thai	*Several good book . . .*	*Several good books . . .*
No relative pronouns	Korean	*The book is on the table is mine.*	*The book that is on the table is mine.*
Different perception of countable/ uncountable	Japanese, Spanish	*I bought three furnitures.* *He has five chalk.*	*I bought three pieces of furniture. Or I bought three chairs.* *He has five sticks of chalk.*
Adjectives show number.	Russian, Spanish	*I have helpfuls friends.*	*I have helpful friends.*
Negative before verb	Spanish	*Jack no like meat.*	*Jack does not like meat.*
Double negatives used routinely	Spanish	*They don't know nothing.*	*They don't know anything. Or They know nothing.*

33 Nouns and Articles

33a Categories of nouns

Nouns in English fall into various categories. A *proper noun* names a unique person, place, or thing and begins with a capital letter: *Walt Whitman, Lake Superior, Grand Canyon, Vietnam Veterans Memorial, Tuesday* (29a, 33f). A *common noun* names a general class of persons, places, or things and begins with a lowercase letter: *bicycle, furniture, plan, daughter, home, happiness.* Common nouns can be further categorized as countable and uncountable.

A *countable noun* can have a number before it (*one, two*, and so on) and has a plural form. Countable nouns frequently add *-s* to indicate the plural: *picture, pictures; plan, plans.*

An *uncountable noun* cannot be directly counted. It has no plural form: *furniture, advice, information.*

<table>
<tr><td colspan="2" align="center">COMMON NOUNS</td></tr>
<tr><td>COUNTABLE</td><td>UNCOUNTABLE</td></tr>
<tr><td>tool, hammer (tools, hammers)</td><td>equipment</td></tr>
<tr><td>chair, desk (chairs, desks)</td><td>furniture</td></tr>
<tr><td>necklace, earring (necklaces, earrings)</td><td>jewelry</td></tr>
<tr><td>view, scene (views, scenes)</td><td>scenery</td></tr>
<tr><td>tip, suggestion (tips, suggestions)</td><td>advice</td></tr>
</table>

The concept of countability varies across languages. Japanese, for example, makes no distinction between countable and uncountable nouns. In French, Spanish, and Chinese, the word for *furniture* is a countable noun; in English, it is not.

33b Uncountable nouns

Some nouns are usually uncountable and are listed as such in a language learners' dictionary such as *The American Heritage ESL Dictionary.* Learn the most common uncountable nouns, and note the ones that end in *-s* but are nevertheless singular:

A mass made up of parts: clothing, equipment, furniture, garbage, homework, information, jewelry, luggage, machinery, money, scenery, traffic, transportation

Abstract concepts: advice, courage, education, fun, happiness, health, honesty, information, knowledge, success

Natural substances: air, blood, cotton, hair, heat, ice, rice, sunshine, water, wood, wool

Diseases: diabetes, influenza, measles

Games: chess, checkers, soccer, tennis

Subjects of study: biology, economics, history, physics

Follow these guidelines when using an uncountable noun:

1. Do not use a number, a plural word like *these* and *those,* or a plural quantity word (such as *many* or *several*) before an uncountable noun. An uncountable noun has no plural form. See 17i.

   ▶ She gave me ~~several~~ ^some^ information~~s~~.

   ▶ The couple bought a lot of new furniture~~s~~.

2. Do not use an uncountable noun with *a* or *an.*

   ▶ Puerto Rico has ~~a~~ lovely scenery.

   ▶ The room needs ~~a~~ new furniture.

   Exceptions to this rule occur when the phrase *a little* or *a great deal of* is used.

   ▶ He has a great deal of antique furniture.

   ▶ She has a little modern furniture.

3. Always use a singular verb with an uncountable noun subject.

   ▶ Their advice ~~are~~ ^is^ useful.

4. Use the following before an uncountable noun:

   • no article (called the *zero article*) for a generalization: *Information is free.*

   • a singular word such as *this* or *that:* *This equipment is jammed.*

   • a possessive: *His advice was useless.*

   • a quantity word or phrase for nonspecific reference (see 17i): *They gave us some advice. They gave us a little advice.*

   • *the* for specific reference (33d): *The information we found was all wrong.*

5. Give an uncountable noun a countable sense—that is, indicate a quantity of it—by adding a word or phrase that indicates quantity.

The noun itself will always remain singular: three pieces of *furniture*, two items of *information*, many pieces of *advice*.

6. Take into account the fact that the concept of countability varies across languages. Japanese, for example, makes no distinction between countable and uncountable nouns. In French, Spanish, and Chinese, the word for *furniture* is a countable noun; in English, it is not. In Russian, the word for *hair* is countable and is used in the plural.

7. Examine the context. Be aware that some nouns can be countable in one context and uncountable in another.

GENERAL CLASS (UNCOUNTABLE)

He loves *chocolate*. [all chocolate, in whatever form]

Time flies.

He has red *hair*.

Life is beautiful.

A COUNTABLE ITEM OR ITEMS

She gave him *a chocolate*. [one piece of candy from a box of many chocolates]

They are having *a good time*.

There is *a long gray hair* on her pillow.

She is leading a hedonistic *life*.

33c Rules for articles (*a*, *an*, and *the*)

1. Use *the* whenever a reference to a common noun is specific and unique for both writer and reader (see 33d).

   ▶ **He loves the museum that Rem Koolhaas designed.**
   [We know that the museum he loves is the specific one that Koolhaas designed.]

2. Do not use *a* or *an* with a plural countable noun.

   ▶ **They cited ̶a̶ reliable surveys.**

3. Do not use *a* or *an* with an uncountable noun.

   ▶ **He gave ̶a̶ helpful advice.**

4. Use *a* before a consonant sound: *a bird, a house, a unicorn*. Use *an* before a vowel sound: *an egg, an ostrich, an hour, an ugly vase*. Take special care with the sounds associated with the letters *h* and *u*, which can have either a consonant or a vowel sound: *a housing project, an honest man, a unicorn, an uprising*.

5. To make a generalization about a countable noun, do one of the following:

- Use the plural form: *Lions are majestic.*
- Use the singular with *a* or *an*: *A lion is a majestic animal.*
- Use the singular with *the* to denote a classification: *The lion is a majestic animal.*

6. A countable singular noun can never stand alone, so make sure that a countable singular noun is preceded by an article or by a demonstrative pronoun (*this, that*), a number, a singular word expressing quantity, or a possessive.

> A (Every, That, One, Her) nurse
> ~~Nurse~~ has a difficult job.
>   ^

7. In general, though there are many exceptions, use no article with a singular proper noun (*Mount Everest*), and use *the* with a plural proper noun (*the Himalayas*). See 33f for more examples.

33d *The* for a specific reference

When you write a common noun that both you and your readers know refers to one or more specific persons, places, things, or concepts, use the article *the*. You can make a specific reference to something outside the text or inside it.

Specific reference outside the text   References to specific people, places, things, or concepts outside the text point to something unique that both the writer and readers will know. In the following sentences, readers will not wonder which earth, sun, moon, door, or dog the writer means.

> ▶ I study *the* **earth, the sun, and the moon.**   [The ones in our solar system]

> ▶ She closed *the* **door.**   [Of the room she was in]

> ▶ Her husband took *the* **dog out for a walk.**   [The dog belonging to the couple, not any other dog]

Specific reference inside the text   A reference to a person, place, thing, or concept can also be made specific by identifying it within the text.

> ▶ *The* **kitten that her daughter brought home had a distinctive black patch above one eye.**   [The specific kitten is the one that was brought home.]

▶ Her daughter found *a* kitten. When they were writing a lost-and-found ad that night, they realized that *the* kitten had a distinctive black patch above one eye.   [The second mention is to a specific kitten identified earlier—the one her daughter had found.]

▶ He bought *the most expensive* bicycle in the store.   [A superlative makes a reference to one specific item.]

33e Which article? Four basic questions

Multilingual writers often have difficulty choosing among the articles *a*, *an*, and *the* and the *zero article* (no article at all). Languages vary greatly in their representation of the concepts conveyed by English articles (see 32e, Editing guide to multilingual transfer errors).

The Key Points box lists four questions to ask about a noun to decide whether to use an article and, if so, which article to use.

KEY POINTS

Articles at a Glance: Four Basic Questions about a Noun

1. PROPER OR COMMON NOUN?
   ↓
   Singular: no
     article (zero article)
   Plural: *the*
                              ↓

   2. SPECIFIC OR NONSPECIFIC REFERENCE?
      ↓
      the
                              ↓

      3. UNCOUNTABLE OR COUNTABLE NOUN?
         ↓
         no article OR
         some, much,
         a little, etc.
                              ↓

         4. PLURAL OR SINGULAR?
            ↓
            no article OR
            some, many,
            a few, etc.
                              ↓
                          a/an

You can use the questions to decide which article, if any, to use with the noun *poem* as you consider the following sentence:

▶ **Milton wrote __?__ moving poem about blindness.**

1. Is the noun a proper noun or a common noun?

COMMON   **Go to question 2.**

2. Does the common noun refer to a specific person, place, thing, or idea known to both writer and readers as unique, or is the reference nonspecific?

NONSPECIFIC   [The reference is not to one specific poem. There is more than one "moving poem" in literature.] **Go to question 3.**

3. Is the noun uncountable or countable?

COUNTABLE   [We can say *one poem, two poems.*] **Go to question 4.**

4. Is the noun plural or singular?

SINGULAR   [The first letter in the noun phrase *moving poem* is *m*, a consonant sound.] **Use *a* as the article.**

Milton wrote *a* moving poem about blindness.

33f Proper nouns and articles

Singular proper nouns: No article   As a general rule, capitalize singular proper nouns (29a, item 4), and use no article: *Stephen King, Africa, Thailand, Tora Bora, Ohio, Cairo, Mount St. Helens, Lake Temagami, Shelter Island, Golden Gate Park, Avenue of the Americas, Cornell University, Thursday, July, Islam, Catholicism.*

There are, however, many exceptions. You should note them as you come across them.

Some exceptions: Singular proper nouns with *the*   Some singular proper nouns use the article *the*: proper nouns with a common noun and *of* as part of the name (*the University of Texas, the Fourth of July, the Statue of Liberty*); highways (*the New Jersey Turnpike, the Long Island Expressway*); buildings (*the Eiffel Tower, the Prudential Building, the Sears Tower, the Empire State Building*); bridges (*the Golden Gate Bridge, the Brooklyn Bridge*), hotels and museums (*the Hilton Hotel, the Guggenheim Museum, the Louvre*); countries named with a phrase (*the United Kingdom, the Dominican Republic, the People's Republic of China*); parts of the globe and geographical areas (*the North Pole, the West, the East, the Riviera*); seas, oceans, gulfs, rivers, and deserts (*the Mediterranean Sea, the Atlantic Ocean, the Persian Gulf, the Yangtze River, the Mojave Desert*); historical periods and events (*the Enlightenment, the Cold War*); groups *(the Taliban, the Chicago Seven, the IRA, the Mafia)*; titles *(the President of the United States, the Chancellor of the Exchequer, the Emperor of Japan)*.

Plural proper nouns: With *the* Examples are *the United States, the Great Lakes, the Himalayas, the Philippines, the Chinese* (people), *the Americans, the Italians.*

EXERCISE 33.1 Use articles, including *the*, correctly.
In each of the following sentences, correct any errors in article use.
(**A** = See Answer Key.)

EXAMPLE:

Many inactive people suffer from ~~the~~ depression.

A 1. Many scientific studies have proved that exercise helps the people sleep better and lose a weight.

A 2. A active lifestyle seems to improve not only a person's health but also his or her mood.

3. Endorphins, which are chemicals in human brain that are linked to feelings of well-being, increase when people get the enough exercise.

4. In West, people who do not exercise are twice as likely as active people to suffer a symptoms of depression.

5. However, the scientists at the Harvard University are not certain whether people do not exercise because they are depressed or whether they are depressed because they do not exercise.

34 Verbs and Verb Forms

34a Forms that cannot function as a main verb

A clause needs a complete verb consisting of one of the five verb forms (16a) and any necessary auxiliaries. However, verb forms such as the *-ing* form and the past participle can never function as the complete verb of a clause. Because readers get so much information from verbs, they have a relatively low level of tolerance for error, so make sure you edit with care and use auxiliary verbs whenever necessary (16c, 34b, 34c).

34b *Do, have,* and *be*

Do, have, and *be* can be used both as main verbs and as auxiliaries to indicate tense and meaning with other verbs. Their forms are irregular.

Forms of *Do, Have,* and *Be*

Base	Present Tense	*-ing*	Past Tense	Past Participle
do	do/does	doing	did	done
have	have/has	having	had	had
be	am/is/are	being	was/were	been

When *do, have,* and *be* occur as auxiliary verbs, use only specific verb forms following them.

Forms Following *Do, Have,* and *Be*

Auxiliary	Form Following Auxiliary	Examples
do	base form	Stern's proposal did not win the competition.
have	past participle	Time has run out. You should have hurried. The plans have been completed.
be	*-ing* (ACTIVE)	They are skating. Someone has been watching. The manager was taking him to the hospital.
	OR past participle (PASSIVE)	The pitcher was taken to the hospital. The book has been sold. The auction will be held next week.

The similarity of sound in spoken English of the forms *been* and *being* sometimes causes confusion. Always edit for the forms that follow *been* and *being*.

Forms Following *Been* and *Being*

Auxiliary	Form of *Be*	Form Following *Be*	Examples
has/have/had	*been*	*-ing* (ACTIVE)	She has been waiting.
		OR past participle (PASSIVE)	They have been arrested.

Auxiliary	Form of *Be*	Form Following *Be*	Examples
am/is/are *was/were*	*being*	past participle (PASSIVE)	The computer is being repaired. Some parts are being replaced.

See 16c on the need to include the *be* auxiliary in present tense forms:

is
▶ His sister ︿working.

34c Modal auxiliary verbs

The nine modal auxiliary verbs are *will, would, can, could, shall, should, may, might,* and *must*. Note the following three important points.

1. The modals do not change form.
2. The modals never add an *-s* ending.
3. Modals are always followed by a base form without *to: could go, should ask, must arrive, might have* seen, *would be* sleeping.

▶ The committee must ~~to~~ vote tomorrow.

▶ The proposal might improve~~s~~ the city.

▶ The residents could disapprove~~d~~.

Meanings of Modal Verbs

Meaning	Present and Future	Past
1. Intention	*will, shall* She *will* explain. [*Shall* is used mostly in questions: *Shall I buy that big green ceramic horse?*]	*would* She said that she *would* explain.
2. Ability	*can (am/is/are able to)* He *can* cook well. [Do not use *can* and *able to* together: *He is able to cook well.*]	*could (was/were able to)* He *could* not read until he was eight. [He was not able to read until he was eight.]

Meanings of Modal Verbs

Meaning	Present and Future	Past
3. Permission	*may, might, can, could*	*might, could*
	May I refer to Auden again? [*Might* or *could* is more tentative.]	Her instructor said she *could* use a dictionary.
4. Polite question	*would, could*	
	Would readers please indulge me for a moment?	
	Could you try not to read ahead?	
5. Speculation	*would, could, might*	*would* or *could* or *might* + *have* + past participle
	If he had more talent, he *could* become a professional pianist. [See also 16f.]	If I had studied, I *might have* passed the test.
6. Advisability	*should*	*should* + *have* + past participle
	You *should* go home and rest.	You *should have* taken your medication. [Implied here is "but you did not."]
7. Necessity (stronger than *should*)	*must* (or *have to*)	*had to* + base form
	Applicants *must* apply for a mortgage.	Theo van Gogh *had to* support his brother.
8. Prohibition	*must* + *not*	
	Participants *must not* leave until all the questions have been answered.	
9. Expectation	*should*	*should* + *have* + past participle
	The author *should* receive a check soon.	You *should have* received your check a week ago.

Meanings of Modal Verbs

Meaning	Present and Future	Past
10. Possibility	*may, might*	*might* + *have* + past + participle
	The technician *may* be working on the problem now.	She *might* already *have* revised the ending.
11. Logical assumption	*must*	*must* + *have* + past participle
	She's late; she *must* be stuck in traffic.	She *must have* taken the wrong route.
12. Repeated past action		*would* (or *used to*) + base form
		When I was a child, I *would* spend hours drawing.

EXERCISE 34.1   Use auxiliary and modal auxiliary verbs correctly. Correct any errors in the use of auxiliary and modal auxiliaries and verbs following them. (**A** = See Answer Key.)

EXAMPLE:

        are   should

Young people who learning to play an instrument would practice if they want to improve.

    A Most people believe that musicians must to have talent in order to succeed. **A** However, a 1998 study by British psychologist John Sloboda may indicates that the number of hours spent practicing affects musical ability more than inborn talent does. **A** The study included musicians aged ten to sixteen years, from both public and private schools. **A** Sloboda investigated how much each young musician practiced, whether parents and teachers involved in helping each musician improve, and how well each student scored on the British national music examination. Young musicians who had practicing most frequently were most successful on the exam; students whose parents and teachers working closely with them also received high scores. After looking at the exam results, Sloboda cannot help noticing that the students with the highest scores practiced eight hundred times more than the students with the lowest scores. According to Sloboda's research, even people who do not believe they have musical talent became excellent musicians if they practiced hard enough.

34d Infinitive after verbs and adjectives

Some verbs are followed by an infinitive (*to* + base form or base form alone). Some adjectives also occur with an infinitive. Such combinations are highly idiomatic. You need to learn each one individually as you find it in your reading.

Verb + infinitive These verbs are commonly followed by an infinitive (*to* + base form):

agree	choose	fail	offer	refuse
ask	claim	hope	plan	venture
beg	decide	manage	pretend	want
bother	expect	need	promise	wish

Note any differences between English and your native language. For example, the Spanish word for *refuse* is followed by the equivalent of an *-ing* form.

▶ He refused ~~criticizing~~ the system.
  to criticize

Position of a negative In a verb + infinitive pattern, the position of the negative affects meaning. Note the difference in meaning that the position of a negative (*not, never*) can create.

▶ He did *not* decide to buy a new car. His wife did.

▶ He decided *not* to buy a new car. His wife was disappointed.

Verb + noun or pronoun + infinitive Some verbs are followed by a noun or pronoun and then an infinitive. See also 18a for a pronoun used before an infinitive.

  V   pron. ┌─inf─┐
▶ The librarian *advised them to use* a better database.

Verbs that follow this pattern are *advise, allow, ask, cause, command, convince, encourage, expect, force, help, need, order, persuade, remind, require, tell, urge, want, warn.*

Spanish and Russian use a *that* clause after verbs like *want*. In English, however, *want* is followed by an infinitive.

▶ Rose wanted ~~that~~ her son ~~would~~ become a doctor.
  to

Make, let, **and** *have* After these verbs, use a noun or pronoun and a base form of the verb (without *to*).

▶ He *made his son practice* for an hour.

▶ They *let us leave* early.

▶ She *had her daughter wash* the car.

Note the corresponding passive voice structure with *have*:

▶ She usually *has the car washed* once a month.

Adjective + infinitive Some adjectives are followed by an infinitive. The filler subject *it* often occurs with this structure.

infinitive

▶ It is dangerous to hike alone in the woods.

ADJECTIVES FOLLOWED BY INFINITIVE

anxious	(in)advisable	sorry
dangerous	likely	(un)fair
eager	lucky	(un)just
essential	powerless	(un)kind
foolish	proud	(un)necessary
happy	right	wrong
(im)possible	silly	

34e Verbs followed by an *-ing* form used as a noun

▶ I *can't help laughing* at Jon Stewart's *Daily Show.*

The *-ing* form of a verb used as a noun is known as a *gerund*. The verbs that are systematically followed by an *-ing* form make up a relatively short and learnable list.

admit	discuss	practice
appreciate	dislike	recall
avoid	enjoy	resist
be worth	finish	risk
can't help	imagine	suggest
consider	keep	tolerate
delay	miss	
deny	postpone	

> inviting
> ▶ We considered ~~to invite~~ his parents.
>   ^

> hearing
> ▶ Most people dislike ~~to hear~~ cell phones at concerts.
>   ^

Note that a negative comes between the verb and the *-ing* form:

> ▶ During their vacation, they enjoy *not* getting up early
> every day.

34f Verbs followed by an infinitive or *-ing* form

Some verbs can be followed by either an infinitive or an *-ing* verb form (a gerund) with almost no discernible difference in meaning: *begin, continue, hate, like, love, start.*

> ▶ She loves *cooking.* ▶ She loves *to cook.*

The infinitive and the *-ing* form after a few verbs (*forget, remember, try, stop*), however, signal different meanings:

> ▶ He remembered *to mail* the letter.   [An intention]

> ▶ He remembered *mailing* the letter.   [A past act]

34g *-ing* and *-ed* forms used as adjectives

Both the present participle (*-ing* verb form) and the past participle (ending in *-ed* in regular verbs) can function as adjectives (see 16a and 16d). Each form has a different meaning: the *-ing* adjective indicates that the word modified produces an effect; the past participle adjective indicates that the word modified has an effect produced on it.

> ▶ The *boring* cook served baked beans yet again.   [The cook produces boredom. Everyone is tired of baked beans.]

> ▶ The *bored* cook yawned as she scrambled eggs.   [The cook felt the emotion of boredom as she did the cooking, but the eggs could still be appreciated.]

PRODUCES AN EFFECT	HAS AN EFFECT PRODUCED ON IT
amazing	amazed
amusing	amused
annoying	annoyed
boring	bored
confusing	confused

PRODUCES AN EFFECT	HAS AN EFFECT PRODUCED ON IT
depressing	depressed
disappointing	disappointed
embarrassing	embarrassed
exciting	excited
interesting	interested
satisfying	satisfied
shocking	shocked
surprising	surprised
worrying	worried

Note: Do not drop the *-ed* ending from a past participle. Sometimes in speech it blends with a following *t* or *d* sound, but in writing the *-ed* ending must be included.

▶ I was surprisê to see her wild outfit.   *d*

▶ The researchers were ~~worry~~ that the results were   *worried* contaminated.

EXERCISE 34.2   Use correct verbs and verb forms.

In the following passage, correct any errors in verbs and verb forms. (**A** = See Answer Key.)

   A Can money makes people happy?**A** A well-known proverb says, "Money can't buy happiness," but some people probably would to agree that money is important for a happy life. **A** A survey by Andrew Oswald and Jonathan Gardner of the University of Warwick in England has investigating the connection between money and happiness for eight years.**A** The results are not surprised. **A** If people suddenly get money that they not expecting—from the lottery, for example—they generally feel more satisfy with their lives.

   In general, according to the study, receiving about $75,000 must mean the difference between being fairly happy and being very happy. However, people who admitted to be miserable before they had money needed to get $1.5 million before they considered themselves happy. But Oswald and Gardner advise to recognize that the study is not finished. They not admit knowing whether the happiness from receiving unexpected money lasts for a long time.

   People who do not expect getting a large amount of money can find other reasons not to despair. The researchers say that money is not the most important factor in whether a person is happy or not. People who married are happier than those who are not: the researchers estimate that a lasting marriage makes the partners as happy as an extra $100,000 a year can. Perhaps looking for love is as important as trying to make—or win—a large amount of money.

35 Word Order and Sentence Structure

Languages structure the information in sentences in many ways. For more on sentence structure, see chapters 12 and 15.

35a Inclusion of a subject

In some languages, a subject can be omitted. In Standard English, you must include a subject in every clause, even just a filler subject such as *there* or *it*.

▶ The critics hated the film because‸was too sentimental.

it

▶ When the director's business partners lost money,‸were immediate effects on the share prices.

there

Do not use *it* to point to a long subject that follows.

▶ We can say that ~~it~~ (does not matter) the historical period of the society‸.

See also 35f for unnecessary pronoun subjects.

35b Order of sentence elements

Expressions of time and place   Put adverbs and adverb phrases of time and place at the beginning or end of a clause, not between the verb and its direct object.

▶ The quiz show host congratulated |many times| the winner.

Descriptive adjective phrases   Put a descriptive adjective phrase after, not before, the noun it modifies.

▶ I would go to |known only to me| places.

Order of subject, verb, object Languages differ in the order of appearance of the subject (S), verb (V), and direct object (DO) in a sentence. In English, the most commonly occurring sentence pattern is S + V + DO ("Children like candy").

▶ *Every* ~~Good grades received every~~ student in the class. *received good grades*

35c Direct and indirect objects

Some verbs—such as *give, send, show, tell, teach, find, sell, ask, offer, pay, pass,* and *hand*—can be followed by both a direct object and an indirect object. The indirect object is the person or thing to whom or to which, or for whom or for which, something is done. It follows the verb and precedes the direct object.

▶ He gave **his mother** **some flowers**.

▶ He gave **her** **some flowers**.

An indirect object can be replaced with a prepositional phrase that *follows* the direct object.

▶ He gave **some flowers** **to his mother**.

Some verbs—such as *explain, describe, say, mention,* and *open*—are never followed by an indirect object. However, they can be followed by a direct object and a prepositional phrase with *to* or *for.*

▶ She explained ~~me~~ the election process. *to me*

▶ He described ~~us~~ the menu. *to us*

Note that *tell,* but not *say,* can take an indirect object.

▶ She ~~said~~ him the secret. *told*

EXERCISE 35.1 Correct errors in inclusion of a subject, order of elements, direct and indirect objects.

Correct any errors in the inclusion of a subject, in the order of elements, and in the use of direct and indirect objects. Some sentences may be correct. (**A** = See Answer Key.)

EXAMPLE:

In the United States, more people are having ~~every year~~

every year   *there*
plastic surgery even though ^ are sometimes side effects
                    ^   ^

from the surgery.

A 1. Cosmetic surgery had in the past a stigma, but now many people consider changing their appearance surgically.

A 2. In addition, the price of such surgery was once high, but it has declined in recent years.

A 3. In 2000, 7.4 million people had for one reason or another cosmetic surgery.

A 4. Were 370,000 African Americans among those 7.4 million patients, and African Americans represent a growing percentage of wanting plastic surgery people.

A 5. Cosmetic surgery gives to some people an improved self-image.

6. However, can be drawbacks to changing one's appearance.

7. Psychologists are concerned that some African American women reject their African features because they accept the most commonly seen in magazines standards of beauty.

8. Such women might say, for example, that it is a universal standard of beauty a narrow nose.

9. Some middle-class African Americans may also consider plastic surgery when they see that certain African American celebrities have changed their features.

10. Many psychologists say a patient considering cosmetic surgery that beauty comes from inside.

35d Direct and indirect quotations and questions

In a direct quotation or direct question, the exact words used by the speaker are enclosed in quotation marks. In an indirect (reported) quotation or an indirect question, the writer reports what the speaker said, and quotation marks are not used. Changes also occur in pronouns, time expressions, and verb tenses. (See also 16e.)

──── direct quotation ────
▶ He said, "I have lost my notebook."

$\overbrace{\qquad\text{indirect quotation}\qquad}$
▶ **He said that he had lost his notebook.**

$\overbrace{\qquad\text{direct question}\qquad}$
▶ **He asked, "Have you seen it?"**

$\overbrace{\qquad\text{indirect question}\qquad}$
▶ **He asked if we had seen it.**

Direct and indirect quotations Usually you must make several changes when you report a direct quotation as an indirect quotation and use an introductory verb in the past tense. You will do this often when you write college papers and report the views of others. Avoid shifts from direct to indirect quotations (15d).

Direct and Indirect Quotations

Change	Direct/Indirect Quotation	Example	Explanation
Punctuation and tense	Direct	The young couple said, "The price *is* too high."	Exact words within quotation marks
	Indirect	The young couple said that the price *was* too high.	No quotation marks; tense change (16e)
Pronoun and tense	Direct	He insisted, "*I understand* the figures."	First person pronoun and present tense
	Indirect	He insisted that *he understood* the figures.	Change to third person pronoun; tense change
Command to statement	Direct	"Cancel the payment," her husband said.	
	Indirect	Her husband *told* her *to* cancel the payment.	Verb (*tell, instruct*) + *to*
Expressions of time and place	Direct	The bankers said, "*We will* work on *this* deal *tomorrow*."	

Change	Direct/Indirect Quotation	Example	Explanation
	Indirect	The bankers said *they would* work on *that* deal *the next day*.	Expressions of time and place not related to speaker's perspective; tense change (16e); change to third person pronoun
Colloquial to formal	Direct	The clients said, "Well, no thanks; *we won't* wait."	
	Indirect	The clients thanked the bankers but said *they would not* wait.	Spoken words and phrases omitted or rephrased; also a tense change (16e)

Direct and indirect questions When a direct question is reported indirectly, it loses the word order of a question (v + s) and the question mark. Sometimes changes in tense are necessary (see also 16e).

DIRECT
QUESTION

                   V   S

The buyer asked, "*Are* the goods ready to be shipped?"

INDIRECT
QUESTION

                     S   V

The buyer asked if the goods *were* ready to be shipped.

DIRECT
QUESTION

                V   S

The boss asked, "What *are* they doing?"

INDIRECT
QUESTION

                S   V

The boss asked what they *were* doing.

DIRECT
QUESTION

     V   S   V

"Why *did* they *send* a letter instead of a fax?" her secretary asked.

INDIRECT
QUESTION

                       S   V

Her secretary asked why they [*had*] *sent* a letter instead of a fax.

Use only a question word such as *why* or the words *if* or *whether* to introduce an indirect question. Do not use *that* as well.

▶ Her secretary asked ~~that~~ why they sent a letter instead of ⸝ a fax.

Direct and Indirect Questions

	Introductory Word	Auxiliary Verb	Subject	Auxiliary Verb(s)	Main Verb and Rest of Clause
DIRECT	What	are	they		thinking?
INDIRECT	Nobody knows what		they	are	thinking.
DIRECT	Where	does	he		work?
INDIRECT	I can't remember where		he		works.
DIRECT	Why	did	she		write that poem?
INDIRECT	The critic does not reveal why		she		wrote that poem.
DIRECT		Have	the diaries	been	published yet?
INDIRECT	The Web site does not say if (whether)		the diaries	have been	published yet.
DIRECT		Did	the space program		succeed?
INDIRECT	It is not clear if		the space program		succeeded.

EXERCISE 35.2 Rewrite direct speech as indirect (reported) speech.

Write the following sentences as indirect (reported) speech, making any necessary changes. In each case, use the given tag followed by *that, if,* or a question word. (**A**= See Answer Key.)

EXAMPLE:

"The soup is too spicy." (She complained)
She complained that the soup was too spicy.

A1. "I cannot abide such pretentious prose." (The critic announced)

A2. "Who is in charge?" (The mayor wanted to know)

A3. "What is the square root of 2209?" (The contestant cannot work out)

A4. "The economy will rebound." (The broker predicted)

A5. "Will I lose all my savings?" (Investors constantly wonder)

6. "I understand the problems." (The candidate assured everyone)

7. "Who knows the answer?" (The game-show host asked)

8. "We will leave early tomorrow." (The guests hinted)

9. "Did my sweater shrink in the wash?" (Her son asked)

10. "We are going to a new French restaurant this evening." (The committee members said)

35e Dependent clauses with *although* and *because*

In some languages, a subordinating conjunction (such as *although* or *because*) can be used along with a coordinating conjunction (*but, so*) or a transitional expression (*however, therefore*) in the same sentence. In English, only one is used.

No   *Although* he loved his father, *but* he did not have much opportunity to spend time with him.

POSSIBLE   *Although* he loved his father, he did not have
REVISIONS   much opportunity to spend time with him.

He loved his father, *but* he did not have much opportunity to spend time with him.

No   *Because* she had been trained in the church, *therefore* she was sensitive to the idea of audience.

POSSIBLE
REVISIONS

Because she had been trained in the church, she was sensitive to the idea of audience.

She had been trained in the church, *so* she was sensitive to the idea of audience.

She had been trained in the church; *therefore,* she was sensitive to the idea of audience.

See 23e for the punctuation of transitional expressions.

35f Unnecessary pronouns

Do not restate the simple subject of a sentence as a pronoun. See also 15g.

▶ Visitors to the Statue of Liberty ~~they~~ have worn the steps down.

▶ The adviser who told me about dyslexia ~~he~~ is a man I will never forget.

In a relative clause introduced by *whom, which,* or *that,* do not include a pronoun that the relative pronoun has replaced. See also 20f.

▶ The house that I lived in ~~it~~ for ten years has been sold.

EXERCISE 35.3 Use correct word order and sentence structure. Correct any errors in word order or sentence structure. (**A** = See Answer Key.)

AMany people fear in China and Japan the number *four.* **A**Is a good reason for this fear: in Japanese, Mandarin, and Cantonese, the word for *four* and the word for *death* are nearly identical. **A**A study in the *British Medical Journal* suggests that cardiac patients from Chinese and Japanese backgrounds they may literally die of fear of the number four. **A**According to the study, which looked at U.S. mortality statistics over a twenty-five-year period, Chinese and Japanese hospitalized for heart disease patients were more likely to die on the fourth day of the month. **A**Although Chinese and Japanese cardiac patients across the country were all statistically more likely to die on that day, but the effect was strongest among Californian Chinese and Japanese patients. **A**Is not clear why Californians are more at risk. **A**However, one researcher suggested that because California's large Asian population includes many older people, the older generation may therefore teach to younger generations traditional beliefs.

Chinese and Japanese patients with other diseases they were no more likely to die on the fourth of the month than at any other time. White patients, whether they had heart disease or any other illness, they were no more likely to die on the supposedly unlucky thirteenth of the month than on any other day. Psychiatrist Jiang Wei of Duke University Medical School said, "She still didn't know the biological reason for the statistical effect" on Chinese and Japanese cardiac patients. David P. Phillips, the sociologist who conducted the study, said that the only explanation that makes sense is that the number four causes extra stress in Chinese and Japanese heart patients. More research may someday prove whether or not the stress on the fourth of the month it can be enough to kill.

35g Order of adjectives

When two or more adjectives modify a noun, they usually occur before the noun in the order listed in the table. Commas separate a series of adjectives of evaluation (called *coordinate adjectives*); their order can be reversed, and the word *and* can be inserted between them. However, do not use commas to separate *cumulative adjectives* (no *and* can be inserted) that describe size, shape, age, color, origin, religion, or material. Read the table across the pages. The comma in the last example occurs between coordinate adjectives of evaluation. See also 23g.

As a general rule, avoid long strings of adjectives. Three or four adjectives of any type after a determiner should be the absolute limit.

Adjective Order

Determiner	Coordinate Adjective of Evaluation	Size	Shape	Age	Color
two				middle-aged	
the		big		old	
a	lovely			antique	
many		little			white
that	beautiful		long		
his	dainty	little			
our			rectangular		
her	efficient, hardworking				

EXERCISE 35.4 Use adjectives in the correct order.

In each of the following sentences, make any necessary changes in the order of adjectives and use of commas. (**A** = See Answer Key.)

EXAMPLE:

> Short, dark winter
> ~~Dark, winter, short~~ days can cause some people to become depressed.^

A 1. In northern states in wintertime, many office workers spend most of the daylight hours indoors.

A 2. Architects are beginning to design some new big buildings to admit as much natural light as possible.

3. A building with features such as Italian round skylights, large windows, or an atrium reduces the need for artificial light, but the most money-saving benefit of outside light is its effect on many workers.

4. A recent architectural study demonstrated that workers in new efficient buildings with natural light were happier, more productive employees than workers in dark or artificially lighted offices.

5. Concerned employers can help their office workers maintain a positive outlook through the winter dreary months by ensuring that workplaces are brightly lit, preferably with natural light.

Region of Origin	Religion/ Architecture/ Design	Material	Noun (or *-ing*) as Adjective	Head Noun
	Catholic			priests
Italian		stone		house
		oak	writing	desk
		ivory		buttons
			kitchen	table
French				poodle
	Art Deco		storage	chest
				assistant

36 Prepositions and Idioms

For language learners, prepositions and idioms can be confusing.
Learn the idioms one by one, as you come across them.

36a Idioms with prepositions

Learn the idiomatic uses of prepositions by writing them down in
lists when you come across them in your reading. Here is a start:

IN

in July, in 2004, in the morning, in the drawer, in the closet, in
Ohio, in Milwaukee, in the cookie jar, in the library stacks, singing
in the rain, in the United States, in his pocket, in bed, in school, in
class, in Spanish, in time (to participate in an activity), in love, the
letter in the envelope

ON

on the menu, on the library shelf, on Saturday, on 9 September
2006, on Union Street, on the weekend, on the roof, a ring on her
finger, an article on education, on the moon, on earth, on occasion,
on time (punctual), on foot, on the couch, knock on the door, the
address on the envelope

AT

at 8 o'clock, at home, at a party, at night, at work

EXERCISE 36.1   Use prepositions in their proper contexts.
In the following passage, fill in each blank space with the appro-
priate preposition, choosing among *in, on,* and *at.* (**A** = See Answer
Key.)

EXAMPLE:

**People should save for retirement, but many workers resist
putting money** _____*in*_____ **the bank for their future.**

A Everyone hopes to retire _____ some time _____ the
future. **A** However, many people fail to invest for retirement,
spending most of the money they earn _____ everyday
expenses and luxuries. **A** The field of behavioral economics tries
to explain why people do not always make rational plans to save
for the future. **A** Behavioral economists also work to find ways to
convince people to save money and to get _____ a schedule

that will allow them to retire. Although most people are reluctant to decrease the amount of money that is _____ their take-home pay, employers can often persuade workers to promise _____ advance to increase the percentage of the paycheck that they contribute to a retirement account. Many employees get an annual raise _____ work, and the increased contribution can take effect _____ the same time as the raise. In this way, people are likely to feel that they are _____ their way to a comfortable financial future without being forced to make ends meet _____ a smaller paycheck. Some people apparently need to play tricks _____ themselves to make sure that they make wise decisions.

36b Adjective + preposition

When you are writing, use a dictionary to check the specific prepositions used with an adjective.

▶ The botanist is *afraid of* spiders.

▶ E. O. Wilson was *interested in* ants.

Some common idiomatic adjective + preposition combinations are the following. Make your own lists to add to these.

Adjective + Preposition Combinations

Preposition	With Adjectives
about	anxious about, excited about, worried about
in	interested in
to/for	grateful to (someone) for (something), responsible to (someone) for (something)
with	content with, familiar with, patient with, satisfied with
of	afraid of, ashamed of, aware of, capable of, fond of, full of, guilty of, jealous of, proud of, suspicious of, tired of

36c Verb + preposition

Learn the following common idiomatic verb + preposition combinations.

> *apologize to* (someone) *for* (an offense or error)
>
> *arrive in* (a country or city); *arrive at* (a building or an event)
>
> *blame* (someone) *for* (an offense or error)
>
> *complain about*
>
> *concentrate on*
>
> *congratulate* (someone) *on* (success or good fortune)
>
> *consist of*
>
> *depend on*
>
> *explain* (facts) *to* (someone)
>
> *insist on*
>
> *laugh at*
>
> *rely on*
>
> *smile at*
>
> *take care of*
>
> *thank* (someone) *for* (a gift or favor)
>
> *throw* (an object) *at* (someone not expecting it)
>
> *throw* (an object) *to* (someone waiting to catch it)
>
> *worry about*

EXERCISE 36.2 Use adjective + preposition, verb + preposition. In each of the following sentences, correct any errors in the choice of prepositions. (**A** = See Answer Key.)

EXAMPLE:

about
Many Americans have been worried ~~from~~ the possibility of
⌃
of
biological terrorism, but some doctors are more afraid ~~from~~
⌃
of
the naturally caused influenza than ~~from~~ any biological agent.
⌃

A 1. Although some Americans wanted to take antibiotics as a precaution against anthrax in the fall of 2001, the percentage of people who asked their doctors of flu shots at that time was no higher than normal.

A 2. Influenza has been responsible to the deaths of many healthy people in the past century, and doctors do not know when a dangerous strain of flu may appear.

3. Doctors in 1918 were unable to prevent the flu epidemic to killing millions of people around the world; more people died of the flu than as a result of World War I that year.

4. Many people may not be aware to the dangers of influenza.

5. Medical specialists are studying genetic samples from people who died with influenza in 1918 to try to find ways to prevent such a deadly flu from recurring.

36d Phrasal verbs

Prepositions and a few adverbs (such as *away* and *forward*) can combine with verbs in such a way that they no longer function as prepositions or ordinary adverbs. They are then known as *particles*. Only a few languages other than English—Dutch, German, and Swedish, for example—use this verb + particle (preposition or adverb) combination, which is called a *phrasal verb*. Examples of English phrasal verbs are *put off* and *put up with*.

The meaning of a phrasal verb is entirely different from the meaning of the verb alone. Note the idiomatic meanings of some common phrasal verbs.

break down [stop functioning]	run across [meet unexpectedly]
get over [recover from]	run out [become used up]
look into [examine]	take after [resemble]

Always check the meanings of such verbs in a specialized dictionary such as *The American Heritage English as a Second Language Dictionary*.

A particle can be followed by a preposition to make a three-word combination:

▶ **She *gets along with* everybody.**   [She is friendly toward everybody.]

Other three-word verb combinations are

catch up with [draw level with]	look forward to [anticipate]
look down on [despise]	put up with [endure]
look up to [admire]	stand up for [defend]

Position of direct objects with two-word phrasal verbs Some two-word transitive phrasal verbs are separable. The direct object of these verbs can come between the verb and the accompanying particle.

▶ She *put off* **her dinner party.** [She postponed her dinner party.]

▶ She *put* **her dinner party** *off.*

When the direct object is a pronoun, however, always place the pronoun between the verb and the particle.

▶ She *put* **it** *off.*

Some commonly used phrasal verbs that follow that principle are listed here. They can be separated by a noun as a direct object; they must be separated when the direct object is a pronoun.

call off [cancel]	give up [surrender]	make up [invent]
fill out [complete]	leave out [omit]	turn down [reject]
find out [discover]	look up [locate]	turn off [stop]

Most dictionaries list phrasal verbs that are associated with a particular verb, along with their meanings and examples. Develop your own list of such verbs from your reading.

36e Preposition + *-ing* form

The *-ing* verb form that functions as a noun (the *gerund*) frequently occurs after a preposition.

▶ **They congratulated him** *on winning* **the prize.**

▶ **Sue expressed interest** *in participating* **in the fundraiser.**

▶ **He ran three miles** *without stopping.*

▶ **The cheese is the right consistency** *for spreading.*

Note: Take care not to confuse *to* as a preposition with *to* used in an infinitive. When *to* is a preposition, it is followed by a noun, a pronoun, a noun phrase, or an *-ing* form, not by the base form of a verb.

┌ infinitive ┐
▶ **They want** *to adopt* **a child.**

preposition + *-ing* form (gerund)
▶ **They are looking forward** *to adopting* **a child.**

Check which to use by trying out a noun replacement after *to*:

▶ **They are looking forward** *to parenthood.*

Note also *be devoted to, be/get used* to (see 36f).

36f *Get used to* and *used to*

For multilingual writers of English, the distinction between *used to* +
base form and *be/get used to* + *-ing* (gerund) is difficult.

▶ **He** *used to work* **long hours.**   [He did in the past but doesn't
anymore. The infinitive form follows *used* in this sense.]

▶ **Air traffic controllers** *are used to dealing* **with emergencies.**
[They are accustomed to it. The *-ing* form follows *be/get
used to.*]

EXERCISE 36.3   Use phrasal verbs, preposition + *-ing*, *get used
to*, and *used to* correctly.

Correct any errors in the use of phrasal verbs, gerunds after
prepositions, and the phrases *get used to* and *used to*. (**A** = See
Answer Key.)

EXAMPLE:

used to be
AIDS ~~is used to being~~ a death sentence, but more people
now survive for years with the disease.

ASince scientists began to learn about AIDS more than thirty
years ago, many people have been counting up a cure for the
disease. **A**The cure has not yet been found, but today many
people with AIDS in this country used to live with the medications and other treatments that allow them to having a reasonably healthy life. **A**In poorer countries, unfortunately, fewer
people can look forward on living with AIDS, but AIDS
researchers are excited about a recent discovery in the central
African country of Rwanda. In Kigali, Rwanda's capital, a
study has been following a group of sixteen people who tested
positive for HIV at least twelve years ago but have neither
taken medicine to treating the illness nor gotten sick. In most

AIDS patients, the virus breaks out the immune system; in many patients in the Rwandan study, however, the virus shows an unusual mutation that seems to allow the body to put the virus up with. Researchers do not yet know whether this discovery will assist them in find a cure for the AIDS virus, but every new piece of information in this puzzle may be helpful in fight the disease.

Research—finding information for a purpose—is the basis of what is called "information literacy." Here is the Association of College and Research Libraries' assessment of the importance of information literacy, from <http://www.ala.org/>:

> Have you ever heard of Data Smog? A term coined by author David Shenk, it refers to the idea that too much information can create a barrier in our lives. This data smog is produced by the amount of information, the speed at which it comes to us from all directions, the need to make fast decisions, and the feeling of anxiety that we are making decisions without having ALL the information that is available or that we need.
>
> Information literacy is the solution to Data Smog. It allows us to cope by giving us the skills to know when we need information and where to locate it effectively and efficiently. It includes the technological skills needed to use the modern library as a gateway to information. It enables us to analyze and evaluate the information we find, thus giving us confidence in using that information to make a decision or create a product.

Part 6 will help you find your way in the Data Smog.

37 Research and the Dangers of Plagiarism

37a Research today: The plusses

Research has gained in scope and excitement. Information is everywhere, in accessible forms, at our fingertips. Researchers used to have to physically trudge off to dusty library shelves to find books and journal articles—sometimes only to find the crucial pages of the journal ripped out. Now researchers can sit in a school computer lab or in their own home and access library catalogs and a vast array of books, reference works, articles, databases, images, and informative Web sites. And the amount of information available online grows day by day. We can all do vast amounts of research as we sit in an armchair with a laptop. The plusses, then, are availability of information and convenience.

37b Research today: The minuses

However (and how often is there a big *however* to frustrate us?), such convenience and comfort is not without its downside. The ease of finding, copying, and downloading information from the screen has its attendant dangers: that researchers lose sight of what is theirs and what isn't, that they forget where they read something, that information seems so prolific that surely it must be there for the taking. Unfortunately, though, that is not the case, especially in the academic world, where presenting somebody else's words or ideas without acknowledging where those words and ideas come from is a punishable offense.

The word for the offense, *plagiarism,* is derived from a Latin verb meaning "to kidnap," and if you use someone else's words and ideas without acknowledging them, you are in effect kidnapping or stealing those words and ideas.

37c Plagiarism and its consequences: The seven sins

KEY POINTS

The Seven Sins of Plagiarism

1. *Intentional grand larceny*   Presenting as your own work a whole essay bought from paper mills, "borrowed" from a friend, or intentionally copied and pasted from an online source (where such a practice may be compared to ordering "a takeout essay"—see 40e)

2. *Premeditated shoplifting*   Using passages from a book, article, or Web site that you intentionally insert in your paper without any attribution (a type of plagiarism differing from point 1 only in that passages, not the whole paper, are copied)

3. *Tinkering with the evidence*   Using unattributed source material, making only a few word changes, and trusting that those changes are enough to avoid charges of plagiarism

4. *Idea kidnapping*   Using ideas written by others (even if you do use your own words) and neglecting to cite the source of the ideas

5. *Unauthorized borrowing of private property*   Using the words or sentence structure of a source and citing the source—but following it too closely and not including actual words from the source within quotation marks

(continued)

(continued)

6. *Trespassing over boundaries*   Failing to indicate in your paper where ideas from a source end and your ideas take over

7. *Writing under the influence*   Being too tired, lazy, or late for an imminent deadline and turning to any of the six previous sins in desperation

Consequences   The types of plagiarism described in items 4 through 6 in the Key Points box sometimes occur unintentionally, but to readers they may constitute sins of plagiarism nevertheless. You have to work hard at avoiding them, especially since the consequences of plagiarism can be severe, ranging from an F on a paper or an F in a course to disciplinary measures or expulsion from college. In the world at large, it can lead to lawsuits and ruined careers. Those are reasons enough to work hard at resisting the temptation to plagiarize.

LANGUAGE AND CULTURE
Ownership Rights across Cultures

The Western view takes seriously the ownership of words and text. It respects both the individual as author (and authority) and the originality of the individual's ideas. Copyright laws define and protect the boundaries of intellectual property. However, even the Western world acknowledges that authors imitate and borrow from others' work, as Harold Bloom notes in *The Anxiety of Influence.* In some cultures, memorization and the use of classic texts are common in all walks of life. And worldwide, the ownership of language, texts, music, and videos is being called into question by the democratic, interactive nature of the Internet. In short, therefore, plagiarism is not something universal and easy to define. In Western academic culture, basic ground rules exist for the "fair use" of another writer's writing without payment, but easy access to music and media sources poses interesting questions about intellectual property and the opportunities to create and remix culture.

TECHTOOLKIT   A Web Site on Plagiarism

For more on the topic of plagiarism, see the excellent Georgetown University Web site *What Is Plagiarism?* at <http://www.georgetown.edu/honor/plagiarism.html> <http://gervaseprograms.georgetown.edu/hc/plagiarism.html>. ∎

37d How to avoid even the suspicion of plagiarism

Research and clear documentation open a channel of communication between you and your audience. Readers learn what your views are and what has influenced those views. They will assume that anything not documented is your original idea and your wording.

Remember that citing any words and ideas that you use from your sources plays out to your advantage. Citing accurately reveals a writer who has done enough research to enter ongoing conversations in the academic world. In addition, citations show readers how hard you have worked, how much research you have done, and how the points you make are supported by experts. So be proud to cite your sources.

KEY POINTS

How to Avoid Plagiarizing

1. Start your research early enough to avoid panic mode.

2. Make a record of each source, so that you have all the information you need for appropriate documentation.

3. Set up a working annotated bibliography.

4. Take notes from the sources, with a systematic method of indicating quotation, paraphrase, and your own comments. For example, use quotation marks around quoted words, phrases, sentences, and passages; introduce a paraphrase with a tag, such as "Laird makes the point that . . ."; in your notes about a source, write your own comments in a different color. Then, later, you will see immediately which ideas are yours and which come from your source.

5. Never include in your own essay a passage, an identifiable phrase, or an idea that you have copied from someone else's work without acknowledging and documenting the source.

6. Never use exactly the same sequence of ideas and organization of argument as your source.

7. When you use a single key word from your source or three or more words in sequence from your source, use the appropriate format for quoting and documenting.

8. Always cite the source of any summary or paraphrase. Not only exact words but also ideas need to be credited.

(continued)

(continued)

9. Never simply substitute synonyms for a few words in the source or move a few words around.

10. Never use in your paper passages that have been written or rewritten by a friend or a tutor.

11. Never buy, find, download from the Internet, or "borrow" a paper or a section of a paper that you turn in as your own work.

EXERCISE 37.1 Detect plagiarism.

The following passage is from page 142 of *His Excellency: George Washington* by Joseph Ellis:

> Whereas Cromwell and later Napoleon made themselves synonymous with the revolution in order to justify the assumption of dictatorial power, Washington made himself synonymous with the American Revolution in order to declare that it was incompatible with dictatorial power.

Consider which of the following passages use the source responsibly and avoid kidnapping its words or ideas. For each passage, explain what is or is not done correctly and what may be considered plagiarism. (If you want to review paraphrase and quotation before you do this exercise, turn to 40b and 40e–40g.) Then compare your results with those of your classmates, and discuss which of the seven sins you find represented here. (**A** = See Answer Key.)

A 1. Joseph Ellis makes the point that whereas Cromwell and later Napoleon made themselves synonymous with the revolution in order to justify the assumption of dictatorial power, Washington made himself synonymous with the American Revolution in order to declare that it was incompatible with dictatorial power.

A 2. Joseph Ellis speculates that whereas Cromwell and later Napoleon made themselves synonymous with the revolution in order to justify the assumption of dictatorial power, Washington made himself synonymous with the American Revolution in order to declare that it was incompatible with dictatorial power (142).

A 3. As Joseph Ellis points out in *His Excellency: George Washington*, Washington was not like Cromwell or Napoleon, who led revolutions in order to become dictators themselves. Washington led the American Revolution in order that no American should ever become a dictator (142).

A 4. Joseph Ellis proposes that whereas Cromwell and Napoleon used their revolutions to justify their assumption of dictatorial power, Washington used the American Revolution to announce that it was incompatible with dictatorial power (142).

5. It is interesting to speculate that Cromwell and Napoleon each led revolutions to become dictators. Washington, on the other hand, led the American Revolution to deny dictatorship to himself and to all other Americans.

6. As Joseph Ellis notes, Washington differed from previous great revolutionary leaders who became dictators by seeing to it that the American Revolution, which he led, "was incompatible with dictatorial power" (142).

7. Cromwell and Napoleon identified with their revolutions so that they could become dictators whereas Washington identified with the American Revolution so that no one could become an American dictator.

8. As Joseph Ellis observes, "Whereas Cromwell and later Napoleon made themselves synonymous with the revolution in order to justify the assumption of dictatorial power, Washington made himself synonymous with the American Revolution in order to declare that it was incompatible with dictatorial power" (142).

9. Joseph Ellis comments that while both Cromwell and Napoleon made themselves identical with the revolution so that they could give good reason for taking on despotic authority, Washington identified with the revolution at home to show that it was irreconcilable with tyranny (142).

38 Planning the Project

38a Strategies for organizing your research

Research brings a heavy load, in more than one way. You will collect and carry around books, papers, notes, and drafts. If there is ever a time in your life when you need to be organized, this is it. If you work mostly on paper, buy several folders of different colors and label them for each part of your research. Keep your research for, say, an English course separate from your notes for a chemistry course. Make a schedule (see 38b), and look at it every day to make sure you are on track.

KEY POINTS

Overview of the Research Process

1. Start early and plan. Allot time to tasks. Fill out the schedule in 38b, copy it, and put it right next to a copy of the assignment in a place where you can look at it every day.

2. Don't be afraid to ask questions of your instructor or librarians. No questions are "silly questions" if you need to know the answer to proceed. All instructors and librarians expect students to feel somewhat bewildered by the size and scope of the task. They know how to help and are glad to help.

3. Gather the tools that you will need: a flash drive, ink for your printer, a pack of paper, a notebook, index cards, highlighting pens, folders, paperclips, money or a prepaid card for the library photocopier, a stapler, and self-stick notes.

4. Do the following to get started, though not necessarily in this order (see the sections listed for more details):

   • Make sure you understand the requirements (1c).
   • Plan which sources to begin with: primary or secondary (38c).
   • Select or narrow a topic (3a, 38d).
   • Compose a purpose statement (4d), a research question (38d), and a tentative working thesis (38d).

5. Find and evaluate sources (chapter 39), make notes (40b), and prepare a working bibliography (40a).

6. Plan your paper and write an outline (4d) and/or a draft (7a, 41f).

7. Evaluate the draft and get feedback (7c).

8. Revise your draft for ideas and organization—as many times as necessary (41f).

9. Prepare a list of works cited (chapters 43, 47).

10. Edit, proofread, and design the format of your paper (7f, 9a, chapters 10–20).

A research notebook Researchers find a research notebook handy, either a paper version or a handheld computer notebook. When an idea occurs to you or you see or hear something relevant to your topic, you can jot down notes. Keep a dated research log so that you keep track of what you find, where, and when. Keep your pencil and notebook next to your bed, too, for those nighttime flashes of insight. Make sure that both on paper and in your computer documents you indicate clearly which words and ideas come from what you find in your source materials and which words and ideas are your own. See chapter 37 for more on the importance of avoiding plagiarism.

Computer files Use your computer not just for writing but also for organizing your work, remembering always the cardinal rule: "Save, save, save."

TechToolkit How to Organize Computer Files

1. In the Save As window, click on Create New Folder and name it "Research Project."

2. Save in that folder all the files you create pertaining to your project: notes on sources, freewriting and brainstorming, ideas for a topic and research question, thesis possibilities, outline, numbered drafts, working bibliography, works-cited list, and so on.

3. If a folder gets unwieldy, move some files into new folders, and rename the first so that you have a system such as "My Drafts," "Notes from Sources," and "Works Cited." ∎

38b Schedule

Get started as early as you can. As soon as a project is assigned, set a tentative schedule, working backwards from the date the paper is due and splitting your time so that you know when you absolutely must move on to the next step. On the next page is a sample time block schedule that you can use and adapt. You will find in reality that several tasks overlap and the divisions are not neat. If you finish a block before the deadline, move on and give yourself more time for the later blocks.

The amount of time suggested in the sample schedule assumes that your instructor gives the assignment five weeks before the paper is due. You will need to recalculate the time allotted to each block of activities if more or less time is available. Go to *The Open Handbook* at <http://college.hmco.com/keys.html>, and click on Research and Documentation for a schedule you can print or save.

RESEARCH SCHEDULE

Starting date:
Date final draft is due:

Block 1: Getting started

Understand the requirements.
Select a topic or narrow a given topic.
Determine the preliminary types of sources to use.
Do preliminary research to discover the important issues.
Organize research findings in computer files.
Write a research question.

Complete by _____

Block 2: Reading, researching, and evaluating sources

Find and copy print and online sources.
Annotate and evaluate the sources.
Write summaries and paraphrases and make notes.
Set up a working bibliography.

Complete by _____

Block 3: Planning and drafting

Formulate a working thesis.
Write a proposal and/or an outline.
Write a first draft.

Complete by _____

Block 4: Evaluating the draft and getting feedback

Put the draft away for a day or two—but continue collecting
useful sources.
Outline the draft and evaluate its logic and completeness.
Plan more research as necessary to fill any gaps.
Get feedback from instructor and classmates.

Complete by _____

Block 5: Revising, preparing list of works cited, editing, presenting

Revise the draft.
Prepare a list of works cited.
Design the format of the paper.
Edit.
Proofread the final draft.

Complete by _____
(final deadline for handing in)

38c Primary and secondary sources

First-year college writing assignments often ask student writers to engage with and respond to *primary sources*—a poem, scientific data, or a photograph. First-year research assignments typically require students to consider and include *secondary sources*—a literary analysis of the poem, an interpretation of the data, an art critic's commentary on the photograph—in order to expand, enrich, and challenge the writer's topic.

Primary sources   Primary sources are the firsthand, raw, or original materials that researchers study and analyze. You can consult historical documents, visuals, journals and letters, autobiographies, memoirs, government statistics and studies, and speeches. You can examine works of art, literature, and architecture or watch or listen to performances and programs. You can study or initiate case studies or scientific experiments and take extensive field notes. You can also conduct interviews and use data collected from questionnaires. The use of such primary sources can bring an original note to your research and new information to your readers.

INTERVIEWS   Interview people who have expert knowledge of your topic. Plan a set of interview questions, but do not stick so closely to your script that you fail to follow up on good leads in your respondent's replies. Ask permission to tape-record the interview; otherwise, you will have to take quick and accurate notes, particularly if you want to quote. Check the functioning of your tape recorder beforehand. Make note of the date, time, and place of the interview.

QUESTIONNAIRES   Designing useful questionnaires is tricky since much depends on the number and sample of respondents you use, the types of questions you ask, and the methods you employ to analyze the data. Embark on questionnaire research only if you have been introduced to the necessary techniques in a college course or have consulted experts in this area.

Secondary sources   Secondary sources are analytical works that comment on and interpret other works, such as primary sources. Examples include reviews, discussions, biographies, critical studies, analyses of literary or artistic works or events, commentaries on current and historical events, class lectures, and electronic discussions.

38d From topic to question to working thesis

At the planning stage, you may not move far beyond establishing a topic and forming a research question. For this, you will turn to sources (see especially 39b and 39e for sources to use to select and narrow a topic). Move toward a research question and a working thesis as soon as you can so that then your search for sources is guided and productive. The secret is to be flexible. If a topic, a question, or a working thesis appears not to be producing good results, be prepared to find a new topic, question, or working thesis. That is why it is essential to start work early.

Searching for a good topic Try these tools and techniques to help yourself find a good topic—usually a more productive approach than lying on the couch hoping for a good idea.

- Look through your college textbooks in various fields for issues worth exploring.

- Consult general and specialized encyclopedias (39b). These sources sketch out the important issues and provide bibliographies for further reading.

- Browse the Web and subject directories (see the TechToolkit that follows) by searching for the keywords that interest you. You may find material that illuminates new issues or new sides of an issue.

- Use the *Library of Congress Subject Headings* (*LCSH*—in the Reference section of your library) to get ideas for topics and the books available on those topics and to learn the terminology used to search catalogs and databases. For instance, in a search for information on "doping in sports," the *LCSH* would provide the search term *anabolic steroids* and many narrower related terms. See more on *LCSH* in 39c.

- Talk, listen, and write. Talk to classmates and your instructors about possible topics. Listen to people around you: what topics engage their interest? Above all, carry your research notebook with you, and jot down any good ideas and leads.

 TECHTOOLKIT How to Find Topics on the Web

1. Log on to the *Librarians' Index to the Internet* at <http://lii.org> or the Internet Public Library at <http://www.ipl.org>. For general-interest topics, use commercial search directories such as Yahoo! <http://www.yahoo.com> or Google <http://www.google.com>. See 39a.

2. Find a subject area that interests you, such as education, literature, health, sports, politics, business, or science. A click on a specific subject area will produce lists of many different topics within that category.

3. Keep clicking on a topic until you narrow the search to one that interests you and is appropriate for your assignment. ∎

Keep the search for a topic in mind as you go about your daily life. Think to yourself, "What would I like to know more about? What am I curious about?" Reading a magazine, watching TV, and thinking about the things that really matter to you—all these simple everyday activities can generate ideas for research. Carry your research notebook with you so that you can jot down every idea that seems promising. Go to *The Open Handbook* at <http://college.hmco .com/keys.html>, and click on Research and Documentation for tutorials on finding and narrowing a topic online.

Selecting a topic   Select your own topic with two criteria in mind:

1. Does the topic interest you? Your topic should engage and sustain not only readers' interests but also your own. Readers recognize a writer who is simply going through the motions.
2. Is the topic appropriate (for example, in terms of the assignment, length, materials available)? Check with your instructor.

Narrowing a topic   You may need to narrow a topic so that it is manageable for the number of pages you intend to write. Narrow by limiting place, time, or issues you will address.

TOO BROAD	NARROWED
Parkinson's disease	Current treatments for Parkinson's disease
Pollution	Remedies for PCBs in U.S. rivers
Genetic engineering	The hazards of genetically altered foodstuffs
Computers	Health issues of computers
Popular music	The appeal of hip-hop to the young

To find a narrow enough topic, you may have to do background reading to discover the important issues. Even if you begin with what you think is a clear response to your topic, make sure you explore any historical background or complexity that you may have overlooked. Spend time looking at what others have said about the issues before you settle on a direction for your research.

If your instructor assigns a topic, make sure you understand the terms used in the assignment, such as *analyze, interpret,* and *argue* (see 1c for definitions). You may also have to narrow a subject area your instructor assigns to a manageable topic for a short paper.

Moving from topic to question   Being assigned a topic or finding an interesting topic and narrowing it gets you on your way, but it is just a beginning. For example, one student, Claudia Esteban, decided to write on automobile safety. She then needed to decide what aspect of this topic to investigate. Here is her brainstorming list on the topic of automobile safety:

Child seats	Restrictions on drinking
Air bags	Punishments for driving while intoxicated
Seat belts	Speeding
SUVs	Using a cell phone while driving

Esteban then did some preliminary reading and research to find out which areas offered useful material. From the narrowed list of topics she framed two possible research questions and concentrated on discovering what material was available in these two areas:

What effects would increasing the highway speed limit to 75 mph have?
What measures would make SUVs less dangerous on the roads?

Designing a research question For a full-scale research paper, design a research question that gets at the heart of what you want to discover. Your question should contain concrete keywords that you can search (see 39a) and not rely heavily on general terms or abstractions. The answer you find as you do research is likely to become your thesis. If you find huge amounts of material on your question and realize that you would have to write a book (or two) to cover all the issues, narrow your question.

QUESTIONS NEEDING NARROWING

1. How important are families? (too broad: important to whom and for what? no useful keywords to search)
2. What problems does the Internet cause? (too broad: what types of problems? what aspects of the Internet?)
3. What are the treatments for cancer? (too wide-ranging: volumes could be and have been written on this)
4. Should prayer be encouraged in schools? (difficult to discuss without relying on personal and religious conviction)

REVISED QUESTIONS

1. In what ways does a stable family environment contribute to an individual's future success?
2. What types of Internet controls would protect individual privacy?
3. For which types of cancer are the success rates of radiation therapy the most promising?
4. If prayer is allowed in schools, how can a multicultural policy be maintained?

A research question will give you a sense of direction. Frequently, as you read and take notes, you will have in mind a tentative response to your question. Sometimes that hypothesis will be confirmed. Sometimes, though, your research will reveal issues you have not previously considered and facts that are new to you, so you will refine, adapt, or even totally change your working thesis (see 4b and 6c for more on a working thesis). If after a few days of research you either cannot find enough material on your topic or discover that all the information is dated, flimsy, or biased, waste no more time. Turn immediately to another topic and formulate a new research question. (See chapter 39 on evaluating sources.)

EXERCISE 38.1 Narrow topics and write research questions. Explore ways in which two of the following topics can be narrowed, do research to identify important issues, and write two possible research questions for each topic. (**A** = See Answer Key.)

A • Materialism
• Truth in advertising
• TV quiz shows

• Edgar Allan Poe
• Sports celebrities
• Recycling

Formulating a working thesis As you do your preliminary work of examining the task, planning which types of sources to use, and moving toward a topic, you will probably have in mind the point you want to make in your paper. If your research question is "Should Internet controls be established to protect individual privacy?" you probably favor either a "yes" or "no" answer to your question. At this point, you will formulate a working thesis in the form of a statement of opinion, which will help drive the organization of your paper.

Internet controls to protect individual privacy should be established.

Or Internet controls to protect individual privacy should not be established.

KEY POINTS
Writing a Working Thesis

1. Make sure the thesis is a statement. A phrase or a question is not a thesis: "Internet controls" is a topic, not a thesis statement. "Are Internet controls needed?" is a question, not a thesis statement.

(continued)

(continued)

2. Make sure the thesis statement is not merely a statement of fact: "NUA Internet Surveys estimate that 605.6 million people were online as of September 2002" is a statement that cannot be developed and argued. A statement of fact does not let readers feel the need to read on to see what you have to say.

3. Make sure the thesis statement does more than announce the topic: "This paper will discuss Internet controls." Instead, your thesis statement should give information about or express an opinion on the topic: "Service providers, online retailers, and parents share the responsibility of establishing Internet controls to protect an individual's privacy."

4. Above all, be prepared to change and refine your thesis as you do your research and discover what your topic entails.

When you have a working thesis, your research becomes more focused. You look for material that relates to your thesis. If you find none, you can revise your thesis. If you find huge amounts of material, that is a signal for you to refine your thesis to make it more narrow and more focused on specific issues. Then you are ready to find sources and evaluate their relevance and reliability (chapter 39). As you read and make notes, you may find that your initial working thesis—"Internet controls should be established to protect individual privacy"—is too broad, and you may decide to narrow it: "Parents need to establish controls to protect their family's privacy on the Internet."

EXERCISE 38.2 Select and revise thesis statements.
Which of the following would make a good thesis statement for a research paper? Show how the others could be improved to make them more effective thesis statements. (**A** = See Answer Key.)

A 1. How to discipline children.

A 2. The advantages and disadvantages of spanking.

A 3. In this paper I will discuss how parents should bring up their children.

A 4. Doctors' advice on the issue of spanking.

5. Children who fear spanking will behave themselves.

6. Disciplining children should involve rewards, removal of privileges, and above all, discussion of right and wrong.

38e Research proposal

While you move from topic to research question to working thesis, you may be asked to submit a proposal to ensure that you are on the right track. View it as a mapping-out of the territory you are exploring as well as a plan for where you need to go. While not as precise as an outline, a proposal helps to focus your research project. It can be written as a narrative or a numbered list, whichever fits your topic. For the research paper assignment in her expository writing course, Diana Fatakhova submitted to her instructor a proposal to research the controversial use of antidepressants for youths.

Depression has been an acute psychiatric disorder for decades, and the emergence of antidepressants has given hope to those diagnosed with this illness. Some of these antidepressants, called selective serotonin reuptake inhibitors (SSRIs), include Prozac, Paxil, Effexor, and Zoloft. They have been taken by adults for years and have also been prescribed for children and teenagers at lower doses as well. However, the use of SSRIs for young people has not been endorsed by the FDA, and recent findings have shown that youths who take these medications are at a greater risk of committing suicide because they exhibit an increase in suicidal thoughts and behaviors.

Background information

This subject is controversial since both benefits and dangers go along with youths taking SSRIs. The use of drugs has resulted in a decrease in suicides, but risk factors had not been previously taken into account. Both scientists and parents are now torn between taking a risk and hoping that the child will be able to refrain from committing suicide by staying on the medication. I plan on researching how antidepressants work and what specific effects they have on young people. For a paper directed to my classmates, instructor, and general readers, my research question is this: Do the risks of antidepressants outweigh the benefits, and if so, what alternatives are available?

Purpose

Audience

Research question

39   Finding and Evaluating Sources

The Internet provides access to reference works, complete texts, and reliable sources such as databases of scholarly articles. It can be seen as a virtual library, available at the click of a mouse. It also provides a means of access to what were once seen as traditional print sources and to information that exists only online.

Using the Internet as a means to access information can lead you to many sources once viewed as traditional—reference works, books, scholarly articles, newspaper reports, government documents, and other traditional reference works, as well as to many reputable sources available only online, such as scholarly online journals and professional sites. Check at your library reference desk and on your library's Web page to find out which scholarly reference works and databases are available to you online and which Web sites might be particularly pertinent to your topic.

However, not everything you need is going to be available to you from a computer. Your search may not be comprehensive if you limit yourself to sources you access online. You may still need to consult reference works, find books in library stacks, check your library's print holdings for articles published more than twenty-five years ago, and then use the library catalog to locate the actual articles in bound print journals or on microform.

The greatest resource of all is the reference librarian, who can direct you to valuable sources and help with the search—a service not available from AOL or from the Internet as a whole. Never be afraid to ask for a librarian's help.

39a   Searching online for print and online sources

Keyword searches   Use keywords to search for any material stored electronically. Keyword searching is especially effective for finding material in journal and newspaper articles in databases such as *EBSCO, InfoTrac, LexisNexis,* and specialized subject-area databases because a computer can search not only titles but also abstracts (when available) or full articles. See 39e for more on searching databases.

Keywords are vital for your Web searches, too. Spend time thinking of the keywords that best describe what you are looking for. If a search yields thousands of hits, try requiring or prohibiting terms and making terms into phrases (see the Key Points box on pages 381–383). If a search yields few hits, try different keywords or combinations, or try another search engine or database. In addition, try out variant spellings for names of people and places: *Chaikovsky, Tchaikovsky, Tschaikovsky.*

Use the results to help tailor and refine your search. If your search produces only one useful source, look at the terms used in that one source and its subject headings and search again, perhaps using those terms with a different search engine or on a different database. Above all, be flexible. Each database or search engine indexes only a portion of what is available in the published literature or on the Web. Once you find a promising reference to a source that is not available online in full text, check whether your library owns the book or journal. If your search yields a source available only on microfilm or microfiche, you might need a librarian's help to learn how to use the reading machines and how to make copies.

URLs If you already know the Web address (the uniform resource locator or URL) of a useful site, type it exactly, paying attention to spaces (or, more often, lack of spaces), dots, symbols, and capital or lowercase letters. Just one small slip can prevent access. Whenever you can, copy and paste a URL from a Web source so that you do not make mistakes in typing. If you ever get a message saying "site not found," check your use of capitals and lowercase letters (and avoid inserting spaces as you type an address), and try again. You may find that the site is no longer available.

Search engines and directories If you do not know the exact Web site you want, you need to use search tools. Some search the whole Web for you; some search selected sites; some search only the first few pages of a document; still others search only a specific site, such as a university library system or a noncommercial organization; or they search other search engines (these are called *metasearch engines*). Some (Google, Yahoo!) offer subject directories to help you search by topic (see 3a). Make sure you try all types to find information on your topic. You will miss many useful sources if you do only a Google search.

A note of caution about using search engines: An article in the *New York Times* has pointed out that searches can perpetuate biases. Geoffrey Nunberg notes how a Google search of the terms *voting machine fraud* will find Web pages that mostly use those words to "support the view that voting machines make election fraud easier," while the search misses sites offering opposing views.

Your Web browser, probably Internet Explorer, Netscape, Firefox, or AOL, will give you access to search engines and other resources that do for you most of the work of rapidly searching Web sites and databases. Whichever browser you use, spending time searching (and playing) is the best way to become familiar with reliable search tools, the types of searches they do best, and the system they use for searching.

TECHTOOLKIT   Advice on Search Engines and Directories

For useful information and search tips, go to <http://www.searchenginewatch.com>.

Here are a few recommendations to get you started with searching the Web:

- Google <http://www.google.com> (the favorite of many academics) searches more than eight billion Web pages and other search engines. It organizes and ranks results by the number of links to a site. Google also offers a directory of sites grouped by topic and an image search. Google Book Search, a new feature, helps you find books addressing your search terms.

- Google Scholar at <http://scholar.google.com> offers searching limited to scholarly content on the Web, though the site's interpretations of what is scholarly may not always agree with your instructor's interpretation.

- INFOMINE <http://infomine.ucr.edu> provides scholarly resources in social sciences, humanities, and general reference, selected and annotated.

- Internet Public Library <http://www.ipl.org> is run by librarians. It includes a guide to subject collections and an "Ask a question" feature, which allows you to e-mail a question about a research project to librarians for evaluation and possible response within three days.

- Metasearch engines extend your search by searching the results of other search engines. Recommended are Dogpile (at <http://www.dogpile.com>), which searches Google, Yahoo! and others, and jux2 (at <http://www.jux2.com>), which searches two chosen search engines at one time and presents "best results."

- WWW Virtual Library <http://vlib.org> is a directory of sources in a large number of academic disciplines.

- Yahoo! <http://www.yahoo.com> is a subject index and directory of the Web. You can keep narrowing down your subjects, or you can use specific keywords. Such a tool is particularly useful when you are trying to find a topic. Yahoo! Picture Gallery finds images.

In addition, consider using subject-specific start pages for more efficient searches than those using general search engines. For government sources, for instance, try <http://www.firstgov.gov>.

KEY POINTS

Doing a Keyword Search

1. *Know the system used by the database or search engine.* Use the Search Tips or Help link to find out how to conduct a search. Systems vary. Some search for any or all of the words you type in, some need you to indicate whether the words make up a phrase (item 5), and some allow you to exclude words or search for alternatives (items 2, 6, and 8).

2. *Use Boolean terms to narrow or expand a search.* Some advanced searches operate on the Boolean principle, which means that you use the "operators" *AND, OR,* and *NOT* in combination with keywords to define what you want the search to include and exclude. Imagine that you want to find out if and how music can affect intelligence. Using only the term *music* would produce vast numbers of hits. Using *AND* narrows the search. The term *music AND intelligence* would find sources in the database that include both the word *music* and the word *intelligence* (the overlap in the circles below).

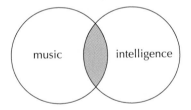

Parentheses can aid in searches, too. The search term *music AND (intelligence OR learning)* would expand the previous search. You would find sources in the database that include both the word *music* and either the word *intelligence* or the word *learning*.

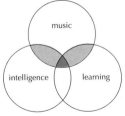

In Boolean searches, *AND* and *NOT* narrow the search: *chicken AND salmonella; tigers NOT Detroit.* The operator *OR*
(continued)

(continued)

expands the search: *angiogram OR angioplasty*. Not all databases and search engines use this system. Google, for instance, deliberately ignores the words *and* and *not* in a search, so there the search string *tigers NOT Detroit* actually produces sites dealing with the baseball team the Detroit Tigers. Google recommends using the minus sign (always after a space) to exclude a term, as in *tigers −Detroit*. Always check the instructions with each search engine or database.

3. ***Do not neglect to check Advanced Search features in a search engine or database.*** Google (<http://www.google.com/help/refinesearch.html>) provides a simple grid to indicate whether you want to find results with all the words, with the exact phrase, with at least one of the words, or without the words (an alternative to using the minus sign). Such a search lets you construct Boolean searches without even being aware that you are doing so. In addition, databases often provide ways to limit results, such as a box you can check to retrieve only "refereed" or "peer-reviewed" articles (scholarly articles, approved for publication by peer reviewers). See Source Shot 2 in 39e.

4. ***Use a wildcard character to truncate a term and expand the search.*** A wildcard allows you to use at the end of a phrase a character that indicates that more letters can be attached. Common wildcard characters are * for several characters and ? for one character. The truncated search term *addict** will produce references to *addict, addicts, addiction, addictive,* and so on. (Google does not provide this feature.)

5. ***Narrow a search by grouping words into phrases.*** You can use quotation marks (or in some cases parentheses) to surround search terms to group the words into a phrase, a useful technique for finding titles, names, and quotations. A half-remembered line from a poem by Wordsworth ("the difference to me") entered as a Google search without quotation marks does not produce a Wordsworth poem on the first page of hits. However, putting quotation marks around this phrase produces a hit to the full text of Wordsworth's Lucy poem right on the first page of results.

6. ***Learn how to require or prohibit a term to narrow a search.*** Many search engines allow you to use a symbol such as + (plus) before a term that must be included in the document

indexed; a – (minus) symbol prohibits a term: + "Civil War" – Gettysburg. Some search engines use these symbols in place of the *AND* and *NOT* of Boolean searching.

7. *Take advantage of the "proximity" search feature if available.* Some search engines and many databases let you indicate when you want your search terms to occur close to each other in the text, a useful feature when you can only remember part of a quotation. Check in the Help or Tips file to determine whether the engine you are using has this feature. Proximity is indicated in various ways in various search engines. *NEAR* or *ADJ* (adjacent) are common: "Virginia Woolf" *NEAR* "Bloomsbury group" would search for the two phrases near each other in the text.

8. *Be flexible.* If you don't get good results, try using synonyms— in Google, type a tilde (~) immediately before the search term, as in *~intelligence.* Or try a different search engine or database.

EXERCISE 39.1   Do a keyword search.
Go to Google at <http://www.google.com>, and do a keyword search to find reliable information on *one* aspect of *one* of the following topics. Discuss your results with classmates.

- nonallergenic dogs
- hamstring injuries
- the digital divide
- mononucleosis
- termites
- titanium

39b Basic reference works

The reference section of your college or local library is a good place to gather basic information. Reference books cannot be checked out, so they are in the library at all times. Also, more and more reference works are being made generally available online, so the accessibility of material from a library or home computer increases.

Reference works provide basic factual information and lead to other sources. However, use reference works only to get started with basic information; then quickly move beyond them. See 39c–39h for details on finding sources other than basic reference works. Check to see if your library subscribes to the huge online database for reference works *xreferplus.*

Encyclopedias   Encyclopedias can help you choose or focus a topic. They provide an overview of the issues involved in a complex topic. Some may also provide extensive bibliographies of other useful sources, so they can also help you develop your research and formulate a research proposal if you are asked to provide one.

General encyclopedias such as *Columbia Encyclopedia* and *Encyclopaedia Britannica* and subject-specific encyclopedias such as the *Internet Encyclopedia of Philosophy* or *Berkshire Encyclopedia of World History* can help you get started.

However, use encyclopedias only as a way to start your investigations; do not rely on them for most of your project. Instead, move on to more substantial sources.

Bibliographies (also known as *guides to the literature*)   You can find lists of books and articles on a subject in online bibliographic databases such as the following: *Books in Print, International Medieval Bibliography, MLA International Bibliography of Books and Articles on the Modern Languages and Literature, New Books on Women and Feminism,* and *Political Science Bibliographies.*

Biographies   Read accounts of people's lives in biographical works such as *Who's Who, Dictionary of American Biography, Biography Index: A Cumulative Index to Biographic Material in Books and Magazines, Contemporary Authors, Dictionary of Literary Biography, African American Biographies, Chicano Scholars and Writers, Lives of the Painters,* and *American Men and Women of Science.* See also *Lives, the Biography Resource* at <http://amillionlives.com>.

Directories   Directories provide lists of names and addresses of people, companies, and institutions. These are useful for setting up interviews and contacting people when you need information. Examples are *Jane's Space Directory* and *Communication Media in Higher Education: A Directory of Academic Programs and Faculty in Radio-Television-Film and Related Media.*

Dictionaries   For etymologies, definitions, synonyms, and spelling, consult *The American Heritage Dictionary of the English Language,* 4th edition; *Oxford English Dictionary* (multiple volumes—useful for detailed etymologies and usage discussions); *Facts on File* specialized dictionaries; and other specialized dictionaries such as *Dictionary of Literary Terms* and *Dictionary of the Social Sciences.*

Dictionaries of quotations   For a rich source of traditional quotations, go to *Bartlett's Familiar Quotations;* for more contemporary quotations, searchable by topic, go to *The Columbia World of Quotations* (both are available online at <http://www.bartleby.com>). Also, consult specialized dictionaries of quotations, such as volumes devoted to chess, law, religion, fishing, women, and Wall Street.

Collections of articles of topical interest and news summaries   *CQ* (*Congressional Quarterly*) weekly reports, *Facts on File* publications, and *CQ Almanac* are available in print and online by subscription. *Newsbank* provides periodical articles on microfiche, classified under topics such as "law" and "education," and *SIRS (Social Issues Resources Series)* appears in print and online.

Statistics and government documents   Among many useful online sources are *Statistical Abstract of the United States, Current Index to Statistics, Handbook of Labor Statistics, Occupational Outlook Handbook,* U.S. Census publications, *GPO Access, UN Demographic Yearbook, Population Index,* and *Digest of Education Statistics.*

Almanacs, atlases, and gazetteers   For population statistics and boundary changes, see *The World Almanac, Countries of the World,* or *Information Please.* For locations, descriptions, pronunciation of place names, climate, demography, languages, natural resources, and industry, consult a gazetteer such as *Columbia-Lippincott Gazetteer of the World* and the *CIA World Factbook* series.

General critical works   Read what scholars have to say about works of art and literature in *Contemporary Literary Criticism* and in *Oxford Companion* volumes (such as *Oxford Companion to Art* and *Oxford Companion to African American Literature*).

EXERCISE 39.2   Use reference works.
Use three different basic reference works to discover several new (for you) and interesting pieces of information about three of the following:

- Afghanistan
- Bloomsbury
- Clarence Darrow
- Islam
- Lyme disease
- Elvis Presley
- the praying mantis
- Algernon Swinburne

Discuss with classmates the works you used and the information you found.

39c Finding and evaluating books and articles

Types of search For library catalogs and periodical databases, decide whether to search by title, author, subject, or keyword. Exact wording and exact spelling are essential for all these searches.

Use keyword searching (39a) when searching for material that is electronically stored, whether in a library catalog, in a database, or on a Web page.

SUBJECT SEARCHES For the more focused subject searching, you need to know the specific subject headings the catalogers used to identify and classify material. Consult a reference source such as *Library of Congress Subject Headings*, or ask a librarian for help. For example, you won't find *cultural identity* or *social identity* in *Library of Congress Subject Headings*, but you can look up *culture* and find a list of thirty-two associated headings, such as "language and culture" and "personality and culture."

In addition, these subject headings show related terms, which can suggest ways to narrow or broaden a topic and can help you in other subject searches, particularly in electronic keyword searches. *Bilingualism*, for example, takes you to topics such as "air traffic control," "code-switching," and "language attrition." An entry in a library catalog will appear with the subject descriptors, so if you find one good source, use its subject classifications to search further. A search in a library online catalog using the keywords *bilingual, education,* and *politics* finds thirty-three records. One of these (on page 387) provides some subject terms to help with further searching: *education and state, educational change,* and *educational evaluation.* Similarly, a keyword search of an online database of full-text articles will produce articles with subject descriptors attached, as in Source Shot 8 (p. 456).

If your college library does not own a book or periodical you want, ask a librarian about an interlibrary loan. This option is helpful, of course, only if you begin your search early.

Finding books

ONLINE LIBRARY CATALOGS The Web gives you access to the online resources of many libraries (actual and virtual) and universities, which are good browsing sites. Some useful sites are *Library of Congress* <http://lcweb.loc.gov>, *LibWeb* <http://sunsite.berkeley.edu/Libweb>, *New York Public Library* <http://www.nypl.org/index.html>, and *Smithsonian Institution Libraries* <http://www.sil.si.edu>.

CALL NUMBER Most college libraries use the Library of Congress classification system, which arranges books according to subject area and often the initial of the author's last name and the date of publication. The call number tells you where a book is located in the library stacks (the area where books are shelved). Write this number down immediately if a book looks promising, along with the book's title and author(s) and publication information (40a). If a library has open stacks, you will be able to browse through books on a similar topic on the same shelf or on one nearby.

INFORMATION IN THE CATALOG The screens of electronic catalogs vary from one system to another, but most screens contain the name of the system you are using; the details of your search request and of the search, such as the number of records found; and detailed bibliographical information.

SOURCE SHOT 1: Library Catalog Screen for a Book

Record Display	Back

Choose format: **Full View | Brief View | MARC**

Record 1 out of 2   Needed for documentation   ◀ Previous Record   Next Record ▶

Call number	All items
Author	＞ Hacsi, Timothy A.
Title	＞ Children as pawns : the politics of educational reform / Timothy A. Hacsi.
Publisher	Cambridge, Mass. : Harvard University Press, 2002.
Description	ix, 261 p. ; 25 cm.
Notes	Includes bibliographical references (p. 217-252) and index.
Contents	Introduction -- What difference does Head Start make? -- Is bilingual education a good idea? -- Does class size matter? -- Is social promotion a problem? -- Does more money make schools better? -- Conclusion.
Subjects	＞ Education and state -- United States.
	＞ Educational change -- United States.
	＞ Educational evaluation -- United States.

Useful subject search terms

—Reprinted with permission of The City University of New York Libraries.

The screen shown here, which extends to links to the call number (LC89.H215202) and the locations of the holdings (locations where the book is housed), provides all the essential information you will need to document the source at the end of your paper: author, title, place of publication, publisher, and date of publication. In addition, it lets you know the number of pages in the book and shows that the book contains a bibliography and an index—useful research tools. The subject search terms shown can help structure further searches.

Once you find a book that seems to be related to your topic, you do not have to read the whole book to use it for your paper. Learn what you can from the catalog entry; then skim the table of contents, chapter headings, and bibliography. Your best time-saver here is the index. Turn to it immediately, and look up some key words for your topic. Read the section of the book in which references to your topic appear; take notes; annotate a photocopy of the relevant pages (40b). A book's bibliography and references are useful, too. The research the author has done can help you in your search. It is a good idea to make a copy of the title page and the page on which the copyright notice appears. If you find nothing remotely connected to your research question, do not cite the book as a resource, even though you looked at it.

BOOKS IN PRINT AND ALTERNATIVES If you want to find a book or to check on bibliographical details, use *Books in Print* (available in print and online). If your library does not subscribe to the online version, you can use the Amazon.com site at <http://www.amazon.com> or any other large commercial online bookseller to look up the details of a book—free.

Finding periodical articles   Find articles in periodicals (works issued periodically, such as scholarly journals, magazines, and newspapers) by using keywords in a periodical database. Use electronic databases for recent works, print indexes for earlier works—especially for works written before 1980. Check which databases your library subscribes to and the dates they cover. Some provide abstracts; some, such as *EBSCO Academic Search Premier* and *LexisNexis Academic Universe*, provide the full text of articles. (See also 39e for more on articles in databases.)

Search methods are similar to those in book searches. If the periodical index does not provide the full text or provide a link to it, you will need to find out first whether your library owns the periodical and then in which form it is available: in bound volumes or in film form, with pages shown in a strip (microfilm) or on a sheet (microfiche), which you will need to read with a special machine. The catalog for your library will tell you on the screen which issues are available in your library and in which format and location.

Evaluating books and articles

BOOKS   Check the date of publication, notes about the author, table of contents, and index. Skim the preface, introduction, chapter headings, and summaries to give yourself an idea of the information in the book and the book's theoretical basis and perspective. Do not waste time making detailed notes on a book that deals only tangentially with your topic or on an out-of-date book (unless your purpose is to discuss and critique its perspective or examine a topic historically). Ask a librarian or your instructor for help in evaluating the appropriateness of sources you discover. If your topic concerns a serious academic issue, readers will expect you to consult books and not limit your references to popular magazines, newspapers, and Internet sources.

ARTICLES   Take into account the type of periodical, any organization with which it is affiliated, and the intended audience. Differentiate among the following types of articles (listed in descending order of reliability, with the most reliable first):

- scholarly articles (see 39d)

- articles, often long, in periodicals for nonspecialist but serious, well-educated readers, such as *New York Review of Books*, *Atlantic Monthly*, *Economist*, *Scientific American*, and *Nation*

- shorter articles, with sources not identified, in popular magazines for a general audience, such as *Ebony*, *Time*, *Newsweek*, *Parents*, *Psychology Today*, and *Vogue,* or in newspapers

- articles with dubious sources, written for sensational tabloid magazines, such as *National Enquirer*, *Globe*, and *Star*

Use the following box to evaluate books and articles (including all sources originally published in print but accessed through an online database).

KEY POINTS

Questions to Evaluate Books and Articles

1. *What does the work cover?* It should be long enough and detailed enough to provide adequate information.

2. *How objective is the information?* The author, publisher, or periodical should not be affiliated with an organization that has an ax to grind—unless, of course, your topic entails reading critically and making comparisons with other points of view.

3. *How current are the views?* Check the date of publication. The work should be up-to-date if you need a current perspective.

4. *How reputable are the publisher and author?* The work should be published by a reputable publisher in a source that is academically reliable, not one devoted to gossip, advertising, propaganda, or sensationalism. Check *Books in Print* or *Literary Market Place* for details on publishers. The author should be an authority on the subject. Find out what else the author has written (in Google, in *Books in Print*, or at <http://www.amazon.com>) and what his or her qualifications are as an authority.

39d How to recognize a scholarly article

Learn to distinguish scholarly from nonscholarly articles. A scholarly article is not something you are likely to find in a magazine in a dentist's office. A scholarly journal is refereed—that is, other scholars read all the articles and approve them for publication.

Just looking at the cover of the journal, noting the length of the article and the length of each paragraph, and scanning the beginning and end of the article should help make the distinction between a scholarly and a nonscholarly periodical obvious.

KEY POINTS

What a Scholarly Article Does

A scholarly article

1. refers to the work of other scholars (look for in-text citations and a bibliographical list of works cited, footnotes, or endnotes)

2. names the author and usually describes the author's credentials

3. includes notes, references, or a bibliography, and may include an abstract

4. deals with a serious issue in depth

5. uses academic or technical language for informed readers

6. appears in journals that do not include colorful advertisements or eye-catching pictures (a picture of two stunning models is an indication that you are not looking at a scholarly article)

When you read scholarly articles, scan any section headings, read the abstract and any section headed "Summary" or "Conclusions," and skim for the author's main idea to find out whether the article addresses your topic. If you are working on a topic related to current events, you probably will need to consult newspapers, magazines, and online sources as well as or in place of scholarly journals. See 44c, item 22, for the cover of a scholarly journal.

Distinguishing scholarly articles in general databases Some databases are specialized and will yield only research articles (or only abstracts) published in scholarly journals. Other databases, such as those hosted by *EBSCO* and *InfoTrac,* are more general, including popular magazines as well as serious and scholarly periodicals. In several databases, you can search for scholarly articles by opting to find "peer reviewed" articles; these are articles that have been approved by an editorial board. *EBSCO* databases provide this feature.

TECHTOOLKIT   Databases of Journal Information

- Genamics JournalSeek at <http://journalseek.net> provides links to help identify journals as scholarly or not.
- The Cornell University Web site *Distinguishing Scholarly Journals from Other Periodicals* at <http://www.library.cornell.edu/olinuris/ref/research/skill20.html> provides definitions and examples of four categories of periodical literature: scholarly, substantive news and general interest, popular, and sensational.   ■

EXERCISE 39.3   Find articles of various types.

In groups of two or three students, go to your college library and to the Current Periodicals section. On the shelves find one example of each of the following:

- an article in a scholarly journal
- an article in a serious but nonspecialist periodical
- an article in a popular magazine, written for a general audience

For each one, write down the name of the author(s) of the article, the title of the article, and other publication data, such as volume number, date, and page numbers of the articles. In addition, make a list of the specific features that helped you distinguish one type of publication from another.

39e   Finding sources in online databases and on Web sites

Online databases   Online databases of journal articles are a wonderful resource for researchers. Start with these. They are comprehensive and easy to use. They also provide sources that have been previously published and referred to by experts.

Online databases and citation indexes owned or leased by libraries can be accessed in the library itself. Many libraries also make the databases they subscribe to available on the Internet through their home pages. For example, many libraries provide online access to the following:

- databases of abstracts in specific subject areas, such as *ERIC* (for education), *PAIS* (for public affairs), *PsycINFO* (for psychology), and *Sociological Abstracts* (for sociology)
- databases of full texts of articles published in the last twenty or thirty years, such as *InfoTrac: Expanded Academic ASAP, LexisNexis Academic Universe,* and *EBSCO Academic Search Premier*

- databases of abstracts (with some full texts) of general, non-specialized magazine articles, such as the Wilson *Readers' Guide to Periodical Literature*

- databases devoted to statistics, such as the Bureau of Labor statistics data at <http://www.bls.gov/data/home.htm> and Census Bureau figures at <http://www.census.gov>, or to images such as works of art at <http://www.getty.edu>

- the *JSTOR* database, providing access to less-recent sources

Access to databases in university library Web sites, from both library and home computers, is often limited to enrolled students, who need to verify their status when they log on. Check with your college library to learn which databases it subscribes to. Articles that you find in a database have for the most part been previously published in print, so evaluate them as print sources for currency, objectivity, and reputation (see 39c).

Before you begin a search, read the instructions on the database to learn how to perform a simple search and an advanced search. Knowing what you are doing can save you a great deal of frustration! Generally, begin a search by using keywords or subject terms, if you know them. Use what the database provides to limit a search as to type of source, date, full-text articles or not, and scholarly, peer-reviewed articles. Source Shot 2 shows a typical search screen.

SOURCE SHOT 2: Search Screen for EBSCO Academic Search Premier Database

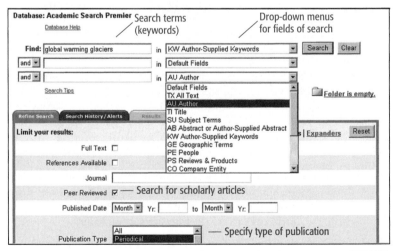

—Reprinted with permission of EBSCO.

Online magazines   Online magazines are proliferating. Here are some examples:

- *Slate* <http://www.slate.com>
- *Salon* <http://www.salon.com>
- *The Atlantic Online* <http://www.theatlantic.com>

Online scholarly journals   Some scholarly journals have no print versions. These are some examples:

- *Early Modern Literary Studies* <http://purl.oclc.org/emls/emlshome.html>
- *Postmodern Culture* <http://jefferson.village.virginia.edu/pmc>
- *Sociological Research Online* <http://www.socresonline.org.uk>

Some online journals are available free; some allow you to view only the current issue at no cost. Many, however, require a subscription through your library computer network or a personal subscription.

 TECHTOOLKIT   Directory of Online Magazines and Journals

Several directories exist. A good one is at <http://library.albany.edu/reference/epub.html>. And see the University of Houston site at <http://info.lib.uh.edu/wj/webjour.html> for a directory of free online journals. ∎

Online literary texts   Literary texts that are out of copyright and in the public domain are increasingly available online for downloading. The following are useful sites to consult, although the versions of texts you see may not always be authoritative: *Project Bartleby* <http://www.bartleby.com>, *Project Gutenberg* <http://www.promo.net/pg/index.html>, *University of Virginia's Electronic Text Center* <http://etext.lib.virginia.edu>.

eBooks   Many books are becoming available as eBooks, either to be read online at a computer or to be downloaded and read in an eBook reader. NetLibrary.com is one of the companies offering eBooks. If your library subscribes to its database, check its offerings when you are looking for a book.

Online news sites   The Web sites of major newspapers, magazines, and television networks provide up-to-date news information; some offer archived information but often only to subscribers. See, for example, *New York Times on the Web* <http://www.nytimes.com> and *CNN Interactive* <http://www.cnn.com>.

Nonprofit research sites Many nonprofit sites offer valuable and objective information. For example, see *Public Agenda Online* <http://www.publicagenda.org>, *American Film Institute* <http://www.afi.com>, and *San Francisco Bay Bird Observatory* <http://www.sfbbo.org>.

Web pages and hypertext links Many universities and research institutes provide information through their own Web home pages, with hypertext links that take you with one click to many other sources. Try, for example, <http://www.refdesk.com> for more than twenty thousand links to reference works and informational sites. Individual Web pages can provide useful information, too, but need careful evaluation since anyone can publish anything on the Web (39f).

E-mail discussions With e-mail, you have access to many discussion groups. Messages go out to a list of people interested in specific topics. Without charge, you can join a list devoted to a topic of interest (51b). However, most of the lists are not refereed or monitored, so you have to evaluate carefully any information you find.

For academic research, personal blogs, Usenet newsgroups, and chat rooms provide little that is substantive. Evaluating the reliability of a contributor's comments can be difficult.

39f Evaluating Web sources: Developing junk antennae

What makes the Internet so fascinating is that it is wide open, free, and democratic. Individuals on a rant, as well as serious government or research agencies, can establish a site. Anyone can "publish" anything, and thousands or millions can read it. For scholars looking for information and well-presented, informed opinion, the Internet can pose a challenge.

If you find an article in a subscription database (*InfoTrac* or *LexisNexis*, for example), you will know that the article has been published in print, so you can use the criteria for print works (39c) to evaluate it. If the article has been published in a reputable periodical or in an online journal sponsored by a professional organization or a university, you can assume that it is a valid source for a research paper.

For works devised specifically for the Internet, use the strategies in the Key Points box to separate the information from the junk.

> ## KEY POINTS
> ### Developing Your Junk Antennae

1. *Scrutinize the domain name of the URL.* Reliable informational Web pages can be found on .gov and .edu addresses, institutionally sponsored (but see item 2). With .com ("dot com") or .org sources, always assess whether the source is informational or serves another purpose.

2. *Assess the originator of an .edu source.* Check that the institution or a branch of it is sponsoring the site. A tilde (~) followed by a name in the URL indicates an individual posting from an academic source. Try to ascertain whether the individual is a faculty member or a student. Increasingly, though, individuals are setting up Web sites under their own domain name.

3. *Check the home page.* Always take the link from a Web site to its home page, if you are not already there. The home page often provides more information about the author, the sponsor, the purpose, and the date of posting.

4. *Discover what you can about the author.* Look for a list of credentials, a home page, a résumé, or Web publications. In Google or Google Scholar, use the author's name as a search term to see what the author has published on the Internet or who has cited the author.

5. *Investigate the purposes of a Web page author or sponsor.* Objectivity and rationality are not necessarily features of all Web pages. You may come across propaganda, hate sites, individuals purporting to have psychic powers, religious enthusiasts, and extreme political groups. The sponsor of a site may want to persuade, convert, or sell. Go to the home page and to linked sites, and in addition, note any postal or e-mail address or phone number you can use to get more information about the page and the sponsor. Even if the message is not pointedly biased and extreme, be aware that most authors write from some sense of conviction or purpose. (Note, though, that a Web site can be oriented toward a specific view without necessarily being irresponsible.)

6. *Evaluate the quality of the writing.* A Web page filled with spelling and grammatical errors should not inspire confidence. If the language has not been checked, the ideas probably haven't been given much time and thought, either. Don't use such a site as a source. Exceptions are discussion lists and

(continued)

(continued)

Usenet postings. They are written and posted quickly, so even if they contain errors, they can also contain useful ideas to stimulate thinking on your topic.

7. *Follow the links.* See whether the links in a site take you to authoritative sources. If the links no longer work (you'll get a 404 message: "Site Not Found"), the home page with the links has not been updated in a while—not a good sign.

8. *Check for dates, updates, ways to respond, and ease of navigation.* A recent date of posting or recent updating; information about the author; ways to reach the author by e-mail, regular mail, or phone; a clearly organized site; easy navigation; and up-to-date links to responsible sites are all indications that the site is well managed and current.

9. *Corroborate information.* Try to find the same information on another reliable site. Also look for contradictory information elsewhere.

 TechToolkit   Web Sites on Evaluating Sources

Useful information on evaluating sources is available at a Widener University (Chester, PA) site at <http://www2.widener.edu/Wolfgram-Memorial-Library/webevaluation/webeval.htm>. An interactive tutorial on evaluating Internet sources is at <http://library.albany.edu/usered/wwwdex/index.html> <http://www.widener.edu/Tools–Resources/Libraries/Wolfgram-Memorial-Library/Evaluate_Web-Pages/659. ■

 Exercise 39.4   Find and evaluate Web sources on a topic.
Use a search engine to do a Web search for information on the topic of *body building* or *dieting*. Find one Web page that offers useful, serious information and another that you would reject as a source of balanced and objective information. Make a copy of each page, bring the copies to class, and explain your evaluation to your classmates.

39g Anatomy of a Web site

Using the table   Use the following table to find on a Web site the information that will help you evaluate its reliability. In addition, if you record the information for every accessed site that you might refer to or quote from in your paper, you will then be able to

How to Read a Web Site

What to Look For and Record; Where and How to Find It	Additional Things You May Need to Do

1. Name of author →
Look at the top or bottom of the page. For Web documents with no author named, look for an organization, government agency, or business that serves as the author.

- Follow any links on the document page to a résumé, publications, purpose statement, or home page. Try to establish the purpose of the site.
- Do a Google search for details about the author, whether an individual, institution, organization, business, or government agency.
- Do not confuse the Web site manager or the person maintaining the site with the author of the information.
- If you cannot find an author, look on the "Home" or "About" page, or go to #2, "Title."

2. Title of document →
Find it at the top of the page. Note, though, that some sites will contain documents with titles, and some will not.

- For online sources previously in print form, record any print publication details provided.
- Record page numbers only for PDF documents, in which page numbers appear on the screen.
- Record the name of the document section in which relevant information appears (e.g., Introduction).
- Record paragraph numbers *only* when they are part of the document and appear on the screen.

3. Name of site →
If it is not visible at the top or bottom of the page, go to "Home" or "About." Or delete the URL progressively back to each single slash, and click to see which part of the site you access.

Also record what you can of the following, if available:

- name of the organization in charge of the content of the site (owner or sponsor)—usually indicated in the root domain of the URL (before the first single slash)
- for an online journal, the volume and issue numbers
- the date when material was posted online or updated (often not available)

4. Your date of access →
Because Web sites come and go and change, always record the exact date on which you access the site.

Save any page that provides you with crucial information or is likely to update or change its content, such as blogs or files ending with *.php*.

5. URL →
Copy and paste this from your browser into your working bibliography. Copying by hand may introduce errors.

If a page is divided into sections (called "frames"), and you want to refer to one frame only, right-click in the frame, and select "Save (or Add) as Favorite"; then retrieve the material in the frame with its own URL.

construct your citation without retracing your steps. (See 40a for the information to record.) Go to *The Open Handbook* at <http://college.hmco.com/keys.html>, and click on Forms and Checklists for templates to download to help you record source information. Although different styles of documentation, such as MLA and APA, ask for different chunks of information in different configurations, the five items listed in the table are common to most of them. Read this table with Source Shot 3, an annotated screenshot of a site with an explicitly stated agenda. It is "dedicated to restoring democratic authority over corporations, reviving grassroots democracy, and revoking the power of money and corporations to control government and civic society."

SOURCE SHOT 3 Web Page

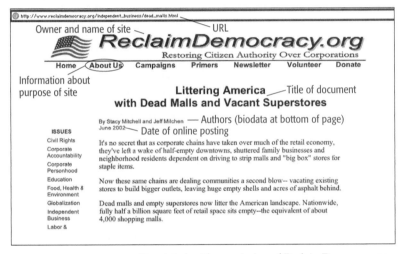

—Reprinted with permission of ReclaimDemocracy.org.

Recognizing the difficulties Note that on many sites, you may have difficulty finding a date of posting, a document title as well as a Web site name, or an exact identification of the author of the material, whether an individual or an organization. Just record whatever you can find on a thorough search of the site. Try using the root domain of the URL—the material just before the dot preceding the first single slash (as in <http://www.library.ucla.edu/>)—to identify the owner, also referred to as the *publisher* or *sponsor*, of the site, who is responsible for its content. If the "Home" and "About" links provide no useful information, consider whether you should use a source if you are unsure about the identity of the author, the author's credentials, or the owner and purpose of the site.

The URL For more on recording URLs and using them in your paper and citations, see 43c.

Always save all Web pages that are crucial to your research. Go to *The Open Handbook* at <http://college.hmco.com/keys.html>, and click on Research and Documentation for an exercise on how to evaluate Web sites.

39h Research sources in 27 subject areas

Twenty-one college librarians from eighteen colleges in thirteen states helped with compiling a list of useful starting points for research across the curriculum in twenty-seven subject areas—from "Art and Architecture" to "Women's Studies." That list has recently been updated and revised by Professor Trudi Jacobson, Coordinator of User Education Programs at the University Libraries of the University at Albany, State University of New York. Go to *The Open Handbook* at <http://college.hmco.com/keys.html>, and click on Research and Documentation for the hyperlinked list, which is regularly updated.

40 Using Sources Responsibly (More Ways to Avoid Plagiarism)

When you use sources responsibly, you not only avoid the slightest hint of plagiarism (chapter 37), but you also bring clarity to your writing. Until you do the research project, you probably are used to wrestling with your own ideas and words and taming them into order on the page. With research, however, introducing others' ideas and words into your writing brings more to wrestle with and much more to tame. Research demands more time and can benefit from the specific strategies detailed in this chapter. With careful citation and smooth integration of source material in your writing, you save time, you gain clarity, and your readers are freed to enjoy the fruits of your labor.

40a Setting up a working bibliography and annotated bibliography

From the first steps of your research, keep accurate records of each source in a *working bibliography*. Record enough information so that you will be able to make up a list of references in whichever style of documentation you choose, though not all the points of information you record will be necessary for every style of documentation.

It may be helpful to think of sorting your sources into four categories: print books, print articles, Web sources, and online database sources. Each category has specific information you will want to collect and record right away. See the table on page 401. Go to *The Open Handbook* at <http://college.hmco.com/keys.html>, and click on Research and Documentation for templates of each source category that you can download and fill in with the information you need.

KEY POINTS

Helpful Hints for Recording Source Information

Print book   Photocopy the title page and the copyright page, where much of the information is available.

Print article   Photocopy the table of contents of the periodical or anthology.

Web source   Save, e-mail yourself a copy, or print out the Web source. Set your computer so that the URL appears on the printout along with the date of access. Use the Copy and Paste functions to copy the URL accurately into your own document.

Online database source   Save, e-mail yourself a copy, or print out the online database source.

Keep your list of sources in a form that you can work with to organize them alphabetically, add and reject sources, and add summaries and notes. Note cards and computer files have the advantage over sheets of paper or a research journal. They don't tie you to page order.

Here is a sample index card for an article accessed in an online subscription database.

Laird, Ellen. "Internet Plagiarism: We All
   Pay the Price." <u>Chronicle of Higher</u>
   <u>Education</u> 13 July 2001 : 5.   <u>Academic</u>
   <u>Universe: News.</u> Lexis Nexis. City U of New York Lib.
   5 May 2003 < http : // web.lexis - nexis.com>.

Source Essentials: What to Record

	Print Book	Print Article	Web Source	Online Database Source
Author(s), editor(s), translator(s) OR Name of company or government agency	✓	✓	✓ (if available on site)	✓
Title and subtitle	✓	✓	✓	✓
Print publication information	✓	✓	✓ (if available on site)	✓
Volume/edition/issue	✓	✓		✓
Call number	✓	✓		
Page numbers of document		✓	✓ (Only for PDF documents) Include number of paragraphs only if numbers appear on screen.	✓ Only for PDF documents. Otherwise include start page if given.
Name of Web site			✓	✓ Name of database and service
Essential information to include	Place: Publisher, date	**Scholarly articles:** Include volume number, issue number, date of publication, inclusive page numbers. **Article in a book:** Include title, editor, place, publisher, year of publication, inclusive page numbers of the article.	**Web site:** Include name of sponsor, date of online publication or update, URL, and date of access. **Article in online journal:** Include volume number. Always include URL and your date of access. **E-mail message or discussion list posting:** Include name of sender, subject line, date of posting, name of list, and your date of access to the list.	**Articles in a database:** Include volume, issue number, date of print publication, and name and location of library. Also include URL of home page of database or persistent URL of article and your date of access.

EXERCISE 40.1 Record bibliographical information.

Select one of the following topics. Find three useful sources (not encyclopedia entries), and prepare a bibliographical record for each source, with some notes on the source that will help you write an annotated bibliography.

- Jean-Michel Basquiat, painter
- Rem Koolhaas, architect
- Rita Dove, poet
- Eleanor Roosevelt, First Lady
- Steven Spielberg, film director

If you need to prepare an *annotated bibliography,* one that summarizes the contents of each source, write a brief summary on the back of the bibliography card or in a computer file.

Here is an entry from Diana Fatakhova's annotated bibliography that accompanied her proposal (see 38e). Notice how Fatakhova's annotations focus on main points and include how the source will help her paper and what type of source it is. She has also evaluated her source here.

Cohan, John Alan. "Psychiatric Ethics and Emerging Issues of Psychopharmacology in the Treatment of Depression." Journal of Contemporary Health Law and Policy, 20 (Winter 2003): Academic Universe: Medical Journals. LexisNexis. City U of New York Lib. 31 Oct. 2004 <http://lexisnexis.com>.

> This lengthy article covers much ground concerning different tests taken to ascertain the risks of antidepressants. It discusses whether or not antidepressants actually provide the cure they are supposedly meant for or if they merely act as placebos. The author poses the question: Is depression due to biology, thus leading to whether it could be cured through drugs? He lists risks associated with these antidepressants, some admitted by drug manufacturers, some by scientific journals, some listed as separate mental syndromes in the DSM-IV, and still others caused by withdrawal. This article will help me identify the risks of taking antidepressants and ascertain what other treatments are possible. This is a reliable source that comes from an academic journal and provides its readers with a number of references.

TechToolkit Annotated Bibliographies

For more information and examples of annotated bibliographies, go to <http://owl.english.purdue.edu/handouts/general/gl_annotatedbibEX.html>. ■

Choose a textbook assigned for one of your courses, and write an annotated bibliography entry, with bibliographical details in MLA style (see Part 7 for more on MLA style) and a brief summary of the work.

40b Keeping track of sources, annotating, and taking notes

The first step toward avoiding plagiarism is keeping track of what your sources are and which ideas come from your sources and which from you. You will find that one of the frustrating moments for you as a researcher occurs when you find some notes about an interesting point you read, but you cannot remember where you found the passage or who wrote it or whether your notes represent an author's exact words. You can spend hours in tedious retracing of your steps. Avoid this frustration by keeping track as you go along. However rushed you are or however little time you have, this saving and recording of source material is essential. See 40a for details on exactly what type of information to record about each source.

Use the Bookmarks or Favorites feature.   Many browsers have a Bookmarks or Favorites feature that allows you to compile and save a list of useful sites you have visited. You can then easily revisit these sites by simply clicking on the bookmark. Bookmarks can be deleted later when you no longer need them. If you work on a networked computer in a lab where you cannot save your work on the hard drive, export your bookmarks to your own computer or try the free bookmark services on the Internet at <http://www.fileitfree.com> or <http://www.mybookmarks.com>.

Record URL and date of access.   Note that bookmarking will not always last with a long URL, such as URLs of online subscription services. To be safe, also use the Copy and Paste features to copy the URL on your hard drive or diskette, along with the date on which you access the source. As a last resort, copy the URL by hand, but take care to get it exactly right: every letter, symbol, and punctuation mark is important.

Highlight, copy, and paste.   As you read material on the Web, you can highlight a passage you find, copy it, and then paste it into your own file. Make sure that you indicate clearly in your new document that you have included a direct quotation: use quotation marks or a bigger font along with an author/page citation. Save as much information as you can about the original document in your working bibliography.

Make photocopies of sources. Photocopying print articles and printing or downloading online articles allow you to devote research time to locating relevant sources and taking notes from reference works and books; you can take the copies of articles with you and use them when you are unable to be in the library. A quick way to make a copy of an Internet source or material in an online database is to e-mail it to yourself. As soon as you have time, though, evaluate the usefulness of your copies by highlighting and commenting on relevant sections or by taking notes.

Annotate and take notes. Printing and saving from online sources make a source text available for you to annotate. You can interact with the author's ideas, asking questions, writing comments, and jotting down your own ideas. Here is a passage from an article by Ellen Laird on plagiarism (see the bibliography card on p. 400). As Laird, a college professor, discusses the case of Chip, a student who has plagiarized, she is considering her own role and her student's explanation. The passage shows student Juana Mere's annotations as she gave the article a critical reading.

But what if her instructions weren't as clear as she thought?
To save face with myself, I must assume that Chip understood that downloading an essay and submitting it as his own was an

Look up egregious act. Why, then, did he do it? *Can she ever really know?*

But it's   Chip explained he had been "mentally perturbed" the weekend *Sounds*
specula- before the paper was due and that the essay he had written failed *like a*
tion on to meet his high standards. But I <u>sensed</u> that Chip felt he had made *very*
her part a choice akin to having a pizza delivered. He had procrastinated *general*
     on an assignment due the next day, had no time left in which to *excuse*
Is this prepare his work from scratch, and had to get on to those <u>pressing</u>
conde- <u>matters that shape the world of an 18-year-old.</u> He dialed his
scending? Internet service provider, ordered takeout, and had it delivered.
Nice analogy Good quotation

Annotating is useful for comments, observations, and questions. You also will need to make notes when you do not have a copy that you can write on or when you want to summarize, paraphrase, and make detailed connections to other ideas and other sources. Write notes on the computer, on legal pads, in notebooks, or on index cards—whatever works best for you (see 40e for sample notes). Index cards—each card with a heading and only one note—offer the advantage of flexibility: you can shuffle and reorder them to fit the organization of your paper. In your notes, always include the author's name, a short version of the title of the work, and any relevant page number(s) whenever you summarize, paraphrase, or quote. Include full bibliographical information in your working bibliography (40a). Then when you start to write your paper, you will have at your fingertips all the information necessary for a citation.

40c What to cite and document and in what style

When you do refer to a source in your work, carefully cite and document it. Systematically provide information about the author, title, publication data, page numbers, Internet address, dates—whatever is available (see 40a for the information you need to collect). You provide such documentation so that readers can locate your sources and turn to them for further information. (Parts 7 and 8 contain guides to specific systems of documentation.) You also document sources so there will be no question about which words and ideas are yours and which belong to other people.

KEY POINTS

What to Cite

1. Cite all facts, statistics, and pieces of information. However, citation is not necessary for facts regarded as common knowledge, such as the dates of the Civil War; facts available in many sources, such as authors' birth and death dates and chronological events; or allusions to folktales that have been handed down through the ages. When you are in doubt about whether a fact is common knowledge, cite your source.

2. Cite exact words from your source, enclosed in quotation marks.

3. Cite somebody else's ideas and opinions, even if you restate them in your own words in a summary or paraphrase.

4. Cite each sentence in a long paraphrase (if it is not clear that all the sentences paraphrase the same original source).

Documenting to fit your discipline Documentation is an integral part of the writing process. Conventions vary from discipline to discipline, but the various styles of documentation are not entirely arbitrary. These styles reflect what each discipline values and what readers need to know.

In the humanities, for instance, many research findings offer interpretation and speculation, so they may be relevant for years, decades, or centuries. Publication dates in the MLA (Modern Language Association) style, therefore, occur only in the works-cited list and do not make an appearance in the in-text citation. Such a practice also serves to minimalize interruptions to the text.

In the sciences and social sciences, however, in APA style, the dates of the works are put at the forefront because timeliness of research is an issue in the fields.

See Parts 7 and 8 for more details on MLA and APA documentation styles.

40d Introducing and integrating source material

When you provide a summary, paraphrase, or quotation to support one of the points in your paper, set up the context. Don't drop in the material as if it came from nowhere. Think about how to introduce and integrate the material into the structure of your paper.

If you quote a complete sentence, or if you paraphrase or summarize a section of another work, prepare readers for your summary, paraphrase, or quotation by mentioning the author's name in an introductory phrase. In your first reference to the work, give the author's full name. To further orient readers, you can also provide the title of the work or a brief statement of the author's expertise or credentials and thesis. Here are some useful ways to introduce source material:

X has pointed out that	According to X,
X has made it clear that	As X insists,
X explains that	In 2006, X, the vice president
X suggests that	of the corporation, declared

The introductory verbs *say* and *write* are clear and direct. For occasional variety, though, use verbs that offer shades of meaning, such as *acknowledge, agree, argue, ask, assert, believe, claim, comment, contend, declare, deny, emphasize, insist, note, observe, point out, propose, speculate.*

40e Summarizing and paraphrasing

Summary Summaries are useful for giving readers basic information about the work you are discussing. To summarize a source or a passage in a source, select only the main points as the author presents them, without your own commentary or interpretation. Be brief, and use your own words at all times. To ensure that you use your own words, do not have the original source in front of you as you write. Read, understand, and then put the passage away before writing your summary. If you find that you must include some particularly apt words from the original source, put them in quotation marks.

Use summaries in your research paper to let readers know the gist of the most important sources you find. When you include a summary in a paper, introduce the author or the work to indicate where your summary begins. At the end of the summary, give the page numbers you are summarizing. Do not include page numbers if you are summarizing the complete work or summarizing an online source; instead, indicate where your summary ends and your own ideas return (see 40f). When you write your paper, provide full documentation of the source in the list of works cited at the end.

After reading the article by Laird on plagiarism, Mere decided to write a research paper on Internet plagiarism. She wrote this 65-word summary of an article of 1,635 words in a computer file headed "Laird on college plagiarism." (She could also have used an index card.)

Laird   Summary

"Internet plagiarism"

College professor Ellen Laird explores the possible reasons why a student might have plagiarized a whole essay. She concludes that Chip, otherwise a good student, knew what he was doing, but taking material from the Internet while at home might not have seemed unethical. Laird connects his behavior to our contemporary culture and laments that teaching will have to change to counteract opportunities for plagiarism.

Paraphrase When you need more details than a summary provides, paraphrasing offers a tool. Use paraphrase more often than you use quotation. A paraphrase uses your words and your interpretations of and comments on the ideas you find in your sources. It is commonly accepted that if you cannot paraphrase information, then you probably do not understand it. So paraphrase serves the purpose of showing that you have absorbed your source material.

A paraphrase is similar in length to the original material— maybe somewhat longer. In a paraphrase, present the author's argument and logic, but be very careful not to use the author's exact words or sentence structure.

KEY POINTS

How to Paraphrase

1. Keep the source out of sight as you write a paraphrase so that you will not be tempted to copy the sentence patterns or phrases of the original.

2. Do not substitute synonyms for some or most of the words in an author's passage.

3. Use your own sentence structure as well as your own words. Your writing will still be regarded as plagiarized if it resembles the original in sentence structure as well as in wording.

4. Do not comment or interpret: just tell readers the ideas that the author of your source presents.

5. Check your text against the original source to avoid inadvertent plagiarism.

6. Cite the author (and page number if a print source) as the source of the ideas, introduce and integrate the paraphrase, and provide full documentation. If the source does not name an author, cite the title.

When Mere was making notes for her paper on Internet plagiarism, she decided to paraphrase one of the key paragraphs from Laird's article, one that she had previously annotated (40b, p. 404).

ORIGINAL SOURCE

Chip explained that he had been "mentally perturbed" the weekend before the paper was due and that the essay he had written failed to meet his high standards. But I sensed that Chip felt that he had made a choice akin to having a pizza delivered. He had procrastinated on an assignment due the next day, had no time left in which to prepare his work from scratch, and had to get on to those pressing matters that shape the world of an 18-year-old. He dialed his Internet service provider, ordered takeout, and had it delivered.

—Ellen Laird, "Internet Plagiarism: We All Pay the Price"

You can use common words and expressions such as "made a choice" or "due the next day." But if you use more unusual expressions from the source ("a choice akin to having pizza delivered," "pressing matters," "dialed his Internet service provider"), you need to enclose them in quotation marks. In Mere's first attempt at paraphrase, she does not quote, but her words and structure resemble the original too closely.

PARAPHRASE TOO SIMILAR TO THE ORIGINAL

Laird   Paraphrase, p. 5, ninth paragraph

Laird knew that Chip was mentally perturbed before he wrote his paper and his high standards prevented him from writing his own essay. But she felt that what he did was like having a pizza takeout. He had procrastinated so long that he could not write an essay from scratch and wanted to enjoy his life. So he ordered a takeout essay from his ISP (5).

Mere gives the name of the author and the page number of the source material (given in the online version) using the MLA style of documentation. Documentation, however, is not a guarantee against plagiarism. Mere's wording and sentence structure follow the original too closely. When classmates and her instructor pointed this out, she revised the paraphrase by keeping the ideas of the original, using different wording and sentence structure, and quoting what she regarded as a unique phrase.

REVISED PARAPHRASE

Laird   Paraphrase, p. 5, ninth paragraph

Laird's student Chip might have felt psychologically stressed
and that might have affected his attitude to the paper he
wrote, forcing him to reject it as not good enough to hand in
for a grade. Laird, however, sees his transgression not so much
as one of high moral principles as of expediency. He chose the
easiest way out. He had left the assignment until the last
minute. He had no time to do the work. He wanted to go out
and have fun. So what did he do? He went on the Web, found
an essay, and "ordered takeout" (5).

EXERCISE 40.3   Paraphrase.
When Michelle Guerra was writing a paper on the English-only
controversy (whether languages other than English should be
banned in schools and government offices and publications) and
looking for the history of the issue, she came across the following
source.

ORIGINAL SOURCE

If any language group, Spanish or other, chooses to maintain its
language, there is precious little that we can do about it, legally
or otherwise, and still maintain that we are a free country. We
cannot legislate the language of the home, the street, the bar, the
club, unless we are willing to set up a cadre of language police
who will ticket and arrest us if we speak something other than
English.

—James C. Stalker, "Official English or English Only,"
English Journal 77 (Mar. 1988): 21

A 1. In the following paraphrase, underline the words and structures
that resemble the original too closely. (**A** = See Answer Key.)

2. Revise the paragraph so that the original source is paraphrased appropriately.

Paraphrase of Stalker, p. 21

As Stalker points out, if any group of languages, Greek or other, decides to keep its language, there is not much any of us can do, with laws or not, and still claim to be a free country. We cannot pass legislation about the language we speak at home, on the street, or in restaurants, unless we also want to have a group of special police who will take us off to jail if they hear us not speaking English (21).

40f Indicating the boundaries of a citation

Naming an author or title in your text tells readers that you are citing ideas from a source, and citing a page number at the end of a summary or paraphrase lets them know where your citation ends. However, for one-page print articles and for Internet sources, a page citation is not necessary, so indicating where your comments about a source end is harder to do. You always need to indicate clearly where your summary or paraphrase ends and where your own comments take over. Convey the shift to readers by commenting on the source in a way that clearly announces a statement of your own views. Use expressions such as *it follows that, X's explanation shows that, as a result, evidently, obviously,* or *clearly* to signal the shift.

UNCLEAR CITATION BOUNDARY

According to a Sony Web site, <u>Mozart Makes You Smarter</u>, the company has decided to release a cassette on the strength of research indicating that listening to Mozart improves IQ. The products show the ingenuity of commercial enterprise while taking the researchers' conclusions in new directions.

[Does only the first sentence refer to material on the Web page, or do both sentences?]

REVISED CITATION, WITH SOURCE BOUNDARY INDICATED

According to a Sony Web site, <u>Mozart Makes You Smarter</u>, the company has decided to release a cassette on the strength of research indicating that listening to Mozart improves IQ. Clearly, Sony's plan demonstrates the ingenuity of commercial enterprise, but it cannot reflect what the researchers intended when they published their conclusions.

Another way to indicate the end of your citation is to include the author's or authors' name(s) at the end of the citation instead of (or even in addition to) introducing the citation with the name.

UNCLEAR CITATION BOUNDARY

For people who hate shopping, Web shopping may be the perfect solution. Jerome and Taylor's exploration of "holiday hell" reminds us that we get more choice from online vendors than we do when we browse at our local mall because the online sellers, unlike mall owners, do not have to rent space to display their goods. In addition, one can buy almost anything online, from CDs, cell phones, and books to cars and real estate.

REVISED CITATION, WITH SOURCE BOUNDARY INDICATED

For people who hate shopping, Web shopping may be the perfect solution. An article exploring the "holiday hell" of shopping reminds us that we get more choice from online vendors than we do when we browse at our local mall because the online sellers, unlike mall owners, do not have to rent space to display their goods (Jerome and Taylor). In addition, one can buy almost anything online, from CDs, cell phones, and books to cars and real estate.

EXERCISE 40.4   Summarize, paraphrase, and indicate a clear citation boundary. (**A** = See Answer Key.)

A 1. Summarize the excerpt below from an article about the Abraham Lincoln Presidential Museum in Springfield, IL. Then compare your summary with those of your classmates.

> The personal is the political: that seems to be the motto of this life "experience." And the political becomes personal, represented not by argument but by shouted insults and condensed formulas, as if the sound bites of 2005 really resembled the political debates of the 1860's.
>
> None of this, of course, undermines the entertainment offered, and it will be surprising if Springfield does not realize its ambitions: the museum promises fun, delivered with at least some insight along the way.
>
> —Edward Rothstein, "Strumming the Mystic Chords of Memory," *New York Times* 19 Apr. 2005: E7

2. Paraphrase the following excerpt from an article about the Abraham Lincoln Presidential Museum. Then compare your paraphrase with your classmates' versions.

> But the new museum, because of technological power alone, risks making invention seem like fact. It also enshrines a notion that the best way to know anything about politics and history is to understand personality, and even then only in a simplified fashion.
>
> —Edward Rothstein, "Strumming the Mystic Chords of Memory," *New York Times* 19 Apr. 2005: E7

3. Revise the following two passages to create clear citation boundaries between the writer's summary or paraphrase and her own commentary.

A

a. Rothstein points out that the museum blurs the line between fact and fiction. This new trend—valuing entertainment and simplification over rigor and complexity—threatens to endanger our collective memory.

b. Rothstein observes, for example, that the viewer's idea of Lincoln is altered forever after seeing the time-line photo display of his face aging through the Civil War years. The way the curators choose to convey history cannot help but impact our own experience of it.

40g Quoting

Readers should immediately realize why you are quoting a particular passage and what the quotation contributes to the ideas you want to convey. They should also learn who said the words you are quoting and, if the source is a print source, on which page of the original work the quotation appears. Then they can look up the author's name in the list of works cited at the end of your paper and find out exactly where you found the quotation.

The Modern Language Association (MLA) format for citing a quotation from an article by one author is illustrated in this chapter and in Part 7. See Part 8 for examples of citations of other types of sources in APA style. For punctuation with quotation marks, see chapter 26.

Deciding what and when to quote   Quote when you use the words of a well-known authority or when the words are particularly striking. Quote only when the original words express the exact point you want to make and express it succinctly and well. Otherwise, paraphrase. When you consider quoting, ask yourself: Which point of mine does the quotation illustrate? Why am I considering quoting this particular passage? Why should this particular passage be quoted rather than paraphrased? What do I need to tell my readers about the author of the quotation?

Quoting the exact words of the original   To understand how to deal with quotations in your paper, consider the following beginning of a newspaper article that a student used as she was working on a paper on the ethics of marketing to children.

> Think your talkative, trendy, Web-surfing 13-year-old might have a future in sales? She might already be in business. New forms of peer-to-peer, buzz-marketing campaigns—ignited and fanned by firms—are growing fast.
>
> In a practice still widely unregulated, marketers enlist youths they see as having real sway over friends. The goal? Solicit the help of these influential kids in broadening sales in exchange for products and the promise of a role in deciding what the marketplace will offer.
>
> Review a not-yet-released CD, score free concert tickets. Talk up a movie at a party, earn a DVD. The stakes are high: The 12-to-19 set reportedly spends about $170 billion a year.
>
> Marketers insist their efforts are transparent, that kids' reactions are unscripted, and that word of mouth, done right, is inherently authentic.
>
> At its first conference this week, the new Word of Mouth Marketing Association (WOMMA) will invite input on an evolving code of ethics aimed, in part, at protecting children.
>
> But opponents call the industry's youth-targeted component the odious next step in the commercialization of childhood, one that eyes ever-younger age groups, bribing them in a bid to cement brand loyalty and prompting them to wring friends for useful market data.
>
> "Some of the forms that [buzz marketing] takes have to do with recruiting kids to be marketers and encouraging them to keep their identities as marketers secret," says David Walsh, president and founder of the National Institute on Media and the Family (NIMF) in Minneapolis. "So kids end up being junior ad people, and they're encouraged not to share this [even] with their friends."
>
> Teens, he says, also often endanger themselves by sharing too much personal information, opening themselves to different kinds

of exploitation. NIMF points out that at one marketer-facilitated online community, kids can create their own Old Spice "Girls of the Red Zone" calendar. And that signing up for membership at Soul-Kool.com, one of a handful of buzz-marketing firms that double as online communities, requires entering an instant-messenger address.

—Clayton Collins, "Marketers Tap Chatty Young Teens, and Hit a Hot Button," *Christian Science Monitor* 30 March 2005: 11

Any words you use from a source must be included in quotation marks (unless they are long quotations) and quoted exactly as they appear in the original, with the same punctuation marks and capital letters. Do not change pronouns or tenses to fit your own purpose, unless you enclose changes in square brackets (see the examples on p. 416–417).

NOT EXACT QUOTATION

WRONG **Collins reports that marketers think "that word of mouth is authentic when it is done correctly."**

EXACT QUOTATION, WITHOUT CITATION

WRONG **"Marketers," Collins reports, think that "word of mouth, done right, is inherently authentic."**

EXACT QUOTATION, WITH CITATION

RIGHT **"Marketers," Collins reports, think that "word of mouth, done right, is inherently authentic" (11).**

Note that if your quotation includes a question mark or exclamation point, you must include it within the quotation. Your sentence period then comes after your citation.

Collins asks, "Think your talkative, trendy, Web-surfing 13-year-old might have a future in sales?" (11).

Quoting part of a sentence   You can make sure that quotations make a point and are not just dropped into your paper if you integrate parts of quoted sentences into your own sentences. When it is obvious that parts of the quoted sentence have been omitted, you do not need to use ellipsis dots.

According to Collins, David Walsh believes that teenagers "endanger themselves by sharing too much personal information, opening themselves to different kinds of exploitation."

Omitting words in the middle of a quotation If you omit as irrelevant to your purpose any words from the middle of a quotation, signal the omission with an ellipsis mark, three dots separated by spaces. See 27e.

> Collins points out that "signing up for membership at Soul-Kool.com . . . requires entering an instant-messenger address."

In MLA style, if your source passage uses other ellipses, place the dots within square brackets to indicate that your ellipsis mark is not part of the original text: [. . .].

Omitting words at the beginning of a quotation If you omit as irrelevant to your purpose any words from the beginning of a quotation, *do not* use an ellipsis.

WRONG   **Collins reports that WOMMA's conference ". . . will invite input on an evolving code of ethics aimed, in part, at protecting children."**

RIGHT   **Collins reports that WOMMA's conference "will invite input on an evolving code of ethics aimed, in part, at protecting children."**

Omitting words at the end of a quotation If you omit the end of the source's sentence at the end of your own sentence, and your sentence is not followed by a page citation, signal the omission with three ellipsis dots following the sentence period—four dots in all—and then the closing quotation marks.

> Alarmed, Collins establishes the role of youths in "broadening sales. . . ."

When you include a page citation for a print source, place it after the ellipsis dots and the closing quotation marks and before the final sentence period.

> Alarmed, Collins establishes the role of youths in "broadening sales . . ." (11).

Also use three dots after the period if you omit a complete sentence (or more). Use a line of dots for an omitted line of poetry (27e).

Adding or changing words If you add any comments or explanations in your own words, or if you change a word in the quotation to fit it grammatically into your sentence, enclose the added or changed material in square brackets (27c). Generally, however, it is preferable to rephrase your sentence because bracketed words and phrases make sentences difficult to read.

AWKWARD	Collins reports that the "practice [is] still widely unregulated [in which] marketers enlist youths they see as having real sway over friends."
REVISED	Collins reports that marketers freely "enlist youths they see as having real sway over friends."

Quoting longer passages If you quote more than three lines of poetry or four typed lines of prose, do not use quotation marks. Instead, begin the quotation on a new line and indent the quotation one inch or ten spaces from the left margin in MLA style, or indent it five spaces from the left margin if you are using APA style. Double-space throughout. Do not indent from the right margin. You can establish the context for a long quotation and integrate it effectively into your text if you state the point that you want to make and name the author of the quotation in your introductory statement.

Author mentioned in introductory statement
> Despite his impartial detachment, Collins gives short shrift to marketers and waxes eloquent when introducing the National Institute on Media and the Family (NIMF):

No quotation marks around indented quotation

Quotation indented one inch or 10 spaces (MLA)

> But opponents call the industry's youth-targeted component the odious next step in the commercialization of childhood, one that eyes ever-younger age groups, bribing them in a bid to cement brand loyalty and prompting them to wring friends for useful market data. (11)

Page citation (only for a print source) after period

Note: After a long indented quotation, put the period before the parenthetical citation.

Avoiding a string of quotations Use quotations, especially long ones, sparingly and only when they bolster your argument. Readers do not want to read snippets from the works of other writers. They want your analysis of your sources, and they are interested in the conclusions you draw from your research.

Fitting a quotation into your sentence When you quote, use the exact words of the original, and make sure that those exact words do not disrupt the flow of your sentence and send it in another direction.

A BAD FIT	It's obvious that Walsh finds the recruiting tactics duplicitous since they "encouraging them to keep their identities as marketers secret."

A BETTER FIT   **It's obvious that Walsh finds the recruiting tactics toward teenagers duplicitous since they encourage the youngsters "to keep their identities as marketers secret."**

A BAD FIT   **Citing another insidious tactic of buzz-marketers, Collins adds "And that signing up for membership at Soul-Kool.com, one of a handful of buzz-marketing firms that double as online communities, requires entering an instant-messenger address."**

A BETTER FIT   **Citing another insidious tactic of buzz-marketers, Collins adds "that signing up for a membership at Soul-Kool.com, one of a handful of buzz-marketing firms that double as online communities, requires entering an instant-messenger address."**

EXERCISE 40.5   Quote.

The sentences below incorporate quotations from the following paragraph by Ben Harder. Correct any errors or inaccuracies in the quotation, and make sure the quotation fits smoothly into the sentence. Some sentences may not need any editing. (**A** = See Answer Key.)

> Using good bacteria to obstruct bad ones—a strategy known as bacterial interference—is one application of so-called probiotics, a field with growing medical promise. The name suggests a twist on antibiotics, which kill disease-causing microbes. Some probiotic bacteria do their work by competing for resources and space with pathogens inside the body and, in effect, elbowing the bad bugs out of the way.
>
> —from "Germs That Do a Body Good," by Ben Harder. *Science News* 161 (2002): 72–74.

EXAMPLE:

Harder calls the word *probiotics* **"~~suggests~~ a twist on antibiotics…" (72).**

A 1. Harder says, "The use of good bacteria to obstruct bad ones is one application of probiotics . . ." (72).

A 2. Harder discusses one strategy of probiotic bacteria, which fight "for resources and space with pathogens inside the body and, in effect, elbowing the bad bugs out of the way" (72).

3. According to Harder, "probiotics is a field with growing medical promise" (72).

4. Harder explains that "antibiotics, which kill disease-causing microbes" (72).

5. Harder notes that probiotic bacteria can "[compete] for resources and space with pathogens inside the body . . ." (72).

> **KEY POINTS**
>
> ## Using Quotations: A Checklist
>
> Examine a draft of your paper, and ask the questions about each quotation you have included.
>
> - [ ] Why do you want to include this quotation? How does it support a point you have made?
>
> - [ ] What is particularly remarkable about this quotation? Would a paraphrase be better?
>
> - [ ] Does what you have enclosed in quotation marks exactly match the words and punctuation of the original?
>
> - [ ] Have you told your readers the name of the author of the quotation?
>
> - [ ] Have you included the page number of the quotation from a print source?
>
> - [ ] How have you integrated the quotation into your own passage? Will readers know whom you are quoting and why?
>
> - [ ] What verb have you used to introduce the quotation?
>
> - [ ] Are there any places where you string quotations together, one after another? If so, revise. Look for quotation marks closing and then immediately opening again. Also look for phrases such as "X goes on to say . . ."; "X also says . . ."; "X then says . . . ."
>
> - [ ] Have you indented quotations longer than four lines of type and omitted quotation marks?
>
> - [ ] Have you used long quotations sparingly?

41 Preparing the Research Paper or Presentation

41a Putting yourself in your paper

You have done hours, days, maybe weeks of research. You have found useful sources. You have a working bibliography and masses of photocopies, printouts, and notes. You have worked hard to analyze and synthesize all your material. You have made a scratch outline. Now comes the time to write your draft.

Get mileage out of your sources. Let readers know about the sources that support your point effectively. Don't mention an author of an influential book or long, important article just once and in parentheses. Let readers know why this source adds so much weight to your case. Tell about the expert's credentials, affiliations, and experience. Tell readers what the author does in the work you are citing. A summary of the work along with a paraphrase of important points may also be useful to provide context for the author's remarks and opinions. Show readers that they should be impressed by the heavyweight opinions and facts you present.

Synthesize your sources; don't string them.   Never get so involved in your mountains of notes and copies of sources that you include everything you have read and string it all together. Large amounts of information are no substitute for a thesis with relevant support. Your paper should *synthesize* your sources, not just tell about them, one after the other. When you synthesize, you connect the ideas in individual sources to create a larger picture, to inform yourself about the topic, and to establish your own ideas on the topic. Remember that the paper is ultimately *your* work, not a collection of other people's words, and that your identity and opinions as the writer should be evident.

41b The importance of your thesis

As you gather information, take notes, and write a draft, always remember to relate what you write to your research question and working thesis. All the notes on your source materials should contribute something to the issue you are researching. As you read and prepare to summarize, to paraphrase, or to record a quotation, ask yourself, "Why am I telling readers this? How does it relate to my topic, my research question, and my thesis?" Those questions should determine the type of notes you take. Then, when you review your notes later, consider what you know about the authors and whether you share their perspectives on the issue and find their evidence convincing. List the ideas and arguments that emerge from your research, and group various authors' contributions according to the points they make, connecting their views to your own thesis.

One way to help keep your thesis in focus is to write it on an index card and stick the card to your computer as you work. Periodically check to see that what you are writing is on target. Remember, though, that a thesis is not set in stone until you hand in your final draft. As you do more research and write more, you may want to tweak your thesis to fit your developing knowledge.

Before you hand in your final draft, check to ensure that your beginning and ending address the thesis and alert readers to what you have to say about the topic.

EXERCISE 41.1 Examine thesis statements.
The following thesis statements appeared in students' research papers. What would you expect to read in each paper? Which statement attracts you as a reader, and why?

1. Distance learning shows all the signs of being just a passing fad.
2. The increase in the numbers of whistle-blowers shows a decline in society's moral values.
3. History belongs in history books, not in the movies.
4. Patriotism does not emerge until there is a crisis.
5. Presidents who have not fought in wars should not be in the position of sending young men and women to defend their country.

41c Driving the organization with ideas, not sources

Let your ideas, not your sources, drive your paper. Resist the temptation to organize your paper in the following way:

1. What points Smith makes
2. What points Jones makes
3. What points Fuentes makes
4. What points Chiu makes
5. What points Jackson and Hayes make in opposition
6. What I think

That organization is driven by your sources, with the bulk of the paper dealing with the views of Smith, Jones, and the rest. Instead, let your points of supporting evidence determine the organization:

POINTS OF SUPPORT FOR THE THESIS:

1. First point of support: what evidence I have to support my thesis and what evidence Fuentes and Jones provide
2. Second point of support: what evidence I have to support my thesis and what evidence Smith and Fuentes provide
3. Third point of support: what evidence I have to support my thesis and what evidence Chiu, Smith, and Jones provide

4. Opposing viewpoints of Jackson and Hayes

5. Common ground and refutation of those viewpoints

6. Synthesis

 ESL NOTE Cultural Conventions about Texts

Be aware that the conventions regarding the use of source materials, especially classic texts, differ from culture to culture. When you are writing in English, readers will expect you to propose and explain your ideas and not to rely too heavily on classic well-known texts from thinkers in the field. ■

To avoid producing an essay that reads like a serial listing of summaries or references ("Crabbe says this," "Tyger says that," "Tyger also says this"), spend time reviewing your notes and synthesizing what you find into a coherent and convincing statement of what you know and believe. Do the following:

- Make lists of good ideas your sources raise about your topic.
- Look for the connections among those ideas: comparisons and contrasts.
- Find links in content, examples, and statistics.
- Note connections between the information in your sources and what you know from your own experience.

If you do this, you will take control of your material instead of letting it take control of you.

41d Making an outline to help with revision

Some people—those who find their way into a paper as they write it—like to make a scratch outline of the points of the paper before they begin to write; then, once they have a draft on paper, they try to make a detailed sentence outline of what they have written to check the completeness and logic of the draft. Other people like to prepare a detailed outline before they start to write—but these are usually the people who have done a great deal of research and have planned the paper before they begin to write. Whichever type of researcher you are, make sure that you do at some point pause to make an outline, especially if your paper is long and your topic complex. It will help you avoid gaps and repetition and will give you a way to see how well you take readers from one point to the next and how well all your points connect with your thesis.

Alternatively, ask a classmate to outline your paper for you to discover any troublespots. You can see an example of an outline in 4d.

41e Including visuals

Consider using visuals to enhance and supplement your content, especially in an oral presentation of your research (11c–11e). Tables and charts (10e) can often show statistics and trends much more clearly than descriptive passages can. If you look at reports issued by government agencies or research organizations, for instance, you will see that they make heavy use of explanatory visuals.

Nowadays, making your own tables and charts is simple. Downloading from the Web is, too, but remember to cite the source and ask for permission if you publish your work online or in print. A well-chosen image can also enhance your written text or presentation, as long as it illustrates or adds something significant to your content and is not just included for decorative value. Remember to introduce the visual in your text and label it with a number and title, such as *Table 1 Minimum Fitness Standards*.

Before your final draft, always assess what you can effectively *show* rather than *tell*.

41f Guidelines for writing research paper drafts

WHAT NOT TO DO

1. Do not expect to complete a polished draft at one sitting.
2. Do not write the title and the first sentence and then panic because you feel you have nothing left to say.
3. Do not constantly imagine your instructor's response to what you write.
4. Do not worry about coherence; a draft by nature is something that you work on repeatedly and revise for readers' eyes.
5. Do not necessarily begin at the beginning; do not think you must first write a dynamite introduction.

WHAT TO DO

1. Wait until you have a block of time available before you begin writing a draft of your paper.
2. Turn off the phone, close the door, and tell yourself you will not emerge from the room until you have written about six pages.

3. Promise yourself a reward when you meet your target—a refrigerator break or a trip to a nearby ice cream store, for instance.

4. Assemble your copy of the assignment, your thesis statement, all your copies of sources, your research notebook and any other notes, your working bibliography, and your proposal or outline.

5. Write the parts you know most about first.

6. Write as much as you can as fast as you can. If you only vaguely remember a reference in your sources, just write what you can remember—but keep writing, and don't worry about gaps:

   As so and so (who was it? Jackson?) has observed, malls are taking the place of city centers (check page reference).

7. Write the beginning—the introduction—only after you have some ideas on paper that you feel you can introduce.

8. Write at least something on each one of the points in your outline. Start off by asking yourself: What do I know about this point, and how does it support my thesis? Write your answer to that in your own words without worrying about who said what in which source. You can check your notes and fill in the gaps later.

9. Write until you feel you have put down on the page or screen your main points and you have made reference to most of your source material.

Now here is the hard part. Do not go back over your draft and start tinkering and changing—at least not yet. Congratulate yourself on having made a start and take a break, a long one. Put your draft in a drawer and do not look at it for at least a few days. In the meantime, you can follow up on research leads, find new sources, and continue writing ideas in your research log.

For more on research papers written about literature or in the sciences or social sciences, turn to chapter 52.

PART 7 MLA Documentation

For research papers and shorter documented essays, you must always provide detailed information about any books, articles, Web sites, or other sources that you cite. Many composition and literature courses ask you to follow the guidelines of the Modern Language Association (MLA) as recommended in the *MLA Handbook for Writers of Research Papers*, 6th edition (New York: MLA, 2003) and on the

MLA Web site at <http://www.mla.org>. Chapters 42 through 45 provide many examples to help you with your citations.

Your college may provide free access to documentation software such as NoodleBib (at <http://www.noodletools.com>), EndNote (at <http://www.endnote.com>), or RefWorks (at <http://www.refworks .com/refworks>); with these programs, you enter details in specific fields, and the program then formats your book or journal citations into a bibliography according to MLA or APA style. RefWorks also transfers the bibliographical references for titles found during a literature search directly into the user's Web-based account. However, whether you use such a program or do the formatting yourself, you still have to know—and type—the information necessary for citations not directly transferred. The examples in the following chapters will help you quickly find the information to include and the format to use.

42 Citing Sources in Your Text

42a Two basic MLA style features

If you follow these simple guidelines and use the samples in 42c and 44, you will not find MLA style too daunting.

KEY POINTS

Two Basic Features of MLA Style

1. *In your paper,* include an author/page citation for each source:

   the **last name(s)** of the author(s) or the title if no author is named and the **page number(s)** where the information is located (unless the source is online or only one page long) but without the word *page* or *pages* or the abbreviation *p.* or *pp.*

   David Crystal , the renowned scholar of language, promotes the idea of "dialect democracy" (168).

2. *At the end of your paper,* include a list, alphabetized by authors' last names or by title if the author is not known, of all the sources you refer to in the paper. Begin the list on a new page with the title *Works Cited.* See chapter 44.

Crystal , David. The Stories of English. Woodstock: Overlook, 2004.

42b FAQs about MLA citations

Frequently Asked Questions	Short Answer	Where to Find Example
What information do I put into the body of my essay?	Give only the name of the author(s) (if available) and the page number (for a print source of more than one page).	42c, item A
Where do I supply that information?	Usually name the author as you introduce the information. Alternatively, put both author and page number in parentheses at the end of the sentence containing the citation.	42c, items A, B
How do I refer to an author?	In your text, use both first and last names (and maybe a brief identification of position or credentials) for the first mention. Use only the last name for subsequent references and within parentheses. If you name the author in your text, you will not need parentheses if the work has no page numbers.	42c, items A, B
What if the work has no author or editor?	Give the title of the work or, in a parenthetical citation, an abbreviation containing the first main word of the title alphabetized in the works-cited list.	42c, item J

Frequently Asked Questions	Short Answer	Where to Find Example
How do I give page numbers?	Do not use "p." or "pp." Give inclusive page numbers for information that spans pages: 35–36; 257–58; 305–06; 299–300.	42c, items C, D, R
When can I omit a page number?	Omit a page number for a reference to a whole work, to an alphabetized entry in a reference work, to a work only one page long, or to an online work with no visible page numbers.	42c, items K, L, M, N, O, Q

See the samples in 42c and 43b to answer other questions.

42c Sample in-text citations (MLA)

AT A GLANCE: INDEX OF MLA IN-TEXT CITATIONS

CITING A WORK WITH INDIVIDUAL AUTHOR(S) NAMED

A. One author named in your introductory text,   429
B. Author not mentioned in your introductory text,   429
C. Work written by more than one author,   430
D. Work by author with more than one work cited,   430
E. Two authors with same last name,   430
F. Author of work in an edited anthology,   431
G. Author of work quoted in another source,   431
H. More than one work in one citation,   431

CITING A WORK WITH NO INDIVIDUAL AUTHOR

I. Corporation, government agency, or organization as author,   431

J. No author or editor named,   432
K. Unauthored entry in dictionary or encyclopedia,   432

CITING A WORK WITH PAGE NUMBERS NOT AVAILABLE (ONLINE WORK) OR RELEVANT

L. Internet and electronic sources with no page numbers,   432
M. Reference to an entire work,   433
N. Work only one page long,   433

CITING SPECIAL TYPES OF SOURCES

O. Multimedia or nonprint source,   433
P. Multivolume work,   433
Q. Lecture, speech, personal communication, interview,   433

CITING A WORK WITH INDIVIDUAL AUTHOR(S) NAMED (MLA)

A. One author, named in your introductory phrase   Naming the author in an introductory phrase allows you to supply information about the author's credentials as an expert and so increases the credibility of your source for readers. Another advantage of naming your source in your text is that readers then know that everything between the mention of the author and the cited page number is a reference to your source material.

For the first mention of an author, use the full name and any relevant credentials. After that, use only the last name. Generally, use the present tense to cite an author. (See 44a, item 1, for the entry in the works-cited list.)

┌─────── author and credentials ───────┐
National Book Award winner Paul Fussell points out that even people in low-paying jobs show "all but universal pride in a uniform of any kind" (5).
            page number

When a quotation ends the sentence, as above, close the quotation marks before the parentheses, and place the sentence period after the parentheses. (Note that this rule differs from the one for undocumented writing, which calls for a period *before* the closing quotation marks.)

When a quotation includes a question mark or an exclamation point, also include a period after the citation:

> Fussell reminds us of our equating uniforms with seriousness of purpose when he begins a chapter by asking, "Would you get on an airplane with two pilots who are wearing cut-off jeans?" (85).

For a quotation longer than four lines, see 40g.

B. Author not mentioned in your introductory text   If you have referred to an author previously or if you are citing statistics, you do not need to mention the author while introducing the reference. In that case, include the author's last name in the parentheses before the page number, with no comma between them.

> The army retreated from Boston in disarray, making the victors realize
>
> that they had defeated the "greatest military power on earth"
>
> author and page
> ┌── number──┐
> (McCullough 76).

See 40g for how to cite the source after a long quotation.

C. Work written by more than one author For a work with two or three authors, include all the names, either in your text sentence or in parentheses.

> (Lakoff and Johnson 42)
> (Hare, Moran, and Koepke 226–28)

For a work with four or more authors, use only the first author's last name followed by "et al." (*Et alii* means "and others.") See 44a, item 2.

> Some researchers have established a close link between success at work
> and the pleasure derived from community service (Bellah et al. 196–99).

D. Work by author with more than one work cited You can include the author and title of the work in your text.

> Alice Walker, in her book In Search of Our Mothers' Gardens, describes
> revisiting her past to discover more about Flannery O'Connor (43-59).

If you do not mention the author in your text, include in your parenthetical reference the author's last name, followed by a comma, an abbreviated form of the title, and the page number.

> comma ┐
> O'Connor's house still stands and is looked after by a caretaker (Walker,
>
> abbreviated title   ┌ page number
> ┌────────┐ /
> In Search 57).

E. Two authors with the same last name Include each author's first initial, or if the initials are the same, include the whole first name.

> A writer can be seen as both "author" and "secretary," and the two roles
> can be seen as competitive (F. Smith 19).

F. Author of work in an edited anthology Cite the author of the included or reprinted work (not the editor of the anthology) and the page number in the anthology. The entry in the works-cited list will include the title of the article, its inclusive page numbers, and full bibliographical details for the anthology: title, editor(s), place of publication, publisher, and date. See 44a, items 5 and 6, for examples.

> Des Pres asserts that "heroism is not necessarily a romantic notion" (20).

G. Author of work quoted in another source Use "qtd. in" (for "quoted in") in your parenthetical citation, followed by the last name of the author of the source in which you find the reference (the indirect source) and the page number where the reference appears. List the indirect source in your list of works cited. In the following example, the indirect source Smith, not Britton, would head an item in the list of works cited.

> We generate words unconsciously, without thinking about them; they appear, as James Britton says, "at the point of utterance" (qtd. in Smith 108).

H. More than one work in one citation Include all the citations, separated by semicolons. Avoid making the list too long.

> The links between a name and ancestry have occupied many writers and researchers (Waters 65; Antin 188).

CITING A WORK WITH NO INDIVIDUAL AUTHOR (MLA)

I. Corporation, government agency, or organization as author Sometimes you will use material authored not by an individual but by a corporation, government agency, or organization. (See 39g on finding the author of a Web site.) Cite the organization as the author, making sure it corresponds with the alphabetized entry in your works-cited list (shown in 44b, item 21). Use the complete name in your text or a shortened form in parentheses. The following examples cite a Web site, so page numbers are not included.

> ┌──────── full name ────────┐
> The United States Department of Education has projected an increase in college enrollment of 11% between 2003 and 2013.

> An increase in college enrollment of 11% between 2003 and 2013 has
> ┌ shortened name ┐
> been projected (US Dept. of Educ.).

J. No author or editor named If there is no stated author of a source, refer to the book (underlined) or article (within quotation marks) by its title. Within a parenthetical citation, shorten the title to the first word alphabetized in the works-cited list (44a, item 7).

> According to The Chicago Manual of Style, writers should always "break or bend" rules when necessary (xiii).

> Writers should always "break or bend" rules when necessary (Chicago xiii).

If you need help in determining the author of an Internet source, see 39f and 39g. For a Web site with no author indicated, use the name of the site.

K. Unauthored entry in dictionary or encyclopedia For an unsigned entry, give the title of the entry; a page number is not necessary for an alphabetized work. Begin the entry in the works-cited list with the title of the alphabetized entry (44f, item 42).

> Drypoint differs from etching in that it does not use acid ("Etching").

CITING A WORK WITH PAGE NUMBERS NOT AVAILABLE OR RELEVANT (MLA)

L. Author or title only for Internet and electronic sources with no page numbers Electronic database material and Web sources, which appear on a screen, have no stable page numbers that apply across systems or when printed unless you access them in PDF (page document format) files. If your source on the screen includes no visible numbered pages or numbered paragraphs, provide only the author's name or the title if no author is named. Be sure the title in your citation matches exactly the word you alphabetize in your list.

> Science writer Stephen Hart describes how researchers Edward Taub and Thomas Ebert conclude that for musicians, practicing "remaps the brain."

With no page number to indicate where your citation ends, be careful to define where the citation ends and your commentary takes over. See 40f for more on defining the boundaries of a citation.

Provide page or paragraph numbers only if they appear on the screen as part of the document. Also include the total number of numbered paragraphs in your works-cited list. See 44e, item 3.

> Hatchuel discusses how film editing "can change points of view and turn objectivity into subjectivity" (par. 6).

You may also locate the information according to an internal heading of the document, such as *Introduction*, *Chapter*, or *Section*.

M. Reference to an entire work and not to one specific idea or page
Use the author's name alone, with no page number.

> Diaries tell about people's everyday lives and the worlds they create (Mallon).

N. Work only one page long   If a print article is only one page long, you may mention the author's name alone in your text, but be sure to include the page number in your works-cited list (44c, item 24). However, a page reference indicates where a citation ends, so you may prefer to include it in your text (40f).

CITING SPECIAL TYPES OF SOURCES (MLA)

O. Multimedia or nonprint source   For radio or TV programs, live performances, films, computer software, recordings, works of art, or other nonprint sources, include only the author (or producer, actor, director, and so on) or title. Make sure your text reference corresponds to the first element of the information you provide in your works-cited list. See 44i, item 56.

> One director shines at capturing political intrigue on the stage (Blakemore).

P. Multivolume work   Indicate the volume number, followed by a colon, a space, and the page number (Stout 1: 25). Give the total number of volumes in your works-cited list (44a, item 10).

Q. Lecture, speech, personal communication, or interview   Give the name of the person delivering the communication. In your works-cited list, state the type of communication after the author's name (44j, items 61–66).

> According to George Kane, Vice President of Infoplease.com, students of all ages increasingly turn first to the Internet when conducting research.

R. Literary work: fiction, poetry, and drama   For well-known works published in several different editions, include information so readers may locate material in whatever edition they are using. Include details in your works-cited list about the edition you use.

FOR A NOVEL Give the chapter or section number in addition to the page number in the edition you used: (104; ch. 3).

FOR A POEM Give line numbers, not page numbers: (lines 62–73). Subsequent line references can omit the word *lines*. Include up to three lines of poetry sequentially in your text, separated by a slash with a space on each side (/) (see 27d). For four or more lines of poetry, begin on a new line, indent the whole passage one inch from the left, double-space throughout, and omit quotation marks from the beginning and end of the passage (see 40g).

FOR CLASSIC POEMS, SUCH AS THE *ILIAD* Give the book or part number, followed by the line numbers, not page numbers: (8.21–25).

FOR A PLAY For dialogue, set the quotation off from your text, indented one inch with no quotation marks, and write the name of the character speaking in all capital letters, followed by a period. Indent subsequent lines of the same speech another quarter inch (three spaces). For a classic play, one published in several different editions (such as plays by William Shakespeare or Oscar Wilde), omit page numbers and cite in parentheses the act, scene, and line numbers of the quotation, in Arabic numerals. In your works-cited list, list the bibliographical details of the edition you used.

> Shakespeare's lovers in A Midsummer Night's Dream appeal to
> contemporary audiences accustomed to the sense of loss in love songs:
>> LYSANDER. How now, my love! Why is your cheek so pale?
>> How chance the roses there do fade so fast?
>> HERMIA. Belike for want of rain, which I could well
>> Beteem them from the tempest of mine eyes.
>> (1.1.133-36)

For a new play available in only one published edition, cite author and page numbers as you do for other MLA citations.

FOR SHAKESPEARE, CHAUCER, AND OTHER LITERARY WORKS Abbreviate titles cited in parentheses, such as the following: *Tmp.* for *The Tempest; 2H4* for *Henry IV, Part 2; MND* for *A Midsummer Night's Dream; GP* for the *General Prologue; PrT* for *The Prioress's Tale; Aen.* for *Aeneid; Beo.* for *Beowulf; Prel.* for Wordsworth's *Prelude.*

S. The Bible and other sacred texts Give the title (underlined), book, chapter, and verse(s) in your text—The Holy Bible, Genesis 27.29 (with no underlining; see 52a)—or abbreviate the book in a parenthetical citation (The Holy Bible, Gen. 27.29). Give the edition of the Bible or other sacred text in your works-cited list. See 44a, item 17.

T. Two or more sequential references to the same work   If you rely on several quotations from the same page within one of your paragraphs, one parenthetical reference after the last quotation is enough, but make sure that no quotations from other works intervene. If you are paraphrasing from and referring to one work several times in a paragraph, mention the author in your introductory phrase; cite the page number at the end of a paraphrase and again if you paraphrase from a different page. Make it clear to a reader where the paraphrase ends and your own comments take over (40f).

U. Historical or legal document   Cite any article and section number of a familiar historical document, such as the Constitution, in parentheses in your text (US Const., art. 2, sec. 4), with no entry in the works-cited list. Underline the name of a court case (<u>Roe v. Wade</u>), but do not underline laws and acts. List cases and acts in your works-cited list (see 44j, item 67).

42d Explanatory footnotes or endnotes (MLA)

With the MLA parenthetical style of documentation, use a footnote (at the bottom of the page) or an endnote (on a separate numbered page at the end of the paper before the works-cited list) only for notes giving supplementary information that clarifies or expands a point. You might use a note to refer to several supplementary bibliographical sources or to provide a comment that is interesting but not essential to your argument. Indicate a note with a raised number (superscript) in your text, after the word or sentence your note refers to. Begin the first line of each note one-half inch (or five spaces) from the left margin. Do not indent subsequent lines of the same note. Double-space endnotes. In footnotes, single-space within each note, but double-space between notes.

<u>NOTE NUMBER IN TEXT</u>

Ethics have become an important part of many writing classes.[1]

<u>CONTENT ENDNOTE</u>

five spaces _____ raised number followed by space
⟵___↘[1] For additional discussion of ethics in the classroom, see Stotsky
799–806; Knoblauch 15–21; Bizzell 663–67; Friend 560–66.

43 Setting Up the MLA List of Works Cited

The references you make in your text to sources are brief—at most only the author's last name and a page number—so they allow readers to continue reading without interruption. For complete information about the source, readers use your brief in-text citation to take them to the full bibliographical reference in the list of works cited at the end of your paper.

43a Format and organization of the MLA list

> **KEY POINTS**
>
> **Setting Up the MLA List of Works Cited**
>
> 1. *What to list*   List only works you actually cited in the text of your paper, not works you read but did not mention, unless your instructor requires you to include all the works you consulted as well as those mentioned in your text.
>
> 2. *Format of the list*   Begin the list on a new numbered page after the last page of the paper or any endnotes. Center the heading (Works Cited) without quotation marks, underlining, or a period. Double-space throughout the list.
>
> 3. *Organization*   Do not number the entries. List works alphabetically by author's last name (43b). List works with no stated author by the first main word of the title (44a, item 8, and 44c, item 28).
>
> 4. *Indentation*   To help readers find an author's name and to clearly differentiate one entry from another, indent all lines of each entry, except the first, one-half inch (or five spaces). A word processor can provide these "hanging indents" (Format/Paragraph/Special—see 9e, item 4).

TECHTOOLKIT   Indentation Online

If you intend to publish on the Internet, it is often preferable to use no indentation at all (HTML does not support hanging indents well). Instead, follow each bibliographical entry with a line space. ■

5. *Periods*   Separate the main parts of each entry—author, title, publishing information—with a period, followed by one space.

6. *Capitals*   Capitalize the first letter of all words in titles of books and articles except *a, an, the*, coordinating conjunctions, *to* in an infinitive, and prepositions (such as *in, to, for, with, without, against*) unless they begin or end the title or subtitle.

7. *Underlining or italics*   Underline the titles of books and the names of journals and magazines. You may use italics instead if your instructor approves and if your printer makes a clear distinction between italics and regular type.

TECHTOOLKIT   Underlining versus Italics

If you write for publication on a World Wide Web site, avoid underlining titles of books and journals; underlining is a signal for a hypertext link. Use italics, or consult your instructor or editor. ■

8. *Page numbers in print sources*   Give inclusive page numbers for print articles and sections of books. Do not use "p." ("pp.") or the word *page* (or *pages*) before page numbers in any reference. For page citations over 100 and sharing the same first number, use only the last two digits for the second number (for instance, 683–89, but 798–805). For an unpaginated work, write "n. pag." See 43d for the problems of page numbers with online sources.

43b How to list authors, months, and publishers (MLA)

Authors

Name of author(s)   Put the last name first for a single author or the first author: *Caro, Robert*. For two or more authors, reverse the names of only the first author: *Engleberg, Isa, and Ann Raimes*.

ALPHABETICAL ORDER Alphabetize entries in the list by authors' last names. Note the following:

- Alphabetize by the exact letters in the spelling: *MacKay* precedes *McHam*.

- Let a shorter name precede a longer name beginning with the same letters: *Linden, Ronald* precedes *Lindenmayer, Arnold*.

- With last names using a prefix such as *le, du, di, del*, and *des*, alphabetize by the prefix: *Le Beau, Bryan F.*

- When *de* occurs with French names of one syllable, alphabetize under *d*: *De Jean, Denise*. Otherwise, alphabetize by last name: *Maupassant, Guy de*.

- Alphabetize by the first element of a hyphenated name: *Sackville-West, Victoria*.

- Alphabetize by the last name when the author uses two names without a hyphen: *Thomas, Elizabeth Marshall*.

AUTHOR NOT KNOWN For a work with no author named, alphabetize by the first word in the title other than *A, An,* or *The* (see 44a, item 7, and 44c, item 28).

Several works by the same author(s) For all entries after the first, replace the name(s) of the author(s) with three hyphens followed by a period, and alphabetize according to the first significant word in the title. If an author serves as an editor or translator, put a comma after the three hyphens, followed by the appropriate abbreviation ("ed." or "trans."). If, however, the author has coauthors, repeat all authors' names in full and put the coauthored entry after all the single-name entries for the author.

Goleman, Daniel. <u>Destructive Emotions: A Scientific Dialogue with the Dalai Lama.</u> New York: Bantam-Dell, 2003.

---. <u>Working with Emotional Intelligence.</u> New York: Bantam, 2000.

Goleman, Daniel, Paul Kaufman, and Michael L. Ray. "The Art of Creativity." <u>Psychology Today</u> Mar.–Apr. 1992: 40–47.

AUTHORS WITH THE SAME LAST NAME Alphabetize by first names: *Smith, Adam* precedes *Smith, Frank*.

Months When you give the date of a journal or newspaper article or of an online source, spell out the months *May*, *June*, and *July* in full. Otherwise, use the following abbreviations:

Jan.	Feb.	Mar.	Apr.	Aug.
Sept.	Oct.	Nov.	Dec.	

Publishers Shorten the names of publishers.

- Omit any articles: *A, An, The*.
- Omit abbreviations such as *Co.* and *Inc.*
- Give only the first name if the name of the company consists of several last names: *Little*, not *Little, Brown and Company, Inc.*
- If the publisher's name includes a first and last name, give only the last name: *Abrams*, not *Harry N. Abrams*.
- Use abbreviations: *Acad.* for *Academy*, *Assn.* for *Association*.
- Use *UP* for *University Press: U of Chicago P, Cambridge UP*.
- Use abbreviations that will be familiar to your readers: *MLA, GPO*.

Some sample abbreviations:

Basic Books	Basic
Department of Education	Dept. of Educ.
The Feminist Press at the City University of New York	Feminist
Government Printing Office	GPO
Houghton Mifflin Co.	Houghton
National Center for Education Statistics	Natl. Center for Educ. Statistics
Simon and Schuster, Inc.	Simon

43c How to list Internet sources (and where to find the information) (MLA)

With whatever system of documentation you use, the basic question is "What information do readers need to access the same Web site and find the same information I found?" The following table shows you how to format the information in an MLA list of works cited. The example illustrating the features in the table refers to Source Shot 4 on page 441. For listing online databases and other online sources, see chapter 44.

MLA (Modern Language Association)

Five Basics for Documenting Internet Sources, MLA Style

Item in Listing	Information to Include
1. Author	Last name, First name, Middle initial, if available. Names of more than one author begin with first name. (Author may also be name of corporation, business, institution, or government agency.)
2. Document title in quotation marks	"Title of Online Article, Story, Poem, or Posting to Discussion List." (Add any print publication, if available.)
3. Name of site underlined + date of posting or update, and name of sponsor if available	<u>Name of Web Site, Project, Online Periodical, Book,</u> or <u>Name of Database.</u> Date of posting. Sponsor.
4. Date of access	Day Month (abbrev.) Year (no period after year)
5. URL	Enclosed in angle brackets, followed by period. Line split only after a slash. No spaces or hyphens inserted. All underscoring is included.

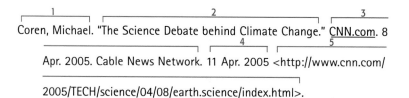

Coren, Michael. "The Science Debate behind Climate Change." <u>CNN.com</u>. 8 Apr. 2005. Cable News Network. 11 Apr. 2005 <http://www.cnn.com/ 2005/TECH/science/04/08/earth.science/index.html>.

Many complex sites need more information. See the Key Points box (below) and the sample entries in Chapter 44 for variations.

MLA (Modern Language Association)

SOURCE SHOT 4: Listing a Web Site Document 5. URL

Bottom of page: 3. Sponsor (Cable News Network)

Reprinted by permission of CNN ImageSource.

KEY POINTS

Beyond the Basics: Special Considerations for MLA

1. *Author*   If no individual author or organizational author is evident, list the source by title of document or name of site, whichever is available. Evaluate a source with no author especially carefully before you use it. See 39f and 39g.

2. *Document title and source*   Sometimes you may find it difficult to differentiate a document title from the name of a Web site. Examining the home page and the structure of the site carefully will often help (39f). Include after the title any available print publication information (as in 44a and 44c) or online journal details such as the journal name, volume number of a scholarly journal, date, and whatever information is

(*continued*)

(*continued*)

provided about the page numbers in a print publication or a PDF document.

3. *Name of site* Underline the name of a Web site or project, an online periodical or book, or the name of a database. Provide, if you can, the date of the online posting and the name of the owner or sponsor of the site, if available. (See 39g, Anatomy of a Web Site.) Abbreviations such as *Assn.*, *Lib.*, and *Dept.* are acceptable. *Note:* A Webmaster is not the owner of the site.

4. *Dates* The last date in your source reference, immediately before the URL or keyword path, should be the date when you found the material. This is called the "date of access." Two dates may appear next to each other, as in 44e, items 38 and 39, but both are necessary; the first is the date when the work was posted or updated; the second is the date when you found the material.

5. *URL* Copy and paste a URL whenever possible to avoid transcription errors. For print presentation of your work, remove all hyperlinks (Tools/Auto Correct/Auto Format/uncheck the box).

43d Page numbers (or lack of) in online works (MLA)

Include in your citation the page numbers for any print version of the source. For the electronic versions, include page or paragraph numbers of the on-screen version *only* if they are indicated on the screen. Page numbers are shown in PDF files, but otherwise they usually are not, so the page numbers on your printout of a source would not necessarily correspond to the page numbers on other printouts. When no page or paragraph information for the online version appears on the screen, include no page numbers in your list of references. For how to cite unpaged online material in your text, see 42c, item L. See also 40f on how to indicate where your citation ends.

44 Sample Entries in the MLA List

How to find what you need

- In the At a Glance Directory, find the type of source you have used and where you viewed it.

AT A GLANCE: DIRECTORY OF MLA SAMPLE ENTRIES

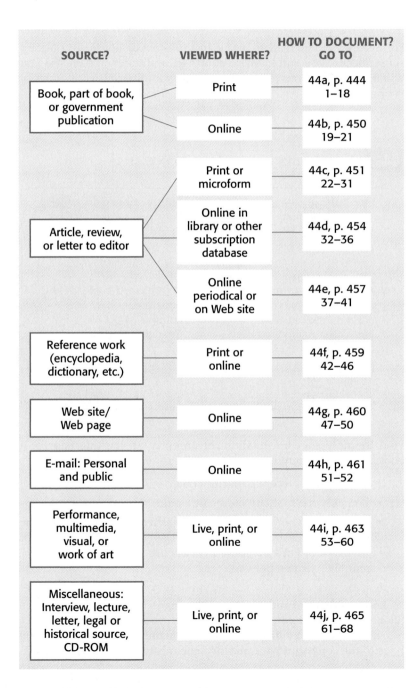

SOURCE?	VIEWED WHERE?	HOW TO DOCUMENT? GO TO
Book, part of book, or government publication	Print	44a, p. 444 1–18
	Online	44b, p. 450 19–21
Article, review, or letter to editor	Print or microform	44c, p. 451 22–31
	Online in library or other subscription database	44d, p. 454 32–36
	Online periodical or on Web site	44e, p. 457 37–41
Reference work (encyclopedia, dictionary, etc.)	Print or online	44f, p. 459 42–46
Web site/ Web page	Online	44g, p. 460 47–50
E-mail: Personal and public	Online	44h, p. 461 51–52
Performance, multimedia, visual, or work of art	Live, print, or online	44i, p. 463 53–60
Miscellaneous: Interview, lecture, letter, legal or historical source, CD-ROM	Live, print, or online	44j, p. 465 61–68

- Follow the line across to the last column.
- Turn to the section and page to find a detailed menu and examples.

For instance, if you read an article in a full-text database your library subscribes to, you will know to go to 44d, and there on page 454 you will find explanations, screenshots, and examples of several types of listings.

44a Print books or parts of books (MLA)

Find the necessary information for an entry on the title page of a book and on the copyright page.

- Use the most recent copyright date.
- List only the first city on the title page.
- Use a shortened form of the publisher's name; usually one word is sufficient: *Houghton*, not *Houghton Mifflin*; *Basic*, not *Basic Books*. For university presses, use the abbreviations "U" and "P" with no periods.

1. Book with one author   The title page of the book in Source Shot 5 shows what you need to include in your documentation.

If the year of publication is not visible on the title page, turn the page to the copyright page and find the most recent copyright date.

MLA (Modern Language Association)

SOURCE SHOT 5   Listing a Book

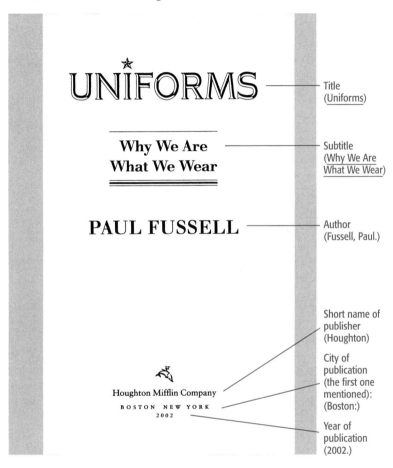

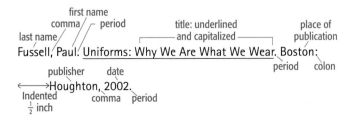

McCullough, David. John Adams. New York: Simon, 2001.

2. Book with two or more authors Separate the names with commas. Reverse the order of only the first author's name.

second author's name
not reversed
comma
Lakoff, George, and Mark Johnson. <u>Metaphors We Live By</u>. Chicago:

U of Chicago P, 1980.

With four or more authors, either list all the names or use only the first author's name followed by "et al." (Latin for "and others").

Bellah, Robert N., et al. <u>Habits of the Heart: Individualism and Commitment</u>
<u>in American Life</u>. Berkeley: U of California P, 1985.

3. Book with editor or editors Include the abbreviation "ed." or "eds."

Gates, Henry Louis, Jr., ed. <u>Classic Slave Narratives</u>. New York: NAL, 1987.

For a work with four or more editors, use the name of only the first, followed by a comma and "et al."

4. Author and editor When an editor has prepared an author's work for publication, list the book under the author's name(s) if you cite the author's work. Then, in your listing, include the name(s) of the editor or editors after the title, introduced by "Ed." ("edited by") for one or more editors. "Ed." stands for "edited by" in the following entry.

name
of editor
author of letters
Bishop, Elizabeth. <u>One Art: Letters</u>. Ed. Robert Giroux. New York:

Farrar, 1994.

If you cite a section written by the editor, such as a chapter introduction or a note, list the source under the name of the editor.

name
of editor editor author of letters
Giroux, Robert, ed. <u>One Art: Letters</u>. By Elizabeth Bishop. New York:

Farrar, 1994.

5. One work in an anthology (original or reprinted) For a story, poem, essay, play, or other work in an anthology, first list the author and title of the included work. Follow this with the title of the anthology, the name of the editor(s), publication information (place, publisher, date) for the anthology, and then, after the period, the pages in the anthology covered by the work you refer to.

author of work in
┌── anthology ──┐
Des Pres, Terrence. "Poetry and Politics." <u>The Writer in Our World</u>.
means   name of editor
"edited by" ┌── of anthology ──┐
       Ed. Reginald Gibbons. Boston: Atlantic Monthly, 1986. 17–29.
                  inclusive page numbers of article or chapter

Alvarez, Julia. "Grounds for Fiction." <u>The Riverside Reader</u>. 8th ed. Ed. Joseph
    Trimmer and Maxine Hairston. Boston: Houghton, 2005. 125–39.

If the work in the anthology is a reprint of a previously published scholarly article, supply the complete information for both the original publication and the reprint in the anthology.

Gates, Henry Louis, Jr. "The Fire Last Time." <u>New Republic</u> 1 June 1992:
    37–43. Rpt. in <u>Contemporary Literary Criticism</u>. Ed. Jeffrey W. Hunter.
    Vol. 127. Detroit: Gale, 2000. 113–19.

6. More than one work in an anthology, cross-referenced If you refer to more than one work from the same anthology, list the anthology separately, and list each essay with a cross-reference to the anthology. Alphabetize in the usual way, as in the following three examples.

                       title of
┌─ author of article ─┐ ┌─ article in anthology ─┐ editor of anthology
Des Pres, Terrence. "Poetry and Politics." Gibbons 17–29.
                              page numbers of article

       editor of
┌── anthology ──┐   ┌── title of anthology ──┐
Gibbons, Reginald, ed. <u>The Writer in Our World</u>. Boston: Atlantic
    Monthly, 1986.

       author
┌── of article ──┐ ┌── title of article in anthology ──┐ editor of anthology
Walcott, Derek. "A Colonial's-Eye View of America." Gibbons 73–77.
                           page numbers of article

7. Book with no author named Put the title first. Do not consider the words *A, An,* and *The* in alphabetizing the entries. The following entry would be alphabetized under *C.*

<u>The Chicago Manual of Style</u>. 15th ed. Chicago: U of Chicago P, 2003.

8. Book written by a corporation, organization, or government agency Alphabetize by the name of the corporate author or branch of government. If the publisher is the same as the author, include the name again as publisher.

Hoover's Inc. Hoover's Handbook of World Business. Austin: Hoover's, 2005.

If no author is named for a government publication, begin the entry with the name of the federal, state, or local government, followed by the agency. See item 21 for an online government publication.

United States. Department of Labor. Bureau of Labor Statistics. Occupational Outlook Handbook 2004–2005. Indianapolis: JIST, 2004.

9. Translated book After the title, include "Trans." followed by the name of the translator, not in inverted order.

Grass, Günter. Novemberland: Selected Poems, 1956–1993. Trans. Michael Hamburger. San Diego: Harcourt, 1996.

10. Multivolume work If you refer to more than one volume of a multivolume work, give the number of volumes ("vols.") after the title.

Stout, Chris E., ed. The Psychology of Terrorism. 4 vols. New York: Praeger, 2002.

If you refer to only one volume, limit the information in the entry to that one volume.

Richardson, John. A Life of Picasso. Vol. 2. New York: Random, 1996.

11. Book in a series Give the name of the series after the book title.

Connor, Ulla. Contrastive Rhetoric: Cross-Cultural Aspects of Second Language Writing. The Cambridge Applied Linguistics Ser. New York: Cambridge UP, 1996.

12. Book published under a publisher's imprint State the names of both the imprint (the publisher within a larger publishing enterprise) and the larger publishing house, separated by a hyphen.

Atwood, Margaret. Negotiation with the Dead: A Writer on Writing. New York: Anchor-Doubleday, 2003.

13. Foreword, preface, introduction, or afterword List the name of the author of the book element cited, followed by the name of the element, with no quotation marks. Give the title of the work; then use "By" to introduce the name of the author(s) of the book (first name first). After the publication information, give inclusive page numbers for the book element cited.

Remnick, David. Introduction. Politics. By Hendrik Hertzberg. New York:
 Penguin, 2004. xvii–xxiv.

14. Republished book Give the original date of publication after the title and the reprint date at the end.

King, Stephen. On Writing. 2000. New York: Pocket, 2002.

15. Book not in first edition Give the edition number ("ed.") after the title.

Raimes, Ann. Keys for Writers. 4th ed. Boston: Houghton, 2005.

16. Book title including another title Do not underline a book title included in the title you list. (However, if the title of a short work, such as a poem or short story, is part of the source title, enclose it in quotation marks.)

Hays, Kevin J., ed. The Critical Response to Herman Melville's

 book title not underlined
 Moby Dick. Westport: Greenwood, 1994.

17. The Bible or other sacred text Give the usual bibliographical details for a book, including the name of any translator.

The Koran. Trans. George Sales. London: Warne, n.d.

(*n.d.* means no date is given.)

The New Testament in Modern English. Trans. J. B. Phillips. New York:
 Macmillan, 1972.

18. Dissertation For an unpublished dissertation, follow the title (in quotation marks) with "Diss." and the university and date.

Hidalgo, Stephen Paul. "Vietnam War Poetry: A Genre of Witness." Diss.
 U of Notre Dame, 1995.

Cite a published dissertation as you would a book, with place of publication, publisher, and date, but also include dissertation information after the title (for example, "Diss. U of California, 1998.").

If the dissertation is published by University Microfilms International (UMI), underline the title and include "Ann Arbor: UMI," the date, and the order number at the end of the entry.

Diaz-Greenberg, Rosario. The Emergence of Voice in Latino High School
   Students. Diss. U of San Francisco, 1996. Ann Arbor: UMI, 1996.
   9611612.

If you cite an abstract published in *Dissertation Abstracts International,* give the relevant volume number and page number.

Hidalgo, Stephen Paul. "Vietnam War Poetry: A Genre of Witness." Diss.
   U of Notre Dame, 1995. DAI 56 (1995): 0931A.

44b Online books or parts of books—found via a Web browser (MLA)

19. Online book or part of book Give whatever is available of the following: author, title, editor or translator, and any print publication information as shown in items 1–18. Follow this with the available electronic publication information: title of site or database, date of electronic posting, sponsor, your date of access to the site, and the URL.

```
      ┌── author ──┐        ┌── title of work ──┐   ┌──── print publication
                                                    information ────┐
Darwin, Charles. The Voyage of the Beagle. London: John Murray, 1859.
```

```
                              date of
                              electronic
   ┌── title of database ──┐  ┌─ publication ─┐  ┌── name of sponsor of site ──┐
Oxford Text Archive. 28 Mar. 2000. Arts and Humanities Data
```

```
            date of            URL enclosed
    ┌──────┐ ┌─ access ─┐  ┌── in angle brackets ──┐
Service. 8 Feb. 2005 <http://ota.ahds.ac.uk>.
```

20. Online poem

$$\overbrace{\text{author}}^{} \quad \overbrace{\text{poem}}^{\text{title of}} \quad \overbrace{\text{source}}^{\text{print}} \quad \overbrace{\text{information}}^{\text{print publication}}$$

Levine, Philip. "What Work Is." What Work Is. New York: Knopf, 1991.

$$\overbrace{\text{title of database}}^{} \quad \overbrace{\text{updating}}^{\text{date of electronic}} \quad \overbrace{\text{of site}}^{\text{sponsor}}$$

Internet Poetry Archive. 4 Apr. 2000. U of North Carolina P.

$$\overbrace{\text{access}}^{\text{date of}} \quad \overbrace{\text{in angle brackets}}^{\text{URL enclosed}}$$

8 Feb. 2005 <http://www.ibiblio.org/ipa/levine/work.html>.

21. Online government publication   Begin with the government and agency and title of the work. Follow this with the date of electronic posting or update, your date of access, and the URL. Government sites often post documents online before publishing them in print form.

United States. Dept. of Educ. Office of Educ. Research and Improvement.

> Natl. Center for Educ. Statistics. Digest of Education Statistics, 2003.
>
> 30 Dec. 2004. 16 Feb. 2005 <http://nces.ed.gov/programs/digest/d03>.

44c Articles in print or microform (MLA)

The conventions for listing articles depend on whether the articles appear in newspapers, popular magazines, or scholarly journals. For distinguishing scholarly journals from other periodicals, see 39d.

- For all types of periodicals, omit from your citation any introductory *A*, *An*, or *The* in the name of a newspaper, magazine, or scholarly journal.
- When giving dates of articles in journals, newspapers, and magazines, abbreviate all months except May, June, and July.
- If a print article is only one page long, give that page number. For a longer article, give the range of page numbers (such as

24–27; 365–72). Your in-text citation will give the exact page on which you found the information. Do not use "p." or "pp." before page numbers.

- Give no page numbers for online articles unless you cite a PDF document.

22. Article in a scholarly journal, continuously paged by volume For journal volumes with continuous pagination (for example, the first issue ends with page 174, and the next issue begins with page 175, and so on), give the volume number, the year in parentheses followed by a colon, and page numbers.

> last name   first name — title of article, in quotation marks —   title of journal, underlined —   volume number
> Brandt, Deborah. "Drafting U.S. Literacy." College English 66 (2004):
>   period   year   colon
> 485–502.
>   inclusive page numbers

SOURCE SHOT 6   Listing an Article in a Scholarly Journal

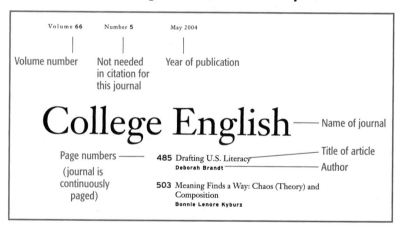

23. Article in a scholarly journal, paged by issue For journals in which each issue begins with page 1, include the issue number after the volume number, separated by a period. (Include the issue number alone if no volume number is given.)

Ginat, Rami. "The Soviet Union and the Syrian Ba'th Regime: From

> Hesitation to *Rapprochement*." Middle Eastern Studies 36.2
>   issue number
> (2000): 150–71.

24. Article in a magazine Do not include *the* in the name of a magazine: *Atlantic* not *The Atlantic.* Give the complete date (day, month, and year, in that order, with no commas between them) for a weekly or biweekly magazine. For a monthly or bimonthly magazine, give only the month and year (as in the first example). In either case, do not include volume and issue numbers. If the article is on only one page, give that page number. If the article covers two or more consecutive pages, list inclusive page numbers. See also items 26–28.

Douthat, Ross. "The Truth about Harvard." Atlantic Mar. 2005: 95–99.

Tyrangiel, Josh. "A *Source* of Discomfort." Time 12 Jan. 2004: 74.

25. Article in a newspaper After the newspaper title (omit the word *The*), give the date, followed by any edition given at the top of the first page (*late ed., natl. ed.*). For a newspaper that uses letters to designate sections, give the letter before the page number: "A23." For a numbered section, write, for example, "sec. 2: 23." See item 39 for the online version of the entry for the following article.

Franklin, Deborah. "Vitamin E Fails to Deliver on Early Promise." New York Times 2 Aug. 2005, late ed.: F5.

26. Article that skips pages When an article does not appear on consecutive pages (the one by Ethan Smith begins on page B1 and skips to page B3), give only the first page number followed by a plus sign.

Smith, Ethan. "How Two Bands, Running Late, Socked EMI's Bottom Line." Wall Street Journal 18 Feb. 2005: B1+.

27. Review Begin with the name of the reviewer and the title of the review article if these are available. After "Rev. of," provide the title and author of the work reviewed, followed by publication information for the review.

Thomas, Kelly Devine. "Conspiracy Theory." Rev. of The Art of the Steal: Inside the Sotheby's-Christie's Auction House Scandal, by Christopher Mason. ARTnews Summer 2004: 130.

28. Unsigned editorial or article Begin with the title. For an editorial, include the label "Editorial" after the title. In alphabetizing, ignore an initial *A, An,* or *The.*

"Four More Years." Editorial. Economist 15 Jan. 2005: 9.

"Not Quite Right." Economist 12 Feb. 2005: 27+.

29. Letter to the editor Write "Letter" or "Reply to letter of . . ." after the name of the author.

Cave, Alice. Letter. <u>Ms.</u> Fall 2004: 6.

30. Abstract in an abstracts journal Provide exact information for the original work, and add information about your source for the abstract: the title of the abstract journal, volume number, year, and item number or page number. (For dissertation abstracts, see item 18.)

Van Dyke, Jan. "Gender and Success in the American Dance World."
<u>Women's Studies International Forum</u> 19 (1996): 535–43. <u>Studies on
Women Abstracts</u> 15 (1997): item 97W/081.

31. Article on microform (microfilm and microfiche) To cite sources that are neither in hard copy nor in electronic form, provide as much print publication information as is available along with the name of the microfilm or microfiche and any identifying features. Many newspaper and magazine articles published before 1980 are available only in microfiche or microfilm, so you will need to use this medium for historical research. However, be aware that such collections may be incomplete and difficult to read and duplicate clearly.

"War with Japan." Editorial. <u>New York Times</u> 8 Dec. 1941: 22. <u>UMI
University Microfilm.</u>

44d Articles in an online library subscription database (MLA)

Libraries subscribe to large information services (such as *InfoTrac, FirstSearch, EBSCO, SilverPlatter, Dialog, SIRS,* and *LexisNexis*) to gain access to extensive databases of online articles, as well as to special-

MLA (Modern Language Association)

ized databases (such as *ERIC, Contemporary Literary Criticism,* and *PsycINFO*). You can use these databases to locate abstracts and full texts of thousands of articles.

The URLs used to access databases are useful only to those accessing them through a subscribing organization such as a college library or a public library. In addition, database URLs tend not to remain stable, changing day by day, so providing a URL at the end of your citation will not be helpful to your readers unless you know it will be persistent. Cite articles in library databases by providing the following information:

- last and first name of author(s)
- title of article, in quotation marks
- print information for the article (name of journal, underlined; date and pages, if the full range of pages is given online; or the starting page followed by a hyphen, space, and period (for example, 26- .). See items 22–29 for sample citations for print articles.
- name of the database, underlined (for example, <u>Academic Search Premier</u>)
- name of the service providing the database (for example, *Lexis-Nexis, EBSCO, InfoTrac*)
- name of library system (add city and state if necessary)
- your date of access
- the URL of the document, enclosed in angle brackets and not underlined as a hyperlink (see 43c), or if the URL is not persistent or is impossibly long, include the URL of the search page or home page—or no URL at all
- a period at the end

32. Magazine article in an online database—with a persistent URL

print publication
information
starting page of article

Gray, Katti. "The Whistle Blower." <u>Essence</u> Feb. 2001: 148- . <u>Academic</u>

database service library date of access

<u>Search Premier</u>. EBSCO. City U of New York Lib. 2 Aug. 2005

EBSCO database provides a persistent URL
<http://search.epnet.com/login.aspx?direct=true&db=aph&an=

4011390>.

The following screenshots show the information you need to include.

SOURCE SHOT 7   Listing an Article in an Online Database

URL is not persistent and is too long for a citation

Name of library system

Online service

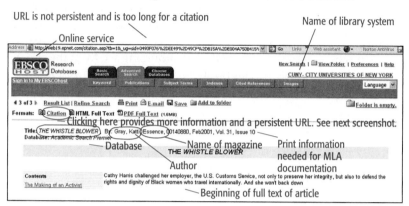

Clicking here provides more information and a persistent URL. See next screenshot.

Title

Database

Name of magazine

Print information needed for MLA documentation

Author

Beginning of full text of article

SOURCE SHOT 8   Citation Link in EBSCO

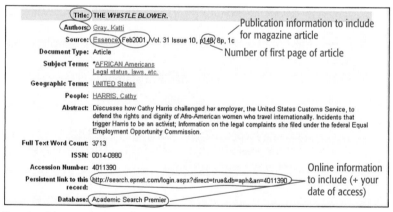

Publication information to include for magazine article

Number of first page of article

Online information to include (+ your date of access)

Reprinted by permission of EBSCO.

33. Scholarly article in an online database—with a persistent URL

Lowe, Michelle S. "Britain's Regional Shopping Centres: New Urban

volume number for print version of scholarly article

Forms?" Urban Studies 37.2 (2000): 261– . MasterFile Premier.

EBSCO. Brooklyn Public Lib., Brooklyn, NY. 20 Feb. 2005

<http://search.epnet.com/login.aspx?direct=true&db=f5h&an

=2832704>.

34. Periodical article in an online database—with no persistent URL

Bailey, Martin. "Van Gogh: The Fakes Debate." Apollo Jan. 2005: 55- .
    Expanded Academic ASAP. InfoTrac. University at Albany Lib., Albany,
    NY. 22 Feb. 2005 <http://www.galegroup.com>.

35. Newspaper article in an online database—with no persistent URL

Weeks, Linton. "History Repeating Itself; Instead of Describing Our
    Country's Past, Two Famous Scholars Find Themselves Examining
    Their Own." Washington Post 24 Mar. 2002: F01- . Academic
    Universe: News. LexisNexis. City U of New York Lib. 3 Aug. 2005
    ┌─── URL of home page ───┐
    <http://web.lexis-nexis.com>.

36. Abstract in a specialized online database—with a long URL
If the URL is impossibly long, as it is for the source below
(<http://md2.csa.com/ids70/view_record.php?id=1&recnum=0&SI
D=b3b289fbf747171aa4acaffaa97a0a6e&mark_id=cache%3A0&mark
_low=0&mark_high=10>), give the URL of the home page of the subscription service.

Kofman, Eleonora. "Gendered Global Migrations: Diversity and
    Stratification." Intl. Feminist Jour. of Politics 6 (2004): 643–65.
    Abstract. Sociological Abstracts. Illumina, CSA. City U of New York Lib.
    28 Feb. 2005 <http://md2.csa.com>.

44e Articles in an online periodical or on a Web site (MLA)

As an alternative to online library databases, you can also find articles on Web sites that you access directly via a URL or a hyperlink.
Sometimes these articles have a print equivalent (as the articles
in databases do), but often they do not. For complete Web sites,
see 44g.

37. Article in an online scholarly journal   Give the author, title of article, title of journal, volume and issue numbers, and date of issue. Include page number or the number of paragraphs only if pages or paragraphs are numbered in the source, as they are for the first example below. End with date of access and URL.

┌── author ──┐   ┌─────────────── title of article ───────────────┐
Hatchuel, Sarah. "Leading the Gaze: From Showing to Telling in Kenneth

name of volume and
online journal issue number
Branagh's Henry V and Hamlet." Early Modern Literary Studies 6.1

date of online   number of paragraphs   date of
publication   (numbered in the text)   access
(2000): 22 pars. 19 Feb. 2005 <http://www.shu.ac.uk/emls/06–1/

hatchbra.htm>.

┌── author ──┐   ┌───────────── title of article ─────────────┐   ┌
Hart, Stephen. "Overtures to a New Discipline: Neuromusicology." 21st

volume and date of
title of online journal   issue numbers   access
Century 1.4 (July 1996). 17 Feb. 2005 <http://www.columbia.edu/
└ date of ┘ └─────── no numbered pages or paragraphs
electronic publication
cu/21stC/issue-1.4/mbmmusic.html>.

38. Article in an online magazine

Landsburg, Steven E. "Save and Save and Then Save Some More." Slate 18
Feb. 2005. 21 Feb. 2005 <http://slate.msn.com/id/2113640>.

39. Article in an online newspaper

Franklin, Deborah. "Vitamin E Fails to Deliver on Early Promise." New York
Times on the Web 2 Aug. 2005. 3 Aug. 2005
<http://www.nytimes.com/2005/08/02/science/02cons.html>.

40. Authored article on a Web site   For the elements that need to be cited, see Source Shot 4, page 441.

Delisio, Ellen R. "No Child Left Behind: What It Means to You." Education
World 24 June 2002. 19 Feb. 2005 <http://www.educationworld.com/
a_issues/issues273.shtml>.

For an article with no author named, begin with the title. If you follow a specific path to reach a document, you may also give details of the path:

"Archeologists Enter King Tut's Tomb: November 26, 1922." HistoryChannel.com.
2005. History Channel. 20 Feb. 2005 <http://www.historychannel.com>.
Path: This Day in History; November 26.

41. Review, editorial, abstract, or letter in an online publication
After author and title, identify the type of text: "Letter," "Editorial,"
"Abstract," or "Rev. of . . . by . . ." (see 44c, items 27–30). Continue
with details of the electronic source.

Raimes, Ann. Rev. of Dog World: And the Humans Who Live There by
Alfred Gingold. Amazon.com. 18 Feb. 2005. 22 Feb. 2005
<http://www.amazon.com>.

44f Reference works—print and online (MLA)

Follow the guidelines below for how to list an encyclopedia, a dictionary, another reference work, or an entry in a reference work. For an
online reference work, include in your citation any date of electronic
publication or update, the sponsor, your date of access, and the URL
(as shown in items 42 and 45).

42. Unsigned entry in a well-known reference work For a well-
known print reference book, begin with the title of the entry. Give
only the edition number and the year of publication. When entries
are arranged alphabetically, omit any volume and page numbers.

"Etching." Columbia Encyclopedia. 6th ed. 2000.

For an encyclopedia online, provide details of the sponsor, your
date of access, and the URL.

```
                                            date of electronic
      ┌─ title of article ─┐   ┌──────── title of database ────────┐  ┌─ updating ─┐
"Bloomsbury Group." Columbia Encyclopedia 6th ed. 7 Nov. 2004.
                        date of
      ┌─ sponsor ─┐   ┌─ access ─┐
Bartleby.com. 20 Feb. 2005 <http://www.bartleby.com/65/bl/
Bloomsbury.html>.
```

43. Signed entry in a well-known reference work   For reference works appearing in many editions, give only the edition and the publication year.

Kahn, David. "Cryptology." Encyclopedia Americana. Internatl. ed. 2001.

44. Entry in an unfamiliar reference work   For reference works that are not widely known, give full details of any editors, number of volumes, place of publication, publisher, and date.

O'Connor, Alice. "Social Security Act." Encyclopedia of the Great Depression.
   Ed. Robert S. McElvaine. 2 vols. New York: Macmillan, 2004.

45. Entry in a dictionary—print or online   For a well-known dictionary, give just the edition and year.

"Heuristic." The American Heritage Dictionary of the English Language.
   4th ed. 2000.

To cite a specific definition, indicate the number or letter, as in "Heuristic." Def. 2. For a specialized dictionary, also provide place of publication and publisher.

   For an online dictionary, give the date of online publication and your date of access.

"Vicarious." Cambridge Advanced Learner's Dictionary. 2004. Cambridge UP.
   20 Feb. 2005 <http://dictionary.cambridge.org/
   define.asp?key=88182&dict=CALD>.

46. An entire reference database online

Project Gutenberg. Ed. Michael Hart. 6 Dec. 2004. 22 Feb. 2005
   <http://www.gutenberg.org>.

44g Web sites and Web pages (MLA)

For online government publications, many of which also appear in print form, see 44b, item 21.

Web sites often comprise many pages, each with its own URL beyond that of the home page. If you are citing a specific article or document (see items 38–41) rather than the whole site, provide the URL for the specific page.

47. Scholarly project online

title of scholarly
——— project ———   ——— editor ———   ┌ publication ┐
Perseus Digital Library. Ed. Gregory Crane. Updated daily. Dept. of
date of electronic

date of
—— sponsor ——,   ┌— access —┐
Classics, Tufts U. 1 Feb. 2005 <http://www.perseus.tufts.edu>.

48. Professional site online

date of
┌——— title of professional site ———┐ ┌— update —┐ ┌——— sponsor ———
MLA: Modern Language Association. 22 June 2005. Mod. Lang. Assn. of
date of
——┐ ┌— access —┐
Amer. 2 Aug. 2005 <http://www.mla.org>.

49. Personal Web site/home page
If a personal Web page has a title, supply it, underlined. Otherwise, use the designation "Home page."

date of
┌— update —┐
Gilpatrick, Eleanor. Home page. Feb. 2005. 21 Feb. 2005 <http://www
.gilpatrickart.com>.

50. Course page
For a course home page, give the name of the instructor and the course, the words *Course home page,* the dates of the course, the department and the institution, and then your access date and the URL.

Raimes, Ann. Expository Writing. Course home page. Aug. 2004–Dec. 2004.
Dept. of English, Hunter Coll. 18 Dec. 2004 <http://bb.hunter.cuny.edu>.

44h E-mail: Personal and public (MLA)

51. Personal e-mail message, 462

52. Online posting on a discussion list, blog, or Usenet, 462

51. Personal e-mail message   Provide the subject line heading.

Kane, George. "Visual Rhetoric." E-mail to the author. 17 Mar. 2005.

52. Online posting on a discussion list, blog, or Usenet   Give the author's name, the document title (as written in the subject line), the label "Online posting," and the date of posting. Follow this with the name of the forum in the discussion list or the title of the Web log (blog), date of access, and URL or address of the list.

Tubbs, Brian. "Washington and Lincoln—Both Great Men." Online posting.
┌─── name of forum ───┐
  21 Feb. 2005. American Revolution. 21 Feb. 2005

  <http://boards.historychannel.com/forum.jspa?forumID=90>.

Brattina, Tiffany. "The *Life* of a Salesman." Online posting. 16 Mar. 2004.
    title of
  ┌── blog ──┐
  Luna Dreams. 22 Feb. 2005 <http://blogs.setonhill.edu/TiffanyBrattina/

  002755.html>.

For a Usenet newsgroup, give the name and address of the group, beginning with the prefix *news:*

Zimmer, Ben. "Eggcorn Database." Online posting. 19 Feb. 2005. 21
    Feb. 2005 <news:alt.usage.english>.

To make it easy for readers to find a posting, refer whenever possible to one stored in Web archives.

Schwalm, David. "Re: Value of an Education." Online posting. 15 Feb. 2005.
    name of
  ┌── archive ──┐
  WPA-L Archives. 21 Feb. 2005 <http://lists.asu.edu/archives.wpa-L.html>.

To cite a forwarded document in an online posting, include author, title, and date, followed by "Fwd. by" and the name of the person forwarding the document. End with "Online posting," the date of the forwarding, the name of the discussion group, date of access, and address of the discussion list.

Gold, Tami. "Update on PSC-CUNY Contract." 16 Feb. 2005. Fwd. by Ken
    Sherrill. Online posting. 17 Feb. 2005. Hunter-L. 20 Feb. 2005
    <http://hunter.listserv.cuny.edu>.

44i Performance, multimedia, visual works, and works of art—live, print, and online (MLA)

53. Film or video, 463	57. Work of art, slide, or
54. Television or radio	photograph, 464
program, 463	58. Cartoon, 464
55. Sound recording, 463	59. Advertisement, 464
56. Live performance, 464	60. Map or chart, 465

Identify online performance, multimedia, and visual sources as you would sources that are not online, with the addition of electronic publishing information (site name and date) as well as your date of access and the URL. Items 53, 54, 57, and 60 include citations of online works.

53. Film or video List the title, director, performers, and any other pertinent information. End with the name of the distributor and the year of distribution.

Million Dollar Baby. Dir. Clint Eastwood. Perf. Hilary Swank. Warner, 2004.

Office Ninja. Dir. Matthew Johnston. iFilm, 2004. 19 Feb. 2005
    <http://www.ifilm.com/ifilmdetail/2659387>.

When you cite a videocassette or DVD, include the date of the original film, the medium, the name of the distributor of the DVD or cassette, and the year of the new release.

Casablanca. Dir. Michael Curtiz. Perf. Humphrey Bogart and Ingrid Bergman.
    1943. DVD. MGM, 1998.

54. Television or radio program Give the title of the program episode; the title of the program; any pertinent information about performers, writer, narrator, or director; the network; and the local station and date of broadcast.

"Seeds of Destruction." Slavery and the Making of America. Narr. Morgan
    Freeman. Thirteen, WNET. WLIW, New York. 22 Feb. 2005.

"My Big Break." This American Life. Narr. Ira Glass. WBEZ, Chicago. 21 Jan.
    2005. 22 Feb. 2005 <http://www.thislife.org>.

55. Sound recording List the composer or author, the title of the work, the names of artists, the production company, and the date. If the medium is not a compact disc, indicate the medium, such as "Audiocassette," before the name of the production company.

Scarlatti, Domenico. Keyboard Sonatas. Andras Schiff, piano. London, 1989.

Walker, Alice. Interview with Kay Bonetti. Audiocassette. Columbia: American Audio Prose Library, 1981.

56. Live performance   Give the title of the play, the author, pertinent information about the director or performers, the theater, the location, and the date of performance. If you are citing an individual's role in the work, begin your citation with the person's name.

Democracy. By Michael Frayn. Dir. Michael Blakemore. Brooks Atkinson Theatre, New York. 18 Jan. 2005.

Blakemore, Michael, dir. Democracy. By Michael Frayn. Brooks Atkinson Theatre, New York. 18 Jan. 2005.

57. Work of art, slide, or photograph   List the name of the artist, the title of the work (underlined), the name of the museum, gallery, site, or owner, and the location. You can also include the date the work was created.

Johns, Jasper. Racing Thoughts. Whitney Museum of Amer. Art, New York.

Christo. The Gates. Central Park, New York. Feb. 2005.

Duchamp, Marcel. Bicycle Wheel. 1951. Museum of Mod. Art, New York. 22 Feb. 2005 <http://www.moma.org/collection/depts/paint_sculpt/ blowups/paint_sculpt_020.html>.

For a photograph in a book, give complete publication information, including the page number on which the photograph appears.

Johns, Jasper. Racing Thoughts. Whitney Museum of Amer. Art, New York. The American Century: Art and Culture 1950–2000. By Lisa Phillips. New York: Norton, 1999. 311.

For a slide in a collection, include the slide number (Slide 17).

58. Cartoon   After the cartoonist's name and the title (if any) of the cartoon, add the label "Cartoon." Follow this with the usual information about the source, and give the page number for a print source.

Shanahan, Danny. "The Lawyer Fairy." Cartoon. New Yorker 7 Feb. 2005: 49.

59. Advertisement   Give the name of the product or company, followed by the label "Advertisement" and publication information. If a page is not numbered, write "n. pag."

Xerox. Advertisement. Fortune 7 Feb. 2005: 1.

60. Map or chart Underline the title of the map or chart, and include the designation after the title.

Auvergne/Limousin. Map. Paris: Michelin, 1996.

Pearl Harbor. Multimedia attack map. Nationalgeographic.com. 19 Feb. 2005
    <http://plasma.nationalgeographic.com/pearlharbor>.

44j Miscellaneous works—live, print, and online (MLA)

61. Personal interview Include the type of interview (telephone, e-mail, personal, etc.).

Gingold, Toby. Telephone interview. 4 Mar. 2005.

62. Published interview Give the name of the person interviewed, followed by the word "Interview" or "Interview with . . .". Include information about the print publication.

Parker, Dorothy. Interview with Marion Capron. Writers at Work: The Paris
    Review Interviews. London: Secker and Warburg, 1958. 66–75.

63. Broadcast interview Provide information about the broadcast source.

Gladwell, Malcolm. Interview with Leonard Lopate. The Leonard Lopate
    Show: Think without Thinking. WNYC, New York. 18 Feb. 2005.

64. Online interview

Gladwell, Malcolm. Interview with Leonard Lopate. The Leonard Lopate
    Show: Think without Thinking. WNYC, New York. 18 Feb. 2005
    <http://www.wnyc.org/shows/lopate/episodes/0218005>.

For a sound recording of an interview, see item 55.

65. Lecture or speech Give the author and title, if known. For a presentation with no title, include a label such as "Lecture" or "Address" after the name of the speaker. Also give the name of any organizing sponsor, the venue, and the date.

Parry, Kate. Lecture. Hunter College, New York. 16 Apr. 2005.

66. Letter: personal or published For a letter that you received, include the phrase "Letter to the author" after the name of the letter writer. Describe the type of any other personal communication ("Telephone call," for example).

Rogan, Helen. Letter to the author. 3 Feb. 2005.

Cite a published letter as you would cite a work in an anthology. After the name of the author, include any title the editor gives the letter and the date. Add the page numbers for the letter at the end of the citation.

Bishop, Elizabeth. "To Robert Lowell." 26 Nov. 1951. One Art: Letters.
    Ed. Robert Giroux. New York: Farrar, 1994. 224–26.

67. Legal or historical source For a legal case, give the name of the case with no underlining or quotation marks, the number of the case, the name of the court deciding the case, and the date of the decision.

Roe v. Wade. No. 70–18. Supreme Ct. of the US. 22 Jan. 1973.

If you mention the case in your text, underline it.

Chief Justice Burger, in Roe v. Wade, noted that . . .

Give the Public Law number of an act, its date, and the cataloging number for its Statutes at Large.

USA Patriot Act. Pub. L. 107–56. 26 Oct. 2001. Stat. 115.272.

Well-known historical documents should not be included in your works-cited list (see 42c, item U).

68. CD-ROM Cite material from a CD-ROM published as a single edition in the same way you cite a book, but after the title add the medium of publication and any version or release number.

Keats, John. "To Autumn." Columbia Granger's World of Poetry. CD-ROM.
    Rel. 3. New York: Columbia UP, 1999.

45   Sample Documented Paper, MLA Style

Here is Lindsay Camp's documented paper written in her required first-year composition course. She chose the topic because she was planning to become a police officer. If your instructor requires a separate title page, see 9c or ask for guidelines.

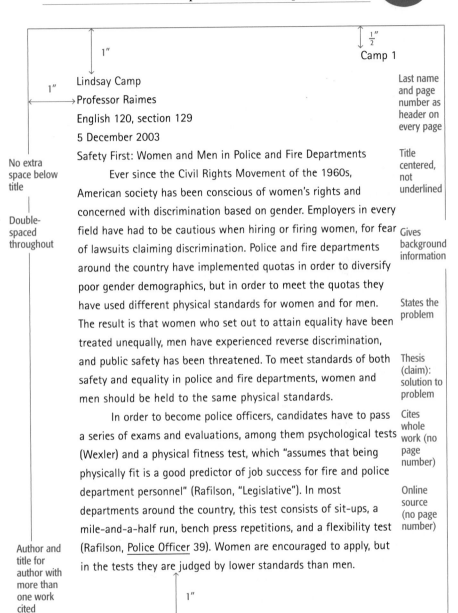

Camp 1

Lindsay Camp

Professor Raimes

English 120, section 129

5 December 2003

Safety First: Women and Men in Police and Fire Departments

    Ever since the Civil Rights Movement of the 1960s, American society has been conscious of women's rights and concerned with discrimination based on gender. Employers in every field have had to be cautious when hiring or firing women, for fear of lawsuits claiming discrimination. Police and fire departments around the country have implemented quotas in order to diversify poor gender demographics, but in order to meet the quotas they have used different physical standards for women and for men. The result is that women who set out to attain equality have been treated unequally, men have experienced reverse discrimination, and public safety has been threatened. To meet standards of both safety and equality in police and fire departments, women and men should be held to the same physical standards.

    In order to become police officers, candidates have to pass a series of exams and evaluations, among them psychological tests (Wexler) and a physical fitness test, which "assumes that being physically fit is a good predictor of job success for fire and police department personnel" (Rafilson, "Legislative"). In most departments around the country, this test consists of sit-ups, a mile-and-a-half run, bench press repetitions, and a flexibility test (Rafilson, <u>Police Officer</u> 39). Women are encouraged to apply, but in the tests they are judged by lower standards than men.

Annotations in margins:

1″

1″

½

1″

No extra space below title

Double-spaced throughout

Title centered, not underlined

Gives background information

States the problem

Thesis (claim): solution to problem

Cites whole work (no page number)

Online source (no page number)

Author and title for author with more than one work cited

1″

Camp 2

Table 1

Minimum Fitness Standards for Entry to the Academy

Female Candidates

Age Group	20–29	30–39
Sit-ups (1 minute)	35	27
Sit & Reach (inches)	20	19
Push-ups	18	14
1.5-Mile Run (minutes)	14:55	15:26

Male Candidates

Age Group	20–29	30–39
Sit-ups (1 minute)	40	36
Sit & Reach (inches)	17.5	16.5
Push-ups	33	27
1.5-Mile Run (minutes)	12:18	12:51

Source: Rafilson, Police Officer 47.

Comments on table and explains data

Table 1 shows that women are given from 2 minutes and 37 seconds to 3 minutes and 15 seconds extra to run a mile-and-a-half. That could mean the difference between catching a suspect and not catching a suspect. Men have to complete 13 to 15 more push-ups than women because women generally do not have the same amount of upper body strength as men. But police officers may need to climb fences, lift heavy items, or carry injured people; certainly firefighters may need to carry injured people and heavy hoses.

Recognizing that the physical fitness tests are flawed, police and fire departments have been turning to a different test, called a physical agility exam, in which the candidate must complete an

Camp 3

obstacle course. For the New York Police Department's agility exam, candidates are required to wear a 10.5 lb utility belt as they run out of a patrol car, climb a six-foot wall, run up four flights of stairs, drag a 160 lb dummy 30 feet, run back down four flights of stairs, climb a four-foot wall, and run back to the patrol car (Rafilson, Police Officer 40–42). Such tasks are seen as relevant to what a police officer actually encounters while on duty. All candidates must complete every part of the obstacle course in the same amount of time in order to pass the exam, regardless of sex, age, or weight. The obstacles in the course and the time allotted may vary between departments, but there is no partiality given based on ethnicity, gender, or age. Women may need to be provided with preparation and training for the test, as an article in The Police Chief points out (Polisar and Milgram), but they should still be required to take and pass it.

Gives page numbers for print source

Online source

More and more police and fire departments are now using the physical agility test instead of the fitness test. According to Dr. Fred M. Rafilson, the fitness model was popular because it "allows fire departments to hire more women because passing standards are adjusted based on a person's age, sex, and weight," but, as he says, a "woman can pass a fitness model test for the fire service and still not be able to perform essential job functions that require a great deal of upper body and leg strength" ("Legislative"). Some programs have been established to help prepare women for the new tests. The program at the University of Victoria in British Columbia, Canada, culminates in having women carry "65-pound pumps and heavy fire hoses across the infield of the warm-up track" (Liscomb). Figure 1 shows a participant in action.

Gives author's credentials

Many see upper body strength as crucial. Firefighters are very much like a family, trust each other like brothers, and in a fire emergency may have to make life and death decisions. They need to know that the person next to them can handle all of the duties

MLA (Modern Language Association)

Camp 4

This visual contributes to the argument

Fig. 1. From Robie Liscomb, "Preparing Women for Firefighting in B.C."

of the job. Thomas P. Butler, a spokesman for the Uniformed Firefighters Association, the firefighters' union, points out that "this is a job where one firefighter's life and safety depends on another. It is important that we attract the best and the brightest" (qtd. in Baker). Any person who cannot perform the tasks of a firefighter poses "a direct threat to human life and safety" (Rafilson, "Legislative") and does not belong on the job.

Work is one page long--no page number necessary in citation

Frances Heidensohn's thorough study of women in law enforcement in the U.S.A. and in Britain does, however, point out that many women have "questioned the relevance and purpose of the physical standards as . . . irrelevant to policing" (170). Women in the police force testified that while they had been tested on doing a "body drag," they never had seen it done or had to do this on the job. And, of course, we all can recognize that having different (and lower) standards for women does allow more women

Considers opposing views

Establishes common ground ("we all")

Camp 5

to be hired as career officers and helps departments with affirmative action requirements.

Those on the job, however, still question the wisdom of different testing criteria. Douglass Mignone, a first lieutenant of the Purchase Fire Department and a New York City Fire Department applicant, for example, sees the situation as one of safety rather than equality of opportunity. When asked in a telephone interview for his view on women in the Fire Department, he replied:

> If you were in a burning building and had the choice
> between my girlfriend Sinead, a five-foot-five, 130 lb
> woman, or myself, a six-foot-two, 200 lb man, to get you
> out alive, who would you choose? I have no problem with
> women being firefighters as long as they meet the same
> requirements and undergo the same training as myself.

This view is the consensus among male police officers and male firefighters, but not that of the general public. The general idea of safety seems to be slipping past the newspapers and television. There are no activists standing outside City Hall crying, "What about our safety?" "Make physical requirements equal" (Rafilson, "Legislative"). There will be no activists, no protests, and no media until someone dies or until there is a tragedy.

Added to the issue of safety is the issue of equality. In 1964, Congress prohibited discrimination based on race, color, sex, national origin, or religion under the Civil Rights Act of 1964 (Brooks 26). In 1991, Congress passed the 1991 Civil Rights Act, which made it illegal to use different standards for hiring men and women. The 1991 Civil Rights Act says it like this:

> It shall be an unlawful employment practice for a
> respondent in connection with the selection or referral
> of applicants to adjust the scores of, use different

Uses evidence from interview to refute the opposing views

Indents a long quotation

Broadens the picture to legislation

Camp 6

cut-off scores for, or otherwise alter the results of
employment related tests on the basis of race, color,
religion, sex, or national origin. (qtd. in Rafilson,
"Legislative")

Cites work in which quotation appears

Title VII under this Act claims the employer accused of "disparate
impact" would have to prove business necessity. This has left police
and fire departments all over the country confused and asking
themselves what to do and whom to hire next. Are police and fire
departments going to claim that the physiological differences
between men and women make different physical standards a
business necessity? According to Special Agent Michael E. Brooks:

Question draws readers into issue.

> The challenge comes when a male cannot meet the male
> standard but can meet the female standard. Such an
> action amounts to express disparate treatment of the
> male. Disparate treatment, like disparate impact, is only
> permissible under the business necessity justification. The
> administrator who uses different physical selection
> standards for female applicants would, therefore, have to
> show what business necessity justifies such a practice. (31)

Controversy and confusion abound, and male applicants are
filing lawsuits claiming reverse discrimination. The Edmonton Fire
Department has a "diversity" policy in which the 12 positions that
were available did not go to the top 12 applicants but to women
and minorities (Champion). Two groups of rejected applicants filed
complaints with the Alberta Human Rights Commission claiming
that "the City of Edmonton exercised race and gender bias in
denying them employment" (Champion).

Summation

The process of applying to be hired in a police or fire
department must be clear to all and equitable to all. Only those
with the highest scores on the written exam should be eligible to
take the physical agility test. Then only the candidates who pass

Camp 7

the physical should qualify for further testing and employment. Men who fail any of the tests should not be hired--nor should women. If police and fire departments lower standards for anyone, they are putting the general public's safety on the line as well as their fellow officers'. Peter Horne, an assistant professor at Meramec Community College, says it succinctly: "Females and males should take the same physical agility test. Then it would not matter whether a recruit is 5'8" or 5'4", or a male or female, but only whether he/she possesses the physical capability to do the job" (33-34). The cost to safety is much too great for women to be held to lower requirements than men.

Reiteration of thesis

List includes only sources actually cited in the paper.

Camp 8

Entries organized alphabetically

Article from a subscription database with URL of home page

Database gives first page number only

Second entry for author

Title centered, not underlined

Article spans consecutive pages

EBSCO provides persistent URL

Published work on Web site

Works Cited

Baker, Al. "Fire Department Looks to Diversify the Ranks." New York Times 3 Apr. 2002: B3. Academic Universe: News. LexisNexis. City U of New York Lib. 25 Oct. 2003 <http://web.lexis-nexis.com>.

Brooks, Michael E. "Law Enforcement Physical Fitness Standard and Title VII." FBI Law Enforcement Bulletin May 2001: 26–33.

Champion, Chris. "Male Honkies Need Not Apply." Western Report 7 Aug. 1996: 24- . Academic Search Premier. EBSCO. City U of New York Lib. 27 Oct. 2003 <http://search.epnet.com/direct.asp?an=9607267865&db=aph>.

Heidensohn, Frances. Women in Control? The Role of Women in Law Enforcement. New York: Oxford UP, 1992.

Horne, Peter. Women in Law Enforcement. 2nd ed. Springfield: ←$\frac{1''}{2}$→Thomas, 1980.

Liscomb, Robie. "Preparing Women for Firefighting in B.C." The Ring 6 Feb. 1998. University of Victoria Sport and Fitness Centre. 28 Oct. 2003 <http://communications.uvic.ca/ring/98feb06/firefighting.html>.

Mignone, Douglass. Telephone interview. 19 Oct. 2003.

Polisar, Joseph, and Donna Milgram. "Recruiting, Integrating and Retaining Women Police Officers: Strategies That Work." The Police Chief Oct. 1998. IWITTS in the News. Institute for Women in Trades, Technology, and Science. 27 Oct. 2003 <http://www.iwitts.com/html/the_police_chief.htm>.

Rafilson, Fred M. "Legislative Impact on Fire Service Physical Fitness Testing." Fire Engineering Apr. 1995: 83- . Academic Search Premier. EBSCO. City U of New York Lib. 23 Oct. 2003 <http://search.epnet.com/direct.asp?an=9505024136&db=aph>.

- - -. Police Officer. 15th ed. United States: Arco, 2000.

Wexler, Ann Kathryn. Gender and Ethnicity as Predictors of Psychological Qualification for Police Officer Candidates. Diss. California School of Professional Psychology, 1996. Ann Arbor: UMI, 1996. 9625522.

Chapters 46 through 48 give details about the documentation style recommended for the social sciences by the *Publication Manual of the American Psychological Association,* 5th ed. (Washington, DC: Amer. Psychological Assn., 2001), and on the Web site for the *APA Publication Manual* (<http://www.apastyle.org>).

46 Citing Sources in Your Text

46a Two basic APA style features

KEY POINTS
Two Basic Features of APA Style

1. *In the text of your paper,* include the following information each time you cite a source: the last name(s) of the author (or authors) and the year of publication. See 46b.

(continued)

(continued)

2. *At the end of the paper,* include on a new numbered page a list entitled "References," double-spaced and arranged alphabetically by authors' last names, followed by initials of other names, the date in parentheses, and other bibliographical information. See 47c–47g for sample entries.

46b Sample author/date in-text citations (APA)

AT A GLANCE: INDEX OF APA IN-TEXT CITATIONS

CITING AN AUTHORED WORK

A. Author mentioned in your text, 476
B. Author cited in parentheses, 477
C. Author quoted or paraphrased, 477
D. Work with more than one author, 477
E. Author of work in an edited anthology, 478
F. Author's work cited in another source, 478
G. More than one work in one citation, 478
H. Author with more than one work published in one year, 478
I. Two authors with the same last name, 478

CITING A WORK WITH NO INDIVIDUAL AUTHOR

J. Corporation, government agency, or organization as author, 478
K. No author named, 479

CITING SPECIAL TYPES OF SOURCES

L. Online source, 479
M. Multivolume work, 479
N. Multimedia or nonprint source, 479
O. Personal communication or interview, 480
P. Classical work, 480

CITING AN AUTHORED WORK (APA)

A. Author mentioned in your text Give the author's last name when you introduce the citation. Include the year in parentheses directly after the author's name. Generally, use the past or the present perfect tense for your citation.

author   year
Wilson (1994) has described in detail his fascination with insects.

(See 47c, item 1, for this work in a list of references.)

B. Author cited in parentheses If you do not mention the name of the author to introduce the citation, include both the name and the year, separated by a comma, in parentheses.

> The army retreated from Boston in disarray, making the rebels realize that they had achieved a great victory (McCullough, 2001).
>   author comma year

C. Author quoted or paraphrased If you include a direct quotation, include in the parentheses the abbreviation "p." or "pp." followed by a space and the page number. All items within parentheses are separated by commas.

> Memories are "built around a small collection of dominating images" (Wilson, 1994, p. 5).

A long quotation (more than forty words) should be indented one-half inch, with no quotation marks (but double-spaced). Put the period *before* the parenthetical citation.

You can also provide page numbers with a paraphrase or summary to help readers locate information easily.

D. A work with more than one author For a work by two authors, name both in the order in which their names appear on the work. Within parentheses use an ampersand (&) in place of *and*.

> Kanazawa and Still (2000) in their analysis of a large set of data showed that the statistical likelihood of being divorced increased if one was male and a secondary school teacher or college professor.

> Analysis of a large set of data showed that the statistical likelihood of being divorced increased if one was male and a secondary school teacher or college professor (Kanazawa & Still, 2000).
>   ampersand in parentheses

(See 47c, item 13, for this work in a list of references.)

For a work with three to five authors or editors, identify all of them the first time you mention the work.

> Jordan, Kaplan, Miller, Stiver, and Surrey (1991) have examined the idea of *self*.

In later references, use the name of the first author followed by "et al." (for "and others") in place of the other names.

> Increasingly, the self is viewed as connected to other human beings (Jordan et al., 1991).

(See 47c, item 2, for this work in a list of references.)

If there are six or more authors, always use "et al." after the name of the first author.

E. Author of work in an edited anthology In your text, refer to the author of the work itself, not to the editor of the anthology, though you will include information about the anthology in your list of references (47c, item 4).

Seegmiller (1993) has provided an incisive analysis of the relationship between pregnancy and culture.

F. Author's work cited in another source Give the author or title of the work in which you find the reference, preceded by "as cited in" to indicate that you are referring to a citation in that work. List that secondary source in your list of references. In the following example, *Smith* will appear in the list, but *Britton* will not.

The words we use simply appear, as Britton says, "at the point of utterance" (as cited in Smith, 1982, p. 108).

G. More than one work in one citation List the sources in alphabetical order, separated by semicolons.

Criticisms of large-scale educational testing abound (Crouse & Trusheim, 1988; Nairn, 1978, 1980; Sacks, 2003).

H. Author with more than one work published in one year Identify each work with a lowercase letter after the year: (Zamel, 1997a, 1997b). Separate the dates with a comma. In the reference list, repeat the author's name in each entry, and alphabetize by the title: Zamel, V. (1997a).

I. Two authors with the same last name Use the authors' initials as well, even if the dates of publication differ.

F. Smith (1982) described a writer as playing the competitive roles of author and secretary.

CITING A WORK WITH NO INDIVIDUAL AUTHOR (APA)

J. Corporation, government agency, or organization as author In the initial citation, use the full name of the organization; in subsequent references, you may use an abbreviation if one exists.

first mention: full name

A survey by the College Board (CB, 2004) shows that in 2004–5, tuition increased 8.7% at two-year colleges and 10.5% at four-year colleges. Further tuition increases are predicted (CB, 2004).

See 47c, item 6, for this work in a list of references.

K. No author named   In your text, use the complete title if it is short, with capital letters for major words. Within parentheses, you can shorten the title. For Web sources, search the site carefully for an author's name (39f).

According to *Weather* (1999), one way to estimate the Fahrenheit temperature is to count the number of times a cricket chirps in 14 seconds and add 40.

Increasing evidence has shown that glucosamine relieves the symptoms of arthritis (*The PDR Family Guide*, 1999).

(See 47c, item 5, for a reference list entry using the complete title.)

CITING SPECIAL TYPES OF SOURCES (APA)

L. Online source   Give author, if available, or title, followed by the year of electronic publication or update. Use "n.d." if no date is given. In order to locate a section of text you quote, paraphrase, or comment on in a source with no page or paragraph numbers visible on the screen, give the section heading, and indicate the paragraph within the section: (Conclusion section, para. 2). (To cite an entire Web site, give the URL in your paper, not in the list of references.)

M. A multivolume work   In your citation, give the publication date of the volume you are citing: (Barr & Feigenbaum, 1982). If you refer to more than one volume, give inclusive dates for all volumes you cite: (Barr & Feigenbaum, 1981–1986).

See 47c, item 8, for this work in a list of references.

N. Multimedia or nonprint source   For a film, television or radio broadcast, recording, live performance, or other nonprint source, include in your citation the name of the originator or main contributor (such as the writer, interviewer, director, performer, or producer), along with the year of production: (Berman & Pulcini, 2003). See 47a, item 31, for this work in a list of references. For online multimedia sources, add your retrieval date and the URL.

O. Personal communication (letter, conversation, e-mail) or interview
Give the last name and initial(s) of the author of the communication
and an exact date. Do not include a citation in your list of references.

> According to Dr. C. S. Apstein, Boston University School of Medicine,
> research in heart disease is critical to the well-being of society today
> (personal communication, January 7, 2005).

P. A classical work If the date of publication of a classical work is not
known, use in your citation "n.d." for "no date." If you use a translation,
give the year of the translation, preceded by "trans." You do not need a
reference list entry for the Bible or ancient classical works. Just give
information about text version, book, and line numbers in your text.

46c Notes, tables, and figures (APA)

Notes In APA style, you can use content notes to amplify information in your text. Number notes consecutively with superscript
numerals. After the list of references, attach a separate page containing your numbered notes and headed "Footnotes." Use notes sparingly; include all important information in your text, not in footnotes.

Tables Place all tables at the end of your paper, after the references
and any notes. Number each table and provide an italicized caption.

Figures After the references and any notes or tables, provide a separate page listing the figure captions, and place this page before the
figures (see pages 497–498 for an example).

47 Entries in the APA List of References

How to find what you need

- On the At a Glance Directory, find the type of source you have
  used and where you viewed it.
- Follow the line across to the last column.
- Turn to the section and page to find sample entries.

For instance, if you read an article in a full-text database that
your library subscribes to, you will know to go to 47e, and there

AT A GLANCE: DIRECTORY OF APA SAMPLE ENTRIES

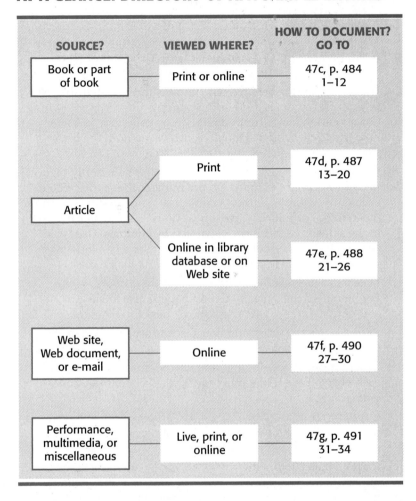

SOURCE?	VIEWED WHERE?	HOW TO DOCUMENT? GO TO
Book or part of book	Print or online	47c, p. 484 1–12
Article	Print	47d, p. 487 13–20
	Online in library database or on Web site	47e, p. 488 21–26
Web site, Web document, or e-mail	Online	47f, p. 490 27–30
Performance, multimedia, or miscellaneous	Live, print, or online	47g, p. 491 31–34

on page 488 you will find a menu followed by explanations and examples of several types of listings.

47a List format and organization (APA)

The APA *Publication Manual* and Web site provide guidelines for submitting professional papers for publication, and many instructors ask students to follow those guidelines to prepare them for advanced work. This section follows APA guidelines. Check with your instructor, however, as to any specific course requirements for the reference list.

> 🔑 **KEY POINTS**
>
> **Setting Up the APA List for Print and Online Sources**
>
> - **What to list** List only the works you cited (quoted, summarized, paraphrased, or commented on) in the text of your paper, not every source you examined.
> - **Format** Start the list on a new numbered page after the last page of text or notes. Center the heading "References," without quotation marks, not underlined or italicized, and with no period following it. Double-space throughout the list. Place any tables and charts after the "References" list.
> - **Conventions of the list** List the works alphabetically by last names of primary authors. Do not number the entries. Begin each entry with the author's name, last name first, followed by an initial or initials. Give any authors' names after the first in the same inverted form, separated by commas. Use "et al." only to indicate authors beyond the first six. List works with no author by title, alphabetized by the first main word.
> - **Date** Put the year in parentheses after the authors' names. For journals, magazines, and newspapers, also include month and day, but do not abbreviate the names of the months.
> - **Periods** Use a period and one space to separate the main parts of each entry.
> - **Indentation** Use hanging indents. (Begin the first line of each entry at the left margin; indent subsequent lines one-half inch.)
> - **Capitals** In titles of books, reports, articles, and Web documents, capitalize only the first word of the title or subtitle and any proper nouns or adjectives.
> - **Italics** Italicize the titles of books, but do not italicize or use quotation marks around the titles of articles. Italicize the names of newspapers, reports, and Web documents. For magazines and journals, italicize the publication name, the volume number, and the comma.
> - **Page numbers** Give inclusive page numbers for print articles, online PDF articles, and sections of books, using complete page spans ("251–259"). Use the abbreviation "p." or "pp." only for newspaper articles and sections of books (such as chapters or anthologized articles). Use document sections in place of page numbers for online HTML articles.
> - **Online sources** Include whatever is available of the following: author(s), date of work, title of work, any print publica-

tion information, and identification of the type of source in square brackets (for example, "[letter to the editor]"). For an online library subscription service, end with the name of the service and the document number (as in items 21 and 22). For an online site, always include retrieval information of the date of access and the URL of the actual document, not simply the home page (as in items 23–26). Do *not* put a period after the URL at the end of your entry. Provide page numbers only for documents accessed as PDF files.

47b Guidelines for listing authors (APA)

Name of author(s)   Put the last name first, followed by a comma and then the initials.

Gould, S. J.

Reverse the names of all authors listed, except the editors of an anthology or a reference work (47c, item 4). If there are six or more authors, use "et al." after the name of the first author.

Alphabetical order   Alphabetize letter by letter. Treat Mac and Mc literally, by letter.

MacKay, M.   D'Agostino, S.
McCarthy, T.   De Cesare, P.
McKay, K.   DeCurtis, A.

A shorter name precedes a longer name beginning with the same letters, whatever the first initial: *Black, T.* precedes *Blackman, R.*

For a work with no known author, list by the first word in the title other than *A, An,* or *The.*

Alphabetize numerals according to their spelling: 5 ("five") will precede 2 ("two").

Individual author(s) not known   If the author is a group, such as a corporation, agency, or institution, give its name, alphabetized by the first important word (47c, item 6). Use full names, not abbreviations. If no author or group is named, alphabetize by the first main word of the title (47c, item 5).

Several works by the same author   List the author's name in each entry. Arrange entries chronologically from past to present. Entries published in the same year should be arranged alphabetically by title and distinguished with lowercase letters after the date (*a, b,* and so on). Note that entries for one author precede entries by that author but written with coauthors.

Goleman, D. (1996a, July 16). Forget money; nothing can buy happiness, some researchers say. *The New York Times*, p. C1.

Goleman, D. (1996b). *Vital lies, simple truths*. New York: Simon & Schuster.

Goleman, D. (2000). *Working with emotional intelligence*. New York: Bantam.

Goleman, D., Kaufman, P., & Ray, M. L. (1992, March-April). The art of creativity. *Psychology Today, 25*, 40–47.

Authors with the same last name   List alphabetically by first initial: Smith, *A.* precedes Smith, *F.*

47c   Books and parts of books—print and online (APA)

On the title page and the copyright page of a print book, you will find the information you need for an entry.

- For the place of publication, give the state (abbreviated) as well as the city (but omit the state when a major city is cited or when the state is included in the name of a university press publisher, as in *University of Illinois Press*).
- Give the publisher's name in a short but intelligible form, spelling out *University* and *Press* but omitting *Co.* and *Inc.*
- Use the most recent copyright date.

For an online book, add to the print publication information your retrieval date and the URL.

1. Print or online book (one author)   Give the author's last name first, followed by the initials.

```
                          periods
        last name  initials / year in parentheses
            \ comma /    / period   title and period italicized
        Wilson, E. O. (1994). Naturalist. Washington: Island Press.
                            place of publication  colon  publisher  final period
```

Darwin, C. (1859). *The voyage of the* Beagle. London: John Murray. Retrieved
February 8, 2005, from http://ota.ahds.ac.uk
⟍ no period at end of URL

2. Book with two or more authors   Reverse the order of all the
names: last name first, followed by initials. Separate all names by
commas, and use an ampersand (&) before the last name. Use "et al."
only if there are six or more authors.

Jordan, J. V., Kaplan, A. G., Miller, J. B., Stiver, I. P., & Surrey, J. L. (1991).
Women's growth in connection: Writings from the Stone Center. New
York: Guilford Press.

3. Edited book   Use "Ed." or "Eds." for one or more editors.

Denmark, F., & Paludi, M. (Eds.). (1993). *Psychology of women: A handbook of
issues and theories.* Westport, CT: Greenwood Press.

4. Work in an anthology or reference book   List the author, the date
of publication of the edited book, and the title of the work first.
Follow this with the names of the editors of the book (not inverted),
the title of the book, and the page numbers (preceded by "pp.") of the
chapter in parentheses. End with the place of publication and the
publisher. If you cite more than one article in an edited work, include
full bibliographical details in each entry.

Seegmiller, B. (1993). Pregnancy. In F. Denmark & M. Paludi (Eds.),
Psychology of women: A handbook of issues and theories (pp. 437–474).
Westport, CT: Greenwood Press.

For a well-known reference book with unsigned alphabetical entries,
begin with the title of the entry, and include the page number(s).

Antarctica. (2000). In *The Columbia Encyclopedia* (6th ed., pp. 116–118). New
York: Columbia University Press.

5. Book with no author named   Put the title first. Ignore *A, An,* and
The when alphabetizing.

The PDR family guide to natural medicines and healing therapies. (1999).
New York: Three Rivers-Random House.

6. Book by a corporation or government organization Give the name of the corporate author first. If the publisher is the same as the author, write "Author" for the name of the publisher.

College Entrance Examination Board. (2004). *Trends in college pricing: Annual survey of colleges.* New York: Author.

If no author is named for a government publication, begin with the name of the federal, state, or local government, followed by the agency.

United States. Department of Labor. (2004). *Occupational outlook handbook 2004–2005.* Indianapolis: JIST.

7. Translation In parentheses, give the initials and last name of the translator, followed by a comma and "Trans."

Jung, C. G. (1960). *On the nature of the psyche* (R. F. C. Hull, Trans.). Princeton, NJ: Princeton University Press.

8. Multivolume work Give the number of volumes after the title. The date should include the range of years of publication, if appropriate.

Barr, A., & Feigenbaum, E. A. (1981–1986). *The handbook of artificial intelligence* (Vols. 1–4). Reading, MA: Addison-Wesley.

9. Foreword, preface, introduction, or afterword List the name of the author of the book element cited. Follow the date with the name of the element, the title of the book, and the page number(s) for the element, preceded by "p." or "pp."

Weiss, B. (Ed.). (1982). Introduction. *American education and the European immigrant 1840–1940* (pp. xi–xxviii). Urbana: University of Illinois Press.

10. Republished book After the author's name, give the most recent date of publication. At the end, in parentheses add "Original work published" and the date. In your text citation, give both dates: (Smith, 1776/1976).

Smith, A. (1976). *An inquiry into the nature and causes of the wealth of nations.* Chicago: University of Chicago Press. (Original work published 1776)

11. Technical report Give the report number ("Rep. No.") after the title.

Morgan, R., & Maneckshana, B. (2000). *AP students in college: An investigation of their course-taking patterns and college majors* (Rep. No. SR-2000-09). Princeton, NJ: Educational Testing Service.

12. Dissertation or abstract   For a manuscript source, give the university and year of the dissertation and the volume and page numbers of *DAI*.

Salzberg, A. (1992). Behavioral phenomena of homeless women in San Diego
County (Doctoral dissertation, United States International University,
1992). *Dissertation Abstracts International, 52,* 4482.

For a microfilm source, also include in parentheses at the end of the entry the university microfilm number. For a CD-ROM source, include "CD-ROM" after the title; then name the electronic source of the information and the access number.

47d Articles in print (APA)

13. Article in a scholarly journal, continuously paged throughout volume   Give only the volume number and year for journals that number pages sequentially for each issue in a volume. Italicize the volume number and the following comma as well as the title of the journal. Do not use "p." or "pp." with page numbers. Use capital letters only for the first word of an article title or subtitle and for proper nouns. See 39d on recognizing scholarly journals.

                              no quotation marks
                        ┌──────── around article title ────────┐
Kanazawa, S., & Still, M. C. (2000). Teaching may be hazardous to your

            journal title, volume number,
    ┌──────── and comma italicized ────────┐
    marriage. *Evolution and Human Behavior, 21,* 185–190.
                              no "p." or "pp." before page numbers

14. Article in a scholarly journal, paged by issue   Include the issue number in parentheses (not in italics) immediately following the volume number.

Ginat, R. (2000). The Soviet Union and the Syrian Ba'th regime: From
hesitation to *rapprochement. Middle Eastern Studies, 36*(2), 150–171.
                              issue number not in italics

15. Article in a magazine Include the year and month and any exact date of publication in parentheses. Do not abbreviate months. Italicize the magazine title, the volume number, and the comma that follows; then give the page number or numbers.

Flora, C. (2005, January/February). Happy hour. *Psychology Today, 38*, 40–51.

16. Article in a newspaper Include the month and date of publication after the year. Give the section letter or number before the page, where applicable. Use "p." and "pp." with page numbers. Do not omit *The* from the title of a newspaper.

Pollack, A. (2005, February 15). The search for the killer painkiller. *The New York Times*, pp. F1, F6.

      p. or pp. used only for newspaper articles

17. Article that skips pages Give all the page numbers, separated by commas, as in item 16.

18. Review After the title of the article, add in brackets a description of the work reviewed and identify the medium: book, film, or video, for example.

Hitchens, C. (2004, December). Survivor [review of the book *The lesser evil: The diaries of Victor Klemperer 1945–1959*]. *The Atlantic, 294*, 140–146.

19. Unsigned article or editorial For a work with no author named, begin the listing with the title; for an editorial, add the word "Editorial" in brackets.

Monetary conundrums [Editorial]. (2005, February 26). *The Economist, 374*, 12, 14.

20. Letter to the editor Write "Letter to the editor" in brackets after the date or the title of the letter, if it has one.

Cruickshank, R. H. (2004/2005, December/January). [Letter to the editor]. *Natural History, 113*, 12.

47e Articles online (APA)

For articles you find online, provide any available print publication information (as in items 13–20). Then put the date when you retrieved the article, followed by either the name of a subscription database or, for a generally available Web site, the URL of the document, with no period after the URL.

21. Article in an online database Universities and libraries subscribe to large searchable databases such as *InfoTrac, EBSCO, ERIC, LexisNexis, Sociological Abstracts, PsycINFO,* and *WilsonWeb,* providing access to abstracts and full-text articles. In addition to print information, provide the date of retrieval and the name of the database. Add the item number if it is provided.

Goldstein, B. S. C., & Harris, K. C. (2000). Consultant practices in two
    heterogeneous Latino schools. *The School Psychology Review, 29,*
    368–377. Retrieved March 3, 2005, from WilsonWeb Education Full
    Text database (0279–6015).

22. Newspaper article retrieved from database or Web site Newspaper articles, as well as journal articles, are often available from several sources, in several databases, and in a variety of formats, such as in a university online subscription database.

Wade, N. (2000, May 9). Scientists decode Down syndrome chromosome. *The
    New York Times,* p. F4. Retrieved March 4, 2005, from LexisNexis
    Academic Universe database.

Eisenberg, A. (2005, February 24). For simpler robots, a step forward. *The New
    York Times.* Retrieved March 2, 2005, from http//www.nytimes.com
                            no period at end of URL

23. Online abstract

Frith, H., & Gleeson, K. (2004). Clothing and embodiment: Men managing body
    image and appearance. *Psychology of Men & Masculinity, 5,* 40–48. Abstract
    retrieved March 2, 2005, from http://content.apa.org/journals/men/5/1

24. Online article with a print source If information such as page numbers or figures is missing (as in HTML versions) or if the document may have additions or alterations, give full retrieval information.

Jones, C. C., & Meredith, W. (2000, June). Developmental paths of
    psychological health from early adolescence to later adulthood.
    Psychology and Aging, 15, 351–360. Retrieved March 3, 2005, from
    http://content.apa.org/journals/pag/15/2/351.html

However, if you access an article in PDF format (with page numbers and charts exactly the same as in the print version), cite it exactly as if you had read it in print, with the addition of "[Electronic version]" after the title of the article.

Campos, G. P. (2004, September). What are cultural models for? Child-rearing practices in historical perspective [Electronic version]. *Culture & Psychology, 10,* 279–291.

25. Article in an online journal with no print source

Holtzworth-Munroe, A. (2000, June). Domestic violence: Combining scientific inquiry and advocacy. *Prevention & Treatment, 3.* Retrieved March 5, 2005, from http://journals.apa.org/prevention/volume3/pre0030022c.html

26. Article in an online site, no author identified

The natural-gas explosion. (2005, February 28). *Economist.com.* Retrieved March 2, 2005, from http://www.economist.com/agenda/displayStory .cfm?story_id-3712621

47f Web sites, Web documents, and e-mail (APA)

27. Web site Give the complete URL in the text of your paper, not in your list of references (46b, item L).

28. Document on a Web site, no author identified Italicize the title of the document (the Web page). Alphabetize by the first major word of the title.

Electronic references. (2003). Retrieved March 4, 2005, from http://www.apastyle.org/elecsource.html

29. Document on a university or government site Italicize the title of the document. In the retrieval statement, give the name of the university or government agency (and the department or division if it is named). Follow this with a colon and the URL.

McClintock, R. (2000, September 20). *Cities, youth, and technology: Toward a pedagogy of autonomy.* Retrieved March 3, 2005, from Columbia University, Institute for Learning Technologies Web site: http://www.ilt.columbia.edu/publications/cities/cyt.html

30. E-mail and contributions to electronic discussion lists   Make sure that you cite only scholarly e-mail messages. Cite a personal e-mail message in the body of your text as "personal communication," and do not include it in your list of references (46b, item O).

Gracey, D. (2001, April 6). Monetary systems and a sound economy [Msg 54].
     Message posted to http://groups.yahoo.com/group/ermail/message/54

Whenever possible, cite an archived version of a message:

Schwalm, D. (2005, February 15). Re: Value of an education. Message posted
     to WPA–L electronic mailing list, archived at http://lists.asu.edu

47g   Multimedia and miscellaneous works—live, print, and online (APA)

31. Film, 491	34. Personal communication
32. Episode from a television	(letter, telephone
series, 491	conversation, or
33. Computer software, 491	interview), 491

Identify the medium in brackets after the title.

31. Film   Give the country where the film was released.

Berman, S. S., & Pulcini, R. (Directors). (2003). *American Splendor* [Motion
     picture]. United States, Fine Line Features.

32. Episode from a television series

Gazit, C. (Writer). (2004). The seeds of destruction [Television series episode]. In
     D. J. James (Producer), *Slavery and the making of America.* New York: WNET.

33. Computer software

SnagIt (Version 7.2.1) [Computer software]. (2005). Okemos, MI: TechSmith.

34. Personal communication (letter, telephone conversation, or interview)   Cite a personal communication only in your text (46b, item O). Do not include it in your list of references.

48   Sample Documented Paper, APA Style

The paper that follows was written for an introductory college course in experimental psychology. Check with your instructor to see whether your title page should strictly follow APA guidelines, as this one does, or whether it should be modified to include the course name, instructor's name, and date.

TITLE PAGE

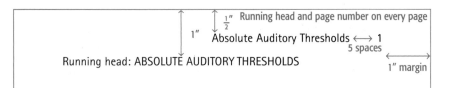

½″ Running head and page number on every page

1″   Absolute Auditory Thresholds ⟷ 1
5 spaces

Running head: ABSOLUTE AUDITORY THRESHOLDS

1″ margin

Absolute Auditory Thresholds in College Students
Todd Kray
Hunter College of the City University of New York

Centered title, writer's name, and writer's affiliation

APA ABSTRACT PAGE

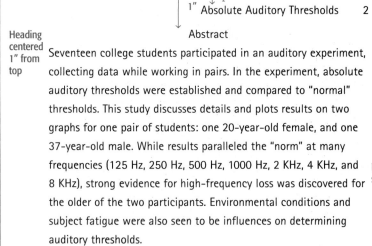

½″

1″ Absolute Auditory Thresholds   2

Heading centered 1″ from top

Abstract

Seventeen college students participated in an auditory experiment, collecting data while working in pairs. In the experiment, absolute auditory thresholds were established and compared to "normal" thresholds. This study discusses details and plots results on two graphs for one pair of students: one 20-year-old female, and one 37-year-old male. While results paralleled the "norm" at many frequencies (125 Hz, 250 Hz, 500 Hz, 1000 Hz, 2 KHz, 4 KHz, and 8 KHz), strong evidence for high-frequency loss was discovered for the older of the two participants. Environmental conditions and subject fatigue were also seen to be influences on determining auditory thresholds.

Passive voice common in accounts of research

Results summarized

Absolute Auditory Thresholds 3

Absolute Auditory Thresholds in College Students

1″ margin

For decades, the branch of psychophysics known as psychoacoustics has concerned itself with the minimum amount of sound pressure level (SPL) required for detection by the human ear. An early landmark study by Sivian and White (1933) examined loudness thresholds by measuring minimum audible field (MAF) and minimal audible pressure (MAP) and found that the ear was not as sensitive as had been reported in earlier studies by Wien (as cited in Sivian & White, 1933). Parker and Schneider (1980) tested Fechner's and Weber's laws, both of which concern themselves with measuring changes in physical intensity and the psychological experiences of those changes (Jahnke & Nowaczyk, 1998; Noll, 2002) and determined that loudness is a power function of intensity, which was consistent with Fechner's assumption. In recent years, loudness thresholds have been measured under various experimental conditions, including quiet sedentary activity, exercise, and noise (Hooks-Horton, Geer, & Stuart, 2001).

An experiment was designed to utilize the method of limits, which establishes the absolute sensitivity (threshold) for a particular sound, to test auditory thresholds in college students and compare them to the "norm." Each threshold is determined by presenting the tone at a sound level well above threshold, then lessening it in discrete intervals until the tone is no longer perceived by the participant (Gelfand, 1981). The present study predicts that, according to Gelfand's (1981) summary of the research on normal hearing, college students' thresholds would be described as "normal."

Method

Participants

Seventeen college students in an introductory experimental psychology course participated in the experiment. The median age of the 5 males and 12 females was 24, with ages ranging from 20

Title centered, not underlined

Brief review of the literature

Date after citation

Ampersand within parentheses

Author and year in parentheses

Hypothesis

Main heading centered

Subheading italicized

1″ margin

Absolute Auditory Thresholds   4

to 37 years old. None of the participants claimed to be aware of any significant hearing loss, and none claimed to have ever participated in this or a similar experiment before. All appeared to be in good overall physical and mental condition, though no formal testing was done in these areas.

Apparatus

Pure tones were generated by a B&K waveform generator. The intensity of the tones was controlled by a Hewlett-Packard 350D attenuator. Tones were gated on and off by a push-button-controlled, light-dependent resistor. This provided for a gradual "ramping" on and off of sound. The tones were presented to the subject through a pair of Koss PRO/99 headphones. The headphones were calibrated at all test frequencies on a Kemar dummy head with a 6 cc coupler.

Procedure

Participants worked in pairs to run and participate in the experiment. In each pair, one participant controlled the waveform generator and attenuator while the other faced away from the tester toward the wall. Participants had been instructed to choose an order of frequencies prior to taking the test. They then administered the tests to each other, trading "roles" after one block of attenuated tones for each frequency was completed. On the first day of testing, the method of limits was utilized to determine a baseline threshold for each frequency. Seven frequencies were generated: 125 Hz, 250 Hz, 500 Hz, 1000 Hz, 2 KHz, 4 KHz, and 8 KHz.

The tests were administered in small cubicles that were quiet but not soundproof. Participants had been instructed to use their "good ear." Tones were heard monophonically, through one side of the headphones.

Eight blocks were run for each frequency, 4 ascending and 4 descending, in a semirandomized order determined by the

---

Margin annotations:

Details of participants

Specialized equipment described

Passive voice common in description of experiment

Details of procedure

Absolute Auditory Thresholds   5

experimenter to help ensure accurate responses rather than the participant being able to "guess it out." Participants were instructed to say "yes" after each audible tone for a descending block, until they could no longer hear the tone, at which point they would say "no" and that particular block would end. For an ascending block, participants were to say "no" for each ascending tone that they could not hear, until the first tone they heard, at which point they would say "yes" and that block would be complete. Each response was recorded on a sheet of paper by the experimenter, handwritten.

Main heading centered

Results

For this pair of participants, 2 audiograms were plotted to display dB SPL (decibel sound pressure level) thresholds for Subject A and Subject B. Threshold ranges for the subjects in one pair were quite different from each other. Subject A's ranged from 5.9 dB to 39.3 dB (Fig. 1); Subject B's ranged from 2.7 dB to 26.6 dB (Fig. 2), resulting in a more "normal" curve than the one for Subject A.

Reference to figures at end of paper

Discussion

Results evaluated with respect to hypothesis

Subject B's absolute threshold levels somewhat resemble those of "normal" hearing, as reported by Gelfand (1981) with a peculiar loss of sensitivity at 2 KHz and extreme sensitivity at 8 KHz. While loss of sensitivity is not uncommon for those who have had prolonged exposure to loud sounds, such as listening to a Walkman being played at the maximum level or attending rock concerts frequently, it seems odd that Subject B, who claimed not to possess these conditions, would experience a loss of sensitivity at 2 KHz, particularly at age 20. In the light of that, it seems even stranger that Subject B would have sensitivity greater than the norm at both 4 KHz and 8 KHz. However, the fact that both subjects had elevated thresholds at 2 KHz could lead to the suspicion of faulty apparatus.

Unusual results analyzed

Causes of results considered

Subject A seems to be a classic example of somebody who would be prone to loss of sensitivity at higher frequencies. He had

Details of causes

constant exposure to loud sounds as a result of over 2 decades spent playing in rock bands, frequently attending rock concerts, wearing a Walkman often in his youth, working in extremely loud nightclubs, and working in recording studios. In addition, he is currently 37 years old and may be experiencing the first symptoms of Presbyacusia--hearing loss at high frequencies due to aging. Subject A showed an extreme loss of sensitivity at 2 KHz (again, apparatus could be at fault here) and the loss at 4 KHz seems real when compared to Gelfand's (1981) norm.

Auditory testing over the years has provided us with no easy answers regarding absolute threshold. Many of the articles cited in this study provide more questions than conclusions. Sivian and White (1933) inquired as to whether ear sensitivity was determined by the actual physiological construction of the ear or if air as a transmitter was responsible. It would be helpful to test for this in the future.

Study related to prior research

Future research suggested

The tests themselves are problematic as well. It is easy to wind up with a masked threshold if thresholds are not measured in absolute silence--not always an easy condition to create. Even under the best conditions that could be achieved in this experiment, demand characteristics and experimenter effects were unavoidable. The dial of the attenuator clicked loudly when turned, providing very definite clues that attenuation levels were being changed. In addition, the test, which took several hours to complete, caused subjects to feel fatigued and restless, making it difficult to concentrate at times.

Problems with research procedures discussed

Despite these hurdles, the experiment produced reasonable estimates for absolute auditory thresholds for college students and a reasonable estimate for a person experiencing symptoms of high-frequency loss due to abuse to the ear in the form of prolonged and excessive exposure to high volume.

Results related to hypothesis

New page for references, double-spaced

Absolute Auditory Thresholds   7

References

Gelfand, S. A. (1981). *Hearing: An introduction to psychological and physiological acoustics.* New York: Marcel Dekker.

Hooks-Horton, S., Geer, S., & Stuart, A. (2001). Effects of exercise and noise on auditory thresholds and distortion-product otoacoustic emissions. *Journal of the American Academy of Audiology, 12,* 52–58. Retrieved March 3, 2005, from EBSCO Academic Search Premier database.

Jahnke, J. C., & Nowaczyk, R. H. (1998). *Cognition.* Englewood Cliffs, NJ: Prentice Hall.

Noll, T. (2002). *Tone apperception, relativity, and Weber-Fechner's law.* Paper presented at the 2002 2nd International Conference on Understanding and Creating Music. Retrieved March 5, 2005, from http://flp.cs.tu-berlin.de/~noll/ApperceptRelativity.pdf

Parker, S., & Schneider, B. (1980). Loudness and loudness discrimination. *Perception and Psychophysics, 28,* 398–406.

Sivian, L. J., & White, S. D. (1933). Minimum audible sound fields. *The Journal of the Acoustical Society of America, 4,* 288–321.

Organized alphabetically

Hanging indents

Year in parentheses after author

Italics extend through volume number and commas

Absolute Auditory Thresholds   8

Figure Captions

Figure 1. Comparison of thresholds for "normal" and Sub. A.

Figure 2. Comparison of thresholds for "normal" and Sub. B.

Figure 1

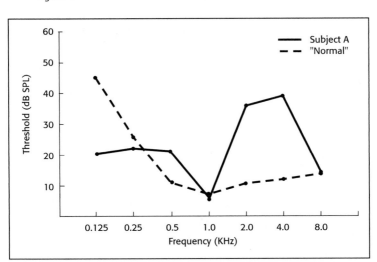

Figure 2

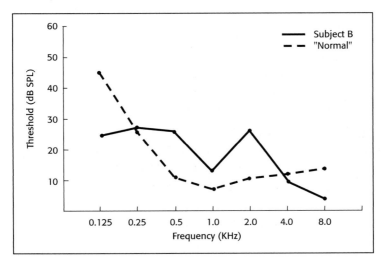

While you are in college, you'll be expected to do a great deal of writing. It is what you do to record what you know, to learn what you need to know, and to show what you have learned. You will continue to write far beyond your first year. Think of all the papers, tests, and exams you will take in all your courses, from humanities and the arts, to sciences, business, and preprofessional subjects. Think, too, of all the online communications you will have with professors, classmates, and college organizations, whether in course-management systems, e-mail discussion lists, or your own personal e-mail accounts.

In addition, while you are a student, you may write to apply for travel grants, internships, scholarships, and so on. You may also be writing letters and reports when you participate in college clubs or community activities. Then, as you prepare to graduate (and you will!), writing plays a large and decisive role when you apply for graduate school or for a job.

49 Writing under Pressure

Pressure is a fact of life in college. Papers are due, exams are looming, you are working, and you have a family crisis. You stay up late night after night trying to get it all done. Unfortunately, this book can't produce a magic formula to make the pressure go away. Remember, though, that most instructors are sympathetic about genuine emergencies (even though they might not accept the "fact" that an aunt breaks a bone three times in one semester). This chapter offers advice that you might find useful in pressured moments.

49a Essay exams and short-answer tests

Essay exams   *Essay exams* are an important part of your life as a student. In an examination setting, you have to write quickly on an assigned topic. Learn how to cope with these tests so that you don't dread them. The advantage of an essay test over a multiple-choice test is that you can include in your answers more of the information you have learned. Knowing the material of the course thoroughly will give you a distinct advantage, allowing you to choose the facts and ideas you need and to present them clearly.

KEY POINTS

How to Approach an Essay Exam

1. For a content-based essay test, review assigned materials and notes; assemble facts; underline, annotate, and summarize significant information; predict questions on the basis of the material your instructor has covered in detail in class; and draft some answers. Go into the exam knowing that you are well prepared with necessary information.

2. Highlight or underline key terms in the assigned questions (see 1c for definitions of terms used). Ask for clarification if necessary.

3. Decide what information is relevant and how the information connects to the assigned question.

4. Think positively about what you know. Work out a way to highlight the details you know most about. Stretch and relax.

5. Make sure you formulate a thesis if it is called for in the essay question. Include key words from the question in formulating your thesis.

6. Make a scratch outline (see 4d) to organize your thoughts. Jot down specific details as evidence for your thesis.

7. Focus on providing detailed support for your thesis. In an exam essay, this is more important than an elaborate introduction or conclusion.

8. Write your essay, using a new paragraph for each new point of support and making connections and transitions between the ideas in the paragraphs. Then check your work for content, logic, and clarity, and make sure you have answered the question.

Short-answer tests   In short-answer tests, use your time wisely. So that you know how long you should spend on each question, count the number of questions, and divide the number of minutes you have for taking the test by the number of questions (add 1 or 2 to the number you divide by, to give yourself time for editing and proofreading). Then for each answer decide which points are the most important ones to cover in the time you have available. You cannot afford to ramble or waffle in short-answer tests. Get to the point fast, and show what you know.

Make sure you do not miss a class before the test. Instructors will often review material that will appear on the test, and if you pay careful attention, you will pick up hints as to the type of questions that will be asked and the material that will be covered. Before a test, familiarize yourself with the terms in essay exams and short-answer tests (1c). For both essay exams and short-answer tests, always read the questions carefully, underline the key terms used, and make sure you understand what each question asks you to do.

In a test you don't have to begin with the first question. Begin with what you know you can do well.

49b   Meeting deadlines

When instructors assign papers or supervisors ask for a report, they usually assign a due date. Note the date, and make yourself a schedule of work to be done and steps to be accomplished, working backwards from the due date to the date the task is first assigned. A sample schedule for writing a research paper is in 38b. Also adapt this schedule for shorter, less demanding papers.

If you don't even start a major paper for a college course until the evening before it is due, you are bound to feel helpless, desperate, and depressed about your dwindling GPA. In short, *get started early*. There is no better way to avoid panic. Then you will be able to say with a degree of confidence as you near the deadline, "The paper doesn't have to be perfect. It just has to be done." Work on finishing a draft to hand in—however rough or "drafty" it is. If you feel you still need additional time to revise, an instructor is likely to be more sympathetic to a request for an extension of the deadline if you show that you have made a genuine effort and have produced a solid draft.

At work, of course, excuses and lateness can damage your prospects, so do what you can to start a project early and complete it on time.

50 Showcasing Your Work: Portfolios and Oral Presentations

50a Preparing a portfolio

Portfolios are used by artists, writers, and job hunters. In a college writing course, selecting work to include in a portfolio gives you and your instructor an opportunity to review your progress over time and to assess which pieces of writing best reflect your abilities and interests. Choose pieces that indicate both the range of topics covered in the course (or in your course of study) and the types of writing you have done. To show readers that you are able to produce more than one type of writing, include pieces on different topics, written for different purposes. If your instructor does not issue specific guidelines for presenting your portfolio, use those in the Key Points box.

KEY POINTS

Presenting a Writing Portfolio

1. Number and date drafts; clip or staple all drafts and final copy together.

2. To each separate package in your portfolio add a cover sheet describing the contents of the package (for example, "In-class essay" or "Documented paper with three prior drafts").

3. Include a brief cover letter to introduce the material and yourself.

4. Pay special attention to accuracy and mechanics. Your semester grade may depend on the few pieces of writing that you select to be evaluated, so make sure that the ones you include are carefully edited and well presented.

50b Preparing an e-portfolio

Increasingly, individual instructors as well as college-wide programs require or strongly encourage students to construct an e-portfolio. They provide space on a server where students can store writing samples and/or documents that they have retrieved from the Web. The specific charges or tasks vary with the course. While an English instructor will probably focus on writing samples, a social science instructor may ask students to locate primary sources about a specific research topic (like the environmental movement or laws and court cases related to civil unions). In education, e-portfolios have become quite common to document a student's progress through a course of study—for example, to file lesson plans, lesson evaluations, and so on.

TechToolkit   E-Portfolios in Action

For examples of college programs that assign e-portfolios, see the following:

- Penn State at <http://portfolio.psu.edu>; this site includes instructions on building e-portfolios and examples of students' e-portfolios (including video and audio clips) that they used when applying for jobs.

- LaGuardia Community College in Queens, NY, at <http://www.eportfolio .lagcc.cuny.edu>; this site includes instructions for developing a portfolio, resources, and student samples. ■

Whatever software your school may use to support e-portfolios, typically you will have control over the material that goes onto your pages of the (Web) server. In your private storage area, you'll be able to make material available to your instructors and/or other students for review so that these "reviewers" can add their comments to the material. Also, you may have the option of making a document (without the reviewer comments) available to a wider audience ("publish it to the Web") so that future employers or friends and family can also see the work. You can make different documents—aimed at different audiences—available for viewing at any time. One advantage to e-portfolios is that you have the flexibility to remix the materials for different purposes. In addition, you can include a variety of materials that you produce, such as HTML documents, graphics, images, sound, and film clips, rather than simply printed college essays that make up more conventional portfolios.

50c Presenting an oral report

You may be asked to give oral reports or oral presentations in writing courses, in other college courses, in community organizations, or in the business world. Usually you will do some writing as you prepare your report, and then you will deliver your report either from notes or from a manuscript text written especially for oral presentation.

Situation, purpose, and audience   Consider the background and expectations of your audience. Jot down what you know about your listeners and what stance and tone will best convince them of the validity of your views. For example, what effect do you want to have on the members of your audience? Do you want to inform, persuade, move, or entertain them? What do you know about your listeners' age, gender, background, education, occupation, political affiliation, beliefs, and knowledge of your subject? What do listeners need to know? In a college class, your audience will be your classmates and instructor. It is often desirable to build a sense of community with your audience by asking questions and using the inclusive pronoun *we*.

Preparation   Making an effective oral presentation is largely a matter of having control over your material, deciding what you want to say, and knowing your subject matter well. Preparation and planning are essential.

KEY POINTS

Tips for Preparing an Oral Report

1. Find an aspect of the topic you feel committed to, and decide on a clear focus.

2. Make a few strong points. Back them up with specific details. Have some points that you can expand on and develop with interesting examples, quotations, and stories.

3. Include signposts and signal phrases to help your audience follow your ideas (*first, next, finally; the most important point is . . .*).

4. Structure your report clearly. Present the organizational framework of your talk along with illustrative materials in handouts, overhead transparencies, Microsoft PowerPoint slides (11d), posters, charts, or other visuals (10 and 11).

5. Use short sentences, accessible words, memorable phrases, and natural language. In writing, you can use long sentences with one clause embedded in another, but these are difficult for listeners to follow.

6. You can effectively use repetition much more in an oral report than in a written report. Your audience will appreciate being reminded of the structure of the talk and of points you referred to previously.

7. Meet the requirements set for the presentation in terms of time available for preparation, length of presentation (most people read a page of double-spaced text in just over two minutes), and possible questions from the audience.

8. Prepare a strong ending that will have an impact on the audience. Make sure that you conclude. Do not simply stop or trail off.

You can make your presentation from notes that you memorize or consult as you talk, or you can prepare a special manuscript.

Speaking from notes   Speaking from notes is the best way. It allows you to be more spontaneous and to look directly at your audience. Think of your presentation as a conversation. For this method, notes or a key-word outline must be clear and organized so that you feel secure about which points you will discuss and in what order you will discuss them. Here is a speaker's key-word outline for a presentation of her views on the granting of paternity leave.

1. Children's needs
   Benefits
   Bonding

2. Issue of equity
   Equal treatment for men and women
   Cost

Your notes or outline should make reference to specific illustrations and quotations and contain structural signals so that the audience knows when you begin to address a new point. You can also use slides prepared with your word processor or PowerPoint slides to guide the direction and structure of your presentation. For a short presentation on a topic that you know well, use notes with or without the visual aid of slides.

Speaking from a manuscript   Writing out a complete speech may be necessary for a long formal presentation, but even if you do this, you should practice and prepare so that you do not have to labor over every word. Remember, too, to build in places to pause and make spontaneous comments. The advantages of speaking from a prepared manuscript are that you can time the presentation exactly and that you will never dry up and wonder what to say next. The disadvantages are that you have to read the text and that reading aloud is not easy, especially if you want to maintain eye contact with your audience. If you prefer to speak from a complete manuscript text, prepare the text for oral presentation as follows:

- Triple-space your text and use a large font.
- When you reach the bottom of a page, begin a new sentence on the next page. Do not start a sentence on one page and finish it on the next.
- Highlight key words in each paragraph so that your eye can pick them out easily.
- Underline words and phrases that you want to stress.
- Use slash marks (/ or //) or color highlights to remind yourself to pause. Read in sense groups (parts of a sentence that are read as a unit—a phrase or clause, for example—often indicated by a pause when spoken and by punctuation when read). Mark your text at the end of a sense group.
- Number your pages so that you can keep them in the proper sequence.

Practice, practice, practice   Whether you speak from notes or a manuscript, practice is essential.

- Practice not just once but many times. Try videotaping yourself, watching the tape, and asking a friend for comments.
- Speak at a normal speed and at a good volume. Speaking too quickly and too softly is a common mistake.

- Imagine a full audience; use gestures and practice looking up to make eye contact with people in the audience.
- Beware of filler words and phrases like *OK, well, you know,* and *like.* Such repeated verbal tics annoy and distract an audience.
- Do not punctuate pauses with *er* or *uhm.*

 ESL Note   Dealing with Nerves in an Oral Presentation

If you have only recently adapted to speaking and writing in English, having to speak in front of others may seem intimidating. Make sure you know your material thoroughly. Practice and make sure you know when to pause and how to pronounce all the words. Ask someone to listen to you practice and give you helpful hints. Then relax. You'll be surprised at how sympathetic and understanding an audience can be—a "foreign" accent can often charm away the perception of errors. ◼

Visual and multimedia aids   If you use any visual aids, check your equipment and practice with it. If you use PowerPoint slides (see 11d–11e), the font size must be large enough for people at the back of the room to read, and the colors you choose should be clear—black on white is best. When you speak, remember to face the audience, not the projector or screen. Do not provide lengthy or complicated visual aids; otherwise, your audience will be reading them instead of listening to you.

Presentation   Most people find that their jitters disappear as soon as they begin talking, especially when they are well prepared.

Look frequently at your listeners. Work the room so that you gaze directly at people in all sections of the audience. In *Secrets of Successful Speakers,* Lilly Walters points out that when you look at one person, all the people in a V behind that person will think you are looking at them. Above all, remember to smile.

51   Communicating Online in Formal Contexts and Public Forums

Writing something like "'Sup, dude? If U cn meet me tnite at skool, that'd be wicked ill, fo shizzle. BTW, wanna chow down 2?" may be usual fare in instant messaging and e-mailing to a friend. But such colloquial code is not recommended for writing to your instructor, boss, or work colleague, or for posting online in a public forum such as a course Web site.

Sam Dillon of the *New York Times* reports that a systems analyst in California wrote this e-mail to her supervisor at a high-tech corporation:

> I updated the Status report for the four discrepancies Lennie forward us via e-mail (they in Barry file)..to make sure my logic was correct It seems we provide Murray with incorrect information . . . However after verifying controls on JBL—JBL has the indicator as B????- I wanted to make sure with the recent changes - I processed today – before Murray make the changes again on the mainframe to 'C'.

Dillon rightly judged this message as "chaotically written." The writer of it paid no attention to her audience and the formal rhetorical context of the workplace. She probably wrote it quickly, treated the communication like speech, and took no time to reread, revise, and edit it. What judgments are her work colleagues likely to make about her?

For e-mail to an instructor, boss, colleagues, classmates in a course discussion forum, or unknown readers in online discussion lists, use the guidelines in 51a to avoid making a negative impression.

51a E-mail netiquette in formal and public contexts

Length and readability   Be brief, and state your main points clearly at the start. One screen holds about 250 words, and online readers do not want to scroll repeatedly to find out what you are saying. Keep paragraphs short or use numbered or bulleted lists.

Capital letters   Avoid using all capital letters in an e-mail message. To readers, it looks as if you are SHOUTING.

Format   To ensure that a reader's e-mail program will not block or jumble your message, use only basic HTML (hypertext markup language) formatting features such as bold and italic fonts. In formal e-mail messages, avoid using multiple colors, special fonts, and graphics until you are certain that your reader can receive and read such messages and you are sure that such features are appropriate.

URLs   To avoid errors in URLs, it is best to copy and paste URLs from a Web page or another document (Select/Copy/Paste) rather than retype them into an e-mail message.

Formality and accuracy   Use a spelling checker, and edit your e-mail before sending if you are writing to people you do not know well and if you want them to take your ideas seriously—for example, your boss, business associates, classmates using a course Web page, or the unknown subscribers to a discussion list. Use slang, abbreviations such as *BTW* ("by the way") and *IMHO* ("in my humble opinion"), and emoticons such as :-) and :-(only when you are certain that readers expect and understand them. Also avoid using nonstandard spelling and verbal shortcuts, such as "RU going 2 the theater w/o her?"

Subject heading   Electronic correspondents often receive a great deal of mail every day. Be clear and concise with a subject heading, so readers will know at a glance what your message is about.

Replies   Pay close attention to who your actual recipient is. If you want to reply to only the individual sender of a message, do not send your message to the whole list; choose "Reply," not "Reply All." In addition, avoid sending a message like "I agree" to many recipients. Make your postings substantive, considerate, and worth reading.

Forwarding messages   Never forward a message indiscriminately. Consider first whether the recipient will need or appreciate the forwarded message. In addition, make sure that forwarding does not violate rules established by your college, business organization, or discussion list. If necessary, ask the original sender for permission to forward the message. He or she can then veto the idea if anyone is likely to be offended or harmed.

Tact   Be careful about what you say and how you say it. Sarcasm and attempts at humor can misfire. Criticism can hurt. In addition, an e-mail message cannot communicate body language. Your reader cannot see a twinkle in your eye or a warm smile. Sometimes a writer fires off a message full of anger and name-calling; such a message is called a *flame*. Avoid flaming.

Signing off   Always put your actual name (not just <cutiepie3@aol.com>) at the end of your online message. You can also construct a "signature file," which will appear automatically at the end of every message you send. Find out how to do this from the Help or Tools menu of your e-mail program.

Attachments It is best to ask someone first if you may send them an e-mail with an attachment. Many individuals and institutions have filters, antivirus programs, or firewalls that automatically screen or quarantine e-mail with attachments. Other people may not accept attachments over a certain size limit. Keep your own antivirus software up-to-date, and open attachments only from known users.

EXERCISE 51.1 Critically assess an e-mail message.
Read the e-mail message. Discuss with classmates your assessment of the message. A sample answer is in the Answer Key.

> To: Joe-mail@company.com
> From: Jane-mail@company.com
> Subject: stuff we need
>
> hey how's is going? :-) listen, I was wondering if you could help me with something regarding a few of our clients. we need to get some information about them, and i think you have the files in your office. the most important one is this guy, larry smith. you should have a sheet with his info on it, if you could fax that over, that'd be great. BTW, we need it yesterday, so please send it ASAP. oh, FYI, and this is **VERY IMPORTANT**, we need the sales figures for March by, get this, 8am Friday, so make sure you have someone fax or mail those over pronto. sorry to dump all this stuff on you :(FWIW, I think we all need a vacation.

51b Online discussion lists, bulletin boards, and discussion boards

Are you interested in Philip Glass, the St. Louis Cardinals, bonsai, beagle puppies, orchids, the Argentine tango, the Battle of Antietam? E-mail discussion lists provide a forum for a virtual community of people sharing an interest in a topic. Since many of the groups and forums may not be moderated or refereed in any way, you must always be careful about evaluating the reliability of a source of information. E-mail lists to which it is necessary to subscribe (not with money, but just by applying to be a participant in the discussion) tend to be more substantive and professional than lists with no access control. You can subscribe to a discussion list and become a regular participant.

Finding discussion lists Use the following directory to find the public lists that are available: CataList, the official catalog of LISTSERV® lists at <http://www.lsoft.com/catalist.html>. As of November 21, 2005, it contained 61,552 public lists out of a total of 407,350 LISTSERV lists.

Subscription lists The administrators of even a public list may screen potential subscribers carefully, even though generally there is no fee for subscribing. (To participate in an e-mail list, you need only an e-mail address and a mail program.) Private lists and professionally moderated lists, especially those with a technical focus, can be reliable sources of factual information and informed opinion. Most discussion lists will direct you to FAQs on how to post messages, unsubscribe, or manage the mail. Make sure you read these. Make sure, too, that you lurk before you post so that you learn the conventions of the list.

Caution: Discussion lists often sell e-mail addresses, so you may get huge amounts of spam. Be careful about giving out your e-mail address. If there is a box you can check to prohibit giving out your address, be sure to check it.

Discussion boards in course management software Colleges frequently use special course management software (CMS) to make it easier for instructors and students to utilize the tools of online courses. Two of the most widely used CMS are Blackboard and WebCT. Such systems provide course Web sites with generally accessible areas (though access is often restricted to students officially enrolled in the course), where the instructor can post the syllabus, course materials, announcements, quizzes, and exams, as well as areas requiring logins by individual students to personally check grades and exam results. These systems also offer a "drop box" where a student can submit files to the instructor and receive files with comments back from the instructor. Increasingly, therefore, if you take Web-enhanced courses, you may be required to produce papers in a Web-suitable format (like HTML) to allow posting and easy access on a course Web site. See 9e for tips on posting academic writing online.

Be sure to consider purpose and audience when you post messages to a class discussion board for a college course. This is not a private e-mail message to a friend but a public document, posted on your course site for all your classmates and your instructor to read. These readers will form judgments about you from what they read. So consider carefully the ideas you express, the language you use, and the level of formality and accuracy that is appropriate. See 3b.

51c Newsgroups and blogs

Newsgroups Tens of thousands of "Usenet newsgroups" cover every imaginable topic. Anyone can post anything on any subject. Messages are archived at <http://groups.google.com>, where you can use a search engine to find subjects and keywords that interest you, and you can read recent postings. As no control exists over the postings, they may contain material that some consider offensive, and they offer little that is useful for scholarly research.

However, reading and contributing to newsgroups is a good way to get engaged in a topic, discover the issues involved, and practice the vocabulary and concepts common in the field in a form with no grade at stake. When you post messages to newsgroups, follow the netiquette guidelines in 51a, and take special care not to be drawn into any flaming.

Blogs Web logs, known as *blogs*, are publicly posted personal diaries. Blogs associated with college courses are public forums hosted on a college server; they are not intended as outlets for personal anecdotes, complaints, or the venting of grievances. The example shown in 3b, written by student Tiffany Brattina, shows how she uses the course blog in her composition course to reflect on an assigned text, connect it to her personal experience, interest her readers, and then draw them into the discussion. Some well-known politicians, academics, and journalists post regular blogs; their views on current topics can therefore be immediately accessible.

52 Writing in the Disciplines and in the Community

52a Writing across the curriculum

One semester you may be writing about *Hamlet*, and the next semester you may move to exploring the census, writing about Chopin's music, discussing geological formations, researching the history of the civil rights movement, or preparing a paper on Sigmund Freud and dreams. You might be expected to write scientific laboratory reports or to manipulate complex statistical data and to use a style of documentation different from one you learned in an English course. As you move from course to course in college, from discipline to discipline, the expectations and conventions of writing will change.

Find out what way of writing and documenting is expected in each of your courses. Although each one may call for some adaptation of the writing process and for awareness of specific conventions, in general you will engage in familiar activities—planning, drafting, revising, and editing.

LANGUAGE AND CULTURE
The Cultures of the Academic Disciplines

Each discipline has its own culture and its own expectations of the people who practice in the discipline and write about it. When you take a course in a new discipline, you are joining a new "discourse community," with established conventions and ways of thinking and writing. Use the following strategies to get acquainted with the discipline's conventions.

1. Listen carefully to lectures and discussion; note the specialized vocabulary used in the discipline. Make lists of new terms and definitions.

2. Read the assigned textbook, and note the conventions that apply in writing about the field.

3. Use subject-specific dictionaries and encyclopedias to learn about the field. Examples include *Encyclopedia of Religion* and *Encyclopedia of Sociology.*

4. Subscribe to e-mail discussion lists (51b) in the field so that you can see what issues people are concerned about.

5. When given a writing assignment, make sure you read samples of similar types of writing in that discipline.

6. Talk with your instructor about the field, its literature, and readers' expectations.

TECHTOOLKIT   Useful Sites for Writing across the Curriculum

Try these Web sites for useful advice on writing in all your courses and for more links to other sites:

The Dartmouth College site with advice to nonmajors on writing in the humanities, sciences, and social sciences: <http://www.dartmouth.edu/~writing/materials/student/toc.shtml>

The George Mason University Writing Center site on writing in public affairs, management, psychology, biology, and history: <http://writingcenter.gmu.edu/resources/index.html> ■

52b Writing about literature

Before you begin writing, pay careful attention to the content and form of the work of literature by reading the work more than once and highlighting significant passages. Work on your own interpretation of the work before you turn to secondary sources (works of criticism). Use the Key Points box to analyze the work systematically.

> **KEY POINTS**
>
> ### Ten Ways to Analyze a Work of Literature
>
> - **Plot or sequence of events** What happens, and in what order? What stands out as important?
> - **Theme** What is the message of the work, the generalization that readers can draw from it? A work may, for example, focus on making a statement about romantic love, jealousy, sexual repression, courage, ambition, revenge, dedication, treachery, honor, lust, greed, envy, social inequality, or generosity.
> - **Characters** Who are the people portrayed? What do you learn about them? Do one or more of them change, and what effect does that change have on the plot or theme?
> - **Genre** What type of writing does the work fit into—parody, tragedy, love story, epic, sonnet, haiku, melodrama, comedy of manners, or mystery novel, for example? What do you know about the features of the genre, and what do you need to know? How does this work compare with other works in the same genre? What conventions does the author observe, violate, or creatively vary?
> - **Structure** How is the work organized? What are its major parts? How do the parts relate to each other?
> - **Point of view** Whose voice speaks to the reader and tells the story? Is the speaker or narrator involved in the action or an observer of it? How objective, truthful, and reliable is the speaker/narrator? What would be gained or lost if the point of view were changed?
> - **Setting** Where does the action take place? How are the details of the setting portrayed? What role, if any, does the setting play? What would happen if the setting were changed?
> - **Tone** From the way the work is written, what can you learn about the way the author feels about the subject matter and

the theme? Can you, for example, detect a serious, informative tone, or is there evidence of humor, sarcasm, or irony?

- **Language** What effects do the following have on the way you read and interpret the work: word choice, style, imagery, symbols, and figurative language?
- **Author** What do you know, or what can you discover through research, about the author and his or her time and that author's other works—and does what you discover illuminate this work?

Guidelines for writing about literature

- Be aware of the distinction between author and narrator. The narrator is the person telling the story or serving as the voice of the poem, not necessarily the author. Often the author has invented the narrator.
- Assume a larger audience than your instructor. Think of your readers as people who have read the work but not thought of the issues you did.
- Make sure that you formulate a thesis. Do not devote a large part of your essay to summary; assume that readers have read the work. Occasionally, though, you may need to include a brief summary of the whole or of parts to orient readers. Make sure you tell them not just what is in the work but also how you perceive and interpret important aspects of the work.
- Turn to the text for evidence, and do so often. Text references, in the form of paraphrase or quotation, provide convincing evidence to support your thesis. But do not let your essay turn into a string of quotations.

Writing about prose fiction or creative nonfiction As you read novels, short stories, memoirs, and biographies or autobiographies, consider these basic questions for thinking about what you read: What happened? When and where did it happen? Who did what? How were things done? Why? Then extend your inquiry by considering all or some of the following factors in detail:

plot: sequence of events in the work

character and character development: main characters, who they are, how they interact, and if and how they change

theme: main message of the work

setting: time and place of the action and cultural/social context

point of view: position from which the events are described, such as first or third person narrator (*I/we* or *he/she/they*), biased or reliable, limited or omniscient

author: relationship to narrator (same or different person?); relevant facts of author's life

tone: attitudes expressed directly or indirectly by the author or narrator

style: word choice, sentence length and structure, significant features

imagery: effect of figures of speech, such as similes and metaphors (see 8e)

symbols: objects or events with special significance or with hidden meanings

narrative devices: foreshadowing, flashback, leitmotif (a recurring theme), alternating points of view, turning point, and dénouement (outcome of plot)

Writing about poetry   In addition to using some of the suggestions relating to prose, you can consider the following factors when you analyze a poem.

stanza: lines set off as a unit of a poem

rhyme scheme: system of end-of-line rhymes that you can identify by assigning letters to similar final sounds—for example, a rhyme scheme for couplets (two-line stanzas), *aa bb cc;* and a rhyme scheme for a sestet (a six-line stanza), *ababcc*

meter: number and pattern of stressed and unstressed syllables (or *metric feet*) in a line. Common meters are trimeter, tetrameter, and pentameter (three, four, and five metric feet). The following line is written in iambic tetrameter (four metric feet, each with one unstressed and one stressed syllable):

Whŏse woóds / thĕse aŕe / Ĭ thínk / Ĭ knów.   —Robert Frost

foot: unit (of meter) made up of a specific number of stressed and unstressed syllables

Writing about drama   As you prepare to write about a play, use any of the relevant points listed for fiction, creative nonfiction, and poetry, and in addition focus on the following dramatic conventions:

structure of the play: acts and scenes

plot: episodes, simultaneous events, chronological sequence, causality, climax, turning point

characters: analysis of psychology, social status, relationships

setting: time, place, and description

time: real time depicted (all action takes place in two hours or so of the play) or passage of time

stage directions: details about clothing, sets, actors' movements, expressions, and voices, information given to actors

scenery, costumes, music, lighting, props, and special effects: purpose and effectiveness

presentation of information: recognition of whether the characters in the play know things that the audience does not or whether the audience is informed of plot developments that are kept from the characters

Figurative language   The writers of literary works often use figures of speech to create images and intensify effects.

simile: a comparison, with two sides stated

Like as the waves make towards the pebbled shore,
So do our minutes hasten to their end.

—William Shakespeare

The weather is like the government, always in the wrong.

—Jerome K. Jerome

A pretty girl is like a melody.

—Irving Berlin

A woman without a man is like a fish without a bicycle.

—Attributed to Gloria Steinem

metaphor: an implied comparison, with no *like* or *as*

The still, sad music of humanity

—William Wordsworth

The quicksands of racial injustice

—Martin Luther King, Jr.

alliteration: repetition of consonant sounds

He bravely breach'd his boiling bloody breast.

—William Shakespeare

assonance: repetition of vowel sounds

> And feed deep, deep upon her peerless eyes
>
> —John Keats

onomatopoeia: sound of word associated with meaning

> murmuring of innumerable bees
>
> —Alfred, Lord Tennyson

personification: description of a thing as a person

> rosy-fingered dawn
>
> —Homer

zeugma: use of a word with two or more other words, forming different and often humorous logical connections

> The art dealer departed in anger and a Mercedes.

For more on using figurative language, see 8e.

KEY POINTS

Common Conventions in Writing about Literature

Tense   Use the present tense to discuss works of literature even when the author is no longer alive (16c).

Authors' Names   Use an author's full name the first time you mention it: "Stephen King." Thereafter, and always in parenthetical citations, use only the last name: "King," not "Stephen," and certainly not "Steve."

Titles of Works   Underline or italicize the titles of books, journals, and other works published as an entity and not as part of a larger work. Use quotation marks to enclose the title of a work forming part of a larger published work: short stories, essays, articles, songs, and short poems.

Quotations   Integrate quotations into your text, and use them for help in making your point (40d). Avoid a mere listing and stringing together: "Walker goes on to say. . . . Then Walker states. . . ." When quoting two or three lines of poetry, separate lines by using a slash (/). When using long quotations (more than three lines of poetry or four typed lines of prose), indent one inch. Do not add quotation marks; the indentation signals a quotation (40g).

52c Writing in the sciences

Most writing in the natural sciences (astronomy, biology, chemistry, and physics, for example) and applied sciences (agriculture, engineering, environmental studies, computer science, and nursing, for example) concerns itself with empirical data—that is, with the explanation and analysis of data gathered from a controlled laboratory experiment or from detailed observation of natural phenomena. Frequently, the study will be a replication of a previous experiment, with the new procedure expected to uphold or refute the hypothesis of that previous experiment.

> **KEY POINTS**
>
> ### A Model for the Organization of an Experimental Paper in the Sciences
>
> 1. Title page
>
> 2. Table of contents: necessary for a long paper or for a paper posted online
>
> 3. Abstract: a summary of your research and your conclusions
>
> 4. Background information: why the study is necessary, your hypothesis, review of other studies
>
> 5. Method: with headed subsections on participants, apparatus, procedures
>
> 6. Results: backed up by statistics in the form of tables, charts, and graphs
>
> 7. Discussion: evaluation of the results from the perspective of your hypothesis
>
> 8. Conclusion and recommendations: implications of the results of the study and suggestions for further research
>
> 9. References: a list of the works cited in the paper

52d Writing in the social sciences

The social sciences include anthropology, business, economics, geography, political science, psychology, and sociology. Social scientists examine how society and social institutions are constructed, how they work (or don't work), and what the ramifications of structures, organizations, and human behavior are.

Two types of writing prevail in the social sciences: scholars can lean toward the scientific approach or can adopt an approach more characteristic of the humanities. Some writers, for instance, use empirical scientific methods similar to those used in the natural sciences to gather, analyze, and report their data, with a focus on people, groups, and their behavior. Then there are writers in the social sciences who are more social philosophers than scientists. Scholars in fields such as public policy and international relations examine trends and events to draw their conclusions. Ethnographic studies are common, too, with researchers taking detailed notes from observing a situation they want to analyze—the behavior of fans at a baseball game, for example, or the verbal reactions of constituents to a politician's tax-cut proposals.

When you are given a writing assignment in the social sciences, it will be helpful if you can ascertain (from the approach taken in class—or just ask) whether your instructor leans toward the humanities or the sciences and whether an empirical study or a philosophical, interpretive essay is more appropriate.

Guidelines for writing in the social sciences

- Understand that the research method you choose will determine what kind of writing is necessary and how you should organize the writing.
- Decide whether your purpose is to describe accurately, measure, inform, analyze, or synthesize information.
- Decide on what kind of data you will use: figures and statistics from experimental research, surveys, the census, or questionnaires; observational data from case studies, interviews, and on-site observations; or reading.
- For an observational study, take careful field notes that describe accurately everything you see. Concentrate on the facts rather than interpretations. Save the interpretive possibilities for the sections of your paper devoted to discussion and recommendations.
- Back up your own observations and research with a review of the literature in the field.
- Use sections and headings in your paper. For an experimental study, see the APA paper written for a psychology course (48).
- Use specialized terminology when appropriate. Examples in psychology include *affect* and *deviance*.

- Report facts. Add comments and expressions such as "I think" only when this is a specific requirement of the task.
- Use the present perfect tense to refer to what researchers have reported (*Smith's study has shown that . . .*).
- Use the passive voice when it is not important for readers to know the identity of the person performing the action: "The participants were timed. . . ."
- Present statistical data in the form of tables, charts, and graphs.
- Follow the APA *Publication Manual* or whichever style manual is recommended.

Types of college writing in the social sciences   Writing in the social sciences can follow much the same patterns and procedures as those of either the humanities or the sciences, depending on your purpose, orientation, and training.

DESCRIPTION OF EMPIRICAL RESEARCH   For a student essay written for an introductory course in experimental psychology and documented in APA style, see chapter 48.

ANALYTICAL REVIEW OF THE LITERATURE AVAILABLE IN A FIELD   See 9e and <http://college.hmco.com/keys.html> for Christel Hyden's review of the literature from 1950 to 2004 on the subject of standardized tests. Her essay was posted online on a sociology course Web site.

52e   Writing in community service courses

Often defined as "experiential learning," service learning projects link college students to their community. For such projects, students volunteer for twenty to thirty hours of community service in a research laboratory, nursing home, hospice, homeless shelter, AIDS clinic, poor neighborhood school, and so on; they relate their work there to the content of a discipline or a particular course. Courses and coursework are oriented to problems in society that students engage with at a personal level in order to attempt to find some solutions. They also are asked to reflect on their service experiences and demonstrate to their college instructor what they learned. These are the three main types of writing in community service projects:

1. writing done initially with the site supervisor to outline the goals, activities, and desired outcomes of the service project
2. writing done during the service work, such as reports to a supervisor, daily records, and summaries of work completed

3. writing done for the college course—usually reflective reports describing the service objectives and the writer's experiences and assessing the success of the project

 TECHTOOLKIT Writing a Reflective Journal

Go to the University of Texas at Arlington site at <http://www2.uta.edu/csl/serve.asp?age=reflection> for instruction on reflective journals and samples of students' writing in service learning courses. ■

The following paragraph is from the reflective journal of a student in a community service course. While enrolled in a microbiology course at Kapi'olani Community College in Hawaii, Joanne L. Soriano worked at an arboretum (a place to study trees) propagating endangered plant species.

> Through Service Learning, I am able to contribute to the Lyon Arboretum's efforts. I made my first visit on February 5th, and was taken to their micropropagation lab. In it, my supervisor, Greg Koob, showed me racks and racks of test tubes filled with plantlets. They were either endangered or native Hawaiian, or both. The endangered ones were clones; in some cases they were derived from only a few remaining individuals. A major function of the lab is to perpetuate these species by growing them in the test tubes and then splitting each individual into more test tubes as it grows. Thus one specimen can become hundreds, under the right conditions. They can be planted on the Arboretum's grounds, or sent to various labs to be studied. I am thrilled to be given the opportunity to participate in the process.

53 What's Next? Writing to Move On

53a Preparing a résumé: Print and electronic

Résumés can be delivered on paper, on the Web, or via e-mail. Designs differ, and no one format works for everyone. However, in all formats, you need to convey to a prospective employer what you have accomplished and when, providing details of your recent education, work experience, honors or awards, interests, and special skills. Above all, you need to show that your qualifications and experience make you suitable for the job you are applying for. Your résumé should show a prospective employer that you are the ideal candidate for a specific job.

KEY POINTS

Writing a Résumé

1. Decide how to present your résumé, or follow a prospective employer's instructions: on paper, on the Web, in the body of an e-mail message, as an e-mail attachment—or all of these. Start with a paper version and save it as an .rtf or .doc file, which you can easily convert to HTML.

2. For a hard-copy version, print on standard-size paper of good quality, white or off-white.

3. Use headings to indicate the main sections.

4. For a hard-copy version, highlight section headings and important information with boldface, italics, bullets, indentation, or different fonts. Use a clear, simple design. Do not use overly elaborate fonts, colors, or design features.

5. Keep a print résumé to one page, if possible. Do not include extraneous information to add length, but also do not cram by using single-spacing between sections, a small font, or a tiny margin.

6. Include information and experience relevant to the job you are applying for. Use reverse chronological order (begin with your most recent work experience and education). Do not include information about your elementary school.

7. Proofread your résumé several times, and ask someone else to examine it carefully as well. Make sure it contains no errors. Avoid howlers such as "rabid typist" and "responsible for ruining a five-store chain."

8. Accompany a print résumé with a cover letter (53c), also carefully checked to avoid an error such as "Thank you for considering me. I look forward to hearing from you shorty."

9. For a Web résumé (HTML), length is not crucial. Put important information on the first page, with navigation links to sections of the résumé or to samples of your materials. List the keywords and provide the date of the latest posting.

Note: Word processors provide résumé templates that set up headings for you—a useful guide.

Sample print résumé   Notice how Aurelia Gomez organized her résumé into clear divisions, using bold headings and a space between sections. This résumé presents the most recent job experience and education first and works backward.*

---

225 West 70th Street
New York, NY 10023
Phone: 212-555-3821
E-mail: agomez@nyu.edu

Aurelia Gomez

Objective:	Entry-level staff accounting position with a public accounting firm	Provides specific enough objective to be useful
Experience:	Summer 2005	**Accounting Intern:** Coopers & Lybrand, NYC •Assisted in preparing corporate tax returns •Attended meetings with clients •Conducted research in corporate tax library and wrote research reports	Places work experience before education because applicant considers it to be her stronger qualification
	Sept. 2001– Nov. 2003	**Payroll Specialist:** City of New York •Worked full-time in a civil service position in the Department of Administration •Used payroll and other accounting software on both DEC 1034 minicomputer and Pentium III •Represented 28-person work unit on the department's management-labor committee •Left job to pursue college degree full-time	Uses action words such as *assisted* and *conducted;* uses incomplete sentences to emphasize the action words and to conserve space
Education:	Jan. 2000– Present	Pursuing a 5-year bachelor of business administration degree (major in accounting) from the Stern School of Business, NYU •Expected graduation date: June 2006 •Attended part-time from 2001 until 2003 while holding down a full-time job •Have financed 100% of all college expenses through savings, work, and student loans •Plan to sit for the CPA exam in May 2007	Provides degree, institution, major, and graduation date Makes the major section headings parallel in format and in wording
Personal Data:		•Helped start the Minority Business Student Association at NYU and served as program director for two years; secured the publisher of *Black Enterprise* magazine as a banquet speaker •Have traveled extensively throughout South America •Am a member of the Accounting Society •Am willing to relocate	Formats the side headings for the dates in a column for ease of reading Provides additional data to enhance her credentials
References:		Available on request	Omits actual names and addresses of references

---

*Sample documents in 53a and 53b are adapted from Scot Ober's *Contemporary Business Communication,* 6th ed. (Boston: Houghton, 2006). Used with permission.

A scannable electronic résumé Companies often scan the print résumés they receive in order to establish a database of prospective employees. They can then use a keyword search to find suitable candidates from those in the database. You may also need to e-mail your résumé to a prospective employer. In either case, you need to be able to adapt a print résumé to make it easy for users to read and scan. You do not need to limit the length of either a scannable or an e-mail résumé.

KEY POINTS

Preparing a Scannable or an E-mail Résumé

- Check any prospective employer's Web site to find its emphasis and important keywords.

- Use nouns as résumé keywords to enable prospective employers to do effective keyword searches (use "educational programmer," for example, rather than "designed educational programs").

- Use a standard typeface (Times New Roman or Arial) and 10- to 12-point type, and for an e-mail document, use "plain text" or ASCII (a file name with a .txt extension).

- Avoid italics, underlining, and graphics.

- Avoid marked lists, or change bullets to + (plus signs) or to * (asterisks).

- Begin each major heading line at the left margin.

- Do not include any decorative vertical or horizontal lines or borders.

- E-mail yourself or a friend a copy of your résumé (both as an attachment and within the body of a message) before you send one to an employer so that you can verify the formatting.

- If you feel that it is necessary, attach a note saying that a formatted version is available in hard copy, and send one as a backup.

- For further advice and examples of online résumés, consult <http://jobsearchtech.about.com/od/resumewriting1/>.

Sample electronic résumé Here is Aurelia Gomez's résumé adapted for e-mailing and scanning.

Begins with name at the top, followed immediately by addresses

Emphasizes, where possible, nouns as keywords

Uses only ASCII characters—one size with no special formatting; no rules, graphics, columns, or tables are used

Uses vertical line spaces (Enter key) and horizontal spacing (space bar) to show relationship of parts

Formats lists with asterisks instead of bullets

```
AURELIA GOMEZ

    225 West 70 Street
    New York, NY 10023
    Phone: 212-555-3821
    E-mail:agomez@nyu.edu

OBJECTIVE
    Entry-level staff accounting position with a public
    accounting firm

EXPERIENCE
    Summer 2005
    Accounting Intern: Coopers & Lybrand, NYC
    * Assisted in preparing corporate tax returns
    * Attended meetings with clients
    * Conducted research in corporate tax library and
      wrote research reports

    Sept. 2001-Nov. 2003
    Payroll Specialist: City of New York
    * Full-time civil service position in the Department
      of Administration
    * Proficiency in payroll and other accounting
      software on DEC 1034 minicomputer and Pentium III
    * Representative for a 28-person work unit on the
      department's management-labor committee
    * Reason for leaving job: To pursue college degree
      full-time

EDUCATION
    Jan. 2000-Present
    Pursuing a 5-year bachelor of business
    administration degree (major in accounting) from the
    Stern School of Business, NYU
    * Expected graduation date: June 2006
    * Attended part-time from 2001 until 2003 while
      holding down a full-time job
    * Have financed 100% of all college expenses through
      savings, work, and student loans
    * Plan to sit for the CPA exam in May 2007
```

```
PERSONAL DATA
    * Helped start the Minority Business Student
      Association at New York University and served as
      program director for two years; secured the
      publisher of BLACK ENTERPRISE magazine as a banquet
      speaker
    * Have traveled extensively throughout South America
    * Am a member of the Accounting Society
    * Am willing to relocate

REFERENCES
    Available upon request

NOTE
    An attractive and fully formatted hard-copy version
    of this resume is available upon request.
```

Runs longer than one page (acceptable for electronic résumés)

Includes notice of availability of a fully formatted version

53b Writing a job application cover letter

Accompany your print or e-mail résumé with a cover letter that explains what position you are applying for and why you are a good candidate. Find out as much as you can about the potential employer and type of work; then, in your letter, emphasize the connections between your experience and the job requirements. (Below is an example of a solicited application letter; it accompanies the résumé on page 524.) Let the employer see that you understand what type of person he or she is looking for. State when, where, and how you can be contacted. As you do with the résumé itself, proofread the letter carefully.

Once you have had an interview, write a short note to thank the interviewer and emphasize your interest in the position.

<table>
<tr><td></td><td>February 13, 2006</td></tr>
</table>

Addresses the letter to a specific person

Mr. David Norman, Partner
Ross, Russell & Weston
452 Fifth Avenue
New York, NY 10018

Dear Mr. Norman:

Identifies the job position and source of advertising

Subject: EDP Specialist Position (Reference No. 103-G)

My varied work experience in accounting and payroll services, coupled with my accounting degree, has prepared me for the position of EDP specialist that you advertised in the February 9 *New York Times*.

Emphasizes a qualification that might distinguish her from other applicants

In addition to taking required courses in accounting and management information systems as part of my accounting major at New York University, I took an elective course in EDP auditing and control. The training I received in this course in applications, software, systems, and service-center records would enable me to immediately become a productive member of your EDP consulting staff.

Relates her work experience to the specific needs of the employer

My college training has been supplemented by an internship in a large accounting firm. In addition, my two years of experience as a payroll specialist for the city of New York have given me firsthand knowledge of the operation and needs of nonprofit agencies. This experience should help me to contribute to your large consulting practice with government agencies.

After you have reviewed my enclosed résumé, I would appreciate having the opportunity to discuss with you why I believe I have the right qualifications and personality to serve you and your clients. I can be reached by e-mail or phone after 3 p.m. daily.

Sincerely,

Aurelia Gomez

Aurelia Gomez
225 West 70th Street
New York, NY 10023
Phone: 212-555-3821
E-mail: agomez@nyu.edu

Provides a telephone number (may be done either in the body of the letter or in the last line of the address block)

Enclosure

TECHTOOLKIT Online Workshop on Cover Letters

Go to <http://owl.english.purdue.edu/workshops/hypertext/coverletter.index .html> for useful information on cover letters. ■

53c Writing a personal statement for graduate school admission

Your personal statement may be one of the most important things you ever write. Graduate school admissions committees read hundreds of such statements, and your aim is to get yours to stand out so that the program of your choice offers you admission. Some basic rules apply:

- Read the instructions carefully, and do specifically what you are asked to do.
- Do not write one statement and send it to several schools.
- Do not send a first draft. Revise until you get it right.
- Show your interest in your field of study, and describe your specific interests and accomplishments.
- Make sure you show why the admissions committee should admit you: What makes you a good fit for that particular school? What makes you better than other candidates?
- Pay special attention to your first paragraph, where you can attract or lose a reader.
- Have someone else check your work, and proofread, proofread, proofread. Mistakes will immediately put a reader off.

TECHTOOLKIT Online Advice on Personal Statements

The Online Writing Lab at Purdue University (at <http://owl.english.purdue.edu/ handouts/pw/p_perstate.html> includes a useful twelve-point bulleted list on questions to ask yourself before you write, as well as general advice, examples of successful statements, and advice from admissions representatives at six institutions. ■

Final note: Take this handbook with you when you move on!

GLOSSARY OF USAGE

Listed in this glossary are words that are often confused (*affect/effect*, *elicit/illicit*), misspelled (*alright, it's/its*), or misused (*hopefully*). Also listed are nonstandard words (*irregardless, theirself*) and colloquial expressions (*OK*) that should be avoided in formal writing.

a, an Use *an* before words that begin with a vowel sound (the vowels are *a, e, i, o,* and *u*): *an apple, an hour* (begins with silent *h*). Use *a* before words that begin with a consonant sound: *a planet, a yam, a ukelele, a house* (begins with pronounced *h*).

accept, except, expect *Accept* is a verb: *She accepted the salary offer. Except* is usually a preposition: *Everyone has gone home except my boss. Expect* is a verb: *They expect to visit New Mexico on vacation.*

adapt, adopt *Adapt* means "to adjust" and is used with the preposition *to*: *Some people adapt slowly to the work routine after college. Adopt* means "to take into a family" or "to take up and follow": *The couple adopted a three-year-old child. The company adopted a more aggressive policy.*

adverse, averse *Adverse* is an adjective describing something as hostile, unfavorable, or difficult. *Averse* indicates opposition to something and usually takes the preposition *to. The bus driver was averse to driving in the adverse driving conditions.*

advice, advise *Advice* is a noun: *Take my advice and don't start smoking. Advise* is a verb: *He advised his brother to stop smoking.*

affect, effect In their most common uses, *affect* is a verb, and *effect* is a noun. To *affect* is to have an *effect* on something: *Pesticides can affect health. Pesticides have a bad effect on health. Effect,* however, can be used as a verb meaning "to bring about": *The administration hopes to effect new health care legislation. Affect* can also be used as a noun in psychology, meaning "a feeling or emotion."

aisle, isle You'll find an *aisle* in a supermarket or a church. An *isle* is an island.

all ready, already *All ready* means "totally prepared": *The students were all ready for their final examination. Already* is an adverb meaning "by this time": *He has already written the report.*

all right, alright *All right* is standard. *Alright* is nonstandard.

all together, altogether *All together* is used to describe acting simultaneously: *As soon as the boss had presented the plan, the managers spoke up all together. Altogether* is an adverb meaning "totally," often used before an adjective: *His presentation was altogether impressive.*

allude, elude *Allude* means "to refer to": *She alluded to his height. Elude* means "to avoid": *He eluded her criticism by leaving the room.*

allusion, illusion   The noun *allusion* means "reference": *Her allusion to his height made him uncomfortable.* The noun *illusion* means "false idea": *He had no illusions about being Mr. Universe.*

almost, most   Do not use *most* to mean *almost*: *Almost* [<u>not</u> *Most*] *all my friends are computer literate.*

alot, a lot of, lots of   *Alot* is nonstandard. *A lot of* and *lots of* are regarded by some as informal for *many* or *a great deal of*: *They have performed many research studies.*

aloud, allowed   *Aloud* is an adverb meaning "out loud": *She read her critique aloud.* *Allowed* is a form of the verb *allow*: *Employees are not allowed to participate in the competition.*

ambiguous, ambivalent   *Ambiguous* is used to describe a phrase or act with more than one meaning: *The ending of the movie is ambiguous; we don't know if the butler really committed the murder.* *Ambivalent* describes lack of certainty and the coexistence of opposing attitudes and feelings: *The committee is ambivalent about the proposal for restructuring the company.*

among, between   Use *between* for two items, *among* for three or more: *I couldn't decide between red or blue. I couldn't decide among red, blue, or green.*

amoral, immoral   *Amoral* can mean "neither moral nor immoral" or "not caring about right or wrong," whereas *immoral* means "morally wrong": *Some consider vegetarianism an amoral issue, but others believe eating meat is immoral.*

amount, number   *Amount* is used with uncountable expressions: *a large amount of money, work, or effort.* *Number* is used with countable plural expressions: *a large number of people, a number of attempts.*

an   See *a*.

and   *And* should be used as a conjunction only, never to mean *to*. For example, <u>not</u> *Try and find me* <u>but</u> *Try to find me.*

ante-, anti-   *Ante-* is a prefix meaning "before," as in *anteroom.* *Anti-* means "against" or "opposite," as in *antiseptic* or *antifreeze.*

any more, anymore   *Any more* refers to quantity; *anymore* means "from now on": *He doesn't want any more pecan pie because he doesn't like it anymore.*

anyone, any one   *Anyone* is a singular indefinite pronoun meaning "anybody": *Can anyone help me? Any one* refers to one from a group and is usually followed by *of* + plural noun: *Any one* [as opposed to any two] *of the suggestions will be considered acceptable.*

anyplace   The standard *anywhere* is preferable.

anyway, anywhere, nowhere; anyways, anywheres, nowheres   *Anyway, anywhere,* and *nowhere* are standard forms. The others, ending in *-s,* are not.

apart, a part   *Apart* is an adverb: *The old book fell apart. A part* is a noun phrase: *I'd like to be a part of that project.*

as, as if   See *like*.

as regards   See *in regard to*.

assure, ensure, insure   All three words mean "to make secure or certain," but only *assure* is used in the sense of making a promise: *He assured us everything would be fine. Ensure* and *insure* are interchangeable, but only *insure* is commonly used in the commercial or financial sense: *We wanted to ensure that the rate we paid to insure our car against theft would not change.*

at   Avoid ending a question with *at*: <u>not</u> *Where's the library at?* <u>but</u> *Where's the library?*

awful   Avoid using *awful* to mean "bad" or "extremely": <u>not</u> *He's awful late* <u>but</u> *He's extremely late.*

a while, awhile   *A while* is a noun phrase: *a while ago; for a while. Awhile* is an adverb meaning "for some time": *They lived awhile in the wilderness.*

bad, badly   *Bad* is an adjective, *badly* an adverb. Use *bad* after linking verbs (such as *am, is, become, seem*): *They felt bad after losing the match.* Use *badly* to modify a verb: *They played badly.*

bare, bear   *Bare* is an adjective meaning "naked": the *bare* facts, a *bare*-faced lie. *Bear* is a noun (the animal) or a verb meaning "to carry" or "to endure": *He could not bear the pressure of losing.*

barely   Avoid creating a double negative (such as *can't barely type*). *Barely* should always take a positive verb: *She can barely type. They could barely keep their eyes open.* See *hardly*.

because, because of   *Because* is a subordinating conjunction used to introduce a dependent clause: *Because it was raining, we left early. Because of* is a two-word preposition: *We left early because of the rain.*

being as, being that   Avoid. Use *because* instead: *Because* [<u>not</u> *Being as*] *I was tired, I didn't go to class.*

belief, believe   *Belief* is a noun: *She has radical beliefs. Believe* is a verb: *He believes in an afterlife.*

beside, besides   *Beside* is a preposition meaning "next to": *Sit beside me. Besides* is a preposition meaning "except for": *He has no assistants besides us. Besides* is also an adverb meaning "in addition": *I hate horror movies. Besides, there's a long line.*

better   See *had better*.

between   See *among*.

brake, break   When we apply the *brake* in a car, we can *break* a window or even get a bad *break*.

breath, breathe   The first word is a noun, the second a verb: *Take three deep breaths. Breathe in deeply.*

bring, take   Use *bring* to suggest carrying something from a farther place to a nearer one, and *take* for any other transportation: *First bring me a cake from the store, and then we can take it to the party.*

can, may   In formal usage, use *can* in reference to ability or capacity, and use *may* to denote permission or possibility: *Climate change may be imminent. Bad weather can ruin farmers.*

can't hardly   This expression is nonstandard. See *hardly.*

capitol, capital   A *capitol* is a building where the legislature meets. *Capital* can refer to a city that is the seat of government: *The capitol is located within the capital. Capital* can also refer to the top of a column, and—as both noun and adjective—to wealth or to uppercase: *He admired the Corinthian capitals in the church aisle. He lost capital in the Enron crash. He made a large capital investment in a risky company. Use a capital letter for a proper noun.*

censor, censure   The verb *censor* refers to editing or removing from public view. *Censure* means to criticize harshly. *The new film was censored for graphic content, and the director was censured by critics for his irresponsibility.*

cite, site, sight   *Cite* means "to quote or mention"; *site* is a noun meaning "location"; *sight* is a noun meaning "view": *She cited the page number in her paper. They visited the original site of the abbey. The sight of the skyline from the plane produced applause from the passengers.*

compare to, compare with   Use *compare to* when implying similarity: *They compared the director to Alfred Hitchcock.* Use *compare with* when examining similarities or differences: *She wrote an essay comparing Hitchcock with Orson Welles.*

complement, compliment   As verbs, *complement* means "to complete or add to something," and *compliment* means "to make a flattering comment about someone or something": *The wine complemented the meal. The guests complimented the hostess on the fine dinner.* As nouns, the words have meanings associated with the verbs: *The wine was a fine complement to the meal. The guests paid the hostess a compliment.*

compose, comprise   *Compose* means "to make up"; *comprise* means "to include": *The conference center is composed of twenty-five rooms. The conference center comprises twenty-five rooms.*

conscience, conscious   *Conscience* is a noun meaning "awareness of right and wrong." *Conscious* is an adjective meaning "awake" or "aware." *Her conscience troubled her after the accident. The victim was still not conscious.*

continual, continuous   *Continual* implies repetition; *continuous* implies lack of a pause: *The continual interruptions made the lecturer angry. Continuous rain for two hours stopped play.*

could care less This expression is often used but is regarded by some as nonstandard. In formal English, use it only with a negative: *They could not care less about their work.*

could of Incorrect usage. See *have.*

council, counsel A *council* is a group formed to consult, deliberate, or make decisions. *Counsel* is advice or guidance. *The council was called together to help give counsel to the people. Counsel* can also be a verb: *We counseled the students to withdraw from the course.*

credible, creditable, credulous *Credible* means "believable": *The jury found the accused's alibi to be credible and so acquitted her. Creditable* means "deserving of credit": *A B+ grade attests to a creditable performance. Credulous* means "easily taken in or deceived": *Only a child would be so credulous as to believe that the streets are paved with gold.* See also *incredible, incredulous.*

criteria, criterion *Criteria* is the plural form of the singular noun *criterion: There are many criteria for a successful essay. One criterion is sentence clarity.*

curricula, curriculum *Curricula* is the plural form of *curriculum. All the departments have well-thought-out curricula, but the English Department has the best curriculum.*

custom, customs, costume All three words are nouns. *Custom* means "habitual practice or tradition": *a family custom. Customs* refers to taxes on imports or to the procedures for inspecting items entering a country: *go through customs at the airport.* A *costume* is "a style of dress": *a Halloween costume.*

dairy, diary The first word is associated with cows and milk, the second with daily journal writing.

decease, disease *Decease* is a verb or noun meaning "die" or "death." *Disease* is an illness: *The disease caused an early decease.*

decent, descent, dissent *Decent* is an adjective meaning "good" or "respectable": *decent clothes, a decent salary. Descent* is a noun meaning "way down" or "lineage": *She is of Scottish descent. Dissent,* used as both a noun and a verb, refers to disagreement: *The dissent about freedom led to civil war. Four judges dissented from the majority opinion.*

desert, dessert *Desert* can be pronounced two ways and can be a noun with the stress on the first syllable (*the Mojave Desert*) or a verb with the stress on the second syllable: *When did he desert his family?* The noun *desert* means "a dry, often sandy, environment." The verb *desert* means "to abandon." *Dessert* (with stress on the second syllable) is the sweet course at the end of a meal.

device, devise *Device* is a noun: *He said they needed a device that could lift a car. Devise* is a verb: *She began to devise a solution to the problem.*

differ from, differ with To *differ from* means "to be unlike": *Lions differ from tigers in several ways, despite being closely related.* To *differ with* means to "disagree with": *They differ with each other on many topics but are still good friends.*

different from, different than Standard usage is *different from: She looks different from her sister.* However, *different than* appears frequently in speech and writing, particularly when *different from* would require more words: *My writing is different than* [in place of *different from what*] *it was last semester.*

discreet, discrete *Discreet* means "tactful": *Be discreet when you talk about your boss. Discrete* means "separate": *They are researching five discrete topics.*

disease See *decease.*

disinterested, uninterested *Disinterested* means "impartial or unbiased": *The mediator was hired to make a disinterested settlement. Uninterested* means "lacking in interest": *He seemed uninterested in his job.*

dissent See *decent.*

dive, dived Be sure to use *dived* for the past tense of the verb *dive. Dove* is nonstandard.

do, due *Do* is a verb. Do not write *"Do to his absences, he lost his job";* instead use the two-word preposition *due to* or *because of.*

drag, dragged Use *dragged* for the past tense of the verb *drag. Drug* is nonstandard.

drown, drowned The past tense of the verb *drown* is *drowned; drownded* is not a word: *He almost drowned yesterday.*

due to the fact that, owing to the fact that Wordy. Use *because* instead: *They stopped the game because* [not *due to the fact that*] *it was raining.*

each, every These are singular forms; use them with a singular noun and verb: *Every child looks happy.* See also 17e, 17g, and 17h.

each other, one another Use *each other* with two; use *one another* with more than two: *The twins love each other. The triplets all love one another.*

effect See *affect.*

e.g. Use *for example* or *for instance* in place of this Latin abbreviation.

either, neither *Neither* is the negative form of *either.* Always use *nor* with *neither. Either Jill or Bob will be here tomorrow, but neither of them will stay long. Neither Joe nor Ed has a reason to come.*

elicit, illicit *Elicit* means "to get or draw out": *The police tried in vain to elicit information from the suspect's accomplice. Illicit* is an adjective meaning "illegal": *Their illicit deals landed them in prison.*

elude See *allude.*

emigrate, immigrate   *Emigrate from* means "to leave a country"; *immigrate to* means "to move to another country": *They emigrated from Ukraine and immigrated to the United States.* The noun forms *emigrant* and *immigrant* are derived from the verbs.

eminent, imminent   *Eminent* means "well known and noteworthy": *an eminent lawyer. Imminent* means "about to happen": *an imminent disaster.*

ensure   See *assure.*

etc.   This abbreviation for the Latin *et cetera* means "and others." Do not let a list trail off with *etc.*: not *They took a tent, a sleeping bag, etc.* but *They took a tent, a sleeping bag, cooking utensils, and a stove.*

every, each   See *each.*

everyday, every day   *Everyday* (one word) is an adjective meaning "usual": *Their everyday routine is to break for lunch at 12:30. Every day* (two words) is an adverbial expression of frequency: *I get up early every day.*

except, expect   See *accept.*

explicit, implicit   *Explicit* means "direct": *She gave explicit instructions. Implicit* means "implied": *A tax increase is implicit in the proposal.*

farther, further   Both words can refer to distance: *She lives farther (further) from the campus than I do. Further* also means "additional" or "additionally": *The management offered further incentives. Further, the union proposed new work rules.*

female, male   Use these words as adjectives, not as nouns in place of *man* and *woman*: *There are only three women [not females] in my class. We are discussing female conversational traits.*

few, a few   *Few* means "hardly any": *She feels depressed because she has few helpful colleagues. A few* means "some"; it has more positive connotations than *few*: *She feels fortunate because she has a few helpful colleagues.*

fewer, less   Formal usage demands *fewer* with plural countable nouns (*fewer holidays*), *less* with uncountable nouns (*less sunshine*). However, in informal usage, *less* with plural nouns commonly occurs, especially with *than: less than six items, less than ten miles, fifty words or less.* In formal usage, *fewer* is preferred.

first, firstly   Avoid *firstly, secondly,* and so on when listing reasons or examples. Instead, use *first, second.*

flammable, inflammable, nonflammable   Both *flammable* and *inflammable* mean the same thing: able to be ignited easily. *Nonflammable* means "unable to be ignited easily." *Dry wood is flammable* or *Dry wood is inflammable. Asbestos is nonflammable.*

flaunt, flout   *Flaunt* means "to show [something] off" or "to display in a proud or boastful manner." *Flout* means "to defy or to show scorn for": *When she flaunted her jewels, she flouted good taste.*

former, latter   These terms should be used only in reference to a list of two people or things: *We bought lasagna and ice cream, the former for dinner and the latter for dessert.* For more than two items, use *first* and *last*: *I had some pasta, a salad, and ice cream; though the first was very filling, I still had room for the last.*

get married to, marry   These expressions can be used interchangeably: *He will get married to his fiancée next week. She will marry her childhood friend next month.* The noun form is *marriage: Their marriage has lasted thirty years.*

go, say   Avoid replacing the verb *say* with *go*, as this is nonstandard usage: *Jane says* [not *goes*], *"I'm tired of this game."*

good, well   *Good* is an adjective; *well* is an adverb: *If you want to write well, you must use good grammar.* See 19a.

had better   Include *had* in Standard English, although it is often omitted in advertising and in speech: *You had better* [<u>not</u> *You better*] *try harder.*

hanged, hung   Both words are the past tense of *hang;* however, *hanged* should be used only when referring to a method of execution, and *hung* is used for all other meanings: *The rope still hung from the gallows. The executioner hanged five men there in one year.*

hardly   This is a negative word. Do not use it with another negative: <u>not</u> *He couldn't hardly walk* <u>but</u> *He could hardly walk.*

have, of   Use *have*, not *of*, after *should, could, might*, and *must: They should have* [<u>not</u> *should of*] *appealed.*

height   Note the spelling and pronunciation: <u>not</u> *heighth.*

heroin, heroine   Do not confuse these words. *Heroin* is a drug; *heroine* is a brave woman. *Hero* may be used for an admirable person of either sex.

hisself   Nonstandard; instead use *himself.*

hopefully   This word means "in a hopeful manner" or "with a hopeful attitude": *Hopefully, she e-mailed her résumé.* Some readers object to the use of *hopefully* in place of *I hope that:* <u>not</u> *Hopefully, she will get the job* <u>but</u> *I hope that she will get the job.*

I, me   Do not confuse *I* and *me.* Use *I* only in the subject position, and use *me* only in the object position. To check subjects and objects using *and,* simply drop any additional subject or object so that only the pronoun remains: <u>not</u> *The CFO and me were sent to the conference* <u>but</u> *The CFO and I were sent* (I was sent); <u>not</u> *Please send copies to my secretary and I* <u>but</u> *Please send copies to my secretary and me* (send copies to me). See 18a.

illicit   See *elicit.*

illusion   See *allusion.*

immigrate See *emigrate*.

imminent See *eminent*.

immoral See *amoral*.

implicit See *explicit*.

imply, infer *Imply* means "to suggest in an indirect way": *He implied that further layoffs were unlikely. Infer* means "to guess" or "to draw a conclusion": *I inferred that the company was doing well.*

incredible, incredulous *Incredible* means "difficult to believe": *The violence of the storm was incredible. Incredulous* means "skeptical, unable to believe": *His colleagues were incredulous when he told them about his daring exploits in the whitewater rapids.*

infamous *Infamous* is an adjective meaning "notorious": *Blackbeard's many exploits as a pirate made him infamous along the American coast.* Avoid using it as a synonym for "not famous."

inflammable See *flammable*.

in regard to, as regards Use one or the other. Do not use the nonstandard *in regards to.*

install, instill To *install* is to "set in position for use" or "establish." To *instill* is to "implant": *She would not have been able to install the fixture if her parents hadn't instilled in her a sense of craftsmanship.*

insure See *assure*.

irregardless Nonstandard; instead use *regardless: He selected a major regardless of the preparation it would give him for a career.*

it's, its The apostrophe in *it's* signals not a possessive but a contraction of *it is* or *it has. Its* is the possessive form of the pronoun *it: The city government agency has produced its final report. It's available upon request.* See also 25e.

kind, sort, type In the singular, use each of these with *this* and a singular noun: *this type of book.* Use in the plural with *these* and a plural noun: *these kinds of books.*

kind of, sort of Do not use these to mean "somewhat" or "a little." *The pace of the baseball game was somewhat [not kind of] slow.*

knew, new *Knew* is the past tense of the verb *know. New* is an adjective meaning "not old."

lend, loan *Lend* is a verb, and *loan* is ordinarily used as a noun: *Our cousins offered to lend us some money, but we refused the loan.*

less See *fewer*.

lie, lay Be sure not to confuse these verbs. *Lie* does not take a direct object; *lay* does. See 16b.

like, as, as if In formal usage, *as* and *as if* are subordinating conjunctions and introduce dependent clauses: *She walks as her father does. She looks as if she could eat a big meal. Like* is a preposition and is followed by a noun or pronoun, not by a clause: *She looks like her father.* In speech, however, and increasingly in writing, *like* is often used where formal usage dictates *as* or *as if: She walks like her father does. He looks like he needs a new suit.*

likely, liable *Likely* means "probably going to," while *liable* means "at risk of" and is generally used to describe something negative: *Eddie plays the guitar so well he's likely to start a band. If he keeps playing that way, he's liable to break a string. Liable* also means "responsible": *The guitar manufacturer cannot be held liable.*

literally Avoid overuse: *literally* is an adverb meaning "actually" or "word for word" and should not be used in conjunction with figurative expressions such as *my jaw literally hit the floor* or *he was literally bouncing off the walls. Literally* should be used only when the words describe exactly what is happening: *He was so scared his face literally went white.*

loan See *lend.*

loose, lose *Loose* is an adjective meaning "not tight": *This jacket is comfortable because it is so loose. Lose* is a verb (the past tense form and past participle are *lost*): *Many people lose their jobs in a recession.*

lots of See *alot.*

man, mankind Avoid using these terms, as they are gender-specific. Instead, use *people, human beings, humankind, humanity,* or *men and women.*

marital, martial *Marital* is associated with marriage, *martial* with war.

may be, maybe *May be* (two words) consists of a modal verb followed by the base form of the verb *be; maybe* (one word) is an adverb meaning "perhaps." If you can replace the expression with *perhaps,* make it one word: *They may be there already, or maybe they got caught in traffic.*

me, I See *I.*

media, medium *Media* is the plural form of *medium: Television and radio are both useful communication media, but his favorite medium is the written word.*

might of Incorrect usage. See *have.*

most See *almost.*

most, most of, the most *Most* means "nearly all": *Most politicians have secret ambitions. Most of* means "nearly all of" and is followed by a word such as *the, this, those, my,* or *their* that makes the noun specific: *She finished most of her homework. Most of the students in the class passed the test.* Use *the most* to compare more than two people or things: *Bill is the most efficient of all the technicians.*

must of Incorrect usage. See *have.*

myself Use only as a reflexive pronoun (*I told them myself*) or as an intensive pronoun (*I myself told them*). Do not use *myself* as a subject pronoun: <u>not</u> *My sister and myself won* <u>but</u> *My sister and I won.*

neither See *either.*

no, not *No* modifies a noun: *The author has no intention of deceiving the reader. Not* modifies a verb, adjective, or adverb: *She is not wealthy. He does not intend to deceive.*

nonflammable See *flammable.*

nowadays All one word. Be sure to include the final *-s.*

nowhere, nowheres See *anyway.*

number See *amount.*

off, off of Use only *off*, not *off of*: *She drove the car off* [<u>not</u> *off of*] *the road.*

oftentimes Do not use. Prefer *often.*

OK, O.K., okay Reserve these forms for informal speech and writing. Choose another word in a formal context: <u>not</u> *Her performance was OK* <u>but</u> *Her performance was satisfactory.*

one another See *each other.*

owing to the fact that See *due to the fact that.*

passed, past *Passed* is a past tense verb form: *They passed the deli on the way to work. He passed his exam. Past* can be a noun (*in the past*), an adjective (*in past times*), or a preposition (*She walked past the bakery*).

peak, peek, pique *Peak* is the top of a summit: *She has reached the peak of her performance. Peek* (noun or verb) means "glance": *A peek through the window is enough. Pique* (also a noun or a verb) has to do with feeling indignation: *Feeling insulted, he stormed out in a fit of pique.*

people, persons Use *people* to refer to a general group, and *persons* to refer to a collection of individuals: *Although many people saw the crime happen, it will still be hard to find the person or persons responsible.*

personal, personnel *Personal* is an adjective meaning "individual," while *personnel* is a noun referring to employees or staff: *It is my personal belief that a company's personnel should be treated like family.*

phenomena, phenomenon *Phenomena* is the plural form of the noun *phenomenon*: *Outer space is full of celestial phenomena, one spectacular phenomenon being the Milky Way.*

plus Do not use *plus* as a coordinating conjunction or a transitional expression. Use *and* or *moreover* instead: *He was promoted, and* [<u>not</u> *plus*] *he received a bonus.* Use *plus* as a preposition meaning "in addition to": *His salary plus his dividends placed him in a high tax bracket.*

pore, pour To *pore* is to read carefully or to ponder: *I saw him poring over the want ads before he poured himself a drink.*

precede, proceed *Precede* means "to go or occur before": *The Roaring Twenties preceded the Great Depression. Proceed* means "to go ahead": *After you pay the fee, proceed to the examination room.*

prejudice, prejudiced *Prejudice* is a noun: *Prejudice is harmful to society. Prejudiced* is a past participle verb form: *He is prejudiced against ethnic minorities.*

pretty Avoid using *pretty* as an intensifying adverb. Instead use *really, very, rather,* or *quite: The stew tastes very* [not *pretty*] *good.* Often, however, the best solution is to avoid using any adverb: *The stew tastes good.*

principal, principle *Principal* is a noun (*the principal of a school*) or an adjective meaning "main" or "most important": *His principal motive was monetary gain. Principle* is a noun meaning "standard or rule": *He always acts on his principles.*

quite, quiet Do not confuse the adverb *quite,* meaning "very," with the adjective *quiet* ("still" or "silent"): *We were all quite relieved when the audience became quiet.*

quote, quotation *Quote* is a verb. Do not use it as a noun. Use *quotation: The quotation* [not *quote*] *from Walker tells the reader a great deal.*

real, really *Real* is an adjective; *really* is an adverb. Do not use *real* as an intensifying adverb: *She acted really* [not *real*] *well.*

reason is because Avoid *the reason is because.* Instead, use *the reason is that* or rewrite the sentence. See 15e.

regardless See *irregardless.*

respectable, respectful, respective *Respectable* means "presentable, worthy of respect": *Wear some respectable shoes to your interview. Respectful* means "polite or deferential": *Parents want their children to be respectful to adults. Respective* means "particular" or "individual": *The friends of the bride and the groom sat in their respective seats in the church.*

respectfully, respectively *Respectfully* means "showing respect": *He bowed respectfully when the queen entered. Respectively* refers to items in a list and means "in the order mentioned": *Horses and birds gallop and fly, respectively.*

rise, raise *Rise* is an intransitive verb: *She rises early every day. Raise* is a transitive verb: *We raised alfalfa last summer.* See 16b.

sale, sell *Sale* is a noun: *The sale of the house has been postponed. Sell* is a verb: *They are still trying to sell their house.*

set, sit *Set* should not be used in place of *sit,* as *set* must always take an object. *He was sitting in his favorite chair* (not *He was setting in his favorite chair*). *When she came in, she sat down* (not *When she came in, she set down*). Conversely, *sit* should not be used in place of *set: Set the bags down there* (not *Sit the bags down there*). See 16b.

should of Incorrect usage. See *have*.

since Use this subordinating conjunction only when time or reason is clear: *Since you insist on helping, I'll let you paint this bookcase.* Unclear: *Since he got a new job, he has been happy.*

site, sight See *cite*.

someplace Prefer the standard *somewhere*.

sometimes, sometime, some time The adverb *sometimes* means "occasionally": *He sometimes prefers to eat lunch at his desk.* The adverb *sometime* means "at an indefinite time": *I read that book sometime last year.* The noun phrase *some time* consists of the noun *time* modified by the quantity word *some*: *After working for Honda, I spent some time in Brazil.*

sort, type See *kind*.

sort of See *kind of*.

stationary, stationery *Stationary* is an adjective meaning "not moving" (*a stationary vehicle*); *stationery* is a noun referring to the paper on which you write letters.

stayed, stood Do not confuse these forms. *Stayed* is the past tense form of *stay*; *stood* is the past tense form of *stand*.

supposedly Use this, not *supposably*: *She is supposedly a great athlete.*

take See *bring*.

taught, thought Do not confuse these verb forms. *Taught* is the past tense and past participle form of *teach*; *thought* is the past tense and past participle form of *think*: *The students thought that their professor had not taught essay organization.*

than, then *Then* is a time word; *than* must be preceded by a comparative form: *bigger than, more interesting than*.

that See *who*.

their, there, they're *Their* is a pronoun indicating possession; *there* indicates place or is used as a filler in the subject position in a sentence; *they're* is the contracted form of *they are*: *They're over there, guarding their luggage.*

theirself, theirselves, themself Nonstandard; instead use *themselves*.

threat, treat These words have different meanings: *She gave the children some cookies as a treat. The threat of an earthquake was alarming.*

thru Nonstandard. Use *through*.

thusly Incorrect form of *thus*.

to, too, two Do not confuse these words. *To* is a sign of the infinitive and a common preposition; *too* is an adverb meaning "also"; *two* is the number: *She is too smart to agree to report to two bosses.*

too, very   *Very* indicates degree, meaning "extremely": *The Volvo was very expensive, but he bought it anyway. Too* indicates "to an excessive degree": *The Volvo was too expensive, so he bought a Ford instead.* Note the pattern *too . . . to* + verb: *It is too hot to sit in the sun.*

undoubtedly   This is the correct word, <u>not</u> *undoubtably.*

uninterested   See *disinterested.*

unique   The adjective *unique* means "the only one of its kind" and therefore should not be used with qualifying adjectives like "very" or "most": *His recipe for chowder is unique* [<u>not</u> *most unique* or *quite unique*]. See 19f.

used to, get (become) used to   These expressions share the common form *used to.* But the first, expressing a past habit that no longer exists, is followed by the base form of a verb: *He used to wear his hair long.* (Note that after *not*, the form is *use to: He did not use to have a beard.*) In the expression *get (become) used to, used to* means "accustomed to" and is followed by a noun or an *-ing* form: *She couldn't get used to driving on the left when she was in England.* See also 36f.

very   See *too.*

way, ways   Use *way* to mean "distance": *He has a way to go. Ways* in this context is nonstandard.

wear, were, we're, where   *Wear* is a verb; *were* is a past tense form of *be; we're* is a contraction of *we are; where* is a relative pronoun, a subordinating conjunction, or a question word. *Hikers wear bells. Bears were roaming. We're afraid. I don't know where the bears are.*

weather, whether   *Weather* is a noun; *whether* is a conjunction: *The weather will determine whether we go on the picnic.*

well   See *good.*

who, whom, which, that   See 20a and 20c.

whose, who's   *Whose* is a possessive pronoun: *Whose goal was that? Who's* is a contraction of *who is* or *who has: Who's the player whose pass was caught? Who's got the ball?*

would of   Incorrect usage. See *have.*

your, you're   *Your* is a pronoun used to show possession. *You're* is a contraction of *you are: You're wearing your new shoes today, aren't you?*

Suggested answers are provided here to exercise items marked with **A**.

PART 1: THE WRITING PROCESS

Exercise 1.1 Match the tone of passages to the intended readers.

Possible answer:
1. Tone: Conversational, informal
   Audience: Readers of magazines. This passage is from the *Saturday Evening Post* (May/June 2000): 12.

Exercise 3.1 Write about your own writing process.

Answers will vary. Here is one example:

The assignment was to write a personal essay on my name. I wrote it the night before it was due, at my desk, a cup of coffee by my side. I felt pressured, stuck, like I had nothing to write about my name. But I just started to brainstorm about when I was born and why I was named after my grandmother. I wrote the essay using the word processing program. I sat at the computer too long, and kept revising it and revising it, then I printed it out. It was late and I went to bed. I got up early, read it, and then made changes—I wasn't happy with it, but I had to leave for class. (I was thinking about asking for an extension, but . . . I just handed it in.) Naturally, I noticed mistakes when I was on the bus, and it was too late to do anything about it and I didn't have whiteout. So, I just neatly crossed out the mistakes and neatly printed the revisions. I write under pressure, not for enjoyment, but because I have to.

Exercise 4.2 Revise thesis statements.

Answers will vary. Sample revisions:
1. Factual statement
   Suggested revision: Among rights sought by gay activists, legalizing homosexual marriage is among the most difficult to achieve because of traditional beliefs about the family and procreation.
2. Too vague
   Suggested revision: Literacy programs enhance the quality of life of individuals and the economy of businesses in the community.
3. Too narrow. Also, subjective statement.
   Suggested revision: Plants not only enhance the beauty of homes and offices but are beneficial to health and wellness. A plant is one of the best air purifiers a consumer can buy.

Exercise 5.1 Identify topic sentences in paragraphs.

1. Topic sentence at the end

Exercise 5.2 Develop paragraphs: examples and narration.

Answers will vary. Sample answers:
1. Mary needs to begin working on her research paper. The deadline is approaching. By conducting research early, she can find out which research materials are available and which are not. She should get a head start on reading the material she finds, so that she can decide on her tentative thesis. Once she has her tentative thesis, she may discover that she wants to change it. Also, if she needs additional material, she may have to go to another library or order a book she cannot locate. In addition, if she encounters any obstacles, she can meet with the instructor and ask for direction.

Exercise 5.6 Consider bases for classification.

Answers will vary. Sample answers:
1. *Students in your class*   Basis for classification: year (freshman, sophomore, junior, senior), age, major, birthplace
2. *Buildings on your campus*   Basis for classification: architectural style, size, comfort, amenities

Exercise 5.8 Identify the transitions in a paragraph.

Although Julia is a returning college student, she has tried hard to blend in with the student population. <u>As a result</u>, she doesn't let the age difference interfere with her relationships with other students. Before she returned to school, <u>however</u>, she had concerns about whether or not she would fit in. <u>Still</u>, after two semesters of interacting with other students, Julia has gained confidence.

Exercise 6.1 Add an emotional appeal.

Some possibilities:

A good opening: In this article, which was published in the *New York Times*, the first four sentences of the article are "What is the most efficient way to raise low-income pupils' achievement? Is it ending social promotion, increasing accountability, or adding more testing? It could be none of those. Improving nutrition might bring a bigger test-score gain."

Language that appeals more to the emotions of the readers: Good nutrition not only helps children grow; it helps them to think well. Don't you want to help our children? They deserve a chance to live up to their potential and not have their futures stunted by poor nutrition.

An anecdote: Discuss the story of an undernourished child whose test scores dramatically increased once the child received the proper nutrition.

A conclusion with a hopeful note: We can do something that will yield results because there is a correlation between nutrition and increases in test scores.

Exercise 6.2 Analyze assumptions.

1. Claim: Steve is wealthy.
   Support/data: Steve wears designer clothing, drives a Mercedes, and has a summer home.
   Assumption/warrant: Since he wears designer clothing, drives a Mercedes, and has a summer home, he must be wealthy.
   Qualifier: . . . unless he is in debt and borrows to keep up the lifestyle. On paper he may be worthless.
   Revised claim: Because Steve drives a Mercedes, wears designer clothing, and has a summer home, he exhibits a wealthy lifestyle.

Exercise 6.3 Examine arguments.

1. Ad hominem: This statement is an attack against a man for being untrustworthy today based on an incident that occurred many years ago while he was in college. It doesn't take into account the details or circumstances or tenor of the times or say if he was convicted of the charges or if he honorably paid his dues for the offense, as may well be the case.
2. OK.

Exercise 7.1 Evaluate introductory paragraphs.

1. Quotation
   Effective because you can hear the voice of the mother

Exercise 7.2 Improve an unsatisfactory conclusion.

Answers will vary. Sample revision:
As we can see, computer users can take several measures to protect their data from dangerous computer viruses. The first and most important measure described above, to invest in an antivirus program, is valuable in screening any questionable documents. The second measure, also sound advice, is common sense: don't open any files, including e-mail attachments, from unknown sources. Perhaps the most important step to take in protecting data is to back up all files at least once a month. Maybe one day there will be early-detection super antivirus warning programs announcing "Virus Detection! Virus Detection!" to unsuspecting data files. Until then, computer users must take proactive steps to safeguard their data.

Exercise 7.3 Try out spelling and grammar checkers.

Answers about existing settings will vary. In both Standard and Formal settings, one student found that Microsoft Word flagged only one error—*there*—and recommended *their* in its place. Grammar checkers often do not catch missing quotation marks.
Correct version: The economist's spreadsheets were simpler than those prepared by competitors. "They were prepared quickly," said the manager. (Is the word "was" a direct quotation or a typo?)
Conclusion: You cannot depend on spelling and grammar checkers. (This assumes that "was" is a typographical error and not part of the original quotation.)

Exercise 7.4 Proofread a passage and use correction marks.

Insomnia is a sleep disorder that effects [ww—*affect*/not *effect*] millions of people. Often they turn to over-the-counter pills to relieve their insomnea. [sp] Medication, especially self-medication, should not be the first course of action. Patients should seek the advice of there physician. [ww—*their*/not *there*]

Exercise 8.1 Make appropriate cuts. [Humanities related]

Answers will vary. Some possibilities:

With computer graphics imaging becoming more lifelike ~~and realistic in today's society~~, filmmakers ~~in the motion picture industry~~ are now able to create animated characters who could conceivably take the place of human beings ~~or people~~ in leading roles onscreen. Nonliving stars are not a completely ~~and totally~~ unknown quantity, of course. Mickey Mouse and Bugs Bunny ~~are cartoon characters who~~ earned millions of fans ~~in spite of the fact that~~ [although] they did not exist ~~in the real world~~ outside of an animation studio. King Kong, ~~who was~~ the first stop-motion animation star, thrilled ~~and delighted~~ audiences beginning in ~~the decade of~~ the 1930s because ~~of the fact that~~ he was ~~believyably~~ [believable] ~~realistic~~ at that ~~point in~~ time.

Exercise 8.2 Check for action. [Science related]

Answers will vary. Some possibilities:

Alzheimer's disease ~~is a terrible affliction of~~ *afflicts* the elderly, ~~terribly~~ in the United States and around the world. ~~People are robbed by the~~ *The* disease *robs people* of a lifetime of memories, and family members often care for patients who no longer recognize them. ~~There can be~~ *Helping an Alzheimer's patient requires* years of round-the-clock, care ~~required to help an Alzheimer's patient, and such care is~~ *expensive.* ~~A~~ *This disease takes a* heavy toll ~~is taken~~ on any stricken family ~~by this disease.~~

Exercise 8.3 Make connections. [Social sciences related]

Answers will vary. Some possibilities:

~~The~~ *When the* Taliban rulers of Afghanistan fell from power in the fall of 2001. ~~An~~ *, an* interim government was formed to rule the war-torn country. ~~and under~~ *Under* the Taliban, the law had forbidden women to hold jobs, reveal their faces in public, or speak to men other than their relatives. ~~and~~ *As a sign that times had changed in Afghanistan,* the interim government included a department devoted to women's affairs ~~in a sign that times had changed in Afghanistan.~~ Dr. Sima Samar, *who had earned a medical degree from Kabul University,* was chosen ~~as the minister for women's affairs. Dr. Samar earned a medical degree from Kabul University.~~ *to head this department.* ~~Dr. Samar~~ *She* had spent years working from exile and from within Afghanistan to improve the conditions for women in her native country.

Exercise 8.5 Avoid biased language. [Humanities related]

1. Some comic strips, such as *Doonesbury,* written by Garry Trudeau, and *The Boondocks*, created by ~~the African American~~ Aaron McGruder, can be considered political satires.

2. Many ~~normal~~ people have found *Doonesbury* offensive throughout its long history, for Trudeau has depicted premarital sex and drug use, championed ~~women's libbers~~ *feminism* and ~~peaceniks,~~ *antiwar efforts,* and criticized politicians from Richard Nixon to George W. Bush.

Exercise 8.6 Revise a draft for style.

Answers will vary. This is how the student who wrote the original draft revised after getting feedback:

The Corner Bistro on West 4th Street in Manhattan is a crowded neighborhood bar and restaurant, where Greenwich Village customers have been enjoying burgers and mugs of beer since the 1960s. They also used to enjoy, or suffer, what the Zagat Survey calls "side orders of cigarette smoke." It is a cleaner, safer environment since smoking has been banned in all Manhattan restaurants and bars. Some of the locals there, however, are outraged. One of them, shouting hoarsely above the noise, gestures with nicotine-stained fingers toward an unnamed enemy: "Who do they think they are, telling me I can't smoke in here? Soon they will be telling me I can't eat and drink in here. They talk about freedom *from* smoke. What about my freedom *to* smoke?" He storms outside to light up. The issue, though, is not just freedom. The issue is the proven danger of secondhand smoke. Out there he will no longer endanger the health of his fellow customers or of the restaurant employees.

PART 2: DOCUMENT DESIGN, VISUAL POWER
Exercise 10.1 Create a pie chart and a bar chart.

Styles of charts may vary. Here are two examples:

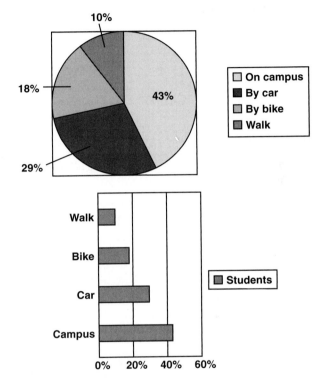

Exercise 11.1 Read an image critically.

Answers will vary. Sample answer:

The spatial organization shows Ms. Kipp, dressed simply in black and white, standing in the center of the picture. A wall shelf holds microscopes to her right and a small child's hands enter the frame from the left. The immediate suggestion is ample resources for study on one hand and easy connection to her child on the other.

The visual focus is, of course, on Ms. Kipp herself. Her image challenges stereotypes of American Indians. She smiles directly at us, with relaxed confidence. The left hand, hidden behind her back, is close to the microscopes; her right hand is relaxed yet supports what we assume are her child's hands, busy at play. Her active, three-quarter stance—one leg seems to step forward—gives a sense of connection but also of freedom. Her long, straight dark hair might connote an image of an American Indian. Her simple black jeans and white button-down shirt avoid a mainstream fashion statement. This image of a young American highlights values that are picked up in the text.

We assume the child is Kipp's because the text has told us she's a "mom." We imagine the microscopes are directly connected to her "biology" major. Knowing that she's a "tutor" underscores achievement, mastery, and dedication. In addition to studying,

Ms. Kipp works, and her job is a vocation. Clearly, she has already given back to her community and has every intention of continuing to do so as she pursues a doctorate specializing in large-animal surgery.

Given the qualities exemplified in both image and text, prospective donors are strongly persuaded to give to the college fund. And economists' predictions that graduates' incomes "will turn over two and a half times" persuade prospective donors that this won't be simple philanthropy but is also a wise investment.

Exercise 11.2 Analyze a visual argument.

Answers will vary. Sample answer:
a.
As diverse and individual as children of the world are, unity can come from love. In this visual, love is the joyous consequence of the connections children make so effortlessly. The balanced symmetries of the children's legs, arms, smiles, and eyes are extensions of the heart that is shaped when they join hands. Even their differences—in this case, hair texture, eye and skin color—become symmetrically distinctive. From the children's point of view, as in this visual, the world is not much bigger than a ball with golden continents.

PART 3: EDITING FOR COMMON SENTENCE PROBLEMS

Exercise 12.1 Identify the subject and verb in a simple sentence. [Social sciences related]

1. Most experts consider some types of debt, such as a mortgage, financially necessary.
2. However, credit-card debt never benefits an individual's long-term financial goals.

Exercise 12.2 Identify parts of speech. [Humanities related]

1. pronoun, verb
2. adverb, pronoun

Exercise 12.3 Identify dependent clauses. [Social sciences related]

1. In 1900, Sigmund Freud, a former neurologist, published a book called *The Interpretation of Dreams*, which discussed the purpose of dreams.
2. Freud believed that dreams reveal the sleeper's unconscious desires in a disguised form.
3. Today modern psychoanalysts are less interested in dream interpretation, and some disagree with Freud's theories.
4. One of these is Dr. J. Allan Hobson, a psychiatrist at Harvard Medical School, who considers dreams simply a byproduct of the sleeping brain.
5. The activity of the brain stem produces dream images, but according to Dr. Hobson, this activity is random.

Exercise 13.1 Identify troublespots. [Science related]

1. In 1983, a mysterious disease ~~attacks~~ attacked sea urchins in the Caribbean and killed most of the species known as *Diadema*.   *tense shift*

2. According to the Smithsonian Tropical Research Institute, ~~they~~ reported
   , researchers
   the biggest die-off ever for a marine animal.   *unclear pronoun ref*

3. ~~In a~~ 3.5-million-square-kilometer area of the Caribbean had once been home to
   millions of *Diadema* sea urchins.   *tangled sentence*

4. Algae began to spread quickly in this vast ocean area, ~~After~~ 97 percent of the *Diadema*
   after
   urchins that had once controlled the algae's growth by eating them died.   *fragment*

5. Soon, the algae had ~~grew~~ over many of the coral reefs, preventing young coral from
   grown
   attaching and building on top of older coral.   *wrong verb form*

Exercise 14.1 Identify and correct dependent clause fragments. [Social sciences related]

1. A group of nuns wrote autobiographies sixty years ago, ~~When~~ they were young
   when
   women.

2. Because the nuns all had similar lifestyles and social status, ~~Psychologists~~ have
   , psychologists
   looked closely at the autobiographies and compared the lives of the writers.

3. Not surprisingly, few nuns reported negative emotions, ~~Since~~ they knew that their
   since
   Mother Superior would read the autobiographies.

4. However, some reported having "very happy" experiences and a positive attitude
   about the future. Others were more neutral. [Sentences are correct.]

5. Psychologists discovered that the nuns who had expressed positive views lived an
   average of seven years longer than the other nuns, ~~A~~ conclusion that indicates that
   a
   looking on the bright side may be good for a person's health.

Exercise 14.2 Identify and correct phrase fragments. [Humanities related]

1. Every country has its own musical styles, ~~Based~~ on the traditional music of its people.
   that are based

2. Having its own tradition as the birthplace of jazz, blues, and rock music, ~~The~~ United
   , the
   States has long been one of the world's leading exporters of popular music.

3. In spite of enjoying enormous popularity in their own countries, ~~Many~~ performers
   , many
   from Europe, South America, Africa, and Asia have had a hard time attracting
   American fans.

4. Some American musicians have championed their favorite artists from abroad.
   Examples include the hip-hop artist Jay Z's collaboration with South Asian artist
   Punjabi MC on the hit song "Beware of the Boys" and Beck's tribute to the late French
   singer-songwriter Serge Gainsbourg. [Sentences are correct.]

5. Although some U.S. music fans pay attention to foreign musical styles, most
   Americans download the music they know from American top-40 radio and MTV.
   ~~Songs~~ also loved by fans around the world for sounding typically American.
   These songs are

Exercise 14.3 Identify and correct fragments resulting from missing subjects, verbs, or verb parts. [Social sciences related]

1. Teachers were once regarded as committed, admirable professionals. ~~People earning~~ (who earned) more respect than money.

2. Today, many teachers feel that they do not command respect. Instead (, they) seem to get blamed when students do not do well.

Exercise 14.4 Identify and correct fragments with no subject after *and*, *but*, or *or*. [Science related]

1. Entomologists, scientists who study insects, often discover new species and get the opportunity to name the creatures that they find.
2. Most people who name a new species either choose a name in honor of someone who assisted with the discovery or describe the species—often in Latin—with the new name.

Exercise 14.5 Correct run-on sentences and comma splices. [Science related]

1. <u>RO</u> Pierre de Fermat was a lawyer by trade, but his passion was mathematics.
2. <u>RO</u> Fermat discussed his ideas in correspondence with other mathematicians; nevertheless, as a modest man, he refused to have his name attached to any published work on mathematics.
3. <u>CS</u> Regarding prime numbers with a special fascination, he formulated a theory about prime numbers in 1640 that later became famous as Fermat's Last Theorem.
4. <u>RO</u> In his notes, Fermat said that the theorem had a "marvelous" proof; however, he claimed that he did not have enough room in the margin to write it down.
5. <u>CS</u> Because some mathematicians believed that a short, elegant answer existed, they struggled to find the proof of Fermat's Last Theorem.

Exercise 15.1 Correct tangled syntax: mixed constructions and faulty comparisons. [Humanities related]

1. Phillis Wheatley's education was remarkable mainly because she received one, a rare luxury for a slave girl in the American colonies.
2. Wheatley was kidnapped from her homeland and sold into slavery when she was about seven, an experience that must have been traumatic.
3. Learning to read and write gave Phillis an opportunity to demonstrate her aptitude for poetry.
4. Like Alexander Pope, Phillis Wheatley preferred the poetic form of iambic pentameter couplets.

Exercise 15.2 Change meaning by changing the position of a modifier.

Only the passenger hurt his arm.

[and nobody else]

The only passenger hurt his arm.

[there were no other passengers]

The passenger only hurt his arm.

[but did not break it]

The passenger hurt only his arm.

[and nothing else]

The passenger hurt his only arm.

[he had only one arm]

Exercise 15.3 Identify dangling modifiers. [Humanities related]

1. __DM?__ When translating literature from one language into another, a writer should strive for both literal accuracy and a similar effect to that of the original work. *Or:* When translating literature from one language into another, it is important for a writer to strive for both literal accuracy and a similar effect to that of the original work.

2. __No DM__ Turning the Greek of the *Iliad* into English in 1997, Robert Fagles managed to translate the words accurately while keeping the poetry lyrical and muscular.

Exercise 15.4 Correct inappropriate shifts: statement and command, pronoun person and number, direct and indirect quotations, and tense shifts. [Science related]

1. When a tourist in Florida wants an underwater adventure, they can swim in the ocean with sharks. __PP__

2. In 2001, a series of shark attacks on the east coast of the United States made Florida Fish and Wildlife Conservation commissioners ask whether swimmers were being too careless or whether tourist attractions that feature swimming with sharks the cause of the problem. __Q__

3. When a tour operators put bait in the water before a shark swim, they may be teaching sharks to associate people with food. __PN__

4. If sharks were fed too frequently by human beings, the commissioners wondered, would the big fish be more likely to endanger swimmers? __T__

5. The curator of the International Shark Attack File told commissioners that the feeding probably didn't contribute to the attacks and that they should tell people more about the good behavior of sharks. __Q__

Exercise 15.5 Avoid errors with logical sequence of subject and verb and with definitions and reasons. [Science related]

1. One reason for farmers to receive subsidies is that they set aside part of their land for wildlife conservation.

2. Conservation, which preserves the land in the most natural state possible, accounts for about 9 percent of farm subsidies in the United States.

Exercise 15.6 Identify omitted words and apostrophes. [Science related]

1. One physicist seriously claims that there are as many universes as or even more universes than the human mind can imagine.

2. This theory, known as the Many Worlds Interpretation, has always been and may always be considered by many other physicists to be nothing more than a poetic way of thinking about quantum mechanics.

Exercise 15.7 Revise for parallelism. [Humanities related]

1. Aimee Semple McPherson was not only the founder of a phenomenally successful ministry but <u>also</u> the first female evangelist to preach on the radio.
2. McPherson's thousands of followers reacted with shock and horror in May 1926 when the evangelist either staged her own disappearance <u>or was captured by kidnappers</u>.

Exercise 16.1 Use commonly confused verbs correctly. [Humanities related]

1. set (<u>set</u> / sit)
2. raise (<u>raise</u> / rise)

Exercise 16.2 Use present tenses correctly. [Science related]

1. Within a few hours of birth, newborn babies <u>show</u> a preference for looking at human faces.
2. Cognitive psychologists determine what <u>interests</u> babies by measuring how long they look at certain patterns or objects.

Exercise 16.3 Use past tenses correctly. [Humanities related]

In 1973, Clive Campbell, a Jamaican immigrant who <u>had been living</u> [or <u>had lived</u>] in the Bronx, New York, since 1967, christened himself "DJ Kool Herc" and <u>began</u> to work as a neighborhood disc jockey. During his childhood in Jamaica, Campbell <u>had seen</u> performers known as *toasters* talking rhythmically over reggae music. At dance parties in the Bronx, DJ Kool Herc <u>chanted</u> rhymes while he played popular records.

Exercise 16.4 Use -ed endings correctly. [Social sciences related]

1. College classrooms <u>used</u> to be seen as places where professors lectured to passive students, with only the most verbal students participating in discussions of the material.
2. Today, however, many professors have noticed the difference computers can make in their students' ability to join in class discussions. [Sentence is correct.]

Exercise 16.5 Use the correct tense in indirect quotations. [Social sciences related]

1. James Chatters, the forensic anthropologist who examined the bones, at first believed that the skeleton <u>was</u> a modern murder victim.
2. He then told authorities that he had noticed a prehistoric arrowhead embedded in the skeleton's pelvic bone. [Sentence is correct.]

Exercise 16.6 Use correct verb tenses in conditional sentences. [Science related]

1. If prehistoric canines <u>had eaten</u> crunchy, bite-sized food, they would probably have lost most of their teeth at an early age. #4 Speculation about the past
2. If dogs eat commercial dog food, plaque <u>tends</u> to collect on their teeth. #1 Condition of fact

Exercise 16.7 Identify active and passive voices. [Science related]

1. __P__ Rice blast, a fungus that destroys the rice crop, often <u>attacks</u> the sticky rice that brings the highest prices in China. *Or* Retain the passive voice to preserve the topic chain: "a thousand pounds of rice" and "the sticky rice."

2. __A__ A farmer in Yunnan province discovered that he could nearly eliminate rice blast by planting alternating rows of sticky rice and long-grain rice. [Sentence is in the active voice.]

Exercise 17.1 Ignore words between the subject and verb. [Science related]

1. An international <u>agency</u> monitoring the air and water quality around the Great Lakes ~~have~~ ^{has} discovered a previously unknown ecological process.

2. Toxic <u>chemicals</u> banned for at least a quarter of a century ~~is~~ ^{are} dispersing from the lakes into the air.

Exercise 17.2 Make subjects and verbs agree. [Social sciences related]

~~Do~~ ^{Does} the <u>government</u> have the right to keep certain kinds of information out of the hands of the public? There ~~is~~ ^{are} no easy <u>answers</u> to this question. When the <u>science</u> of cryptography was being developed, the National Security <u>Agency</u> wanted to restrict access to powerful, unbreakable codes. After all, <u>using</u> codes ~~are~~ ^{is} one way that a government keeps information from its enemies, and <u>breaking</u> codes allows a government to find out what its enemies are planning. NSA <u>agents</u> worried that unbreakable <u>codes</u> would allow enemies of the United States to conceal their activities from U.S. intelligence.

Exercise 17.3 Make verbs agree with tricky subjects and collective nouns. [Humanities related]

1. To play soccer, a <u>team</u> ~~need~~ ^{needs} few things other than a ball, a field, and a group of opponents.

2. When medieval British warriors defeated a Danish chieftain on the battlefield a millennium ago, their <u>kicking</u> the loser's head around the bloody fields ~~were~~ ^{was} the origin of soccer, according to a hard-to-prove legend.

Exercise 17.4 Use correct subject-verb agreement with compound subjects. [Humanities related]

1. In the Bamiyan valley of eastern Afghanistan, a 150-foot <u>Buddha</u>, believed to have been the largest standing Buddha in the world, and a 120-foot <u>Buddha</u> ~~was~~ ^{were} carved out of sandstone cliffs in the fourth or fifth century.

2. During that period, when the Silk Route wound through the mountains of Afghanistan, <u>wandering Buddhist monks or a caravan</u> of silk or ivory merchants was a common sight in the Bamiyan valley, which was home to Buddhist monasteries until the arrival of Islam in the ninth century. [Sentence is correct.]

Exercise 17.5 Use correct subject-verb agreement with indefinite pronouns and quantity words. [Humanities related]

1. <u>Many</u> of the small, hand-lettered, meticulously illustrated books by Edward Gorey (~~concerns~~ / concern) macabre events, yet <u>most</u> of Gorey's stories (~~is~~ / are) hilarious.

2. In the story "The Wuggly Ump," for example, <u>every human character</u> (ends up / ~~end up~~) being eaten by the title monster, yet the tale itself looks and sounds like a Victorian nursery rhyme.

Exercise 18.1 Use the correct form of personal pronouns. [Science related]

Marie Curie, born Maria Sklodowska in Poland in 1867, devoted her life to pure science in the hope that humans would benefit from what she discovered. Her parents, poor teachers, wanted ~~she~~ *her* and her siblings to get an education. Marie went to Paris to study at the Sorbonne when she was twenty-four; her work as a governess had earned her enough money to educate ~~she~~ *her* and her older sister. Marie struggled to learn French and overcome her deficient early education in physics and mathematics—subjects that girls in Poland such as ~~her~~ *she* and her sister had not been allowed to study. When she completed her master's degree in physics in 1894, she placed first in her class. Pierre Curie, who was doing research on magnetism, and ~~her~~ *she* met when Marie was searching for a laboratory she could use. Although Pierre did not have space for Marie in his lab, ~~him~~ *he* and ~~her~~ *she* fell in love and married.

Exercise 18.2 Use the correct possessive pronoun form. [Humanities related]

1. When Dietrich Bonhoeffer was a visiting pastor at Harlem's Abyssinian Baptist Church in 1931, the congregation was pleased with ~~him~~ *his* learning to love gospel music.

2. As a white German Protestant among African American worshippers, Bonhoeffer at first worried that his life was too different from ~~them~~ *theirs*.

Exercise 18.3 Use clear pronoun reference. [Science related]

1. Any food supplement or vitamin can obtain a patent, but ~~it~~ *the supplement or vitamin* may not be effective.

2. The U.S. Patent Office's purpose is to help inventors lay claim to their unique creations, but ~~it~~ *the office* does not investigate whether a creation actually does what its inventor claims.

Exercise 18.4 Use correct pronoun-antecedent agreement. [Humanities related]

1. If ~~a historian studies~~ *historians study* World War II, they will learn how important intelligence was for the Allied victory.

2. At first, however, U.S. intelligence was unable to identify the risk of a Japanese attack, and ~~their~~ *this* failure brought the country into the war.

Exercise 18.5 Avoid gender bias. [Social sciences related]

1. In the past, ~~a~~ first-grade ~~teacher~~ *teachers* might teach ~~her~~ *their* students to read by asking them to sound out letters.

2. In the last two decades of the twentieth century, many ~~a principal~~ *principals* asked ~~his school~~ *their schools* to teach reading using new theories.

Exercise 18.6 Maintain a consistent point of view, and use *you* appropriately. [Social sciences related]

Some possibilities:

Several municipalities around the United States—from small towns to the city of Chicago—have been trying a new method to establish a sense of community: All residents are encouraged to read the same book at the same time. When ~~we~~ _people_ read a book that ~~you~~ _they_ can discuss with ~~your~~ _their_ neighbors, ~~we~~ _they_ have a common ground for discussion. In the summer of 2001, ten thousand or more Chicagoans were reading Harper Lee's classic novel, _To Kill a Mockingbird_.

Exercise 18.7 Correct errors in pronoun use. [Science related]

By some estimates, 70% of all of the antibiotics produced in the United States are used to promote growth in healthy livestock. In 1998, ~~in~~ a report by the National Research Council and the Institute of Medicine ~~,they~~ said that feeding antibiotics to farm animals contributed to the rise of some antibiotic-resistant bacteria and ~~that this~~ _these bacteria_ could make human beings sick. Papers published in a 2001 issue of the _New England Journal of Medicine_ also concluded that ~~we~~ _people_ should be concerned about the use of antibiotics to make livestock grow more quickly and about the bacteria that are becoming harder to kill as a result.

Exercise 19.1 Use adjectives and adverbs appropriately. [Social sciences related]

Participating in a team sport can teach many good lessons to high school students. They can learn sportsmanship, the value of practicing to improve skills, and the strength that comes from working ~~good~~ _well_ together. However, many administrators, teachers, alumni, and students take high school athletics too ~~serious~~ _seriously_. When students are forced to practice football in full uniforms in ~~real~~ _really_ hot weather at the beginning of the school year, the coaches' priorities are misplaced.

Exercise 19.2 Use compound adjectives correctly. [Humanities related]

1. Lady Gregory's ~~twelve-years~~ _twelve-year_ marriage ended with her husband's death, and afterward she began to finish her husband's incomplete autobiography.
2. Her friendship with the ~~well known~~ _well-known_ poet W. B. Yeats was profitable for both of them: they inspired each other and collaborated on one act plays.

Exercise 19.3 Position adverbs correctly. [Humanities related]

In the nineteenth and twentieth centuries, polar exploration <u>usually</u> attracted courageous and foolhardy explorers. Many of these explorers kept journals or wrote books, and even today their writings are popular. Why would modern people want to read them? Perhaps the charm of these tales for modern readers lies in the strangeness of the quests. The early polar explorers <u>seldom</u> gave satisfying reasons for their journeys: on one British expedition to the South Pole, biologists endured weeks of the coldest weather ever recorded in order to collect specimens that scientists at home did not want. Another fascinating feature of polar exploration adventures is that they frequently were fatal: the most celebrated heroes of polar exploration have <u>often</u> been those who failed.

Exercise 19.4 Use comparative and superlative forms correctly. [Social sciences related]

In the United States, the first people to have cellular telephones were the ~~most rich~~ [richest]
members of the population. In India, in contrast, many poor and working-class people
have been among the people who have adopted cell phone technology the ~~most fast~~ [fastest].
Many of these people live and work in remote areas that are not served by traditional
land telephones, and they are finding that cell phones are one of the ~~usefullest~~ [most useful] inventions
for improving a small business. Fishermen in western India, for example, have no other
access to telephones from their boats, and calling the markets before heading to shore
with the day's catch allows them to find the ~~most high~~ [highest] prices. Growers of produce in rural
areas are also beginning to rely on cell phones to find the ~~most high~~ [best] prices for their wares.

Exercise 20.1 Use relative pronouns correctly. [Humanities related]

When George Lucas made the movie *Star Wars* in 1977, he told people ~~whom~~ [who] asked
about the film's box-office prospects that it would make sixteen million dollars. In fact,
the original *Star Wars*, the story of which was based on old movie serials and comic book
adventures, went on to become the second-highest-grossing film of all time. However, the
real money-making potential of the *Star Wars* films lies in the merchandise [that] accompanies
them.

Exercise 20.2 Make the verb and antecedent of a relative pronoun agree. [Science related]

1. Most people ~~whom~~ [who] participate in group insurance plans now use some form of
   managed care.
2. Many insurance companies require any patients who ~~participates~~ [participate] in managed care
   plans to get a referral from their primary care physician before seeing an expensive
   specialist.
3. This practice, which ~~are~~ [is] known as "gatekeeping," often infuriates both patients and
   physicians.

Exercise 20.3 Identify restrictive and nonrestrictive clauses. [Humanities related]

1. __R, R__   When a person <u>who speaks only English</u> and a person/<u>who speaks only
   Spanish</u> must communicate, they will find common ground by using the simple
   grammar and vocabulary of pidgin.
2. __NR__   Pidgin <u>which is not spoken as a native tongue by anyone</u> is different from
   creolized language.

Exercise 20.4 Correct errors in relative clauses and relative pronouns.

The QWERTY typewriter and computer keyboard, ~~that~~ [which] is named for the first six letters
on the left-hand side, was invented in the late nineteenth century. That keyboard came
into common use precisely because it prevented typists ~~which~~ [who] used it from typing fast.
The typewriter keys ~~which~~ [that] were used in those days became tangled if they moved too

quickly, so slow typing was actually beneficial. However, the situation soon changed. The
typewriters, ~~which~~ *that* were in use in the 1920s, were more mechanically sophisticated and
faster, so the QWERTY system was holding typists back instead of allowing them to type
their fastest. At that time Dr. August Dvorak, ~~whom~~ *who* taught at the University of
Washington, began to research keyboard layouts.

PART 4: EDITING FOR PUNCTUATION, MECHANICS, AND SPELLING
Exercise 22.1 Use end punctuation correctly. [Social sciences related]

1. A
2. B

Exercise 23.1 Identify commas: yes or no. [Social sciences related]

The notion of artificial intelligence, [×] is one of the most intriguing, [√(6)] controversial ideas in
computer programming today. Anyone, [×] who studies computers, [×] has probably wondered
whether modern computers are learning to think. Alan Turing, [√(3)] who helped to develop
computers during and after World War II, [√(3)] believed that the only way to tell if a computer
could think was to ask it questions. According to him, [(2)√] if the computer gave answers that
were indistinguishable from those of a human, [(2)√] the computer could be considered
intelligent. John Searle, [√(3)] a philosopher at the University of California at Berkeley, [√(3)] argued
that a computer that was able to create intelligent-sounding answers to questions need
not actually understand anything, [×] it might simply be popping out replies based on the
rules it had absorbed.

Exercise 23.2 Use commas before coordinating conjunctions connecting independent clauses. [Humanities related]

1. Patrick O'Brian once said that he was a derivative writer, for all of his information
   came from "log books, dispatches, letters, memoirs, and contemporary reports" from
   two centuries ago.

2. O'Brian wrote about adventure on the high seas and naval battles, but he also brought
   the manners and customs of naval society to life.

Exercise 23.3 Use commas after introductory material or with nonrestrictive elements. [Science related]

1. Realizing that laboratories and medical facilities around the world all needed to
   dispose of biohazards, researchers wanted a symbol that would indicate to everyone
   which material was infectious.

2. Designers who create symbols want them to be memorable. [Sentence is correct.]

Exercise 23.4 Use commas with transitional expressions, items in a series, coordinate adjectives, and direct quotations. [Science related]

The Department of Energy has proposed to recycle scrap metal from weapons and
research plants that are going to be demolished in Tennessee, Kentucky, Ohio, South
Carolina, and Colorado. Radiation has, unfortunately, contaminated the surface of the

metals that the DOE plans to recycle. Over a million tons of the contaminated metal will be available for recycling in the next fifteen years if the proposal is accepted.

First, however, the DOE is/funding an environmental study of the plan, analyzing the feasibility of recycling and reusing only those metals that meet lower radiation standards, and scheduling public hearings around the country. On one side, scrap metal dealers have expressed preliminary support for the proposal. Citizens who live near steel-recycling plants, on the other hand, have asked the DOE to reject the proposal as an irresponsible, environmentally unsound/idea.

Exercise 23.5 Use commas correctly. [Humanities related]

"All men are created equal," wrote Thomas Jefferson, but his deeds did not always match his eloquent words. Like most of the other aristocratic landowners in Virginia, Jefferson, the author of the Declaration of Independence, founder of the University of Virginia, and third president of the United States, owned slaves. One of them was a woman named/Sally Hemings, who was one-quarter African/and was probably the daughter of Jefferson's father-in-law and a half-African slave. If this genealogy is correct, Hemings was the half-sister of Jefferson's late wife, Martha. Indeed, observers at the time noted that/Hemings looked remarkably like Martha Jefferson, who had died on September 6, 1782, when Jefferson was thirty-nine.

In 1802, a disgruntled former employee reported that President Jefferson/ was the father of Hemings's three children. Jefferson never responded publicly to the charge, but/ many people noticed the resemblance between him and the Hemings children.

Exercise 24.1 Use semicolons and colons correctly. [Social sciences related]

Japan has long been one of the most homogeneous of the modern industrial nations; many Japanese protect their cultural identity so strongly that foreigners are rarely allowed to feel a part of Japan, no matter how long they and their families remain in the country. Foreign nationals who make Japan their home are not required to send their children to school as Japanese parents must; in addition, non-Japanese are not covered by Japan's national health insurance. Many foreign nationals, consequently/consider Japan only a temporary home. However, the Japanese population is/ getting older, with more retirees than new babies throughout the country; currently, the Japanese birthrate is one of the lowest in the world. To keep the economy alive and pay for pensions for retired workers and their families/Japan must find more workers. The United Nations now recommends that Japan begin to encourage immigration.

Exercise 25.1 Use apostrophes to signal possession. [Science related]

1. Doctors and healers' ideas about useful treatments for people infected with the AIDS virus sometimes conflict with each other.

2. For example, traditional healers often prescribe emetics to cause vomiting, and if a patients' treatment also includes retroviral drugs, the patient may expel the drugs before they take effect.

Exercise 25.2 Use apostrophes correctly. [Social sciences related]

Vermont's legislature passed a law in 2000 that recognizes gay and lesbian civil unions in its state as the equivalent of marriage. Since it's passage, the law has attracted gay tourists to Vermont, which along with Massachusetts is currently one of the few states that grant's gay and lesbian couples the right to all of the benefits of marriage. In the first year of the new law's existence in Vermont, two thousand gay and lesbian couples got civil-union licenses (in the same period, about five thousand heterosexual couples got traditional marriage licenses).

Exercise 26.1 Use quotation marks correctly. [Humanities related]

Child psychologist Bruno Bettelheim wrote that fairy tales, with their archetypal evil characters, terrifying situations, and improbable happy endings, could tell children a great deal "about the inner problems of human beings and of the right solutions to their predicaments in any society." In a newspaper article called Old Theory Could Explain Love of Harry Potter, Richard Bernstein argues that Bettelheim's analysis of fairy tales reveals the reasons for the staggering popularity of J. K. Rowling's books. Although Bernstein sees the book *Harry Potter and the Sorcerer's Stone* as "a fairly conventional supernatural adventure story," he admits that children find the books "as powerful as the witch of Hansel and Gretel." Bernstein analyzes the narrative and concludes that, "Harry's story, . . . with its early images of alienation, rejection, loneliness and powerlessness leading to its classically fairy tale ending, contains the same basic message that Bettelheim described."

Exercise 27.1 Use other punctuation marks correctly. [Humanities related]

1. George Harrison—the most reclusive member of the Beatles and the one who urged most strongly that the band stop playing live shows died on November 29, 2001.

2. Beatles fans from all over the world mourned the death of the second member of the most famous rock band in history John Lennon had been murdered more than twenty years before Harrison died of cancer.

3. Harrison (known to fans everywhere simply as "George" whose songwriting took a back seat to that of Lennon and McCartney, still wrote some of the Beatles' biggest hits, including "Something," "While My Guitar Gently Weeps," and "Here Comes the Sun."

4. Obituaries noted Harrison's interest in Eastern music and religion (at the time of his death, he remained a follower of a form of Hinduism he called Krishna Consciousness).

Exercise 28.1 Use italics and underlining correctly. [Science related]

Note: Italics are often used in place of underlining.

In the nineteenth century, phrenology—the study of bumps on the skull and their relation to the personality—was a popular pseudoscientific practice, and one of the best-known phrenologists was Lorenzo Fowler. Along with his brother Orson, Lorenzo Fowler headed the Phrenological Institute in New York City, where the two trained other phrenologists, and Lorenzo gave readings to celebrities such as Julia Ward Howe, author of "The Battle Hymn of the Republic." The Fowler brothers saw themselves as leaders of a progressive movement; they ran the publishing company that put out the first edition of Walt Whitman's <u>Leaves of Grass</u>. They also published the <u>Phrenological Journal</u>, hoping that phrenological analysis could lead people to correct defects of character that had been revealed by their cranial protrusions.

In 1872, Samuel Clemens, who had written <u>Huckleberry Finn</u> and many other works under the nom de plume Mark Twain, visited Fowler under an assumed name and obtained a reading and a phrenological chart.

Exercise 29.1 Use capital letters correctly. [Humanities related]

1. Biological warfare may strike modern Americans as ~~Barbaric~~ barbaric, but during the French and Indian ~~war~~ War, smallpox-infected blankets given to Native Americans helped to decimate their numbers.
2. ~~in~~ In the 1860s, Dr. Luke ~~blackburn~~ Blackburn tried the same tactic, giving or selling clothing from patients with ~~Yellow~~ yellow fever to ~~Soldiers~~ soldiers in the Union Army.

Exercise 29.2 Use abbreviations and acronyms correctly.

1. An early adopter—someone who buys new devices and gadgets as soon as they are available—probably owned ~~CD's~~ CDs when most people still bought records, rented ~~DVD's~~ DVDs while others still watched videos on their ~~VCR's~~ VCRs, and picked out ~~CD-ROM's~~ CD-ROMs as holiday gifts.
2. The acupuncturist's receptionist referred to him as ~~Doctor~~ Dr. Loren Selwyn, but I later discovered that he was Loren Selwyn, ~~doctor of philosophy~~ PhD, not Loren Selwyn, ~~medical doctor~~ MD.

Exercise 30.1 Use correct spelling and hyphenation. [Science related]

Recently, researchers who study chimpanzees have come to the ~~suprising~~ surprising conclusion that groups of chimpanzees have their own traditions that can be ~~past~~ passed on to new generations of chimps. The chimps do not ~~aquire~~ acquire these traditions by instinct; instead, they learn them from other chimps. When a scientific journal published ~~analysises~~ analyses of chimpanzee behavior, the author revealed that the ~~every day~~ everyday actions of chimpanzees in ~~seperate~~ separate areas differ in significant ways, even when the groups belong to the same subspecies. For instance, in one West African group, the chimps are often seen ~~puting~~ ^{putting} a nut on a stone and using another ~~peice~~ ^{piece} of stone to crack the nut open, a kind of behavior never observed in other groups of chimpanzees. ~~Sceintists~~ ^{Scientists} have also observed the chimps teaching ~~there~~ ^{their} young the ~~nut-opening~~ ^{nut-opening} method, and chimps in other places that crack nuts ^{differently} differentally teach their young ~~they're~~ ^{their} own way. Researchers have ~~therefor~~ ^{therefore} concluded that chimpanzees have local traditions.

PART 5: EDITING FOR WRITERS WITH OTHER LANGUAGES (ESL), OTHER ENGLISHES

Exercise 33.1 Use articles, including *the*, correctly. [Science related]

1. Many scientific studies have proved that exercise helps ~~the~~ people sleep better and lose ~~a~~ weight.

2. ^{An} ~~A~~ active lifestyle seems to improve not only a person's health but also his or her mood.

Exercise 34.1 Use auxiliary and modal auxiliary verbs correctly. [Humanities related]

Most people believe that musicians must ~~to~~ have talent in order to succeed. However, a 1998 study by British psychologist John Sloboda may ~~indicates~~ ^{indicate} that the number of hours spent practicing affects musical ability more than inborn talent does. The study included musicians aged ten to sixteen years, from both public and private schools. Sloboda investigated how much each young musician practiced, whether parents and teachers _∧ ^{were} involved in helping each musician improve, and how well each student scored on the British national music examination.

Exercise 34.2 Use correct verbs and verb forms. [Social sciences related]

Can money ~~makes~~ ^{make} people happy? A well-known proverb says, "Money can't buy happiness," but some people probably would ~~to~~ agree that money is important for a happy life. A survey by Andrew Oswald and Jonathan Gardner of the University of Warwick in England has ^{been} investigating the connection between money and happiness for eight years. The results are not ~~surprised~~ ^{surprising.} If people suddenly get money that they ^{are} not expecting—from the lottery, for example—they generally feel more ~~satisfy~~ ^{satisfied} with their lives.

Exercise 35.1 Correct errors in inclusion of a subject, order of elements, direct and indirect objects. [Science related]

1. Cosmetic surgery had ~~in the past~~ a stigma ^{in the past}, but now many people consider changing their appearance surgically.

2. In addition, the price of such surgery was once high, but it has declined in recent years. [Sentence is correct.]

3. In 2000, 7.4 million people had ~~for one reason or another~~ cosmetic surgery *for one reason or another*.

4. ~~Were~~ *There were* 370,000 African Americans among those 7.4 million patients, and African Americans represent a growing percentage of *people* wanting plastic surgery ~~people~~.

5. Cosmetic surgery gives ~~to~~ some people an improved self-image.

Exercise 35.2 Rewrite direct speech as indirect (reported) speech.

1. The critic announced that he (*or she*) could not abide such pretentious prose.
2. The mayor wanted to know who was in charge.
3. The contestant cannot work out what the square root of 2209 is.
4. The broker predicted that the economy would rebound.
5. Investors constantly wonder if they will lose all their savings.

Exercise 35.3 Use correct word order and sentence structure. [Science related]

Many people ~~fear~~ in China and Japan *fear* the number *four*. ~~Is~~ *There is* a good reason for this fear: in Japanese, Mandarin, and Cantonese, the word for *four* and the word for *death* are nearly identical. A study in the *British Medical Journal* suggests that cardiac patients from Chinese and Japanese backgrounds ~~they~~ may literally die of fear of the number *four*. According to the study, which looked at U.S. mortality statistics over a twenty-five-year period, Chinese and Japanese *patients* hospitalized for heart disease ~~patients~~ were more likely to die on the fourth day of the month. Although Chinese and Japanese cardiac patients across the country were all statistically more likely to die on that day, ~~but~~ the effect was strongest among Californian Chinese and Japanese patients. ~~Is~~ *It is* not clear why Californians are more at risk. However, one researcher suggested that because California's large Asian population includes many older people, the older generation may ~~therefore~~ teach to younger generations ~~traditional beliefs~~ *traditional beliefs*.

Exercise 35.4 Use adjectives in the correct order. [Social sciences related]

1. In northern states in wintertime, many office workers spend most of the daylight hours indoors. [Sentence is correct.]
2. Architects are beginning to design <u>some big new</u> buildings to admit as much natural light as possible.

Exercise 36.1 Use prepositions in their proper contexts. [Social sciences related]

Everyone hopes to retire __*at*__ some time __*in*__ the future. However, many people fail to invest for retirement, spending most of the money they earn __*on*__ everyday expenses and luxuries. The field of behavioral economics tries to explain why people do not always make rational plans to save for the future. Behavioral economists also work to find ways to convince people to save money and to get __*on*__ a schedule that will allow them to retire.

Exercise 36.2 Use adjective + preposition, verb + preposition. [Science related]

1. Although some Americans wanted to take antibiotics as a precaution against anthrax in the fall of 2001, the percentage of people who asked their doctors ~~of~~ *for* flu shots at that time was no higher than normal.

2. Influenza has been responsible ~~to~~ the deaths of many healthy people in the past
   ^for
   century, and doctors do not know when a dangerous strain of flu may appear.

Exercise 36.3 Use phrasal verbs, preposition + *-ing*, *get used to*, and *used to* correctly. [Science related]

Since scientists began to learn about AIDS more than thirty years ago, many people

have been counting ~~up~~ a cure for the disease. The cure has not yet been found, but today
                  ^on
                                                              ^are   ^living
many people with AIDS in this country used to ~~live~~ with the medications and other
                                                          ^have
treatments that allow them to ~~having~~ a reasonably healthy life. In poorer countries,
                                                          ^to
unfortunately, fewer people can look forward ~~on~~ living with AIDS, but AIDS researchers

are excited about a recent discovery in the central African country of Rwanda.

PART 6: WRITING A DOCUMENTED RESEARCH PAPER

Exercise 37.1 Detect plagiarism. [Humanities related]

Passages 3, 6, and 8 use the source responsibly.
1. The author is cited, but the exact words of the source are not put within quotation marks. In addition, no page number is given. This would be considered plagiarized.
2. Here the page number is given but the writer uses exact words from the source as if they were her own. This would be considered plagiarized.
3. The writer of this passage gives author and page number and uses her own words to paraphrase the content. This is not plagiarized.
4. Here the writer uses exact phrases from the original without putting them in quotation marks. This would be considered plagiarized.

Exercise 38.1 Narrow topics and write research questions.

Answers will vary. Some sample answers:
1. Materialism: Topic could be narrowed to country, society, industry (clothing, electronics), time period (When did it become an issue? What events might have instigated it?), gender (Is one gender more stereotyped as materialistic and why? Is there truth to the assumption?), the reverse—antimaterialism movement (Is there really one?). Possible research questions:
   a. Are women stereotyped more than men as being materialistic, and, if so, what societal, patriarchal, and media-related factors contribute to this stereotype?
   b. How does materialism relate to crime? As the pressure to equate material wealth with personal worth and success increases, is there a correlating increase in crime to accrue more materials quickly and when lacking legal means?

Exercise 38.2 Select and revise thesis statements. [Social sciences related]

Possible answers:
1. "How to discipline children," 2. "The advantages and disadvantages of spanking," and 4. "Doctors' advice on the issue of spanking" are topics, not statements.

"How to discipline children" is too broad. One possible solution would be to narrow the topic to one type of discipline, such as spanking. "The advantages and disadvantages of spanking" and "Doctors' advice on the issue of spanking" are narrower topics but need to be designed into research questions to get at the heart of what needs to be discovered. For example, "What are the advantages and disadvantages of spanking?" and "What do doctors advise on the issue of spanking?" Depending on the success of preliminary research, the research question could be revised and formulated into a working thesis such as: "While spanking modifies a child's behavior, it ultimately undermines trust in adults."

    3. "In this paper I will discuss how parents should bring up their children" merely announces a topic. It fails to provide readers with information about the topic or express an opinion about it.

Exercise 40.3 Paraphrase. [Humanities related]

1. As Stalker points out, *if any group of languages, Greek or other,* decides to keep its language, there is not much *any of us can do, with laws or not,* and still claim *to be a free* country. We cannot *pass legislation about the* language *we speak at* home, on the street, *or in restaurants,* unless *we* also want to have a group *of special* police who will *take us off to jail if they hear us not speaking English* (21).

Exercise 40.4 Summarize, paraphrase, indicate a clear citation boundary. [Humanities related]

Sample answers:

1. Rothstein laments the museum's aim to offer entertainment first and insight second as it reduces the underlying arguments of the 1860s political debates into shouting matches.
3a. Rothstein points out that the museum blurs the line between fact and fiction. Sadly, his commentary points to a new trend—valuing entertainment and simplification over rigor and complexity—that threatens to endanger our collective memory.

Exercise 40.5 Quote. [Science related]

1. Harder says, "Using good bacteria to obstruct bad ones . . . is one application of so-called probiotics . . . " (72).
2. Harder discusses one strategy of probiotic bacteria, which fight "for resources and space with pathogens inside the body and, in effect, [elbow] the bad bugs out of the way" (72).

PART 9: WRITING THROUGHOUT COLLEGE—AND BEYOND

Exercise 51.1 Critically assess an e-mail message.

    The e-mail is disorganized and unprofessional; the subject line is vague; the e-mail embeds important information late in the body of the message, amid a jumble of urgent requests; and it uses too many distracting emoticons and acronyms (*BTW* for "by the way," *ASAP* for "as soon as possible," *FYI* meaning "for your information," and *FWIW* meaning "for what it's worth").

Text Credits

Photo Credits

Index

An asterisk denotes the Glossary of Usage.

NOTES

ESL NOTES

TECHTOOLKIT

SOURCE SHOTS

For a list of 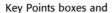 Key Points boxes and  Language and Culture boxes, see page ii.

COMMON EDITING AND PROOFREADING MARKS

Note: Numbers refer to chapters and sections in the book.

Abbreviation	Meaning
ab or abbr	abbreviation, 29b
adj	adjective, 12c, 19
adv	adverb, 12c, 19
agr	agreement, 17, 18d
art	article, 33c
awk	awkward, 8, 15
bias	biased language, 8e, 18e
case	case, 18a
cap (<u>tom</u>)	use a capital letter, 29a, 37, 33f
comp	comparison, 15a, 19f, 19g
coord	coordination, 8c, 23b
cs	comma splice, 14g, 14h
dic	diction, 8e
db neg	double negative, 19e
dm	dangling modifier, 15c
doc	documentation, 40–48
-ed	error in -*ed* ending, 16d
frag	sentence fragment, 14
fs	fused sentence, 14g
hyph	hyphenation, 30h
id	idiom, 36
inc	incomplete, 15f, 35a
ind quot	indirect quotation, 15d, 16e, 35d
-ing	-*ing* error, 16c, 34
ital	italics/underlining, 28, 42a, 46a
jar	jargon, 8e
lc (M̶e)	use a lowercase letter, 29a
mixed	mixed construction, 15a
mm	misplaced modifier, 15b
ms	manuscript form, 9
num	faulty use of numbers, 29c
p	punctuation error, 22–27, 31
pass	ineffective passive voice, 8b, 16g

Abbreviation	Meaning
pron	pronoun error, 18
quot	quotation error, 40g
ref	pronoun reference error, 18c
rel cl	relative clause, 20, 23d
rep	repetition, 8a
-s	error with -*s* ending, 17a
shift	needless shift, 15d
sp	spelling, 30
s/pl	singular/plural error, 17a
sub	subordination, 8c, 12e, 23c, 35e
sup	superlative, 19f
s-v agr	subject-verb agreement, 17
trans	transition, 5e, 8c, 23e
und	underlining/italics, 28, 42a, 46a
usg	usage error, Glossary
vb	verb error, 16
vt	verb tense error, 16c, 16e
wc	word choice, 8e
wdy	wordy, 8a
wo	word order, 35
ww	wrong word, 8e

Symbol	Meaning
??	unclear
¶ or par	new paragraph
no ¶	no new paragraph
//	parallelism (5e, 15g)
⌒	close up space
#	add space
∧	insert
___ℓ	delete
∽	transpose (reverse order)
⊙	needs a period
. . .	stet (= let it stand = do not change)

CONTENTS

A complete table of contents appears on the first page of each part.